Scenes of Seduction

Scenes of Seduction

Prostitution,
Hysteria, and
Reading Difference
in Nineteenth-Century
France

Jann Matlock

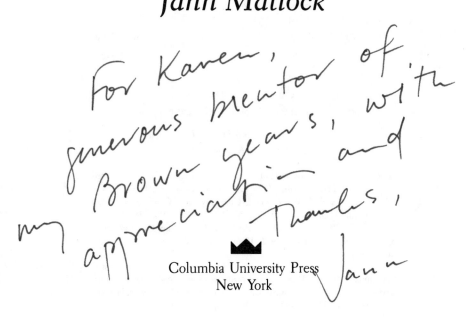

For Karen,
my generous mentor of
Brown years, with
appreciation and
Thanks,
Jann

Columbia University Press
New York

Columbia University Press

New York   Chichester, West Sussex

Copyright © 1994 Columbia University Press

All rights reserved

Library of Congress Cataloging-in-Publication Data

Matlock, Jann, 1955–

Scenes of seduction : prostitution, hysteria, and reading
difference in nineteenth-century France / Jann Matlock.

p.   cm.

Includes bibliographical references and index.

ISBN 0–231–07206–6

ISBN 0–231–07207–4 (pbk)

1. French fiction—19th century—History and criticism.
2. Women and literature—France—History—19th century.
3. Books and reading—France—History—19th century.
4. Prostitution—France—History—19th century.   5. Prostitutes
in literature.   6. Seduction in literature.   7. Hysteria in
literature.   8. Sex in literature.   I. Title.

PQ653.M36   1994

843′.709353—dc20   93–13966

CIP

∞

Casebound editions of Columbia University Press books are
printed on permanent and durable acid-free paper.

Printed in the United States of America

c 10 9 8 7 6 5 4 3 2 1

The lines from "The Burning of Paper Instead of Children" are reprinted
from *Collected Early Poems*, 1950–1970, by Adrienne Rich, by permission
of the author and W. W. Norton & Company, Inc., Copyright © 1993
by Adrienne Rich. Copyright © 1967, 1963, 1962, 1961, 1960, 1959,
1958, 1957, 1956, 1955, 1954, 1953, 1952, 1951 by Adrienne Rich.
Copyright © 1984, 1975, 1971, 1969, 1966 by W. W. Norton & Company, Inc.

Columbia University Press wishes to express its appreciation of assistance
given by the Department of Romance Languages and Literatures, Harvard
University, toward the publication of this book.

Pour mes parents

Back there: the library, walled
with green Britannicas
Looking again
in Dürer's *Complete Works*
for MELANCOLIA, the baffled woman

the crocodiles in Herodotus
the Book of the Dead
the *Trial of Jeanne d'Arc*, so blue
I think, It is her color

and they take the book away
because I dream of her too often

love and fear in a house
knowledge of the oppressor
I know it hurts to burn
   —Adrienne Rich, "The Burning of Paper
      Instead of Children" (1968)

Contents

PART FOUR: SCENES OF INTERPRETATION

List of Illustrations

Preface

"Here, my ladies, don't close this book," Georges Grisson begged his readers at the beginning of the chapter on prostitution in his *Paris horrible* (1881). "Aunts may permit their nieces to read this book," declared Maurice Alhoy in the epigram to his 1841 *Physiologie de la lorette*. In the preface to the English edition of her *Mémoires*, Marie Cappelle-Lafarge invoked the "ladies of England" who might "give a tear to her griefs." Hippolyte Régnier-Destourbet, writing under the pseudonym of the "Abbé Tiberge," dedicated his 1830 *Louisa; ou, Les douleurs d'une fille de joie* (*Louisa; or, The Sorrows of a Prostitute*) to "charity ladies," insisting that "this true story cannot corrupt the morals of those who read it."

Despite the inviting tone, these epigrams and prefaces function in a context of surveillance. Women might be goaded to read on because they have so long been disciplined for their reading. The euphemistic physiology can tease "aunts" about what they should permit their nieces to read only in the context of endless similar epigrams that warn mothers to keep their daughters away from books. Marie Cappelle-Lafarge elicits the support of her female readers despite widespread insistence upon the corruption her message might spread. The "Abbé Tiberge" even claims to have given a "licentious" title to his book so as to warn away "those people for whom this reading may be improper." As I will show in this book, these works invoke women readers in a gesture that is part of the same continuum that denies women and workers access to literacy and literature.

This study began with injunctions against books, with the intrigues that the books contained, and with the complicity between censors of texts and those who censored people. In a poem that has long served me as an antidote to the proscriptions that placed books in the *"enfers"* of libraries and people in the closed systems of tolerated prostitution, asylums, and prisons, Adrienne Rich writes "And they take the book away because I dream of her too often . . . I know it hurts to burn." My search for what it meant to be inflamed by books, for what happened to those who were inscribed in the tolerance system, and for the silences of those who disappeared into the asylum system in nineteenth-century France has taken me into places I never dreamt existed. It has spurred me on beyond fantasies into a space of representation that gives way to more than "knowable reality."

During my own explorations, many people urged me on, shared their friendship and their wisdom, and insisted that I should not close these books. They are the ones whom I now imagine reading this book. I therefore thank them with my own invocation to read.

Research and writing of this project was made possible by a Gilbert Chinard Scholarship from the Institut Français de Washington, a Humanities Research Grant, and a Dean's Special Research Award from the University of California, Berkeley, and a Deutscher Akademischer Austauschdienst Dissertation Fellowship. Final revisions were completed with the help of a J. Paul Getty Postdoctoral Fellowship in the History of Art and the Humanities. The Clark Fund of Harvard University provided timely assistance for the reproduction of visual materials.

D. A. Miller, R. Howard Bloch, Avital Ronell, Susanna Barrows, and Catherine Gallagher, the members of the committee that read the dissertation that became this book, listened as this work took shape, imagined its completion even when I could not, and provided generous and sensitive readings of early drafts. I owe a very special debt to Howard Bloch for his confidence in me, wisdom, and friendship from my first year of graduate study to the present. Two other mentors from my graduate study have become cherished colleagues and interlocutors, Charles Bernheimer, with whom I studied when he visited Berkeley in 1980–81, undertook his own book on prostitution around the same time I began this project. Unfailing in his interest in my research, generous in both challenges and support, he has relayed enthusiasm to me about our common pursuits when I most needed it. Alain Corbin, who welcomed me into his study in Paris in 1983, continues to inspire me with his keenly crafted prose and desires for a truly interdisciplinary cultural history.

The generous readings and encouragement of colleagues and friends enabled me to radically improve the original manuscript. I am grateful to Jan Goldstein, Sarah Winter, Anne Higonnet, Margaret Cohen, and Alain Corbin for their readings of the whole manuscript, and for comments on drafts of individual chapters, to James Smith Allen, Nancy Armstrong, Janet Beizer, Peter Brooks, Marie-Noëlle Duclaud, Christine Froula, Peter Sahlins, Vanessa Schwartz, Ann Smock, Rebecca Spang, Leonard Tennenhouse, and Richard Terdiman. Colleagues at Harvard University, the University of Rochester, and the Whitney Humanities Center at Yale University provided friendship and suggestions during periods of revision. I am particularly grateful for the input and encouragement of Nadine Bérenguier, Norman Bryson, Angela della Vacche, Luis Fernández-Cifuentes, Caroline Ford, Patrice Higonnet, Michael Holquist, Linda Nochlin, Per Nykrog, Craig Owens, Pierre Saint-Amand, and Bonnie Smith. At Harvard, I have been inspired by the examples of my senior female colleagues, among them Marjorie Garber, Mary Gaylord, Alice Jardine, Barbara Johnson, Doris Sommer, and Susan Suleiman. Without the provocative work of two scholars in French studies and feminist theory, this book would never have been possible. I would be honored to imagine that this book repays in part my debt to Nancy K. Miller and Naomi Schor.

In addition to my dissertation committee and colleagues, a series of mentors from my undergraduate and graduate careers have taught me how to ask hard questions and encouraged me to believe in the importance of those questions. They include Michel-André Bossy, Alison Elliot, Karen Romer, Arnold Weinstein, and Susanne Woods at Brown University; Friedrich Kittler at the Universität-Freiburg; and Thomas Laqueur and Anne Middleton at the University of California, Berkeley. Several professors with whom I worked at Berkeley—Bertrand Augst, Leo Bersani, Marie-Hélène Huet, Joel Fineman, Anton Kaes, Leo Löwenthal, and T. G. Rosenmeyer—gave encouragement and criticism at crucial stages of this work.

During my fieldwork in Paris, Michelle Perrot, Geneviève Fraisse, and Christine Buci-Glucksmann offered time, suggestions, and encouragement. Doctor Jacques Postel welcomed me into his research seminar at the Hôpital Sainte-Anne and made it possible for me to use the resources of the Bibliothèque Henri Ey. Yannick Ripa offered friendship, introduced me to colleagues, and shared her wealth of knowledge and materials. Laird Boswell coached me on the Paris archive and library system. Eglal Errera and Malka Marcovich opened her home and heart.

In the libraries of Paris certain people transformed my research with their generosity: Florence Greffe at the Archives de l'Assistance Publique made my work there the best of experiences. Véronique Leroux-Hugon of the Bibliothèque Charcot helped me meet others of like concerns. The staff of the Bibliothèque Médicale Henri Ey at Sainte-Anne provided research assistance and a superb collection of materials. The staff of the Bibliothèque Historique de la Ville de Paris, especially Odile Sanson, helped me unravel obscure references in a congenial environment. Jean-Luc Rancelli of the Archives de l'Assistance Publique and Emmanuel Gingembre at the Bibliothèque Nationale made easier long weeks of reading crumbling manuscripts. I am especially grateful to my many friends on the staff of the Bibliothèque Nationale for their help and kindness over the years. Invaluable research assistance came from David Devine, Paul Franklin, Elizabeth Galaznik, Sharon Haimov, and Lynn Love.

My mother, Mildred B. Matlock, gave generous support at all stages of my graduate work. Tony Daley, F. Edward Daley, Joan Daley, and Antoinette Powers believed in me in special ways.

It is always hardest to tell about the friends whose presence sustained more than just research. Let each of their names hold the place of narratives of magnanimous proportions: Emily Apter, Faith Beasley, Margaret Cohen, Frédéric Cousinié, Marie-Noëlle Duclaud, Eglal Errera, Anne Feibelman, Jay

Feldman, Robin Gaster, Anne Higonnet, Paul Holdengräber, Ewa Lajer-Burcharth, Nancy Laughlin, Salim Lekouaghet, Michael Levine, John Marry, Diane Rothenburg, Juliana Schiesari, Abigail Solomon-Godeau, Rebecca Spang, Charles R. Taylor, Rebecca Walkowitz, Diane Wine, Susan Winnett, Sarah Winter.

I dedicate this book to the memory of my niece, Anne Courchesne (1969–1992), who would have known that its other dedication—*pour mes parents*—includes her.

Versions of three chapters of this book have appeared elsewhere in slightly different forms. I thank the editors for permission to use this material. A version of chapter 8 was published in French translation as "Lire Dangereusement: Les Mémoires du diable et ceux de Madame Lafarge," in *Romantisme* 76, no. 2 (1992): 3–21. A version of chapter 9 appeared in *Representations* 34 (Spring 1991): 166–95. Portions of chapter 7 will appear in "Censoring the Realist Gaze," in *Realism, Sexuality, and Gender,* ed. Margaret Cohen and Chris Prendergast (Minneapolis: University of Minnesota Press, 1994).

All translations, unless otherwise noted, are my own. In quotations, I have made no distinction between my ellipses and those of the author, although almost all ellipses are mine. In the rare cases when both an author's ellipses and mine appear in the same passage, I use square brackets around mine.

Abbreviations Used in Text and Notes

AAP   Archives de l'Assistance Publique de Paris

AMP   *Annales médico-psychologiques*

AN   Archives Nationales, Paris

APP   Archives de la Préfecture de police de Paris

Br   Pierre Briquet, *Traité clinique et thérapeutique de l'hystérie* (Paris: Baillière, 1859)

CB   Honoré de Balzac, *Cousine Bette* (1847; Paris: Gallimard Folio, 1972)

CD   Honoré-Antoine Frégier, *Des Classes dangereuses de la population dans les grandes villes et les moyens de les rendre meilleures*, 2 vols. (Paris: Baillière, 1840)

Corr.   Marie Cappelle-Lafarge (Madame Lafarge), *Correspondance*, 2 vols., ed. Boyer d'Agen, 2d ed. (Paris: Mercure de France, 1913)

DC   Alexandre Dumas fils, *La Dame aux camélias* (1848; Paris: Garnier-Flammarion, 1981)

DP   Michel Foucault, *Discipline and Punish*, trans. Alan Sheridan (New York: Vintage, 1979)

DSM   *Dictionnaire des sciences médicales*, 60 vols. (Paris: Panckoucke, 1812–22)

EC   Alfred Nettement, *Etudes critiques sur le feuilleton roman*, 2 vols. (Paris: Perrodil, 1845).

FL   Ulysse Trélet, *La Folie lucide étudiée et considérée au point de vue de la famille et de la société* (Paris: Adrien Delahaye, 1861).

FPP   F. F. A. Béraud, *Les Filles publiques de Paris et la police qui les régit* (Brussels: Meline, Cans, 1839)

Frémy	Arnould Frémy, *Les Femmes proscrites*, 2 vols. (Paris: Delessart, 1840)
HR	Hersilie Rouy, *Mémoires d'une aliénée* (Paris: Ollendorff, 1883)
HS	Michel Foucault, *The History of Sexuality, Volume I: An Introduction*, trans. Robert Hurley (New York: Vintage, 1978)
JLB	Jean-Louis Brachet, *Traité de l'hystérie* (Paris: Baillière, 1847)
Mdd	Frédéric Soulié, *Les Mémoires du diable*, 8 vols. (1837; Paris: Ambroise Dupont, 1838)
Mém.	*Mémoires de Marie Cappelle, Veuve Lafarge, écrites par elle-méme*, 4 vols. (Paris: A. René, 1841–42)
ML	Victor Hugo, *Marion de Lorme*, in *Oeuvres complètes* (Paris: Club Français du livre, 1967), vol. 3, no. 2
MP	Eugène Sue, *Les Mystères de Paris* (1942–43; Paris: Robert Laffont, 1989)
PdF	Antony Méray, *La Part des femmes*, published in *La Démocratie pacifique*, May–August 1847, cited by date of publication
PD	Alexandre-J.-B. Parent-Duchâtelet, *De la Prostitution dans la ville de Paris*, 2d ed., 2 vols. (1836; Paris: Baillière, 1837)
PD, 3d ed.	Alexandre-J.-B. Parent-Duchâtelet, *De la Prostitution dans la ville de Paris*, 3d ed., 2 vols. (Paris: Baillière, 1857)
PM	Honoré de Balzac, *Physiologie du mariage* (1829; Paris: Garnier-Flammarion, 1968)
Sand	George Sand, *Lélia* (1833; Paris: Classiques Garnier, 1960)
SMC	Honoré de Balzac, *Splendeurs et misères des courtisanes* (1838–47; Paris: Garnier-Flammarion, 1968)

Introduction:

Scenes of Seduction

A "well-born girl, nineteen years of age, strong and tall," was stricken with hysterical fits. Her convulsions, reported one of the authors of the *Dictionnaire des sciences médicales* in 1813, were violent and continuous. Jean-Étienne-Dominique Esquirol, specialist in mental illnesses at the Salpêtrière asylum for women, was called in to help the hysterical young woman. After a long and completely unsuccessful treatment, she disappeared one day from her parents' house. Every attempt to find her proved futile, and Esquirol heard nothing further about her. A few months later, the young doctor happened to be spending the evening "in a rather remote quarter of Paris," when the very woman he had been treating stopped him in the street.

"What are you doing here?" he asked her. "I am curing myself," she answered.

A stint of prostitution apparently was not enough for the hysterical girl. According to the narrator of this account, "This unfortunate victim of an overly passionate constitution went on for ten months as a courtesan of the lowest class; she had two miscarriages.... Finally she went home, perfectly cured, to her father's house." To the analyst of this case, the proof of her recovery lay in the kind of life she there embraced: "This woman is today married, the mother of a family, and follows the most orderly of conducts."[1]

The author of this story of miracle cures was not prescribing prostitution for the hysterical daughters of the upper classes—despite appearances to the contrary. Rather, Antoine François Jenin de Montègre was attempting to demonstrate the perils of what he called *la continence*.[2] As far as he was concerned, the "shameful abasement" to which this girl's nature was "reduced" (*DSM*, 6:364) resulted from the self-restraint to which she had been subjected, and *not* from what theorists would later call the innate degeneracy of those driven to prostitution. Her problem, he believed, was unfulfilled sexual desire. Her solution, although drastic, returned her to the fold. The doctor's acceptance of her choice of cures—and his willingness to see her delivered from prostitution's ranks—made him an exception among medical experts of his era.[3] His overriding concern, however, with the flooding of sexual energies through defenseless bodies positioned him squarely in the midst of the most fervent debates of the nineteenth century.

Continence requires a combat and a victory, explained de Montègre, who defines it as an "effort to resist the penchant that carries us to the pleasures of love." Pain seems inherent in this process that derives, we are told, from a word (*continere*) defined with some hyperbole as "to do violence."[4] Unlike the chaste who freely choose to follow their "natural dispositions," the continent are those forced by circumstances beyond their control to resist their desires: pubescent girls, widows in the prime of life, neglected spouses, young men who seek to enter the Church to please their parents but whose nature is ill-suited to the chastity required of priests (*DSM*, 6:355). For the medical community of the nineteenth century, the pain of sexual continence bodies forth terrifying specters. The convulsive figure of the sexually continent haunts doctors' writings as the prostitute haunts those of health inspectors and police bureaucrats. But while the prostitute may appear containable, the ills of the sexually continent prove baffling: any victorious combat against sexual desire threatens continually to precipitate the continent into further perils. The bodies of the sexually continent cannot be contained—except by the satisfaction of their desires. And those desires are always out of line. Driven to masturbation, adultery, and prostitution when they fail to contain themselves, the sexually continent slide into hysteria and madness when they cannot master the contradictions in their body.

The overwhelming desires de Montègre evokes were believed all the more problematic because they surged up naturally—in adolescents whose "organs" were not yet ready for marriage, in widows constrained by a husband's premature death, and in spouses lacking an "intimate union" with their husbands.[5] While the hysterical girl who became a prostitute found an extreme solution to a widespread problem, de Montègre urged fellow doctors to seek ways to help their patients dissipate these natural urges. Dietary changes and herb teas might work, he advised, but only if medical efforts were "backed up by the scrupulous care to remove all lewd ideas," combined with a flight from idleness and an attempt to live an active life (*DSM*, 6:382). The resulting continence, though dangerous over long stretches of time, could even turn productive: the body would grow stronger; the mind, "gently excited," would become sharper; pleasures, when at last attained, would be delirious and all-satisfying (*DSM*, 6:378).

De Montègre invoked Hippocrates in approval of his hysteric's miscarriages: *Si concipiant sanescunt* (If they conceive, they will be cured) (*DSM*, 6:364). Yet even as the doctor's account fell back on the ancient notion that a reproductively active womb would not "misbehave," it also emphatically endorsed regular sexual activity as a cure for hysteria. Most amazing, the doctor insisted on the power of the prostitute's activities to bring about a change in the continent girl's maladies. Although he would have preferred to see parents and doctors help such girls avoid the ravages of hysteria, when they failed, he accepted radical cures. What de Montègre wanted in place of continence was a better regime for controlling and channeling desires. He would make hard choices to ensure that desires did not go unsatisfied for long if he could, in turn, save families from the deluges brought on by unchecked sexual desire.

As de Montègre's anecdote suggests, nineteenth-century hysteria takes shape through the stories told by medical and psychiatric experts. It is far less the diagnostic name for a set of symptoms than a category for perceptions. In an era of obsessive attempts to categorize and classify bodily disorders, it marks efforts at understanding the very real suffering of a large group of individuals. Yet the understanding of "hysteria" evidenced in these narratives is always only partial. While doctors with radically different views reported similar phenomena—paralyses, fainting, coughing fits, convulsions, impressionability, and hypersensitivity to physical and emotional stimulation—the range of symptoms for this disorder was so great that some doctors refused to categorize it at all except as an exacerbation of whatever made women different from men. The search for ways to prevent and cure hysteria gave a focus to the stories told by nineteenth-century medical and psychiatric analysts. How such prevention was envisioned depended in large part on the theories about gender, class, heredity, and sexuality underlying the perceptions of any given doctor. In the course of this book, I will show that these theories far transcended the day-to-day care of women diagnosed as hysterical. Through their embodiment in proliferating medical case studies, the narratives of hysteria radically transformed the social and cultural perceptions through which difference was understood.[6]

Sexuality, Michel Foucault contended, served as a privileged point of support for nineteenth-century power relations. Through the bodies of individuals, the workings of power became intelligible and transformative. Foucault elaborated "four great lines of attack along which the politics of sex advanced" in the nineteenth century, each combining regulative methods with disciplinary techniques (*HS*, 146). Four figures emerged in his *History of Sexuality* as the targets and supports for this deployment of sexuality: the hysterical woman, the masturbating child, the Malthusian couple, and the perverse adult (*HS*, 103–5). Each of these "privileged objects of knowledge" was invested with a discourse that claimed to speak its truth and through which strategies of power could be anchored. "The hysterization of women," Foucault explained, "involved a thorough medicalization of their bodies and their sex." Women's bodies were regulated "in the name of the responsibility they owed to the health of their children, the solidity of the family institution, and the safeguarding of sex" (*HS*, 146–47). The discourse of hysteria attempted to contain the desires of the bourgeois woman so that they could be productively channeled in the service of society. It sorted female bodies by investing them with sexual meanings, endowing "normal," "healthy" women with a difference that separated them from working-class women.

Foucault might have argued that the hysterization of women's bodies required the participation of the prostitute. In this book I go a step further by arguing that the prostitute became a privileged object of knowledge in her own right and that prostitution generated a "great line of attack" all its own. At about the same time as doctors honed in on the exuberant desires of hysterical women, another group of social theorists and medical professionals turned their attentions to the desires invested in prostitution. In 1836 Alexandre Parent-Duchâtelet transformed the methodology of the social sciences with his detailed documentation of the world of registered prostitutes.[7] In the later years of the July Monarchy (1830–48), doctors, police officials, and state bureaucrats agreed with his view that regulated legal prostitution worked "in the interest of morals and the preservation of social order" (*PD*, 1:503). The nineteenth-century investigation of the prostitute's body thus provides a key to the power mechanisms through which female difference could be produced and desire contained. In the closed spaces of the brothel, hospital, prison, and refuge, as I shall show, the prostitute's own excesses could be held in check. In the strategical order of the regulationist system, she could contain — and therefore help police — potentially disruptive desires.

What Foucault called the hysterization of women's bodies was achieved in the nineteenth century by differentiating orderly bodies from those perceived as disorderly. The hysteric and the prostitute provided opposite models against which an orderly body could be measured — the one tormented by desires welling up from the inside, the other transformed into a holding tank for desires that might contaminate society from the outside. The fantasies out of which each of these bodies was created, differentiated, and understood required a delicate balance keeping the two kinds of women separate. Yet the barrier between them, as the anecdote with which I began suggests, constantly threatened to collapse. In a myriad of ways, the hysteric became the prostitute, the prostitute taught the hysteric her tricks, and the desires invested in their differences generated new stories of contagion and collusion.

Proponents of tolerated prostitution — as the Parisian system was called — justified their methods by insisting that the physical needs of men might overload social circuits if prostitution were outlawed entirely.[8] Doctors who imagined continence breeding a plethora of ills depended on a similar fantasy of irrepressible desires. Each fantasy churned up uncontrollable desires as the basis for elaborate plots of containment. Whatever might leave desires unchecked became suspect and dangerous. Containing desires often required choices between imagined evils — as in the anecdote from de Montègre, between prostitution and hysteria — or between masturbation and potential madness, between adultery and convulsions, and between the stimulations of illicit books and terror-filled privations of the senses.[9] Theorists imagined scenarios in which one plot seemed preferable to the other while nevertheless insisting on the dangers of both.

While de Montègre and his followers argued that continence led to hysteria and madness, other theorists of the body argued that sexual indulgence bred idiocy and mental illness. Masturbation, adultery, and prostitution sowed sickness in the body and mind, said other medical writers, who only occasionally noted that the last of these "scourges" also spread contamination with body-eroding and mind-deforming illnesses such as syphilis.[10] Despite his fears of containing desire, de Montègre's interests lay uncannily close to those of theorists who sought to distance bodies from desire. Both groups of thinkers invested *their* desires in "well-born" bodies that might be constrained through imaginative intervention for the service of society. As the rest of de Montègre's article on continence makes clear, he wanted to ensure that men and women marry, conceive, become parents, and "follow the most orderly of all conducts."

Should bourgeois girls be promptly married to ensure that they avoid the dangers lurking around them? Was hysteria really bred from unsatisfied sexual needs or were there other factors that one could isolate and control? If sex was all one needed, then why did so many married women suffer from nervous disorders? Were prostitutes really less prone to hysteria than "normal" women? Was there a secret that linked the one "female ill" to the other? Those were the questions repeatedly asked by the medical profession in the nineteenth century. The answers to these questions staked out three general camps in the understanding of female sexuality.

Some, like de Montègre, his contemporary J. B. Louyer-Villermay, and later Hector Landouzy, Émile Mathieu, and Auguste Debay, believed the repression of sexual urges was so dangerous that even prostitution might be justified as a cure. These analysts held that continence led to hysteria or other mental illnesses, such as nymphomania and erotomania. Some believed that prostitutes were rarely, if ever, mentally ill and that the majority of the mentally ill women in society could be found in the bourgeoisie among the ranks of young unmarried girls or neglected spouses.[11] The working classes, they intimated, not only lived frequently from an early age in healthy concubinage but were far less inclined to nervous disorders because their sensitivities were not as developed as those of the upper classes. [12]

Others—for example, Étienne Georget and Pierre Briquet—sought to divorce hysterical afflictions from their perceived connection to female reproductive organs. Hysteria, they argued, was not the price of illicit desire but rather the result of a plethora of conditions ranging from a poor education to poverty. The womb was no more to blame for the mental illnesses of women than it was at fault for women's fall into prostitution. For each of the ills of women, these thinkers offered a range of explanations, many of them ideologically loaded but at least not based on the fallacious reasoning of *post hoc ergo propter hoc*. Just because a girl stopped being hysterical after a stint of prostitution did not prove, they contended, that prostitution, orgies, masturbation, regular sexual activity, or even conception could mitigate women's nervous disorders. These thinkers also sought to undermine theories about endangered bourgeois girls by studying prostitutes and working-class women. In fact, asserted Briquet, prostitutes are more likely to suffer from hysteria than other women precisely *because* of the poor conditions in which they have been raised and forced to live (Br, 123–26).[13]

A third group believed prostitutes frequently hysterical because they were inherently degenerate. Some said that such women had been driven into prostitution because of overactive sexual drives that made them, in turn, crazy. Others argued that a line of degeneracy could be traced between the mentally ill and their sick offspring. They might become alcoholic, devoured by sexually transmitted diseases, nervous, mad, criminal, or sexually aberrant—drawn to prostitution, homosexuality, and masturbation.[14]

Although the continence debates initially raised questions about male as well as female desires, they increasingly focused on hysteria and thus became an inquiry into the regulation of female sexuality. Fears about the restraint of male sexuality were increasingly played out in arguments about the policing of prostitution. There, too, however, the bodies under surveillance were almost exclusively female. The discussions of prostitution generated out of the continence debates provided a new focus on the nature of these female bodies. By exploring the link between hysteria and prostitution, the continence question forced issues of gender, class, and education into the open. It challenged assumptions through which sexual and social relations had been regulated since the ancien régime. And although old fantasies about female sexuality were frequently merely replaced with new justifications for old prescriptions, the ensuing debates radically transformed the ways in which female subjects entered into discourse.

The continence debates brought questions about internal containment into a realm where external containment became possible. Those who contended that continence endangered no one nevertheless repeatedly argued that women needed to be placed under close surveillance lest sexual excess drive them to hysteria and madness. Those who argued that prostitutes and working-class women suffered more frequently from nervous disorders in turn sought to extract bourgeois women from the heinous influences that had predisposed their poorer contemporaries to these afflictions. The very individuals who sought to put sexual excesses under surveillance themselves engaged in a fervent combat to ensure that men and women would not entirely repress sexual urges. Internal conflicts had been put into observable spheres of restraint. Fears about desire had been shifted from inside bodies to outside bodies.

Perhaps not surprisingly, the continence debates paralleled and linked a series of debates about external containment. From the time Georget (1824) locked horns with Louyer-Villermay (1816) and throughout the era when Briquet (1859) disputed the findings of Landouzy (1847), regulationists sought to contain prostitution's contagion and doctors sought new ways to regulate and treat mental illnesses. Reformists' attempts to contain excesses inside spaces such as prisons, state-regulated brothels, asylums, and hospitals found uncanny equivalents in the sexual self-restraints encouraged by the clergy and the radical solutions proposed by doctors like de Montègre.

This book is about the process that moved terrors about desire from inside bodies to outside bodies. It is an analysis of three nineteenth-century plots of containment: the structures of regulated prostitution, the discourse of the hospital system that created spaces for mentally ill women, and the novel. At the center of each of these plots of containment was a scene of danger — a fantasy of uncontrollable and overwhelming desires. Each of these scenes, as I will show, evoked a fantasy of seduction. This book tells the story of those scenes of seduction and the plots of containment they engendered.

This book focuses on the nineteenth-century discourse that attempted to know and regulate desire. Because the bodies of the prostitute and the hysteric served fantasmatically as the polar vanishing points through which this discourse was constructed, I concentrate on the discursive plots that created and surrounded these two entities. I argue that neither the prostitute nor the hysteric exists as an ahistorical being outside of the flood of texts that surrounded their bodies. Rather, both the prostitute and the hysteric are textual products, elaborated into case studies, codified into narratives, emplotted into fantasies. Like the hysterical girl in the *Dictionnaire* article on continence, the bodies of these women were given medical stories that had corollaries in prescriptions for a better society. Their desires were provoked so that they could be channeled and controlled. Their differences were interpreted and labeled so that they could be easily recognized and kept in check.

This process entailed a kind of fantasmatic reading: hysterics and prostitutes came to be interpreted, defined, and endowed with social significance in new ways in the early nineteenth century. For the first time in the course of the July Monarchy (1830–48), theorists emphasized their confrontations with the individual under analysis. These thinkers believed they could, through close observation, read the body and its desires into the framework of their theories. I call this process *reading difference* (1) because central to this enterprise were finely tuned investigations of gender, class, and race, and (2) because this process engaged methods of analysis and interpretation for the purposes of sequestration and exclusion. As my study will show, these readers of difference brought with them preconceived notions of the categories they used for analysis, just as they insisted on predetermined ways of channeling desire. Much of the process of *reading difference* emerged, I will argue, as an inscription of indelible otherness upon bodies.

The plots these writers embraced had much in common with the story with which we began. The discourse of tolerated prostitution depended on a fantasmatic scene in which a man, prohibited from seeking satisfaction with prostitutes, sought to relieve his urges. This primal scene of prostitution struck terror into the hearts of the bourgeoisie: driven by desires beyond his control, he would begin to seduce well-bred daughters, to corrupt servants, and to lead working-class girls into the depths of depravity.[15] A corollary view focused on the "seduction" into prostitution of innocent young girls and argued that their fall could be prevented by instituting a more efficient system of morals.[16] If men knew *who was appropriate* to their needs, other girls might be spared. If better morals were instilled in girls, women would not so easily fall prey to the "seductions" of men. Whether the readers of prostitution believed prostitutes inherently depraved or simply led astray, they repeatedly insisted that when the prostitute filled her "necessary" role, she helped contain dangerous desires. The fantasy of seduction evoked by these writers required a clear boundary between "good girls" and those who could be sacrificed to the former's virtue. It anchored a framework of surveillance and control that lasted for most of the nineteenth century.

The discourse that read the hysteric's difference also depended upon a fantasmatic scene. At its center was a horrible scene of bodily convulsions brought on by unchecked engagements with sensation and desire. The hysterical girl was imagined to have been seduced into illness by excessive stimulation. Exactly what stimulations could seduce her became the subject of intense debate. Regardless of the individual theorist's views on the dangers of continence, almost all of them postulated a scene of dangerous desires. Whether they believed the hysteric's problems could be relieved through marriage, conception, or sexual activity, the readers of hysteria unanimously agreed that this malady could be prevented through a closer surveillance of the education and experiences of young women.[17]

The "scenes of seduction" conjured up by these readers of difference had their equivalents in yet another set of debates over the dangers of written texts. Although good girls might wind up hysterical because of natural sexual development, doctors argued, they might also fall prey to a lively imagination. Early in his dictionary entry, de Montègre fretted over the dangers these pages might create for his more innocent readers: "Let the common reader stop now! This article is suitable only for those who want to see man in all his nudity!" (*DSM*, 6:355). The specter of the hysterical girl, convulsing over a specialized medical volume, would haunt the nineteenth century. The authors of the feminist newspaper *L'Opinion des femmes* warned girls away from Mathieu's study of female maladies. Debay, the author of popular books on "marital hygiene," worried that most scientific works on "what is physical in marriage" might "alarm the modesty" of young women. Freud blamed Frau K. for compromising Dora's innocence with "big books," among them Paolo Mantegazza's *Physiology of Love* and a German medical encyclopedia resembling the *Dictionnaire des sciences médicales!*[18] Doctors imagined even greater dangers emanating from the novel.

"If your daughter reads novels at age fifteen," the eighteenth-century Swiss physician Samuel Tissot is quoted as declaring, "she will be hysterical at age twenty."[19] This injunction echoed throughout the nineteenth century, casting an aura of titillation over literary works portraying the social world. The novel was targeted as dangerous because it allegedly awakened affections and sensitized the overly impressionable female nature to the world of sexual experience. What had changed from the eighteenth to the nineteenth century was not so much the novel but its accessibility to an ever growing number of readers. As the literacy rates rose substantially for the working classes and women, so did the kinds of texts at their disposal. New printing techniques, paper-making processes, and reading rooms brought literature to almost anyone with a desire to read.

Novels like those of Honoré de Balzac, Frédéric Soulié, and Eugène Sue were directed *at* women by a growing book market that relied as much on women readers as the police depended on registered prostitutes in regulated brothels. Criticism of the novel emerged from camps as diverse as workers, feminists, Catholic journalists, police bureaucrats, state censors, physicians, and the emerging psychiatric community. One would have thought that by devouring fictions the newly targeted audience of women readers had joined the ranks of the registered prostitutes in the police depot. At the very least, critics contended, those women readers risked being taken in by novelistic *scenes of seduction* that exposed them to hysteria or worse.

The fact that in those novels the prostitute became a very special narrative lure for the early mass-market publishing business, convinced doctors, educators, and moralists that she did so at the expense of the *nerves* of her female readers. In this book I argue that these *scenes of seduction* had a great deal in common with those embraced in the discourse about prostitution as well as with those evoked in the debates over hysteria. In each of these scenes, the prostitute summoned fantasies of seduction and in turn produced plots of containment. Her body became a matrix for a struggle aimed at reading women. It was also at the center of a contest through which women could be made readable.

I began this study with questions about the entanglements of proscriptions against people and those against texts. I wanted to understand what gave texts — novels in particular — a reputation as dangerous in precisely the same era as they engaged in debates about marginals. The nineteenth-century French novel not only suffered scorn from critics and deprecation from educators, doctors, and moralists but also experienced harassment from the state. Few critical studies of the novel have accounted for the fears and outrage that surrounded the genre in the era when it first became accessible to the masses. Even fewer studies of nineteenth-century culture account for the rich legacy of popular fiction that reached its pinnacle in the course of the July Monarchy. In privileging canonical authors like Stendhal and Flaubert, we have lost sight of the processes that swept aside their rivals. We have become equally blind to the cultural context in which such canonical authors positioned their works and their values.

I have therefore sought to understand how certain kinds of people, under certain circumstances, were censored for reading. I have considered how these processes of censorship resulted in differences that were read even more insistently out of those people's bodies. I have tried to rethink our readings of novelistic marginality through an examination of how new scientific ways of looking and codifying bodies transformed the plots that could be given to those bodies. I have sought to reposition the 1857 trial of *Madame Bovary* in a framework that encompasses the censorship of Victor Hugo's *Marion de Lorme* during the Restoration (1814–30), the trials of a Fourierist newspaper novel on the eve of the Revolution of 1848, the banning of *La Dame aux camélias* from the stage throughout the Second Republic (1848–51), and the terrors that incessantly surrounded popular novels. I have read Balzac alongside his critically maligned rivals Sue and Soulié and in turn read scandal back into Balzac. I have taken a new look at the cultural battlefield of the Revolutions of 1830 and 1848. I have used the memoirs of a woman whose trial shook France in 1840 to examine how gender became a central category in monitoring reading. From the memoirs of a woman who escaped the asylum, I have sought counsel on the ways in which writing might enable one to transgress imprisoning theories of reading and interpretation. Finally, I have tried to expand our own interpretative categories to include new ways of looking at a variety of discourses—medical case studies in archives, psychiatric analyses, police reports, prison records, trial transcripts, newspaper editorials, advice manuals for women, nineteenth-century literary criticism, memoirs, and, of course, novels.

This work began with an observation that informs the first chapters of this book: the nineteenth-century novel has a peculiar dependence upon the prostitute as the center of its disciplinary regime. Like D. A. Miller, who was exploring the possibility of a "radical entanglement between the nature of the novel and the practice of the police,"[20] I wished to consider the circumstances of an equally significant collusion between nineteenth-century fiction and the prostitute. Alain Corbin's rich study of prostitution between 1851 and 1914 laid out the historical framework in which such literary complicity evolved in the social sphere.[21] Like Miller and Corbin, I too looked to Foucault for ways of explaining the modalities of power through which bodies were ordered and known.

Jeremy Bentham's imaginary figure of the Panopticon represents, in Foucault's view, the crystallization of a program of disciplinary power that worked to differentiate, analyze, and distribute bodies (*DP*, 200–9). The Panopticon consists of a building composed of individual cells arranged in a circle around a central watchtower. From that tower one can see into each cell, observe whatever is happening there, and yet remain absolutely invisible. Confined alone in a cell, each individual is exposed to the gaze of the supervisor in the central tower but unable to tell whether at any given moment someone is actually watching. Separated from the inhabitants of the other cells by windowless walls on either side, fixed by the imagined gaze of someone who might be looking on, the prisoners are trapped into policing themselves. The divisions between cellmates preserve order: these separated individuals will not devise plots, harm one another, or collude in misconduct. Their potential visibility traps them into disciplining themselves. Their certain invisibility to one another preserves this order: "a real subjection is born mechanically from a fictitious relation" (*DP*, 202). Bars, chains, and locks suddenly become superfluous in this imaginary enactment of power on and through its objects. The imprisoned "inscribe in [themselves] the power relation in which [they] become the principle of [their] own subjection" (*DP*, 203). They put *themselves* under restraint.

For Foucault the Panopticon of 1791 was also a project for a laboratory, "a privileged place for experiments on men, and for analyzing with complete certainty the transformations that may be obtained from them" (*DP*, 204). Its every result contributes to the very efficiency of the processes enacted there. What Foucault has called the "generalization of discipline" presumes a paradigmatic shift around the time of Bentham's imaginary program for the Panopticon. Bentham's "inspection-house" emerged as a theoretical paradigm that had analogies in the practices of nearly every disciplinary regimen from the late eighteenth century onward. The Panopticon turned out to be far more than "a perverse dream" or an isolated architectural moment (*DP*, 225): nineteenth-century surveillance functioned at all levels of society — and in a striking variety of forms — in "panoptic" ways. Explicitly invoked as a model for building nineteenth-century prisons (*DP*, 249–50), Bentham's Panopticon functioned according to specific principles that became generalized in other social spheres: "surveillance and observation, security and knowledge, individualization and totalization, isolation and transparency" (*DP*, 249). No wonder, as Foucault reminds us, prisons came to resemble "factories, schools, barracks, hospitals, which all resemble prisons" (*DP*, 228).

Perhaps not surprisingly, the date Foucault chooses for the birth of the carceral system — January 22, 1840, the day of the opening of Mettray reformatory — falls within the same decade as the laws for cellular detainment (1844), as the Law of 1838 that reorganized the psychiatric asylum system, as the publication of Parent-Duchâtelet's *De la Prostitution dans la ville de Paris* (1836), and as the first medical prize for a treatise on hysteria (1833). The decade of the carceral also witnessed popular journalistic accounts of trials as well as the birth of the newspaper serial novel and the rise of reading rooms. People were learning to read in droves; spaces to contain their drive to read proliferated. We should not be surprised, then, that this very reading came to be placed under the disciplinary surveillance of panoptic mechanisms. We should not be astonished that the differences between readers were invoked as ways of differentiating, analyzing, and distributing bodies.

I differ radically with Foucault, however, regarding the workings of the novel in the midst of these panoptic practices. For Foucault in *Discipline and Punish*, the nineteenth-century novel embraced its own versions of marginality (criminality and madness, for example) in a move parallel to that of the *fait divers*, or true-to-life crime tale, that gained popularity in the early nineteenth century. The novel's role, argued Foucault, was to set delinquency apart, to assert the strangeness of the criminal world (*DP*, 286). With the creation of a literature of crime, popular broadsheets disappeared: "the people was robbed of its old pride in its crimes; the great murders had become the quiet game of the well behaved" (*DP*, 69). Foucault imagines the novel in the hands of the bourgeoisie and casts its readers as primarily male. To explain the paradigm shift in the representation of discipline, Foucault calls upon a crime literature centering on sharp-witted male criminals and revolving around the confrontation between (male) murderers and (male) detectives. From Gaboriau to Vidocq, from *Les Mystères de Paris* to *Rocambole*, from Thomas de Quincey (published in France in 1849) to Charles Baudelaire to Arsène Lupin, Foucault traces a trajectory that insists upon certain arts of crime committed by certain kinds of criminals and appreciated by particular kinds of readers. The trajectory I trace begins with one of these novels, Sue's *Mystères de Paris*, but it turns on quite a different set of arts practiced by quite a different kind of criminal and appreciated by a much broader readership. I have sought to write women back into stories that depended on gender difference. I am not so much turning Foucault's vision of the novel on end as insisting on its multivalence. I want a history of literary bodies that takes into account the differences between readers and the fantasies surrounding those differences.

My quarrels with Foucault on the subject of the nineteenth-century novel replicate in many ways the disagreements I have with his work elsewhere. In a compelling moment of *The History of Sexuality*, Foucault gives an account of the way the discourse about sex invested nineteenth-century bodies. As Foucault tells the story, a farmhand named Jouy was arrested in 1867 for having "obtained a few caresses from a little girl, just as he had done before and seen done by the village urchins round about him." The man was imprisoned, examined by doctors, acquitted as mentally ill, and institutionalized in the asylum at Maréville for the rest of his days. For Foucault, "the significant thing about this story" is "the pettiness of it all; the fact that this everyday occurrence in the life of village sexuality, these inconsequential bucolic pleasures, could become . . . the object not only of a collective intolerance but of a judicial action, a medical intervention, a careful clinical examination, and an entire theoretical elaboration" (*HS*, 31). Although one cannot help but be shaken by Foucault's descriptions of Jouy's examination and eventual asylum death sentence, another story seems to have been left by the wayside here, not only by Foucault but also by the doctors and legal experts called in on the case. This story belongs to the little girl whose parents reported the "game" and who, undoubtedly, was as much silenced by the experts as by Foucault. I would like to see an archaeology of silence that accounts for that little girl as well as for the victimized farmhand. Yet, in the attempt to give voices to the silences Foucault so eloquently invoked, I have chosen to refocus the concerns of such an endeavor. The history of bodies I have chosen to write allows, therefore, for more than one story of victimization.[22] But it also insistently attempts to move beyond accounts of victimization to a history of resistance.

Foucault's system accounts brilliantly for the workings of power on bodies and through bodies. His accounts of power, knowledge, and sexuality leave us, however, with lapses in vision: gender, racial, and often class differences too disappear through panoptic grids. His system also fails to account for the resistances to power and to the transformations in the carceral system. It leaves us trapped by panoptic power, unable to free ourselves from the restraints of our own investigations. For these reasons, a history of bodies in nineteenth-century discourse has required a revision of Foucault's imaginary models.

I argue here that the disciplinary structure of the Panopticon has analogies, first, in the system of tolerated prostitution institutionalized in the nineteenth century and, second, in the novel that embraced similar systems of *tolérance*. The tolerance system (which I describe in chapter 1) functioned in panoptic ways but with two striking differences. First, it worked in specifically gendered ways and through optics that entailed questions of class. Second, and even more important to my overall argument, this disciplinary mechanism became not only the dominant perpetrator of ideological control in the nineteenth century but also the guarantor of its own displacement. The processes through which the prostitute was investigated and marginalized were even more discreet and thus more effective than the penitentiary mechanisms Foucault described, but, strangely, they were also capable of generating resistance in ways that threatened to topple the entire panoptic system. Likewise, the other nineteenth-century plots of containment I examine here—the asylum system and the novel—work to forestall resistance even as they anticipate new strategies that might forever undermine the old. Panoptic in their disciplinary strategies, "tolerant" in their views of class and gender differences, and consuming in their powers, the prostitution system, the asylum system, and the novel inscribed their subjects into power struggles over desire.

"Where there is power, there is resistance," Foucault declared (*HS*, 95), yet his every analytical move installed him more fully in the bonds of panoptic power. Foucault showed the extent to which the perceptual grids of panopticism are as much a part of our modern investigative practices as of our penal codes. My goal in this work is to reexamine those grids. My critique of Foucault's notion of power insists upon the ways strategies of resistance might arise out of even the most containing discourse. For this reason, I have organized each chapter around a containing plot and the possible reversals it engenders.

Part 1 of this book revolves around plots around prostitutes and explores the interrelations of female sexuality and representation in a series of literary, political, social scientific, and medical studies between 1829 and 1851. Chapter 1, "Traffic in Mystery: The *Roman-Feuilleton* and the Tolerance System," begins with an analysis of Parent-Duchâtelet's monumental study of prostitution of 1836. Arguing that the novel of prostitution depends on a system of controlled illegality, such as the system of legalized prostitution (*tolérance*) Parent's work helped to fortify, this chapter reads the most popular novel of the July Monarchy, Sue's *Les Mystères de Paris* (1842–43) for its interest in the prostitute's body. Like the other chapters in this book, this one attempts to read nineteenth-century literary, medical, and social scientific discourses for their entanglements in common power plays and, especially, for the forms of resistance to which they gave rise. In chapters 2 and 3 I explore the relationship of prostitution to revolution in the period between 1829 and 1852. Chapter 2, "Censored Bodies: Plots, Prostitutes, and the Revolution of 1830," reads a series of incendiary pamphlets from the Revolution of 1830 together with two of the final scandals of the Restoration, the censorship battle over Hugo's *Marion de Lorme* in 1829 and the police crackdown on Paris prostitution in the spring of 1830. Chapter 3, "Taking Liberties: Plots Around Prostitutes in 1848," takes up the political culture of the Revolution of 1848 in relation to Alexandre Dumas fils' *La Dame aux camélias* to explore the emergence of alternatives to the discourse of fear surrounding revolutionary women.

Part 2 of this book, "The Hysteric's Difference," sets out to refigure the problem of hysteria in the context of debates during the July Monarchy. I argue here that hysteria was a much more common diagnosis in the July Monarchy and early Second Empire (1852–70) than has hitherto been acknowledged. Chapter 4, "Telling the Difference: Hysterics, Prostitutes, and the Clinical Gaze," therefore returns to one aspect of the continence debate, the question of the prostitute's mental stability, as a key to exploring the creation of female subjectivity in the discourse that sought to differentiate the madwoman from the hysteric. Chapter 5, "Pathological Masterplots: Hysteria, Sexuality, and the Balzacian Novel," takes up the imbrication of plots around hysteria and those around prostitution through a reading of Honoré de Balzac's *Cousine Bette* and Jean-Louis Brachet's *Traité de l'hystérie*, both published in 1847.

Part 3, "Seduction under Surveillance," returns to theories of endangered reading and endangered readers. Chapter 6, "Dangerous Reading: The Trials of the Nineteenth-Century Novel," examines the fears of the novel both before and after the explosive popularity brought to it during the July Monarchy. The censorship of a *roman-feuilleton* in a small Fourierist newspaper on the eve of the Revolution of 1848 focuses our analysis in chapter 7, "The Politics of Seduction: Trying *Women's Share*." Chapter 8, "Reading Dangerously: The Memoirs of the Devil and Madame Lafarge," considers the memoirs of this woman tried for poisoning her husband alongside the novels that critics imagined might have driven her to murder.

Part 4, "Scenes of Interpretation," posits a space for reading and interpretation that the concluding chapter and epilogue can only begin to suggest. Chapter 9, "Doubling out of the Crazy House: Gender, Autobiography, and the Insane Asylum System," reads the memoirs of Hersilie Rouy, who was incarcerated in Charenton in 1854, for possibilities of resistance within nineteenth-century systems of marginalization. Substituting the powers of critical analysis for the fears of seduction that have haunted this study, the epilogue asks questions about the legacies of nineteenth-century theories of difference for the reading strategies we bring to texts.

This project began as an exploration of literary texts that, in one way or another, did not fit into the critical categories traditionally used to analyze them. It quickly became a work of interdisciplinary boundary-crossing. I formulated this research by asking how one could tell the story of the representation of female sexuality in nineteenth-century France. Although I knew that literary texts raised provocative questions about these issues, I was certain that they could not tell that story by themselves. I sought, therefore, to write a new "comparative literature," one that—instead of "comparing" texts from different cultural or linguistic backgrounds—would engage historical as well as literary problematics at the same time as it questioned such categories. I sought to enlarge the framework of literary and historical analyses by reclaiming questions of discourse and power that each discipline on its own might leave unanswered. For decades, literary study eschewed questions of context. Historians have only recently begun to consider cultural representation as a productive arena for the study of ideological and political struggles. This is not just a work of "new historicism," but rather a project in feminist cultural history.[23] I have taken Foucault's invitation to write a "history of bodies" and sought to make sense of the discourses through which the silence of certain bodies had been transacted. In doing so, I hoped to give a voice to those bodies. I wanted to find a new methodology for speaking of the power of their desires. The history I have ultimately written is therefore perhaps less one of silent bodies than one of the resistances to silence.

When I began this study, I thought that what we traditionally call "historical primary texts" might provide powerful models for the workings of "literary texts." I believed that one could lay "historical works," like the *Dictionnaire des sciences médicales*, side by side with cultural representations of the same period—the novels of Balzac or Sand, for example—and see analogous structures of containment and resistance. I soon discovered, however, that the relationships between literary and nonliterary materials were not so straightforward. Although I found remarkable analogies between "literary" and "nonliterary" discourse, I also discovered the imbrications of the scientific, social scientific, and cultural, the interactions of the explicitly "fictional" and the implicitly "real." Literary texts were as much part of the historical primary material I sought to analyze as they were a separate phenomenon, held up by nineteenth-century critics and moralists as potentially more disruptive than supposedly "scientific" and "factual" texts. The very extent to which this distinction riveted the attention of nineteenth-century commentators suggested a need for new methodologies to contest such distinctions. As I worked with novels, memoirs, social scientific documents, medical studies, and hospital archives, I discovered that the tools I had long used for reading literary texts were frequently blunted by the new tasks I had set myself. Historians volunteered techniques that often helped but just as frequently failed me in the face of the new questions I wished to answer. My trajectory has been one, therefore, of allowing my texts to teach me new questions and of seeking new interpretative methods through which to answer them.

Most important, I have learned that the tensions between what are traditionally called "historical" texts and those labeled "literary" can teach us productive new ways of seeing and interpreting. Through the process of juxtaposing what I initially believed were radically different kinds of texts, I saw the distinctions between "history" and "culture" disappear. My entire project became one of unraveling those interpretative distinctions. By breaking down the barriers between fields, I discovered, we can reexamine the perceptual grids of the past without mystifying them once again. We can understand how we learned to read without losing sight of the desires we invest in reading.

PART ONE
Plots Around Prostitutes

1

Traffic in Mystery:
The *Roman-Feuilleton* and the Tolerance System

*T*wo women in fake fur slouch against a tenement wall, disinterestedly dangling cigarettes from their rhinestone-bedecked hands. Men drift by. Some pause only long enough to cast a prurient glance; others stop to ask the price. The women continue to lean wearily against the wall, barely mustering a seductive smile as interested passers-by linger to catch their eyes. The credits come up. We are in the realm of postmodernist studies in scarlet—a Newgate fiction for the nuclear age that draws all the strands of the nineteenth-century novel tradition into one-hour shots at the dangerous classes lurking in the mean streets of America. We can expect everything—suspense, action, titillation, and even realism—in episodes as contained and as repetitive as those of the penny dreadfuls. The main characters have hardly changed: criminals, victims, and saviors still inhabit the Manichean universe of melodrama that depends upon oppositions between virtue and vice. Television, the ultimate surveillance device of the postwar era, provides a vantage point through which America can reform morals, preserve health, invigorate industry, diffuse instruction, and lighten public burdens[1]—all from the living-room couch. Technology has not ceased to refine the instruments of power that allow for the separation of the deviant from the normal. This perceptual grid provides order, relieves tension, tempers threats, and occasionally even consoles. Yet this contemporary version of the *roman-feuilleton* seems to have changed the rules of an old game.

A scream rings out from an upper story of the ramshackle boardinghouse. These modern-day "Nanas" toss cigarettes aside, clutch at their bags, and race through the crowd. Somewhere nearby, the Forty-Second-Street Ripper skulks in the shadows, savoring his success. The women know they are close on his trail, badges and guns tucked in the pockets of their fake-fur garb. Unscrupulous in their response to demands for more women on the screen, network executives have given us the ultimate in vice, the ultimate in vulnerability: john-duty with a Ripper on the loose. Viewers grow used to the curious collusion of police and policed and change the channel. No one, except possibly the cops in question, who really want to be detectives, complains that john-duty degrades the women in the policing profession.[2]

Such scenes evoke no surprise because we know these strategies are now commonplace on the red-light beat. Yet, the recent excursion of metropolitan police into the dens of iniquity to nab the buyer and not just the bought set off rumblings of protest throughout the country.[3] The apparatus through which deviance could be differentiated had changed its hierarchy of norms. We might say that its field had simply been enlarged, for the prostitute's lot has remained a tarnished one throughout our century. Her movements continue to be a subject for study—by passers-by, vice squads, medical inspectors, psychologists, and academics. Her position in the crime world remains a privileged one, and the stigma attached to her, hardly alleviated by the supposed sexual permissiveness of the 1970s, has only become more pronounced in the wake of AIDS fears.[4] Nevertheless, she continues to maintain a kind of order in a society that has long saved face by looking the other way, and the discourse circulating around her depends on that order to avoid accountability. To arrest those she taints is to acknowledge that the excesses she exudes remain unchecked by the strategies that would quarantine them. Placing a cop in her shoes not only threatens the men who depend on her discretion, but also upsets a balance of power dating at least from the late eighteenth century, which requires that whatever is marginal, abominable, or uncanny be identifiable and easily relegated to its proper place. Yet, such a ploy also tallies the account of a discourse that stretches back to Augustine and makes visible the ways in which that discourse has asked her for special services.

If the ubiquity of television crime tales, rising crime rates, and anxiety about sexually transmitted diseases have spurred a new concern with vice and the mechanisms we use to control it, the literary profession has hardly remained outside the intrigues. Studies in the crime and mystery novel have proliferated.[5] The underside of the literary canon—from domestic melodrama to scandal sheets—has escaped relegation to the domains of social history and sociology of culture. We have gazed profitably at the ideologies of the perpetrators of disciplinary technologies, at the way they impose discipline, and at the way these strategies have infiltrated the networks of the culture that produced it. However, we have remained frequently one-sided in our concerns with policing mechanisms that require (if we accept Foucault's appraisal) the policed to participate fully in the disciplinary technology that engulfs them.[6] Our preoccupation with the powerful in these ideological maneuvers has regularly aligned us with the perpetrators of repression, as if we might share in the discourse of the nineteenth-century reformers who depended upon the maintenance of order from the bottom up even as they imposed order from the top. We have learned to see how we are all put under restraint, but we have seen few of the responses to those restraints.

I propose an inquiry into the objects of these disciplinary mechanisms, into the networks established between these objects and those who govern them, and into a discourse that inevitably taints those who try to contain it. In the following three chapters I explore the discourse that surrounded the prostitute and its connection with other nineteenth-century plots of containment in order to investigate a collusion between nineteenth-century fiction and the prostitute. This first chapter produces testimony on a series of encounters between the novel and the *fille de joie*, played out over the tumultuous years of the July Monarchy and surrounding the publication of Eugène Sue's *Les Mystères de Paris*.

In the first part of this chapter, I look at the discourse of regulationism, what I call the discourse of *tolérance* because it depended upon an elaborate system of closed spaces in which prostitutes were compelled to circulate: brothels (called *maisons de tolérance*), prisons, where unregistered prostitutes were sent if they were caught, prison hospitals where from 1836 on prostitutes were sent when they were found to have *visible* signs of venereal infection, and refuges, where prostitutes were encouraged to reside after they withdrew from their trade. In the latter part of this chapter, I turn to the novel that explicitly appropriated the concerns of this tolerance system. Sue's *Mystères de Paris*, arguably the most popular novel of the nineteenth century, not only thematizes the circulation of women through the prostitutional system of the July Monarchy, but it also elaborates a critique of that system and explores ways of transforming it. The powers appropriated by the popular novel and perceptions of those powers will serve as a means to examine the struggles for meaning in which the nineteenth-century novel was engaged. Central to my argument, as my reading of the discourse of *tolérance* will show, is an analogy between nineteenth-century disciplinary systems and the novelistic discourse. I argue that the tolerance system and the novel alike engaged in a moral economy that depended on complicity between delinquency and the networks that sought to police it. And as my reading of Sue's novel will demonstrate, that moral economy was racked by paradoxes that simultaneously impeded change and promoted it.

Throughout this chapter, I attempt to engage the prostitute as a way of gaining access to the positions through which nineteenth-century discourses of containment could be transformed. She has left us few traces, little writing, certainly no novels of her own. The writings of the regulationists, like the asylum reports of the *aliénistes* we see in chapter 4, do little more than recycle her silence. The texts of novelists like Sue, Hugo, Dumas fils, Frémy, Balzac, Méray, Soulié, and Sand, all of which we consider in this book, find varying ways of appropriating her position and procuring her voice. Images of her world, proliferating in the late nineteenth-century work of Manet, Degas, and Toulouse-Lautrec, have distanced her from the shadowy spaces of *tolérance* where one could not even be sure what a prostitute might look like, and, certainly, one could not be sure what visions she might evoke. Even the few texts in which prostitutes supposedly recounted their stories—for example, the 1830 "protest" documents examined in chapter 2—smack of a sensationalism that casts doubt on their authenticity.[7] We will not find memoirs of women who escaped the tolerance system and lived to tell its tale. But throughout the nineteenth century, I argue, we find the traces of women who fought that system, women whose lives were somehow structured by the existence of such a system, women who could not—no matter how honorable they claimed to be—escape the ravages of *tolérance*. These are the texts through which the prostitute's own story can perhaps begin to be heard.

Ordo Occultus Rerum: *The Traffic in Women*

"The prostitute is, for me, an impenetrable mystery," wrote the socialist-feminist Flora Tristan in 1840 in a diatribe against the social conditions that exposed women to this "most hideous of afflictions."[8] Even as she wrote these words, others were seeking to penetrate that mystery, to insinuate themselves into the "horrible unknown regions" of the closed societies of crime thriving in their midst (*MP*, 31), so as to emerge, triumphantly armed with "useful lessons" (*PD*, 2:586). With an almost fanatic intensity, peculiarly characteristic of the scientific researchers of their era, the investigators of the July Monarchy plunged into the world of the "barbarians" in their midst (*MP*, 31). Doctors, police agents, philanthropists, and journalists turned a deaf ear to the public outcry against their pursuits and demanded to know "what exists" (*PD*, 2:586). Conditions of female degradation alone could not satisfy these indefatigable cataloguers of manners. "In order to know the good that remains to be done, to enter successfully onto the path of improvements, . . . it is necessary to know the truth," wrote Alexandre Parent-Duchâtelet as he concluded his momentous study of prostitution (*PD*, 2:586).[9]

Prostitution had become a central issue—if not *the* social issue—by the early years of the July Monarchy. The estimated numbers of clandestine prostitutes in Paris grew from the prefect's guess of nine thousand in 1820 to twenty-two thousand in 1831 and to another observer's estimate of thirty-four thousand in 1850.[10] Closely regulated since the time of Napoleon, prostitutes met with new sanctions in the last years of the Restoration. The administration's attempts to clamp down on unregistered prostitutes resulted in a sharp increase in the number of registered prostitutes, new registrations, and officially sanctioned brothels.[11] The cholera epidemic of 1832 had focused attention on the relationship of prostitution to disease. An increased medical understanding of syphilis and gonorrhea led to merciless crackdowns on those who did not make their required regular visits to the police dispensary doctors. For the investigators who sought to quantify, classify, and regulate it, prostitution united a set of vital concerns: poverty, disease, criminality, and debauchery. At the same time, it provided a closed circuit of spaces in which its practitioners could be observed. Because women believed to be prostitutes lost their rights under the Penal Code, investigators could penetrate their interior worlds without warrants or hearings. Their police records, their houses, and their bodies were at the disposal of any man who could muster the "right" proof of his interests.

No one gained more privileged access to this world than Parent-Duchâtelet, author of the study of prostitution that would influence a century of theory and regulation of prostitution. Parent, as his contemporaries called him, became a figurehead in the public health movement and a martyr to its cause. His statistical research earned him the nickname the "Newton of Harlotry" and a place among the fathers of modern social science.[12] Trained as a doctor in Napoleon's Paris, Parent had abandoned medical practice for the study of "moral hygiene." A respected member of the Paris Health Council (*Conseil général de salubrité*), he joined alienists Étienne Esquirol and C. C. H. Marc, physician Louis-René Villermé, and toxicologist Mateo Orfila in 1829 to found the *Annales d'hygiène publique et de médecine légale*, a journal that led the field for decades with its analyses of public health issues.[13] By the early 1830s Parent's studies of water pollution, sewers, dissection rooms, and longshoremen's diseases had made him an esteemed "physiologist of excretion."[14]

In 1827, according to Parent's own account, he turned at a friend's request to investigating prostitutes. His friend had hoped to help "those prostitutes whose hearts were not yet entirely perverted" to escape "disorder" and repent (*PD*, 1:3). Parent's work would take him far from these noble goals to the study of "a cesspool of another kind"—one he called "more vile than all the others" (*PD*, 1:7). Though he never abandoned the exhilarating belief that his work could help its subjects, Parent wound up producing a blueprint for their more efficient repression. About the same time as his friend died, leaving him alone in his humanitarian labor, Parent was asked by Brazilian bureaucrats to document how the Parisian police administered their regulation of prostitutes. Suddenly he found himself plunged into a flood of surveillance data, medical cases, registration information, and arrest reports. His two concerns—helping prostitutes repent and recording the workings of the Parisian *Bureau des moeurs* (Morals Police)—merged into a single quest. Parent sought the cooperation of the police of the *Bureau des moeurs*, of prison supervisors, of hospital attendants, and of dispensary doctors who performed the required examinations on registered prostitutes. Assiduously gathering whatever information he could obtain, Parent gained access to the private world of Paris prostitution. The study he completed only weeks before his death in 1836 combined the statistical data of years of research with a theoretical justification of the current regulatory system. His two-volume work challenged the current regime to reassert the fundamental regulationist project of collecting all *filles* into closed *maisons de tolérance* where they could ply their trade under the watchful eye of the police. What had begun as an allegedly charitable proposal for the reform of prostitutes became the guidebook for those who wished to hold them fast in the regulatory system.

That system, commonly referred to as the system of *tolérance* after the houses where the police compelled prostitutes to reside, was already fully institutionalized by the time Parent began his research. Ministerial directives and police circulars had woven a tight web around the prostitute, progressively denying her civil rights, freedom of movement, and especially self-determination. Under the Directory, Consulate, and Empire (1795–1814), police decrees demanded that all women practicing prostitution submit to regular medical examinations at their own expense. During the Empire and Restoration periods, the police kept lists with increasing efficiency and were thus able to keep an eye on suspected prostitutes and to arrest those who failed to appear for medical inspection. By 1823, when the police commissioner circulated an order to the prefects of each Parisian district asking them to encourage the establishment and existence of brothels, the tolerance system had become fully established. "The police would believe it had done a great deal to advance morality and public order if it succeeded in enclosing prostitution in tolerated brothels, which it could act upon constantly and uniformly and which could not escape its surveillance," wrote the commissioner in a paradigmatically panoptic gesture.[15] If prostitutes could be convinced to sign up with the *Bureau des moeurs*, make their regular visits to the dispensary, and live in tolerated brothels under the strict watch of the police, then no one would have to worry about disease or disorder. If prostitutes policed themselves, then the police would not have to worry about falsely imprisoning "honorable" women. If prostitutes would simply learn the rules and help enforce them, they in turn could help the police bring other aberrant groups in line. In the utopic form Parent and his followers gave it, the tolerance system gained its power from the uncanny collusions it enforced between the prostitutes of Paris and the police who ruled them.[16]

Parent's study made three major contributions to the *tolérance* system: it powerfully demonstrated the uses of statistical analysis for knowing and controlling groups of people; it described in detail the current workings of the regulatory system and made proposals to improve it; and it elaborated the theoretical framework for that system. Even more important, Parent led the way for other excursions into the "vile cesspool" of prostitution. F. F. A. Béraud, a former police agent in the Restoration Morals Police, supplemented Parent's work from a legal perspective in 1839. Honoré-Antoine Frégier, a departmental head at the Prefecture of the Seine, adapted Parent's methodology to a broader sphere—*Des Classes dangereuses de la population dans les grandes villes* (1840). Dr. Ariste Potton extended Parent's work to Lyon in 1842. Alphonse Esquiros, in his *Les Vierges folles* (1840), took issue with the proposals of his predecessors but nevertheless adopted Parent's statistics to bolster his demands for improving the lot of prostitutes. Others followed, offering their investigative tools to society in a self-congratulatory gesture of martyrdom.[17] Some observers applauded, heralding Parent's methodology as the inauguration of "a new era in this science."[18] Others, like the literary critic Jules Janin, were shocked by the audacity of these new social scientists:

> In his *Histoire de la prostitution publique*, Mr. Parent-Duchâtelet, the learned gentleman who, out of pure charity, lived amid filth, that rigid Port-Royal Christian who lived out his whole life in haunts of ill fame out of sheer virtue, tells us that in order to perfect his frightful knowledge of Parisian vice he was once taken to

a house where five-score ladies of the night were sleeping promiscuously with thieves on a great pile of rags gathered from all the garbage heaps in the kingdom. Mr. Parent-Duchâtelet saw it; he tells us so; and we must credit him.[19]

Despite public embarrassment, moral outrage, and disgust, Parent and his followers did receive "credit": they had discovered and documented "the truth."

This new preoccupation with "urban barbarians" played directly into a proliferating discourse of fear—of the city, disease, political agitation, criminal violence, the lower classes—as the bourgeoisie saw "the unknown" overflowing the boundaries of the criminal districts. However, this obsession with "urban barbarians" also secured force and influence by means of new strategies of analysis and infiltration, observation, and quantification. The new breed of explorers learned to transform the inhabitants of this mysterious republic of crime into objects of knowledge. Most remarkable, these investigators found ways to obtain the participation of their objects. The prison and the hospital, eventual stopping-points for most *filles publiques*, offered privileged vantage points from which to amass data on their family history and choice of occupation, to document their physiology, and to investigate "what is happening in [their] souls" (*PD*, 1:17–24, 104).

Parent's detailed analyses of the prostitute's body, psyche, and manners make it all the more surprising that in his enormous evaluation of the committed prostitute he never recorded his own conversations with any of his subjects. At most, prostitutes are accidentally overheard. Usually, however, their words are recounted as hearsay derived from those who manage the enclosures in which the prostitute dwells. Ultimately, she never speaks for herself. Parent was no oral historian of "lost girls." Rather, he was a scientist, intrigued by the possibility of using his new tools to reach a territory fouler than the sewers: "In collecting and editing all my materials, I have done my utmost to arrive at numerical results on every point that I undertook to consider" (*PD*, 1:22).[20] Statistics imbued him with the voice of authority, legitimated his intrusion into the spaces of infamy, and ratified his summary judgments. He collected his numbers in places where no one else wished to go but in a way that anyone could respect: from the *Bureau des moeurs* he solicited names and files; from prison-heads and chaplains he collected "brand-new information of the greatest interest." Doctors, guards, and selected informants verified what he had learned in the prisons; doctors, nurses, charity workers, and "a few intelligent pupils" gave him hospital tales. Accompanied by doctors or police officers, he observed "the houses in question" (*PD*, 1:17–19, 21). His inquisition reached only so far as specially gifted *mangeuses*[21]—never to the objects themselves.

The distance Parent maintains from his objects, even as he catalogues minute details of their habits and tastes, lends credibility to the stories he tells and grants importance to the discourse only a professional investigator could appropriate. No one else is equipped to obtain *useful* information from the prostitute. No one else has the perceptual tools to discover what differentiates her from other women. No one else can penetrate the privileged spaces of her internment and obtain the cooperation of eager informants—among them the most moral of the lost. Codified and classified, she can now be collected and segregated.[22] Invested with quantifiable meaning, she can now be possessed through stereotypes. Her private world has been penetrated and made public; yet it remains no less mysterious or intriguing than before.

The mystery of the prostitute seemed to lie somewhere other than in what could be measured by statistics and eyewitness reports. Most of the studies that followed Parent's persisted in the certainty that these women, lurking on the margins of society, represented a danger that required more thorough study.[23] Each set out to supplement the others. Each claimed to have new evidence that could unlock this tantalus in which one could see clear forms but for which no key could be found. Three factors seem to have generated this dilemma: (1) The investigations did not provide the researchers with evidence that might have enabled them to differentiate prostitutes from "honorable women"; (2) they consistently failed to explain the needs and motives that led women into prostitution, enabled them to adjust to it, and allowed them to disengage themselves from it; (3) and, furthermore, these investigations failed to locate the *order* to which the prostitute belonged. In what follows, we look at how these stumbling blocks affected the results of the investigations and, in turn, the theories that defined the tolerance system. A close look at Parent's study will enable us to analyze the paradoxes that racked the regulationist project. Although Parent's work cannot possibly stand in for the voluminous nineteenth-century discourse on prostitution, it offers a privileged perspective because of its centrality to that discourse and also because of its importance as a reference point for the very workings of the tolerance system.

The Prostitute's Difference

At the height of a series of crackdowns on street solicitation toward the end of the Restoration, a proposal surfaced that prostitutes begin to wear a costume to help clients and police agents to identify them on sight (*PD*, 1:361–62). Widespread protest forced the abandonment of a plan that, as Parent explained, would have "infect[ed] public spaces with the mobile signs of vice" (*PD*, 1:362). Instead, the police, like Parent, promoted a system that would allow prostitutes to slip unnoticed among the general populace. Carefully draped and decently covered, *filles publiques* would be indistinguishable from *femmes honnêtes* to any but the most knowing observer.[24]

The dilemma for the police as well as for Parent resided in the contradiction between their desire to be able to differentiate prostitutes from other women and their wish to keep prostitutes as invisible as possible. In order to arrive at the utopian moment where the prostitute would elude all but pertinent glances, investigators had to be able to identify the woman they wanted to single out for special invisibility. And even before that, they had to decide who they were actually talking about. Like the moral economists who would follow them in the field of social science,[25] these researchers based many of their claims upon unsupported or unexamined premises derived largely from preconceptions and fantasmatic notions. Parent's definition of a narrow field of study, *les filles publiques* (as opposed to women who engaged in other kinds of sexual exchange), remained shockingly vague. At best defined by their mobility and clientele, *filles publiques* were differentiated from *les femmes débauchées* in that the latter represented "the passage from an honest life to the state of abasement of a class that separates itself from society, that renounces society, and that, through scandalous, brazen, and constantly public habits, forswears that society and the common laws governing it" (*PD*, 1:26–27). *Filles publiques* were the repeat offenders in the eyes of the law, yet nowhere do we learn what constituted grounds for arrest or how one might identify a *fille publique* in order to arrest her.[26] Despite Parent's insistence that subtle distinctions existed between degrees of debauchery, his evidence does not grant him support for more than a few random stereotypes.[27] In fact, he was all too frequently constrained to admit that in temperament, habits, dress, attitudes, and physique, prostitutes were as varied and as unremarkable as other women. Even those women given over to what Parent viewed as the "abominable vice" of lesbianism showed no particular identifying features (*PD*, 1:222). Outside of the prostitute's routinely syphilitic state, her health proved remarkable. She even appeared less susceptible to the nervous disorders afflicting her bourgeois peers (*PD*, 1:261–62).

Investigators worried even more about their discovery that these women were as likely to seep back into the midst of honorable society as to remain either in the streets or in correctional institutions. Prostitution, the researchers were obliged to conclude, was only a "transitory state" (*PD*, 2:16). Unless these "dangerous elements of the vicious classes" (*CD*, 1:44) were placed under surveillance by an entire corps of social servants, their excesses would contaminate the whole of society. "They return to society . . . they surround us . . . they insinuate themselves into our houses and gain access to our homes," wrote Parent in terror of women who would slip unseen out of prostitution (*PD*, 2:18). Despite his humanitarian claims, Parent shied away from any plans to reform the degraded.[28] Although their statistics and observations had granted investigators like him power over their objects, that power was only sufficient to reinforce a myth of marginality. The lack of clear guidelines for identifying future, present, and past offenders accentuated the fragility of the laws this scientific discourse would impose. Somehow, these investigators were convinced, prostitutes must be compelled to participate in the discourse that would screen them from those they endangered. The prostitute thus had to be forced to mark herself or risk previously unthinkable penalties for her refusal to come in from the shadows of clandestinity.

The Prostitute's Desires

Parent attributed the women's seduction into prostitution to a series of misfortunes: poverty, low wages, abandonment by lovers, and loss of parents; however, he could produce no direct causal links (*PD*, 1:99). Instead, he fell back on age-old stereotypes, backed up more by the circumstances of the trade than by evidence: "Laziness can be placed at the top of the list of determining causes of prostitution; it is the desire to procure pleasures without working" (*PD*, 1:91). One has to wonder how this implacable detective, circulating among his informers in prisons and hospitals, arrived at a conclusion that he himself concedes is "proverbial." Perhaps not surprisingly, he ignores this deduction in his plan for refuges for repentant prostitutes as if the recognition of their abominable state (already a marked attribute of the women he observed in prisons and hospitals) comports with it a submission to the work ethic.[29] What Parent seems to lack—despite the choice language of the above pronouncement—is a verified documentation of the prostitutes' *desires*. Although the prostitute *is* the question, she cannot be a speaking subject in the discourse that surrounds her.[30] Like the charity workers and nuns whom Parent believes are diverted from hard facts by a self-indulgent blindness, the prostitute cannot escape her marginal status to join in the clamor of a disciplinary science. Others on the inside must speak in her place. We cannot assume that "modesty" alone motivated Parent and his followers to ignore the nature of the prostitute's involvement with her clients. While those clients' own status defines her, Parent makes no attempt to refine that definition with the aid of statistics on services performed.[31] What, indeed, separates such potentially useful data from Parent's unabashed specifications of the size of the prostitute's clitoris, shape and state of her anus, and regularity of her menstrual cycle? Nothing, it seems, menaced the authoritative discourse more than desire.

"Where there is desire, the power relation is always present," Foucault has insisted, since the desire of one conditions and effects the desire of the other (*HS*, 81). To depict the prostitute as *desiring* and not simply as wanton, unstable, and susceptible to "ardors" and "transports"[32] implies objects of *her* desire— men who must themselves desire, men like the calculating investigators except that they do not go to brothels "always accompanied by an inspector,"[33] men whose needs lie outside the reign of authority and beyond the propriety of Parent's articulations. In fact, Parent addresses those needs only in the hypothetical case in which they might be *unmet* by prostitutes. For the investigator to depict her as desiring implies that the investigator himself might desire—her or anyone else, as he probes the recesses of her body with his metal speculum.[34] His investigation can only be carried out in the pristine margins of desire because the desire that circulates in and around her body is perceived as tainted. If the factmonger concedes its existence, he will also be conceding the possibility that his facts have been drawn into that orbit. He might even be conceding that she, too, enjoys power.

The Prostitute's Order

The language of the regulationists betrays an obsession with order: Parent advanced his proposal for improved *maisons de tolérance "in the interest of morals and the preservation of social order."*[35] Clandestine prostitution had to be suppressed "in the interest of sanitary surveillance as well as of good public order" (*PD*, 1:353). Although many held that the prostitute should be abandoned to her syphilitic state in an effort to let "the order of things" stand, Parent took issue with the belief that "it sets a good example when vice itself is seen to punish vice" (*PD*, 2:41). Too many could be contaminated by that vice. Syphilis, lesbianism, and "disorder" could spread too easily into all reaches of society.

In order to prescribe methods of surveillance that might bring this "unstoppable torrent" into "the line of duty" and ensure "passive obedience to the regulations of the police," the regulationists were obliged to identify not only the influences that made the prostitute an "inexhaustible source of disorders, of misdemeanors, and of crimes," but also the characteristics that had disposed her to this marginality.[36] Parent was more intent upon cataloguing indications of disorder in her past and present state than in defining the disorderliness itself. Her frequently "ignoble" origins, in households themselves marked by "disorder," predisposed her to a disorderly life even before she gave herself up to prostitution. At best we might derive from his statistics and summaries a notion that this "disorderly" past implied no more than sexual relations outside of marriage (*PD*, 1:90, 94–95). Vile seducers and libertines are cited as parties to her initiation into "debauchery," but we find almost no mention of abandonment and betrayal by "normal" men. Unlike the girl with a bent for immorality, those who were "really honorable" would surely always find someone who would take an interest in them, find them a job, or pay their way home (*PD*, 1:94–95). Girls might be seduced by other prostitutes or *maîtresses de maison* in hospitals, boardinghouses, or cafés, but only "a certain kind of girl" would be prone to seduction (*PD*, 1:94–95; 90; 490; 533ff). Such a girl was imagined as independent, needing movement and agitation so much that she abandons herself to a "derangement of her passions" and to "all the excesses of a dissolute life."[37] Parent dodges the specifics of these women's disorderliness, contenting himself with evaluating at length the problem of syphilis and the surveillance that might diminish it. We learn at most of the prostitute's drunkenness and quarrelsome nature, her inability to maintain a "fixed abode" or save what she earns. She is depicted as disorderly in and of herself—and, therefore, as threatening to "honorable women" and young girls from whom she should be rigorously segregated (*PD*, 1:362–63; 2:422–24). In fact, Parent would have us believe that disorder does not dwell in any other part of society outside of unregulated prostitution—with one exception: the Revolution. It, too, generated "disorders" and, indeed, led to further "disorders" on the part of prostitutes (*PD*, 1:291–92).

While clinging to silence on issues that might actually evoke this sex object's sexuality, Parent steadfastly evades any implication that *her* disorder might be related to other disorders in the society at large. No, he tells us, advanced civilization has not given us this ill, for the "barbarians" of the Middle Ages, the "uncivilized" peoples of America and Africa, and the provincials of the countryside have also shared it. Even when he admits, "No doubt that our social conditions are the cause of the ruin of many girls; but these same social conditions procure for others the resources they would not otherwise have had and enables them to preserve their honor and practice the rules of virtue" (*PD*, 1:99), Parent exonerates his own social "order."

Throughout the texts of the regulationists, we find the same disavowals: no one and no social order can be held responsible for the prostitute's situation. One would think that the prostitute engaged in debauchery without a partner— or at most with partners as prone to libertinage as she. While Parent conjures up images of the wanton student and the irrepressible professional libertine, he nevertheless appeals to society to check the spread of syphilis into the *family*. Facts betray what he would happily leave unsaid: "We will obtain . . . the sad evidence that married and mature men are not sheltered from these illnesses and that they have almost always contracted them with prostitutes" (*PD*, 2:44). The state therefore has a responsibility to the wives and children of these men whose desires are treated with more tact and more understanding than those of the libertine. Although Parent's study focuses on ways to check prostitutes' excesses, the overflowing desires of these family men are considered inevitable: "The administration . . . cannot make men virtuous; it cannot correct their judgment and repress the impetuosity of the passions, which speak too loudly to leave men conscious of their duty" (*PD*, 2:47–48). No one so much as whispers that something might be amiss in that bastion of order, the bourgeois family or, worse, in the social order that marginalizes women by means of low salaries and untenable working conditions before they have had a chance to find their places in it.

A yet more radical disavowal marks Parent's conception of the prostitute's place in the social order. Although he claims to take issue with the current belief that, in his words, "prostitutes are necessary, and . . . they contribute to the maintenance of order and tranquility in society," he spends an entire section of his work amassing evidence of just such a necessity (*PD*, 2:525). Though he shrinks from an explicit conclusion that society might *need* prostitutes by insisting on the ubiquity of prostitution in society, his analysis nevertheless points in another direction. What would a man do, he asks, if the fear of illness turned him away from the prostitute's door?

> He will not appeal to courtesans, indeed, but will instead pervert your daughters and your servants; the most innocent and the most virtuous will be the ones he will choose to besiege and against whom he will use every imaginable means of seduction; he will bring trouble into households; he will bring misfortune to a throng of fathers and children, and in turn to all of society. (*PD*, 2:45–46)

Because uneducated and lower-class girls are most prone to enter into prostitution when seduced by a libertine, to bar the man from prostitutes would only "multiply the number of these unfortunates and precipitate beings who otherwise would have remained innocent into the most dreadful abyss." His more elevated conquests would be disposed to turn to abortion and infanticide, if not to suicide as well (*PD*, 2:44–46). The logic of this scenario leads to an affirmative answer to the question, "Are prostitutes necessary?," yet this is an answer Parent will not openly express.

Rather than admitting that prostitutes are indispensable to the social order, he appeals to his readers to acknowledge that

> prostitutes are as inevitable, in an agglomeration of men, as sewers, garbage-heaps, and refuse-dumps; the conduct of the authorities ought to be the same with regard to one as to the other; its duty is to watch over, to diminish by all possible means the inconveniences inherent in them, and, certainly, to hide them, to relegate them to the darkest corners, to make their presence as unnoticed as possible. (*PD*, 2:526–27)

Fearful that he has not sufficiently justified a regime of *tolérance*, he answers his detractors with one of Augustine's examples of the "secret order of things" (*ordo occultus rerum*):

> What is more sordid, more miserable, more shameful and dishonorable than the condition of prostitutes, of pimps, and of all the other plagues of the same kind? Cast prostitutes out and passions will disrupt everything. In this way, therefore, these people have, with respect to their morals, a completely impure life, but the laws of order assign them a place, albeit the vilest of places.[38]

Only at this point does Parent declare openly what he has elsewhere evaded: the prostitute is a repository for violent passions; she can be neither *given up* nor *fixed up*. Like the sewer to which he compares her, she is polluted once she has been used. Though Parent tries to draw a boundary between the prostitute and the men who use her, he can assign her neither an order nor a disorder in and of herself. To avoid positioning her in relation to what is *proper* to him, Parent launches her into a *secret* order where her lack of propriety has its place.

Nevertheless, this displacement cannot diminish the enigma the prostitute poses in the first place. She remains disquieting because even when contained she profits from the incontinence of men. Even though she personifies disorder, she also preserves order by satisfying potentially disruptive desires. Because she threatens the social order from its margins with disease and degradation, she must be brought under surveillance. Because the salary she earns by selling herself tempts other women to seek the same "pleasures," she must be required to come under the power of the state and to share her earnings with those who want to clean her up. The "correction" provided by this administration of discipline will not, however, repair her for life in the social order. Her duty, like that of a nun, necessarily lies elsewhere—it is to the *useful* profession she has elected. If she would serve, she must participate in the moral economy that seeks to govern her industry. If she opts not to serve, she will be referred to an order that will press her even more vehemently into duty. She is, in short, delivered into the social sphere that requires order, economy, and obedience so that she can be still more marginalized from it.

Because investigators like Parent-Duchâtelet and the Morals Police could not differentiate the prostitute from other women, they provided her with the means to differentiate herself. Because they could not express *her* desire, they implanted her even more fully with theirs. Because they could not locate *her* order, they created one to contain her. Ultimately, they endowed her with differences, desires, and an order other than those articulated by Parent. Yet no one spoke of what she *got*, for that lay, like her, on the margins the reformists so feverishly patrolled. Although the regulationists circumvented the issue of the economy in which the prostitute participated, they remained deeply concerned with it, for, inevitably, it became their own. Their attempt to award her a *social economy* through which they could prevent the waste of resources she occasioned could not also provide her with an *economy of the body* that would eliminate the wasteful use of her body.[39] At best, they could target her as a privileged object of knowledge that might be transformed into a strategic point of support for their assaults on other unproductive elements in their midst. They gave her a *moral economy* in which their good would become her reward.[40]

We would be mistaken, however, to read Parent's opus as a diatribe against unrestrained sexuality or as a prescription for repression. As both Foucault and Jacques Donzelot have suggested, the theoretical apparatus of the nineteenth-century reformists was far more complex, comprehensive, and calculated. Reformism was located somewhere between the overburdened state and private initiative in coercive mechanisms that would give both a measure of control over what threatened their interests. It also had to assure its targets that they, too, would reap benefits and share in control. Donzelot locates the family as the space making these transformations possible by reabsorbing potentially disruptive individuals and conveying the state's norms into the private sphere. Yet as the family gradually embraced the autonomy and duty with which the reformists endowed it, it became a repository of fears and demands increasingly in conflict with the desires invested in it.[41]

The prostitute thus served as an ideal "local-center"—a place where a discourse of investigation as well as subjugation could mediate conflicting interests in this process of transformation.[42] She threatened family values, yet she was a direct product of them. She threatened the state, yet she was necessary to prevent a threat to the family. She embodied everything that could potentially thwart state reformists: sexuality, poverty, disease, criminality, and subversion. She represented, at least nominally, all the groups threatening bourgeois ideals—the working class, the "dangerous classes," revolutionary insurgents, domestic help, and women who did not remain within the boundaries of duty.[43] In a sense, the prostitute was seen as even more marginal than the most heinous criminal because she could be neither suppressed nor reformed.

Foucault has shown how the nineteenth-century state fostered forms of delinquency and invested them with power. The panoptic system he described continues in the twentieth century to thrive on "controlled illegalities": arms and drug trafficking still serve to draw other illegal practices into a field where supervision and manipulation become possible. Well before the French Revolution of 1789, the police had called on informers and *agents provocateurs*. Beginning in the early nineteenth century, the police built up clandestine police forces to infiltrate political parties and workers' associations. The police also promoted a network of tolerated prostitution that enabled it to gain a hold on other potentially aberrant bodies.

Prostitution emerges for Foucault as a "characteristic" development in the manipulation of delinquency: "police checks and checks on the prostitutes' health, their regular stay in prison, the large-scale organization of the brothels, the strict hierarchy that was maintained in the prostitution milieu, its control by delinquent-informers, all this made it possible to canalize and to recover by a whole series of intermediaries the enormous profits from a sexual pleasure that an ever more insistent everyday moralization condemned to semiclandestinity and naturally made expensive" (*DP*, 279–80). I would argue that prostitution was far more than "characteristic" of the uses of delinquency. Nineteenth-century prostitution became paradigmatic for the condoned illegalities used to assimilate and differentiate other illegalities. It became the nodal point of a struggle to develop mechanisms of power in those marginal to power and a struggle to defuse the power of those marginals.

Prostitution does not serve as the basis of the era's most radical developments in the social sciences by some quirk of fate. The prostitute could be made an accessory to every crime against nature, against the family, and against the state—adultery, homosexuality, bastardy, infanticide, abortion, rebellion against parental authority, theft, alcoholism, refusal of the work ethic, and political insurgency. No other social element could present so many dangers or prove so costly to the state. No other element could so threaten the boundaries between the familial and the sexual considered so necessary by Donzelot to the consolidated interests of the bourgeoisie and the liberals.[44] Yet, no other element could be so useful in the implementation of a policing network that would maximize collective and individual forces.

In the body of the prostitute, reformists lodged the moral economy they believed could protect them from the specters lurking in urban poverty. Yet the basis of that moral economy was deceptively tenuous in spite of the massive research and concentrated effort it required. Unlike other "criminals," the prostitute was a known quantity who could easily be contained, segregated, and observed. However, one aspect of her remained inexpressible and unquantifiable, for she could also be desired.

Filles perdues *in the Panopticon: The* Maison équivoque *of the Novel*

The nineteenth-century French "popular" novel comes on as the *fille perdue* of the literary canon. Strictly differentiated from "good" literature, defined in relation to the market economy that encouraged its proliferation, and denounced for its refusals of literary and political order, the *roman-feuilleton*, along with its maligned romance cousins—*romans noirs, romans d'aventure,* and *romans sentimentaux*—has been treated as a conduit of excesses that neither readers nor scholars should approach without scruples. Like the *filles publiques* investigated by Parent, the literature that "the unsophisticated reader has chosen for pleasure"[45] offers a facile escape to those it captivates. It turns its tricks at "the right moment" in order to give the *most* for the *least.*[46] Cheap thrills and easy gratification characterize its means and mode as it entraps undiscriminating buyers and leads them to satisfaction. Popular melodrama at its best manipulates its reader, achieving closure by routing all desire[47] and sending its consumers on to other, perhaps more productive, pursuits.

Like the streetwalker, the *roman-feuilleton* and its melodramatic relations resist censorship and repression,[48] confronting observers with the unrestrained desires its readers bring to it. As a result, such texts have been sentenced to relative obscurity in the pages of literary history and left largely to the study of social historians and sociologists of popular culture. Scholars have sought in popular literature an access to knowledge about the people depicted in them, but they have too frequently read these texts as representations of a transparent social reality. They have sought an account of those who read them, but they have too frequently taken the appeals of a text for a blueprint of its actual workings. The nineteenth-century "popular" novel did far more than just appeal to the people. It did more than simply reflect the problems of the people. Rather, it was transformed *by* the people and offers not only a means to gain knowledge *of* them, but an access to *their knowledge* of themselves.[49] By reconstructing the ways a text tendered readings in the context of the readings given to it, we can begin to write a new history of the workings of those texts. "Popular culture," Stuart Hall has argued, "is one of the sites where the struggle for and against a culture of the powerful is engaged."[50] Like the prostitute, the "popular" novel served as a local-center that mediated conflicting interests. It was a transfer point for relations of power. And even as it bolstered and anchored the strategies of the powerful, it exposed the conflicts inherent in those practices.

The most popular *roman-feuilleton* of its day, Sue's *Les Mystères de Paris,* elicited almost as much moral outrage in the 1840s as the prostitutes investigated by Parent-Duchâtelet. Like the regulationists of prostitution, these critics were not so much concerned with the economic conditions of the production of such texts as with the results of their widespread diffusion. Their deepest concerns revolved around the moral turpitude of what Balzac called a *littérature bâtarde,*[51] and the debauchery it might engender: "Contemporary literature has acted as *provocatrice* to the public spirit; in all things it has deliberately flattered evil passions and exploited dangerous changes. . . . It has played the role of those nameless women whose depravity is encouraged by the industry that exploits it."[52]

The troubled book market of the 1820s had given way, under the July Monarchy, to demands from an increasingly literate public. In the 1830s it sought to reach a wider audience and to gratify the tastes of the largely self-taught working classes. Enterprising bookdealers and publishers cultivated the urban readership whose "rage to read"[53] made it the perfect target for new distribution techniques, mass advertising campaigns, and cheaply produced literature. From 1830 on, books appeared in installments in magazinelike installments (*livraisons*). In 1836, with the publication of *La Presse*, book publishers turned to cheap newspapers as a means to reach a wider public. Instead of depending upon subscriptions, these shrewd businessmen drastically lowered subscription costs and single-issue prices to a level affordable even for many day laborers and turned to advertising to cover publishing costs.[54] Serial novels became the means to attract and keep a large circulation, and despite Balzac's contempt for their maneuvers, his own *Vieille Fille* was the first to appear in *feuilleton* form.[55] Writing serial novels became good business for more than the successful entrepreneurs. Sue's *Mystères de Paris* earned him 26,600 francs. His next novel, *Le Juif errant*, brought him one hundred thousand francs. When the conservative *Journal des débats* began running Sue's *Mystères* on June 19, 1842, it sold three thousand copies the first day, ten thousand after a few days, and tens of thousands during the course of its sixteen-month appearance.

With that kind of readership—and money—at stake, it is hardly surprising that the novel Sue had originally planned as a two-volume work grew to more than ten. Even then, readers as "reputable" as Victor Hugo, George Sand, and Alphonse de Lamartine, expressed their appreciation of Sue's work and critics dreamt of an endless version of the novel: "If I were King Louis-Philippe, I would give an annual income to Alexandre Dumas, Eugène Sue, and [Frédéric] Soulié so that they might continue forever *The Three Musketeers*, *The Mysteries of Paris*, and *The Memoirs of the Devil*; there would never again be a revolution; France would just read newspaper novels."[56] Others, however, were not so sanguine about the effectiveness of such novels as deterrents. They saw these works not only as products of aesthetic "prostitution" but also as corrupters of the masses, threats to the moral fiber of the nation, and, worst of all, invitations to revolution:

> First striking society at its triple foundation: religion—which it replaced by the free satisfaction of carnal appetites; morality—which it broke down by attributing vices and crimes to fate or society; and the family—by proclaiming the equal liberty of spouses, Mr. Eugène Sue finished his work by exciting the working classes to the most terrible of all wars, social warfare. . . .

For twenty years, in every form and in every novel, Mr. Eugène Sue has by degrees inoculated the people with these ideas, these calumnies, these excitations, these calls to revolt and to war.

When on June 24, 1848, society had to defend itself against the most formidable of insurrections, what did these people say who attacked it with a superhuman courage? They said and thought what Mr. Sue had said and thought. They were putting his novels into action. Tired of suffering and of working, they came, arms in hand, to reclaim their share of pleasures and bliss: Didn't God, according to Mr. Sue, create man to be happy, and if he is not, isn't it society's fault?[57]

The conservatives' complaints were little more than a response to the claims the working class made on Sue and his writings. The dandy who was converted overnight to socialism had hardly intended to appeal so widely to such an audience. Nonetheless, as later commentators have noted, the writer who (according to legend) had intended initially to refuse the project because he didn't like "what is dirty and smells bad," rose to the task put to him by an impassioned audience and eventually blundered upon his "mission."[58] In the third book he offered a Fourierist utopia. Beginning with the fifth book, he reveled in long, moralizing lectures and no longer apologized for scandalizing his audience. He disguised himself—playing his hero Rodolphe disguised as a laborer—and haunted *tapis-francs* (dives) and *garnis* (boardinghouses).[59] Not surprisingly, one of his correspondents compared him to the social scientists of his era, referring to his exploration of "this heredity of crime whose horrors had already been revealed in the learned works of Parent-Duchâtelet and Monsieur Frégier."[60] Sue garnered a following that seems to have embraced the whole of Paris, rich and poor. Letters poured in, offering him advice on how to deal with his characters—particularly Fleur-de-Marie—and begging him for help and money. One worker even hanged himself in the vestibule of Sue's home, leaving behind a note that declared: "I am killing myself out of despair; it seemed to me that death would be less hard if I died under the roof of the one who loves us and defends us."[61]

The dialogue around this novel, from the aftermath of 1848 to our own day, has been largely concerned with its role as the novel of the "people." From Marx and Engels' claim that the text was an "ideological hoax" to V. G. Belinski's critique of Sue as a "sensationmonger," to Antonio Gramsci's evaluation of the novel's appeal to the working-class imagination, and to more recent attempts by Marc Angenot, Umberto Eco, and Marcelin Pleynet to uncover the ideology of the work, critics have focused primarily on one question: How could a novel with so many reactionary implications so successfully take in the working classes that they would rise in revolt against their oppressors?[62] The answer to that question lies somewhere between Jean-Louis Bory's claim that "February 1848 was the irresistible saturnalia, laboring classes and dangerous classes mixed together, across the Paris of *Les Mystères* and of the heroes of Sue" and Foucault's contention that novels like Sue's sought above all "to show that the delinquent belonged to an entirely different world, unrelated to familiar everyday life." We will not find the answer in the novel's descriptions of the working classes, or in Sue's letters from his adulating fans. Rather, we will find it in the novel's *practices*, for they expose what Stuart Hall has called the "double movement of containment and resistance" that seems inevitably to transpire on the "battlefield" of popular culture.[63]

Sue's works so worried the Second Empire government that it taxed him out of circulation and into exile. His *Mystères du peuple* (1849) was repeatedly seized and banned and its publishers sentenced to prison. The earlier *Mystères de Paris*, by contrast, survived the July Monarchy unscathed, despite critiques holding it responsible for every imaginable ill. Sue's *roman-feuilleton* about the Paris underworld may well have been the most closely watched uncensored novel of the nineteenth century. Nearly every critical study of the 1840s and 1850s places it at the top of a hit-list of dangerous fictions. Yet it was allowed to circulate into all levels of society and into the hands of all kinds of readers. In this respect, it resembles the controlled illegalities put in motion by panoptic discipline. Despite its declared subversive agenda, it was drawn inexorably into the service of a government of censorship that feared this novel almost as much as it despised the working-class agitators who claimed to see themselves mirrored in its pages.

Although such a government, along with Sue's conservative contemporaries, may have seen *Les Mystères* as a flagrant attack on bourgeois values, its "ugly facts" were in reality the *exposed facts* of the public courts, the police reports, and criminal trials. "Artfully and cleverly dressed up and aided by the depraved pencil of an artist skilled in depicting the sensual and the horrible" to "fearfully stimulate the animal propensities of the young, the ardent and the sensual," facts as much propelled Sue's project as they had that of the regulationists.[64] The sensations of the serial novel were the same as those of the lawmakers. The criminal heroes of the broadsheets had become the messengers of those wielding power. The "ideological control" effected by the late eighteenth-century literature of crime had simply been rerouted. While the earlier "scaffold literature" ostentatiously justified justice as it glorified criminality (*DP*, 67–68), this later literature performed its maneuvers in apparent clandestineness.

The surreptitious manipulation effected by Sue's work was not, however, what worried the majority of Sue's critics. Rather, they lashed out at what Sue called "the power of contrasts" (*MP*, 32)—at Sue's juxtaposition of alluring charms with sequences they saw as shockingly immoral. The journalist Alfred Nettement imagined a scene of seduction with compelling repercussions. Sue, he wrote, had found a way to lure the curious into his novelistic scaffolding, "He made of his book not quite one of those infamous houses (*maisons infâmes*) where no one dares tread, but one of those questionable houses (*maisons équi-voques*) where many people still go, taking care not to look beyond appearances, because, after all, as long as one does not have delicate tastes, one has fun there" (*EC*, 1:332). Nettement's comparison of Sue to an architect of *maisons équivoques* suggests the complexity of the new genre's operations. In one sense, Sue *was* a "new Restif de la Bretonne," looking at his century "through the keyhole of a wicked bordello"[65] and tempting others to follow him into abysses of sin and crime. In another sense, however, Sue was a regulationist reformer consciously following in the steps of Parent, recording the statistics of the netherworld and offering solutions to diffuse its danger. His novel, originally bearing the subtitle "or the Converter," began as a kind of vigilante scaffold and ended as a kind of *maison de tolérance*. If it succeeded in converting either its characters or its readers, it did so not because of the laws it pronounced so loudly from beginning to end, but rather because it joined forces with *both* the police and the policed of a society that had moved beyond scaffold spectacles to panoptic surveillance.

Behind the conversions achieved by *Les Mystères de Paris* and behind the strategic alliances designed to put the prostitute in her place stands a complex modality of power for ordering and knowing bodies. Foucault has proposed Jeremy Bentham's Panopticon as the model for "power reduced to its ideal form" (*DP*, 205), for it discreetly enlists its prisoners to put themselves under surveillance. The panoptic apparatus achieves its success proportionate to its ability to hide its own mechanisms, and it works upon the little things through which it cunningly gains a hold on larger bodies (*DP*, 138–40). It is intentional: it names targets and seeks out points of support to forestall resistance—yet, it *will* generate resistance, not outside itself, but from everywhere within.

The effectiveness of the uses of controlled illegality derives from this very process. By investing the prostitute's body with particular meanings, the nineteenth-century state elicited and contained resistance. Through a careful enlargement of the powers of the prostitute, other bodies could be attracted into her field. Through an enlistment of the prostitute's participation in policing mechanisms, the subversive potential of other elements could be defused. The nineteenth-century *roman-feuilleton*, however, exposes the paradoxes in such a paradigm and gives us a view of the ways in which panopticism could lose its hold. I have chosen Sue's *Mystères de Paris* for discussion because it explicitly thematizes the concerns to which, as Foucault would say, the Panopticon was an answer and for which it became a strategical program. It also thematizes the concerns answered by the *maison de tolérance*. As the most popular *roman-feuilleton* of its day, it provides a literary model of disorder and excess not only in the context of its own rambling structure, but in terms of its political and moral interactions as well. Finally, it purports to undermine the undisciplined elements of its content and structure alike by means of lawless invocations of the law, moral appeals to its audience's desire for intrigue, and invitations to a debauch that might impose a new order. Its conflicting signals thus make it a likely space in which to see modifications in power relations that escape the ideally functioning paradigm proposed by Foucault.

Sue's novel is far too naïvely scaffolded to present anything like a coherent strategy of discipline. It incorporates too many of the public's own demands to participate wholly in the ideological controls that strive for a clear separation between the body of the policer and that of the policed. It remains too conscious of the regulation of informers either to serve as an informer itself or to induce its readers so to serve. However, in the tensions between the novel's overt strategies and covert tactics, between its direct attacks and its oblique manipulations, between its defined moral economy and its implicit ordering of mysteries, between its consoling closure and its errant middles, transformations are played out indicating that the matrix of the nineteenth-century power structures through which power and knowledge are produced might be even better represented by the *maisons closes* of *tolérance* than by the modern penitentiary.

Foucault's choice of the Panopticon as a paragon for contemporary disciplinary technologies derived from a historiographic operation that privileged one paradigm in order to expose the workings of others. As Michel de Certeau has suggested, other technological practices existed alongside these privileged panoptical ones. These other practices may well lack the coherence of the "final formation or 'full' form" of panopticism. They may not "organize discourse itself." They may not possess a space of their own. Instead, these other practices may "merely persist, preserving the premises or the remnants of institutional or scientific hypotheses that differ from one society to another." They may even exist as *part* of a coherent series of practices, colonizing an institution such as the Panopticon with their silent resistances. De Certeau has posited the existence of such "tactics," operating "in the place of the other," and against the strategical power of the dominant classes. Through such an opposition between dominant *strategies* and the resistant *tactics* that gradually come to replace them, de Certeau gives us a compelling model for imagining social change.[66]

Foucault's claim that discourse not only "transmits and produces power . . . but also undermines and exposes it, renders it fragile and makes it possible to thwart it," (*HS*, 101) holds forth promises he was unable to realize in his work. "Resistance," he wrote only a few pages earlier, "is never in a position of exteriority in relation to power" (*HS*, 95).[67] Foucault's panoptic strategies are forever recuperating the moments of resistance they themselves elicit and produce. De Certeau's critique of Foucault allows us to imagine *oppositional practices* that are not recuperated by dominant power structures. It allows us to imagine movements beyond panopticism, investigations in which we do not find ourselves in the tower watching ourselves confined below.

The tactics imagined by de Certeau perform metaphorically, inhabiting the space of the other (the object of knowledge, Foucault might say) without possessing it and exploiting this shift in place without losing themselves in the process. De Certeau takes pleasure in imagining that the novel effects just such tactical maneuvers even as it narrates the arts and practices of everyday life.[68] The tactics of popular culture "fool" the order of things and make it the "field" for their subversive action. They derive their arts from its power. The discourse surrounding the prostitute seems to have grown, in this way, out of the same *mentalité* as the Panopticon to become both the dominant perpetrator of ideological control in the nineteenth century and the guarantor of its own displacement. Unlike the Panopticon, the *tolérance* system is racked by paradoxes, by tactical maneuvers that constantly threaten to displace it. Because it explicitly evoked desire, sexuality, and roles of gender and class, it created a series of oppositional discourses that threatened to topple the disciplinary structures on which it was based.

My goal here is not to find a better paradigm for understanding nineteenth-century power relations but rather to imagine how those power relations mutated. If the Panopticon has served us, through Foucault, as an enlightening vantage point through which to see a paradigm shift (between spectacular discipline and more discreet uses of power) and as an ideal model through which to see our own connections to the most egregious uses of power, it remains nevertheless *ideally* all-consuming. It obscures any view to its overhaul or to its subversion precisely because its power both as a theoretical model and as a model prison depends on seeing all its subjects entranced. When nineteenth-century disciplinary power discovers the usefulness of delinquency, it exposes the fragility of the power relations on which it is founded. The significance of prostitution as a model for controlled illegality does not derive, as Foucault suggests, simply from the *profit* the police (and society) reaped from these delinquent bodies. Rather, in the tolerance system we see the power of panopticism at work as well as the fragility of that power. What made it *necessary* for the police to collude with prostitutes—what made it perhaps even necessary for prostitutes to ally themselves with the police—derived from the delicate moral economy on which tolerance was based. In that economy, panoptic surveillance was not enough. Someone or something always seemed to be slipping out of bounds. The subsequent nineteenth-century authorization of the powers of delinquency was tactical, in de Certeau's sense, and it in turn empowered tactical maneuvers that could not be recuperated by police power.

Foucault suggests that even these maneuvers—even the resistance of abolitionists, philanthropists, and feminists—were part of that power, generated to defuse revolutionary demands, strategically produced to draw momentum from those tactical maneuvers. I am not convinced. This is where Foucault's "non-subjectivity" of power becomes problematic. For, as Nancy Fraser suggests, Foucault's discourse makes it hard to differentiate illegitimate and coercive forms of power from those that do not involve domination and enslavement. If everything is within power and no one can know who is dominating whom, then we can neither know who is resisting nor who is submitting.[69] The system of tolerance forces us to know—and see—just that.

While the Panopticon blinded us to its potential failures, its analogue, the tolerance system, has a specific *history* that reveals how it has participated in power relations and how it has prepared the field for their mutation. Portions of this book specifically address those changes. Other portions take the negotiations around *tolérance* as a model for examining other containing strategies—the asylum system, the hysterization of women's bodies by the nineteenth-century medical profession, the nineteenth-century novel, and the censoring discourse that surrounded it. This book imagines a field of power relations where resistance is not contained, where social change occurs, where *subjects* stake out claims to a space in which to express their desires.

In the remainder of this chapter I look at the way the novel appropriates the paradigms of tolerance, the way one novel in particular explicitly evokes and thematizes the tolerance system and mimes its workings. Sue's novel—because it is both about tolerance and *in* its model, struggling with and against panoptic discipline—shows us how the tolerance system adopts these normative disciplinary strategies and how it authorizes tactical maneuvers within and through them. Because its theoretical field so closely resembles that of Parent-Duchâtelet's system, *Les Mystères de Paris* gives us a privileged view of the ways disciplinary systems were put into practice, transformed, and displaced. Because we have so much evidence about the way Sue's novel was received, we can also begin to imagine how a disciplinary system like *tolérance* maintained its force and generated resistance.

Women Inflamed: Eugène Sue's Charitable Intrigues

When Emma Bovary discovered her new husband could not initiate her into the *"mystères"* of passion, she turned instead to literature: "In Eugène Sue, she studied descriptions of furnishings; she read Balzac and George Sand, seeking in them imaginary satisfactions for her own desires."[70] Already she projected her dreams of romantic fulfillment and fantasies of adultery into the pages of these works that would supposedly lead her astray. Although Gustave Flaubert made Sue's novels into upper-class furniture catalogues beside the more sensual appeals of a Balzac or Sand, when Emma did give herself over body and soul to adulterous passion, her partner's name was Rodolphe—the same as the literary alter ego of the man who died the year *Madame Bovary* appeared in bookstores.

During the July Monarchy critics credited women with the success of the newspaper novel. Some moralists worried that novels like Sue's would corrupt these otherwise "pure" women who flocked to public reading rooms to devour segments of *Les Mystères de Paris*. Others lambasted Sue for sacrificing propriety to please an especially corrupt audience. These women, Charles-Augustin Sainte-Beuve contended, were already inflamed, and Sue *knew* what they liked:

> I imagine that Sue wanted to see—in a sort of wager—just how far this time he could lead his pretty readers . . . and whether the great ladies would not recoil from the *tapis franc*. . . . He speculated well; some mysteries of this genre have their allures, and occasionally they inflame: *"Quaedam feminae sordibus calent,"* Petronius said energetically of the noble Roman women of his time. "Those women get inflamed by filthy things."[71]

The filth Sainte-Beuve thought had inflamed nineteenth-century women was the story of a girl, registered as a prostitute at the police *Bureau des moeurs*, and her seemingly endless trajectory through an underworld of lower- as well as upper-class crime. If the novel heated women up, it did so at the expense of lower-class women who had entered the profession of heating up men.

To listen to nineteenth-century critics, when women of their era had nothing to do, they read novels of intrigue and committed crimes of passion. To listen to regulationists of prostitution like Parent or Béraud, when men had nothing to do, they went whoring. Statistics bear out these fantasies in uncanny ways. In 1840 there were 189 registered *cabinets de lecture* in Paris. Women in particular flocked to these spaces to rent books and newspapers by the sitting for less than the price of a kilo-loaf of bread.[72] Of the estimated three hundred thousand "potential readers" James Smith Allen has counted in Paris during this period, an astonishing percentage could actually have read a novel that sold as many as ten thousand copies a day during its sixteen-month appearance.[73] While we cannot know how many of these readers may have been women, we do know that the rise of the *roman-feuilleton* corresponds directly to a marked increase in literacy among women and the working classes.[74] In the days when "nearly all of France was occupied . . . with the adventures of Prince Rodolphe before going about its work,"[75] women ventured into public reading spaces, frequently created *by* women with women's pleasure in mind.[76]

At the same time as the police were registering the reading rooms that made the new genre of *feuilleton* novels accessible to the masses, the vice squad also set about registering brothels. The number of official *maisons de tolérance* grew throughout the July Monarchy from 198 in 1830 to 235 in 1845, decreasing gradually after the 1848 Revolution.[77] At the end of the July Monarchy thirty-four thousand prostitutes were estimated to be working in Paris.[78] Even if each of these prostitutes had only ten clients, their total "audience" would have been larger than the potential readership of Paris. If literature kept the women busy, the prostitute may well have occupied the men. And as useful as novels and prostitutes seemed in containing desire, both nevertheless produced excesses and thereby generated further attempts at containment.

Les Mystères de Paris not only attracted swarms of adulating female readers, it thematized that attraction and put it in terms that inextricably linked the prostitute and the idle *bourgeoise*. The mysteries of Sue's gigantic novel posed, in fact, as direct offerings to women. They were also, however, presented as the means through which the idle housewife might redeem herself from romance. This novel explicitly serves up its mysteries as alternatives to a number of less productive activities—among them the reading of novels. The first fictional *roman policier* delegated the duty of detection to its female characters and posed them as models for a "police of virtue" (*police de la vertu*). The sordid mysteries of Paris were deployed for their investigation.

"Reward the good, pursue the bad, relieve those who suffer, probe all the wounds of humanity in order to try to wrench several souls from perdition, that is the task that I have given myself" (*MP*, 1116). Sue's hero Prince Rodolphe de Gerolstein sets himself a task that sounds like a description of policing in the era of the Panopticon. In a defense of the novel against its critics, Sue insists that his novel seeks to embrace precisely the same mission: "We are one of the most humble, but among the most convinced, propagators of these two great truths: That it is the duty of society to prevent evil and to encourage and reward the good however that may be possible" (*MP*, 705). The concurrence of the novelistic project and its protagonist's quest in a single *"pensée morale"* (*MP*, 705) lets Sue delegate the novel's social responsibility to its represented agents. If Sue can legitimate the uses of power by the philanthropic prince, he will likewise justify the narrative mechanism that not only makes those uses possible but *depends upon them* to achieve its own goals. Ultimately, then, the novel generalizes a self-promoting disciplinary power by investing it at every level. Not only will Rodolphe carry out this program of rewarding and punishing, but each meritorious figure assembled in the novel's panoptic gallery will join its forces in search of even more sublime rewards. Thanks to this confederation of the virtuous, the novel's disciplinary power is disseminated everywhere—in the bars of the underworld, in the households of both the aristocracy and the working class, in the marketplace and the workplace, in the prison, in the boardinghouse, in the city police force, in the pastoral country farm, in the hospital, in the insane asylum, in the distant colonies of America and Algeria, in the institutions of charity, in the crowd at a public execution, in the convent, in the government of the German state, in the family, and also in the spaces of prostitution.

Sue's novel condemns the *law* that dishes out an inegalitarian, hypocritical, and duplicitous brutality, but it substitutes a justice that is no less crafty in spite of all its accessibility:

> JUSTICE should hold a sword in one hand and a crown in the other, one for striking the wicked, the other for rewarding the good. The people would see that even when there are terrible punishments for evil, there are dazzling triumphs for good; whereas now, in their naive and primitive common sense, they vainly seek the judgments of the courts, jails, galleys, and scaffolds. (*MP*, 645)

Though the present criminal "justice" system masquerades as singular, unified, and consistent (*MP*, 991), it double-deals, victimizing those who cannot afford it (*MP*, 510, 978), extracting a "tax on the soul and the body" from the poor (*MP*, 617). The "justice" this text puts in its place will ostensibly no longer perpetuate cleavages between the rich and the poor, the thief and the murderer, the adulterous victims of arranged marriages and the criminals who entrap them in those arrangements, the child of the guillotined and the child of the prince. Rodolphe's dispensation of justice according to the true leanings of the heart will supposedly erase these contrasts. What Christians dream of attaining in heaven can, we are told, be achieved on earth, in a utopia that remunerates virtue wherever it may be unveiled.

Such a system needs envoys, go-betweens, proctors, informers, and secret agents to accomplish its mission of consolation and salvation. It solicits the collaboration of a veritable army of surveillants and none too discreetly promotes them as "spies of virtue" in the tradition of the state police apparatus. Even as a replacement for the delinquent-producing injustice of institutionalized "law," this "radical" model abides by the latter's rules. Sue's narrator contends that just as "society" had imagined the surveillance of the "high police" in the interest of incessantly controlling the conduct of the dangerous classes, the delegates of an "ideal justice" will engage in a "surveillance of high moral charity"—a tutelary vigilance designed to enlist the exemplary advocate in every sphere (*MP*, 679). Although all virtuous souls drawn into this struggle will be endowed with the power of observing, identifying, differentiating, hierarchizing, excluding, and reforming their fellow souls, they will never become plenipotentiaries of disciplinary power. They can administer the law, but they cannot make it. Nor can they make the ultimate decisions about who should become objects of this justice. They can solve mysteries, but they cannot determine what mysteries are fit for solution. In short, the law will always be invented elsewhere and, with it, the criteria that make certain "mysteries" profitable, expedient, and desirable.

In his zeal to procure champions for his new religion of detection, Rodolphe goes so far as to fantasize himself as a kind of proto-Emma Bovary:

> If I had been a woman (and between us, I fear I would have been both very charitable and very flirtatious [*légère*]), the day after my marriage, I would have assumed the most mysterious demeanor [*les allures les plus mystèrieuses*] in the most innocent possible way.... I would have artlessly enveloped myself in the most compromising appearances [. . .] in order to be able one day to visit my poor ... or my lover. (*MP*, 417)

It is precisely upon these "allures" that Rodolphe will capitalize in his attempt to transform the best of his potential converts.

In order to ruin the one woman Rodolphe secretly loves, his scheming first "wife" Sarah has staged an adulterous liaison between the bored and misused wife of the Marquis d'Harville and a man for whom her "impassioned charitable interest" might have fatal consequences (*MP*, 280). Rodolphe, who has managed until now, out of friendship with the marquis, to resist his attraction to Clémence d'Harville, overhears the scheme and understands. He has already learned about Clémence's near-fall at the boardinghouse where he has recently rented a room. Now he manages to substitute for the spectacle of adultery a new scene, this time one that is indeed charitable. The marquis's suspicions are eliminated; Clémence is saved. Yet Rodolphe must still redeem Clémence and set her upon a new path.

"Judge my life! Judge my cruel deceptions!" she begs him as she shares the "fatal secret" of her husband's epileptic condition, the "horrible *mystère*" that has made her marriage an "odious union" as she suffers from "that cruel contrast between what is and what seems to be" (*MP*, 409–13). Because Rodolphe has an almost preternatural understanding of women, he knows that "love's greatest charm is the enticing attraction of forbidden fruit" (*MP*, 415). Without the fears and the dangers inherent in adulterous affairs, *he* knows there would remain no temptation. What women like Clémence need, then, is that excitement provided by mystery, for mystery, in this novel, is always somehow forbidden fruit.

In reforming Clémence, Rodolphe sets himself a task that will tenuously meet the conditions of his program for justice, except that he will be rewarding the good and pursuing the bad *through* Clémence as well as *in* her. She will be his vicarious means to console the suffering and save souls from perdition, and she will do so by saving her own soul, as Rodolphe explains in terms of what he "knows" are women's needs:

> If I find the way to make you feel these fears, this anguish, these anxieties that entice you, if I use your natural taste for mystery and for adventures, your penchant for dissimulation and trickery (there you see my abominable opinion of women which breaks through in spite of me!) . . . won't I change into noble qualities these imperious, inexorable instincts that can be so excellent when used well, and fatal when used badly? (*MP*, 416)

What's more, in satisfying her female taste for mystery and intrigue, he will also satisfy his own—and legitimate a "shady association" with her. They will both have access to *jouissances:*

> If you were to become my accomplice in several of these shady intrigues, you would see . . . that besides even the nobility of action, nothing is ever more interesting, more engaging, more alluring . . . sometimes not even more entertaining than these charitable adventures. [. . .] Tell me, would you like it if we wove together all sorts of charitable tricks and beneficent plots in which we would be the *victims*, as always, of very good people? We would have our appointments, our correspondence, our secrets . . . and especially we would hide ourselves well from the marquis. [. . .] If you want, we would have a regulated intrigue. (*MP*, 415–16; my emphasis)

Together they will play "at providence," *victimizing* deserving citizens as they give themselves over to "a passion so profound and so incurable, so pure and so noble all at the same time" (*MP*, 414, 419). Their "good works" will not only give Clémence a goal and distractions but will provide "*tout le piquant d'un roman*" (all the heat of a novel) (*MP*, 414).

This "*roman*" seems to share motives with the one that contains Clémence, as she herself remarks of the working-class family that has provided her access to "*une adorable jouissance*": "Poor people! their horrible misery gave him a pretext for saving me" (*MP*, 616). This "*roman*," these "mysteries," these "miseries" of the people are nothing more than a way of keeping the idle *bourgeoise* in her place.

Foucault has pointed out that one of the first figures to be sexualized as a result of the strategical disciplinary alliance of the state and the family was the one most protected from the disorder and perversion running rampant in the streets of the city, namely, the bourgeois woman (HS, 121). "It is not necessary to be a husband or father," wrote Parent, "to feel all the baleful effects of prostitution. It is enough to have a mother and to ponder how the sex to which she belongs finds itself degraded by the circumstances and the practices of prostitution" (PD, 2:526). Alain Corbin and Theodore Zeldin have pointed out that the idealization of the descendants of Jean-Jacques Rousseau's Sophie, the angel-mother of the bourgeois household, may well have rendered prostitution all the more necessary. Although the popular medical writer Auguste Debay counseled French women in 1849 to fake orgasm to obviate the inevitable "disorders" should their husbands turn to more amorous mistresses, the cult of purity that elevated the mother to sainthood necessitated quite another attitude toward sexual pleasure.[79] She was to find her *"jouissance,"* if not also her hysteria, in more productive activities, as Jules Michelet contended: "Woman is a religion . . . an altar . . . a living poetry for lifting up man, for raising children, for sanctifying the family. . . . Her maternal instinct dominates everything else . . . because, from the cradle, woman is mother, crazy for motherhood."[80] The passionate, instinctual, maternal woman was already halfway to hysteria, contended the major nineteenth-century theorists of female physiology.[81] Nevertheless, doctors, philosophers, and reformists alike presented the weakness of her disorderly nature as an innate power.[82]

In the same moves that restructured power relations around what Foucault calls the "administration of bodies and calculated management of life" (HS, 139)—the same moves that compelled occasional prostitutes to register themselves permanently with the Bureau des moeurs and to enter into regulated brothels under strict police surveillance—the bourgeois woman was invested with new powers over her own sphere. As the supreme rulers of the household, bourgeois women guaranteed familial order even as they were deprived of their previous influence outside the home. Because a "good woman" was expected to "purify all around her with her own purity,"[83] it was indeed imperative that she avoid contact with anything—such as workers or prostitutes—that might sully her. As Erna Olafson has noted, her virtues, "involuntarily displayed, could only be held, guarded, or . . . lost." Woe to that woman accused of prostitution—for she would be responsible for proving that her virtue had not been lost under any condition—whether she had been paid or not.[84] While men like Sue's Rodolphe could penetrate into the disorderly world of the city's streets and remain untainted, a woman like Clémence was obliged to retreat, in the words of a journalist of the 1840s, to "a narrow and often unhealthy prison," to which she was expected to "bring well-being, order, and joy."[85] She set the norms against which bourgeois society judged the targets of its reformism. She clarified the boundaries between the public world and the private one: "Ultimately, what she was doing was defining a society of those whose lives were structured, while the others, those outside, were perceived as living without structure, in sickness, or uncontrolled passion, or rude necessity, states that were seen as forms of disorder."[86]

Yet, as Rodolphe's projects for the marquise indicate, the ideology of domesticity, so often *actively adopted* by these women, did not exclude a missionary function. Moralists believed they had already instituted that function by giving the bourgeois woman the all-important responsibility of educating her children.[87] Beginning in the 1830s, however, and increasingly throughout the 1840s and 1850s, women returned to the streets in a role made to order for their "maternal, angelic nature." The Catholic Church already offered the auspices for their charity work, with organizations such as the *Société de la charité maternelle* (founded in 1784) and the *Société de St.-François Régis* (founded in 1826).[88] Similarly, leisured women, like those in Lille studied by Bonnie Smith, engaged in charity work according to explicit ideological norms. They carefully screened those who came to them for help, requiring not only "virtue," but also conformity to the family code. Central to their ideology was a standard by which they judged their own deeds and the deeds of their peers — indeed, the same standard that Rodolphe invokes in order to titillate the *"curiosité romanesque"* of the marquise: discretion. "It is true charity that conceals from the protégé his benefactor's identity," one *dame patronesse* wrote in her diary.[89] Smith notes that domestic novels were even based on whether such carefully concealed divine acts would finally be discovered and openly praised. Clémence d'Harville never quite gets that far; in fact, she provides for a substantial extension of the novel's "excitement" by receiving credit for charity she never even accomplishes (*MP*, 831).

From the strictly regulated charitable societies that refused fallen women and bastards to the more lenient philanthropic societies that sought to uphold the family by reaching out to its most malleable members — women and children — these groups offered the bourgeois woman new prisons to which she could spread order. The charitable societies gave gifts. The philanthropists gave advice and material aid attached to a "legitimate moral influence." The former sought out "spectacular suffering" in the midst of genuine Christian virtue. The latter pragmatically sought to moralize those whose loose ways would cost society in the long run.[90] It was not only pragmatic but also tactical for the protectionist societies to grant women a place in this sphere, as Barbara Corrado Pope explains:

> The female charity worker served her society — at least the most conservative elements in it — very well by teaching the poor how best to survive *within* their lower-class standing. Women probably succeeded in reaching more people than the men of their class because the poor did not identify them so conclusively with political power or economic exploitation. The volunteers thought of themselves not so much as purveyors of the dominant value system but as peacemakers. Fully aware of the class hatreds and the conditions that bred mutual distrust, they put themselves in the middle, mediating — often through mothers, girls, and chil-

dren—between the men of the lower and their own class. Indeed, the role of the angel on the outside was very much like her role in the home: to conciliate, to make people happy, to exemplify the moral standards of her society. [91]

Like the novel, then, and indeed less "dangerously," "good works" could serve the interests of the bourgeois family and, by extension, those of the state, by siphoning off the excessive energies of the idle matron. In the same location as the first correctional institute for prostitutes, the Salpêtrière Hospital stood awaiting those whose naturally impressionable minds could not even withstand the pressures of the private sphere.[92] The desire of the *bourgeoise* was much more usefully channeled out of the *"prostitution légale"* of marriage[93] and into prisons, out of the "narrow prison" of the household and into the havens of prostitutes.

Les Mystères de Paris not only represents this process and extols the non-fictional *"femmes courageuses"* who leave behind "chosen" society to confront the "vulgar indifference and criminal purposes of the thieves and prostitutes" at Saint-Lazare Prison; this novel even aspires to *emulate* them. The circular reasoning that saves these *bourgeoises* from crimes of passion by plunging them into the midst of crime and passion emerges as the same reasoning the novel itself adopts as a subterfuge against critical accusations of immorality:

> Without daring to establish an ambitious parallel between their mission and ours, may we say that what sustains us too in this long, painful, and difficult work is the conviction of having awakened some noble feelings for these upright, courageous, undeserved unfortunates, for these sincere Magdalens, for simple, naive decency; and of having inspired the disgust, aversion, horror, and salutary fear of all that was absolutely impure and criminal? (*MP*, 606–07)

Even as Sue's novel deploys this female detective force as a "police of virtue" in place of the *Bureau des moeurs* it so viciously condemns (*MP*, 636), it assumes the motivations of *tolérance*. Like the police who put into effect the reforms proposed by Parent, the novel's narrator remains more concerned with inspiring "salutary fear" than with actually saving those feared by the novel. Even as the narrative explicitly condemns the police registration that fixes prostitutes forever in the "abyss of infamy" (*MP*, 88, n1), its charity workers do little more than register the conditions of the degraded.

In the novel, these philanthropists function much like the police envoys of a system of tolerated prostitution: they serve the narrative apparatus by extracting the stories of those who deserve to be rewarded or punished. These accounts are the novel's answer to the economic requirements of selling its morality: the more lives it registers, the longer it can hold out and the more revenue it will generate. In this way it resembles the police informer, as described by R. C. Cobb, who must "convey the inestimable and unique value of his information, for, to be successful, he needs to prove that he has access to secrets that would otherwise be unknown to the authorities, and, in order to make money, he needs to provide a great deal of information, whatever its worth, information generally being paid for by bulk." Like the informer, the *feuilletoniste* pads his reports, claims to have undergone extraordinary difficulties to obtain information, and all too frequently provides data on characters marginal to the central "plots." To tell all he knows in one "snitch" would be to commit "professional suicide" and to risk being himself taken in by the scandalmongers. According to Cobb, "even the repressive authorities would not like it: from their point of view, too, a 'plot' must be made to last as long as possible, in order to bring in certain groups of people, one group after another, over a matter of months or of years. . . . Always some men would have to be kept over, for use later, because convincing death labels and useful categories of suspects could not be allowed to circulate for as long as [that plot] drew an audience and provoked a ready response."[94] Sue even admits that the "exigencies" of his "multiple narration" require this kind of capitalizing on postponement (*MP*, 385).

Even the immoral characters bolster the extravagant economy of narrative "exigencies" and sustain the work of extracting information. The duplicitous Cecily "had only one goal, that of incessantly inflaming the passion of [Jacques Ferrand] without satisfying it, of provoking him that way to the point of madness, in order then to be able to execute the orders she had received"—to procure the facts of his secret crimes. The double agent Badinot provides almost every address necessary to the salvation of souls and meanwhile furthers the plots of the evil Ferrand. The irredeemably monstrous Maître d'École ministers to the justice of the one who has blinded him as he equates the grill of justice with the torment of the audience of crime tales. Just as he has served his "executioner" Rodolphe (*MP*, 343) by defending Fleur-de-Marie against La Chouette, he will promote the same insurgent justice by meting out punishment to the woman who has twice wronged that girl, as he explains to his former mistress before mutilating her: "You surely feel . . . that I don't want to finish right away. Torture for torture! You made me suffer enough. I have to talk to you for a long time before killing you . . . yes . . . for a long time . . . that is going to be horrible for you . . . what agony, eh? [. . .] She will have only what she deserves . . . a profitable lesson" (*MP*, 885–86).

Like the charity whose most sublime heights it pretends not to attain, this novel dishes out lessons on exemplarity. Decidedly unlike that philanthropy, however, it does not presume to reform. None of those enlisted in the ranks of this "surveillance of virtue"—least of all Madame d'Harville—actually *rehabilitates* anyone. At best, they provide enough information to Rodolphe that he can exercise vengeance upon those who have wronged the good as they meanwhile urge those virtuous ones to find more virtue in their lot. At best, they satisfy the supreme audience for these fictions, Rodolphe, who, though he stands in judgment, nevertheless keeps his distance and, "impatient to know" (*MP*, 906) how each tale turns out, always somehow lies in wait. Even as the novel condemns the strategies of the penitentiary system, it adopts them wholesale to sell itself: "Instead of ameliorating, it worsens. . . Instead of curing mild moral ailments, it renders them incurable" (MP, 984).

The "imperious exigencies" of narration (MP, 32) require its perpetrator to take the reader to one prison after another (MP, 385); yet he depends upon that "timorous curiosity that these terrible spectacles sometimes excite"—for in this moral economy, fear alone can save. Even as the novel condemns the strategies of police *tolérance* (MP, 88, 636), it praises "the precious work of Dr. Parent-Duchâtelet, work of a philosopher and a great man of good" (MP, 88), as if Parent had not himself backed, refined, and expanded those strategies. Like Parent, the narrator believes in "the power of contrasts" (MP, 32), for once the prostitute and the criminal are registered, marginalized, and differentiated, they will become "more timorous," abandon themselves less to "disorder," and dispense with the kind of disguises that keep the pronouncers of the law safe from discovery (PD, 1:370–71).

At its best, *Les Mystères* deploys its tactics thriftily and profits as much from the tales told about crime as from the techniques of clandestine prostitution itself, described by Parent as "that which is practiced in the shadows, supporting itself by trickery, swindling, and lies" (PD, 1:492). If the prostitutes and criminals awaiting salvation are nothing more than expedients to get bourgeois women all fired up and no more than feints to contain the excesses of the upper classes, they nevertheless anchor the same "secret order of things" advertised by Parent. Yet this excitation is induced so flagrantly and these excesses are contained so ostentatiously as to make us suspect the novel has other objects in view.

The disguised prince of *Les Mystères de Paris* haunts the "foul cesspools" of the urban wilderness, himself a kind of outlaw amid outlaws. In his attempt to discover the secrets of these men with "morals of their own, women of their own, a language of their own," he appropriates their "mysterious language, filled with baleful images and metaphors dripping with blood" (MP, 31). He reproduces what makes these marginals mysterious by affecting it. He becomes like them, "hideous and frightful" (MP, 31), in order to share their secrets. He stages himself in these "terrible spectacles" (MP, 32) in order to procure the *stories* required by the "imperious exigencies of narration." He dons the guise of mystery in order to unearth mysteries.

He will not, however, perform "that moral activity that disentangles."[95] Although Rodolphe seeks the display of results "in truth," he produces that truth not in display but in concealment—in his very choice of enigmas. Instead of being revealed, those enigmas remain mysterious precisely because the detective agents who work on them do so without access to the truth they produce. The novel's lone plenipotentiary performs a feat much like that of Parent and the regulationists. He sets a new truth in the place of the impenetrable conundrums confronting him. He marks the good and the evil so they can be more easily differentiated. He invests the objects of his investigation with his own desire (even as he grants them investigative powers) and contains them in his own order, attesting to his belief in the "power of contrasts" by mystifying even more fully whatever is different, otherly, and enigmatic. In an ironic reversal, the mysteries upon which he puts his double-dealing talents to work are transformed into mysteries in their etymological sense: as coveted secrets that *cannot* be understood, as private rituals that exist to solidify bonds, and as unspeakable privileges of the initiated. Since the word *mystery* comes from the Greek word *mysteron* meaning "to close," we can infer that anyone who would divulge what he has seen (i.e., anyone who would divulge the "mystery") would be subject to justice, for such an indiscretion implicates the others sharing in the secret. Guilt is inscribed in the moment of revelation, just as it underwrites the project of the one who infiltrates the "mysteries of Paris."[96]

"I was patricidal in deed," confides Rodolphe to the monstrous woman who drove him to an attempt on his father's life:

> "Since that day, I have been pursued by an inexorable remorse. Soon I left Germany for long journeys; that was when I began to impose the atonement on myself.... Even as I wanted to aid honorable unfortunates, I wanted to know those classes whom misery crushes, brutalizes, and depraves, realizing that help given in the nick of time—even a few generous words—are often enough to save the wretched from the abyss. In order to judge for myself, I adopted the appearance and the language of the people I wanted to observe." (*MP*, 1116–17)

There amid mystery, wearing the apparel of mystery, speaking the words of mystery, and judging the mysterious, Rodolphe has discovered a mystery that reflects so much on the origins of his guilt that it is, for him, unspeakable. He recoils from it even as he pursues it with a vengeance. He appropriates it, imbues it with his powers, and evades the consequences of his appropriation. He disperses his forces to act upon it and discovers, at last, that he is acting upon himself.

That mystery takes the form of a sixteen-year-old café girl whom Rodolphe rescues in the first scene of the novel. Sent to the countryside to be reformed by Rodolphe's Fourierist emissaries, the girl flourishes, despite some lingering moodiness and the chastisement of a moralizing priest. Just as Rodolphe's plan to redeem Fleur appears to be working, her former employer, the Ogresse, kidnaps the girl and plunges her back into a cycle of victimization. Clémence meets Fleur in Saint-Lazare Prison and seeks to help the girl whom the prostitutes treat as special (*MP*, 609–10). But Clémence does not know what we have learned several hundred pages earlier—that Fleur is really Rodolphe's own daughter, born of his illicit union with the girlfriend his father opposed (*MP*, 256). Clémence's jealousy of the girl prevents her from intervening to save Fleur. Instead, Fleur sets about saving everyone around her—the working-class prostitute La Louve, the *grisette* Rigolette, the apparent infanticide Louise Morel, and, ultimately, her own mother and father who are brought together in the discovery that their daughter is not dead, as was long believed, but very much alive. Fleur's reappearance gives Rodolphe the chance to learn what we have known since the second of the novel's eleven parts, namely, to recognize his daughter, to sanctify at last his union with her mother (who promptly dies), and to reclaim his heritage, with daughter and new spouse (Clémence, whose husband has expired in an epileptic fit) in tow. Though what becomes a mysterious source of intrigue for Rodolphe and his delegates of virtue has long since been demystified, Fleur's mysteries do ultimately save Clémence d'Harville. "What novel would give me these touching emotions or excite my curiosity to this extent?" asks the charitable lady upon meeting her future step-daughter (*MP*, 616). Perhaps only a novel that knows the power of mysteries, Sue's *roman-feuilleton* seems to respond.

Those who complained that the early revelation of the family ties between Rodolphe and Fleur destroyed the novel's suspense missed the thrust of this work's entanglement with mystery. When Sue's socialist contemporary Eugène Faure remarked that "the entire scaffolding of the novel reposes . . . on this character [Rodolphe] around whom all the events enchain themselves, and all the other figures move like so many satellites,"[97] his appropriation of the language of prepanoptic punishment—*échafaud(age)*, *enchaîner*—recalls a spectacular suffering that the novel initially abets. Yet Faure's metaphor as a whole points to the panoptic nature of the novel: around Rodolphe circulate all those who are seen and judged. Like the "formidable tribunal" that irresistibly attracts the dangerous classes (*MP*, 32), Rodolphe engenders a system of discipline that virtually magnetizes the criminals whose stories it tells. Yet even more strikingly, it puts them to use. The novel *tolerates* them so that it can cash in on their take. That profit will always grow in proportion to their ability to further multiply plots, as was the case in the police informer system. Even more so, however, that profit depends on a further mystification of mystery. The novel can let the cat out of the bag and tell us Fleur is Rodolphe's daughter precisely because her real mystery lies elsewhere, and *that* mystery is the one the text invests most discreetly, for its interest lies in what is *not* disclosed.

Although *Les Mystères de Paris* recoils from the vicious uses of punishment and torture it begins by endorsing, the structures of tolerance in which it ultimately lodges its stakes are no less cruel. Like the system to which Parent's work adheres, this novel is intent upon entrapping those who register with it— either as "dangerous elements" or as readers. It will decide when they should pass from one locus of investigation to another. It will determine when they should be let loose. Just as Parent's narrative traces the harlot's progress from street to brothel to hospital to prison and, at long last, to final refuge in an almost novelistic layering of suspense, Sue's work pursues its mysteries of iniquity into each of the spaces of *tolérance*. Like Parent, who in a decidedly novelistic way begins by sketching his subjects' physique and character, proceeds by detailing their crimes and dangers, then produces their threat as a means to provide a spectacle of acceptance, resignation, and repentance, so Sue carefully plots the investigation of his central mystery. The revelation of Fleur's aristocratic background thus generates the more attentive interest of an audience that

might otherwise leave the surveillance of such figures to statisticians and po-
licemen. It justifies the *nobility* of her character in the same way that the
disorderly backgrounds of Parent's *filles* legitimate his tally of their danger. It
cannot, however, erase the past that stretches between Fleur's beginnings and
her ends. That "past" nevertheless grants tenure to the dangers of desiring.
Unless its secrets are exploded—which is done only in the most tactical of
manners—their dangerous excesses will be conserved. This text's evasion of
any such revelations upholds the same order as Parent's system, for the authority
of both is equally menaced by desire.

What remains untold in *Les Mystères de Paris* is precisely the sort of account
Parent elides as well: decisive details about the activities of the girl whom we
first see among those women "who lie in wait under gloomy vaulted porches
as deep as caverns" (*MP*, 33). Despite the conflicting testimony the text provides
with regard to her purity, no one who has analyzed the novel has ever questioned
the worst of these insinuations. What everyone infers—that Fleur-de-Marie has
exchanged sex for money—is nowhere articulated in the course of this narrative.
The novel neither gives her an explicit label nor provides undeniable evidence
of her circulation. For all of its verbosity on every other matter, with regard to
this one affair the novel keeps mum. No one—not Rodolphe, not Madame
Georges, not the reproving Abbé de Bouqueval, not her friend the Chourineur,
not the Ogresse who owns and enslaves her, not the Maître d'École who holds
keys to her past, not the Abbesse who blesses her remains, not even Fleur
herself—ever documents her acts. Outside of the reprehensions of those who
rescue her, we have little to go on that is not simply circumstantial. Even the
one damning detail, that she is *"inscrite à la police"* (registered with the police,
MP, 655), proves absolutely nothing. We know too well from reading Parent
that the *Bureau des moeurs* arbitrarily registers the suspicious.[98] Sue's narrator
himself implies that registration is the first step toward prostitution (*MP*, 636)—
more the authorization for the act than its commission. Still, we must ask why
it matters when the innuendo is condemnatory enough.

It matters, I believe, because in the system of tolerance erected by this novel
what is *not* spoken is what both preserves desire and expels it. What is not
spoken is what sustains narration and ensures the triumph of the disciplinary
system that shirks responsibility for reforming. Fleur sells as long as we don't
know she solicited. She can be punished for her "crimes" as long as she appears
the innocent victim through whom others must pay for their crimes. She must
always seem only to mediate that for which she is in fact the source and the
object. Shrouded in mystery, she surrounds the ploys of *tolérance* with shadows
in which they can play out their malicious business.

Fleur-de-Marie is the shared secret of all the guilty who inhabit this text.
She is the unbound element who must be bound—into her family, her birthright, and her past—if the novel is to end. She is the error that produces
seemingly endless deferrals, yet she ultimately confirms the right judgment of
the mysterymonger. She is the unnamed who waits for the "name of the father"

inherent in the law of this reformist genre. She is the loss produced to create a communality of crime,[99] for she focuses anger and elicits discussion. She is the matrix from which both vengeance and charity issue. Even more important, she is the exemplar of *tolerated* prostitution. Operating in the open without lies or double-dealing, she proselytizes for Rodolphe in each of the closed spaces of tolerance—the carefully watched *garni*, the hospital, the prison, and the refuge.[100] He registers her to save himself and promote his own goals, and she thereby produces more converts than all the other charity workers put together. Paradigmatically, she becomes the novel's emissary of delinquency: under the gaze of the law, she makes possible every ruse, every lie, and every shady deal the novel contrives.

She is the offering the law makes to the undisciplined for she can help them discipline themselves. She alone of all the army of virtue *actually* reforms those she encounters. She is the lone object upon whom Clémence successfully plays out her charitable novel. She binds the lawgiver to those he tries. Like the prostitutes Parent investigates, Fleur points up the tenuous links between the "dangerous classes" and laboring classes and enables the more competent disciplinarian to differentiate between them. She serves as a kind of condoned "illegality" within the text, for despite her potentially deviant past practices, she proves too useful to be forborne. As Foucault has pointed out, the kind of "controlled illegality" represented by the likes of Fleur made it possible to "canalize and recover" profits from sexual pleasure (*DP*, 280). Collusions between moralists and prostitutes fortified the structures of tolerance and reinforced police powers. However, the tolerated prostitute not only guaranteed the secrecy shrouding condoned illegalities, she also proved to be the best informer a policing apparatus could want.[101] Her natural trajectory as a prostitute is reproduced according to accidents and errors, yet it nevertheless takes her into every reach of dangerous society and makes her a chance witness of nearly every possible crime. Ultimately, her victimization makes a far better story than Rodolphe's punishment of her enemies. The tales she brings back seem far more truthful than the ones obtained by those who lurk disguised in the shadows. Yet, for all of their "truth," for all of the danger she undergoes to reveal it, she cannot and will not be redeemed.

In order for a *fille publique* to be "radiated"—dismissed from the registration rolls of the administration of *tolérance*—she must tell her story to the authorities. Everything must be done, Parent explains, to assure that she is not asking for *radiation* in order to escape "sanitary visits, the regulations imposed on her, or the danger of being locked up in a hospital or prison" (*PD*, 1:408–09). For the safety and the health of the public, it is "of the greatest importance" to require extensive formalities and proof that the woman can attain an "honorable existence" (*PD*, 1:409). Even after she has provided a marriage contract, a doctor's excuse, proof of her family's willingness to have her return, or documentation that she has a job, she must be watched for several months (*PD*,

1:409–10). Although Parent contends that "it would be contrary to justice and to good morals to want to retain [these women] on the paths of prostitution" (*PD*, 1:408), he sees few ways out for even the least hardened *filles publiques* (*PD*, 1:403ff). At best, he proposes to teach them to sew and to surround them by middle-aged female philanthropists who will make "virtue" agreeable to them (*PD*, 2:573–74)—and as far as he is concerned, they will be safest and therefore best off by remaining permanently in such enclosures. Undoubtedly, Augustine's "order" would thus be maintained. After serving their purposes—as containers for society's excesses—old whores would just fade away into sweet repentance.

Fleur-de-Marie meets quite the same end. The girl who declared that her fate came from not economizing her money is given a moral economy by both the novel and the tolerance apparatus. Although the extent to which she is tainted is shrouded in the *"mystère"* of the chagrins she won't express (*MP*, 299–300, 822–23, 1245, 1280), she judges herself enough to become the biggest selling point of the novel.[102] Later editions of the novel in translation went so far as to leave her alive for fear of cutting down on sales.[103] While the detours of narration can forestall violence with promises of a rewarding ending, violence nevertheless erupts. The charitable little girl who had neither the presence of mind to economize her prison earnings nor the sense to seek out charitable souls (*MP*, 301, 834) is finally condemned to the ultimate reaches of marginality—death—without any chance to tell her own tale.

When Fleur remembers at the conclusion of the novel "what she had almost forgotten," she does try to narrate *for* herself in order to make herself more worthy before her fellow nuns. However, the person who has the greatest investment in her silence, the father whose task so closely resembles that of the novel, will ward off this danger by invoking the shared pact of mystery: "she had understood that I was destined to share the shame of that horrible revelation. . . . She had understood that after such an avowal, they could accuse . . . me, of lying . . . for I should always have let it be believed that Fleur-de-Marie had never left her mother. . . . At this thought, the poor child believed herself guilty of a foul ingratitude to me. . . . She did not have the strength to continue" (*MP*, 1303).[104] Even guiltier for *trying* to speak, Fleur succumbs within the same day to her shame. The day of the attempted patricide becomes also the day of her martyrdom: in an ironic reversal, she dies *for* her father.

In the moral economy of this charitable work, we have learned that "the means of good and of evil are often just about the same" (*MP*, 415). If, as Rodolphe assures Clémence, "only the end differs," Fleur-de-Marie's end suggests that she belongs to the order of evil. She is indeed the only major "good" character who does not survive the narrative, and few of the evil escape severe retribution. Yet we should consider that the closure of this work does far more than punish the spent prostitute and her guilt-ridden father. In a backlash from its own disciplinary system, the narrative of tolerance is itself put on trial.

Mysterymongers and the Novel:
Taking Up with Whores

Near the beginning of Marx and Engels' *Die Heilige Familie* (*The Holy Family*, 1845)—a study of Sue's novel constituting their only full-length work of literary criticism—Engels attacks the Young Hegelian Edgar Bauer for his failure to disclose his own vantage point on the subject of the work he is reviewing:

> Herr Edgar who for once takes pity on social questions, meddles also in the "affairs of whores" [*Hurenverhältnisse*].
> He criticizes Paris Police Commissioner Béraud's book on prostitution because he is concerned with the "point of view" from which "Béraud considers the position of prostitutes [*Freudenmädchen*, or joy-girls] in society." [Bauer] is surprised to find that a policeman has a police viewpoint, and he gives the masses to understand that this point of view is completely perverse. But he does not reveal his own point of view. Of course not! When criticism takes up with *Freudenmädchen*, one can't expect that it do so in public.[105]

Like the prisoners in Bentham's Panopticon, from which Marx and Engels accuse Sue of having borrowed his principles,[106] the works upon which the Bauers speculate become "objects of information, never subjects in communication" (*DP*, 200). The works of Béraud, Sue, and even Flora Tristan become, for Marx and Engels, just so many more mysteries deployed to make way for critical judgment. Because the Young Hegelians have lavished praise on Sue's novel by elevating it to the status of Critical Epic,[107] Marx and Engels castigate Sue as a way of getting at them: Critical Critics become *Geheimniskrämer*, or "mysterymongers"[108] who speculate on the affairs of prostitutes for questionable profit. Like Marx, Engels, and those they reproach, I too have been concerned in this chapter with the "affairs" of nineteenth-century prostitutes, seeking a perspective on the "points of view" from which the investigations of prostitution proceeded. This concern has led me to question the usefulness of a model of panoptic power for thinking about nineteenth-century power relations and to insist on other vantage points from which to seek out tactical points of resistance to the strategical powers of *tolérance*. Central to my argument here has been the contention that the prostitute serves both as a source and as a compulsion of narrative and social panopticism in the nineteenth century. As a kind of vanishing point for the apparatus of *tolérance*, the prostitute is effaced when desire is successfully mediated through her. Yet she leaves behind an imprint of desire that nevertheless threatens to tumble the entire system. Within the structure of *tolérance* she anchors the perceptual grids through which other deviants are investigated and normalized. Outside of it—either because she has escaped it or because she has been expelled from it—she forces us to focus on the crimes committed on her behalf and with her voluntary complicity.

In the economy of the novel, the prostitute is indeed a *fille de noce*, as she has been called since the eighteenth century. Just as she offers the pleasure associated with the slang word *noce*, she also makes good its association with marriage. She prepares the hymen that both distinguishes between inside and outside of the text and nevertheless shows up their inextricable commingling.[109] She engages the novel in a social discourse and involves radically different social interests (the state, regulationist followers of Parent, the Republican opposition, doctors, *aliénistes*, and critics of varying persuasions) in surveillance of the novel.[110] Within *Les Mystères de Paris*, she paves the way for the weddings between Rodolphe and Sarah and between Rodolphe and Clémence (meanwhile fortifying numerous other bonds). In the one case, she enables her father to purge his guilt—even as she becomes the evidence he uses to indict and torture her mother. In the other, she serves as the *"intrigue"* upon which Clémence goes to work. Her narrative and perils bind the two justice-seekers and make possible a love that intensifies Rodolphe's dominant urges: "I love . . . all my faculties for loving have increased. . . . I feel better, more charitable. . . . However, my hatred for evil has also become more intense." That same bond, however, increases Rodolphe's tormenting pain at the loss of his daughter (*MP*, 916). When that daughter has been truly and inexorably lost at the conclusion of the novel, nothing will remain for Rodolphe except that pain-producing bond and the sense of guilt that set him on his search for mysteries in the first place. His intrigues have not, in themselves, expiated that guilt. He pursues his mystery one step further in the telling of loss: "The thirteenth of January . . . an anniversary which is now doubly sinister!!!! My friend . . . we have lost her forever! Hear this story! It is so true . . . recounting a horrible sorrow makes us feel an *agonizing pleasure*" (*MP*, 1299–1300; my emphasis). The novel, the tracing of this central mystery, becomes the penance for what must be told. It is also the conduit of a maliciously exacted *jouissance*.

The closure of a text that so resembles the enclosures of controlled illegality cannot help serving the interests of those who manipulate the tools of domination. Nevertheless, the lawless invocation of the law that destines Fleur-de-Marie to a prefabricated secret order, that differentiates her by sanctifying her, and that makes her the agent of her own demise, cannot mask the violence it triggers. Nor can it disavow the intentional nature of its cruel strategies. Just as the ruses of the evil characters in the novel have been successively exposed each time they threaten to implicate the mysterymongers, the violence of closure undermines the ploys the novel has used at the moment they seem to accede to a permanent guarantee of order. We are reminded of what the narrator told us some eight hundred pages earlier: "What was slowly killing Fleur-de-Marie was analysis, it was the incessant examination of what she reproached herself for; it was especially the constant comparison of the future that the inexorable past imposed on her and of the future of which she would have otherwise dreamed" (*MP*, 380). The spirit of analysis, we have learned, leads proud individuals to doubt and revolt against others and delicate souls to doubt and revolt against themselves (*MP*, 380). With or without the disciplinary strategies of a text or a society that condemns the first and absolves the second (*MP*,

380), the spirit of analysis that killed Fleur-de-Marie inevitably arouses both doubt and revolt. The mystification coordinated by the apparatus of *tolérance* is both the guarantee of panopticism and its most dexterous achievement. In short, to traffic in mystery is to propel the spirit of analysis to new heights. At the same time, however, trafficking in mystery elicits doubt and protests. The violence produced by mystery ultimately propagates new ends in view: out of the *Hurenverhältnisse* submitted to analysis comes a movement of feminist resistance Donzelot chooses to discredit if only because its beginnings are located in an alliance with both philanthropy and reformism.[111] Yet the feminist movement whose significant force helped bring an end to the abuses of tolerance also incited new doubts and instigated new revolts against those very groups who had initially offered the *bourgeoises* forming it paths of escape from the prison of the household.

Taking up with whores simultaneously endangered and reaffirmed the ideology that most fervently embraced analysis, observation, and disciplinary technologies.[112] To preserve itself, the apparatus of *tolérance* condoned illegalities and ultimately invited resistance. One set of novel readers put down their books to come to the aid of those contained by intrigues.[113] New alliances were forged that crossed class boundaries and took aim at different groups, as one prostitute's complaint to a feminist abolitionist suggests:

> It is *men*, only *men*, from the first to the last, that we have to do with! To please a man I did wrong at first, then I was flung about from man to man. Men police lay hands on us. By men we are examined, handled, doctored, and messed on with. In the hospital it is a man who makes prayers and reads the Bible for us. We are up before magistrates who are men, and we never get out of the hands of men.[114]

The female subculture that developed around the prostitute[115] enabled these strategists to take aim—like the reformists did before them—at an entire series of social ills. Yet, these were the ills perpetrated by those who sought to fix the prostitute in their order. Most important, however, the feminists' attempt to penetrate the "impenetrable mystery" of prostitution led to demands that implied the beginning of a new order, as Tristan so passionately declared two years before the publication of *Les Mystères de Paris*:

> Prostitution is the most hideous of the afflictions produced by the unequal distribution of the world's goods; this infamy blights the human species and bears witness against the social organization far more than does crime; prejudices, misery, and ignorance combine their baleful effects to bring about this revolting degradation. Certainly, if you had not imposed the virtue of chastity on woman without compelling man to observe it as well, she would not be repulsed by society for giving way to the feelings of her heart, and the seduced, wronged, abandoned girl would not be reduced to prostituting herself. Certainly, if you allowed her to receive the same education, to exercise the same jobs and professions as man, she would not be overtaken by poverty any more often than he. Certainly, if you

did not expose her to every abuse of power due to the despotism of paternal power and the indissolubility of marriage, she would never be in the position of having to choose between oppression and infamy. . . . Thus, this monstrosity ought to be blamed on the state of your society, and woman ought to be absolved! As long as she is subject to man's yoke or to prejudice, as long as she receives no professional education, as long as she is deprived of her civil rights, there can be no moral law for her![116]

Although it has the ring of an appealing call to arms, Tristan's diatribe does not take the place of a statement of my own point of view. Rather, it provides for a sobering afterthought as I attempt to "radiate" myself from *Les Mystères de Paris* and the structures of *tolérance*. If the moral law of Sue's novel is a bogus, counterfeit one, it has served us no less profitably as a means of putting panopticism, *tolérance*, and the narrative of mystery on trial. The final line of Tristan's paragraph makes for even more disquieting reflection: "And we can affirm that, until the day that women are emancipated, prostitution will continue to increase." Should we assume that on that day, we will all be subject to a "moral law" that we will have helped to create? Should we hope that such a "moral law" will depart completely from the laws that forced us to clamor for an end to prostitution? Or should we lodge our hopes in mysteries not explored by the *roman-feuilleton?*

The prostitute's story remains, here and elsewhere, to be told. Yet even if we found her point of view, as some believed they had in the pamphlets we examine in chapter 2, could we tell a different story? We have come here, not unlike the mysterymongers whose texts we have read, asking for names for her desire. We have occupied her spaces so that we might find our point of view in hers. Must we find, then, that the only point of view we can impute to her is that of the police who gave her their desires in order not to know hers? Would we ask her to police *us* if only to know that in her view, none of our desires would be put under restraint? Have we put on her garb only to discover that no one among us would wear chains if we could, instead, be cops?

2
Censored Bodies:

Plots, Prostitutes,
and the Revolution of 1830

*I*n April 1830, a "revolution" in morals was announced in the city of Paris. "Prostitutes are expressly prohibited from appearing in public," proclaimed Police Prefect Jean-Henri Mangin on April 14, 1830. His ordinance banned *filles publiques* from the Palais-Royal garden, long renowned as their haunt, as well as from all other gardens, passageways, and streets. Prostitutes were now expected to practice their trade exclusively in the *maisons de tolérance*.[1] Any woman who failed to observe the law would meet with severe sanctions. Rewards were promised to every inspector who discovered clandestine places of debauchery. Bounties placed on the heads of minors rapidly increased the numbers of arrests.[2] Changes were transpiring that promised, regulationists claimed, a "revolution in this important arena of public order" (PD, 1:559). For the first time in history, Parent-Duchâtelet boasted, prostitutes were forced off the streets, out of sight, and into the closed spaces of tolerated brothels. This "revolution" in morals came nevertheless suddenly to a halt in late July of 1830 when a revolution of quite another sort rocked Paris.

Historical accounts have repeatedly linked one revolution to the other. Outraged by their loss of livelihood, the pimps of the prostitutes now banned from the streets are supposed to have risen up to give force to the revolutionary cause. "Imprudent Mangin!" writes historian Guillaume de Bertier de Sauvigny, "Emotions ran high in that sphere. . . . The first riots of the revolution were to take place at the Palais-Royal" — in the very garden from which prostitutes had been banned only months before.[3]

The myth that cracking down on prostitutes was a catalyst for the political protests of the Revolution of 1830 seems to have been supported by two sets of documents: the first, a series of contemporary accounts of the liberation of prostitutes from prisons during the July Days, and the second, a set of short texts published in 1830 that constituted almost the entire pamphlet production of the July Revolution. The prison liberation stories require that one believe the so-called dangerous classes of 1830 were ready for insurrection in part because of their desire to liberate their wrongfully imprisoned *filles*.[4] They depend upon the fantasy that criminals, pimps, and the unemployed waged the revolution of 1830, moved into position by the Mangin ordinance if not mobilized directly as a result of it. The pamphlets likewise transform Mangin's "revolution" into a call for political activism. They do so, however, in ways distinctly different from those to which they have been lent by previous interpreters. While these pamphlets — of uncertain origin and unknown readership — threatened that the repression of prostitution would lead to political turmoil, commentators attributed origins, readership, and motives to them, refiguring their intrigues in already prefabricated plots. Because many of the pamphlets purported to speak in the voices of the "oppressed" parties, commentators recast their accounts as the authentic voices of prostitutes and pimps.[5] Reread through an optic of the July Revolution, these pamphlets produced a stir in the regulationist discourse of their era that continues to resonate in recent historical interpretations. Warning of a revolution to come if some "50,000 pimps" cannot go back to living off their ladies, these pamphlets have long been read as portents ignored by the Restoration state.[6]

This chapter seeks to reevaluate the relationship of prostitution to the political struggles of 1830. Through an analysis of the pamphlets and their accounts of the unrest in Paris in spring 1830, I argue that although the Mangin ordinances in no way *led* to the revolution of 1830, they evoked responses that inevitably empowered those who demanded political change. Claiming to speak in opposition to the Mangin ordinances, the pamphlets appropriated the voice of the prostitute to raise a set of broader political concerns in the turbulent weeks before the revolution. While these pamphlets mimed regulationist discourse in unexpected ways, they nevertheless played on tensions about the "dangerous classes" to open up a space in which the demands of the working classes and the disenfranchised might be heard.

The prostitute's body took a central position in these struggles because she mobilized a series of old obsessions about revolution, libertinism, sexuality, gender, and class. Viewed as marginalized, she could be made to stand in for other members of the disenfranchised classes. Seen as victimized by her gender and her class, she could be transformed into a martyr for the desires of the upper classes. Depicted as degraded, she could be associated with movements feared and hated by opposing groups. Censored, literally as well as figuratively, by laws banning her body from the stage and from the streets, she could be lent to plots that demanded the representation of all who lacked voices, any who lacked power.

A burning question of 1830 is, therefore, the starting point for my readings: What plots circulated around the prostitute? This chapter takes issue with the tendency in recent historiography to read the prostitute's body metaphorically, as a figure for all women or all marginals.[7] Rather than read the relationship of revolution to *all female bodies* through the body of a prostitute, I wish instead to read narratives that surrounded the prostitute *through revolution*. I want to see how the prostitute became a significant figure in debates over political and social change. This chapter therefore turns to the ways different interest groups used their narratives about prostitutes to make varied and frequently conflicting demands. Because a central issue of the revolutions of 1830 and 1848 was the representation of the people, each revolution was wracked by clashes over how one might put that representation into practice. In both revolutionary moments, the representation of groups hitherto unrepresented came into conflict with a series of fears about what representing women and workers might entail. The prostitute came to figure those conflicts both metaphorically and politically. Demands for the representation of prostitutes evoked aesthetic and political debates that resonated far beyond the spheres of the *maisons closes*.[8]

The following two chapters therefore contribute answers to a series of questions about representation and revolution: What representational practices are put in motion in a moment of radical change? What is the relationship between those aesthetic representational practices and the political practices at stake at the barricades? How do literary works like plays and novels participate in those political practices, and how do they assume authority in their midst? The literary works of 1830 and 1848—those read *in* the years of revolution as well as those through which we read those revolutions—stake out the fantasmatic space through which the nineteenth century conceived of social change. In order to *represent* a revolution, however, the novel or play must give it a plot—a narrative, a temporal dimension, a story.[9] This chapter therefore considers narratives about prostitution within their historical framework as debates over representation— of political interests, of people, of desires. In order to reconstruct the ways nineteenth-century revolutions mediated interests through the body of a woman labeled a prostitute, I turn to source materials that deliver more fantasies than facts: archival texts, contemporary newspapers, memoirs, critical studies, theatrical works, censors' reports, and visual imagery. By unraveling the workings of representational practices in a variety of discursive spheres, this chapter seeks to plot the possibilities for political representation in the mid-nineteenth century.

Three interwoven stories take shape here: (1) the investments of the nineteenth century in containing disorderly bodies in texts and spaces through which they could be controlled and excluded. We might call this the battle over censored bodies and censored texts. (2) the struggle over representing women— the battle over how to represent marginalized women and how to give those women a space where they could be seen and known; and (3) the struggle over how women might represent themselves despite their relegation to the spaces of censored people and censored texts. This is the story of women's activism in the nineteenth century and of its relationship to women's desires. These are the voices of the nineteenth-century subaltern speaking in the interstices of the very texts that might seem to codify their silence.[10]

In order to explore the relationship of prostitution to the political struggles of 1830, this chapter considers the discursive remnants of the police crackdown on prostitution in 1830 alongside another one of the final scandals of the Restoration, namely, the censorship battle over Victor Hugo's *Marion de Lorme*.

Like the pamphlets of 1830, *Marion de Lorme* implicated the prostitute in the tensions of the revolutionary moment. Written in June of 1829 and rejected by the state censors that August, Hugo's play bears an uncanny relationship to the frenetic surveillance of its era as well as to the myths about the Revolution of 1830. First, its censors—in the government of Charles X, in the July Monarchy audience who saw it at last performed in 1831, and among its contemporary critics—reread the prostitute's plot through the revolution. Second, this play used the interests of a woman labeled a courtesan to articulate political concerns of the late Restoration. Because this play both thematized Restoration proscriptions against people and was itself censored, it gives us a view of the concerns that linked prostitution to revolution and the overcoming of censorship to libertinism.

What emerges in *Marion de Lorme* as well as in the pamphlets of 1830 is far less a revolutionary discourse than the fantasmatic fears about the possibility of the successful uses of such a discourse. Like the pamphlets, Hugo's play sets the terms for what was at stake in the revolts of 1830 and later reactions to those revolts. The fantasies that came to surround the play's censorship and eventual performance, like the myth that Mangin's crackdowns on prostitution caused the revolution, tell a bizarre story of fears about sexuality, about dangerous literary texts, about the rights of workers and women, and about political protest.

Censored Exchanges

"One day, July 1830 will be as much a literary date as a political date," announced Hugo in his 1831 preface to *Marion de Lorme*. "Without the July Revolution," Hugo declared, "[this play] would never have been performed." But July 1830 did not so much mark the opening of the stage to this melodramatic tragedy as it seemed, in 1831, to have transformed the spaces into which one wrote and the plots one had the right to insert there. A regime of censorship had surrounded the theater for so long that people remembered the moments of freedom more clearly than the specifics of banned plays. The July Revolution promised to change all that. It vowed to transform the possibilities for literary representation as surely as it pledged new ones for political representation. For Hugo as well as for his public, these were heady days: "Now art is free: it must now remain worthy" (*ML*, 729–30).

Hugo's melodramatic tragedy about a young courtesan and her doomed lover had met with determined resistance from Charles X's censors in August of 1829. The board of censors had been presented with the manuscript of *Marion de Lorme*, as required by law, in anticipation of its production at the Comédie-Française.[11] They found it lacking on several counts.[12] First, it revolved around a prostitute, and all prostitutes had been banned from the stage during the Empire and Restoration periods.[13] Second, the portrayal of Louis XIII, with whom Marion is rumored to have been involved, was deemed politically dangerous. As one critic noted, his "incontestable greatness failed to be acknowledged."[14] Few could fail to recognize in him the impotent Charles X. Even fewer would miss the embodiment of Polignac, Charles's hardline minister, in the vicious Richelieu who swept virtually unseen in and out of the play, asserting his bloodthirsty, intransigent will.[15] Third, Hugo balked at changing his play, publicly challenging the censors and chiding them for their concerns. By the conclusion of the affair, Hugo had managed to create such a furor that the government may have felt the only way to quiet things down was to deny him a further forum in the shape of a play.

The 1829 version of Hugo's play told the story of a renowned seventeenth-century courtesan, Marion de Lorme, rumored to have consorted with Louis XIII, Richelieu, and a number of other Parisian noblemen. Even before the curtain opens, however, Marion has stopped trading on her body. Now monogamously attached to man named Didier, she has taken up residence with him in Blois, far from the pointing fingers of her previous courtiers. Back in Paris, nevertheless, her charms have not been forgotten. One of her former lovers, the Marquis de Saverny, has tracked her to her new home and tries to seduce her, unconvinced of her change of terms. By the end of act 1, he has been saved from thieves by Didier and has pledged himself to his rescuer.

The remainder of the play then turns on an ambiguous debt described by Saverny at the opening of act 2: "I had six robbers, he had Marion de Lorme. . . . My debt is enormous! And I will pay him for it with my very blood" (*ML*, 762). Saverny soon meets up again with Didier, mocks the less educated man for his stumbling reading of a just-posted edict, and accepts Didier's challenge to a duel. Whether Saverny is seeking to pay with his blood for Didier's rescue or rather to pay Didier off for stealing Marion matters very little in what follows. Though the duel is interrupted by Marion, its consequences cannot be erased: because dueling has been outlawed by Louis XIII and Richelieu, Saverny and Didier are sought by the state for their violation of royal edict and ordered to be executed. In a moment of male bonding induced by their outlaw status, Saverny reveals Marion's "true identity" to her lover, opening Didier's eyes to his own "betrayal." When the magistrate charged with arresting the duelists finds Didier, the distraught lover turns himself in, as does the honor-bound Saverny. Desperate to save her one true love, Marion meanwhile gives herself to Magistrate Laffemas in exchange for Didier's freedom. But when she arrives to help him escape, her beloved refuses to flee. Upbraiding her venomously for her past prostitution, Didier induces her confession that she has again bartered her body to free him. Merciless, Didier rejects her pleas for forgiveness. Embracing instead Saverny, who has likewise refused to accept the freedom purchased by his family's power, Didier goes to his execution.

The play was finally performed in 1831, but it was not the overwhelming success its author had hoped for. Less popular than *Hernani*, which had made it past the censors in February 1830, *Marion de Lorme* struggled to gain audience approval.[16] Its assured position in the months after the revolution was now threatened by the plethora of plays that challenged the old rules and pressed at the limits of the new government's liberties. Hugo's amazement at the freedom with which he could now stage his work marks the preface he published that summer. Everything, it seemed, had changed: the play's prostitute, its slurs on the king and his ministers, and its description of quasi-revolutionary fervor were now given free rein by the new government. Just as the Revolution had liberated prostitutes from Mangin's restrictive regime, it seemed to have freed the stage for new social questions. In the spirit of the new freedom, Hugo even wrote a new ending for his play, one that afforded Marion the forgiveness of her lover. While the 1829 version left Marion spurned for her attempts to save her beloved from the abuses of an authoritarian state, the 1831 version added several hundred lines in which Didier threw himself weeping into Marion's arms and begged her forgiveness. Her "fault" is now excused as the result of a family tragedy not unlike the one that marginalized the foundling Didier:

> If you deceived me, it was by loving too much!
> —And your fall, besides, have you not atoned for it?
> —Perhaps your mother forgot you in your cradle,
> As mine did. Poor child! when you were so young, they must have
> Sold your innocence! (*ML*, 854)

Hugo's changed plot did more than respond to critics' complaints that the original play had made Didier too cruel.[17] In a shift that responded to the changed politics of the moment, the new version allied its hero with the working classes and gave a transformed revolutionary value to his death. As a foundling of unknown parentage in a world dependent on the power of the father's name, Didier had been doomed to a life of isolation and poverty (*ML*, 742–43).[18] His relationship with Marion has, he claims, given him a destiny. "Make use of my heart and of my life," he tells her, offering to buy with his blood anything she might desire (*ML*, 743). In the 1829 version, Didier transferred this loyalty to his dueling partner, the aristocratic Marquis de Saverny. By having Didier forgive Marion in the 1831 version, Hugo gave a new valence to the heroism of his protagonist. Whereas in the earlier version Didier threw in his lot with the aristocrat rather than live through prostitution, now Didier allies himself with the plight of the prostitute to free her from opprobrium. "You will love me better dead" (*ML*, 856), Didier tells Marion before climbing the scaffold. These dying words suggest a story of heroism that the Revolution of 1830 has inserted between the writing of these two versions. Hugo seems to have learned that a dead hero has powerful currency in revolutionary memory. Alive, Didier would have been just a man. Dead, he could confer a new plot upon the living. By forgiving Marion, he has made good on his earlier offer and bought her freedom from prostitution with his blood. He has gone to his death to give her a plot like his own.

But censorship was just around the corner. On opening night the audience hissed at Marion's description of the love that had "remade her virginity" (*ML*,

860). Disappointed that the audience had misunderstood the passage that contained what he called the play's "essential explanation," Hugo now censored himself. Marion's new lines lamented her fall from sublime love into depths as vile as those of Laffemas.[19] There was no further mention of "remade virginity." The second revised version no longer insisted on the new plot that Didier's love had forged for the former prostitute. Instead, Hugo bowed to the plots of public opinion.[20]

The play's critics did not need state censorship to condemn it. As far as they were concerned, *Marion de Lorme* was *the* play of 1830. The furor over its censorship had, indeed, spurred public opposition to the monarchy. The substance of its plot, already well-known in 1829, had given rise to expectations of political change. Critics claimed its 1831 performance proved the revolution had unleashed scandals into public spaces: "We saw the poet ... in *Marion de Lorme* make Cardinal Richelieu submit to the curses of a prostitute, we saw the poet present to a whole audience of young people the dangerous spectacle of debased greatness and rehabilitated vice." For prize-winning essayist Jules Jolly, "insurrection" had been forced to retreat after 1830, but it had found a home in literature. "Riots" had been chased from the streets, but they had "changed costume and face, and taken new names," such as Romanticism, Saint-Simonianism, and Fourierism. Jolly saw Hugo as the "head of the new school," who was all the more dangerous because of his genius, which he had turned from Christianity and Royalist leanings to revolutionary sentiments. The July Revolution had changed Hugo in the eyes of his disappointed critic: "It was from that era ... that he made himself the apostle of all the doctrines subversive of the social order."[21]

That *Marion de Lorme* might serve as the basis of "a whole theater" as Hugo proposed in his 1831 preface worried critic Charles Menche de Loisne:

> What! this impure courtesan who prostituted herself to everyone, who, after having belonged to Cinq-Mars, gave herself to Richelieu, then to that this corrupt judge who sells justice, and at what a price! this Didier, a wastrel typical of our modern socialists; this imbecile king, that "red man" who passes by, they all paint a forever glorious era for France, and make up a vast, simple, true national theater through history!.... Oh! you insult our land.

This is no way to give history lessons, Menche de Loisne fulminates. More important, you cannot "moralize the people" by painting as worthy of interest and sympathy a prostitute who leaps from the bed of the victim to the bed of the executioner.[22] What worries Menche de Loisne even more is that Marion has not truly reformed:

> But what has this woman in fact done to redeem her past? Does she feel remorse? Does she drag herself, a repentant Magdalen crying to the foot of the cross? No. She loves Didier; if she regrets her previous life, it is because Didier has contempt for her: she would like to be pure to be worthy of him. It is not virtue that speaks in her, it is her love. The tears she sheds, she does not shed them on the feet of

Christ, but instead on the hand of her lover. Let Didier pardon her and she will have quickly forgotten, and without worry, without remorse, she will abandon herself to the passion that dominates her.

For critics like Menche de Loisne, Hugo's play lacked "a *conception morale.*" It cannot be enough that "love washes all stains, erases all marks." It cannot be acceptable that society pardon a *fille de joie* who falls in love with "the first man to come along." This version of morality is like Hugo's version of history— "handled with impropriety and cheek."[23]

The battle over Marion de Lorme's remade "virginity" was, as becomes clear in light of our reading of Parent-Duchâtelet and Sue, a struggle over the conditions under which a woman could be released from prostitution's ranks. Closing in narrowly on women in the months before July 1830, these structures of tolerance prevented a woman's release from servitude unless she could prove she had work, a family, a place to live, and an array of individuals ready to testify that she had already been living a new life for six months or more.[24] That a woman might redeem herself through love seemed possible enough. That she would fall a second time—even to buy the life of her lover—seemed to justify condemning her forever, as Hugo chose to do in the first version of the play. In fact, some regulationists demanded that a radiated woman arrested anew on suspicion of prostitution should *never again* be allowed to remove her name from the police registers (*FPP*, 2:156). Like Marion de Lorme in Hugo's first version of the play, such a woman was seen as unforgivable, unrehabilitated even by love, duty, or a new calling.

To be registered with the police is to fit already within a known plot. To be *inscrite* is to belong to that choice group of 3,131 prostitutes whom the police knows it has in hand.[25] It is to work for the police, with the police, under the auspices of the police. The plots of the police give meaning to a woman's inscription, even if her body and soul have not given their assent.

But the prostitute can equally circulate outside the police economy as, for example, does Marion de Lorme for whom there would have been no police registry in 1638. Such a woman might have several choices: she can be a *femme galante* or *courtisane*, the kept woman of a rich man. She can be a *lorette*, a kind of middle-class prostitute, born of the 1840s, who is kept by several men at the same time. She can be a *grisette* or needle-worker, who, like Rigolette in *Les Mystères de Paris*, has come to Paris to seek her fortune and is obliged to take up life with a student to make ends meet on her meager salary. She can be a *femme du théâtre*, like Balzac's Coralie or Josépha, would-be courtesans who stake their hopes on the stage and circulate freely in search of better roles. Or she can be just a *fille*: trafficking her body on the sly, or only occasionally, the *fille* does her best to make a living in an era of rampant poverty and below-subsistence-level wages for women. If she has not written her name into the books of the police, the *fille* is imagined to plot the destruction of all order. *Insoumise*—as she was called for refusing to submit herself to the order of the regulationist system—she always risks being brought into the plots of the police. Operating under cover, the *clandestine* always risks being recognized for what she really is or for who she has become.[26]

But who is she? And how has she become that monster of the streets tracked by the police and shunned by passers-by? What makes her circulate in the plot that names her a whore? Suspicion, for one thing. Or maybe a few well-placed slurs, carefully reported to the local police commissioner: "That woman is up to no good." "That woman takes customers into her boardinghouse room." "That woman has a lot of male friends."[27] The woman named a *fille* must, by definition, be selling her body for money. She must be giving herself over for the price of a loaf of bread, for the money to pay her landlord, for the cash to cover rapidly rising debts. Only she and her clients can really know what she is, or what she has become, or why she chooses to circulate. The police do not include her reasons in their plots. The arrest records, like the requests for "radiation," revolve around police evaluations of her situation.[28] Once they have her in their plots, *they* will decide when she can call herself by another name. They will pick the moment her plot takes a new turn. They will choose the shape of her reform.

For decades after her appearance on stage, Marion de Lorme's name will give a plot to prostitutes. In their turn, Esther Gobseck of Balzac's *Splendeurs et misères des courtisanes*, Marguerite of Dumas's *Dame aux camélias*, and even Émile Zola's *Nana* will have to circulate in relation to her plots.[29] The plots of 1830—both the literary representations and the representations of what supposedly went on in the streets that year—equally marked the real women who circulated in the real streets of Paris in subsequent decades. Just as *Marion de Lorme* could not escape the censorship that her theatrical inscription had prepared for her, the women of July Monarchy Paris would shoulder the burden of fantasies about impossible radiation, irretrievable virtue, unregenerable "virginity," and irrepressible revolutionary debauchery.

The pamphlets published in the weeks before the July Days fostered these fantasies with a vengeance. They even purported to embody the actual demands of prostitutes and pimps and to mediate fervent warnings to the police, monarchy, and bourgeoisie. Although these pamphlets marketed titillation to anyone willing to lay down the cash, they nevertheless articulated central issues in the debates over *tolérance*. Invoking the demands of workers and women alike, they mounted their own unique resistance to the tolerance system. The changes in the 1831 versions of *Marion de Lorme* suggest how much the stories the pamphlets told had marked revolutionary discourse. The critical response to Hugo condemned him as a dangerous coconspirator in the revolutionary discourse despite his willingness to moderate the politics of his message. By rereading the story of the prostitute through revolutionary demands, critics evoked the discursive power of the myths of 1830.

Throughout the July Monarchy, accounts proliferated about how libertinism had flooded into the streets after the July Days, where it was rumored still to hold court unchallenged. Fears circulated about what might happen if the imagined champions of Eugène Sue ever took to the barricades. The press colluded with literature to create the specter of individuals who might disseminate their dangers in every possible social sphere. Terror rose that these individuals might learn to evade being noticed. By the mid-1830s, partially in response to such fears, censorship of "dangerous" books, plays, imagery, and reportage had been restored. But even so, said those on the watch for social aberrations, it seemed that nothing could be done with those *insoumises* who swept through the streets, spreading their immorality and revolutionary passions.[30]

In both its pre- and postrevolutionary versions, *Marion de Lorme* is about precisely this kind of recognition. It is the story of men who follow the tracks of a prostitute, who name her for what they say she is, who trace her passage between men, and who pass her portrait between themselves as proof of her unmistakable identity. It is far less a story of what a woman might do for love than a story of what transpires between men. Didier is sentenced to die because he has fought a duel despite an edict threatening to make an example of men who use swords to settle quarrels. He actually dies, however, because he refuses to escape from prison with his lover. However, his death does not ensue from his refusal to accept this sacrifice from one who has exchanged her body for his life: in all three versions he refuses to escape *even before* he realizes how she has won his freedom (*ML*, 846–49). He refuses to flee because the man with whom he has dueled, Marion's former lover Saverny, has given him a portrait of the woman who passed between them. Saverny has named the portrait Marion and claimed it represents Didier's own Marie.

Didier has always known what the name Marion de Lorme signified. Like the followers of Hugo, *he* knows what it means when that name resonates from "infamous books": "Do you know," he asks his girlfriend when he finds she owns a book inscribed with a dedication to Marion de Lorme, "Do you know what Marion de Lorme is? A woman, beautiful of body and deformed of heart. A Phryne who sells herself to every man, in every place. Her love shames and horrifies" (*ML*, 746). To Saverny the aristocrat, however, Marion de Lorme is a trophy whose portrait one exhibits with pleasure:

> She's a good girl
> who never loves anyone but sons of good families.
> Of such a mistress, one has the right to be proud,
> It's honorable; and then, it looks classy,
> It's in good taste; and if someone asks who you are,
> Then speak up: the lover of Marion de Lorme! (*ML*, 787)

Such a mistress carries too high a price for the foundling Didier whose unknown parentage allows him to be treated by the marquis as a potential nobleman (*ML*, 765).

"I have no name. But it is enough that I have blood to shed," announces Didier of the duel for which he will lose his life (*ML*, 765). Small wonder Didier was compared by Menche de Loisne to the revolutionary "socialists" who demanded representation on the basis of their demonstration of worth instead of in relation to their family fortunes. Yet like the bourgeois revolutionaries of 1830, the Didier promoted by the play's final staged version of 1831 is willing to sacrifice his life to prove he deserves to be treated like a nobleman. Perhaps even more like the revolutionaries of 1830, this Didier wants nothing to do with prostitutes whose pathetic exchange has been unveiled by those who seek even greater social change. Let them practice their trade, the 1831 play ultimately asserts, but don't expect revolutionaries to put much store in their representation. These men want change, but for a chosen group who would know how to use it. They want freedom, but only for those who, as Hugo suggests in his preface to *Marion de Lorme*, are worthy of it. They want an end to censorship, but only for those who censor themselves.

Conspiracies over Liberty

"Oh! I beg of you, have pity on us!" reads the epigraph of one of twenty pamphlets protesting Mangin's 1830 crackdown on prostitution. Citing this line from the censored *Hernani*, written by Hugo just after *Marion de Lorme* and not performed until February 1830, the pamphlets told their version of a story of the censorship of people and texts as well as their fantasies of containment and resistance. Mushrooming suddenly in the spring of 1830, this series of pamphlets claimed to speak on behalf of the disenfranchised prostitutes—indeed, it even purported to let them speak for themselves.[31] Like the libelous pamphlets of the Revolution of 1789, these small brochures of six to forty pages were priced above the means of most workers—30 centimes to one franc—and seem to have been distributed as well as published by the bookdealers of the Palais-Royal. Also like the pamphlets that condemned Marie-Antoinette, these texts played on sexual innuendo, sexual anxieties, and fantasies about the impropriety of telling a titillating story. These texts made demands on the current government and warned of dangers if these demands were not met.[32] In pamphlets with titles like *Doléances des filles publiques, sur l'ordonnance de M. le Préfet de Police*, the women themselves claimed to expose the Mangin ordinances to public scrutiny and called for a change in the regulations (see figure 2.1). In parodic poems and prayers like *La Paulinade* and *Prière romantique de Laure, dite la séduisante*, the "joyous nymphs" of Paris summoned their courtiers to their defense. In yet more fantastic works, like *Le Vrai Motif de la capitivité des femmes soumises et leurs plus grands ennemis dévoilés* and the provocative *50,000 Voleurs de plus à Paris*, narrators claimed to speak from the world of crime and libertinism to threaten grave consequences if the ordinances were not repealed and the liberties of prostitutes reinstated.

Figure 2.1

The color frontispiece to the most elaborate of the pamphlets.
*Plainte et Révélations nouvellement addressés par les filles de joie
de Paris* . . . (1830), which depicted the "Central Committee" of
Paris prostitutes uniting to oppose the Mangin ordinances barring
them from the streets. (BIBLIOTHÈQUE NATIONALE)

The scandals of censorship that had surrounded the monarchy's treatment of Hugo had made him a fantasmatic fellow victim as well as a logical choice of ally in revolt. One pamphlet claimed to speak "in the genre adopted by the author of *Hernani*."[33] Another described the distress of a pimp who had been obliged to turn away from his usual activity of theater-going to plot new ways of supporting himself now that his *fille* had been driven from the streets. Naturally, that spring of 1830, "Isidore the romantic" was "crazy about *Hernani*" and had attended every performance until Mangin's ordinances "plunged [him] into distress."[34] Although this same pamphlet pokes fun at the playwright by noting that Isidore's preference for the drama derives from the fact that "one could make a tragedy like *Hernani* without even knowing how to write the French language correctly," it nevertheless takes a far more serious cue from the words of Hugo's heroine. "I throw myself at your feet," it appeals in the epigraph cited above, appropriating the entreaty of the play's female martyr, Doña Sol.

No one in Paris in the spring of 1830 could have missed the significance of such an alliance. In February, *Hernani*'s account of the devastation wrought by the older generation's laws on the younger generation's lives had managed to break through the wrath of the censors where *Marion de Lorme* had failed.[35] Its "oedipal protest"[36] rallied opponents to Charles X's reign by drawing further attention to the censorship battles that had repressed *Marion de Lorme* and by further emphasizing the antagonisms that racked the elderly monarch's realm. Mangin's ordinances, like the absurd pledge of honor to which the play's hero is held, derived from outworn aristocratic notions and tired moral scruples. As the pamphleteers were all too pleased to use Hugo to point out, unless the repression of such a regime were to end, dire consequences would result for the future. Even Marion de Lorme's appeal to Laffemas would not have resonated so deeply in the minds of the pamphlets' readers, for unlike Marion, Doña Sol does not survive the cruel law of the fathers.[37] Because no one pays attention to her entreaty, Doña Sol wrenches the poison from her lover's hand and kills herself, making way for the suicide he has pledged to the older man to whom he owes his honor. The only way the younger man will enjoy union with his beloved is in death—in the very bed where they were to spend their wedding night. By using her plea, the pamphleteers can insist on both the tragedy of the women for whom they spoke and the potentially dangerous results for the men with whom they might wish to sleep.

Just as Hugo's critics saw *Marion de Lorme* as the emblem of the debauchery unleashed by the July Revolution, conservatives like Alfred Nettement, Menche de Loisne, and Jolly pointed to the staging of *Hernani* as the straw that broke the back of the Restoration government. Not only had *Hernani* suffered the wrath of the censors as it staged its confrontation between the older and younger generation, but it thematized the censorship with which its author had met— both for *Hernani* and for *Marion de Lorme*—in its account of the costs of the older generation's laws. Like *Marion de Lorme*, it offered little hope for change:

its young heroes were dead, its aging autocrats still in power. Nevertheless, like *Marion de Lorme*, it scared conservatives. Such a play, argued the censors, would show the public "how far astray the human spirit can go."[38] Instead, it seems to have urged opponents of the monarchy to believe that the human spirit had, indeed, gone dangerously astray. The pamphleteers who used its words, appropriated its story line, and imitated its style had recognized the coincidence of their aims with those of Hugo in his two 1829 plays. They had equally and uncannily tapped into the anxieties that surrounded censorship of people and texts as well as into the fervor of the revolution that temporarily brought an end to that censorship.

"The Paris crowd in the 1830 Revolution . . . was above all else for liberty," Edgar Newman has argued. The workers wanted good jobs and national independence. They identified with the army, loved their nation, and held dear the Napoleonic legend. Their liberty meant "dignity for themselves and glory for France."[39] They were able to translate this desire into goals of guaranteed "jobs, higher pay, a shorter workday, lower taxes, protection from foreign workers, from machines, and from the new large-scale methods of production and distribution, government regulation of prices, wages, and work rules, an end to the reign of the priests and nobles, and a new and aggressive national foreign policy." Their success testified to their alliances and well-formulated ideals. Liberty, as far as the revolutionaries were concerned, could only be claimed if people came together to demand it. Their actions in July 1830 and in subsequent protests of the July Monarchy indicated how successfully they had already laid claim to those demands.

The liberties at stake in 1830 for the unskilled and marginalized members of the Paris population were of a very different kind. A government report of 1828 advised the police to stem the tide of unrest: "Put a stop to usury. . . . Expel five-sixths of the beggars. . . . Clear Paris of a crowd of vagrants who do nothing but spread theft and crime. . . . Halt the proliferation of common prostitutes."[40] As July Monarchy studies like those of Parent, Béraud, Honoré Frégier, Louis-René Villermé, and Eugène Buret suggested, the years surrounding the July Revolution (1828–1833) saw rampant poverty, increased arrests for vagrancy, clandestine prostitution, infanticide, a high visibility of homelessness and mendacity, soaring numbers of abandoned children, worker suicides, and asylum admissions. As critics of Louis Chevalier have pointed out, the figures on these working class "plagues" collected by the moral economists of the July Monarchy are as much indications of the new phobias of this era as they are proof of a genuine swelling in the population of marginals.[41] One thing, however, remains certain. If public perceptions of misery grew in the years leading up to the July Revolution, no one—not the people, their champions, their critics, or the police—seemed to believe the government had made any significant changes. To the police, violent revolution seemed just around the corner:

"People are saying . . . that the people must assemble and march on the Tuileries to demand work and bread and that they do not fear the soldiery. This exasperation on the part of the workers has been noted ever since the recent rise in prices, and professional agitators . . . are trying to exploit it to incite the workers to indulge in excesses."[42]

But when the excesses of the Revolution of 1830 came, the marginals and unskilled workers of Paris did not lead the battles. Despite the myths, the fighters of 1830 were not the "*50,000 voleurs*" and "*25,000 filles publiques*" who, the pamphlets claimed, had been left destitute by Mangin's repression.[43] Rather, as David Pinkney has shown, those at the barricades were mostly skilled workers and artisans—masons, locksmiths, carpenters, and especially printers. Two groups were surprisingly absent from the reports on dead and wounded civilians: first, the middle and upper bourgeoisie—the supposed inheritors of the so-called "bourgeois revolution"[44]; and second, the ever growing numbers of unskilled workers left penniless, homeless, and hungry by the social and economic crises of the late Restoration. These were not the revolutionaries who fought in the streets to bring Louis-Philippe to power.[45]

The fact that skilled craftsmen turned up in hordes at the barricades during the July Days tells a story more about who was *prepared* to protest than about who was actually *suffering* in mid-1830.[46] They came, as François Guizot would attest, to raise *political* questions. Their protests made way for others, less prepared in July 1830 to represent themselves, to ask *social* questions.[47] Out of the artisans' revolution of 1830 grew a process of working-class revolution that culminated in 1848. The July Monarchy became a period of "resistance" in which the disenfranchised would learn to arm themselves.[48] It became an era in which the marginals imagined by the pamphleteers came forward to make claims for representation. The first step in their articulation of these demands was made possible through expectations—and fears—that these marginals had demands to make.

While the "dangerous classes" of Paris did *not* serve "in the insurrectionary army that defeated the royal troops,"[49] they cannot have been oblivious to the insurrectionaries' success and to hopes that the revolution would bring changes in their lives. In the subsequent months they asserted their needs in ever more compelling ways. More important, the indigents of Paris had become a presence so disturbing to the *bourgeoisie* and nobles that they might as well have demanded their own liberties on the barricades. The fact that the public perceived the threat of these marginals as so devastating and that texts like the pamphlets so readily capitalized upon this threat propelled the fantasy of criminals raging in the streets to make violent revolution. "In any critical trial of strength with its political opponents the established government could certainly not count on [the] support" of the men and women who lived "in desperate poverty," writes Pinkney.[50] Small wonder that politicians worked to end this struggle before that fantasmatic body of unskilled laborers, prostitutes, pimps, and thieves joined the others at the barricades. It was bad enough that the prostitutes had spilled from their prison back into the streets of Paris to make claims on the passions of Parisians without their pimps making claims on the state. No group of texts contributed so persuasively to this fantasy as the 1830 pamphlets on prostitution.

"A vast Conspiracy has risen up against the rights, the fortune, and the liberty of a large class of society," claimed one of the first pamphlets published in May 1830.[52] Mangin's ordinances, the pamphlets argued, had abrogated the freedoms guaranteed by law to all French citizens and threatened the very foundations upon which that society was based.[53] Some sixty-five thousand women had found their livelihoods threatened.[54] Some fifty thousand men who had lived off them were about to turn Parisian society upside down: "By devil, Monsieur Prefect," one pamphlet warned Mangin, "you have just created one hell of a reinforcement for the thieves, swindlers, tricksters, crooks, vagabonds, etc. who infest the most beautiful capital of the world; and when I say fifty thousand more thieves, I am proudly certain of being quite modest."[55] "This threat is a warning," wrote Béraud, "that the agents of power will use to their advantage to purge society forever of a scourge that it cannot much longer tolerate without abdicating all sense of dignity" (*FPP*, 2:92). For Béraud, pamphlets like these unveiled a "most disgusting baseness" that could only spur "honorable citizens" to action (*FPP*, 2:92). That Béraud would print an abridged version of one of the pamphlets nine years later as proof of the threat of prostitution to the people of Paris demonstrates the enduring anxiety these texts produced.[56] Perhaps even more powerfully, it reveals the anxiety aroused by the fantasy of the prostitutes' resistance to policing.

The narrators of the pamphlets claim a unified goal: to describe the odious effects of Mangin's ordinances on all of Paris. According to their accounts, the *filles* themselves, unable to work the streets, have been forced either into clandestine operation or entirely out of work. The pimps who depend on them have lost their income and begun plotting new ways to make a living. The men who buy their favors are having trouble satisfying their desires. Fathers who wish to educate their sons cannot find teachers.[57] Working women, for example, seamstresses and embroiderers, have come under suspicion by the police.[58] Innocent women have been detained.[59] Honorable women are now at risk of rape.[60] Men who do succeed in finding sex are all the more jeopardized by disease.[61] "Infamy cannot be abolished by police ordinance," warns the "Nouvelle Pétition" "signed" by some 261 *filles publiques:* "Passions always run their course."[62] Whether Mangin likes it or not, this group of women plans to liberate itself. They will take clients in their boutiques, put on their own surveillance of the police, circulate according to their own whims, and avoid required "sanitary visits": "Syphilis, which was beginning to disappear from France, will expand such that, in spite of the ordinances of Mr. Mangin, it will be very difficult to check."[63] They will make Mangin sorry he ever fantasized about clearing prostitutes from the streets of Paris.

The liberties to which these pamphlets lay claim are not just sexual liberties, though the narrators manage to load their demands with innuendo. Rather, they are the specific liberties guaranteed by the first article of the Charter of France: "The French are equal before the law, whatever their titles and their rank may otherwise be."[64] The Civil Code invoked by the "thieves" and "prostitutes" who purport to speak here is one they claim protects their rights as well as those of the clients the prostitutes serve. "The question is whether *filles publiques*, who are in the service of all nations, can claim the rights of French women," asks Rinaldo Rinaldini who, the pamphlet claims, is "head of the thieves of the capital." After all, this "Rinaldo" concludes, "why did [they] become *filles publiques* if it was not to enjoy the individual liberty guaranteed by the Charter?"[65]

One pamphlet raises particularly compelling questions about civil liberties in hopes that its addressees, the lawyers of France, will give counsel and defense:

> Is there in the charter, an article that deprives us of the benefit of equality before the law? . . . Doesn't this liberty consist of the right to go and come, without being submitted to any constraint or any impediment? Isn't this right violated for anyone held by the police according to its own private charter? Isn't it an abuse of authority to prevent people from leaving their homes outside of late-night hours?[66]

One need not look very hard at the police ordinances of April 1830 to see how these regulations pushed at the limits of the French Charter. By interpreting prostitutes as outside the law, the police (and the ministers who supported them) created a fantasmatic category of women with whom and to whom one might do as one pleased.[67] Ambiguity reigned about whether arrested prostitutes had rights to a public hearing under the Penal Code, about whether they could demand a jury trial, about whether their protests could be heard in any legal framework. "When the police officer has established the facts of the case by an official report of the offense," wrote a police bureaucrat of the Restoration, "the women thus legally recognized as being prostitutes find themselves placed outside the law."[68] Under the Mangin ordinances, a woman found anywhere in public and suspected of prostitution could be hauled into the police depot for "questioning." Once the report on her suspicious behavior had been filed, she would forever after be read as a prostitute and would therefore be denied all rights under the law that might have been accorded any other *française*. The woman could find herself shipped off to prison without further ado.[69] Under Mangin's ordinances, she did not have to be caught dressed indecently or using foul language. She did not have to be caught soliciting. As the pamphleteers persuasively demonstrate, the new laws could victimize almost anyone for simply venturing into the streets.[70] The liberties of thousands of French women had, indeed, been abrogated by the new ordinances. One did not have to be a prostitute, a pimp, or a thief to question the legality of such a move.

Although the pamphlets made powerful arguments about the rights of all French citizens, men and women, to liberty, their most compelling maneuvers revolved around an issue crucial to the disenfranchised of 1830—what we might call the politics of visibility. The liberties and rights claimed by the pamphlets were given metaphorical and rhetorical meaning through discussions of the specific terms of the Mangin ordinances and challenges to the regulationists who, before and after 1830, sought to push prostitutes into the shadows. The recurrent discussions of the pamphlets in regulationist and police discourse from Parent-Duchâtelet to Lombroso suggest how powerfully these texts worked their messages of fear. Yet strangely enough, most of the pamphlets tacitly supported the tolerance system, replicating in frequently contradictory ways the arguments of regulationists who would separate "honorable women" from those *"demoiselles."*

Herein lay, I would argue, the power of the pamphlets' rhetorical as well as fantasmatic tactics. By linking liberty to a politics of visibility, the pamphlets' messages resonated throughout the July Monarchy each time prostitutes were pressed back out of sight—by reminding those who held state power that others lurked in the same shadows. The story the pamphlets evoked kept recurring in the literature of tolerance. As even the pamphleteers remark, the free circulation of *filles publiques* "keeps mothers inside, obliges girls to lower their eyes."[71] A decade after the revolution, Béraud would call for a return to laws like Mangin's to spare youths, girls, and "honorable women."[72] Yet as the pamphlets were quick to note, ordinances like Mangin's could only succeed in sweeping all spectacles of prostitution from the streets if they managed to catch women who were not yet registered. The police might be able to imprison its 3131 *filles inscrites* in closed brothels, but it could hardly hope to sequester the other twenty-two thousand (*FPP*, 1:33) or twenty-five thousand or sixty-two thousand clandestine *filles* of Paris.[73] To do so, even to preserve the honor of mothers and daughters,[74] was ultimately to put the latter at risk of arrest. Béraud himself proudly notes that the late Restoration ban on prostitutes in the Palais-Royal brought a marked increase of honorable women to shop there (*FPP*, 1:266–67). But how could he be so sure of these women's honor? Were the "sisters and children" he saw accompanying them really such convincing evidence that they did not circulate? What if they were just smart cookies who knew a good cover when they saw one?

In plays of irony and parody, the pamphleteers capitalized on the concerns of the regulationists, turning issues of public decency into matters of liberty for more than just the *bourgeoisie*. Mangin's ordinances, argued the pamphleteers, were part of a plot to repress their fashion rivals:

> For quite a long time didn't the nymphs of the Palais-Royal and other prettily kept women give the tone, the style, and often the good taste to our women of fashion? It seems this displeased the ladies of the court, as well as the mannered women of the Faubourg Saint-Germain, and that all those great ladies . . . wanted to appropriate for themselves an advantage that rightly belongs to *those young ladies*.[75]

The public presence of prostitutes had given them a reputation as models for Paris fashion.[76] But any prostitute who wanted to keep out of the clutches of the police had long since known that she had to keep her elegance within narrow bounds. Until Mangin's 1830 ordinances, as soon as she distinguished herself, through gestures, looks, or apparel, from the women around her, she could be arrested for soliciting. Parent opposed giving her a costume for precisely this reason: as soon as she could be recognized by others in the crowd, her dangerous spectacle would become apparent to all (PD, 1:362–63).

The pamphleteers and the regulationists alike worried about honest women being mistaken for prostitutes, about upright women forced to mingle with prostitutes, about honorable women running the risk of attack by less-than-honorable men in search of satisfaction. "Despite its immorality, prostitution is the safeguard of the major part of that sex worthy of our respect and of our homage," wrote Béraud (FPP, 1:107). If these restrictive laws are not revoked, warns a fille publique in the pamphlets, "we'll be counting the victims."[77] As we saw in chapter 1, Parent assented to the necessity of prostitution on one score alone: to protect the bourgeois home from the devastation of a desperate man who would help himself to virtuous daughters (PD, 2:45–46). But unlike the pamphleteers, Parent dreamt of a "perfected" system that would spare these victims and, "all the while tolerating prostitutes, . . . would make them disappear completely from the street" (PD, 1:553–54). He demanded debauchery out of sight, libertinism beyond the field of vision, seduction within confines. "Women of pure morals" (FPP, 1:106) would not have to witness these spectacles anymore; their dignity would remain intact. As for the women whose sex made them "worthy of respect and homage" but whose rights were not "safeguarded by prostitution," of course, the police would take care of them. No one worried what spectacles they might see or cared what rights they lost when the prostituted body was forced underground. No one asked if they needed to be safeguarded—for, of course, they already were, in the closed spaces of tolerance.

Though the rhetoric of the pamphleteers frequently resembled that of the regulationists who championed Mangin's 1830 ordinances, their goals were far from similar. Nevertheless, the pamphlets mimicked and thus ultimately upheld the fundamental rationale for tolerated prostitution. Whether these pamphlets were intentionally satiric and parodic is hard to say. What is certain, however, is that these pamphlets drew upon public fantasies about prostitution, and that in some cases they played on these fantasies in any way promising to increase their sales. Perhaps the pamphlets were aimed at a disgruntled clientele who, finding the Palais-Royal empty, could be convinced to buy cheap little books that expressed its displeasure. Perhaps the first pamphlets were marketed by the prostitutes themselves in hopes of gaining support for their protests against Mangin. Such a scenario might have continued with the publishers capitalizing on the success of these first brochures with anything they could come up with to feed a purchasing public—much as they had during the heady days of pamphlet-publishing in the Revolution of 1789 and much as they would in the early 1840s with the *Physiologies*.[78]

What we *do* know about the pamphlets marks them as an extraordinarily significant body of texts in the months before the Revolution. The twenty-one prostitution pamphlets constituted over four percent of the entire book (and pamphlet) production of France in the month of their publication—and that production included a boom in new and expensive reeditions of classic works as well as large numbers of devotional materials. In the ten weeks before the revolution, these texts about prostitution constituted nearly the entire pamphlet discourse of Paris.[79] Of the eighty printers in Paris, eight published one or more pamphlets in the period between the weeks of May 15 and June 5. One printer, Poussin, published a total of eight pamphlets, several of which cost more than the average fifty centimes. Another, Gaultier-Laguionie, published four pamphlets, including one in two different editions.[80]

In view of the near absence of other political pamphlets in the months preceding the revolution, the prodigious quantity of these pamphlets suggests that they may have served far more interests than those of the prostitutes, pimps, and thieves whose voices they appropriated. What we know of the pamphlets' circumstances of publication suggests that they came from other sources than the brothels out of which they claimed to speak. All the pamphlets seem to have been reported to the French Interior Ministry despite rampant censorship of similar subjects in the theater and the press. Only one pamphlet (*Réponse à M. Engin aux pétitions des filles publiques*) was published by a printer known for its less than innocent involvement with colportage.[81] Most of the pamphlets seem to have emerged from printers with Orleanist ideals (Gaultier-Laguionie), close ties to the Palais-Royal trade (Poussin), and purely pecuniary interests (Sétier).

One further circumstance suggests that the pamphlets had close ties with opposition journalism willing to exploit the crackdown on prostitution for unrelated political ends. In the week of the publication of the first pamphlets, on May 10, 1830, a letter appeared in the newspaper *Le Corsaire*, known for its satirical barbs, posing as the protest of one "Suzanne Prudence Desvertus, *demoiselle tolérée*," and addressed to "*Monsieur le Préfet de Police*." Whether this article actually originated the strategies, tone, and content of the pamphlets, or only imitated the first ones, we can be certain that this newspaper heartily endorsed the pamphlets.[82] The small liberal paper's backing of the prostitutes' cause was as charged with ambivalence as many of the pamphlets themselves. Initially applauding Mangin's resolution to rid the capital of "hideous public prostitution," the paper quickly moved to condemn police abuses of authority. Of the pamphlet *Plainte et révélations*, it acknowledged that "This *nouveauté* will make some laugh and plague others. Everyone has to live."[83] By the time of the government crackdown on the press on June 16, 1830, *Le Corsaire* was using the Mangin ordinances as a metaphor to protest increasingly narrowing rights of free speech.[84]

Despite the alliances we can conjecture between the opposition press and the pamphleteers, we cannot say who wrote these texts, or even whether prostitutes—not to speak of pimps and blackguards—had any hand in their composition. The petition to the ministers, which bears some two hundred signatures with first names and addresses of prostitutes, reads convincingly enough as an accurate portrayal of the concerns of a group of *filles*. Far less convincing are the *Paulinade* or the *Prière romantique*, both of which seem hatched for the purpose of profiting from the popularity of the genre. Even less convincing is the alleged response by Mangin published in the pamphlets, which mocks the prefect with his supposed responses to the accusations about abrogated liberties. Equally unconvincing is the petition claiming to speak for the fifty thousand pimps driven to theft by their women's lack of livelihood. Depicting the suffering pimps as torn from their habitual activities, this pamphlet sketches a fantasy of kept men who ordinarily dash from their writing tables to dances to public promenades to the theater—all of whom are now constrained to turn to crime: "You realize of course that a pimp is a moral being, useful to society, and you have just forced him to become its scourge, by forcing our special women to limit their commerce to the inside of their houses."[85] Least convincing of all is the witty pamphlet that offers a canny proposal for resolving the moral dilemmas of prostitution: "As to honorable women, if you say they ought not to mix with loose women, that's easy enough: they can just stay home." Safe in their houses they would be spared the indecent dress and manners of the fallen women in the streets. After all, writes the narrator, "a truly honorable woman always finds something to do in her house, without showing herself at the window or running around in the streets." Imprisoned in their homes, they can profit from the liberties guaranteed them in the Charter to choose how to live: "Why did they stay honorable if it wasn't to endure slavery in their households?" Even if they die of boredom, they will win our esteem, while those other women, "the shame of their sex, will be pointed out in the streets. Oh those pretty little rascals, people will say, ... How embarrassing for them!"[86]

Regardless of who *wrote* these pamphlets, they tell one particularly persuasive story: the seclusion of prostitutes in *maisons de tolérance* aroused vehement opposition. They address themselves to an audience that would embrace the prostitutes' cause—because they were frustrated to find no women in the Palais-Royal, or because they believed that Charles X's ministers had gone too far this time, or because they worried about the implied threats of a revolt of prostitutes and pimps. Regardless of who *bought* the pamphlets, their proliferation testifies to the following the genre garnered. Regardless of who *read* the pamphlets, the bookdealers of the Palais-Royal profited. Regardless of who actually distributed them, these texts circulated.[87] No matter whose voices are actually recorded in them, these pamphlets articulated the terrors and the anxieties of two conflicting groups, the bourgeoisie and workers. Because the pamphlets claim to speak for the "dangerous classes," they produce an image of what dangers the bourgeoisie may have fantasized as lurking in the wilds of Paris. At half a franc each, these texts were not, after all, being sold to workers or prostitutes, but rather, like the *roman-feuilleton* of 1836, mostly to the middle classes. Because the regulationists evidently read these pamphlets as articulating the "real" views of the groups they were trying to police, these texts support the theory that the state of 1830 was as concerned about the fomentation that might be spread by prostitutes as about the protests of bankers and skilled workers.

Yet, at the same time, the pamphlets manage to make articulate claims about police oppression and to threaten convincingly a series of reprisals and misfortunes should the police not back down. The pamphlets may not have been written or read by any of the groups whose livelihoods would have been endangered by the ordinances of 1830, but they stunningly demonstrate the fallacies in the ways the police interpreted French law. All the prostitutes depicted there seem to want is to be treated as French citizens. All the pamphleteers—whoever they were—are demanding is a little liberty.

Ruptured Plots

Revolutions change the plots possible for narrative, Ronald Paulson has argued.[88] In such a moment of *rupture*, the laws that govern representation are as much disrupted as the laws that govern society. The fact that the prostitute is already seen as outside the law and therefore as ungovernable makes her a privileged handmaiden to revolution. When the laws that regulate society are overthrown, debauchery is imagined to spill into the streets. "The revolution brought an abuse of unrestrained liberty; under the pretext that we were a free people, we outstripped the most scandalous behavior of the absolute monarchy," Maxime Du Camp proclaimed of the Revolution of 1789.[89] "The excess of liberty engenders licentiousness," declared police chief Louis Canler of the Revolution of 1848.[90] Although the Revolution of 1830 lasted only a few days, its effects were imagined to be devastating in the police realm where the prostitute and the criminal circulated. The fantasy of rampant venality, crime, and debauchery haunted the July Monarchy like an ever growing specter. Social analyses and statistical studies sought to contain this phantom of unrestrained lawlessness. Novels capitalized on giving it free rein and played at containing it. The theater, caricatures, and racy lithographs tested the boundaries of the new laws that guaranteed freedom of speech. The press speculated on what power it might actually have picked up along the way. At all levels of society, and in all kinds of texts, representations of unrestrained sexuality, uncontained prostitution, and lawlessness prevailed.

The plots that emerged took a number of forms. Some, like *Marion de Lorme* and *Les Mystères de Paris*, speculated upon the tragedy that women who have fallen do not have the right to elevate themselves again and used those plots to complain about contradictions racking their society. Others, like

Napoléon Landais's *Une Vie de courtisane*, depicted the trajectory of a young woman from her seduction into prostitution and, ultimately, death, insisting on her mistakes as well as her tragedy. Others, like Balzac's *Splendeurs et misères des courtisanes*, portrayed criminals and whores who managed to insinuate themselves into polite society or even into the police network itself.[91] Still others, like George Sand's *Lélia*, imagined the powers that accrued to the woman who had chosen the dissimulating plots of prostitution. Others, such as the pamphlets, capitalized on imagined threats of lawless prostitutes and criminals rising up to avenge themselves.

Contemporary opponents of the revolution gave the pamphlets a revolutionary value: the protests of prostitutes and their pimps were imagined by police commentators and regulationists as genuine voices raised against the Restoration government, inadequately restrained and ultimately debilitating to both state and moral order.[92] Leftist commentators like Alphonse Esquiros capitalized on the supposedly revolutionary message of the pamphlets, using them to remind the July Monarchy government of the political power of the marginalized.[93] We cannot make the assumption, however, that any one of these plots worked in a specifically revolutionary or counterrevolutionary way. Rather, as Richard Terdiman suggests, culture is a "field of struggle" where the very plots possible for narrative become "contested terrain."[94] The revolutionary moment breaks with previous representational strategies and tactics in such a way as to exacerbate the struggles that transpire over and through language. Lynn Hunt has analyzed the cultural formations of the Revolution of 1789 to demonstrate how "the discursive structures of politics shaped the possible political outcomes." New rhetorical and narrative strategies paved the way for new possibilities of social participation and social conflict. The "texts" of revolutionary political culture "configured the context."[95] Likewise, the discourse linking the prostitute and revolution in the Revolution of 1830 changed the stakes for political demands, for conceptions of class, and for understandings of gender.

"Discourse is rhetorical, . . . rhetoric is a form of persuasion, and . . . persuasion is a form of power, an instrument of social manipulation and control," writes Giles Gunn.[96] The kind of discourse at stake in the Revolution of 1830 used fantasies about a world out of control to reinstate controls. It generated fears about powerlessness to insist upon the need for new mechanisms of power. It dreamed up the manipulations of whores to make demands for new plots that might hold them in check. The strategies of containment[97] employed by the discourse of 1830 do not derive exclusively from the bourgeois or state discourse. Rather, they emerge from all levels of literary discourse and from all social positions. The "double movement of containment and resistance"[98] is not just part of the struggle of popular culture. Rather, it is a necessary constituent of the so-called high culture of art and literature as well as of the criticism that grows out of it. This double movement is at the same time a product of revolutionary political culture and of the interpretations generated by it.

"The representations of the social world themselves are the constituents of social reality," Roger Chartier has argued, "Instruments of power, the stakes of struggles as fundamental as economic struggles, the systems of classification, or images of social order are all transformers of this very order."[99] The struggles played out on the battlefields of culture give us a view not only of what is at stake in them but also of the transformations in social order negotiated through those struggles. By looking at the cultural texts of an era of revolutionary change, we can therefore see what changes are at stake as well as how those very texts participated in the renegotiations of revolutionary politics. By reading for the plots of the revolution, we can define the terms of revolutionary contests. By considering how certain signs were invested with such significance in revolutionary plots, we can define what powers were ratified through those plots.

The discourse of 1830 seemed already to have embedded within it the possibilities of several counter-discursive formations. The strategies of containment that emerged at the moments of revolution were as much embedded *in* the prorevolutionary discourse (as we saw in our reading of *Marion de Lorme*) as they were imposed upon discourse that appeared to represent the interests of workers and marginals (as we saw in our reading of the pamphlets). The tactics of resistance were at the disposal of those who wrote "social novels," but they were extended to the people by the texts that countered the revolutionary movements with a discourse of fear. The creation of plots of delinquency, as we saw in chapter 1, necessarily empowers the resistances of the delinquents. New plots become possible. In revolution the resistances of delinquents, working tactically, become most visible.

The discourse generated by these late Restoration scandals lent itself conveniently to a myth that prostitutes and their pimps led the revolts of the July Revolution. Such a myth focused on the demands of the supposedly dangerous classes as a way of ridiculing revolutionary activity. It simultaneously scapegoated the "outrageous" demands of the "criminal classes" as a way of furthering the more modest goals of the bourgeoisie. But in doing so, it warned of an unrest that, it would seem, took the form of the very real liberation of prostitutes from their prisons in the July Days. The pamphlets gave a plot to the prostitute in which, as in *Marion de Lorme* and other literary works of the same era, her rights are publicly asserted. Her self-determination was demanded in a way bearing upon the rights of others to self-determination. Tragically, however, the rights of marginalized women—whether registered as prostitutes or not, whether named as censored or not—were evoked in ways that dissipated the force of the demand. The woman was made to ventriloquize the demands of those who spoke through her. She seemed to gain a voice, yet her interests were articulated for purposes that incessantly positioned her in someone else's plot. We could argue that her voice was only suspended, awaiting the amplifiers of those who would come in 1848 to champion her cause and who would come again repeatedly until her rights were written into law and her representation put into practice. New plots had become possible, even if only fleetingly.

The image through which we have come to read July 1830 reminds us of the power of those plots to go on signifying and of the potential of those plots to open up spaces for representation of a political as well as aesthetic kind. Displayed in the 1831 Salon the same spring as *Marion de Lorme* went into rehearsal, Eugène Delacroix's *Liberty* (figure 2.2) is no more the portrait of the revolution than Hugo's play. Yet the painter's attempt to translate his regret for not having fought at the barricades into artistic activism was not only embraced by the forty-eighters but has become the image through which subsequent generations would envision the Revolution of 1830.[100]

Commentators from the July Monarchy on demanded to know if Delacroix's painting had models for its depictions and if those models were specific individuals or only general types of the revolution.[101] Through its failure to respond to these questions, Delacroix's painting promoted a fantasy about who participated in the revolution, and this, like the fantasy of the pamphlets and the myths they engendered, and like the critics' fears of *Marion de Lorme*, generated

Figure 2.2

Eugéne Delacroix, *Liberty on the Barricades* (1831).

(Musée de Louvre)

anxieties about what liberties might be demanded—and taken—in a moment of revolution. Like the pamphlets and Hugo's drama, *Liberty on the Barricades* helped to generate a counter-discourse that worked corrosively upon the containing discourses of the nineteenth century.

One description of a "real" Liberty makes her a woman named Marie Deschamps who, dressed only in a slip, dashed into the streets of July 27 in search of her brother, found him dead, and shot nine men before she was herself felled.[102] To this reading of Delacroix's model as a "real" woman has been opposed an allegorical reading that makes her "a piece of living beauty, formed from class warfare." This Liberty is *only* an idea, *only* a representation of an allegorical dream of freedom and dignity, at most *like* a "sister or beloved of one of the fighting young men."[103] She derives from poems or from myths of Amazon warriors; she is the legacy of the symbolmongering of the Revolution of 1789.[104] She circulates with allegorical power, Marina Warner suggests, only *because* women of 1830 had neither vote nor voice.[105]

The salon critics of 1831 were only prepared to see revolutionary women as allegories—and this one was too real for her own good. Like the audience of the Hugo play that went into rehearsals about the same time, Delacroix's critics refused to imagine that such a woman could serve as an emblem of a struggle, as a figurehead for battles against censorship and greed, as an allegory of all that was noble in humanity. *Liberty*'s critics fretted over the figure's bare breasts, her dirtiness, her underarm hair, and her possible relation to Saint-Simonian sexual emancipation.[106] As soon as the figure of a woman was introduced into a picture that purported to show real people in real battle at the moment of a real revolution, the allegorical possibilities of that body entered into tension with the fantasmatic plots given to that "real" moment. Whatever allegorical plot Liberty may have imported into the salon painting, she also dragged behind her the plot that surrounded real bodies.[107]

This Liberty looks like she has just escaped from Saint-Lazare prison, claimed one contemporary critic, making a place for her among the prostitutes supposedly liberated during the July Days of 1830.[108] Such critical disdain returned Liberty to the spheres of prostitution in a move that crystallizes the conflicting stories read through the represented bodies of revolutionary women. Giving Liberty a fleshly body implicated her in the struggles over such bodies in the days surrounding the revolution. Even more strikingly, it invoked a very specific story about the liberation of prostitutes from Saint-Lazare prison during the revolts of the *trois glorieuses*. Like the criticism that made *Marion de Lorme* a lesson in the immorality derived from revolutionary mores, the fantasy of Liberty as an escaped prostitute was a convenient way of denigrating both the revolution and its representatives. It nevertheless also forced a rereading of the episode of the revolution in question. It suggested that the liberation of the prostitutes aroused enduring fears that the revolutionary days of 1830 had not yet come to an end.

July Monarchy commentators tell conflicting stories about that liberation. One version of the story has the very pimps of the pamphlets breaking open the doors of the prisons to liberate their *filles*.[109] In another version, the liberated prostitutes swept through the streets, spreading renewed debauchery, flaunting their new freedom in violation of Mangin's ordinances, returning in hordes to the spaces from which they had been banned.[110] Still another version of the story gave the last laugh to regulationists, prison officials, and cops:

> When the prison doors were broken open on July 30, the pimps and other ruffians who broke in had to use force to drive out half the inmates who persisted in wanting to stay. These women were thrown into the street where they met up with the prison doctor, Mr. Jacquemin, stopped him, and explained the misfortune and trouble in which they found themselves. Already that evening most of them came back on their own to reenlist as prisoners. (*PD*, 2:300)

In prison, wrote July Monarchy historians, "they had at least found some bread."[111] Yet even this cynical version of the crackdowns had a peculiarly revolutionary message: Mangin's ordinances were not the only reason the prostitute prison of Paris was full; widespread poverty had given a certain appeal to the regular meals of sequestration.

As soon as Liberty was imagined escaping from Saint-Lazare, she circulated in a network of stories, only one of which degraded her or the revolution's efforts. To imagine her freed from the prostitutes' prison is necessarily to evoke the structures of containment that imprisoned her in the course of the Restoration. It is to summon the image of a poverty so overwhelming that jail would seem preferable to freedom. It is to imagine that battles might yet be fought in which women so disenfranchised, so powerless, and so desperate might march forth, arms raised in triumph. If such a fantasy evokes the potential dangers of revolution, it conjures up all the more powerfully the potential demands of what the pamphlets called "a large class of society." Censored bodies, these people had a showing to make in more than just texts.

The story of Liberty in 1830 cannot be reduced to an allegory, but it is even less the story of a single real, heroic female body. As such, it underlines what I have argued from the beginning of this chapter: we need to reread the representations of 1830 and those of 1848 for their engagements with the conflicting discourses about female sexuality, marginality, and political representation. Like *Marion de Lorme* and the pamphlets, Delacroix's *Liberty* articulated a fantasy about who was on the barricades that was anything but representative. Neither young boys, nor women, nor even unskilled workers loomed large on the real barricades of 1830. Nevertheless, the questions about gender, class, and marginality raised by this painting would endure through decades of revolts. Though women's rights were barely an issue for the revolutionaries of 1830, *Liberty* forced questions about the political representation of women to which the revolutionaries of 1848 would be obliged to respond. Her body remained: female, sexual, towering amid revolt, challenging anyone who would reduce her to a symbol, looming up to warn anyone who would read her as only a figure.

3
Taking Liberties:
Plots Around
Prostitutes in 1848

*I*n 1876, an aging Maxime Du Camp told how he had met Gustave Flaubert on the evening of February 24, 1848. Together they proceeded to the Palais-Royal where, in the wake of the king's abdication, they witnessed a moment of popular triumph:

> An armed band of around fifty people came running down the rue Saint-Honoré. Leading them marched a woman who was covered only by a shirt and a petticoat; her hair, dark and very long, had rolled down onto the small of her back; she walked in slippers worn down at the heels and one of her stockings fell in a spiral around her ankle; her arms, her shoulders, and almost all her chest were bare; she was shouting as she brandished a butcher knife; men threw themselves on her and kissed her. She did not even notice them.[1]

Unlike Delacroix's *Liberty* upon which Du Camp seems to have based his "recollection," this exultant woman of the people marches headlong into a scene of sexual desire. No matter that she doesn't notice; she *is* noticed. As leader of the parade, representative of the masses, goddess of reason for this opening festival of the new revolution, she no longer rises in virginal solemnity to be revered.[2] Whether she notices it or not, this Liberty can be *had*.

Maurice Agulhon has pointed to the importance of an "emotional and mystical aura" surrounding the Second Republic and insisted that without a comprehension of this "new religion" we cannot understand how the masses were won over to the revolutionary cause. This aura, he contends, explains the "strength and ardor that sustained the republican party from 1849 to 1851" and elucidates its involvement with allegorical and figurative expression.[3] Every revolution has its symbolic practices and that of 1848 did not differ in its impulse to rid itself of the trappings of the last regime in order to make way for the ideals of the new order. Central to the symbolic practices of the forty-eighters was the figure they called Marianne.

Although the revolutions of 1789 and 1830 contributed to the invention of this woman of the people as allegory of the Republic, the revolutionaries of

1848 were the ones to define her, draw her, popularize her, and baptize her Marianne.[4] What distinguished this gesture from earlier representative practices was that the nature of the body this revolution baptized had itself become an issue. If the allegory of the people was to be *representative* of the people—spontaneous, moving, vehement, strong, heroic—she had to *resemble* in some way a woman of the people. The problem with Marianne was that, unlike the earlier allegories, she might be *desired*.

Lynn Hunt has described those "symbolic practices, such as language, imagery, and gestures" that conferred in 1789 a unity and coherence to political practices and, after the fact, to our perceptions of events:

> Through their language, images, and daily political activities, revolutionaries worked to reconstitute society and social relations. They consciously sought to break with the French past and to establish the basis for a new national community. In the process, they created new social and political relations and new kinds of social and political divisions. Their experience of political and social struggle forced them to see the world in new ways.[5]

Du Camp's story of the February 24 procession brings together the symbolic practices of revolutionary political culture with the hopes and fears it would evoke. In his account of the forty-eighters' jubilant march through Paris, Du Camp represents the convergence in one body of three female figures traditionally embraced by populist struggles between 1789 and 1871: the allegory, the processional flag-carrier, and the fighter.[6] Accounts by witnesses of the February Days refer to a live allegory like the one described by Du Camp, perhaps mounted on horseback, perhaps carrying a red flag, but nevertheless heading a parade along the Quai.[7] Like the female standard-bearers chosen by revolutionaries to cheer on insurgents, Du Camp's woman exults in her role as *leader*. Du Camp has, however, exchanged her flag for a prop more consistent with the view of revolutionary women he embraces elsewhere. Like the women he describes as "bellicose viragos," pathologically crazed, who held out longer than the men of the Commune,[8] this female revolutionary could prove dangerous. No longer allegorizing the excesses of revolution, this woman rebel has become a repository of violence: she brandishes a butcher knife.

Her weapon propels this woman into a role outside the realm of allegory—that of *actual* participant in the battles of the revolution. Because women had rarely appeared in the revolutionary struggles of 1789 and 1830, their increased participation in 1848 was both fascinating and suspicious.[9] Tocqueville looked back on the involvement of women in the battles of 1848 as a new development signifying widespread participation, "the revolt of one whole section of the population against another."[10] Republican satirists deployed caricatures and spurious reportage mocking women who took up arms to defend the Republic.[11] The presence of women at the barricades stood out: women were fighting, women were *making* demands, women took liberties, and, inevitably, liberties were being taken with women.

Each representation of women's participation invested their gender with greater significance. At this moment of obsession with biological difference, it was hardly surprising that gender became a "primary way of signifying relationships of power," or that accounts of the gendered body entailed fantasies about a sexualized body.[12] Neil Hertz has suggested that the Revolution of 1848 would crystallize an equation of sexual and political threats. Eric Hobsbawm has discussed the ways political participation and sexual freedom were linked in the nineteenth century. Michelle Perrot and Geneviève Fraisse have pointed to the ways in which women's physical presence on the barricades of 1848 would signify rebellion against the repressive authority of patriarchy.[13] Yet none of these accounts tells the whole story. Although women's presence has frequently been recounted as a way of denigrating popular revolutionary movements,[14] it has also proved a significant rallying point. To describe the ardor of women in battle in 1848 insists, above all, on the enormity of the stakes in the revolutionary conflicts. It emphasizes the fervor of the class conflict that pitted the working class against the bourgeoisie in a battle intent on *social* change, not just a change of government.

Du Camp's vision of Liberty tells us nothing of this woman's story, of her past, or of her profession. Unlike other chroniclers of the revolution, from Daniel Stern to Hugo to Flaubert, Du Camp will not speculate on the morals of the woman of the people. He points instead with subtlety to the crowd around her: "men threw themselves on her and kissed her." The sexual content of their desire is left to our imagination: do they kiss her because she marches forth as Liberty, or because she is one of them, rejoicing in their victory—or because she is one of those women with whom men can take liberties?

For the chroniclers of 1848, telling of a woman's participation in the revolution necessarily meant giving a story to her sexuality, putting a value on her gender, assigning a plot to her sexual difference. Women's bodies might emerge as incitement to revolution, as in Stern's account of the *Promenade des cadavres* of February 23, which will be discussed below. They might serve as a reminder of the people's victory, as in the exultant amazons of the Tuileries, also discussed later. They might become symbols of protest, as in accounts of women's bravery at the barricades. Yet all of these moments suggest ambivalence about what a woman's presence in revolution might mean. As soon as Liberty's body becomes sexualized, the knife the *femme du peuple* carries can be turned against the people who would have her represent them.

The popular revolutions of 1789 and 1830 had solicited female participation for their rituals, imagery, and discursive plays. The revolution of 1848 involved women at its barricades and in its insurrections as well. Distinctions between public and private spheres continued, nevertheless, to define the moral code for female participation in these new struggles, for chroniclers of the 1848 revolution seemed to assume that if a woman was *in* the streets, she belonged there anyway. Participation in revolts was tantamount to solicitation. What changed in 1848, however, were the implications of having been bought. This revolution's Liberty, sexually besieged, carries her weapon onward, continuing to lead the people. Even put to task by the chronicler least likely to excuse her for being desired by men, she moves forward, somehow unscathed by the uses to which her body is put: *"elle ne s'en apercevait pas."*

The plots of the revolution of 1830 had invoked prostitution as a way of conceptualizing revolutionary dangers and demands. The women on the battlefield of that revolution were always seen as circulating without a license. Although revolutionary investments were channeled through their bodies, their plots had already been written. The revolution of 1848 transformed those plots. Caught up in fervent hopes that any change might be possible, the forty-eighters took up the cause of the woman blamed for whoring. They gave her new liberties and demanded that she in turn help them take theirs. They had read the works of those who investigated her plight and made up their own minds about what might be done. They imagined they might gain by inducing her complicity. What they had not counted on was that their counter-discursive strategies might play right back into the discourse of fear that, as I argued in chapter 2, lent them momentum. For anxieties about class, sexuality, and morality still surrounded any woman involved in revolutionary acts or revolutionary culture. And the forty-eighters would have to contend, like it or not, with the ways their representations transformed their social order.

Avenging Liberties

On the night of February 24, 1848, the rejoicing masses poured into the Tuileries palace to celebrate the triumph of the people. The king had taken flight earlier in the day. At the Palais Bourbon that afternoon and at the Hôtel de Ville that night the insurgents proclaimed the Republic. Politics—even the declaration of "Liberty, Equality, and Fraternity"—seemed of little concern in the halls of the abdicated royal palace. According to Stern, the multitude delivered itself to every excess of a delirious imagination. The chateau became "the theater of an immense orgy, of an indescribable saturnalia."[15] Some of the invaders set about to destroy the remnants of the opulence of the routed monarchy. Others turned the fallen regime into a satirical comedy, playacting receptions, imitating gamblers and chess players, making themselves into princesses with the finery and perfume left behind.

In such an atmosphere of "moral chaos," we should hardly be surprised to find a burlesque of traditional revolutionary symbols. The throne was carried away for destruction. Scraps of tapestry served to construct "Phrygian caps." This moment of symbolic triumph[16] needed its live allegory. From among the people, Liberty would rise up: "One of them, a pike in her hand, a red cap on her head, posted herself in the great entrance-hall and remained there for several hours, immobile, her lips closed, staring fixedly, in the pose of a statue of liberty: it was a *fille de joie*."[17] Stern's descriptions of the people's excesses suggest her discomfort, even as a strong proponent of the republic, with the spectacle they produced in the name of victory. Not surprisingly, Stern's account of the sacking of the Tuileries has frequently served a counterrevolutionary discourse: those opposed to the republic could point to the perversion of revolutionary imagery and could view this Liberty's profession as a profanation of republican goals.

In his 1869 "fictionalization" of the events of 1848, Flaubert makes only minute changes in the fragmentary moment he appropriates: "In the waiting room, upright on a pile of clothing, stood a *fille publique* posed as a statue of Liberty—immobile, wide-eyed, terrifying."[18] Flaubert's account of the Tuileries is remarkable for the content he ascribes to the people's actions. Like the "criminals" Flaubert's narrator will describe rolling about in the princesses' beds "as a consolation for not being able to rape them," the *fille publique* has changed valence. One word alone reminds us that this woman on display has a spectator who confers meaning upon her. The prostitute of *L'Éducation sentimentale* stands, like Stern's, immobile, eyes staring straight ahead of her, playing statue of Liberty. Flaubert's prostitute, however, is *"effrayante."* Her actions, unlike those of the criminals, are not given motivation. She remains simply *seen* and therefore terrifying.

But why terrifying? What has come together in her body that makes this pose more than theatrical and takes it beyond the ironic to the unsettling and horrifying? We might have first asked—and that even of Stern—what identified this woman as a prostitute? And once that identification had been made, why should her profession be significant here? Is a woman of the people more burlesque as an allegory of liberty when her contemporaries know she is for sale? Does she tell us more about the tensions inherent in revolution if we know she is a prostitute? In the shadows of the cavernous antechamber of the palace, wouldn't any live statue seem a bit uncanny? Should we assume that her gender, class, and profession represent each in turn exacerbations of that uncanniness? What is at stake when Liberty, *"effrayante"* to the spectator, can be taken for a price?

In a kind of mythic distillation, the live allegory of Liberty as a whore recurs as a symbol of the agony of the republic, the worm in the bud of the "beautiful revolution."[19] She codifies the blame that would be cast upon the people, the sorrow of the republicans that good ideas would be put to bad uses, and the counterrevolutionary disgust with the entire revolutionary movement.[20] Her appearance in the Tuileries nevertheless generates stories other than those equating her with a denigrated popular movement. The prostitute's body has a forceful way of involving others in the plots that circulate around her. At the same time as Stern provided the source for myths to mock the republic, she suggested other employment for their symbols. Once she has described the prostitute's pose, Stern pulls back from the condemnation she seems to have been making of the people's revelry:

> It was a *fille de joie*. They march past her with all the signs of profound respect.
> Sad image of the capricious laws of fate: the prostitute is the living sign of the

degradation of the poor and of the corruption of the rich. Insulted by [the rich] in supposedly "normal" times, she has the right to her hour of triumph in all of our revolutionary saturnalia. La Maillard, travestied as the Goddess Reason, is the ironic symbol of the insulted, brutalized popular honor that awakens with a start in the intoxication, and revenges itself.[21]

Suddenly we are in a realm where women's bodies rally popular revolts. This figure has the power to remind us that other battles remain to be fought.

Stern's account of the parade of the cadavers on the preceding night suggests what those battles might entail. Just as she has used sexuality to give significance to the gender as well as class of the woman of the Tuileries, here her depiction of the call to action emphasizes the significance of the gender of the body. In a carriage conveying sixteen cadavers, a child of the people throws his torchlight on

> the body of a young woman whose livid neck and breast were stained with a long trail of blood. From time to time another worker, positioned at the back of the wagon, clasps this inanimate body in his muscular arms, and raises it as he shakes his flaming, sparking torch. He throws fierce glances to the crowd and cries out: "Vengeance! Vengeance! They are slaughtering the people!" "To arms!" answers the crowd.[22]

When the people's interests are involved, naming a victim's sex as female seems an appeal for vengeance. Regardless of how that vengeance was evoked — whether in revolutionary demands for change or in fantasmatic depictions of its threat — it became a powerful vehicle of desire and fear, both in the political culture of the revolution of 1848 and in the chronicles that sought to give it meaning. Small wonder that Flaubert, who based his own representation of the Tuileries Liberty on Stern's chronicle, would stop short of the respectful parade past her, and comment in shorthand on the vengeance called for in her name: *effrayante*.

Plots Around Prostitutes

As the masses reveled in the Tuileries on February 24, others made a historic pilgrimage — to the prisons of Paris. On the previous night, the cry *"à la Bastille"* had set the insurgents in motion toward the symbolic site of the liberation of 1789. The gunshots of the Boulevard des Capucines had impeded their trek. For the night and day after their triumph, the revolutionaries left behind symbolic displays in search of action. Their attention focused on three prisons: Clichy, a small debtors' prison holding fewer than two hundred occupants, Sainte-Pélagie, where political prisoners were incarcerated (394 in 1846), and Saint-Lazare, an enormous structure with a resonant history, holding about a thousand female prisoners, most of them for infractions or illnesses relating to prostitution.[23] In an attempt to quell rumors that the entire prison population of Paris had stampeded into the streets, the republican newspaper *Le National* provided the following account:

> Mistaken reports are circulating that could worry the population. Rumor has it that the prisons have been broken open and that criminals have spread into all areas of Paris. To deny these rumors, we need only cite the facts:
> Only the doors of the debtor's prison have been opened. Saint-Lazare Prison has equally been evacuated with the exception of 120 sick women and those who didn't want to take advantage of the liberty offered them. But the revolts that took place at the Force and Conciergerie Prisons were immediately suppressed, and, in order to prevent any further attempts of this kind, the doors of these prisons were reinforced. The woman found guilty in the affair of the rue des Moineaux has been kept imprisoned.
> Yesterday at 4:00 P.M., the political prisoners held in Sainte-Pélagie Prison were liberated by the National Guard of the 12th Legion. Mr. Delaroche, director of *Le National*, who had been imprisoned for six days, was enthusiastically embraced by his liberators and carried triumphantly by the people.[24]

Several concerns converged here. Tales of disorder, crime, and prison revolts had quickly erupted and spread, but the truth of these tales was not at issue. The real story was one of fear. Criminality struck terror in the hearts of the notables because, as Chevalier has illustrated, they believed criminals dangerous.[25] Criminality frightened the bourgeois republicans because they believed any disorderly conduct could be used to topple their entire victory. Criminality threatened the revolting workers because they knew how easily the label of criminal found its way onto their own bodies. It could be used to condemn them to prisons for crimes they had not committed, to marginalize them socially, to deprive them of work, to assail them morally, and to vilify any popular movement with which they were involved.

Le National therefore had a vested interest in dispelling rumors of dangerous criminality. The first impulse of the republican press was to draw a clear boundary line between the successfully contained dangers and the nondangers that did not need containment. The story of these revolts was quickly transformed into a tale of dangerous criminality bridled and damaging rumors quelled. Yet, for all its attempts to focus attention on the republicans' orderly containment of prison revolts, the paper nevertheless evoked dangers the revolutionaries could not contain.

Prisoners *had* indeed revolted in La Force, La Roquette, and the Conciergerie, as we learn from other reports authenticating the republican account. These revolts belonged to a tradition of prison uprisings in moments of populist struggle just as rumors about their success derived from an equally long tradition of fear of disorder, vengeance, and savagery.[26] Suddenly what had been—for better or worse—marginalized behind prison doors could, when those doors flew open, tear at the seams of civilized, orderly society. The revolutionaries had good reasons to fear the disturbances such revolts could wreak. Fear of disorder, they knew well from 1789 and 1830, could become a powerful weapon against their cause. Like revolting prisoners, thieves—plunderers of untended stores and abandoned palaces—focused concerns about controlling illegality. Republican newspapers overflowed with touching stories of working-class children who saved the wealth of the Tuileries from the pillaging mob and of combatants who shot thieves on the spot, announcing, "You are not one of us, we disavow you."[27] If the republicans were to demonstrate themselves worthy of the provisional government they had just declared, they had to convince everyone that the new republic would maintain order.

At the same time, however, the republicans insisted on the misery that drove these men to crime. When Eugène Sue's *Les Mystères de Paris* depicted the horrors leading to the prisons of Paris, it did not seek to demonstrate that the inmates of La Force belonged to distinguishable dangerous classes.[28] Rather, like the republicans of 1848, it had sought to depict the trajectory of "honest" and "moral" citizens into crime and to make them emblems for demands for social change. The republicans' immediate impulse was to embrace this logic. "We are all workers," a republican law professor announced in the euphoric rhetoric of that February. He demanded for dayworkers an end to poverty, for each child an education, for each man work, and for each man unable to work "rest" and the means of living. "Because otherwise," he declared, "what would you have these men do? Die? Or become criminals?"[29]

Newspapers recounted fears that legitimists might organize criminals against the provisional government, rumors that the pillage resulted from plotting by counterrevolutionaries, and horror of what might spring from these disorders: phantoms of the Terror fed the counterrevolution and came to haunt the barricades of the June Days: "The fearsome images of the 'dangerous classes' of the forties fused with those of the September Massacres and the Terror."[30] By June, the republicans' hard-won order would be shaken by imagery, fables, and myths given momentum by the republicans' own rhetoric. Though the republicans could demonstrate that prison inmates had not broken out, they could not dispel fears that workers without wages, means, or education were *already* criminals who lay in waiting in the streets.

The decade preceding 1848 had prepared the stage for a new definition of the people, for new concerns with workers' salaries and education, and for a growing need to separate the laboring classes from the dangerous ones reportedly lurking in the urban wilds. Social reformers like Honoré Frégier, Louis-René Villermé, and Eugène Buret catalogued the experiences of the working classes, claiming that their procedures of scientific observation could uncover not only the conditions but also the causes of the problems they unveiled.[31] "Morality based on facts" would replace what they scorned as philosophical speculation (CD, 1:xiv). The new methodologies uncovered the "truth" of those who lived in squalor in the newly industrialized cities. They produced statistics through which a moral order could be imposed on those individuals whose disorder threatened bourgeois values and property. Parent-Duchâtelet's study of prostitution enabled the new moralists to justify already existing systems of discipline and surveillance. Regulationists' speculations over the role of prostitutes in the "decadence" and revolts of 1789 and 1830 further fueled fears of popular protests.

The work of utopian socialists like Charles Fourier, Prosper Enfantin, Alphonse de Lamartine, and Louis Blanc registered new concerns with the fate of the man of the people and also with his wife, daughters, and concubines.[32] Workers joined together to print their own newspapers, among them *L'Atelier* and *La Ruche populaire*, which sought to educate other workers about the lives they might hope to lead.[33] The woes of their sisters became an unequivocal call to arms as the workers' collectives pitted themselves against low wages and poor working conditions. The editors of the early feminist press, like the charity workers they frequently resembled, sought to provoke concern with the social conditions of workers and their families.[34]

The stories told by these scientific and philosophic moralists focused the attention of the bourgeoisie and working classes alike on the problems of overlapping categories of dangerous and laboring classes.[35] Certain images, terms, and concerns recur in radically different kinds of texts. We find reflected there a common currency of assumptions about what mattered—a recurrent list of problems requiring solutions—in texts as different as those of the bourgeois investigators and those of workers. The images, buzzwords, and cast of characters could be lent to many causes.[36] Each time, the *story* would differ, and in that story we begin to see the ideological investments that conditioned events and the perceptions of those events.

For moralist investigators, utopian socialists, and the workers of *L'Atelier* alike, the issue was policy. The investigators wanted to regulate the bodies they sought to know. The socialists demanded better conditions through changes in state-implemented actions. The workers echoed demands for changed conditions but vehemently insisted on their own meritorious nature—as *different* from the barbarians with whom they had so far been too easily confused. Both in its February and June Days, the Revolution of 1848 rearticulated the terms of the discourse on social marginality and saw the policy issues at its center turned into the battlefield on which the republic would rise and fall.

The transformation of these issues into political questions did not, however, wrench them from the fantasmatic aspects of the discourse itself. At most that transformation gave rise to new distortions while seeming to liberate certain of its actors from the condemnations to which they were accustomed. If the worker was to be elevated as the deserving hero of the republic in government attempts to find some new means of putting him to work, his fellows in misery would quickly find themselves relegated to roles of sloth, lush, and wastrel. For every worker who gained a voice or a means of support from the revolutionary change in agenda, another would find himself the subject of a plot that depended on his silence and poverty. Because the working-class woman had even less of a voice and made far less money, she could be lent with extraordinary ease to those plots that silenced her. Yet the investigators, socialists, workers, and republicans were intent on spreading tales about her.

Perhaps the most frequently told tale made her a whore. As we saw in chapter 1, prostitution had become a central social question in the eighteen years of the July Monarchy. Although the prostitute had been investigated, counted, and classified by the new reformists of the 1830s and 1840s, she still continued to fascinate. The investigators had induced her complicity in their differences, their desires, their order, and therefore, in their disciplinary system — up to a point — for she always seemed to escape their gaze and their plots. Even when she collaborated to help police others, she remained dangerous, potentially disruptive, and provocative.

To transform the woman of the people into a prostitute always exaggerates whatever other terms one would associate with her. To tell the story of female poverty in terms of the inevitability of prostitution is to call for higher wages for women. To tell the story of female victimization in terms that relate the bourgeois seduction of working-class girls to their fall into prostitution is to call for a better ordering of bourgeois sexuality.[37] To tell the story of the fall of a working-class girl into vice is to call for better moralization of workers.[38] To speak of female depravity in terms of prostitutes is to insist upon the irredeemable quality of these women's mores and to suggest that, in fact, the working class cannot be redeemed either. If the *femme du peuple* is unnatural, the prostitute is even more removed from woman's special goodness.[39] If the working-class woman lacks scruples, the prostitute has never conceived of belonging to moral society. If the working-class woman slips with ease into a turbulent world of "dangerous" souls, the prostitute entangles others in the world she seems to get blamed for inventing. If women of the people become easy concubines, prostitutes should never be allowed to marry into "normal" society. If working-class women engage in violent behavior, prostitutes erupt as veritable monsters, uncontrollable and berserk.

Prostitution thus served as a metaphor for an entire range of concerns and fears.[40] A label assigned at random to a woman, it allowed stories to be told without so many explanations (statistics or documentation) as might otherwise be required. Just as the legal system of nineteenth-century France denied the prostitute equal protection under the law, abrogating her rights to a hearing and ignoring her complaints when violence was perpetrated against her,[41] few would defend the prostitute against the representational intrigues in which she was implicated. Some of these plots discredited her. They censored her either as a prostitute or as a woman or as a worker and did so as a means of censoring the groups with which she was associated. Others, however, like Stern's account of the Tuileries, turned her occupation into yet another kind of currency. The episode at the beginning of this section, the freeing of the women of Saint-Lazare by the people of February, enables us to elaborate on the power of that currency.

Saint-Lazare Prison in 1843 held between 1250 and 1300 women, divided into five categories: (1) *"prévenues"* or *"accusées"* — women arrested but not yet charged as well as those already indicted for crimes but not yet tried, amounting to 300–350; (2) prisoners condemned to less than a year, also about 300–350; (3) prostitutes detained by discretionary power of the police prefect, numbering 300; (4) young girls held according to Articles 66 and 67 of the Penal Code, and young prostitutes held by administrative order, amounting to 50–60; and (5) "sick" prostitutes — those women diagnosed syphilitic during a medical visit, numbering 250–300.[42] In 1846 a history of the Paris prisons characterized Saint-Lazare in terms that must have approximated the popular view: "The majority of its prisoners are high-class and low-rate swindlers, women of gaming whose salons were discovered by police spies, minors under police supervision, and prostitutes imprisoned by the authorities." Saint-Lazare was hardly the prison of the hardened criminal. Rather, it held either the victims of poverty, popularly seen as driven into occasional prostitution by circumstances beyond their control, or women "whose greed and predatory nature excite them to steal the property of others."[43] When the republican press excused the liberators of the women of the Saint-Lazare prison, it did so by evoking visions of the prostitute as victim. Within days of that liberation, however, the stories told about these women changed drastically. While the republicans had temporarily treated the escapees from Saint-Lazare as women who deserved the liberty of revolution, they just as quickly reassigned them to a clan marked irredeemable, immoral, and dangerous.

What had driven the crowds to Saint-Lazare on that occasion of victory? What encouraged them — either traditionally or on this specific occasion — to rally around a prostitutes' prison? Why liberate the prostitutes but not all the prisoners there? Why was it so important to reassure the public that the *Femme Delannoy* had been left behind in her cell? Or that the sick prisoners had not been liberated?

Strangely enough, none of the contemporary histories of the February Days deems this episode worth mentioning. For nearly 150 years this story has been treated with strange indifference by the chroniclers of 1848.[44] In works like those of Stern, Alexis de Tocqueville, and Du Camp, the revolts put down by students of the École polytechnique take their place beside accounts of thieves shot by the people. Order has its story as does fear of disorder. The plot around the prison prostitute seems to balance on the delicate borderline between these two stories. Yet this episode, which seems to have resulted in neither vengeance nor moral chaos, highlights the fragile differences on which the revolutionaries of 1848 depended.

The people may have gone to Saint-Lazare for any of five reasons: (1) out of solidarity with women victims whose stories had recurred in workers' press and social-science moralizations alike; (2) because the people were convinced of the innocence of their own kind; (3) because the insurgents wanted to free their own family members; (4) because pimps wanted their women and livelihood back;[45] and (5) because they may have feared reprisals against imprisoned women like those of the September massacres. To imagine this liberation as acceptable during days when order was fervently sought, we must suppose that the republicans viewed these women as fundamentally harmless—as victims of police repression, bourgeois seduction, or denunciations. We must assume that neither the liberators nor the press saw any *difference* between the prisoners set free and women who were already at large.

When *Le National* reported the story of the liberation of Saint-Lazare, its reporter was quick to establish a contrast between the "good" women who were liberated and those *others* left behind in Saint-Lazare. Those "120 sick women" who were kept in the prison found themselves in the company of *la Femme Delannoy*, "the woman found guilty in the affair of the rue des Moineaux," a woman the boulevard press had labeled a "heinous criminal." A revolutionary figurehead had to deserve respect or pity. Working-class people had to be able to identify with her. She *could* be a prostitute, but she could not be syphilitic or dangerous. The comurderess of her elderly employer, the sixty-seven-year-old charwoman Delannoy had conspired with the porter and their relatives in a crime considered so brutal that her own son hanged himself in his cell to escape punishment. Delannoy had stolen the woman blind, executed her, and set her on fire.[46] The trial, detailed daily in the *Gazette des tribunaux*, must have so permeated the public imagination during late 1846 and early 1847 that the very mention of Saint-Lazare recalled the evil servant's presence there. The revolutionaries and their press champions assured the public that *she* would not be allowed to roam free. With her syphilitic sisters she would be kept under carceral observation, safe from revolution and insurgents. The differences of each—in the one case the perceived depravity of a servant who murdered her mistress and, in the other, the more verifiable contamination of disease—shoved these prisoners beyond the realm of the people's concerns. The *other* women of the prison could be liberated because they were somehow *like* their champions. As long as their differences were not noticed, they could be left at liberty.

"Every revolution is, more or less, a reinterrogation of the law,"[47] Michelle Perrot has noted. Because the law is in flux, any "illegality" is quickly perceived as the handmaiden to the revolution. As we have seen, the specter of disorder haunted both revolution and prostitution in the nineteenth century. Accounts of the Great Revolution proliferating in the mid-nineteenth century repeatedly emphasized its moral chaos.[48] What had changed in 1789, remarked one historian, was that the libertinism of the aristocrats had descended into all ranks of society.[49] Regulationists claimed that ordinances regulating prostitution derived from the revolutionaries' attempt to stem the tide of debauchery they saw as a threat to their cause (*FPP*, 1:80–82). Each nineteenth-century revolution would have its trial for depravity. The uses made of those fantasies of debauchery seemed, indeed, to change more than the stories of loose morals themselves.

Writing in the shadow of myths about prostitutes and the Revolution of 1830, Parent promoted tough prison conditions: only prison could "keep prostitutes in the line of duty and repress their disorders" (*PD*, 2:253). For Parent, a disorderly prostitute was a disobedient prostitute: an *insoumise* who turned her tricks outside the tolerance system of regulated medical visits and taxed registration. The illness she might spread was only nominally at issue. When she was *soumise* —submitted to a registered state—the violence perceived as emanating naturally from her character could be channeled into "proper" uses. *Insoumise*, she might disseminate violence in unlikely places. Because the clandestine prostitute so resembled women who did not sell their bodies, the disorder Parent projected upon her bolstered the regulationists' views that she was, indeed, inherently different. Her disorder, then, resulted from her circulation in a system of exchange outside the law. Her challenge to the law, like her challenge to a traditional system of values, became a central issue in both the politics and the representations of 1848.

Within days of the prison liberations, the minister of justice of the provisional government begged the people to cooperate in the name of liberty, equality, and fraternity: "Order in the utmost liberty, that is the spectacle that Paris has just given the world. The most insignificant disorder must not come to disturb this admirable situation. Those who would try to compromise it with their excesses are not only bad citizens but delinquents who veil dangerous criminal plots in the interests of a revolution that disavows them."[50] Suddenly, despite over a week's silence about the hundreds of women freed from Saint-Lazare, the press began to remind Parisians of their presence—and of their recall to order. Minister Crémieux demanded the arrest of these disavowed criminals, reminding the people that "our popular revolution, achieved in the name of justice, must assure and wants to assure the reign of the law."[51] Within two days, the reigning law encompassed the people's women: "Two women found behaving suspiciously in the surroundings of the palace were arrested because they were recognized by the head of the police as habitual offenders who had escaped Saint-Lazare Prison in the middle of the confusion of February 24."[52] Unlike the prostitutes of 1830 who, according to legend, begged to return "home" to Saint-Lazare the day after their liberation, these women circulated freely until the law came after them.[53] They simply tried to become like everyone else. Perrot has remarked that the scattered press accounts of their brushes with the law suggest attempts to "live differently," to break with family and past, or to establish themselves in a new trade. She points in particular to the attempt by one group to set up a laundry, an endeavor that was ultimately put down by the police as successfully as though it had been a riot.[54] The republicans had learned that order depended on knowing that your local *blanchisseuse* did not have stains on her past. It suddenly had become more important to contain her as disorderly than to represent her freedom.

Saint-Lazare Prison would again swallow its marked creatures. There, in the spirit of the revolution, they would be forced to serve out their time *without* working. The provisional government sought to make sure these women did not jeopardize the wages of *honest* women with prison work that, it argued, would at best teach them discipline.[55] The revolutionaries seem not to have considered that in prison these women might have learned a trade and thus found a means to change professions. They too depended on the difference between disorderly and orderly women, dishonest and honest women, bodies sold and labor exchanged. The ordered body of the woman had quickly become one of the revolution's most valuable commodities.

The revolutionaries of 1848 touted two seemingly antithetical representations of the prostitute in the months between February and June. The first crowned her with pity, making her a victim, one of the reasons why a revolution had been necessary. The second surrounded her with terror, insisting on her danger, and making her one of the reasons why strict order was essential to the republican cause. These two portraits, though deriving from completely different impulses, began to overlap and blur in a way that confused the original impulses and endangered the goals.

In 1840, in a small book seized by the censors (figure 3.1), socialist Alphonse Esquiros conflated these two stories in a way that set the stage for revolutionary representations to come:

> Prostitution is, know it well, in the present state of things, a source of agitation and disorders. It always becomes dangerous in the long run, for a state to allow its members to separate from the center in this way: it is these divided and marginalized forces who, in a given time, make revolutions. There are two bastard sisters in the world: prostitution and revolt. This poor creature, rejected with disgust and horror by society, sets against it with resistance, rebellion, and hatred. Like all those suffering and uncomfortable, the prostitute dreams of an upheaval; she engages all those who surround her in this spirit of revolt. Those smoky hovels and these dubious passages are the ones, in fact, that, on the day of the tocsin, vomit fighters into the street. Vengeance and the hatchet come out of there with [feverish] kisses.[56]

The union forged between prostitution and revolt may not have engendered either the streetfighters or the imagined "kisses" of 1848. What it did produce, however, was a series of fantasies — of dangerous bodies in circulation, of violated bodies in search of change, of marginals whose interests could be championed, of women whose desires could be profitably represented.

Emplotting Difference

The logic of the tolerance system required that prostitutes be distinguishable from honorable women. Regulationist logic further required that good prostitutes be separable from bad prostitutes, that those capable of repenting would be helped to repentance, that those worthy of charity would benefit from its gifts. The discourse of the Revolution of 1848 struggled with the contradictions inherent in this logic — for if good women could be separated from bad, then

Figure 3.1

The frontispiece from the 1841 edition of Alphonse Esquiros's *Les Vierges folles* depicts two "crazy virgins" whose vengeful "kisses" are imagined to spread into the streets in revolutionary moments.

surely revolutionaries could help women who deserved it. However, if good women had already been perverted by the evil influences of the previous regimes, then it might not be possible to tell them from the inherently perverted. It might be impossible to know whether a prostitute was worth fighting for. It might not even be possible to know if the working-class women on the side of the revolution were worthy of their mission.

Clémence d'Harville's first charitable quest in *Les Mystères de Paris* takes her into the same prison that aroused such anxiety in 1848. In Saint-Lazare, Clémence finds her first *"roman"* (MP, 609)—none other than Fleur-de-Marie who after her disappearance from Rodolphe's farm has been arrested for loitering on the Champs-Elysées (MP, 608). Recognized by the police, Fleur has been sent to prison because her name still appeared on the registers (MP, 609). The proof of Fleur's worthiness of the interest of charitable ladies such as Clémence, we learn, lies not just in her timid and respectful manner, but also in her influence upon the other prisoners (MP, 609). Quickly becoming the champion of the prison's downtrodden, she has even conquered the heart of the most "violent, audacious, and beastlike" prisoner in their midst. La Louve is "a girl of twenty, tall, virile, with a rather pretty but hard face," known for terrorizing her companions to get whatever she wants (MP, 610). During a scuffle over a piece of bread for a pregnant prisoner, Fleur has taken on La Louve and begun to work a strange magic on the vicious woman: "The worst characters sometimes experience good changes of fortune" (MP, 611), the novel informs us. Thereafter La Louve will not only defend Fleur but will confide her story and dreams to the young prostitute-turned-philanthropist.

Sue's Saint-Lazare is a place where goodness and evil can be spied at a glance. The prison's female philanthropists are physiognomists of sorts who instantly "classify" prisoners "according to their degree of immorality" (MP, 608). Like these charity ladies, the incarcerated prostitutes engage in a behavioral determinism that tells them that Fleur is not "one of them" (MP, 611).[57] The novel is quick to perform its own classification of prisoners and to arrange them before us so that we, too, may judge their worth. Like the discourse surrounding the prisoners liberated from Saint-Lazare, Sue's novel leaps to establish the difference between (Princess) Fleur and the common prostitute the text nicknames "She-Wolf." La Louve is represented as inherently tainted: a model of the dangerous, irredeemable prostitute, she is contrasted with Fleur and her fundamental goodness. But despite her "dangerous influence," she is given yet another chance. Fleur's "salutary influence" works so well on La Louve that the seemingly dangerous prostitute shows signs of rehabilitation. Like Fleur, La Louve will now be given an excuse for her situation, a fantasy of a background that makes her present state understandable if not also excusable. Abandoned by her mother at age eleven, raised by her abusive father and his mistress, she found herself obliged to sleep in the same bed with the two sons her father's mistress brought into their one-room household. La Louve, we learn, did not enter into prostitution for any of those perverse reasons listed by regulationists. She sought neither luxury nor libertinage. Rather, she was forced on her sixteenth birthday by her father's ex-mistress to register with the police. She has simply never known any other way of life.

Just as surely as the novel uses La Louve's depravity to foreground Fleur's goodness, it now uses her rehabilitation to promote its philanthropic success stories. Dreaming only of returning to the man she loves, renouncing prostitution, and making a home with him, La Louve leaves prison to arrive at her lover's island just as the delegates of the evil notary, Jacques Ferrand, are using its waters to hide their crimes. The body she fishes from the deep turns out to be that of Fleur—just barely alive. La Louve's rescue brings her even greater rewards: along with her new husband she is given passage to Algeria to a farm Rodolphe has purchased for them. Safely transported to the colonies, these former criminals are invited to make new lives. Separated from the world in which their stories mark them, they can be allowed to live. Fleur, meanwhile, like other prostitute heroines of the July Monarchy, must pay her dues for aspiring to reform within her *own* society.

But Fleur had entered the hearts of the thousands who followed her story, her rehabilitation becoming as important for Sue's readers as the punishment of the evil characters who continually jeopardized her safety. Sue's fan mail advised him in particular on how to save the adolescent girl about whose past the novel gave only one detail: that she was *inscrite* on the rolls of the police. The *souteneurs* who wanted to rescue her did not, however, stop at writing letters to her author demanding her safe passage beyond the tolerance system of this novel.[58] When she did not survive, they registered the meaning that had been circulated through her body. They demanded social change, prison reform, better wages for women, education for girls, divorce rights, and the vote for women. Over her dead body, safely entrapped in the novel that registered her plight but not the extent of her sexual exchange value, other stories began to be told that suggested there were prostitutes for whom one could fight. If women could be represented, these stories hinted, then social change might become more than the stuff of novels.

In the editions of *Les Mystères de Paris* of the 1840s and 1850s, La Louve was depicted setting out to save Fleur, rising up like Delacroix's *Liberty*, breast bared, raging forward, unstoppable (see figure 3.2).[59] The woman freed from Saint-Lazare and the one imagined by its critics as belonging there have in common a fantasy of liberty that might include more than just symbols. The July Monarchy illustration reminds us that La Louve has battles yet to fight. Unlike Sue's critics, we can hardly credit him with inciting the working class to social warfare. Yet his novel opened up spaces in which the demands of the previously silenced might be heard. It gave novel readers like Clémence d'Harville something better to do with their time than committing adultery. It reversed its initial condemnation of the *femme du peuple* by insisting that the conditions in which she had lived did not leave her any other option. Most important, it

Figure 3.2

"La Louve," the rehabilitated prostitute of Sue's *Mystères de Paris*, was depicted in the 1851 edition of the novel in a pose drawn from Delacroix's *Liberty on the Barricades*.

(BIBLIOTHÈQUE NATIONALE)

imagined that the individual who would come to the prostitute's defense would do so in the guise of a female revolutionary.

The stories Sue's novel set in motion may well have existed as much in the minds of his critics as in the dreams of his readers. Unlike the stories of this novel, the new stories made possible in 1848 laid claim to radically new ways of representing women, of representing the working class, and of imagining change. And Sue would be blamed for every moment of violence or tension that resulted. Like the legends about the prostitutes and the Revolution of 1830, the familiar story about Sue and the people may well have been a convenient myth, told to demonstrate how gullible the people were and spun by those who sought to denigrate the revolution or to condemn the violence of the June Days. It may well have lost sight of the extent to which the bourgeoisie became impassioned by this novel.[60] Yet it assigns a power to this novel and to the prostitute at its center that nevertheless reminds us of the fears and desires lodged in literature.

Throughout the July Monarchy, and even more so after the June Days of 1848, conservative critics like Alfred Nettement, Charles Menche de Loisne, and Eugène Poitou raged against Sue's attempts to excuse criminals and prostitutes for their offenses: "[Sue] makes them so sympathetic that we are truly tempted to see them as oppressed people exposed to social persecution" (*EC*, 1:307). The workers of *L'Atelier* complained similarly of Sue's attempt to "hold society responsible for the mistakes and crimes committed by some of its members." After all, they argued, every man must choose between good and evil and "each person must bear the responsibility for his acts." Only a moral system in which the evil are punished and the good rewarded could suit the workers. It would not do to imagine that the criminal or the prostitute might be "victims of blind fate."[61] Both conservatives and workers worried that literature broke down the fragile boundaries by means of which revolutionary representation had been achieved. They were afraid that if prostitutes and criminals could not be held accountable for their evils, even "virtue" might go unrecognized.

The novelists of the July Monarchy tried to resolve these dilemmas by generating intricate plots in which some criminals, like Balzac's Vautrin or Sue's Ferrand, were rotten to the core, while others, like Lucien or the Chourineur, managed to redeem themselves—usually through a repentant and ennobling death. For the prostitutes in these novels, the choices narrowed. Elvire of Napoléon Landais's *Une Vie de courtisane* (1833) pledges to go straight after the Revolution of 1830 but dies instead of hunger in the arms of the man who first seduced her. The repentant prostitute of *Louisa: ou, les douleurs d'une fille* (1830) expires in the presence of the priest who "publishes" her memoirs. *Splendeurs et misères des courtisanes* (1838–43) allows Esther a noble suicide in the face of a return to prostitution. The novel I examine in chapter 7, Antony Méray's *La Part des femmes* (1847) bans its fallen woman, virtually unseen, to Saint-Lazare without giving her a chance to repent. Each text goes about the task of "purifying prostitutes" (*SMC*, 83) and transforming the aberrant, all the while threatening its readers with the dangers of the impure, the unrepentant, or worse yet, the undifferentiated.

The literary works of this period seek to give their prostitutes a past that could excuse their wrong turns and establish their inherent worth. The stories of July Monarchy prostitutes have peculiar ways of becoming *Bildungsromane* with a twist: novels of educationlessness. If we are to learn that a prostitute is truly a good girl, then we must also discover that she was cruelly seduced and abandoned. If we are to learn that she is really rotten to the core, then we must become privy to her poor choices—to her refusals to go to school, for example, in the case of Landais's Elvire—or to her twisted nature—as in Pulchérie's description of herself as a young girl in George Sand's *Lélia* (1833). In this way, July Monarchy narratives of prostitutes' lives resemble the stories given to hysterics and other asylum inmates in the same period, as I show in chapter 4. Medical and social scientific advances during the July Monarchy seem to have converged in obsessions with naming the origins of social and personal maladies. By giving a primal scene to prostitution, these texts seem to argue that the prostitute is not only worth representing but also *worth fighting for*.

Most surprising is the extent to which these texts ensure that their prostitutes function within the tolerance system. Despite the differences between them, La Louve and Fleur-de-Marie are both registered with the police. Vautrin/Herrera blackmails Esther with her radiation from the rolls of the *Bureau des moeurs* (*SMC*, 83). Elvire signs herself Coralie after her fall onto the police registers.[62] Of the major literary studies of prostitution between 1830 and 1848, only three allow their heroines to circulate without a permit. One of these, Balzac's *Cousine Bette* (1847), discussed in chapter 5, depicts the clandestine acts to which a housewife maliciously lends herself. The other two, Hugo's *Marion de Lorme* and Dumas fils' *La Dame aux camélias*, both of which attracted enormous critical attention in theatrical versions, represent women whose occupation is listed as *courtisane*. Hugo's Marion, as we have noted, could hardly have been expected to sign up with a "Morals Brigade" in the France of Louis XIII. Yet she might as well have been on the books for all the individuals who try to police her back into circulation.

Unlike Hugo's play, Dumas fils' *La Dame aux camélias* makes no efforts to stage its novelistic or theatrical drama in any historical past. Rather, it sets its story in 1847, the year before its publication as a novel. Shockingly, it dared to send its whore into the streets without first signing her up in the police army of libertinage. It gave her a plot without first ensuring that she would represent either the interests of the state or those who feared the breakdown of the clear demarcations conferred by tolerance. It sent her into the debacle of the June Days without first attaching her to traditional structures of containment.

Over Her Dead Body

"The prostitute is . . . a monstrosity," declared police commissioner Béraud in 1839 (*FPP*, 1:127). The most monstrous of all prostitutes, according to July Monarchy regulationists, was the courtesan. Solutions for coping with her dangers varied widely. Parent chose to concentrate his energies on the women he believed the police could control. His study placed kept women (*femmes galantes*) in a class apart from that of common *filles en cartes* and *filles en numéro*.[63]

Béraud saw only one difference—her presentability. To Béraud, the courtesan was the most dangerous of all prostitutes because one could not tell her apart from women of polite society: "she often combines personal charms with the attractions of the most brilliant and most well-rounded education: music, singing, dance, pure language, a refined spirit, exquisite taste, and the most pleasant abandon" (*FPP*, 1:131–32). Thanks to her charms she "prepare[s] the ruin" of "honorable men" and compromises the fortune, honor, and happiness of families. Although he agreed that courtesans are "the most dangerous beings in society," Parent abandoned any attempt to restrain them administratively. The doctor seemed resigned that one could tell no stories about a *femme galante*—after all, she had a home, she paid taxes, she seemed to conform to every rule of decency. Like the honorable women she resembled, she enjoyed her political rights; she even had the power to sue anyone who called her a prostitute (*PD*, 1:176). Béraud would have insisted that the courtesan's decent mask was precisely what required stories to be told. Just like the *insoumises* whose clandestine debauchery "paralyzes police action," the courtesan neglected her health and threatened to ravage the health of those enjoying her company (*FPP*, 1:138–39; *PD*, 1:176). And nothing, but nothing, would bring her under the wing of tolerance.

The only virtue of a courtesan, argued Béraud, is that "the triumph of vice is short-term. Her fall is rapid: it is impossible to escape the horrible consequences of a life of depravity and immorality" (*FPP*, 1:133). Béraud might well have been writing the outline for Dumas fils' 1848 novel. Like the publishing coup of that same year, a new edition of *Manon Lescaut* priced at less than a loaf of bread,[64] Dumas's short novel traced the trajectory of a high-class prostitute from her heady days of gallantry to her purification through love to her melodramatic death. Like Prévost's novel, *La Dame aux camélias* was to become one of the sensations of its era, enjoying an immense popularity throughout the Second Empire. Not surprisingly, this story of a whore who frequents the theater became a *succès de scandale* not in its novelistic form of 1848 but in its stage version. Like many other novelistic works of its era, including *Les Mystères de Paris*, *La Dame aux camélias* was prepared almost immediately for the theater and submitted to the Second Republic Board of Censors for approval. But the play was just as quickly rejected in 1849. Although the July Monarchy had fallen in part due to its too-frequent, vindictive, and unpredictable use of the censor's privilege, the new government—founded on the principles of rights and equality so dear to July Monarchy opponents like Hugo—proved quickly unable to make good on its promises. This play, wrote the censors of 1851, had the audacity to reproduce the life of a recently dead *femme galante*. Unlike the more circumspect *Marion de Lorme*, *La Dame aux camélias* traced the contemporary life of a prostitute—and worse yet, everyone knew this prostitute had actually lived.[65] No matter how many changes Dumas made, the censors informed him that his play remained the "same painting of the manners and intimate life of kept women" and that nothing he could alter would change its thrust. The play did not open until after the *coup d'état* of December 2, 1851—when the Second Empire censors were able to overturn the morality of the republicans who had once spurned all censorship.

Dumas's novel and play have a curious position among the stories of prostitution in the mid-nineteenth century and an even stranger place among battles over censorship. Just as the Second Empire government laid down a formidable newspaper tax on all papers carrying *feuilleton* novels, they made way for the staging of a long censored drama about a contemporary prostitute and her youthful bourgeois lover. Even as the government of Louis-Napoléon sought to bring an end to the sinuous plots of novels like the one that contained the death of reformed prostitute Fleur-de-Marie, it broke the bonds that kept Marguerite Gautier out of circulation. At the same time as the new government began to seize and prosecute "immoral" texts like Sue's *Les Mystères du peuple*, Xavier de Montépin's *Filles de plâtre*, Flaubert's *Madame Bovary*, and Baudelaire's *Fleurs du mal*, it bowed to the excesses of the very kind censors had been throwing out of theaters for decades.[66] The obtuse resistance of the Second Republic's censors to Dumas's play may well have amounted to an attack on its author, a known opponent of the Republic, or upon the society the play depicted (the *haute bourgeoisie* and their women). We could nevertheless read this repeated censorship as another segment of the story we have been telling. Condemned by the same conservative critics who assaulted Sue, Hugo, Balzac, Sand, and Soulié, Dumas's novel aroused anxiety, anger, and fear. Censored by the very republicans who had promised changes in the circulation of texts and in the liberties of the people, *La Dame aux camélias* clearly challenged the techniques the new government had implemented to represent its people. Applauded by a bourgeois audience throughout the Second Empire, Dumas's work hardly played to the same crowds as Sue's. Caught up in the stories, the rhetoric, and the plots of the Revolution of 1848, *La Dame aux camélias* could not help participating in the cultural struggles that were to transform the social order. And strangely, though this text wears the guise of the bourgeois reaction of the June Days (just after which it was published), it encodes powerful resistances to those trappings.

Like the theatrical censors of 1851, Dumas's champion Jules Janin insisted upon the *true* story that lay behind *La Dame aux camélias*. Applauding its "touching story" and "sincere emotion of youth," Janin produced his own reflections on the woman whose "entirely true and bleeding representation" served as the basis for the novel.[67] Once the public had realized that Marguerite was based on a real courtesan, Janin noted, the popularity of the work had soared. Everyone wanted to read back into this "novel" what they knew of her real name, real lovers, real fortune, and real position in society. Everyone wanted to know what truth lay behind this "woman apart" (DC, 493). Suddenly the "interest in her story" lodged in who and what she had really been—and not in the terms the novel might have given her.

But the "real" Marie Duplessis died on February 3, 1847, *not* on February 20. She was buried within days of her death and *not* on February 22. The coincidence of the dates the novelist chose for his heroine's death and burial with the events of the year in which he published his text must be read as far more than fortuitous. The fatal decision of Louis-Philippe's regime, namely, to ban the opposition banquet scheduled for February 22, had been announced on February 21, the anniversary of the day following Marguerite's death. She had in some sense died with the regime and been buried with the insurrection of February 22.[68] Marguerite's (and her model Marie's) connections to the July Monarchy bourgeoisie are so tight that we have no choice but to read these dates as a commentary on the Revolution of 1848. Throughout the novel she associates with dukes and counts, with the rich and influential men of Paris. Her social standing depends as much on theirs as it does on her ability to pass for "honorable." Her companions, the novel suggests, are so powerful that even when people know *what* she is, no one says a word. If people talk, they do so with discretion: Armand Duval has nourished a crush on this well-known lady of the theater for years before he figures out she has a price.

Should we therefore read her connections to the bourgeoisie as evidence that this novel is just another representation out of the tolerance system? Can we imagine this novel to be anything more than a counterrevolutionary backlash to the February Days—a kind of literary version of the June Days? Like the plots around the prostitutes we have analyzed in the last two chapters, Marguerite Gautier's body turns out to be lent to a series of different concerns. The censorship that surrounded her—both as prostitute and as text—testifies to the anxieties as well as the desires lodged in her body.

The novel *of* 1848 trades the endless detours of the *roman-feuilleton* for a plot that guarantees from the outset that its heroine has already met her end. The suspense will, therefore, not revolve around the novel's play at rehabilitating its heroine but rather around the "mysteries" (*DC*, 52) that surround her ends. Peter Brooks has contended that the French Revolution is the "epistemological moment" of melodrama: "The Revolution attempts to sacralize law itself, the Republic as the institution of morality. Yet it necessarily produces melodrama instead, incessant struggle against enemies, without and within, branded as villains, suborders of morality, who must be confronted and expunged, over and over, to assure the triumph of virtue."[69] Like the melodrama of 1789, the revolutionary moral system instituted in 1848 established decisive structures of expectations. Aspiring to the melodramatic "logic of the excluded middle," described by Brooks, this text explicitly refuses deviance. Its "outlaw," the prostitute, is already dead by the time the story begins. Yet in place of the melodramatic battles that would exclude her, this text installs the oedipal conflict between father and son. In the place of the jealous lover with whom Armand imagines himself in competition for his beloved Marguerite's actions, the novel reveals his own father. The lure of the novel—why Marguerite abandons Armand just as she has undergone rehabilitation—is answered in the final pages: Armand has been competing with his own father for the loyalty of his lover.

This description of the plot gives a kind of twist to the conflicts of this novel in order to emphasize the extent to which the novel expels one kind of desire (to know what happened to Marguerite) in exchange for another (to resolve the oedipal conflict). Everyone—from the novel's narrator to its youthful bourgeois whose story is framed by that of the narrator he befriends to Armand's father—wants Marguerite's story. Everyone wants to make sense out of her remains. Like a murder mystery, this text produces a dead body out of which its plots might spring. Beginning with the announcement of the prostitute's death and a proclamation that her effects will be sold at auction, the novel invites us to want stories. Like all those who have come to peruse the objects for sale, we are invited to seek "the traces of this courtesan's life about whom one had heard, without a doubt, such strange tales" (DC, 52). This novel's representation will be an effect of the prostitute, meant to be sold, like her garments, her furniture, her *objets de toilette*. What the narrator chooses to buy at the sale—a book with an inscription, *"Manon à Marguerite: Humilité"* (DC, 64)—provides a generous return on the investment. No sooner has this gentleman pocketed his copy of *Manon Lescaut*, another gentleman appears at his door—the very Armand Duval who gave the dead courtesan the novel. In exchange for the artifact, the narrator gets Marguerite's story. He even gets a look at the body he seeks to represent and finds it, not surprisingly, rotting in its tomb (DC, 86).

Marguerite's story, told man to man as Armand lies in bed suffering the aftereffects of shock from digging up her still recognizable corpse, will extract her from the market in which she sold herself. Her cadaver enables Armand to set in motion representations of virtue in her name. The plot around her will soon reveal that she has only reprostituted herself to save Armand. At the entreaty of her lover's father, Marguerite has agreed to prove her love by sacrificing it "to Armand's future" (DC, 234). She has left his son to become a martyr for the protection of bourgeois values. But what of the idyll between the high-class prostitute and the young bourgeois? Are we to forget that Marguerite gave herself in a moment to the youth who proclaimed his undying love? Are we to forget her willingness to two-time him with her wealthy lover, the duke? Should we put aside our recollections of the clandestine underworld of covetous desires and greed in which Marguerite and her friends circulated? Armand's story of Marguerite's pure love cannot undo the bonds of courtesanry that have made her so intriguing.

Marguerite must therefore be shown to pay for her immorality with the wages of sin—her death by slow and painful disease. Consumption, that nineteenth-century euphemism for syphilis, ensures what Béraud called the "horrible consequences of a life of depravity and immorality." But it also infuses her increasingly with melodrama, rendering her increasingly pathetic and all the more deserving of the lover who was the first to "pity her" (DC, 161).[70]

Like most of the prostitutes whose stories preceded her in the July Monarchy gallery of harlots, Marguerite is given a past that might explain, if not excuse, her fall into prostitution. A poor farmgirl whose mother beat her (*DC*, 161), Marguerite learned to write only after joining the world of Paris gallantry (*DC*, 147). But like Fleur-de-Marie, she quickly shows signs of a higher nature. "Who would believe that a kept woman wrote that!" Armand exclaims of Marguerite's last letter (*DC*, 73). Even if this young woman was *not* a colonel's daughter schooled at Saint-Denis (*DC*, 147), she has gained the education and the morals necessary to become the emblem of a greater good. Caught by her lover annotating her copy of *Manon Lescaut*, Marguerite has come to bear the mark of humility that might differentiate her from her double. In the idyllic countryside of Bougival, one would no longer have known she had traded on her body. If from the beginning "we recognize in this *fille* the virgin that a trifle made into a courtesan," far from Paris, purified by love, "the courtesan disappeared" (*DC*, 110, 170). This novel demands that we take pleasure, like Armand, in her redemption and that we read her not for the story of her deviation but for the story of her goodness (*DC*, 66–67).

In a time of revolution, the prostitute can rally support for three reasons: (1) because the people want to save her since they see the rich as her oppressors; (2) because she is one *of* the people and therefore *like* the insurgent working classes; and (3) because even the rich and the bourgeois can pity *her*, as Armand does: poor creature, so much a victim, so clearly out of her natural order as a gentle, moral woman.[71] Dumas's novel allows for a new kind of support to gather around the prostitute, for its heroine is hardly a pitiable *femme du peuple*. Rather, she has put on all the trappings of the bourgeoisie—its luxury, its garments, its values, and its desires—and insinuates herself as a spectacle of honor into the midst of the bourgeoisie. She can indeed prove touching,[72] but she cannot draw support in the name of women like herself, driven into prostitution by the pathetic plight in which the labor market leaves them. Rather, she rallies support for bourgeois values, for a cover-up of the violence at the heart of the Revolution of 1848. Her pitiful death transforms her into a commodity to preserve family values, property values, promised wage values for men, and most of all, men's liberties. This novel surrounds her, it would seem, with the plots of tolerance, ensuring that if she circulates, she will do it only as pure representation, as a story in the place of a body. *La Dame aux camélias* therefore puts Marguerite on the books just as surely as a novel that would have shown her registered with the police. Coerced into submission by a love greater than her own desires, Dumas's prostitute has become a *soumise* in her turn.

Yet Dumas's courtesan left moralists as well as republicans reeling from the dangers they saw depicted in his book. The play's censors complained of the "feverish life without discretion, without modesty, of these *femmes galantes* who sacrifice everything, even their health, to the intoxications of pleasure, of luxury, and of vanity."[73] Moralist critic Poitou railed against its mockery of the meaning of virtue.[74] Socialist Adèle Esquiros complained that such "literary" courtesanry was more dangerous than "real" courtesans. Not only did it exalt "wicked instincts," she insisted, but it seduced poor women onto the road to dishonor: "these books make people believe in a life of display and easy-to-obtain pleasures. It's a lie." Women like Marguerite trade badly on their expensive tastes and simple reasoning. "Fatal creature who takes all and gives only nothingness!" Esquiros complains: What if, instead of dying *young*, Marguerite had died *old*? Would she have then inspired so many tears?[75]

Marguerite's critics, like her champions, insisted on the extent to which she must be read as "an exception" (*DC*, 250). Yet those who wanted to put a hold on the circulation of her text insisted equally upon the dangers that she might pose to others. Whether she was imagined as a seductress, as a redeemed Magdalen, or simply as a poor girl sacrificed to the desires of those around her, Marguerite's story was read as potentially endangering to its audience. Even represented within the strict network of tolerance, which exacts punishment as well as repentance, this prostitute aroused anxiety. Behind her story seemed to lie other stories that her critics feared might, because of her, be told. Over her dead body, this novel threatened to resurrect the fervor and hopes of the February Days.

Romanesque Theories

"The free woman is dead, but her venom is not," declared Ernst Legouvé, a republican historian invited in spring 1848 to lecture at the Collège de France.[76] The prostitute whose text moved into rapid circulation in the summer of 1848 survived the massacres of the June Days to make a series of scandalous demands. Marguerite did not want money, her novel reminds us repeatedly. She only wanted security. To get it, she set conditions for her relationships, called the shots in her sexual life, made her own financial decisions, and repeatedly demonstrated her capacity to run her own show. This woman has attained a kind of independence that only a handful of her married sisters could achieve.[77] She doesn't need charity to keep her busy. She has the theater, balls, and lavish dinners. She doesn't wait around for someone to escort her into the streets: she always travels alone in her carriage. Even when she is dying, she makes the choices that make her plot intriguing and redeem her past excesses: she withholds the truth about her "deception" from Armand until she has been lost to him forever.

The life Marguerite leads and the demands she makes on the men around her suggest that she has achieved freedoms of which the women revolutionaries of 1848 had only begun to dream. With the abolition of the press censorship of the July Monarchy and an end to restrictions on public meetings, the women of 1848 had begun to hope for radical changes in their own lives as well as in those of male republicans. Beginning in March, Eugénie Niboyet, Jeanne Deroin, Désirée Gay, and Suzanne Voilquin joined forces to produce *La Voix des femmes*, "a socialist and political newspaper, organ of the interests of all women."[78] Women's clubs called for women's right to vote and a reinstitution of divorce, improved compensation for women's work, women's right to conduct their own business affairs, and above all, women's right to education. "A woman is a free person," argued Pauline Roland, "She must build her life by means of her own work, her own love, her own intelligence."[79] The woman worker, argued *La Voix des femmes*, had a right to revolt: "What she wants is no longer organized charity, but justly distributed work."[80] Only education, fairly paid work, and political rights could extract women from the misery, hunger, and debasement that had constrained them. "Many single women are in desperate straits," a delegation of workers told republican Louis Blanc in March, "you would not want them to continue to be exposed to misery and disorder."[81]

The "disorder" these feminists summoned to call attention to their rights, education, and salaries, might have been lifted directly out of regulationist reports. Just as the victimization of working-class women had served republicans in the days just after February, feminists summoned their fall into prostitution as an inevitability that only changed conditions could prevent. While Legouvé called for legal controls on the men who seduced women and left them, fallen, pregnant, and shamed, the feminists of 1848 placed far more emphasis on increasing the liberties of women to prevent such eventual victimization.[82] "People complain about the immorality of women," wrote a woman worker to the new government, demanding other options than starvation or prostitution:

> How do you expect it to be otherwise when, after having worked all day, she finds she has earned twelve, fifteen, or at most twenty sous? What courage, what virtue can hold up against such a state of affairs? A poor girl fights a long time against misery; she hangs on against the seductions that surround her, but a day comes when she lacks work, and having nothing to put aside during good times to provide for the needs of bad times, she gives way to the demands of necessity and accepts dishonor to hide her intolerable misery. From the day she sets a foot on the path of vice, she is lost, prostituted![83]

For the editors of *La Voix des femmes*, the solutions to the degradation in which so many women found themselves could come only from economic, legal, educational, and political changes. Yet they made these appeals under the cover of tactical plots to moralize the new republic: "The morality of a nation depends especially on the morality of women," they wrote in their first issue.[84] Only if the state helps women to become moral can it expect mothers to raise "good sons" and "good citizens." Like men, women "want their country free but without profligacy, without licentiousness."[85] The feminists were all too aware, as an editor of the earlier *Tribune des femmes* had noted in 1832, that when society hears women speak of liberty, it becomes indignant, "because outside of slavery, it knows only prostitution."[86]

The *femme libre* of Saint-Simonianism had left a dangerous stain on all demands for women's freedom. Twisted into a rapacious sexual monster by conservatives and antifeminists, she had endangered whatever liberties republicans might hope to take in the name of women. Soon enough, the ghosts of "free women" returned to haunt the feminists of 1848. On June 28, women's clubs were banned. Deroin's *Politique des femmes* was obliged to change its name to *L'Opinion des femmes* because, the government informed her, women had no right to politics.[87] Women found themselves suffering from unemployment and low wage levels even worse than in the late July Monarchy.[88] The revolutionary Jacques-Étienne Chénu portrayed the radical feminists of 1848 as whores who joyfully "followed the common law" of the new government that required them to share their beauty with all.[89] Two of the most visible feminists of 1848, Deroin and Roland, were arrested in May 1850 for plotting against the republic. Roland's arrest report charged she was "the enemy of marriage which, since it subjects women to the authority of their husbands and sanctions an unacceptable inequality."[90] Censored for their idealism and values, Roland and Deroin were imprisoned for six months each. Devastated by the failures of feminist republicanism, Deroin sought exile in England. Roland was again apprehended as dangerous to the state after the *coup d'état* of December 1851. Deported to Algeria, she died before being able to return to her homeland.

Aware that one kind of emancipation of women was being demanded at the barricades, the republicans proposed their own. In the place of woman's catching violence, they set out to install a relay of morality.[91] For the better wages they demanded in her name, they provided her with academic elegies. As Police Prefect Caussaudière worked overtime to clean up the streets, the new minister of public instruction authorized Legouvé to open a course that would help women find their role in the new society. Legouvé's course would have at its root a justification of the family so like that of the July Monarchy moralists that one might expect that his demands for women's improved conditions—hailed by bourgeois feminists[92] as a "radical new development," were as much a concession to bourgeois ideology as was the bloodshed of the June Days. Legouvé was intensely aware of the threat other theories circulating around the revolution's women posed to the traditional patriarchal family:

> The condition of women requires many fundamental improvements, but in the presence of novelistic (*romanesque*) theories and socialist theories produced and reproduced on this subject, honorable minds nourished by hard study ought to come together to talk in the name of liberty and in the name of morality, to reconcile the woman's indefensible rights to self-possession with her character and duties as spouse, mother, daughter, and woman. (My emphasis)[93]

Lurking behind this history was another one, more violent perhaps, and more threatening than the disorders of the women who were not spouses, mothers, or daughters. Hertz has accurately pointed to the recurrent terror induced by representations of the bellies of prostitutes.[94] His psychoanalytical explanation nevertheless loses sight of the fact that a prostitute's belly produces new stories:

from her womb comes not just more disorder but rather a semblance of order. If she could evade recognition, her progeny would bear no sign of its history. It might, however, claim to belong to another family's plot. And the forty-eighters came dangerously close to changes that would have given that undifferentiated, unmarked child some rights to signs of respect.[95]

Like the feminine allegories adopted by the revolutionaries of the French Revolution in the wake of the Terror, where, according to Hunt, "the violence of the Revolution was conventionalized and to a large extent repressed,"[96] the stories the forty-eighters gave to women failed to represent their political and social interests. Designed to stem whatever violence might accompany women, these representations demonstrated with a flourish the investments of the forty-eighters in keeping their figureheads out of circulation. Unlike the figureheads of the earlier revolution, these symbolic women had begun to move into places where virtue might be compromised and where violence could erupt. Increasingly visible, increasingly vocal, they seemed no longer to allegorize that violence but instead to provoke stories about it. These were women in need of representation.

"Honorable women want to know how other women live and die," wrote Jules Janin of the stage success of *La Dame aux camélias*.[97] Finally throwing off the yoke of the censor to play to packed audiences, Dumas's *femme libre* reassured these women's husbands even as it insinuated tactical reminders of the powers the women might claim. Sixteen years later Dumas would lament the encroachment of women like his heroine onto the fortunes of the bourgeoisie as a kind of revolution of prostitutes: "For a long time women have complained, cried out, called for help. No one has answered them. They are finally waging their revolution" (*DC*, 521). The women he imagines encroaching upon society are elegant, ostentatious, indistinguishable from honorable women. They seek fortune in the garb of the most luxurious ladies, and, unlike Marguerite, they do not sacrifice themselves to save their bourgeois counterparts and young lovers. Instead, they redistribute the riches of the upper classes into the ranks of the working classes from which they rose. In the name of what Dumas calls "women's rights," they reclaim liberties long denied them. They devour everyone in sight. Dumas's image of "universal prostitution" summons a vampiric Marguerite from her unquiet grave. But Dumas does not imagine her gratified by changes in the conditions that led to her "revolt." Whatever needs may have led these women to their "revolutionary" prostitution, Dumas is less concerned with meeting those demands than with summoning a specter of terror. Just as he obfuscated the circumstances that bound his heroine in 1848 to a life of prostitution and a painful, tragic death, in 1868 he condemned the society that empowered its luxury courtesans instead of projecting an end to the suffering that drove them into servitude.

Not all those who represented prostitutes would so easily quell the stories that circulated around these women's bodies. Julie Daubié, the first French woman permitted to take a *baccalauréat* examination, reminded her readers in *La Femme pauvre* that the audacity of texts like those of Dumas "reflect our morals," and therefore show us how much must change.[98] Active in the 1860s in the campaign to end government regulation of prostitution, Daubié called for paternity suits, legal equality for "illegitimate" children, and penalties for men involved with prostitutes. According to Daubié, clandestine prostitution was the result of the "irresponsibility of men in the face of seduction." Only when men were penalized for pimping, haunting bordellos, and seducing women, she argued, could one hope to relieve the misery afflicting women.[99] Daubié's contemporary, feminist Maria Desraismes particularly attacked male dependence upon courtesans. Upholding family values, for Desraismes, meant insisting upon women's rights within that family, upon their sexual fulfillment, and upon an education equal to that of men. Depicting the courtesan as a victim of men who sought her to meet needs they could not satisfy in the marriages they had rendered sterile, Desraismes called for a return to love in marriage and for an end to notions of essential difference upon which inequalities were based.[100]

Only after the establishment of the Third Republic in 1871 did voices like Daubié's and Desraismes's begin to transform the ways society saw women, working women, and prostitutes. By the 1870s the prison that had rallied the forty-eighters had become a symbol for the abolitionists who sought to bring an end to the tolerance system. Desraismes became a leader in the *Association française pour l'abolition de la prostitution réglementée*, joining together with the philanthropic women of the *Oeuvre des libérées de Saint-Lazare* to seek the demolition of the prostitutes' prison and the suppression of the Morals Police.[101] "We must give a trade to all women," declared in 1869 the "diary" of a woman working under cover to expose the conditions of the prisoners of Saint-Lazare.[102] Like Clémence d'Harville, the author of these memoirs believed she could identify those women capable of repenting. Unlike either Sue's charity workers or the forty-eighters who embraced their cause, this woman did not seek proof that the inhabitants of Saint-Lazare were not themselves guilty of crimes. She embraced instead an ethic that would dominate republican feminism for the next decades: she argued that *all* these women deserved help, for the conditions that led to their victimization were beyond their control. But unlike the abolitionists of the Third Republic (1871–40), this author seemed to resign herself to those conditions. By the Third Republic, the feminists who followed her into Saint-Lazare had begun to resemble more and more the prison liberators of 1848. Refusing to be content with a system that victimized the poor, the marginal, and the working class, these activists sought solutions that would both free prisoners and abolish the conditions that led to their arrests. Change came slowly. Saint-Lazare's last prisoners would not go free until the late 1930s. Nearly a century passed before the liberties demanded by the feminists of 1848 became a reality. Married women attained full legal rights in 1938. Women received the right to vote in 1944. Equal pay for women was not legislated until 1946.[103]

The nineteenth-century women who championed prostitutes' causes have been criticized as embracing, even in their counterdiscursive undertakings, fundamentally conservative goals.[104] Such views imagine the engagements of feminism and philanthropy as a kind of mating of the values of Clémence d'Harville, La Louve, and Armand Duval—charity ladies, poor women workers, and male bourgeois socialists—and condemn their emphasis on morality as a further extension of the policing of sexuality. Critics of these feminists lose sight of the complexity of their goals and the breadth of their interests: for a century after 1848, the prostitute's plight gave a focus to battles for women's liberties. For some who fought in her name, those battles required the kind of moralization embraced by Legouvé. For others, motherhood gained primacy over the rights of women workers. Some became obsessed with retaining essential differences between men and women. Still others became paralyzed by anger and fear. The nuances of these struggles are as much a legacy of 1848 as the prostitute's plight. If we are to make sense of the successes of feminism, we must also understand the struggles through which its tactical positions were achieved. By studying the tensions under which that feminist discourse was wrought, we can begin to see what is at stake in women's representation. This chapter has traced a segment of that history.

The battles fought over the prostitute's body allowed bourgeois women an alternative to charity work. The struggles for working women's rights generated spaces through which women of all classes began to make themselves heard. Even though at times these feminists struck notes uncannily similar to those of reformists who sought to police women out of the work force and into the home, they resoundingly rejected compromises to the rights they sought.[105] Through the union of feminists and philanthropists around the issue of prostitution, the conditions of all women were called into question. Through crusades uniting workers and bourgeois women, feminist goals were articulated. Through the tactical alliances of republican revolutionaries, feminists, and prostitutes, the tolerance system was at last dismantled. In 1946 the regulated brothels were closed. With the end of police plots around prostitutes, the promises of 1848 had at last been fulfilled.

The readers of the plots of 1848 left a curious legacy of fear and hope. Conservatives' studies of the "influence of literature and theater on public spirit and morality" reread works like those of Hugo, Sand, Soulié, Sue, Balzac, and Dumas fils back into the events of the revolution. Disappointed republicans sought excuses for the revolution's failures in literature as well as in the causes it championed.[106] In his 1857 assessment of July Monarchy literature, Poitou worried in particular about "an extremely large class of people whose half-education has placed them halfway between ignorance and knowledge." Many of these people, he insisted, got their opinions from novels: "It is on this kind of reader . . . that bad literature has exerted a great influence. It has corrupted some and seduced others. . . . By exalting in all a pride in individual reason, it has especially augmented the moral anarchy from which we are suffering."[107] He saw works like *Marion de Lorme, Les Mystères de Paris,* and *La Dame aux camélias* as the "zealous accomplices" of "the revolutionary spirit." Most dangerously, he argued, they have incited people to believe in "equality"—"the secret evil, the disintegrator of democratic society." The pride and envy born of this "love of equality" have driven the people to embrace "popular courtesanry."

According to Poitou and other critics of this literature of immorality, the literary tradition that began with *Marion de Lorme* had to be brought to an end.[108] For such moralists, the "immorality" of *La Dame aux camélias* was not attenuated by her noble goals or by her punishing illness. That this text gained such popularity simply proved that something was deeply wrong with France. In fact, Poitou contended, every time plays like this regaled the public, the police were obliged to double their surveillance efforts over a "trembling crowd, always ready to bring into reality the passions that [plays] inflame in them."[109] The censorship he tacitly embraced would put people as well as texts under wraps. The story that bound fears of literature to terrors about marginals gained a life of its own in nineteenth-century France. It was, as I have argued in the last three chapters, an outgrowth of battles over morality, gender, and power.

Beginning with the crackdowns against Hugo's *Marion de Lorme* in 1829 and against prostitutes in 1830, that story recurred in ever-changing ways over the course of the next decades. It linked the four stories about representation we have traced in the discourse of 1848: a story of ambivalence and fear, insisting on women's dangers; a story of women's victimization, calling for change; a story that sought to imbue a woman with values worth fighting for; a story that plotted women's need for representation. As we have seen throughout this chapter, literature became one of the battlefields on which the struggles over these stories were played out. It rechanneled fears as well as tensions. It incited censorious moralism. Yet it also produced a space for aesthetic representations when political representations were beyond reach.

The critical stir over *La Dame aux camélias* represented the culmination of the censorship battles over Hugo's prostitute. It generated another set of struggles not only over culture but over the way culture mediates the social and political. It engaged battles not just over the signs of prostitutes but over the very possibility of representing the working classes and women. The struggles played out around nineteenth-century prostitutes had become contests over the plots possible for people as well as for literary texts.

The stories we have traced in the discourse of 1848 cannot be categorized as revolutionary or counterrevolutionary or even as appealing to the *mentalités* of the aristocrat, bourgeois, and worker. We cannot confine one version of the prostitute's story to one group, one way of seeing women to another. Rather, because all representation—and therefore all stories—lay in the balance, especially in the months between February and June 1848, we can point to the astonishing way that stories changed hands. Accounts of women dying courageously on the battlefield serve as cases in point. Stern left her female fighters standing triumphantly amidst the fray, in spite of widespread knowledge that they had *met* death as well as risked it: "On the barricades, raised as much with speed as with knowledge . . ., stood women and children, waving flags, defying death, and inflaming the rebellion with their shouts."[110] Tocqueville tells of brave women who were the last to give in on the barricades of June.[111] Leftist newspapers give details of the death of a rallying *fille publique* at the hands of the brutal National Guard.[112]

Hugo makes the deaths of two more prostitutes on the June barricades into a sensationalistic staging of their "barbaric" gestures that has as much to do with the profession it assigns them as with the women's teasing of the soldiers. Like the live allegory of the Tuileries in Stern's chronicle of February, like the escapees from Saint-Lazare, these women are marked, from their first appearance, as whores:

> The June uprising, from the first day, presented strange features. It showed suddenly, to a horrified society, monstrous and unknown forms. The first barricade was raised by Friday morning the 23rd at the Porte Saint-Denis. It was attacked the same day. The National Guard advanced resolutely upon it. . . . When the attackers, who arrived by the boulevard, came within range, a formidable volley went forth from the barricade and scattered the road with guardsmen. The National Guard, more irritated than intimidated, charged the barricade at a run. At that moment, a woman appeared on the crest of the barricade, a young woman, beautiful, disheveled, terrifying. This woman, who was a *fille publique*, raised her dress to her waist and shouted to the National Guard, in that dreadful whorehouse language that one is always forced to translate: "Cowards, fire if you dare, at the belly of a woman!" Here things turned dreadful. The National Guard did not hesitate. A fusillade toppled the miserable creature. She fell with a great cry. There was a horrified silence at the barricade and among the attackers. All of a sudden a second woman appeared. This one was younger and still more beautiful; she was practically a child, barely seventeen. What profound misery! She lifted her dress, showed her belly, and cried: "Fire, you bandits!" They fired. She fell, riddled with bullets, on the body of the first woman. That was how this war began.[113]

If the label *fille publique* might explain the rage of the National Guardsmen at the public display of these women's social threat, it hardly explains Hugo's own use of the women in his memoir. Nor does it tell us how Hugo knew these women sold their bodies. Like an officer of the *Bureau des moeurs*, Hugo seems to depend for his myths on the notion that a female body's circulation is knowable. Differentiated as a prostitute, she could incur the fascination of those who pitied her, but she could also justify the fears through which her martyred body might be riddled.

Here and elsewhere in 1848 prostitutes take the fall for revolutionary women's quest for rights, for the demands of workers for self-determination, for the dreams of those who demanded an end to censorship. Champions of failed revolutionary plots, these Mariannes invite speculation, fear, and protest. Yet behind the plots that brought sexuality into a fantasmatic rapport with revolution lay ideological investments that no allegory could contain. Behind plots around prostitutes lurked the anxiety that sexual threats might have political consequences and that, over the dead body of the prostitute, other liberties, perhaps this time those of women, might be taken.

PART TWO
The Hysteric's Difference

4

Telling the Difference:

Hysterics, Prostitutes, and the Clinical Gaze

*P*rostitution drives women mad, argued Alphonse Esquiros in 1840. Although the socialist reformer acknowledged that some prostitutes showed a natural strength of soul "against the sufferings and disgrace that afflict them," he believed many were unable to hold their own: "the habit of vice makes [them] fall unfeelingly into a sort of childhood." This is, he contended, where they got the nickname *filles folles* (crazy whores) and why he chose to call his own analysis of their plight *Les Vierges folles.* His proposals for changes in the conditions of prostitutes would, he declared, grant them the respect they deserved. "Society's lost children" would be "returned to society." Instead of taking chances on the alliance of prostitutes and revolution we saw in chapter 3 and "putting ideas of war and rebellion into the heads of women," Esquiros called for society to "rehabilitate them through submission and patience." If something were not done soon for these crazy women, he warned, their disorders would overwhelm society.[1]

Parent-Duchâtelet warned just as fervently of the dangerous disorders of prostitutes, yet the *health* of these women left him baffled. Although he found prostitutes beset by afflictions relating to venereal diseases, they suffered from so few other illnesses that Parent began to think that "the trade practiced by prostitutes is not as dangerous for the health as one might believe" (*PD,* 1:270). In fact, prostitutes seemed to have so many fewer ailments by comparison to "honest women workers" that Parent wondered if "an absolutely sedentary life might be more harmful than an active life of disorder" (*PD,* 1:281). He nevertheless made one surprising discovery: a disproportionately large number of the women entering public asylums were prostitutes. The figures from which he drew this conclusion, statistics from the Salpêtrière admissions registers, fueled intense debates in the course of the nineteenth century. Parent found that an average of twenty-one prostitutes were admitted annually into the Salpêtrière between 1811 and 1815, a figure corresponding to Esquirol's estimate that one-twentieth of all Salpêtrière patients suffering from mental illness were *filles publiques:* "These miserable women live separated from society in the greatest abandon; they have nothing to lean on in their weakness; after giving themselves over to all kinds of excesses, they generally fall into the deepest misery, and consequently, into paralytic dementia."[2] Far more than continence, which, argued Esquirol, caused mental illness only in a few rare cases, "libertinage" was the most frequent cause of madness—especially among women of the people.[3]

A glance at the Salpêtrière registers tells a somewhat different story. In 1845, for example, needleworkers and seamstresses were the largest group admitted into the asylum (130 women out of 552 or 24 percent), followed by domestic servants (47 women or 8.5 percent), laundresses (22 women or 4 percent), and other day laborers. Women identified as prostitutes represented only 2.54 percent, or fourteen total involuntary admissions, certainly a substantial number but hardly the most prevalent of professions.[4] Parent and Esquirol might just as well have counted the seamstresses in the Salpêtrière and drawn the conclusion that detail work leads promptly to madness. Other factors may, however, explain the discrepancy between medical concerns and statistics. Asylum registrations surely underrepresent prostitutes in the same way that police registers would have: a woman would no more automatically volunteer *fille publique* as her profession upon entering the asylum than she would have announced it to the police. We know, too, that poorly paid needleworkers, domestic servants, and laundresses frequently turned to occasional prostitution to make their "fifth quarter" of wages.[5] The doctors may well have leapt to their own conclusions that many of these women circulated on the side. Nevertheless, the doctors clearly had some more compelling reason than asylum statistics for fussing over crazy prostitutes.

A reformer like Esquiros had a far more philanthropic concern over prostitutes' madness than did medical authorities like Esquirol and Parent. All three, however, shared a common assumption—that if a sick woman *was* a prostitute, her lifestyle must surely have caused her illness. Like the author of the article on continence in the *Dictionnaire des sciences médicales*, these three observers believed in a causal relationship between a prostitute's activities and her mental state. But the agreement between them ended there. For de Montègre, as we have seen, the problem was dangerous desire. Esquiros's concern revolved around the conditions in which an entire segment of the working class was obliged to live. For Esquirol, the problem was a society that predisposed upper- and lower-class women alike to vice, excess, and misery. Parent's concern was defining disorders that made prostitutes different. Each of these writers wanted to bring an end to a series of ills he saw in the society around him, and to do so, he read his own unique logic into the relationship between prostitutes and mental disorders. The story of a prostitute's tendency to mental illness could be lent to a variety of concerns. Just as easily, the account of her impermeability to nervous disorders became part of a much more complicated plot.

Yet one more twist knotted the debates about prostitution and madness. While Parent unquestioningly accepted the information Esquirol provided about the melancholia, mania, and dementia of prostitutes, he balked at the idea, equally a part of Esquirol's teachings, that all madness in women is complicated by hysteria.[6] Instead, Parent embraced the medical assumption of his era—a mainstay of the *Dictionnaire des sciences médicales*—that prostitutes almost *never* showed signs of hysteria. Even after a long detention, he noted, prostitutes remained untouched by nervous ailments—surely due to the "vices and solitary maneuvers" to which they turned during hospital and prison stays. The "voluptuous ecstasies" to which these women were accustomed assured that their nerves functioned right on the money (*PD*, 1:261–62).[7]

Debates recurred throughout the nineteenth century over the mental health of prostitutes. The question of these women's hysteria became, in some ways, more consequential than the question of their madness because it had a greater impact upon the understanding of women of every class, circumstance, and way of life. While doctors largely accepted the correlation between madness and prostitution, they were far more hesitant to see hysteria as resulting from the conditions, either social or sexual, of prostitution. And yet clinical studies increasingly showed that prostitutes suffered as much or more than bourgeois women from the nervous ailments catalogued under the heading of hysteria. Thus, for more than a century, doctors' attempts to unravel the relation of hysteria and prostitution represented a key inquiry in the understanding of women's nature, sexuality, and predisposition to mental illnesses.

The hysteria of prostitutes mattered because it focused a series of debates in the first decades of the nineteenth century. As shown in the introduction, debates over continence fixed the prostitute and the hysteric as opposite models against which an orderly body could be measured: the prostitute was promoted as a septic tank for the excessive desires of society, while the hysteric was seen as victimized by desires overflowing from the inside. The continence debates also laid out a series of questions for medical, social, and moral analysis. The three theoretical camps on continence we identified in the introduction shared a common set of concerns. Those who believed that repression of sexual urges was dangerous, those who sought to divorce hysteria from accounts of sexuality, and those who believed that prostitutes and most of the mentally ill, including hysterics, belonged to a class of inherent degenerates *all* used questions about desire and sexuality to articulate positions on gender and class. If the prostitute became the center of heated debates about the dangers of the working classes, the hysteric focused similar debates about the dangers lurking around bourgeois women. Yet as studies of both prostitution and hysteria made increasingly clear, the differences between these two entities could not be drawn in such simple class terms. As I will show in this chapter, the hysteria diagnosis was practiced and elaborated in clinical notes and case studies *not* on the upper classes but on the same working-class women who were imagined as prone to prostitution. The studies that resulted from these diagnoses had a major impact on three spheres: (1) they affected global views of female marginality, particularly of women's mental and nervous illnesses; (2) they influenced conceptions of class that in turn affected social and cultural policy; (3) they were translated into moralizing practices that came to affect women of all classes.

The question of the prostitute's hysteria forced, therefore, a much more compelling question: that of the hysteric's *difference*. If analysts could make sense of the link between prostitution and hysteria, they might arrive at answers to some of the most pressing questions about hysteria's causes. These questions revolved around four general issues, the first and foremost of these was that of sexuality. What was the site of hysteria? Did it come from a lesion of the uterus, the genitals, or the nerves? Did the absence of sexual experience cause or contribute to hysteria? Could regular sexual contact—even when excessive—bring an end to hysterical ailments? The second was that of gender difference. Were women more prone to madness than men? Was hysteria an ailment that affected only women, as had long been believed, or could it equally affect men? If men could suffer from hysteria, what kind of men were prone to this affliction and under what circumstances were they afflicted? What was the role of gender in the origins and development of mental illnesses? The third major issue was that of class. Were certain kinds of women predisposed to such illnesses? Did the advantages of the upper classes protect women, or did they instead predispose women to such ailments? Were lower-class women less disposed to hysteria because of their inherent natures, or because of their regular sexuality activity, or rather because a difficult life had inured them to stress? Were poor women and especially prostitutes driven to madness because of the difficult conditions of their lives or for hereditary reasons? Could education or close supervision of women alter their chances of becoming hysterics? The fourth issue was that of heredity—an issue that grew out of questions of gender, race, and especially class. Were nervous illnesses and madness simply different versions of the same hereditary taint? Were the mentally ill inherently doomed to suffer—unable to extract themselves from their hereditary fates? Did social influences further exacerbate these hereditary ailments? Could either madness or nervous illnesses be prevented through the manipulation of environmental influences?

The same questions recurred for a century in studies of hysteria: What could be done to stem the tide of hysteria? How could doctors, moralists, and parents protect girls from this blight? In order to answer these questions, doctors first had to differentiate the hysteric from women suffering from other kinds of mental and nervous illnesses *and* from "normal" women. The medical discourse of the nineteenth century was as desperate to distinguish the hysteric from other women as police bureaucrats were to give a difference to the prostitute. Just as Parent and Béraud foundered on the difficulties of *separating* women who did *not* traffic in their bodies from those who did, their medical contemporaries battled valiantly to find ways of *differentiating* hysterics from women suffering from other kinds of maladies. Telling the difference of the hysteric meant far more than listing symptoms. It required elaborate observations and calculated narratives—what we might call a *poetics* of hysteria in which doctors articulated the relation of gender, class, sexuality, and heredity to the politically charged plots they had already become accustomed to telling.[8]

At the end of the eighteenth century, according to Michel Foucault, the discourse of medicine changed: "A new alliance was forged between words and things, enabling one *to see* and *to say*." The "birth of the clinic" occurred when the ploys (and language) of "positive science" took the place of theory, systems, and philosophy. The "gaze" of the clinic "is no longer reductive, it is rather that which establishes the individual in his [or her] irreducible quality."[9] At about the same time, Peter Brooks has argued, "narrative—the interpretation of human plots, especially the understanding and justification of their generalizable patterns, became a task of prime urgency."[10] Through the gaze of the new clinic, doctors sought to give a narrative meaning to the female bodies they placed under surveillance.

While hysteria had simply served as a sign of femaleness in the eighteenth century, the birth of the clinic forced new ways of looking and, in turn, new ways of accounting for what was seen.[11] Like other diagnostic categories of the nineteenth-century asylum, the label of hysteria separated women into categories according to the histories given to their impressionability. In order to do so, doctors had to establish a history for the epithet they so desperately wished to define. Beginning with the symptoms they could observe in the clinic, they gave a story to the woman under surveillance. Telling the hysteric's difference in gender terms meant extrapolating a relationship between a subject's gender and visible symptoms, manifest suffering, and observable trauma. It meant trading on any of the three sources doctors staged for her illness, two of them explicitly gendered—her uterus and her genitals—and the third, the nerves, implicitly understood as different because of her gender. Telling the hysteric's difference in class terms meant deciding if the wages of poverty were mental illness. It meant returning to the streets—where Esquirol was reputed to have found his former patient—to ask if the women who came there to ply their trade were more likely hysterical than their upper-class sisters. Telling the hysteric's difference in hereditary terms meant deciding whether a woman's illness had a plot of its own or simply fit into a grand design of hereditary degeneration. Telling the hysteric's difference in sexual terms required that doctors decide if there was, as Charcot would deny in the later years of the century, a *"chose génitale"* of hysteria[12]—or only a concern that the *"chose génitale,"* if left untended, would develop into an excess about which no one—not even doctors themselves—dared speak. Whether doctors called the hysteric's malady the result of her sexual organs or denied its sexual origin, their diagnoses repeatedly centered on her *sexual difference*. As such, their stories always sought to locate her desire.

This chapter focuses on the ways the difference of the hysteric came to be told in order to get at the plots that put women's bodies under surveillance. As subsequent chapters will show, the moralization of women outside the clinic was directly dependent upon the observations produced inside it. Hysteria provides a privileged key to this process because it linked practices of several different disciplinary spheres—hospitals, prisons, asylums, the tolerance system of prostitution, *and* the bourgeois family. It connected discussions about the sexuality of the upper classes to those about the sexuality of the lower classes. It related fears about social change and urbanization to debates over education, culture, and censorship. Because in the course of the nineteenth century hysteria was at the center of what Jan Goldstein calls a "boundary dispute"—a struggle by the medical profession to define the territory over which it would hold uncontested sway[13]—we will use it as our touchstone to consider the concerns doctors brought to mental illness. This will enable us to articulate the struggles out of which a psychiatric subject came into existence. Because the hysteric's difference became intimately connected to the difference of the prostitute, looking at debates over their common trajectory can help us to formulate the desires invested in the marginalization of both. Because, the hysteric, like the prostitute, haunted attempts to control desire, we can use fantasmatic readings of her desires to envision nineteenth-century investments in her difference. Out of the processes of telling the differences of hysterics and other mentally ill women grew theories that would for decades bolster proscriptions against people as well as against texts. At the same time, those processes created possibilities through which those excluded from discourse might begin to be heard and, ultimately, through which they might tell their own stories.

Hysterical Fantasies

Hysteria was the collective fantasy of the medical profession of the nineteenth century. A contagious fascination in itself, hysterical illness represented a central focus not only for debates over gender, class, sexuality, and heredity, but also over criminality, marriage age, religion, politics, and clinical methods. The later years of the July Monarchy and the early years of the Second Empire in particular saw a burgeoning interest in hysteria.[14] Medical academies held competitions for the best studies on the subject. Gynecological manuals proliferated, all containing major sections devoted to this malady. New printing processes made possible widely distributed collections of analyses of cases of hysteria.

More medical theses on hysteria were written during the nineteenth century than on any other kind of psychiatric problem. Throughout the century, theses on hysteria constituted between one-fifth and two-fifths of those written on mental, nervous, and emotional disorders. Most striking, nearly as many theses were written during the July Monarchy and the Second Empire as during the "golden age of hysteria," the Charcot regime of the Salpêtrière, between 1872 and 1893.[15] Goldstein has shown how Charcot's Salpêtrière developed its diagnostic categories in a climate of anticlericalism and republican politics.[16] This chapter provides an account of the hysteria diagnosis in the fifty years before Charcot began his *Leçons du mardi* (1872) at the public asylum. While Charcot's Salpêtrière depended upon a codifiable hysteria for its photographic and theatrical spectacles, in the preceding decades doctors had *negotiated* the forms hysteria might take in textual as well as symptomatic terms. Through an exploration of these negotiations we can begin to see the fantasies projected into the diagnoses of hysteria. We can also see the masterplots of gender, class, heredity, and sexuality, to which these diagnoses were lent.

We can find the traces of nineteenth-century hysteria in a series of texts left by the doctors who diagnosed and treated it. The Salpêtrière asylum has left us a legacy of psychiatric records, particularly detailed for the July Monarch and the early Second Empire, of the women who passed through it. But as Goldstein discovered in her explorations of the admissions registers of the public asylum, the hysteria diagnosis was not widely prevalent there until Charcot took over its administration. Indeed, as she found, in 1841–42, only 7 out of 648 (about 1 percent) of the women admitted involuntarily to the Salpêtrière were recorded as suffering from hysterical illnesses. Forty years later, a decade after Charcot had turned the asylum into a gallery of somatizing bodies, the proportion of women diagnosed as hysterical approached 18 percent. Yet in this interim period, theses and medical treatises on hysteria proliferated, made possible by research in another set of institutions—public hospitals such as La Charité and La Pitié. Throughout the decades when the hysteria diagnosis was used relatively infrequently in the public asylum, hospital doctors like Jean-Louis Brachet, Piorry, Lisfranc, C. M. S. Sandras, and Pierre Briquet pursued their own exploration of the histories, symptoms, and treatment of hysteria in the patients in their institutions. The number of women they may have treated in this period appears to have exceeded substantially that later examined in the Salpêtrière.[17] For this reason, we must read the histories of hysteria that came from the public hospitals both in relation to asylum practices during the July Monarchy and the Second Empire and in a continuum with the psychiatric practices of Charcot's era. For this reason also we cannot study hysteria in isolation but must look at it in the context of the views of mental and nervous illnesses that constituted differential diagnoses.

Two dates are particularly significant for the nineteenth-century understanding of hysteria and mental illness. In 1838 a major new law separated mental patients from prisoners and formalized the processes for the incarceration and treatment of asylum inmates.[18] The Law of 1838 created spaces in which the new psychiatric profession could study the patients for whose treatment it claimed to have special skills. This seems to have resulted in a pronounced separation of patients defined as mentally ill from those suffering only from nervous illnesses. The former found themselves transported into the public asylum. The latter, especially those defined as hysterics, were admitted into public *hospitals*, such as La Charité or La Pitié.

Sometime between the late Second Empire and the early Third Republic, the asylum was again restructured to encompass an increasing number of women with nervous disorders. This may have resulted from changing emphases on the part of asylum doctors like Charcot or from a transformation in the physical spaces in which mental illnesses were observed. We know that in 1871 the Salpêtrière underwent bureaucratic reorganization due to the dilapidation of several of its buildings. According to Pierre Marie, this resulted in a wing made up entirely of hysterics and epileptics.[19] Evidence suggests that Charcot used this new division to reclassify patients admitted as epileptic. Patients who would have been brought from the police depot as deranged because of epileptic fits must have been defined, in this new Salpêtrière, as hysterics or hystero-epileptics (those who only *seemed* to have epilepsy).[20] From this date on, there was only one Parisian space for reading the hysteric's difference. The *consolidation* of the spaces of hysteria brought an end to the negotiations that concern us in this chapter.

The Law of 1838 was the result of years of campaigning by the new profession of doctors who called themselves *aliénistes* after the *aliénié(e)s*—or estranged of mind—they treated.[21] Beginning with the *aliéniste* followers of Philippe Pinel at the turn of the nineteenth century, doctors sought to define the causes of mental illnesses in a far more "scientific" way than their eighteenth-century predecessors. The changes in the way doctors observed and the ways they recorded those observations were consolidated by the asylum transformations of 1838. As a result, studies of hysteria produced after the Law of 1838 differ radically from those of the earlier years of the nineteenth century. Out of the attempt to explain the symptomatology of hysteria and to isolate the factors that might predispose women to this scourge, doctors began to tell *stories* of more than just bodies in crisis. Whatever their investments in producing a narrative account of their observations, doctors began to flesh out the *subjects* of their narrations. They implicated families, friends, social influences, reading, and sensory stimuli. Above all, they asked what difference sexuality made in the constitution of a hysterical body.

The women who emerged from these case studies found themselves part of a much larger narrative—about the relationship between female sexuality and social disorders. But in spite of their imprisonment in these cases, the girls became subjects in their own right. No longer just bodies, no longer reduced to symptoms they could not control, no longer implicated in their own disorders, these women gained a social sphere that, for the doctors, began to insinuate that other forces were at work besides a disorderly body. Rather than subjecting the young women to torturous treatments, the doctors began to talk with them, to encourage them to tell their own stories, and to let them account for their own symptoms. Although these women remained in the thrall of the medical profession—doctored into cases, observed in obsessive detail—increasingly in the course of the century, they left on these cases the imprint of what must have been their own desires.

The label of prostitute, as we have seen in the last three chapters, gave an order to the bodies of women.[22] Like the police registration of *filles publiques*, the diagnoses of nineteenth-century medicine served a differentiating function for those preoccupied with observing and ordering bodies. In this chapter we look at what doctors meant when they called a patient hysterical. Did their propensity to use this diagnosis change in the course of the century? Did the medical fascination with the sexual aspects of hysteria affect the way doctors used the diagnostic category? Who were they most likely to label hysterical? What women turned up in their published observations? Were these the same women whom the doctors claimed they wanted to help achieve their "true role" of wife and mother—or women of a different sort entirely? By looking at a series of texts, both in the unpublished archives of the Salpêtrière hospital and in published reports on women's mental and nervous illnesses—in particular, at those of hysteria—I will trace the patterns in the way female sexuality was constituted in the course of nineteenth-century France.

In the eighteenth century, medical folklore had made every woman a hysteric and elevated hysterical symptoms into signs of an aristocratic femininity.[23] In the nervous ailments of their hysterical patients, doctors had found evidence for a *moral* perspective they represented as science. The nineteenth-century clinic, which found its origins in the hysteria of women,[24] claimed to change those processes of representation. Yet nineteenth-century observers remained equally obsessed by the "moral treatment" and "moral causes" of the illnesses they observed.[25] Even the most reputable analysts of hysteria embraced the values that served as the underpinning of much of late eighteenth-century physiology. Despite the tendency of even the most "scientific" observers—such as Briquet[26]—to discount the descriptive techniques of earlier medical practices, doctors emphasized the predisposition of *all* women to nervous disorders. Those who idealized women's reproductive function made the assumption that any women who did not bear children would eventually suffer from a body out of control. In this view, both the hysteric and the prostitute emerged as categories with which a female body outside its "fulfilled" state could be understood. The paradox of hysteria was that it named the malfunctioning of the bodily sites seen as marking the most elevated qualities of this romanticized woman: "Good and evil emanate from the same source in woman," wrote Joseph-Julien Virey in 1823. The evil, for Virey, was visible in her extravagant passions and oversensitivity. Yet that same sensitivity ensured that she made a better mother, wife, and daughter.[27] Her "natural" predisposition marked her from the outset for disorders. It set her up to have her difference read.

"Most women become hysterical," claimed Brachet in the epigraph to his 1847 *Traité de l'hystérie*: "The basis of woman's character lies in her physical and moral sensitivity." Woman's defective education *and* her native sensitivity were the sources of her hysterical ailments as well as the reasons for her descent into prostitution, adultery, incest, and infanticide: "Her life is all sensations and feelings. She therefore lives principally through her nervous system: one feels consequently how much these qualities when exaggerated or too often activated must excite her system and predispose her to pathological nervous depravities" (JLB, 93, 95). According to Brachet, once a woman became a *femme galante*, she could no longer control herself. She would seek to destroy others since her own esteem was lost: "Her life becomes nothing more than a succession of passions and storms." Each additional descent into passion wrought further havoc on her nervous system (JLB, 93).

Brachet's explanation of the relationship between mental illness and prostitution embraced a recurring concern of virtually every analysis of hysteria in the nineteenth century. Brachet wanted to protect women from the kinds of symptoms he detailed in the observations of his book, but he was equally interested in ensuring that they stayed clear of what he called "degradation." This required, he argued, that women be sheltered from the influence of passions and from society's "vices." The underlying emphasis in the work of Étienne Georget, Esquirol, Brachet, Briquet, Ulysse Trélat, and Jacques-Joseph Moreau de Tours—to name just a few prominent observers of women's mental disorders—was the definition of a role for women that is safe, ordered, and, above all, "moral."

Reducing women to their bodies meant assigning them a bodily function and certain *symptoms* of their failure to fulfill it. Hospital and asylum observations codified the aberrant body in terms of the sensual stimuli it appeared unable to tolerate. Reducing women to their emotions meant, in fact, accounting for those reactions in terms of what might *move* them. The analysis of hysterics, then, required inquiries into the dangers of the outside world. The *story* of what might drive a woman to hysteria was therefore a narrative of her relationship to that outside world. Out of these stories, a semantics of femininity came to be generated whose influence went far beyond the asylum. Like the differences of prostitutes, the hysteric's desires—or those the medical observers gave her—came to anchor political as well as interpretative systems.

Spaces for Reading Difference

The archives of the Salpêtrière harbor a wealth of accounts of mental illness. In large, black, leather-bound registers, secretaries inscribed the patient's name, age, birthdate, birthplace, address, profession, marital status, admission date, name of the authority who was institutionalizing her, and the diagnosis made upon admission. Unlike published case studies, which were harnessed to a purpose and given meaning in retrospect, the running accounts of the treatment of Salpêtrière inmates are not doctored into cases. They were not produced as texts through which to transmit knowledge about patients to other doctors but rather as records of the crisis in view: the pain and confusion of a woman deemed *aliénée* by at least two doctors. The register reports do not tell these women's stories so much as *represent* their crises. Yet it is that very representation that makes possible the narration of these women's *otherness*.

The Law of 1838 created the conditions for observation that shifted the study of hysteria (and mental illness in general) from philosophical generalization to scientific analysis.[28] The law required an "immediate certificate," a "fifteen-day certificate," and monthly observations of the patient's condition.

Each patient entering the asylum was immediately observed by a doctor. Two weeks later a second observation was recorded. But neither the registers nor the few remaining volumes officially called *"dossiers"* —patient files—actually conform to the kind of monthly observations required by the Law of 1838. The best these women could hope for was release before another month went by. If they were not let out within that first six weeks, their chances of leaving the hospital became increasingly slim.[29] The registers were not optimistic even in the categories offered to the scribe: next to the almost always blank area meant for later observations is a column entitled "Declaration of maintenance or cure." It was filled in only if the patient was released or transferred. Under those circumstances, the patient's departure date and her release order are recorded along with the name of the person who took the patient away. In the far right column, a space awaited those for whom the right-hand page of the register held no other indications: the date of death.

Charcot's Salpêtrière defines the fantasmatic space for so much historical and literary work on hysteria that we need to pass through it in order to see what preceded it. The Salpêtrière of the *fin de siècle* was a place of spectacle in every imaginable sense, a theatrical space into which women—and also men—would be brought for clinical observation.[30] Brouillet's image of one of the celebrated *leçons* (figure 4.1), dating from 1887 and depicting Blanche Wittman collapsing in Joseph Babinski's arms as Charcot lectures to his disciples, transforms into salon iconography the plays of desire set in motion by the Salpêtrière clinic of those years: the eyes of the men in this audience fall as much on Charcot—on the master of ceremonies—as on the woman who drapes herself arrestingly in the arms of the disciple, her nearly exposed breasts thrust forward, the top of her dress dangling around her waist. From his appointment as resident in 1862 until his death in 1893, the Salpêtrière would be a space of *display* for the master showman. "We are . . . in possession of a sort of *living pathological museum*," wrote Charcot of the clinic in which he produced his own form of performance art.[31] Its lectures drew the attention of writers, intellectuals, and dandies—the Goncourts, Guy de Maupassant, Alphonse and Léon Daudet, and Freud, who would memorialize his French master as *"un visuel."*[32] Its public *bals des folles* became a subject of newspaper society columns.[33] Most important, as Georges Didi-Huberman has shown, its women came under the gaze of a new visual machinery, capable—for the first time in history—of recording their expressions as well as their likenesses.[34]

With the *Iconographie photographique de la Salpêtrière* of 1876, the asylum moved from written to visual observation, and with this leap from the formulation of *aliénation* in *cases* to the articulation of a new kind of knowledge, translatable through the image. *"Voilà la vérité,"* Charcot would declare in 1887 of the photographs that inscribe his observations of hysteria. Responding to criticism that "hystero-epilepsy," on which he had made his reputation, existed only in France—or only at the Salpêtrière—he announced: "It would be a truly marvelous thing if I could thus create maladies according to my whim and fantasy.

Figure 4.1

André Pierre Brouillet, *A Clinical Lesson of Dr. Charcot at the Salpêtrière* (1887).

But in truth, I am no more there than the photographer; I inscribe what I see."[35] With the inscription made possible by the photograph, Charcot would contend that he had taken hold of that Protean form defined by his predecessors as "ungraspable."[36] From the moment the snapshot memorialized them, his patients would join the ranks of Christian visionaries, debunking the legends of Catholicism with their ecstatic conversions to hysteria.[37]

"It is not a novel: *hysteria has its laws*," proclaimed Charcot. With the photograph, the *aliénée* passed from "storied body" into icon.[38] Whether invented as spectacle, or simply made up of the clinical gazes that converged in individual photographic sessions, the woman of the Charcot Salpêtrière exists for us as a phantom mediated by visual images. The *Leçons du mardi* that surround her emerge, in turn, as theatrical scripts accompanied by the master's own drawings. By the 1880s the spectacular world of the Salpêtrière had left behind the kind of narrations that assured hysteria a unique place in the literary production of nineteenth-century *aliénisme*. The case history as it had been practiced in asylum registers, in the *Annales médico-psychologiques*, and in the volumes of Charcot's predecessors—Georget, Esquirol, Brachet, Briquet, Trélat, Moreau de Tours—would give way to the documents of the "living pathological museum." In this Third Republic gallery of madness, symptoms were transferred by looks, not narrative.

In Charcot's Salpêtrière, the admissions registers defer to the *Leçons de mardi* and *Iconographie photographique*. The published and unpublished reports of the master create a silence in the daily surveillance records, as if no one but Charcot might have anything to say about these patients. Their cases are reduced to epithets: "hysteria," "is afflicted with hystero-epilepsy," "appears to be affected by general paralysis."[39] There are no causes, no descriptions of symptoms, no records of what the women might have had to say about these bodies out of control. The differential diagnoses give no space to accounts of what may have brought these women into the asylum. They have become, instead, *inscrite* like the prostitutes at the *Bureau des moeurs*. Their names in the volume gave the doctors license to practice on them. Their diagnoses, exchanged for their names, authorized a certain kind of gaze upon their symptoms.

Charcot's Salpêtrière gave a material body to hysteria, but it did not invent the clinical observation that permitted hysterical bodies to be read and known. If we are to come to grips with the hysterized women whose bodies anchored both the tolerance system of prostitution as well as widespread practices of literary and press censorship, we must imagine a space for clinical observation where there were no cameras watching the hysterical patients, where no women were put on display to an audience of men, where none of the paintings on the walls told women what symptoms they should mime.

Jeanne Adélaïde G. arrived at the Salpêtrière in May 1845, delivered by the police of the *Bureau central* with a "certificate" signed by a doctor named

Gillette. Her admissions record gives few clues of what convinced the police and the depot doctors to send her to an asylum. The fifty-eight-year-old cook was diagnosed as "afflicted with hysteria with mental trouble during attacks that recur about monthly." The admitting doctor, Jean-Pierre Falret, seemed in no hurry to send her home, though he reported that she underwent a marked improvement between her arrival and her second week at the hospital. Two years later, for reasons equally obscure, he would declare her "cured" and let her return to her family. For the police of the *Bureau central* to have sent her to the Salpêtrière, two doctors had to decide that she needed to be "treated for the malady with which she is afflicted." Two physicians had to testify in writing that she had shown signs of illness "manifested by extravagant acts." From Falret's diagnostic report, we can assume that Jeanne Adélaïde had had one of her hysterical attacks. What the doctors saw as extravagant about her acts is figured only in the euphemism of "mental trouble."[40]

Like Jeanne Adélaïde, the women delivered into the Salpêtrière from the July Monarchy through the Third Republic arrived there out of shocking destitution. Most were either domestics or day laborers, such as shoe-stitchers, laundresses, or linen-maids, who might have earned two and a half francs a day in good times.[41] In 1845 fifteen percent of those admitted were unemployed or unemployable: the registers list them as "*sans état*" (without position) or leave blank the space for profession.[42] Of these, half were single or widowed, many of them children or elderly, unable to support themselves in the best of circumstances.[43] The patients of the Salpêtrière came with pedigrees that predisposed them to the experimentation of the *aliénistes* who worked there: poor and alone, abandoned figuratively or literally by their families,[44] physically ill or aged, they had been collected by the police and herded from a brief medical examination in the depot into this place of no return.

"It takes two to make a diagnosis," Goldstein has demonstrated: the doctor and a set of symptoms in the patient.[45] The bureaucratic circumstances that bring those two together in the clinic are equally important in determining how the symptoms will be read. The doctors of the police depot had certain orders to follow—those of the Law of 1838 and whatever interpretations were presently being given to it—but they also had certain interests. Yannick Ripa reports that a change in the politics of social assistance caused a decline after 1843 in the number of mental patients who were not deemed *dangerous*.[46] The public asylums were jammed full in the 1840s; low wages for women and squalorous conditions for the working classes made the Salpêtrière a logical way station for many of the Parisian poor. What brought a hysterical woman like Jeanne Adélaïde into its walls was a decision by the police depot doctors that she would be placed under better surveillance in the asylum. There, whatever the "*chagrin*" listed as the cause of her malady, she would be kept where her "mental trouble" could cause no harm. Someone had decided that she would be better off disciplined in the asylum than doctored in a hospital.

The world of the Salpêtrière between 1838 and 1871 revolved around a series of preoccupations concerning the nature of the women admitted there. The first involved the monomania diagnosis and the intervention of *aliénistes* in legal cases. The second, increasingly prevalent during the 1850s, concerned a patient's potential danger to self or society. The third, hysteria, exploded into the Salpêtrière registers in the 1860s. By that time the *aliéniste* followers of Pinel and Esquirol had transformed the Salpêtrière of the 1840s and 1850s into a laboratory for the exploration of the diagnostics that anchored the doctrine of monomania on which they had built their professional standing.[47] The *aliéniste* journal, *Les Annales médico-psychologiques*, ensured the importance of these individuals' research by staking out a field of expertise: legal testimony about an individual's fitness to be tried. In 1845 of 607 women who entered the Salpêtrière fifty-three (8.7 percent) were diagnosed as monomaniacs.[48] By 1854, about 15 percent of all patients were admitted under this diagnosis.[49] By the mid-1860s, however, the monomania diagnosis had virtually disappeared and had increasingly been replaced by medical testimony about the patients' dangers.[50]

During the July Monarchy and the Second Empire, hysteria interested the *aliénistes* of the Salpêtrière far less than the various manias on which they set their professional reputations. Yet the diagnosis maintained a steady and even increasing presence. In 1845 the admitting doctors found that 15 of the 607 (2.5 percent) women admitted involuntarily to the Salpêtrière suffered from hysterical symptoms.[51] In 1854, when the monomania diagnosis was in its heyday, a survey of one hundred entering "involuntary placements" found three (and therefore 3 percent) with hysterical symptoms.[52] In the first five months of 1865 thirteen patients with hysterical symptoms entered the hospital—out of a total of 196 patients, amounting to 8.1 percent.[53] In 1869 out of 269 total involuntary admissions, 17 were diagnosed as hysterics or "hystero-epileptics"—6.3 percent.[54]

For the presence of hysteria in the asylum to rise to 17.8 percent in 1882–83, as Goldstein discovered, a major change had to have occurred: doctors had to reconceptualize what kind of symptoms indicated a woman belonged in an asylum. As Goldstein has shown, what made Charcot's Salpêtrière the dominant space for the unveiling of hysteria resulted from a complex set of political, social, and medical transformations in the Third Republic. It hinged on the administrative reorganization of the Salpêtrière itself and on Charcot's politics and personality. It required, above all, a change in the thinking of the doctors cooperating in the system that linked the police depot to the asylums, to the hospitals, and to the prisons. For the Salpêtrière to become the central laboratory for the study of hysteria, *aliénistes* had to usurp a role previously entrusted to doctors in public hospitals.

"Placed by the fact of circumstances at the head of a department where it had long been the practice to put those afflicted with hysterical ailments," wrote Briquet in 1859, "I was obliged, for the relief of my conscience, to give all my attention to this kind of patient toward whom my taste for the study of positive science hardly drew me" (Br, v). The resident of La Charité made no bones about his disgust with the patients he was obliged to treat. Like Parent, Briquet summoned images of his colleagues' distaste for the kind of women whose maladies he studied, and elevated himself into a martyr to the facts.[55] Contending that hysteria had never before been studied methodically, "first by observing and then by drawing conclusions," Briquet set out to accumulate observations of all the "patients afflicted by hysteria who should appear in my wards" (Br, vi). Seconded by student interns, he was able to bring together observations about "their previous history, their actual condition, and the results of treatment," and to submit well-known theories to the test of observation: "everything was finally set up so that all things came from facts" (Br, vi). His radical reformulation of the etiology and treatment of hysteria derived from the hundreds of clinical observations he collected—seventy-one of them detailed in his enormous treatise. But though Briquet was a source for many of the *aliénistes* who followed him—Moreau de Tours, Henri Legrand Du Saulle, Charcot, and Pierre Janet, for example—unlike them, he worked in a public hospital. La Charité's immense population (some fifty thousand annual admissions, male and female) afforded Briquet a wide variety of victims of neurological and uterine disorders, enabling him, over a period of only a few years, to tabulate 430 publishable observations of hysteria.

We know far less about the women of public hospitals than about those inscribed into the Salpêtrière registers. The Law of 1838 did not require hospital doctors to keep records of regular observations of the women's condition. In the large black registers of the medical institutes that harbored the suffering poor, only the names, occupations, ages, marital status, gender, length of stay, and a few words of diagnosis stand in for the stories that brought these people to seek medical care. Alongside those suffering from bronchitis, tuberculosis, and syphilis entered those diagnosed with "hysteria." Beside them came others whose ailments sound strangely similar to those described under the heading of hysteria in medical textbooks and dictionaries: "nervous affection," "nervous cough," "displacement of the uterus," "antiflexion of the uterus," simply "uterus"—and still others with ailments frequently confused with hysteria: "chlorosis" (whose victims were 90 percent female) and "neuralgia," whose victims (like Freud himself) were often young men in their twenties or thirties.

The hospital doctors who treated hysteria drew on a combination of sources for their work—gynecological studies, eighteenth-century pseudo-scientific treatises about women's nature, the work of early *aliénistes* like Pinel, Georget, and Esquirol, and analyses of madness and nervous disorders published in the medical journals of their era—the *Union médicale*, *Gazette des hôpitaux*, and *Annales médico-psychologiques*. Their studies combined the analytical methods made famous by the *aliénistes* of the Salpêtrière with the fantasmatic assessments of women's nature so familiar in gynecological treatises. Not surprisingly, their work was reviewed with interest and cited regularly by the asylum doctors.[56]

Perhaps because of the similarity of their concerns, or because of the similarity of their patients, the emphases of medical cases left by the hospital doctors dovetails with the work of those who practiced in the Salpêtrière and other asylums for the mentally ill. Even the minimal data we can cull from the hospital registers show patterns similar to those of the asylum. The fifteen involuntary patients diagnosed at the Salpêtrière as suffering from hysterical symptoms in 1845 were young—ages fourteen to twenty-nine, and nearly all single. Even the forty-five-year-old exception to this rule entered under circumstances that made her a model candidate for disorders of the uterus: this woolens worker was in a state of "hypochondria that drove her to suicidal acts." Fifteen days later a second doctor would find that she had symptoms closer to "hysteria than epilepsy." In the column where causes are marked, the admitting physicians inscribed the reasons they used to explain her unruly body and not her suicidal desires: "abandonment by her husband."[57]

About two hundred women entered La Charité in that same year with hysterical symptoms. They too were young, frequently unmarried, but above all, like their counterparts in the madhouse, the hysterics of the public hospital were working-class women: domestics, seamstresses, laundresses, shopkeepers, upholsterers, colorists. Hysteria seems to have ranked especially high among medical diagnoses given to women in their twenties. Of 225 women who entered La Charité in January 1845, twenty-two were diagnosed specifically as suffering from hysteria, eighteen as having bronchitis, thirteen as suffering from pneumonia. Only three had syphilitic conditions; only one was believed to suffer from epilepsy. Only chlorosis and neuralgia were more frequently used diagnoses for female patients, represented by fifty-five and twenty-seven patients respectively. These three categories represented particularly significant diagnostic groups for young unmarried women.[58] Unlike the Salpêtrière women, those diagnosed as hysteric in La Charité stayed rarely more than a few days before returning to the life in which they had fallen ill. While at the Salpêtrière of the 1840s hysterics risked eternal imprisonment or death, at La Charité, at least, hysteria was not a fatal illness.

The Salpêtrière and La Charité were spaces where bureaucratic conditions and professional ambitions converged to create certain nosological emphases. The medical observations of the Salpêtrière ensured a perpetuation of the philosophies that governed the clinical gaze. In the golden age of the monomania diagnosis, the 1850s, one finds it constantly used as a diagnostic reference point. In the peak years of the Charcot Salpêtrière, the hysteria diagnosis recurred to such an extent that one wonders if other ailments even existed. These two diagnoses in particular seemed to usurp the place of descriptive information and theories about causality. The labels became political vehicles upon which the Salpêtrière doctors could transport themselves into notoriety. In the registers these two labels take the place of observations. They displace the accounts that allow for reinterpretation.

The stories told in the July Monarchy registers of the Salpêtrière and in the hospital studies of Brachet and Briquet express the tensions in the uses of diagnoses. They report the labels, the nosological categories in current usage, but they also struggle with the cases that do not fit. Some of these, like that of Jeanne Adélaïde B., tell little about the diagnostic conditions that brought the patient into an asylum rather than into a public hospital such as La Charité. Others, like those we discuss in the next section, report the symptoms of a woman's condition in ways that begin to account for her presence in the institution. The diagnostic certificates recorded in the Salpêtrière registers are a kind of shorthand marking the trajectories of pain of working-class women. When these texts become stories—and not just labels—they set the terms for debate concerning both the monomania and hysteria diagnoses. The interpretative gestures of those who observed women's disorders generated new ways of seeing gender—and new ways of keeping it in view.

Doctored into Narrative

"Psychoanalytic understanding involves reconstructing a story, tracing a phenomenon to its origin, seeing how one thing leads to another," writes Jonathan Culler.[59] If a case study is to have exemplary power, it must provide more than mere observation and description. It must narrate the history of an individual in such a way as to enable others to generalize from that individual case. To say that "the king died, then the queen died," does not make a plot. These two events (what the Russian formalists called *fabula*) become narrative only when a connection is made between them: "the king died, then the queen died of grief."[60] Once the narrator has assigned the events to a system of causation (the presentation of events called *sjuzhet*), the history gains meaning. Psychoanalysis produces narratives of human experience to which it assigns meaning based on an investigation of causes.

The texts in the registers of the Salpêtrière oscillate between simple labels ("is afflicted with hysteria," "is in a state of partial delirium," "is afflicted with monomania") and stories—sequences of events or descriptions of symptoms. Occasionally those texts have plots. Most of the time these texts only verge on an explanation of what brought the woman into the institution. What interests me about these texts is their struggle to represent their confrontation with individuals in crisis. Whether they articulate a fluctuating set of diagnoses or achieve a certainty about what ails a patient, these texts produce the closest existing account of a doctor's attempts to read the disorder of a woman assigned to him.

These texts are our only key to the texture of everyday reality in the Salpêtrière of the July Monarchy. They provide our only access to the distressed bodies of confined women. Because they are not written as *exempla* (unlike published case studies), they strive to reconstruct the story of a life for the purpose of treating the *aliénation* at hand. They produce only the evidence that would be used to decide whether to keep a patient, where to keep her, and, in the best moments of the crowded asylum, how to help her. These texts testify to the fragility of the diagnostic categories in the asylum, to the fantasies the doctors bring to their work there, and to the obsessions that influence the interpretations of women's mental conditions. In the conventions of these readings of otherness, we begin to see patterns for constructing sexuality, gender, and class.

Of all the patients brought into the asylum from the police depot, the hysteric proves the most baffling to the *aliéniste*. He has learned from Esquirol that hysteria degenerates and frequently becomes madness. He knows the arguments about its bodily seat. But whether he believes hysteria is a disease of the uterus, genitals, or brain, when a patient is brought before him, his only resource is a decoding of her symptoms. Because the hysteric's symptoms can mime other diseases, the doctor must differentiate her from other patients on the basis of his belief in what she says.

"Pain comes unsharably into our midst as at once that which cannot be denied and that which cannot be confirmed," writes Elaine Scarry. "To have great pain is to have certainty; to hear that another person has pain is to have doubt."[61] The unrepresentability of pain is nowhere more apparent than in these asylum observations. Clarisse Charlotte M., age seventeen, is subject to "convulsive attacks that do not have the character of epilepsy, that seem more to resemble hysteria." Marguerite Joséphine H., age twenty-four, is "exalted, turbulent, hysterical, bothering her asylum companions." Babet S. is "afflicted with spasmodic convulsions that appear in the form of attacks and seem to have more the character of hysteria than of epilepsy."[62] Hysteria has an appearance, but no materiality. Its symptoms can be catalogued, their frequency registered, but it remains always beyond understanding. Without the visibility of a lesion — some part of the body that would bespeak the ravages of the disease — its name marks the frustration of the doctor. It labels his inability to read the patient's pain.

The observations of the Salpêtrière record a legacy of medical doubt in the evidence put forth by patients. We have the traces of what the women may have said, recorded in a register of suspicion. One woman suffers from monomania and hallucinations, says the doctor: "She was frightened, she said, when the rebels broke into her house" during the Revolution of 1848.[63] Although the doctor reports her words in indirect discourse, he insists on assigning them to her (*"dit-elle"*). He thus casts doubt on their believability. He takes her testimony, records it, relegates it to some system in which it gains meaning for him. The result no longer holds the meaning of her utterance. It is primarily in the face of a woman's failure to respond that her actual engagement in the dialogue is reported: Aglaé F., seamstress, age twenty-six, enters in January 1849 and "appears to be in a kind of dementia. She only vaguely hears the questions that are asked of her. She answers only slowly and incompletely, and doesn't know where she is or where she comes from." Two weeks Jules later

Mitivié judged that she suffers from "hysterical monomania with hallucinations."[64]

Confronted with their patients' stories, these doctors trace their own impressions of the extent of the hallucinations. Most of the time they simply record whether the patient is seeing or smelling things. Occasionally they are so taken by the story that it becomes the subject of their report. Marie B., for example, entered on Christmas Day of 1848 with the predominating ideas that "someone wants to assassinate her, someone is constantly stealing from her, someone killed her two husbands out of jealousy, and yet she does good deeds for everyone, for the poor as well as for the rich, she constructs railways with her own money." Mitivié reproduces without narrative intervention the declarations of Geneviève L., a widowed ragpicker, age sixty-three: "She claims to be an extremely popular author. She is awaited at the Théâtre de La Gaiété for the first performance of the new play she has composed. Her public awaits this performance with impatience." Occasionally, the results of the patient's delusions are so apparent that the doctor reconstructs her story from an event she reports: Suzanne thinks she hears a voice accusing her of taking part in the revolution, and of having "an evil tongue." "This accusation," writes Falret, "leads her to mutilate her tongue."[65]

The Revolution of 1848 seems to confer a particular value on the explanations the women give of their problems. Whether the doctors actually give credence to this particular woman's account of being asked to denounce insurgents from the June Days, or treat as "incoherence with exaltations" another woman's insistence that she deserves "the Honorary Cross," the observers nevertheless report with frequency the "predominating ideas" of those who connect their *aliénation* to the uprisings of February or June. They even give the revolution as a source of the mental illness of a number of women.[66]

These texts betray the doctors' notions of the limited range of sexual expression available to women. Erotic thoughts are recorded frequently as signs of *aliénation*. Woe to the woman who has acted upon her thoughts. Jeanne Henriette V., an eighteen-year-old flower-girl is described in unusually vivid terms: "She appears to be completely lacking in control over her senses, runs after men, tries to pervert her little brothers." Two years after her admission she died in the asylum. Trélat diagnoses Genny Anne M., an eighteen-year-old lacemaker, as suffering from mania. Like the prostitutes tabulated by Parent, she suffers from "extreme mobility." The symptom of her illness is her masturbation, to which she "abandons herself with fury."[67]

The doctors readily draw their own conclusions about *filles publiques*. They even question the sexual trades of women who say they have *real* jobs.[68] Whatever a prostitute suffers, the registers indicate, is the result of her "debauchery."[69] Her past marks her. It tells the only story these registers will give her. Joséphine Cathérine B., age thirty-six, comes from Saint-Lazare prison, and Doctor Mitivié knows how to read that sign. He reports her illness in that same staccato that marks these register observations. His account omits her name and leaves behind no pronoun that would mark her as a subject. She is reduced, as are so many of these women, to predicate nominatives that name her plight: "Is ravaged, broken, as one is after debauchery or a dissolute orgy." In a rare move for these short observations, he inserts himself into the narrative frame, staging her condition in terms of his interpretation of her profession: "I am drawn to attribute the delirium that motivated the admission of this woman to the Salpêtrière to a similar agent: this delirium appears no longer to exist."[70]

Those diagnosed as hysteric are rarely heard telling their own stories. The teacher admitted with the improbable name "Marie Antoinette Charlotte Alexandrine" on the day after Christmas 1848 is an exception. The doctor's report finds her "in a state of manic exaltation with a predominance of ideas of pride. She thinks she is a great lady, a poet. She recites verses with the expression of someone inspired; she has symptoms of hysteria."[71] The woman diagnosed as hysterical gains her story from a body out of control. The symptoms themselves are rarely named; the attacks, described in vivid detail in published case studies, are summed up by their presence or their frequency. They have few results: unlike melancholia, they rarely drive a patient to suicidal acts; unlike "mania" or "monomania," they rarely unleash fits of passion upon the patient's family or neighbors.[72] One case of a rampaging hysteric glaringly betrays the doctor's refusal to see beyond appearances to find a source for family violence: Louise Georgette M., age twenty-four, a "day laborer" is diagnosed as "afflicted with deafmuteness, according to police documents. She is hysterical and has recently undergone character changes such that she wanted to kill her sister-in-law who gave her hospitality. She indulges in indecent acts."[73]

"Hysteria" marks the space of an absence of knowledge—either on the part of the attending physician or on that of the patient herself. Unlike those suffering from "partial delirium," the hysteric neither identifies her causes nor conceives of their results. She is referred to a system in which her symptoms would be "characteristic"—yet no existing textbook in the 1840s could tell a doctor what characterized hysteria.[74] In the Salpêtrière registers, the hysteric's symptoms garner few plots.

In the registers of the mid-1840s, the doctors record what their textbooks call "moral agents" (*causes morales*) for the conditions of their patients. These range from "family problems" to "menstrual irregularity" to small plots in themselves like "sorrows caused by the death of her husband," "loss of money, bad treatment by her husband," and "sorrows caused by prostitution, loss of a child."[75] Occasionally, the doctors produce a *cause morale* that suggests something of their prejudices. A number of women have a problem with "misunderstood religion"—but who decides what the correct understanding of religion should be? Masturbation appears as a source of madness—testimony to the widespread eighteenth- and nineteenth-century terror about nonreproductive use of sexual energy.[76] Some of the *causes morales* tell the story of the professional allegiances of the doctors. Heredity and fear are given as frequent sources of women's problems—opposing views about whether the constitution of an individual or some accident in her life could be the origin of mental illness. Frequently the causes refer to her female body: problems of menstruation, lactation, and childbirth correlate her madness with her difference. One origin in particular seems to go without saying: *"misère"* (poverty).[77]

The shorthand of these entries tells a story about the easy marginality into which the lots of working-class women were cast: One woman is ill because she believes her neighbors are saying she has venereal disease. Another thinks her neighbors are accusing her of trying to murder her child. Still another does not know her own sex. In a rare case where the admitting doctor listens to — and actually records — the words of a patient, one woman announces "I do what I can, but I must not suffocate."[78] Though the doctor apparently chooses not to paraphrase her words, he nevertheless provides no account of what has made these words compelling enough to record — or of the circumstances against which the patient believes she struggles.

The fragility of the female constitution, so often projected in texts about women's maladies — and even listed as a *cause morale* for several women's *aliénation* — is given little consideration in the squalorous conditions of the Salpêtrière. The lucky woman gets her walking papers because she is "orderly, calm, hardworking."[79] But even working hard is no guarantee that the doctors will deem a woman sane enough to go home: the registers record that a forty-two-year-old seamstress is "quiet, she works, she speaks little: she is without a doubt under the influence of some fixed idea, but she hides it." No record exists of her release.[80] What seems to count in this inferno of catalogued manias is becoming "reasonable." The patient with a neurological disorder, like epilepsy or hysteria, will be judged fit to depart if the doctors decide that she has her wits about her — or at least that someone will watch over her to see that any lapses in her reason will not be offensive. The "release certificates" frequently note that the patient is "much better and can be released without danger into society."[81] How that society will construct the stigma of her institutionalization remains a question beyond the concern of the physicians who have found a category into which they can fit the patient.

The recording of *causes morales* in the column below the patient's name makes her story a *narrative* or *plot*. The few words jotted down there testify that her illness is narratable. If it has origins, then it must also have a meaning. Yet madness and hysteria, like pain, resist language.[82] These women's ailments resist the meanings doctors try to impose on them. Their stories remain in that space of unreason prowled by the doctors, outside understanding, or at least outside empathic dialogue. The meanings these doctors give to their patients ultimately derive from the systems the former hold dear, from their ordering of difference into representations they can leave behind in books. But the desires of the patients remain somehow outside the texts of the doctors' narratives.

The codes that govern the production of *aliénation* in the Salpêtrière texts are those of plot and interpretation — what Roland Barthes calls the proairetic code, "the code of actions," and the hermeneutic code, "the code of enigmas and answers."[83] But the hermeneutics of the women institutionalized there almost always come up short in the production of their own plots. These big black books make the women's histories into a master narrative that refers only remotely to their inexpressible suffering, only generally to their obstinate "unreasonableness." What remains nevertheless extraordinary is that their plots exist at all, and that they occasionally become narratives of a richness that even the doctor's interpretative gestures cannot obscure.

Virginie Joséphine L., age twenty-four, was a hysteric with a story we'll see recur. Her case stands out both as a narrative, and because it suspends its account of causality. Initially diagnosed as *"hystérique,"* she was then described as "subject to convulsive attacks (*sujette à des attaques convulsives*) that have more the character of hysteria than of epilepsy. Their onset goes back to her tenth year and appears to be connected to an accident in which she was bitten by a dog. The attacks are of an extreme violence and continue often for an entire day. In the intervals, her reason is not troubled."[84] Virginie Joséphine's case stages a scene of confrontation between the physician and the patient, leaving traces of his suspicious gaze in his account of the "apparent" cause of her convulsions. Like many Salpêtrière observations, Lélut's report reduces her to her convulsive body, producing only the shadow of a woman who suffers the intense pain of day-long fits. Like many of the cases above, the report demurs before the task of tracing the origins of her hysteria. Instead it refers the reader to the account the girl has apparently given. In its refusal to make a plot out of her story, it has performed a surprising twist on the process of disciplinary observation it inscribes. It has embedded her story without commentary. It has faithfully reproduced the metaphor she has given to the scene of her malady's origins. Whatever the meaning of that metaphor, whatever the value of that scene, it has made her the subject (*"sujette"*) of her own convulsions. By giving the benefit of the doubt to a story of an attack Virginie must have told on one of those days when her reason was not troubled, Lélut allows Virginie to retain her own plot. By positioning her within a register of possible truth, the doctor has opened the way for a woman like Virginie to tell her own story.

Scientific Plots

A quarter of all women are afflicted with hysteria, Briquet contended in 1859, and yet another quarter have serious nervous disorders. The male hysteric is rare, though by no means nonexistent.[85] Woman's difference, he concluded, could be attributed to "the particular constitution of her genital organs," to "the special state of the whole of her organization in general," and to the special state of her nervous system in particular (Br, 37). Her uterus governs the *economy* of her body, but it is not the source of her afflictions. Rather, proclaimed Briquet, the source of her propensity to hysteria lies in her special *"sensibilité."* Briquet located women's susceptibility to hysteria in their "noble and most important mission" — raising children and caring for the elderly (Br, 51). Sexual difference, according to this tabulator of clinical observations, is the effect of the providential destiny of men and women: "Woman is made to feel, and feeling is nearly hysteria. Man, on the contrary, is made to act, and he suffers the inconveniences of action" (Br, 50).

Briquet wanted to rescue hysteria from the cloak of shame with which earlier interpreters had surrounded it. What his predecessors had called "instability," "mobility," "nervous weakness," or "susceptibility," Briquet intended to elevate into noble sentiments — the best maternal feelings a woman might have: "I recognized finally that hysteria was not that shameful malady whose name alone reminds doctors and laymen alike of those lines from our great tragic poet Racine — 'It is Venus tooth and claw attached to her prey.' Rather, hysteria was due to the existence, in a woman, of noble and admirable feelings, of feelings that only a woman is capable of feeling" (Br, vii). But Briquet's *Traité de l'hystérie* is not a volume full of admiring portraits of noble female sentiments. Unlike Rousseau's Sophie or Virey's ideal dictionary *"femme,"* this hospitalized hysteric was in pain.

The Freudian case history, contends Michel de Certeau, destroys the individualism of the scientific observation: "It substitutes another history in returning . . . to the system of tragedy."[86] The tragedy of *Phèdre*, summoned by Briquet, is one of desire unsatisfied — continence leading to an uncontrollable passion.[87] The poetics of hysteria in Briquet escape those of tragedy precisely because the physician believes that out of his scientific plots come solutions to the maladies of his patients. Out of a concatenation of possible hysterogenics, other bodies may be spared. What separates Briquet's narratives from the tragic plots of his philosophical predecessors — or the Freudian masterplots discussed by de Certeau — is his insistence upon a female constitution that can be successfully managed. And unlike those who were content to sprinkle their texts with secondhand anecdotes of women who were saved, Briquet brought science to his plots.   •

When a doctor believes that hysteria is caused by an unruly uterus or unfulfilled sexual desire, he can tell a story of clear causality: the hysterical girl of the *Dictionnaire* cured herself with prostitution and pregnancy. In the irrational logic of *post hoc ergo propter hoc*, she had hysterical fits because of her sexual continence. When woman's innate *sensibilité* is seen as the source of her malady, the doctor is harder pressed to produce a narrative to account for her symptoms. What can he say to translate the language of her body when he believes that the hysteric is communicating in her natural mother tongue? How can he presume to treat symptoms he deems an exacerbation of her most noble destiny? How can he tell the difference between her illness and her health when he believes her hysteria is the constitutional mark of her sexual difference?

Briquet's claims to the new "positive science" lend him an authority for assigning disorderly bodies to a system. He calls his predecessors' observations faulty because they rarely worked from *personal* observation but rather from books and previously collected material, because doctors were overly concerned with an upper-class clientele, and because the spaces from which doctors drew their observations limited their scope.[88] The Salpêtrière's admission of "only incurables" inevitably had prevented the likes of Georget from seeing the larger picture of the development of hysteria (Br, 54). Briquet transforms ideas about hysteria because of his rich original observations, the diversity of his clientele, his knowledge of earlier work, and his awareness of his contemporaries' work in diverse clinics and asylums. His study also represents a turning point in the study of hysteria because he took up debates long dividing not only those working on hysteria but also those concerned with women's roles in society. Though he embraced myths about femininity that had thwarted observations of female illness, he nevertheless confronted the fantasmatic discourse of the era before the clinic and attempted to use new insights to treat and prevent women's nervous disorders.

Because of his detailed observations, Briquet believed he could see a continuity between predisposing causes and hysterical symptoms in the 430 "scientific observations" he collected in his *Traité*. His case studies are therefore a catalogue of responses to these central debates, a set of stories in which certain influences will be listed, analyzed, and positioned in relation to other influences. By locating the precipitating conditions, he believed he could give the suffering body a reality deserving a cure. His case studies produced plots for his philosophical views, and in these plots he cast himself as savior. Unlike the patients in the Salpêtrière, these are curable bodies, bodies in flux, sensibilities momentarily exacerbated by a crisis. Instead of creating a fantasmatic "other" beyond help or cure, Briquet looks for configurations of crisis in any female body he comes across.

Taking a set of broad symptoms of hysteria as his guide, Briquet produces a study of the fifteen agents (*causes prédisposantes*) influencing an individual's hysterical symptoms: gender, age, her parents' health, her physical constitution and "moral disposition," the climate, her social position, the location and nature of her education, her diet, her profession, the passions, continence, her menstruation, earlier and present illnesses. Any one of these categories may be filled by a story of circumstances that could, eventually, predispose a woman to hysterical illness. Briquet's ostensible goal here is to accumulate scientific evidence about each of these categories so that women's chances of becoming hysterical may be significantly reduced. He contended that by relying on new evidence about factors that might predispose a girl to hysteria, doctors could supervise women into normality.

Two problems quickly arose. First, Briquet became a kind of *entrepreneur* of hysterical behavior, finding problems in nearly every woman he encountered. Because he believed that not all hysterics actually have attacks, he managed to equate a predisposition to hysteria with actually *being* hysterical. He discovered women's susceptibility to hysteria around every corner, making normality harder to achieve than a hysterical temperament. Though he offered an immense amount of detail about the women he observed, Briquet's stories wound up mirroring the concerns of the predecessors he sought to supplant. Eighteenth-century medical philosophers like Pierre Roussel and Cabanis, along with their obsessive nineteenth-century follower Virey, provided Briquet with a framework for defining the "true nature" of the women whose hysterical symptoms he scrupulously observed (Br, 48). Drawing on such views, Briquet ultimately trivialized his patients' complaints: "Hysteria is a very common malady among women; it is necessary to know this in order to be always on guard against the possibility of its intervention in illnesses and in order to reassure women who, preoccupied with their sufferings, believe themselves gravely ill, when they are really only afflicted with a nervous ailment" (Br, 37).

Second, Briquet did a better job of accumulating predisposing agents than he did of actually drawing conclusions from his observations. His enormous *Traité* provides an elaborate blueprint for supervising women's daily lives, but it offers little empathy to those already afflicted with hysteria. Although Briquet touted his observations as putting an end to the tragedy of Racinian hysteria, the cases he actually reported (71 out of the 430 he has observed), back away from relating specific *causes prédisposantes* to the patients' symptoms. His examples seem somehow at odds with his masterplot—as if there were con-nections he refused to see. Despite his attention, in the theoretical portions of this work, to the circumstances that might render an individual susceptible to hysteria, his case studies tell remarkably little about the patients' pasts. Instead, they leap from issue to issue, almost as if they were responding to questions on a preprinted form listing all the possible categories of *causes prédisposantes*. Most of Briquet's case studies tell the stories of bodies—of vomiting attacks, stomach cramps, anorexia, headaches, palpitations, paralysis, and delirium—and of medical treatment. The following cases are not typical, but they provide particularly elaborate accounts of the patients' histories. They are also among the cases Briquet endowed with a particular exemplarity, using them to illustrate the issues central to his understanding of hysteria. For this reason, they give us a privileged look at the obsessions, the narrative ploys, and the inconsistencies of the stories of hysteria produced in the hospital clinic.

Marie Gaudin was especially vulnerable to hysteria because her mother suffered from the same malady, claimed Briquet. He produced this case as evidence that hysteria frequently affects girls too young to be infected with the dangers of desire.[89] Other clues to her hysterical condition, we learn, lie in her siblings' problems, in her own impressionability, and in her overreaction to emotions. The events of her adolescence are shadowed forth without com-mentary:

> At eighteen years, a painful pregnancy, frequent vomiting, frequent attacks, and because of many contraventions, a normal delivery: the child is alive and in good health.
>
> She took refuge in Paris at age nineteen, in order to flee the reproaches leveled at her because of her pregnancy. Dating from this period, she had many problems. (Br, 58)

Unlike the women's stories that are embedded in the short narratives of the Salpêtrière registers, Marie Gaudin's tale is recounted with diffidence. The *passé simple* of "A vingt-trois ans, elle dut se marier, plus par raison que par goût" (At age twenty-three, she had to get married, more for convenience than by choice), enforces a distance between this laundress's account of her past and the meaning Briquet attached to it. We cannot know how he arrived at the reason for her marriage. Did he determine that her family's insistence that she marry was against her will? Did she tell him? That her family was contraried by her "dispositions" is reported as a fact that leads to symptoms. Whatever affect may have been attached to her account has been dissipated by the gaze of science. From this and other cases like hers, Briquet drew the conclusion that hysteria in childhood is always produced under the influence of "moral emotions" (Br, 67). Small wonder, then, that he tried to capitalize on Marie's impressionability as a means to a cure: when she sees a paraplegic in the next bed get better under the same medical regime as her own, Briquet "energetically" steps up the treatment.

"Hysterical paralysis has nothing mysterious about it," writes Briquet in the chapter discussing the case of Eugénie Pontois. "It results, like other symptoms of hysteria, from a problem in the organs through which passions are manifested" (Br, 442). Eugénie was driven over the edge by "vivid and sudden moral feelings." Her impressionable character has exposed her to the crises of a body that becomes the rhetorical figure of emotions too intense for her to express. With a dead body on his hands, Briquet can demonstrate better than ever that Eugénie's symptoms have no organic origins. In a twisted affirmation of Eugénie's exemplarity, the physician informs us that all the incidents together *did not leave the least doubt* about the existence of a hysterical illness and that "there was little doubt that the incidents of paralysis arriving so suddenly after a moral emotion were not likewise of a hysterical nature." His elliptical wavering about his causal logic returns the reader to the scene of that *"émotion morale."* Eugénie is not shown *feeling*, but rather—as though Briquet were only good at describing bodily functions—flying off the handle: "the sick girl flew into a passion, becoming agitated. There was an epigastric impediment, suffocation, strangulation, and it all ended with shouts, cries, and sobbing" (Br, 454–56).

Stranger still, Briquet seems to struggle with the beginnings of this agitation: "She was very jealous about her husband, who committed numerous infidelities; this resulted in frequently repeated violent scenes and acts of violence." But whose *"voies de fait"* were repeated frequently? We learn that Eugénie's once happy personality became "irritable and irascible." When there were scenes, *"elle s'emportait"* (she flew into a passion). A paragraph later, another version of this scene of violence emerges: "After a heated quarrel during which she had been more mistreated than usual, she was seized with a fever." What we know of this husband, we learn only by filling in the gaps in this narrative: he was unfaithful and *there were scenes* in which *she* was mistreated. Briquet's evacuation of the male agent of the *"émotion morale"* he obstinately refuses to name is only one of many moments in this study when he demurs before a scene of violence embedded in his text. Whatever may have been narratable in Eugénie's story, her physician will only bring forth what he needs to make her a case. Whatever the predisposing causes named here, Eugénie's case winds up conforming to a masterplot in which "woman is made to feel and . . . [man] suffers the inconveniences of action."

Céline Tonnelle's case proves the exception to Briquet's practice of either subsuming his observations into a litany of symptoms or integrating them into a romantic masterplot of pseudoscience. Unlike either Marie or Eugénie, Céline gets the benefit of the doubt. Her case is presented as an example of the gradual and successive manifestation of all phases of hysteria. As in the case of Marie, her family history evaporates into a cavalcade of convulsions. The family violence reported by Briquet is considered as only the first in a chain of predisposing causes. Yet Briquet cites it in the sentence that makes a central causal connection: "Constantly mistreated by her mother and frequently beaten by her, Céline Tonnelle became morose and very impressionable, the smallest thing affected her" (Br, 197–99). Despite the fantastic quality of a story that recalls Virginie Joséphine's in the Salpêtrière, Céline's story is reported without commentary: "This young girl had her menstrual period for the first time when she was deeply frightened by the sudden invasion of a mad dog, who ran out of a bush to throw himself on her at a time when she was alone in the country. At that very moment, she lost consciousness, and she had her first hysterical attack with convulsions." While Briquet recounted Marie's case by coyly casting doubt on her motivations and not letting us know what she may have told him, he insists on the believability of the story he narrates about Céline. His appropriation of a position of omniscient narrator—"elle fut vivement effrayée . . . elle perdit connaissance"—assures us that this scene of violation by a raging dog is as real to him as the hysterical symptoms he observes as its result.

Because everything for a woman is "an occasion for sensation," and all emotions stress her "internal organs," she lingers ever on the border of hysteria. Her impressionability may make a cure more effective, as in the case of Marie. Alternatively, it may make her more likely to suffer attacks from sexual experiences, as Briquet suggests is the case of Désirée Pelletier who set out to cure herself with public balls and all the other pleasures "that young girls of her sort take" (Br, 471). It may dispose her to an improvement in her condition through religious experiences (Br, 434). Or it may make her more likely to overreact to the religious fervor of others (as in hysteria epidemics). Briquet's observations make an elaborate show of the effects of female sensitivity on women's bodily symptoms. Yet they never make any case—not even that of Céline Tonnelle—representative. Instead, they promote a fantasy that would put all women, representative or not, under surveillance.

Briquet claims to give exempla, yet the specific histories of these women fail to yield lessons on ways to avoid hysteria. The causes morales amassed by Briquet are so extensive it is hard to imagine a hysteria patient who had not suffered one or more of them. The scenes he theorizes as leading to hysterical attacks are not negligible events in the life of a woman—battery as a child, abuse by a husband—but Briquet gives them a content that generated his stories and obfuscates those of the patient. These *causes morales* become reduced to moral values no different from those that marginalized the patient in the first place. Ultimately, they become the source for the doctor's fantasies about prophylaxis and for his participation in debates larger than the treatment of an individual patient. They allow him to spin a story of a representative woman who will not suffer from hysterical symptoms, who will serve society in productive ways, and about whom no tales are told.

Briquet's study supported the policies of healthy, happy mothering embraced by almost every social reformer of his era.[90] Yet unlike reformers who were convinced of the moral depravity of the working classes, Briquet insisted upon the importance of caring for the health and education of women of all classes. By rejecting the sexual etiology of hysteria, he managed to give new honor to the women whose bodies were out of control. However, he did not extricate these women from their marginal status. Rather, by developing a model in which nearly all women may become hysterical, he produced the justification for hereditary models that marginalize individuals on the basis of their family history.[91] By refusing to name sources for hysteria's invasion, he opened the floodgates to endless fantasies about what incidents in a patient's life may have caused her suffering. By multiplying "causes" and treating elliptically a patient's account of her *"émotions morales,"* he created a virtual minefield of dangers that would permit women hardly more activity than one would expect of a porcelain doll.

Briquet did not assign blame—except perhaps to dogs. The doctor did not chide these girls' educators or batterers for their mishandling of this future mother. Rather, he emphasized identifying the moment when the sickness began—as if nothing could really have been done differently, but at least now that the facts are known, some lessons for the upbringing of others may be drawn. Women who are prone to hysteria, according to Briquet, show remarkable sympathy for others. They break down in tears whenever moved by pity. Sad stories make them weep (Br, 355). The hysteric-to-be is always in danger of internalizing the scenes of the outside world.[92] This is why she must be kept away from anything that would overpower her with affect. This is why she must neither go to the theater nor read novels. This is why she should not have contact with anyone who will stir her feelings—like girls her own age or, heaven forbid, young men. This is why "one must abstain from showing feelings in their presence; one must speak to them with reason and never with feeling," and show them that their "excessive sensitivity" is a weakness that "makes them ridiculous" and "submits them to the power of those who surround them" (Br, 609-10).

Submitted into Briquet's power, the women in this *Traité* never get a chance to show their feelings. Doctors, it would appear from this work, never feel. Or at least they never show they are affected by their patients. To let the mask slip would be to risk becoming like the women themselves—hysterical, suffering, out of control. The narrative preserves the doctors' position of action, of authority, of power. But it is also syncopated by acknowledgment of the gaze that has connected them to the bodies they fear. The case studies can no more eliminate the presence of the doctor than they can lose the patient in a morass of symptoms. He is there, like the women he examines, holding on to his position by insisting that what he knows is different. For what separates him from the bodies he treats is not some recognizable lesion, some bacteria, some fever, but the difference he creates in the telling.

The meanings the doctors of the Salpêtrière and La Charité assigned to their hysterical patients betray their investments in certain social and moral values. The fantasies they spin of the origins of these maladies give narratives to women who would otherwise only suffer the convulsions of their bodies. Yet those stories are bound by conventions and codes. They participate in larger systems that make possible prescriptions for behavior. While the codes differ and the impulse to narrate changes from analyst to analyst, from space to space, the poetics of hysteria nevertheless remain a strikingly consistent process of reading difference. These doctors sought in the symptoms of their patients an account of moral, not physical, lesions. Out of the most detailed representations of physical symptoms, they extrapolated an account of female difference that is only tangentially related to the actual cases. They affirmed an essential feminine with a "positive science" that gave her a name, a body, and a past.

These cases nevertheless threaten to break down the system they ostensibly support. Given a history, an individuality, and a voice—even if embedded in another's text—these women become subjects in their own rights. No longer just the source of generalizations, they stand apart from the text intended to serve as their masterplot. Reduced to symptoms and treatment, given only a shadow of a history, they testify to little more than their narratability. But that shadow of a history invites further interpretations. The stories given to these women seem to allude to other stories that are *not* told. The fantasies the doctors assign them suggest other fantasies we can only reconstruct provisionally.

Hysteria became the ultimate enigma for these doctors. When the doctors let go of their theories of a single center for the hysterical malady, they began to produce narratives of the patient and her pain. Because they could not find a lesion, they sought a pattern. Because they did not find a clear pattern, they sought a set of symptoms. Because they did not find a consistent set of symptoms, they sought a set of predisposing causes. The gender of the patients stands out as the most visible consistent sign. To that gender, the doctors added their masterplots.

The doctors at the Salpêtrière and La Charité believed they could generate narratives that would demonstrate their patients' otherness: unproductive, dangerous, depraved, or abused, these women had not enjoyed the kind of life girls needed to make them virtuous and maternal. The doctors assigned motives to the women to replace the desires they could not understand. Predisposing agents would let the doctors moralize the desires of women: if the patient's history suggested her problem came from a pattern of misdirected interests, the doctors would attempt to redirect them. They would make examples of those patients so that other women would stay in line. These doctors failed to discover an order for hysteria—despite all their protests to the contrary. In the end, they managed to order the hysteric in their institutions and in their texts. They gave her their orderly fantasies of the origins of her ills. Her femaleness became the lure for those fantasies. It seduced those who looked upon her into betraying *their desires* for her *difference.*

Hysterical Dangers

In 1849 the doctors of the *Annales médico-psychologiques* reprinted the case of a girl suffering from chronic chorea. Her limbs were semiparalyzed: "Having undergone an insult to her modesty, she saw the weakness of her legs increase." Something about the girl's account of her condition must have drawn the doctor's attention to this detail of her history—the only one reported. Whether the girl actually insisted that her ailment resulted from an "insult to her modesty," or whether the doctor pressed her for details of her sexual experience and got this result, the girl must have encoded her own sexuality as somehow violated.[93] In the resulting case study, the doctor and patient have jointly participated in the construction of a fantasy about vulnerable female sexuality. Together they must have read female sexuality as capable of transmitting messages to the body in ways that can even cause death (the outcome in this case). No matter who insisted on the importance of this event, in the logic of *post hoc ergo propter hoc* that informs this account, the moment of violation becomes a transformative one. Moreover, it is a transformative moment not just in terms of this narrative, but in terms of the understanding of the illness. Once such an observation is disseminated, it serves as a touchstone for other readings of illness. It endlessly refers doctors to scenes of seduction in the past lives of their patients. It correlates incidents of sexualization with the sufferings of women.

Such a narrative depends upon the truth of what the patient says. It requires that she provide a believable and true account of her past. This is precisely what hysterics are rarely believed capable of doing. "These sick women are usually sensitive, bizarre, preoccupied, and sad," wrote Georget in 1824. "It is not always easy to discover pains of the heart, especially among women, and if one does not watch out, one risks being taken in by false narratives, and of being tricked about the origins of the illness one sees."[94] By the first years of the Second Empire, *aliénistes* presumed that whatever hysterical patients say would have little truth to it. According to Bénédict-Auguste Morel, hysterics "drown in the most bizarre, the most false, the most ridiculous, and the most unfair suppositions." They are masters at subterfuge: "Since the love of truth is not the dominant virtue of their personalities, they never show facts as they are in reality, and trick their husbands, parents, friends, confessors, as well as doctors." The infamous Marie Jeanneret, who was found guilty of poisoning nine people in 1868, was analyzed before and after her crimes as a hysteric: "She was always fickle in her tastes, lacking in judgment, with an obstinate will, a need for fervent emotions and a taste for intrigue and falsehood." Jules Falret, second-generation Salpêtrière doctor, likened hysterics to the fiction-writers of his era: Hysterical madwomen are *romanesque* and dreamy with a "spirit of duplicity and falsehood" that leads them to "put on or travesty" even their convulsions: "They compose veritable novels in which they frequently mix up the true and the false, interpolating them artfully and inextricably so that they trick even the most clearsighted. In a word, the life of hysterics is nothing but a perpetual lie."[95] Beginning in the 1850s the authors of the *Annales médico-psychologiques*, most of them doctors at the Salpêtrière—Falret, Trélat, Baillarger, Moreau de Tours, and later Legrand Du Saulle—would spin elaborate theories of the hysteric's deceiving, dissimulating nature. Out of her symptoms, they created a monster who malingers and only masquerades as mad.

This fantasmatic dangerous hysteric became the flip side of the impressionable endangered girl in the course of the 1850s and 1860s. Unlike the cases of hysterics in Brachet or Briquet, these cases of hysteria are no longer staged as *exempla* out of which prescriptions might be derived for the population at large. Rather, these dangerous, duplicitous, and frequently depraved women become examples of quite another kind. The cases in which they appeared resulted from a long struggle by the Salpêtrière doctors to differentiate their hysterics from those whose cases proliferated in public hospitals. Through these women the doctors created a different kind of hysteria, arising particularly out of the lower classes, a hysteria that had nothing to do with femininity but that was rather a *perversion* of femininity. Out of the plots they gave to their patients' difference, they created a traitor whose tales could be dismissed without a second thought. The hysteric's stories now served only to further justify the system to which she was assigned: because she could so successfully manipulate all but the most adept *aliénistes*, she needed their order all the more.

The hysterics of the 1850s and 1860s continue to be read in terms of gender, class, heredity, and, above all, sexuality, but with one striking difference. The doctors were no longer willing to conceive of these hysterics' sexuality as violated. Accounts of attacking dogs no longer held the place of a scene of sexualization. In these later cases, the women were seen as engaging in acts of debauchery themselves. Baillarger reports the case of a woman who has prostituted her older daughter and forced her own ten-year-old daughter to perform sexual acts with her. In 1860 Legrand Du Saulle recounted the case of a hysteric who accused a health inspector of raping her and whose testimony was initially discounted because of "the minimal confidence inspired by the testimony of a hysteric." Jules Falret described the obscene remarks, violent scenes, and "most disorderly acts" in which hysterics indulge: "they put on airs of piety and devotion and succeed in passing themselves off as saints, all the while abandoning themselves secretly to the most shameful acts." In 1882 Henri Huchard wrote about the sexual appetites of hysterics that drive them to nymphomania and even prostitution.[96] Hysteria named these women's absence of a sense of morality, the doctors contended. It marked these women's difficulties with the boundaries the doctors constructed in the world. Out of the *causes morales* that might provoke hysteria, the doctors of the Salpêtrière had created "moral lesions" resulting from it.

The hysteric brings about a short circuit in such a system of truth and consequences because—if we are to believe many of the doctors who treated her—she thrives on lies, or, at the very least, she cannot distinguish truth from falsehood. Her problem, as doctors from Virey to Briquet pointed out, is that she is so impressionable that she does not know where reality stops and impressions begin.[97] She transforms everything into feeling because her imagination knows no limits. Her body, as Freud will later show, figures metaphorically what she knows, but cannot tell. In this respect, the hysteric's duplicity becomes just a further kink in a system of essentialized femininity. Coupled with her hereditary circumstances, class background, and sexual behavior, the *romanesque* nature of the hysteric becomes a potent signifier of danger. Doctors sought less to cure such women than to separate them from anyone they might harm. The intrigues around these women's duplicity quickly included debates over the mental state of prostitutes. After all, both were intensely related to concerns about women's roles, behavior, and potential aberrations.

Containing Desires

In order to save prostitutes from the mental problems afflicting them, Esquiros imagined a better world of harlotry. He imagined improving the education of working-class girls and making marriage easier for men and, above all, transforming the conditions of prostitution—the brothels, the surveillance, and even the choice of girls. He believed that with more luxurious houses, the "abundance and luxury that recommend good will come to educate the morals of prostitutes and render them capable of arousing love." Illnesses would then diminish, and women would have an easier time reverting to marriage. In these finer houses, prostitutes would spend their days reading instructive and amusing books: "They prefer in all their readings tragic scenes, virtuous deeds, animated emotions, maternal courage, pity, and filial feelings." Such readings might in fact include a novel published in the same year as Esquiros's own *Vierges folles* and praised fervently in its last pages, namely, Arnould Frémy's *Les Femmes proscrites* (The Banned Women). This novel stakes out the spaces of rehabilitation imagined by Esquiros to reach out to adulteresses as well as prostitutes.[98] Like Esquiros, it imagines horrendous conditions under which women are driven to desperate acts, squalorous places where the banned are sequestered, and tragic ends for lost lives. Drawing on evidence culled from Parent-Duchâtelet and Esquirol, it paints a bleak landscape of women's lives in July Monarchy France and connects the fates of bourgeois women to those of the prostitutes and madwomen populating the prisons and asylums of Paris. This novelistic appropriation of the scientific observations of the 1830s centers on a character who has devoted his life to the study of women. This *"homme martyr"* has watched from a distance as the girl of his youthful dreams is seduced by another. He devotes himself to exploring the secrets of marginalized women:

> He wandered without respite in the circle of unpardonable miseries: hospitals, prisons, places of detention and of penitence. He was more than once surprised to find in the midst of this infamy that woman who was formerly his supreme happiness and the glory of his desires. He took pleasure in mentally disfiguring this idol of a rejected religion and in destroying the last vestiges of the touching and noble deeds that the unfortunate woman might have left in his heart. (Frémy, 1:194)

His study and observation (Frémy, 1:190) takes him into two of the spaces that confine marginalized women during the July Monarchy. The novel views those places as two stops along the same trajectory:

> Saint-Lazare is a prison for women and the Salpêtrière a hospital for women. Although these two establishments can hardly be confused, they nevertheless have certain similar features and are held together by a common bond of misfortune and penitence. They form the two extremes of the life of a woman caught up in misery and degradation. At Saint-Lazare, an incarcerated woman, often still extremely young, begins in some ways her repentance, and sheds her first tears along the accursed road onto which she has thrown herself. She comes to the Salpêtrière to fade away, feeble, paralyzed, mad, or incurable, she sheds her last tear and utters her last moan. (Frémy, 1:113)

Henri's reflections "on the origins and consequences of [these women's] debasement" have an uncanny way of replicating many of the interpretive moves we have traced in this chapter. Like the Salpêtrière doctors and Briquet, the novel's protagonist seeks a story to explain the degradation of the women he studies. But this text is far more explicit about the origins of *his* motives. The charitable work of his observations dovetails with the "pleasure" he takes in seeing as *"proscrites"* the very women he might have loved. This text makes Henri into a case in order to see what drives men to their obsessions for these "creatures of salvation and nothingness, of abjection and idolatry" (Frémy, 1:233).

This novel's exploration of the link between prostitution and madness evokes momentous debates about women's place in society. As we have seen, the suggestion that prostitution might *lead* to hysteria or some other form of madness threatened those who believed that sexual desire, if left untended, was fundamentally destabilizing to society. If male continence was not dangerous, then all the justifications for prostitution crumbled. Those concerned about the dangers of continence, like Antoine de Montègre, J. B. Louyer-Villermay, Hector

Landouzy, Émile Mathieu, and Auguste Debay, articulated this concern in terms of female, not male desire. They raised their voices as much against rampant sexual energy as against sexual repression. Far less a plea for a "sexual revolution" than a way of controlling sex through discourse, tirades against continence targeted the church and upheld a morality that attempted, above all, to raise the birth rate. The views of these doctors presented an entire series of contradictions. They saw masturbation, which they opposed, as the inevitable result of a philosophy of continence. They abhorred women's refusals to participate in the requisite conjugal "duties," yet some insisted on a need to coax her into such duties. Debay, for example, embraced the importance of women's orgasms in a strange return to the Aristotelian folklore that both partners' sexual pleasure might be necessary to conception—but with a twist, advising women to fake sexual satisfaction if their husbands left them cold, as if a husband's certainty of his wife's orgasm was far more important than anything she might herself have felt.[99] They produced endless accounts of the anguish suffered by unmarried women—Saint Teresa of Avila, Théroigne de Méricourt, and Olympe de Gouges were particularly targeted[100]—yet they ignored the social and philosophical contributions of these women. They questioned any reinstitution of divorce, yet acknowledged that the sexual excesses of unsatisfied married women led them to accesses of hysteria as severe as any suffered by unmarried younger women or widows. They would not have granted Emma Bovary a divorce; nor would they have left her to books and adulterous affairs. Rather they would have demanded that Charles Bovary find a way to convince her to like sex with him. And if that had been impossible, they would have simply assumed that she would find some way to contain her displeasure *and* her desire.[101]

Those who imagined hysteria to be the result of continence created an elaborate fantasy about the power of desire. Those who insisted that continence had nothing to do with hysteria set about to cope with the powers of agents in the outside world. "We should be driven to think about hysteria as more frequently the result of moral influences than of physical causes," wrote an anonymous doctor of the Hôtel-Dieu Hospital in 1843. Sexual appetites and the needs of the uterus are unlikely to bring about hysteria, argued this doctor when confronted with a young woman in a kind of ecstatic coma. The moral cause in this woman's case derived again from an attack by a dog: "One day while she was in the fields, far from home, she was assailed by a mad dog who did not actually harm her; but she was seized by a terrible fright." Several doctors had suggested sexual activity as a remedy for the nervous symptoms she suffered since the dog attacked her. "*Ces conseils sont absurdes,*" declares her attending physician. He is sure that her hysteria "was produced by a moral cause, by a terrible fear that violently shook up her nervous system." The sexual relations advised by these other doctors risk harming her physically as well as morally, he asserts. Unlike de Montègre, this doctor refused to conceive of sexual activity as a form of cure.[102]

In place of the specifically sexual desire early nineteenth-century doctors had imagined overloading the hysteric's system, analysts now saw a myriad of desires. Whether they called these desires *causes morales, causes prédisposantes*, or *influences morales*, they repeatedly imagined kinds of emotions and social conditions that harkened back to traditional views of gender, class, and sexuality. The stories through which they allowed their hysterics to feel—and thus to become subjects in their own right—remained caught up in masterplots that confined women of all classes. The desires contained in these stories derived from honest attempts on the part of the doctors to hear and report the conditions of women's suffering. Yet at a certain point it was hard to know whose desires— those of the women or those of their doctors—had been given narrative shape. What was certain, nonetheless, was that these doctors had found ways to formulate their own fears about the working classes, prostitutes, and sexual excess. For despite their attempts to minimize the importance of the sexual in the exegesis of hysteria, they nevertheless remained obsessed with the mental state of prostitutes and, as such, with the relationship of prostitutes' sexuality to hysteria and madness.

Those who worked in the Salpêtrière, like the doctors of the public hospitals, needed only to look around their wards to see whether the sexual activity of prostitutes was a shield against hysteria and other forms of mental illness. Parent had embraced the familiar myth that only upper-class women suffered from the nervous problems of hysteria. Prostitutes were too base, he contended, somehow hardened by their experiences in the streets (*PD*, 1:280–82). Yet prostitutes were omnipresent among the mental patients of the 1830s through 1850s, steadily one of the larger professional groups of inmates in the Salpêtrière. Esquirol had paved the way for views opposed to those of Parent and de Montègre when he declared that nearly all mental problems in women were complicated by hysteria and that five percent of those in the Salpêtrière with mental problems were prostitutes. But the correlation between hysteria and prostitution would not become a widely accepted fact until Briquet brought his skills of observation to the prostitutes in the Hôpital Lourcine. In a flourish meant to end all debate over continence, Briquet used the tools of scientific observation to determine that over half of all prostitutes suffered from hysteria (Br, 124–25).[103]

By removing hysteria from a direct causal relationship to sexual activity, the Salpêtrière doctors and Briquet made possible a new evaluation of the madness of the prostitute. "Will people now invoke the overexcitation of the genitals [as the source of hysteria]?" asks Briquet of his astounding findings that 106 out of 197 prostitutes were hysterics and that 28 more were "impressionable" (Br, 125). According to Briquet, prostitutes avoid orgasms. Should one assume, he asks, that mechanical excitation of the genitals is enough in itself to cause hysteria? His answer would not satisfy those seeking ways to discourage women from clandestine prostitution:

In reflecting on the life led by these women and on the multiplicity of painful experiences and sensations to which they are prey, one will not be surprised that hysteria is so common among them. Poverty, nights spent without sleep, alcohol abuse, constant fears of the demands of the police or of bad treatment by the men with whom they live, the forced imprisonment occasioned by the illnesses they contract, the unbridled jealousy and violent passions that animate them—all this explains well enough the frequency of hysterical problems among them. (Br, 125–26)

Briquet's findings would nevertheless satisfy those who could not believe a working-class woman capable of the exalted sensibilities of the *bourgeoise:* "This frequency would probably be even greater," he continues, "if it were not for the strength of the constitution of these women and the moral insensitivity their profession has given them" (Br, 126). Concerns that prostitutes might not be sufficiently different from their betters have, with Briquet's treatise, been put completely to rest.

Those who debated the comparative dangers of continence and prostitution in the making of hysteria drew increasingly upon statistical information and observations. Stanislas Rossignol's thesis on the inmates of Saint-Lazare furnished further evidence that prostitution does not help nervous maladies.[104] His contemporary, Legrand Du Saulle vehemently argued that continence did *not* cause hysteria. Rather, what predisposed a woman to hysteria related far more to "moral influences" that were in turn affected by class, education, and profession. Working-class women and prostitutes were therefore particularly prone to hysteria.[105] Those who believed sexual activity irrelevant to hysteria posited a new paradigm in which class and education mattered far more. The new fantasies of the origins of hysteria consistently invoked the suffering of girls who earned so little they were forced to sell their bodies and ultimately their mental health.[106] The novelist Frémy prefigured the fight against prostitution that came out of this new paradigm. If prostitution could not be eliminated, then at least it could be given even more of a difference than it presently had: "To destroy prostitution is a utopia whose immediate achievement would be not only impossible but probably dangerous. It is rather a matter of limiting it, of regulating it, of rescuing the poorer classes from it to confine it uniquely to the vicious classes" (Frémy, 1:154). Like the *aliénistes* who increasingly depicted their hysterical charges as duplicitous, those who sought a greater difference for the prostitute would make her ever more criminal.

Meanwhile, de Montègre's case of the hysteric cured by debauchery, conception, and miscarriages was passed along in dozens of editions of Auguste Debay's marriage manuals and popular gynecological handbooks for women. Popular medicine took up most fervently the fight against continence, spinning endless prescriptions of ways to keep bourgeois daughters away from anything that might make them desire and therefore send them into hysterical battle against those desires. In these manuals, the endangered girl turned up again, curing herself this time not of hysteria or of continence, but of lubricious acts.

This time, Jean-Louis Alibert, well-known physician of the Saint-Louis Hospital in Paris during the Restoration, was called in to care for a young aristocratic woman afflicted with nymphomania. His advice to her parents followed that of the gynecologists of his era: "marriage—as soon as possible." The eavesdropping nymphomaniac made a quick escape from her parents' house. Several weeks later, of course, Alibert happened to recognize, "despite her disguise," the young aristocrat in her new occupation as a *"fille d'amour."* The rest of the story might have been drawn from de Montègre: "I'm following your prescription and curing myself," she announced with a smile. "And so it was," reported Debay, since "a month later, satisfied by venal pleasures, the young girl returned to her parents completely cured." One more prescription remained to be filled: "A quick marriage buried forever in oblivion the shame of her escapade."[107] Strangely enough, the prescriptions created by popularizers like Alibert and Debay differed little from the ones elaborated by the supposedly more scientific Brachet or Briquet. Girls were advised to avoid excitement, emotional stimulation, and passion. Novels, plays, and of course racy pictures were to be eschewed at all costs. Girls were not to be spoiled, caressed, or indulged. Rather, advised Briquet, "If you see a young girl dreaming and launching herself into the land of chimeras, make her put herself at her piano and the castles in Spain will quickly collapse" (Br, 608). This life of simplicity, emotional restraint, and repression of pleasure should surely breed better wives, mothers, and caretakers.

With the midcentury shift away from a belief in the dangers of continence and toward a certainty that *causes morales* were to blame for prostitutes' mental problems came few changes in the masterplots in which hysterics and prostitutes were subsumed. Whether they circulated in the streets or simply into the theater, women's sensibilities were seen as endangered. The spaces into which they might travel continued to be circumscribed. No matter what their sources, women's desires seemed always in need of containment.

With the advent of the clinic, new ways of looking, seeing, and telling the difference of the hysteric had emerged. It was no longer possible to make the single body part stand for the whole: uterus, genitals, or even the brain came up short as the locale of the disorder. The woman with sick nerves had problems deriving from her entire constitution. What the mythmakers most praised in her came to be read as the source of her pain. Her sensibilities had become a justification for constraints on her movements and feelings alike. Her internal and external involvement with the world of the senses could equally disrupt her delicate equilibrium. From the moment that she was seen suffering because of her *organisation morale* and not because of an unruly womb (or overactive genitalia), she became a *subject* who could be fantasmatically read by the medical profession.

"Freud's discovery of the unconscious is the outcome of his *reading* of the hysterical discourse of his patients," writes Shoshana Felman.[108] The author of the *Studies on Hysteria* was not the first to discover this "new way of reading." The woman his medical predecessors came to treat was, they thought, victimized by her body. Instead of seeking to know her, the earlier doctors had sought to master the symptom, to tame the unruly uterus or savage genitals. These doctors found her in new spaces of observation. She was working class and poor. She did not have the education or the knowledge to read her own difference. In the spaces of the public asylum and public hospital, the doctors gave her their readings. Made observable by the places to which the police and medical doctors brought her, she allowed them to make narrations out of her symptoms and her history. Her body would be seen as representing her lapses in *moral* spheres. In those spheres, and in those narrations, she was forced to give up the habits that jeopardized her body. Otherwise she risked becoming dangerous herself. And when that happened, she became the subject of novels.

5
Pathological Masterplots:
Hysteria, Sexuality,
and the Balzacian Novel

"   _T_he story of the mental state of hysterics has been . . . travestied by journalists and novelists to their content," complained
aliéniste Henri Legrand Du Saulle in 1883. "They have gone spreading the
most unscientific and false ideas among the public, both about the causes and
the manifestations of neurosis—resulting in prejudices, erroneous opinions, and
unfounded preventive measures—against which it is important that the doctor
fight each day." For these "unscientific and false ideas," Legrand claimed to
substitute clinical case studies that analyzed "the extremely important changes
in the hysteric's personality and desires." His collection of observations became
his private battle against novelists, novels, and the *"romanesque."*[1] Yet as he set
out to supplement a hundred years of hysteria studies, his own goals seemed
scarcely different from those of the novels he condemned.

Only a few years before Legrand published his observations, Émile Zola's
Son Excellence Eugène Rougon (1876) provided its own reflections on novelistic
as well as clinical versions of hysteria. In a scene near the beginning of the
novel, Minister Rougon finds himself confronted with the seductions of his
future nemesis Clorinde Balbi. Their chat turns to contemporary literature and
provides Rougon an opportunity to flaunt his knowledge of literature as well
as of science before the teenage seductress:

> A novel had just appeared [. . .] a work of the most depraved imagination, affecting
> a regard for the exact truth, dragging the reader into the excesses of a hysterical
> woman. That word "hysteria" seemed to please him, for he repeated it three
> times. When Clorinde asked him its meaning, he refused to give it, overtaken
> by extreme modesty.
>
> —Everything can be said, he continued; only there is a way to say every-
> thing. . . . Thus in government service, one is often obliged to tackle the most
> delicate subjects. I have read reports on certain women, for example, you un-
> derstand me? Well! Very precise details were recorded there in a clear, simple,
> honest style. But the reports remained in fact chaste! Whereas the novelists of
> our day have adopted a lubricious style, a way of saying things that makes them
> live before you. They call it "art," but it's really indecency, that's all.

Whatever combination of medical, psychiatric, juridical, or police reports Rougon is describing, he embraces a notion that *scientific* studies preserve their readers' honor. Such texts seem to hide their "real" story behind shared codes. They convey meaning because doctors, lawyers, and *aliénistes* transmit to state administrators some knowledge that can go *without saying*. Reports about "certain women" remain "chaste," it seems, because they elide what might have been represented by a *definition* of the word "hysteria." As soon as someone asks for more information, as Clorinde does here, a wall of modesty blocks the story.

The novel, however, is allied in this scene both with the pornographic[2] and with the hysterogenic, for we learn that Clorinde, "had a horror of books": "As soon as she forced herself to read, nervous attacks made her put herself to bed." Neither Rougon nor the young seductress can tolerate literature. Only science and its "chaste" scenes seem appropriate to the seduction in the works here: "Even as he spoke, he maneuvered with great skill to get behind Clorinde's chair without her noticing. Her eyes closed, she murmured, 'Me, I've never read a single novel. It's dumb, all those lies.' "[3]

The novel to which Rougon alludes in the above passage hardly goes without saying. The critical and administrative horror surrounding *Madame Bovary* (1857) resonated into the Charcot era of hysteria and beyond, leaving the novel repeatedly indicted for its failure to mince words.[4] In 1858 the critic Eugène Poitou assaulted Flaubert's novel as heir to the depravities of July Monarchy literature and to the methods of the nineteenth-century clinic:

> *Madame Bovary*, with its brutal paintings, its coarse sensualism, its flattering pictures of libertinage, its poetry of vice and of the ugly, has been the delight of great ladies and honorable *bourgeoises*. What do you expect? In the marasmus where souls have fallen, in the resulting need for violent distractions and strong emotions, only that sort of thing still pleases us. Nothing succeeds today in the novel, drama, or comedy like those studies of depraved morals, like those corruptions stripped bare.

Railing against "that school that calls itself realist," Poitou likened the literature that would "expose our secret maladies" to the Musée Dupuytren, the pathological anatomy museum whose wax figures shared knowledge of the diseased body with medical students. "Anatomy, physiology . . . there is the muse of the new school," ranted Poitou, imagining that these novels, like the feared museum, bring "together the terrifying images of the most hideous afflictions of humanity."[5] Unlike Rougon, Poitou saw the intervention of science into literature as deeply traumatizing, but he also bemoaned the new literature's "loving" analysis of the likes of hysteria—"the transports of the senses, the brutalities of passion, and the bloody and nervous phenomena that set off or accompany outbursts." Like many critics of his era, he claimed this new realist literature owed its very lifeblood to the "father of physiological literature," Honoré de Balzac, admired for his exaggerations, excesses, mixtures of physiology, anatomy, and "repulsive studies of monstrosities and mental illnesses."[6]

Legrand's hostility toward the novel, Zola's thematized tensions over literary hysteria, and Poitou's anxieties about Balzac and Flaubert dovetail with a series of concerns that plagued France from the July Monarchy to the early Third Republic. The birth of the clinic, it seemed, had begun to work its magic upon literature as well. The concerns of the new *aliéniste* profession—ranging from monomania to hysteria—had increasingly become matters of public fascination and literary convention. Prescriptions of medical researchers concerning the health and morality of French men and women had begun to filter through a wide range of sources, translated into directives for behavior as well as into ironic plays on what we have called the masterplots of fear and, more tenuously, into further channels for anxiety and censorship.

In this chapter we look at the relationship between hysteria and the novel. We ask what happens when the novel engages medical debates about nervous disorders and particularly how the novel picks up on debates over hysteria and continence, madness and sexuality, and hysteria and prostitution. While the nineteenth-century novel even in its earliest manifestations—in novels like *Atala* (1801), *René* (1802), and *Adolphe* (1816)—explicitly evoked female marginality as the representational terrain out of which a fully constituted (male) subject could be imagined,[7] only with the advent of the July Monarchy *roman social* do we see that marginality articulated in terms that correspond to the medical, psychiatric, and "hygienic" concerns of the clinic. As we have seen, the July Monarchy novel obsessively exploited prostitutes: Janin's *L'Ane Mort; ou, La Fille guillotinée* (1829), the "Abbé Tiberge's" *Louisa; ou, Les Douleurs d'une fille de joie* (1830), Landais's *Une Vie de courtisane* (1833), Sand's *Lélia* (1833), Soulié's *Mémoires du diable* (1838), Frémy's *Femmes proscrites* (1840), and Méray's *La Part des femmes* (1847) inscribed prostitutes as vigorously as Sue's *Mystères*, Balzac's *Splendeurs et misères*, and Dumas fils' *Dame aux camélias*. At the same time, the July Monarchy novel had far less explicit dealings with the clinics where hysterics circulated.[8] Since the hysteric herself remained a medical rather than psychiatric problem through the 1850s, we should perhaps not be surprised that the literature of hysteria stayed largely outside the space of the asylum until Charcot's ascension.[9] A shift in literary emphasis nevertheless occurred at the beginning of the Second Empire just as doctors and critics began to complain of novelistic incursions into the psychiatric. By the 1860s, following *Madame Bovary*, nervous crises and psychiatric disorders proliferated in literary works resembling case studies.[10] The novels that engaged hysteria during the second half of the century did so with medical intertexts[11] and with increasing diagnostic exactitude. Although nowhere in *Madame Bovary* did Flaubert call his heroine "hysterical," he greeted Baudelaire's diagnostic critique with pleasure and wrote elsewhere of his interests in women's nervous disorders.[12] Edmond de Goncourt's *Fille Elisa* (1876), Zola's *Nana* (1880), Jules Clarétie's *Les Amours d'un interne* (1881), and in England and Austria, M. E. Braddon's *Lady Audley's Secret* (1862) and Arthur

Schnitzler's *Therese* (1928), all explicitly invoked hysteria in their contributions to debates about gender, class, heredity, and sexuality.

This description of novelistic clinical engagements might suggest that hysteria remained outside the novel's thematic scope until the Second Empire. This is not in fact the case for, like prostitution, hysteria entered the literature of the July Monarchy as a problem of labels and categories. Rather than appearing, as it would by the Third Republic, as a knowable entity with clear nosological properties, hysteria emerged in the literature of the 1830s and 1840s with all the diagnostic ambiguity that had marked debates from Louyer-Villermay to Briquet. Since all women in this era were read as potentially hysteric, the symptoms of the disorder recurringly materialized as personality traits of female characters. Since hysteria in the first half of the century was coded far more in terms of debates, the novels of this era explored the subjects of debate rather than posing, as would novels in the Charcot era, as clinical case studies of a knowable psychiatric disorder. Unlike the novels of the late century that even purposely resembled case studies, works of the July Monarchy approached women's nervous disorders far more euphemistically. Fiction that took up women's ailments—Soulié's *Mémoires du diable*, Méray's *La Part des femmes*, and Balzac's *Wann-Chlore, Physiologie du mariage*, "Adieu," and *Le Lys dans la vallée*—engaged hysterical symptoms to explore the myth of dangerous continence or to interrogate the relationship between nerves and passions. As a result, these texts frequently upheld the logic of de Montègre and Louyer-Villermay, making marriage a container for hysteria and questioning women's traffic with novels, despite the genre's dependence upon its women readers.[13] Women's nervous disorders therefore constituted not only a central concern for the July Monarchy novel, but served also as a touchstone for the very circulation of the novel in society.

The novel at the center of our discussions in this chapter, Balzac's *Cousine Bette* (1846–47), deals with hysteria in more subtle ways and took the brunt of critical and even psychiatric outrage in the course of the nineteenth century. Like *Elisa, Nana*, and *Therese*, as well as Jules Barbey d'Aurevilly's "La Vengeance d'une femme," *Cousine Bette* explicitly engages the relationship of prostitution to nervous disorders and madness. But unlike these later works, which make one woman into a kind of case, Balzac's 1846 *roman-feuilleton* expands its vista to reflect upon fallen men and women of all classes (from the aristocratic Hulots to the bourgeois Marneffes to working-class *arrivistes* like Josépha). I argue here that *Cousine Bette* articulates the conflicts racking novelistic appropriations of hysteria even as it serves as the conduit for a series of other tensions in the society that reads, interprets, proscribes, and is in turn embattled by literature.

Legrand Du Saulle did not, anymore than Rougon, name the novels that have tormented him. But we can guess what they might have been. "Disseminating to the public the most unscientific and false ideas" came, in quick succession, the works of Balzac, Flaubert, Barbey, the Goncourts, and Zola.

The *littérature physiologique* of the July Monarchy summoned by Poitou fast became a literature attacked for its dissections and medical intrigues. It quickly gave rise to a series of novels obsessed with pathology. In the previous chapter I showed how medical and psychiatric narratives told the hysteric's difference — a difference, I argued, that was used to moralize all women. In this chapter, I ask how the plots embraced by mid-nineteenth-century doctors were read into and through the novel. Just as the doctors gave shape to fears about the working classes, prostitutes, and sexual excess, the novel found itself caught up in these same processes. Its central role in debates over hysteria, prostitution, mental illness, and sexuality derived, of course, from the themes it explored, from its new strategies of narration, and above all, from its investments in theories about observation.[14]

The Novel of Spasms

"Mr. Balzac is a refined novelist who tackles spasms, malaises, neuralgias, and all those little affectations of that closed society that spends its life horizontally and in silk," wrote critic Janin, echoing attacks that began as early as 1830 and reverberated throughout the nineteenth century:

> [Balzac] is the novelist of women. . . . For Mr. Balzac, woman reigns and rules. . . . [He] whispers, he works on the sly. In his books, one never hears the sound of violence; he purposefully constructs the scene of his drama. Everything is prepared in advance: the house, the door, the bedroom, the wall hangings, the furniture, the paintings; he acts gently, in silence. Even murders, when he commits them, happen like very natural and very simple things. . . . Mr. Balzac is Doctor So-Much-The-Better, that physician with the orange perfume who cures all pains with a glass of sugared water. Mr. Balzac is himself often the dupe of his heroines. To see them so simpering, so wheedling, so *vaporeuses*, with such a velvet eye, such a white hand, a throat so artfully hidden that one sees it without it being shown, Mr. Balzac lets himself be moved.[15]

Janin's description of this "king of the modern novel" brings together three complaints about Balzac's work that dominated critical discussions between 1835 and 1860. First, Balzac was seen as obsessed with the medical. Critics labeled him the novelist of physiology, of anatomical dissection, and especially of convulsions and spasms. Second, his political ambivalence irritated critics of all political persuasions. Just as Janin rebuked Balzac for failing to question his heroines, critics ranging from conservatives to Fourierists complained that his novels left a gap between theory and practice and a tension between their subject matter and political ends. Third, he was berated as the "lady's man" of July Monarchy literature. Not only did his appeal to female *readers* gall critics, but his concentration on female *subjects* generated countless attacks. Throughout the July Monarchy and Second Empire, Balzac's female readers figured in discussions of the dangers of the novel as well as in accounts of the novel's hysterogenic potential. These three accusations are intricately bound up with the theorizing of realism and the practices of the "realist" novel in the mid-nineteenth century.

"Realism is that paradoxical moment in Western literature when representation can neither accommodate the Otherness of Woman nor exist without it," writes Naomi Schor.[16] Eugénie Grandet, "the woman who is in the world but not of the world" becomes for Schor the prime example of the woman of Balzacian realism. Bound by the law of the Napoleonic Code, Balzac's women "submit to the laws of exchange enforced by [their] capitalistic father[s]." They suffer in a world that represents them only to deny them a subject position. They seem to exist only to be confined, outlawed, expelled, or bound. Telling their difference emerges as a process ensuring that difference can be held in check. These novelistic women's desires are evoked and given significance in gestures that seem intent on dissipating their force, individuality, and meaning. The "realist" novel, like the nineteenth-century clinic, is founded on the representation of women as potentially desiring. Yet, as Schor reminds us, "male subjectivity and its representations in the nineteenth century" are also "grounded in the denial of woman as subject of desire."[17]

The term *realism* has had a strange way of loading the canonical dice for our readings of nineteenth-century literature. While the word invokes an important story of theoretical debates about painting (Courbet, Daumier, Millet) in relation to the literary and critical practices of Champfleury, Duranty, and Baudelaire in the 1850s, it hardly refers to either a literary *school* or a *movement*. In fact, the term functioned in the 1830s, 1840s, and 1850s primarily as a watchword for denigration. Sainte-Beuve attacked Sand's *Lélia* (1833) for its lack of realism.[18] Balzac's contemporaries assaulted him for his physiological mode, for his dissections of the human psyche, and for his obsession with detail. The trials of the nineteenth-century novel frequently turned, literally as well as figuratively, on complaints that texts too zealously reproduced the world. This was true of Méray's *La Part des femmes* (1847), which I discuss in chapter 7 and even more so of Flaubert's *Madame Bovary* (1857), whose "lascivious pictures" were exposed in court so that their dangerous detail might be contained.[19]

The debates about the dangers of "realistic" depictions of the world resounded throughout the nineteenth century, beginning long before Duranty named his review *Réalisme* in 1856 and continuing well after novelists themselves began to speak of "naturalism." Significantly, the novels targeted as indulging in this imagined *pathological realism* were those revolving, like the ones by Balzac, around the sufferings of women. The laws that came to bind these women were not only the laws of the Napoleonic Code, but also those of scientific observation and of political as well as literary representation. Balzac became, in myth and in practice, the novelist of spasms and convulsions, the writer of literary pathology, and the author of ladies' desires, but his works remained deeply conflicted about the implications of these appeals, subjects, and desires. Balzac's politics were thus entangled with a moral vision that embraced the clinical gaze but, at the same time, his mission was repeatedly in conflict with that gaze. His handling of these conflicts came to resemble a kind of literary hysteria in its turn, threatening in peculiar ways to dismantle dominant modes of medicalized representation. In what follows, I trace the ways Balzac generated, answered, and played on the three criticisms leveled at him by his contemporaries. I show how he thematizes hysteria and prostitution and how he problematizes the very concerns circumscribed by these two labels.

"To teach women or not to teach them, that is the question," winks Balzac in his *Physiologie du mariage* (1829) (PM, 42). Fifty years later, Paolo Mantegazza recommended Balzac's *Physiologie* to the women he hoped would teach men "that love is neither lust nor a business of sensual pleasure but the highest and most serene joy."[20] The possibility that Balzac might serve as a lady's tutor in matters of love terrified moralists, literary critics, and, in fact, analysts of hysteria. As I discuss in more detail in part three, fears about the novel's dangers for girls, women, and the working classes mobilized attacks on it and anchored strategies for placing these groups under surveillance. Balzac became central to these practices not only because he appealed to women and seemed to take their part, but also because he thematized medical debates over hysteria. "Woe to the girl who devours novels before she knows the world!" wrote Jean-Louis Brachet in his 1847 *Traité de l'hystérie*. "Her exalted imagination will trick and lead her astray, and she will create for herself a world that will bring her many disappointments." Brachet's advice differed from that of his predecessors only in the detail with which he advised parents and doctors to protect girls from hysteria. "Teach girls, therefore, don't just nourish them with shameful ignorance that will later make them blush," the Lyons doctor seemed to be responding to Balzac's earlier question, "But keep that instruction within appropriate limits, and make sure it always leads back to the goal of nature." Above all, Brachet warned, make sure they read nothing but "useful and interesting works" (JLB, 505).

Like Balzac's narrator in the *Physiologie du mariage*, Brachet worried that education failed to train women for their "duties" (JLB, 505). He likewise condemned boarding schools, preferring home schooling since it allowed optimum "surveillance" of girls (JLB, 508). Surveillance mattered, for it ensured that girls never had a chance to do, see, or learn anything that might make tongues wag. Even so, Brachet reminds his readers, girls will be girls: "In spite of the most active surveillance, girls teach each other things of which they should long remain ignorant. Their lively minds, so desirous of impressions, so curiously avid for forbidden things, yet excited by their accumulation, never miss a chance to teach each other the ways of love." How does Brachet know this? Why, he's been reading Balzac:

> One girl knows something, so she lifts the corner of the mysterious veil and becomes the teacher for the others. Their secret little chats, their caresses so naive in appearance, those Balzacian virginal nibbles (*ces friandises virginales de Bal-*

zac), this pussying about excites their senses, fills them with anticipation, and leads almost always to the knowledge of illicit pleasures, which is the beginning of depravity. Thus are lost chastity, innocence, and moral virginity—that sweet flower, that delicious perfume—without which physical virginity leaves you only a woman's body. (JLB, 509)

Brachet is referring here to one of the "meditations on conjugal happiness and unhappiness" collected by the anonymous "celibate" and "eclectic philosopher" who served as Balzac's mask in the *Physiologie du mariage*. "A girl may leave her boarding school a virgin, but never chaste," cautions the narrator, for she will have almost inevitably engaged with her girlfriends in secret sessions "where honor is lost in advance" (*PM*, 94). Even if she has not participated in what the Balzacian narrator calls *"ces friandises virginales,"* she will have befriended two or three girls who could at any time lead the adult woman into intrigues. The man who marries her "will therefore have four women to keep watch over instead of one" (*PM*, 95).

Although Brachet happily used Balzac as a reference point for the dangers of certain kinds of education, he ignored Balzac's proposals for educating girls in the ways of sexuality and disregarded the novelist's parody of fears of women's reading (*PM*, 142–47). In fact, Brachet might as well have been reading Balzac's critics: of all the agents predisposing women to hysteria, wrote Brachet, *"the most common and most aggravating is the reading of novels"* (JLB, 213, my emphasis). Would that the potential hysteric avoid books "where one finds unveiled the darkness of the human heart or the greatest woes, odious denunciations, destitution, unjust persecutions, secret plots, etc." (JLB, 236)! And where might she better find such books than among the novels of Balzac, contemporary critics howled.

"The woman belongs to Mr. Balzac," wrote Sainte-Beuve in 1834, "she belongs to him in all her finery, in her nightgown, in the smallest details of her home; he dresses her and undresses her." Sainte-Beuve claims that by putting in action the knowledge exposed in the *Physiologie du mariage*, Balzac has become the confidant of the women of France: "he knows a lot about women, their sensitive or sensual secrets; in his stories, he asks them bold, familiar questions, equivalent to taking liberties. He is like a doctor who is still young and who gains entrance to the alleys and the bedchambers; he has claimed the right to hint at those mysterious private details that charm the more modest with embarrassment."[21] Women flocked to Balzac, claimed Sainte-Beuve, Janin, Al. de C. of the *Chronique de Paris* (1835), Chaudes-Aigues (1836), Louise Ozenne (1843), Eugène Pelletan (1836 and 1846), Charles Menche de Loisne (1852), Alfred Nettement (1854), Armand de Pontmartin (1857), Poitou (1857–58), and Sirtema de Grovestins (1859).[22] According to Sainte-Beuve, something had changed with the Revolution of 1830 to permit a novelist like Balzac to insinuate himself into women's hearts. Somehow the July Revolution and "Saint-Simonian promises" had "awakened" their imaginations and left something "broken and vanished in women's condition." Balzac, Sand, and the Saint-Simonians had changed the tenor of discourse about women and for women.[23]

Horrified that his contemporaries might have Balzac's number, Armand de Pontmartin portrayed women blushing at the very thought of reading such novels: "if women really had an incorrigible preference for this cold corruptor, then that would be the end of it. The education of future society, the dignity and honor of private life, the safety and the sweetness of the home, all this is in their hands. We can easily predict what they would do with Balzac as counselor and teacher." Like many of Balzac's critics, Pontmartin most feared the novelistic woman's duplicity: "Phryne or Aspasia beneath the lying label and the false blazon of a great lady . . . that is Mr. Balzac's type, there she is in a hundred different editions, the figure he offers for the admiration and emulation of his female readers."[24]

In 1843 Louise Ozenne described "the perfect emblem of the talent of Mr. Balzac" as one of "those women who simulate beauty, love, and all elevated feelings." Working her seductions in the privacy of the bourgeois or aristocratic home, such a woman has cultivated "a calculating force, a knowledge of the human heart, a capacity for ruse and disguise that would shame the most consummate spy." She has learned how to give herself saintly intentions, how to speak of morality and virtue, how to use the most honorable discourse to stir up "all that is impure in the depths of a man's heart." Beneath her decent words and her front of a *"femme comme il faut"* lurks a poisonous intoxication which she knows how to manipulate without anyone even noticing that she has broken every man around her. Ozenne's critique suggests further stakes for all this fulminating about Balzac's women readers. Balzac's "perfidious and corrupt science" may indeed work on "innocent and new souls" as well as upon "hearts advanced in debauchery," but the society woman who has devoured his works has found there models of duplicity bent on *corrupting men*: "[she] knows that she has to inebriate him with subtle and delicious poisons that will kill his moral sense, weaken his will, and destroy his discrimination between good and evil."[25] Like the male prey of prostitutes, or the husbands of hysterics, the victim of the Balzacian novel loses out because the women around him have tried to break out of traditional molds. Men are taken in because women have educated themselves with novels.

While these critics seem convinced that Balzacian novels would drive women to desert wifely and motherly duties, to take to adultery and prostitution, and to develop even more frightening arts of dissimulation, Brachet and his contemporaries imagine a mind given over to passion and a body out of control. The hysteria described in the eighteen detailed observations of the work crowned by the *Académie Royale de Médecine* in 1847 is hardly that of the manipulative criminals later represented by Bénédict Morel, Jules Falret, and Legrand Du Saulle. Like the convulsive bodies we saw in the July Monarchy Salpêtrière and in Briquet's La Charité, Brachet's collection of hysterics, accumulated in a public hospital and in private practice in Lyons between the late 1820s and

1847, demonstrates most insistently these women's loss of power over their bodies, lives, and destinies. Although Brachet's 1847 edition of observations was published the year after *Cousine Bette* finished its *feuilleton* run and therefore could not have directly influenced the novel, it nevertheless provides a striking account of the same obsessions.[26] Most important, Brachet's work provides a parallel narrative of both hysteria and prostitution that we can juxtapose with Balzac's own discourse in this volume of the *Parents pauvres*. I have chosen, therefore, to read these two texts side by side in order to show the imbrication of the novel of spasms with the pathological realism of the clinic.

Pathological Realism

"There is a very dangerous thing in literature," wrote Eugène Maron in his 1847 review of *Cousine Bette*, "and that is the excess of truth. That excess leads to a method of observation without ideals or poetry, which recounts every fact and scrutinizes every feeling indiscriminately, randomly, and without a thought to whether they are by nature worthy of study." Maron insists that he does not question either the "truth of manners" described by Balzac in *Les Parents pauvres* nor the "exactitude of his observations." There are, however, things Maron just does not want to see: "Is it really necessary to paint such morals? Isn't there a corner of life that we should carefully hide and never unveil? Aren't there things in this world that we should hush about because they are bad in themselves and because we already know too much about them?" Like many of Balzac's critics over the previous decade, Maron saw *Cousine Bette* as an example of "incessant, merciless observation" that reduced the world to "a barren and practical reality."[27] Balzac, "father of physiological literature" became, for his contemporaries, the emblem of the observer whose truths exceeded all desire.

Cousine Bette is indeed a novel of observation, but not just by Balzac who claims in his preface to be a "doctor of social medicine."[28] Rather, this is a novel that multiplies investigations, engages spies in every court, and proliferates interpreters, analysts, and observers. In one sense, *Bette* is the panoptic novel pushed to its extreme limits: the power of observation has been so thoroughly delegated and invested at all levels that it is hard to know who is watching whom, when they are doing so, and in whose interests. Everyone is under scrutiny, and almost everyone is scrutinizing someone. The characters who successfully master the gaze steadily gain power and wealth. Those who fail to investigate are duped, impoverished, and compromised by illness and neuroses. All this up to a point—and at that point Balzac's narration almost magically reinstates order. In one gesture, the novel seems to reappropriate the panoptic gaze it spent four hundred pages disseminating. And in the final pages of a novel that needs a deus ex machina to reach closure, everyone who has used the gaze for devious purposes is dispatched with hideous punishments or grievous suffering—with one exception. In the reading that follows, I consider how

Cousine Bette delegates its scrutinizing gazes, how it uses methods of clinical observation to engage questions of class and sexual difference, and how Baron Hulot comes to be the exception to its rules.

"The physiologist may observe the entire gamut of women's emotions, from aversion, through indifference, to Phèdre's declaration to Hippolyte," writes the Balzacian narrator as he details his observation of Valérie Marneffe serving tea.[29] "There is a whole language in the way a woman performs this function, but women are well aware of it. It is a curious study to watch their movements, gestures, looks, intonations, and accents when they perform this apparently so simple act of courtesy" (*CB*, 253). While Hulot is content to remark, "Woman is an inexplicable creature!" the narrator of this text, like Crevel, responds "I can explain her" (*CB*, 224). But while the majority of the male characters of this novel, including Crevel, seem stumped by the language of women's performances, the novel invests *women* with knowledge of their own physiology and the power to observe and manipulate the physiology of others. "We women are like that," writes Valérie to Hulot (*CB*, 292), engaging in her turn in the generalizations about gender for which the Balzacian novel is famous. Valérie alone in this novel presumes to know and hold forth on "the whole truth about woman" (*CB*, 252), taunting men like Hulot, Crevel, Montès, and Steinbock with it to such an extent that they become her puppets.

Yet this novel is not billed as the story of Valérie Marneffe—despite her expansive ability to attract the attention of the narrating physiologist and, decades later, to incarnate female corruption in Cesare Lombroso's *Donna Delinquente*.[30] Rather, according to its title and preface, this novel is the story of that beastly relative, Cousin Bette, who delegates to her friend Valérie the powers to see, interpret, and manipulate appearances: "Bette plotted, Madame Marneffe acted," the narrator explains, "Madame Marneffe was the axe, Lisbeth the hand that wielded it" (*CB*, 187). Together these two had concocted "a prodigious machine" (*CB*, 180) designed by Bette to demolish the Hulot family whom she held responsible for the departure of her beloved Wenceslas. On the urging of Valérie, who has told her of Wenceslas's traffic with the Hulots, the two women have sworn to be each others' "spies" (*CB*, 127). Banding together in a friendship to which the narrator gives lesbian overtones, Bette and Valérie plot intrigues that would mortify even the most unchaste boarding school girlfriends. Bette confides that Hulot has put her up to becoming Valérie's neighbor and Valérie sets out to use the information she wheedles from "*her* Cousin Bette." Bette meanwhile seeks to fix Hulot by putting his rival Crevel up to stealing Valérie from the baron. Valérie plots to become rich and powerful. Bette arranges to marry Hulot's brother, the marshal.

Working under cover, the two women become a kind of industry in gallantry. Valérie gains both Crevel and Hulot as lovers, so successfully drawing on their pocketbooks and favors that she amasses a fortune in three years. Meanwhile, Bette becomes the "good angel" of the Hulot household (*CB*, 155). Since Hulot has again abandoned his wife Adeline for the sexual blisses he finds elsewhere, Bette uses the family's vulnerability to insinuate herself into their confidence. Beloved and trusted in their midst, Bette weaves plans for both her future and her revenge. Even as she campaigns for their support of her marriage bid, she stokes the fires that impoverish them by serving as cheerleader, "lady's companion," and pimp for Valérie's courtesanry—and, even more devastatingly, by bringing Wenceslas under Valérie's charms. Working panoptically, Bette gains hold of a clinical viewpoint, which she, like the Balzacian narrator, mercilessly exploits: "Lisbeth, like a spider in the center of her web, observed every physiognomy" (CB, 194).

The machine of Bette's vengeance gains such force that it, like the novel, works almost independently of her. Mobilized by Bette's thirst for revenge, Valérie helps her husband engineer Hulot's arrest by the police, prevents Crevel from lending Adeline the two hundred thousand francs Hulot needs to save his wife's uncle after the failure of Hulot's plot to embezzle money from state interests in Algeria, and makes way for Hulot's subsequent disgrace in the government and with his brother, the marshal. The courtesan's actions, although motivated by Bette's initial plots, ultimately undermine the desires of the vengeful cousin. Broken by his brother's crimes, the marshal dies shortly before his marriage to Bette. Just as it seems Hulot's dandling has cost the family its fortune, house, and honor, the marshal's death brings them financial security, a steady paid position as Lady Welfare Visitor for Adeline, and lucrative appointments for her son Victorin.

Through her alliance with Bette, Valérie's power has grown to such an extent that her courtiers dream of using her to increase their own prestige. Although Hulot has been cured of *his* passion by his discovery of her involvement with his arrest, Wenceslas pursues the model for his Delilah instead of putting himself to work. Montès patiently awaits the marriage he has been promised since his return to Paris. Crevel imagines that her influence will make him deputy: "She's a proud locomotive, a woman like that," he boasts to Adeline, "she'll be one of the secret sovereigns of Paris" (CB, 326). She will not get the chance, for as soon as she has married his father-in-law, Victorin Hulot will contract with Vautrin's ally, Madame Nourisson, to bring an end to this engine of destruction. Consumed by the hideous disease Montès has infused into her bloodstream, transformed into a disfigured mass of sores, Valérie repents, leaving even more money and property to the Hulot family. Crevel's death from the same disease ensures the future of Victorin and Célestine Hulot. In the place of the "spectacular death scene that should by rights have been [Bette's],"[31] Balzac gives us the spectacular demise of Valérie Marneffe. And it is precisely at this point that the novel engages outside observers to investigate—scientifically—and report on the contagion at work in these spaces.

"The true doctor . . . has a passion for knowledge," explains Bianchon, omnipresent physician of La Comédie humaine, "He sustains himself as much by this feeling as by the certainty of its social utility" (CB, 436) In fact, explains the doctor to the Hulot family, he is presently engaged in such scientific ecstasy for he is observing "a lost disease," a medieval plague incurable in the West. Heartlessly, he realizes the coincidence of his "find" with the family relations to whom he speaks: "For the past ten days I have been thinking constantly of my patients, for there are two, a wife and husband! Are they not related to you, since, Madame, you are Monsieur Crevel's daughter?' he said, turning to Célestine" — who knows nothing of her father's impending death (*CB*, 436). Balzac delegates to Bianchon the role of observer, which, in the space of this novel, only Bette, Valérie, and, to some extent, Marneffe have fully mastered. With Marneffe dead, Valérie dying, and Bette laid up with tuberculosis, the novel has a practical need of the clinician's gaze. But his intervention here has a more significant resonance. Capable of speaking in "medical" terms of the devastation wrought on Valérie by the rare disease, Bianchon produces a supposedly objective vision of a terrifying death, grounding the astonishing repentance of the dying Valérie. Relieved even of the task of observing her decaying partner, Bette is left impotently figuring her own visions of vengeance (*CB*, 441).[32]

For Bianchon, the house of Hulot hides secrets that even the keen observer's eye cannot bring into the open. Although he succeeds in tempering Adeline's nervous fits, Bianchon cannot save the virtuous baroness from the scourge her body wreaks upon her. For several hundred pages and nearly a decade, Adeline has suffered from the kind of out-of-control body nineteenth-century doctors associated with hysteria. Although she manages, at long last, to use her position as Lady Welfare Visitor to wrench her husband from the arms of his current adolescent lover, she is as powerless against his satyriasis as against her own convulsions.

Because Adeline Hulot serves as the virtuous force against whom the vicious of this novel are measured, her nervous fits, convulsions, paralysis, and tremors invoke scrutiny. Like Bianchon, we are invited to make sense of her suffering, to give a meaning to this exemplary life, and to decode the symptoms that rack it. Like the doctors whose observations we saw in chapter 4, we are engaged by this novel in diagnostic practices that elicit our interpretative gaze and at the same time force us to hypothesize about what the medical community calls *causes morales* and *causes prédisposantes*. What has led to Adeline's hysteria? What has predisposed her to these problems? What might have been avoided? How might her plight serve as an example to the women who Balzac knows clamor for his teachings?

Cousine Bette seems to demand our diagnostic readings precisely because it poses so fiercely as "social medicine." "Could there be in this house a source of contagious madness?" asks Bianchon in a gesture that suddenly convokes all the moments of madness, nervous illness, criminal rage, and sexual mania accumulated in this text (*CB*, 407). What could possibly explain the bonds that link this family in common suffering? The Balzacian narrator would argue, in his steadfastly royalist and Catholic voice, that the revolutionary devastation of the family has generated this contagion of pain (*CB*, 133). A decade after the publication of this novel, Morel would advance a theory of hereditary degeneration that developed July Monarchy assumptions that mental and nervous illnesses, criminality, and even prostitution could run in the family.[33] Doctors of 1846–47 had some theories of their own. *"Instruire ou non les femmes,"* Balzac had joked in 1829, but women's education had become one of the central issues in debates about familial relations. Indeed, much of the July Monarchy attempt to stem the tide of hysteria revolved around ensuring that girls would grow into good mothers, tutors, and *surveillantes* for their own children. Nowhere is this concern more apparent than in the observations interpreted by Brachet.

Plots Around Hysteria

In the clinic of the late eighteenth century, claimed Foucault, a domain opened "in which each fact, observed, isolated, then compared with a set of facts, could take its place in a whole series of events whose convergence or divergence was in principle measurable." Each element perceived by the clinical gaze became a recordable event that might be placed in what Foucault calls an "aleatory series," or a progressive set of contingencies, a history that stretched backward and forward from the observed symptoms in relation to all other similar incidents, all other potentially relevant signs, all other analogous aberrations. The "individual in question" was no longer a sick person, but rather "the endlessly reproducible pathological fact to be found in all patients suffering in a similar way,"[34] or in Brachet's words, a "type . . . around whom all other types could easily be grouped" (JLB, 196).

Prior to Brachet's *Traité de l'hystérie*, we can find philosophical treatises on hysteria (Frédéric Dubois d'Amiens), theoretical analyses with lists of supposed symptoms, influences, and causes (Louyer-Villermay, Georget, Félix Voisin), and even a collection of observations from other sources (Landouzy). Before 1847, however, no work provided such a rich collection of personal observations, such an adept fulfillment of the promises of the clinic, or such a daring appropriation of the challenges of the clinical gaze:

> Medicine ought more than ever today to proceed from observation. . . . We are bordering on an era where clinical observation and the study of facts will be the only paths for teaching medicine. It is the sick person under our gaze who will be able to describe and make his illness understood. It is by comparing him to the sick person next to him that one can establish nuances and differences. It is by watching the changes effected by medication and other remedies that we can prove therapeutic action. (JLB, 196)

Brachet's method, predicated on his belief in the paradigm of clinical observation, consists of reconstructing the conditions that *surround* his patients. Rejecting scientific methods that isolate individuals from family, class, and order, Brachet insists on the "true spirit of deduction and generalization," which he combines with "talent and a pleasure in observation" (JLB, 198). Out of clinical exposition—the analysis of facts and deeds—Brachet presumes to deduce the description of hysterics: "Everything left for us to say is only and can only be the consequence of observations. Already we can form an idea of the illness, its character, and its nature. It will therefore be easy for us to make our general history. We just have to relate each phenomenon to its source so that the whole may be in complete harmony" (JLB, 200). Brachet's clinical plots depend on an initial question that he believes can be answered only through careful observation. Before asking "What makes that so?" Brachet's doctor must first ask, "Is it so?" (JLB, 198). In order to become "architects" of the clinic's materials (JLB, 197), he urges, doctors must adopt a skeptical gaze, admit there may be things one does not know, and doubt apparent realities.

In this insistently "objective" account of scientific methodology, the observer of hysterics lets us in on his secret: these women lie. "Since these brilliant lies embellished by the charm of an ardent imagination can very easily seduce, we must never forget that the false sometimes comes so close to the true that one struggles to see how to hold back one's scorn" (JLB, 199). Woe to the doctor who does not ask if he has been seduced. Woe to the observer who does not begin by doubting whatever these women show or tell.

"Most women become hysterical, more from the results of the vices of their education than from those of their constitution," declares Brachet's work from the outset. Brachet's study provides the stage on which eighteen women will help him validate this assessment. He situates his observations of the facts of their cases in the context of specific generalizations he claims to have arrived at in clinical ways. But like a Balzacian narrator, Brachet is a master of unfounded generalizations, a strident protector of traditional notions about women's nature, and a careful recorder of data that correlate with the plots he has already embraced. He will work through the histories and current suffering of these women to arrive at prescriptive narratives about women of all classes and circumstances. Yet the plots in which they emerge produce their subjectivity in a way closely resembling that of the fictional representations of their era. We see them accede to subjectivity only so that their desires may be placed under restraint. As Brachet's methodological discussion suggests, these women are meticulously represented in a register that proceeds from a presumption that they cannot be believed.

The disparity between appearances and reality is not just a problem for the medical observer, according to Brachet; it is at the very root of women's problems. Resulting from the kind of education women most often receive, it is in turn the source of their disorders. In the traditional masterplots on which Brachet draws, women are destined for feeling, but not for either working or thinking. Women "subjected" to men's work have been degraded, for they have been wrenched from their natural sphere (JLB, 69). Women who seek to "acquire knowledge" only embarrass their gender, for Brachet believes women have "never invented anything, discovered anything, or perfected anything" (JLB,

73). Fortunately, he declares, most women seek knowledge only as part of their adornment, much as they would put on make-up or change their clothes: "through learning, she wants more to please than to have, and more to amuse than to educate herself" (JLB, 73). Yet it is this kind of "ornamentation" that most worries Brachet:

> Woman's personality . . . is constantly modified . . . even spoiled by customs and education. Our customs require that woman disguise her feelings. We make it a crime, or at least shameful, for her to reveal the love that someone might have inspired in her before she is wed. We therefore teach her early if not to master her true feelings, at least to hide or disguise them. Reprimands and often ridicule reward her candor or innocence. Such is the origin of this appearance of falseness for which we reproach her. Our morals and our demands force her into it. (JLB, 87)

This kind of education wears on a woman's nerves:

> Thus tossed between customs and feelings, her mind lacks stability. She makes only half confessions and half revelations. She becomes the most profound enigma of the universe; her heart is a mystery even she does not know. . . . Her weakness, her shyness, and her false shame are even further sources of dissimulation. (JLB, 87)

And sooner or later, the doctor has a hysteric on his hands:

> Despite her care, she is almost never able to hide entirely her inclinations; they always betray themselves. This perpetual restraint that a dissimulating woman is obliged to impose on herself requires efforts that further act on her nervous system and exaggerate her sensitivity. Thus one evil leads to another. (JLB, 87)

According to Brachet, women are most grievously exposed to the dangers of dissimulation when deserted by the men they love—or, worse yet, when educated above their station. The company of girls of a higher class than their own almost always makes women vain, presumptuous, and prone to dissimulation. Brachet paints a horrific portrait of girls returning overeducated from boarding schools to indulgent bourgeois parents who are soon bankrupted by their daughters' demands and to husbands whose fortunes are risked by the haughty young women they have married (JLB, 89–90).

The boarding school is not the only place where girls develop such educational vices. According to Brachet, the family prepares its daughters just as easily for pathological states (JLB, 90). By indulging girls' vanity and encouraging them to live above the family's station, parents expose their own daughters to hysteria. Social practices that create for women an "atmosphere of seduction and of rivalry" virtually finish the job of transforming women into nervous wrecks: "Each wants at least to equal her rivals by her dress, spirit, and amiability. And soon, poor of virtue and rich in illusions, she throws herself, a lost body, into the abyss of pleasures" (JLB, 91–92). Once accustomed to intrigue, such a woman seeks "pleasure for its own sake," strangling her nervous system with an ever growing appetite for sensations (JLB, 92). Nothing will stop her now.

Brachet's lessons speak loud and clear: parents should live within their own means, accept their station, grant their daughters only the education appropriate to their class, and reject any aspirations for social mobility. A family should keep its daughter at home, educated privately under the mother's surveillance, preparing her for a life in which she, too, can temper the expectations of her husband, sons, and daughters.[35] Brachet upholds a masterplot of sexual difference designed to maintain class divisions. His descriptions of the dangers of women's dissimulations mask his own behavioral determinism. Like Parent-Duchâtelet, Frégier, and later Morel, he clings to a myth that people have their class background imprinted in their genes. Theories of hereditary madness, criminality, libertinism, and nervous illness are anchored by theories of gender difference not only because women are the obvious link in the relay of procreation, but because women's own constitution is believed fundamentally unchangeable — either by environmental influences or education. Just as theorists of prostitution rejected hopes of rehabilitating old whores, proponents of hereditary pathology harbored few expectations that the lower classes could better themselves. Optimally, studies like Brachet's suggested, such people could keep their daughters in line. They could rein in their expectations and survey their daughter's every move. With luck, she might marry a man who would appreciate her natural virtues. If she succeeded in avoiding all the pitfalls disposing her to hysteria, madness, prostitution, and criminality, she could become his guardian angel and the devoted tutor of their children. Hysterized by the medical profession, the woman born into the working or artisan class waltzed through a minefield of dangers, ever more tightly contained by plots claiming to set her free.

To read *Cousine Bette*, one would think Balzac had been privy to the case studies and commentary accumulated by Brachet in the 1830s and 1840s. Just as *Bette* thematizes observation, it also accumulates its own set of clinical cases. And while this novel puts the power of the gaze into the hands of diabolically scheming women, it nourishes its own observations on the masterplots of gender difference we have seen in medical studies of nineteenth-century hysteria.

The suffering bodies of dissimulating women litter the landscape of *Cousine Bette*. Bette plots revenge behind an angelic veneer and is ravaged by misfired schemes and tuberculosis. Valérie works her seductive intrigues behind the mask of the proper *bourgeoise* and is stricken with venereal plague. Hortense Hulot connives the theft of her cousin's artist boyfriend, loses him to an even more seductive schemer, and is wracked by nervous convulsions (CB, 290). But of all these women, Adeline Hulot is given the novel's most privileged nod as master of the cover-up. She also suffers most steadily from a body out of control. Of these four, only Adeline will be ennobled by the narrative's endorsement of her virtue. But like each of the others, Adeline has visited upon her the scourges of a diseased body. Despite her virtue, the novel makes her into a case.

Adeline's medical problems might have been fished out of almost any early nineteenth-century analysis of hysteria. Marrying well above her station, self-educated above her class, this woman has left behind the pastoral sweetness of the countryside for the decadence of Parisian aristocrat life.[36] A voracious reader, even if apparently only of "safe" books like the *Imitation of Christ* (*CB*, 189), Adeline espouses a sedentary and—especially dangerous—a dissimulating life: "From the first days of her marriage . . . the baroness had loved her husband . . . with an admiring love, a maternal love, with abject devotion." Although she has known for twenty years that her husband cheated on her, "she had veiled her eyes with lead; she had wept silently, and no word of reproach had ever escaped her lips" (*CB*, 49).[37]

Adeline was willing to put on such a fine show because, the narrator tells us, "for the young peasant girl, this marriage was something like an Assumption." Leaving behind her "village mud," Adeline entered the "paradise of the Imperial Court," granted by her marriage to the baron all the makings of a fairy story: the title of baroness, a fine house, a carriage, diamonds from the Emperor, and fame (*CB*, 51). From the time she detected her husband's infidelity, she pretended it didn't exist, practicing the "contagious" deception of worshiping her husband despite his faults, treating him like a spoiled child, and suffering in silence. Only the devastation of her daughter's marriage plans—and her realization that Hulot is compromising her children's future along with the family honor and fortune—shakes Adeline's noble front.[38] Just at that moment, as if she were following a script out of Brachet, the baroness begins to show signs of the hysteria that ravages her throughout this novel.

Adeline's nervous ailments punctuate the pivotal events of the novel. She faints at Crevel's proposition, claiming she has only had an attack of nerves (*CB*, 111), but worse is yet to come. When she learns of her husband's embezzlement of funds in Algeria, "she experienced a nervous shock so violent that her body eternally kept its mark. Within a few days she had become subject to a continuous tremor" (*CB*, 312). When her offer of her virtue to Crevel fails, she is found unconscious. For a month, she lies "in a nervous fever suspended between life and death" (*CB*, 358). Strengthened by her family's recovered fortune, Adeline again suffers a nervous attack when she visits Josépha in search of her husband (*CB*, 380, 388). Threatened by Valérie's discovery of her offer to Crevel, Adeline is seized with "horrible convulsions" (*CB*, 406). Bianchon's treatment pays off only when Adeline manages to bring her husband home again (*CB*, 459). But her body will finally get the better of her when she overhears her husband promising the kitchenmaid his wife is not long for this world: Adeline fulfills her husband's wish and drops dead almost on the spot. Given a death scene of martyrdom less spectacular but far nobler than that of Valérie, Adeline finally gets her chance to reproach her husband—but in a gesture of benevolence that seems as duplicitous as the front she has put up all these years: "A moment before expiring she took her husband's hand, pressed it, and whispered in his ear: 'My friend, I had nothing left but my life to give you. In a moment you'll be free, and you will be able to make a Baroness Hulot'" (CB, 461).

Like Adeline, Brachet's Madame A. was a rejected wife humiliated, in her own way, by the behavior of her husband (JLB, 100). Like the baroness, the hysterical women on whom Brachet collected evidence differ in one striking way from those discussed by his predecessors and contemporaries: many are married and even sexually active when hysteria begins to shake their lives. In fact, of Brachet's eighteen observations, thirteen show apparently married women.[39] Their symptoms suggest that Brachet is formulating a bold rejection of the continence theories that held that only *unmarried and unsexualized* women suffered from hysteria. Madame F., for example, had an adoring spouse and a darling daughter whose illness set off a chain of hysterical attacks (JLB, 109–10). Madame L. was the working mother of two children whose sedentary job in a dark, unpleasant store predisposed her to nervous fits that disappeared only when she sought refuge in the countryside. Madame G. lived the kind of life Brachet believed protected women from hysteria: "Confined by the cares of raising her family, of overseeing a workshop, and of keeping her house," this mother of three became hysterical after she lost her shop and encountered personal sorrow because of a reversal of fortune (JLB, 119–121).[40]

Though he hardly reaches de Montègre's or Louyer-Villermay's conclusions, Brachet does dwell on the relationship between sexual relations and hysteria. Madame V. had the good fortune, Brachet noted, to marry a man "who appreciated her good qualities and whose fondness and sensitive attentions were the source of all her happiness" (JLB, 129–30). Could "conjugal duties" have brought about her hysteria, Brachet asks, concerned that if this were the case, all young women might endure such suffering (JLB, 132). He nevertheless concludes that the cause of Madame B.'s hysteria *was* coitus (JLB, 172). Should we assume then, that Brachet is more worried about the hysterogenic properties of sexual activity than about the dangers of continence? What explains his recurrent concern with the hysteria of married women? How do these cases of hysterically convulsing matrons relate to Brachet's obsession with the education of *girls*? How are we to read the prescriptive plots that these cases set into motion for parents, doctors, and moralists?

"Marriage will be the surest guarantee against the invasion of this neurosis," wrote Louyer-Villermay in 1816.[41] Married women are rarely hysterical, theorists had argued for decades, for either reproductive activity, sexual activity, or orgasm protects them from the ravages of this disease of desire. Although in 1824 Georget rejected theories about the dangers of continence, Brachet's is the first comprehensive study of hysteria to use clinical observations to challenge such views. His proposed alternative—a theory focused on women's nervous system and constitution and not on their genitals or reproductive organs—is nevertheless wrought with contradictions. While Brachet argues that continence may cause hysteria (JLB, 175), he allows that it may also cure it. Coitus, orgasm, and childbirth seem as likely to cause nervous ailments as celibacy or the continence of widowhood. According to Brachet, "Any agent that causes a keen excitement and a specific change in the cerebral nervous system becomes or may become a source of hysteria" (JLB, 175). Any sexual activity or its absence can potentially disrupt the delicate nervous systems of women. Marriage may cure hysterics or it may worsen their symptoms (JLB, 176). Continence may trigger hysteria or it may rescue women otherwise disposed to nervous fits.

The differences in women's constitution provide the key to what treatment Brachet believes a doctor should choose. Although Brachet embraces some certainties (holding, for example, that common prostitutes almost never become hysterical, that *femmes galantes* and *grisettes* are especially disposed to hysteria, and that masturbation never cures hysteria), his observations offer few remedies. If married women are as likely to suffer from hysteria as old maids, if women who have given birth to children are just as prone to nervous fits as widows, if sexual activity is as likely to send a wife into convulsions as abstinence, Brachet's readers cannot glean lessons from his examples. They can only be sure that sexuality and reproduction forcefully influence the nervous system (JLB, 176). If they want to know how that influence works, they had better call in a professional.

Like the Balzacian novel, Brachet's hysterogenic family needs an omniscient observer who can take an objective position, give order to the events of the ailment, and "refrain from intervening."[42] Each of the families in which a wife, mother, or daughter has sought his assistance has already been disrupted, if not by some precipitating event, then by the woman's illness itself. Despite his apparent inability to advise his patients *before the fact* how to avoid hysteria, he vaunts his ability to give them and their families relief. He applauds his own capacity to generalize from these extremely specific cases, and, especially, to derive substantial advice for families about how to decrease their predisposition to such pain. Brachet's chapter on prophylaxis, containing his guidelines on education, pursues many of the plotlines he has sketched in his introductory physiological and moral portrait of women and in the reflections on his observations. But this is far more a chapter about educating girls than a formula for the safe nerves of wives and mothers: "Give the body a constitution to protect it from a thousand dangerous influences, and the soul the strength and guidance to bolster it against the whirlwind of moral trials (*causes morales*) with which it is constantly assailed, that is the whole secret," he declares. Medicine should turn its attention to helping parents raise girls steeled against hysteria by means of "a well-reasoned education" (JLB, 492). Even if we cannot change the fortunes that besiege us, we can, according to Brachet, fortify our bodies and souls.

This fortification begins for girls at birth and consists of the most careful training for that single "goal to which nature has destined them": "By teaching them early the duties of a wife and mother that they will one day be called to fulfill, we assure their happiness and spare them many torments, the source and cause of a thousand nervous ailments" (JLB, 503). Brachet's young woman should gain whatever knowledge can "develop, adorn, and embellish her mind"; she should learn to complement her husband without envying his prerogatives lest she become a "virago or impotent hermaphrodite"; she should learn to put up with boredom, aggravations, and even irreparable wrongs, seeking always to bring her husband back to the fold. Such a woman knows both how to please *and* how to keep her husband interested. She knows how to forgive his inconstancy as well as spark his desire. She also knows her own health depends on it: "The more she makes trouble and sorrows, the more nervous illnesses will come raining down upon her" (JLB, 502, 503, 504, 505).

The well-educated girl can become this kind of devoted, forgiving, and ever desirable spouse only if her parents listen to doctors like Brachet. Her body should be strengthened with exercise, her mind busied with music and art. Her imagination should be kept under close watch lest her dreams give her hopes of escaping the life for which she has been destined by nature, gender, and class. "To love and please, that is almost the entire life of a woman," explains Brachet: "Give her therefore all the amiability that she must bring to society in order to please everyone. Inspire in her at the same time the qualities that should make everyone esteem and cherish her. Inspire in her especially modesty and prudence, which embellish all women and without which a woman is incomplete." In short, Brachet suggests, teach her to put up a *desirable front* without it masking anything besides modesty and complacence, amiability and forbearance, virtue and tolerance. The woman in Brachet's utopia has never had any other self but the one she effaces. She has never known any other desire but self-denial.

This model daughter, wife, and mother becomes, through Adeline Hulot of *Cousine Bette*, the ideal of Balzacian realism as well. But she achieves this position of applauded martyrdom only by being framed in a plot that dissipates any power her ideals may seem to have bolstered. She is caught in a network of intrigues that do not allow her to become an example for others. Even her attempts to become a charitable lady dispose her to nervous tremors and the mockery of those she would reform. Unlike *Les Mystères de Paris*, *Cousine Bette* does not succeed in making its noble *bourgeoise* into a model for its female readers. Rather, despite the lip service it gives to her virtue, it seems to have other ends in mind.

Brachet's account of hysteria names two principal demons—ambition and vanity—that imperil even the most virtuous married women. A woman can become hysterical, his observations suggest, if she is too proud to put up with her husband's ill manners, or if she wants more than her parents or husband can offer. She risks grievous maladies when she disguises her real feelings or when she puts on a show to gain approval. At the same time, Brachet expects his girls to master arts of charm, modesty, and innocence. He expects them to further their husbands' ambitions even if it means putting on false fronts and to flatter their husbands' vanity even if it means choking on their own sorrows.

Even as Brachet worries about women's nerves when they are forced to hide their *real* feelings, he plots an education for girls in which their every thought is harnessed to appearances—their own, their husband's, their family's. He would artfully mold the feelings of women to make them part of masquerades that fit so well as to seem innate. He would instruct women to forget the differences that give men "prerogatives," assuring them that their own "role" has its virtues. He would teach them to ignore what they cannot change—to put up a front to protect family honor and to use their own powers of intrigue to tempt their men away from vice. The contradiction that racks Brachet's plots of hysteria also troubles Balzac's accounts of female virtue. Doomed by her very attempts to model herself on social norms, to protect her husband's name, her family's tranquility, and "appearances," a woman like Adeline winds up, in both Brachet and Balzac, tormented into convulsions: "Despite her care, she is almost never able to hide entirely her inclinations; they always betray themselves" (JLB, 87).

Adeline's hysteria might be traced to any number of fantasmatic *causes prédisposantes* projected by medical writers of Balzac's era—urban life, society appearances, sedentary living, forceful emotions, excessive reading, marriage above her class, self-education above her family's illiteracy, or even continence, for after all, she clearly hasn't had much sex in twenty years. None of these potential agents can, however, dissipate the force of the indictment the narrative uses Adeline's hysteria to further: through its gradual erosion into convulsions, Adeline's virtue becomes, as Crevel reminds her, nothing more than "*une maladie mal soignée.*" Even as this novel mobilizes Adeline as its exemplary presence,[43] it pathologizes her virtue. Despite its promotion of her as a touchstone for nobility and goodness, the narration targets her for an illness as debilitating as those that destroy its two embodiments of evil, Bette and Valérie. Ultimately, the Balzacian narrative diminishes its own respect for the woman who anchors it by assimilating her into the very system of evil it purports to abhor.

Hysterical Plots

The world of the Balzacian novel is subsumed in a struggle between good and evil "played out under the surface of things," as Peter Brooks has persuasively argued. The "melodramatic mode" embraced by Balzac's narratives exists primarily to open paths to what Brooks has called "the moral occult." The moral truths these novels seem to enact occur in a theatrical realm where nothing is left unsaid and everything contributes to the dramatization of the moral struggles of social life: "Man is seen to be, and must recognize himself to be, playing on a theater that is the point of juncture, and of clash, of imperatives beyond himself that are non-mediated and irreducible."[44] The melodramatic theater of the Balzacian novel seems to depend particularly upon a staging of what Thomas Laqueur has called "theatrical" gender—socially defined roles through which gender differences are expressed.[45] The Balzacian novel is built not only on a polarization between good and evil, but its polarizations are specifically gendered and then further nuanced by class. As Fredric Jameson has suggested, the allegorical attributes divvied up by *Cousine Bette* among its characters fall almost exclusively to the women: to the schemers and prostitutes on the one side— Valérie, Bette, Josépha, Madame Nourisson, and Atala, and to the devoted wives on the other—Adeline, Hortense, and Célestine.[46] The men of the novel—Hulot, Crevel, Fischer, the marshal, Victorin, Wenceslas, Montès—are distinguished by their absence, blindness, and impotence. Emerging only when called up by the schemes of the women, each of these figures seems at most to hold the place of victim—like the legendary Samson imagined by Valérie— caught up in the passion of the moment, unable to think, act, or defend himself. It is through its observations of women and through the pathologizing of women's desires, actions, and even—in Adeline's case—inaction, that the novel claims to articulate its "moral occult." But it is also through these observations of women that this novel ultimately implodes upon itself, collapsing its own allegorical categories and becoming, in turn, a hysterical narration.

If Adeline Hulot personifies the well-intentioned and virtuous cover-up, Valérie Marneffe becomes within the framework of this novel the embodiment of evil duplicity. The entire novel emerges as a kind of morality play in which "innocent souls" are permitted "to guess at the various havocs that the Madame Marneffes of this world may wreak in families, and by what means they can strike at poor virtuous wives, apparently so far beyond their reach" (*CB*, 289).[47] From the moment she enters its theater, Valérie serves as this novel's vision of the satanic (*CB*, 378), steadily opposed to the virtuous Adeline. This text will spare no venom at each of her entrances, regularly inviting us to witness her perfidy.

Even as the emissary of Bette's plots, hatchet woman for the poor cousin's vengeance, Valérie is shown overplaying her roles. From the first moment of her collusion with the peasant woman, Valérie is depicted as a schemer who will betray even the "friends" with whom she plots. The novel sets Valérie to work her evil, much as a plague might be unleashed in a city, and, at an appointed time, finds an antidote—the illness of which she dies—to rid itself of her physical presence. While Adeline embraces self-sacrifice for the sake of the family, cheerfully maintaining a front to protect her husband, and weeping behind a curtain that spared her children the spectacle of their father's scandals (*CB*, 262), Valérie plots to force men to sacrifice themselves, their riches, and their family honor for the sake of desires her society deems outside women's "prerogatives." While Adeline seeks to hold the family together at all costs, Valérie looks for ways to secure her own future without regard for her husband. While Adeline seeks the friendship of her poor cousin, Valérie is shown repulsed by the peasant she claims to love as her own family. Yet despite the novel's insistence upon the evils of this "ambitious married courtesan who from the start accepts moral depravity with all its consequences" (*CB*, 173), it repeatedly revels in the art of her triumphs. The narrator even goes so far as to assign her projects like his own—"thinking, dreaming, conceiving beautiful works" (*CB*, 231).[48] More disturbing within the context of its apparent moral framework, this text gives her a voice that constantly upsets this moral universe. Despite its attempts to condemn her as vice personified, this text cannot stifle the chilling observations she makes on the society around her, the indictments of gender and class relations she uses to empower and enrich herself, and the desires for freedom, self-possession, and sexual liberty she articulates.

Valérie's version of freedom strangely resembles the one embraced by proponents of tolerated prostitution: because her husband satisfies himself with common prostitutes, he preserves her from his syphilitic condition. She finds further benefits in her marriage to this "walking disease": "By preferring to me the dirty monkeys of the street-corner he leaves me free. If he takes his whole salary for himself, he never asks me to account for the way I make money" (*CB*, 180, 131). This means that in practice, Valérie has the freedom enjoyed under the Napoleonic Code only by widows and that is, in fact, what she calls herself (*CB*, 132). As long as she can keep her husband happy with his promotions, she may revel in personal and financial liberty. She has mastered the art of holding property independently of her husband (*CB*, 176). She has found ways to get men to give her what she wants without ever seeming to have asked for anything (*CB*, 322). She has learned that a woman like herself is protected only by the appearances of her good reputation (*CB*, 215). She knows she can always summon the specter of her raging husband reasserting his rights (*CB*, 292). She even knows how to manipulate men with the hysterical fits from which virtuous women like Adeline so often suffer (*CB*, 293).

Despite her apparent virtue, however, Adeline is quickly caught up in the same system Valérie uses for her own purposes. Putting on a front of one of "those women" (*CB*, 316), the baroness offers to prostitute herself to Crevel in exchange for the two hundred thousand francs her husband needs to save her uncle and his own neck. "They're not all walking the streets," the police remind Hulot when they arrest him for consorting with Valérie (*CB*, 305). Adeline, though rebuffed by Crevel, only provides further evidence of the widespread nature of Paris prostitution. "I belong to Art, as you belong to Virtue," Josépha tells the baroness who has come to her seeking Hulot (*CB*, 389); yet they have equally set out to use men's sexual desires for their own ends. Though the novel ultimately exonerates its "sublime courtesan" (*CB*, 318) since her proposition is never accepted, it nevertheless draws parallels between the kind of appearances she maintains and the ones put up by the text's "real" courtesans. Like Adeline, Valérie is shown as a charity worker, churchgoer, and spinner of illusions for the men in her life (*CB*, 175, 177). Like the peasant girl whose beauty tantalized a baron into marrying her, Valérie banked on her looks to get the men she wanted (*CB*, 171). Just as Adeline once flirted with Napoléon to further her husband's ends, Valérie trades favors for her husband's advancement. "I have all the appearances of honorability," Valérie tells Bette. Like Adeline, whose husband's infidelities relieve her of spousal responsibilities, Valérie rejoices in her freedom to live as she pleases: "I am a married woman and I am my own mistress" (CB, 131).

Although Valérie maneuvers, schemes, and prostitutes herself, she never commits any crimes for which the police could arrest her. Working, as Jameson notes, more like the covert police of the 1840s,[49] Valérie's worst offenses are plotting with her husband the arrest of Hulot, and conning Crevel into giving *her* and not Adeline the two hundred thousand francs. Hulot, after all, is the one who rigs promotions for Marneffe, dissipates his family's fortune, embezzles state money, and even plays pimp to his wife's "fake courtesan" (CB, 325). He commits adultery with married women, traffics in minor girls, falsifies his identity, and hides from the police. Valérie does little besides desire. We cannot call her a thief, since she is freely given everything her lovers take from their families. We hesitate to call her a prostitute, since she asks favors rather than cash for her affections—and accepts money to please her admirers. We can barely call her a homewrecker, since the men she entraps come to her of their own free will. We cannot even call her a blackmailer, since her little "slip" to Adeline about the two hundred thousand francs names neither price nor threat.

But we *can* see Adeline as the force behind the murder of both Valérie and Crevel, arranged by her son Victorin because, as he explains, "with one single sentence that woman has endangered my mother's life and reason." At the very moment when the only words the hysterical Adeline can utter are "a lifetime of virtue," her own delegates are plotting murder to preserve her front of goodness (CB, 407–08). "Virtue cuts off the head, Vice only cuts our hair," declares Valérie in her perverse reading of the legends of Judith and Delilah, but she has somehow hit upon the paradox of this novel's plots (CB, 252). Ironically, the most virtuous characters are those who unleash the most devastating destruction. Small wonder then that Adeline suffers from a body out of control. The contradictions racking the novel are somehow channeled through the nerves of the woman it uses to represent its ideals.

"Noble sentiments pushed to extremes produce results similar to those of the greatest vices," the narrator comments upon Adeline's "fanatism" (CB, 104). The baroness's mistake, suggests the narrator, is that she never becomes one of those "honorable and prudish women in the world's eyes and a courtesan to her husband" (CB, 317). She indulges his inconstancy without ever trying to tempt him back. She has missed a lesson known to clinicians and prostitutes alike: "It is in her interest," writes Brachet, "to leave always a few sparks of desire and not to extinguish them" (JLB, 504). "If only," Josépha tells the desperate wife, "you could have had a little of our knack, you know, you would have kept him from running around, for you would have been what we know how to be—*all women* to a man" (CB, 388). Adeline, shown pathetically adorning herself to tempt Crevel, has not learned how to "possess the seductions of Vice." As the narrator reminds us, "One isn't a courtesan for the wishing!" (*CB*, 316). Adeline lacks what the narrative calls the "genius" to keep her husband's desires inflamed (*CB*, 317). She fails in the task this text sets her— to "save a family from the horrors of hunger, depravity, and misery, by bringing its members back to work, and back to life in society" (*CB*, 435). In the Manichean universe of the Balzacian novel, all the women have somehow failed to anchor true virtue. Despite the artful appearances the novel allows them to put on, all the women have been compromised.

In the "drama of morality" this novel enacts, the existence of a moral universe is asserted only so that it can be unmasked as out of range. Its "presence and categorical force among men" is asserted in a gesture that simultaneously unveils women's capacity to pervert that force.[50] Virtue does not emerge victorious because, along the way, virtue has been shown corrupted, emptied out, indistinguishable from evil. What the novel promoted as desirable has turned out, like Adeline's body, to be overrun by contradicting signals. Its plot has become as hysterical as the character it used to promote its values.

Ironically, this collapsing of the moral universe of the Balzacian novel is precisely what critics of all political persuasions cited when they protested that the Balzacian novel does not practice what it theorizes. "Let's have a look at how the author of the *Parents pauvres* punishes vice, avenges virtue, and reconciles us with religion," invites the Fourierist Alexandre Weill. According to Weill, the "charming" characters whom Balzac associates with vice, especially Valérie and Josépha, succeed in seducing everyone and in accumulating extraordinary riches. "What is therefore the reward for the sufferings of abnegation and virtue of Adeline?" he asks, noting that the emblem of virtue must wait years for vengeance risking in turn her son's neck as the accomplice of Valérie's murderer.[51] One does not show one's Catholicism, Weill argues, in whining like Adeline or in imposing upon herself "continual sacrifices for a spendthrift like the baron who has neither head nor heart."[52] The ideas of the resulting novel "have degenerated into paroxysms." "In all your works," Weill taunts Balzac, "the portraits created are inconsistent with the principles with which you accompany them, and that proves your genius is more progressive than your science and your will."[53]

While leftist critics winked at Balzac's contradictory convulsions of virtue and vice, conservatives railed at the decadence one must pass through to get to an otherwise Catholic moral.[54] Pontmartin sees Balzac as a man who puts on a show of being Catholic when he is really "materialistic and atheist."[55] To listen to conservatives, no one is more vulnerable to Balzac's put-ons than women: "With what impatience our ladies await these . . . works," wrote Al. de C., "His immorality is not a vice that belongs to him, it is the atmosphere which penetrates [his work]. All his women, in the midst of an ultrarefined delicacy, are subject to egoistical penchants, more sensual than voluptuous, physical without the ideal, penchants that they disguise skillfully beneath the silk and velvet of their words."[56] The kinds of "bad examples" through which

Balzac plies his moralities[57] seem particularly to tempt women into believing he is their champion. Balzac was seen as the master of the "immoral sophism, developed artfully in a great number of novels where the talent of observation and descriptive analysis is pushed to the exactitude of a daguerreotype." According to Alfred Nettement, such theories had so much "success with women" Balzac "applied this maxim to literature."[58] Balzac endangers, these critics conclude, by offering women lessons that seem to spare their modesty but that lure them into an even more perfidious realm of pseudomorality. The novelist whom Janin called "the dupe of his heroines" winds up attacking their "spasms" by giving them plots ravaged by "malaises."

The Lady's Man

Rumors that twelve thousand letters from women poured into Balzac's mail during the July Monarchy bolstered critics' fears about the seductive powers of his novels.[59] Whether such a figure is as apocryphal as the lithographic scene of Balzacian seduction depicted in figure 5.1, we will never know. Only a hundred letters from Balzac's supposedly voluminous fan mail have survived, some two-thirds bearing female signatures.[60] The majority of these letters, almost all dating from the 1830s, come from strangers who share effusive appreciation of his literary contributions to their lives, request his response to their inquiries, and invite him to private rendez-vous. "They say, Monsieur," writes Madame Adrien in 1833, "that when an author publishes a book, lots of women write him. Is this true? Are these women right in doing so? I don't know. But just as we all do things to follow our desires, I so empower myself to write you. To me, Monsieur, you are the most lovable author whose works most please and seduce me."[61] Madame Adrien confesses her dreams, not only of a reply to her letter, but of meeting her beloved author in person. Enticed by his literary works, these women have set about imagining real-life seductions in which they might take the initiative.

Balzac's appeal to women, it would seem from these letters, depended on his remarkable ability to convince them that he understood their sorrows, their emotional entrapment, their diminished rights, and the pain of the vacuous existence the nineteenth-century hysterizers wished upon them. In his novels he granted them voices and the skills of observation and interpretation. He empowered them to resist the confinement of bourgeois life and to reject the aspersions cast on those who strayed from virtue's path. He gave them a subjectivity, which, although limited by the conflicting morality he channeled through them, nevertheless made their desires central to the struggles of social life. Perhaps most important, he authorized their dissimulation, their tactical maneuvers, and their schemes to improve their existence. He wanted them reading novels for, as he pointed out to future husbands in the *Physiologie du mariage*, as long as they did so, their spouses would at least know what they were up to (*PM*, 145).

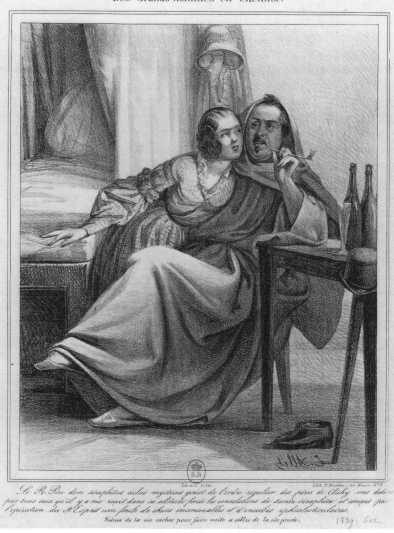

Figure 5.1

Edward Allet's lithograph from 1839 claims to represent "Scenes from hidden life intended to follow Scenes from Parisian life." The easily recognizable Balzac is mocked as a Saint-Simonian priest with a way with women. (BIBLIOTHÈQUE NATIONALE)

Despite Balzac's ability to convince his female readers that he had reclaimed "the right of liberty . . . for the daughters of France,"[62] the moral universe of the Balzacian novel upholds a tolerance system similar to the one we saw in Parent, Sue, Hugo, and Dumas. Like these other works, it deploys its criminal women and prostitutes as a force capable of keeping its *bourgeoises* in line. Yet there remains a significant difference in the way the moral economy of *Cousine Bette* functions. Whereas Sue and others delegated policing powers to the prostitute to help inflame their female readership back into virtue, Balzac dismantles the kind of restricted female subjectivity on which these writers depended. Even as he embraces the legends of intemperate male passion—Samson, Holofernes, Hulot—Balzac promotes paradoxical coping strategies for the women his works would seduce. He authorizes them to work the system in whatever way they can, using clever covers to preserve whatever desires they see fit. For unless Balzac's ladies go on desiring, the male subjectivity he promotes will have no one to uphold its privileges. Unless these girls go on dreaming of seductions, male fantasies will have no bearers.[63]

Jameson has argued that *Cousine Bette* is the "sign of the exhaustion of substitute formation and of the return of the repressed, the reemergence of the purely instinctual and the ultimate dissolution, as a consequence, of the narrative form itself."[64] I want to argue that such an exhaustion of the alternative "languages of social and economic motivations" and such a dissolution of narrative transpires precisely through the kind of *reading of sexual difference* that made Balzac a favorite of women. Balzac's moral universe breaks down because his narration can no longer support the theories of difference with which it flirts. The lady's man has become a hysteric at the expense of the sexual difference that props up the melodramatic "theater of gender."

By 1835, in a preface to the Werdet *Père Goriot*, Balzac acknowledged his female interlocutors, those "sincerely virtuous women" to whom he promised the model of "a woman virtuous by taste" who would assuage their alarm over his steady stream of adulterous women.[65] That woman materialized in 1836 as Madame de Mortsauf, heroine of the immensely popular *Lys dans la vallée*, whose virtues are offered up to readers with a caveat that the author is neither the "accomplice of the feelings he attributes to his characters" nor a double for the narrator Félix de Vandenesse.[66] Not surprisingly, critics constantly evoked this novel as one that had ensnared Parisian ladies. While Balzac's female fans most frequently cite the *Physiologie du mariage*, *La Vieille Fille*, *La Femme de trente ans*, and *Eugénie Grandet* in the extant letters of the 1830s, the *Lys* also turns up in the fan mail. Perhaps more important, this novel generated a heated correspondence between Balzac and another of his female interlocutors, his mistress Laure de Berny, whose objections to the original edition culminated in Balzac's own self-censorship of some fifty lines of the text.[67] Ironically, the *Lys* was also caught up in a trial between Balzac and the *Revue de Paris*. Although the trial had no relation to either the work's morality or its audience and although Balzac triumphed, the legal battle nevertheless framed the novel's appearance with intrigue and a long explanatory preface. By the time Balzac published the 1838 edition, the novel had been triply tried—in the courts, by his women readers, and by critics.

Balzac's *Lys* incurred attacks for its indelicacy of observation,[68] for its moral ambivalence, and above all, for its flattery of women's desires.[69] Théodore Muret complained that its omnipresent immorality was all the more dangerous because it emerged carefully disguised. The woman of adulterous desire, Henriette de Mortsauf, is held up, Muret fulminated, as a "model for wives and mothers": "When she dies of that adulterous passion . . . she is hailed as a saint. Consider such lessons!" The women invoked as "sincerely virtuous" were imagined duped by an ambiguous painting that sought nothing less than to put their virtue on the line.[70]

Later critics like Pontmartin, Poitou, and Sirtema claimed that with *Le Lys dans la vallée*, Balzac's writing had taken a turn for the worse that would culminate in novels like *Splendeurs et misères* and *Cousine Bette*.[71] Critics of the *Lys* called Balzac a *séducteur*, yet they saw only the dangers of his appeals to women without noticing how this novel promoted male fantasies of power, prestige, and virility. The *Lys* was, after all, the story of a man for love of whom a woman denied herself, became hysterical, and died. Critics ignored the fact that Madame de Mortsauf's desires, suffering, and convulsions are narrated by a man. Instead they focused on how the hysteric's plight appears in a letter destined to seduce yet another woman. Terrified of what female readers might learn from such a novel, critics failed to see that its thematized woman reader was only metaphorically in possession of the text and, as such, only fantasized as controlling the effects of its seductions: after all, the recipient of Felix's narrative, Natalie de Manerville, has responded to his letter with a rejection. By the novel's conclusion, the narrative of seduction lies in his hands, answered and once again within his power.

Critics of the *Lys* also overlooked Balzac's self-censorship between the editions of 1836 and 1838. The passage Balzac claimed "marred" Madame de Mortsauf had been substantially tempered. In the earlier version, Balzac had the dying woman decry her chastity at length, but in the later version, she simply reproaches herself for lying.[72] What galled critics from 1836 through the 1850s was the overwhelming passion evoked in its chaste heroine, as a Second Empire critic explained, citing his contemporary:

> Mr. Eugène Poitou reproaches [Balzac] for speaking of woman without modesty, for having only painted the desire she excites, without ever having felt the respect she inspires—in short, for having seen her too often with only materialistic and libertine eyes, whereas he should have seen her with the eyes of a moralist and a poet. We find the proof of this in *Le Lys dans la vallée*, the novel where Balzac . . ."worked to paint what he has never understood, alas! ideal and chaste love. . . . Coarse ideas clothed in precious language, mystical expressions, and lascivious thought; refined materialism, musky libertinism, there's the book. Let it thus be judged."[73]

Sirtema and Poitou emerge scandalized from Henriette de Mortsauf's final regrets of earthly passion. Both describe in detail the sequence in which, dying and delirious, she bewails her error in espousing virtue:

> It is as if the cry of the flesh triumphs, as if a frenetic hymn to sensuality takes its revenge. . . . This is nothing but physical love, sensual love; it is the love of antiquity, like that which devoured Phèdre, "It is Venus tooth and claw attached to her prey" (*C'est Vénus tout entière à sa proie attachée*), but Venus without the intervention of divine fate that excuses it and partially veils it; it is the *ardor of the blood*, what the author himself calls *the boiling up of sensations and carnal fits*.

Poitou's objections to this presentation of female desire mirror his shock at its moral ambiguity: "to connect in one soul the purest mysticism, to put those furies of the senses in an angelic nature, to thus couple the idea and the sensual, isn't it a loathsome idea?" To his mind, such contradictions do not exist in humanity. Instead, one finds the "contrasts" of moral oppositions, clear-cut disparities between idealism and the call of the flesh, visible differences between good (i.e., exemplary, pure women) and evil (i.e., desiring, sexualized women). Women racked by the contradictions expressed by Madame de Mortsauf can only exist in dangerous fantasy: "They are not human beings; they are monsters, half women, half reptiles."[74]

The line Poitou cites here, "*C'est Vénus tout entière à sa proie attachée*," originally used by Racine's Phèdre to describe her passion,[75] had become a watchphrase by the time of these critiques for a debate I have repeatedly evoked in this book. Although I would not want to venture an original source for medical references to Phèdre's plight, we can be certain that when Briquet cited this line in 1859, its associations were well known. As we saw in the introduction, from the middle of the eighteenth century to the Second Empire, medical studies had relayed concern over the relationship between hysteria and sexual desire. Summoning the same line from Racine to describe traditional explanations of hysteria as a "shameful malady," Briquet promises to undermine the association of hysteria with the wages of illicit desire in women's bodies (Br, vii). Poitou's use of this same line to describe Madame de Mortsauf's passion evokes a story of hysterical desire that by the 1850s has made its way from medical treatises back into literary debates.[76]

Henriette de Mortsauf is coded under the sign of hysteria, not only for Balzac's Second Empire critics, but for Peter Brooks and Nancy K. Miller in the 1970s, because her somatizing body can be read diagnostically as enacting the passion she has been unable to consummate.[77] For a woman like Henriette, continence alone might not lead to hysteria, but excitation added to sexual frustration would certainly place her at risk. Superficially at least, the *Lys* inscribes a medical-dictionary paradigm of hysteria as a lure to readers who would see Henriette repressing her adulterous desire for Félix. Such a diagnosis furthers an appraisal of Madame de Mortsauf as a saint from those who see her nobly clinging to the bonds of marriage. Both Brooks and Miller have argued, however, that her desire becomes so overwhelming that it destabilizes the novelistic system it is explicitly evoked to anchor. Virtue only triumphs at the expense of the self. Félix's account of Henriette's martyrdom can only signify at the expense of the seduction (of Natalie) it was designed to achieve. Hysterical passion disintegrates the exchanges it is narrated to produce. Nevertheless, even if the moral system of the *Lys* is undermined by Henriette's expression of her desires, this heroine offers no lessons in selfhood to enterprising female readers. She gains a voice to express little more than her self-abnegation and dependency.[78]

Despite the fact that a novel like the *Lys* promotes a moral system that ultimately negates the female subjectivity it so expansively elaborates, critics like Pontmartin, Poitou, and Sirtema evoke Madame de Mortsauf's hysteria to attack the novel for educating women in passion. For these conservative critics, the novel endangered its readers because it gave space to female desires and invited women to believe such passions worth coveting. These critics saw the hysterical passion of the novel's heroine expanding uncontrollably and contagiously beyond the novel.[79]

Ironically, the same Racinian line that encodes for Balzac's critics the dangers of Madame de Mortsauf's hysteria will enter *into the Balzacian novel itself*, though not into the one with which critics here associated it. Rather it appears in the very novel we have read in this chapter as an interrogation of the medical discourse on hysteria—*Cousine Bette*. For critics of *Le Lys dans la vallée*, the plight of Phèdre describes a woman's destructive, adulterous passion. In the 1846 *roman-feuilleton*, it is also cited to describe desire out of control, unrepentant lasciviousness, and overwhelming passion, but not on the part of its female characters—nervous, hysterical, or prostituted. Rather, Josépha the courtesan uses the expression to reproach the *male* character whose desires power this novel's intrigues, the Baron Hulot:

> "You have only ruined your own family; the only property you've given up is you! And then, you have excuses, both physical and moral." She struck a tragic pose and said: " 'It is Venus tooth and claw attached to her prey.' . . . That's how it is!" she added, with a pirouette. (*CB*, 359–60)

What are we to make of the fact that this expression, legion in the description of the troubles of (female) hysterics, comes in the Balzacian novel to frame the trials of the *male* character—and, in fact, virtually to exonerate him: "Hulot found himself absolved by Vice. . . . The immensity of the crimes was there, as it is for members of a jury, as an extenuating circumstance" (*CB*, 360)? How are we to read the hysteric's etiquette when it offers not only absolution but praise to the pedophiliac, whoremongering, embezzler Hulot? Should we reject Josépha's preference for "a real spendthrift, mad about women" like Hulot as little more than an acknowledgment of her own much needed patrons, or does such a line resonate beyond the mock tragedy of this interaction to other spaces of this novel so obsessed with uncontrollable passion, sexuality, and hysteria? I want to argue that this moment of intertextuality between literary criticism, medical discourse, and the novel is not only remarkable for the significance of the discursive crosscurrents it inscribes, but also represents a pivotal moment in this novel's implosion on itself. When the novel places its lady's man, Hulot, under the sign of the hysteric, it effectively explodes the gender — if not also class — differences on which its moral system has depended.

Although Brachet's 1847 study was one of the first to include a case study of a male hysteric, decades would pass before Charcot created a special wing at the Salpêtrière for the study of hysterical men.[80] As late as the 1980s, psychoanalysts insisted on the gendered quality of the hysteria diagnosis.[81] The masterplots of hysteria would themselves be discredited before the theory detached itself from the sexual and reproductive organs of woman. Brachet's male hysteric, like those of Briquet and Charcot after him, was a feminized man, a kind of vulnerable androgyne, unable to cope in the gender-role nature had assigned him. Antidotes would include a reeducation in the behavior and prerogatives of masculinity, a kind of progressive retooling designed to restore his virility and bodily integrity (JLB, 98, 190–95).

Balzac's male hysteric is no such pathological sissy. Rather, excused by Josépha, forgiven by his wife, cultivated by Valérie for his power, and adored by his adolescent concubines, this chubby geriatric aristocrat baffles with an inexplicable charm. Power, wealth, and savvy cannot alone have lured the likes of Josépha or enslaved the saintly Adeline. The je-ne-sais-quoi, which Dorothy Kelly aligns with a (Lacanian) phallus, sets loose decades of mishaps for family, fortune, and state.[82] Freed at the novel's conclusion by his wife's martyrdom, Hulot reverts to the antics that have made him the talk of Paris: the kitchenmaid he weds, while described as coarse and buxom, is nevertheless some sixty years his junior.

Much of Hulot's prowess works through rumor, as we could assume do reports of his wealth, prestige, and power. The kinds of interactions that Eve Sedgwick has called "homosociability" mobilize social and sexual relations in this novel.[83] The exchange of Joséphas and Bijoux (not to mention Adeline) feeds a kind of "male malady" in which male privilege is bolstered through interactions over the bodies of women. What Balzac's narrator calls a search for "that mysterious androgyne" "both the ideal and pleasure," seems to send men like Crevel and Hulot in search as much of one another as of women partners. Such men, intent on finding "that rarity" (CB, 307), depend on female objects to further their exchanges with male objects. Such male hysteria depends upon the distinct gender roles that mark these female objects and in turn upon the hysterization of the bourgeois women who do not circulate, but who instead — distinctly female — keep up appearances.

Despite the novel's failure to indict Hulot, either for his crimes or for his passions, Cousine Bette transforms him into another case of uncontrollable nerves. By likening its male mover to its female hysterics, the Balzacian novel threatens to dissolve the very gender differences on which its narrative system seemed to depend. By launching Hulot into the same sphere as its aberrant female characters, the novel rattles the foundations that anchor literary homosociability and its equivalent clinical masterplots. Hulot's hysteria emerges as a part of the novel's erosion of narrative codes and moral oppositions. Although *Cousine Bette* flirts with the clinical methods that upheld theories of strict gender differences, this novel continually chips away at these theories. Its involvement with pathological realism, narrative spasms, and women's desires leave it pinioned between the theater of gender appropriate to its moral occult and the paradoxes inherent in the clinical theories it mimes. Characters like Hulot may escape the novel intact, but they cannot evade pathologization. Even what may have seemed, in Hulot's case, to prop up the novel's very definitions of masculinity and femininity, falls prey to clinical scrutiny. The theories that bolster the clinical gaze collapse under the pressure of contradictory observations.

Nowhere do we see these gender differences more shaken than in the novel's representation of the lessons of its diabolical prostitute. Alone of the women of this novel, Valérie Marneffe suffers no nervous disorders—though she does threaten to go mad and, on one occasion, feigns nervous fits to drive away the indefatigable Hulot. Her crime and her narrative force derive from her ability to manipulate appearances without lapsing into hysteria. In contrast to Adeline or Madame de Mortsauf, she has learned to channel desire without being possessed by the passion of Phèdre.

"I want to tell you the secret feelings of us other hidden women (*femmes cachées*)" wrote one of Balzac's female *lectrices* in the year after the publication of *Le Lys dans la vallée*. "We all have for you the fondest admiration, and if the inquisitors of the world force us sometimes to condemn a few chapters of your works, as soon as two of us are together in private, we whisper, 'I love Balzac! Balzac knows all the miseries of women's condition.' "[84] The very women feared by Balzac's critics and by Brachet are the ones marginalized by the Balzacian narrative—the hermaphroditic Bette, the criminally manipulative Valérie, the *femme galante* Josépha. For they are no less capable of providing lessons than emblems of virtue like Madame de Mortsauf and Adeline Hulot. They alone of the Balzacian universe attain the desirable status of being artful. They are all observers, master readers of the sphere in which they function as marginals, but Valérie in particular offers up lessons the novel would hope to emulate (*CB*, 122, 231). Perhaps, through Valérie, the novel recognizes its own limitations. Or perhaps, in comparing novelistic maneuvers to those of its bedeviled courtesan, *Cousine Bette* once again unfurls hysterical plots for the delectation of whatever *femmes cachées* might find solace there.

In the sphere of the clinic, under the gaze of astute observers like Brachet and Bianchon, the nineteenth-century woman was obliged to give up the habits that jeopardized her body. She was forced to educate herself on appropriate forms of dissimulation lest she risk her husband's honor or family fortune. She was directed to adhere to her assigned gender role lest she become an "impotent hermaphrodite." She was taught to covet her virtue lest "appearances" dissolve into scandal. Otherwise, as we have contended, she risked becoming dangerous. Otherwise, she chanced becoming like Valérie Marneffe, Emma Bovary, or the Fille Elisa—the subject of novels.[85]

Narrative, claims Todorov, derives from the desires invested in difference.[86] Theories of gender difference propelled the mid-nineteenth-century novel to the same extent that they obsessed the clinic of that era. The novel of spasms, from *Cousine Bette* to *Madame Bovary* to *La Fille Elisa*, problematizes the very possibility of telling that difference, of holding it in check, of guaranteeing the moral system it anchors. Romanticized by Baudelaire as a *male* hysteric, Emma Bovary will emerge as that androgyne who does not know "difference."[87] Contained by the novel that made her a case, like Madame de Mortsauf, Adeline, Elisa, and Nana, Emma Bovary would provide a corpse on which her narrative clinician could perform an autopsy and scrutinize the effects of that difference. What makes Emma a "poet" for Baudelaire, however, lies more in her hysteria than in her explosion of difference. It is, in fact, precisely what got the novel she inhabits tried for immorality—her "excessive taste for seduction."[88]

"Watch out especially for seduction," warned Brachet (JLB, 506). The world surrounded women with so many dangers. This is perhaps why the nineteenth-century French state assumed responsibility for protecting honorable women from those less honorable. As I will show in the next section, government censors increasingly invested the project of keeping women from hysterics and other "cases" lurking in novels. Refusing to know difference, rejecting appearances, rebuffing the masterplots of gender difference relayed by nineteenth-century medicine, these novels disseminated hysteria of yet another kind. They expanded a vista around women under surveillance. They opened lookout points from which difference, however tentatively, might begin to dissolve.

PART THREE
Seduction Under Surveillance

6

Dangerous Reading:

The Trials of
the Nineteenth-Century Novel

" $\mathscr{I}$ f your daughter reads novels at age fifteen," cautioned Briquet and Legrand Du Saulle, "she will have nervous attacks at age twenty."[1] The warning they paraphrased, first articulated by eighteenth-century physician Samuel Tissot, echoed through educational, medical, and moral tracts in the nineteenth century. Relayed by doctors and *aliénistes*, Tissot's advice to parents supported elaborate theories about the fantasy life of women. More important, it served as a mandate for strategies of surveillance that targeted reading women. In the next three chapters, we will explore how the novel came to be represented as a danger as well as what dangers it in fact contained.

Our story begins with an account of what a woman might be driven to do in bed:

> He exercised definite control over my reading. If I had a book that seemed to him improper for a girl of my age, he would say, "Anna, it is too early to read that book now." When I was fifteen, I remember, he felt that I should not read Balzac and Dumas. I read them, of course, notwithstanding, hiding the forbidden volumes among the linens.[2]

Although Freud was only three years older than his sister Anna, at age eighteen he had already appropriated the fears of Tissot's followers. And, indeed, those worst fears would be realized as the adolescent girl learned her lessons between the sheets.

Almost magically, books are invested with desires we cannot hope to tell. Freud's prohibition underlines the extent to which there might be something in books that *affects* the world outside of books. To attempt to locate that stimulus is to become partner in a relay of fantasy. Yet because no one ever quite tells the driving fantasy, with each relay it gains new values, shifts locales, becomes ever more difficult to know. In the space of the prohibition it must remain untellable lest its power be lost. Freud at eighteen set out to control his younger sister's reading, believing fantasmatically that some peril lurked in those pages. With a desire inflated by the taboos surrounding French novels in fin-de-siècle Vienna, Anna Freud defied her brother and read. We cannot know if Balzac and Dumas fulfilled the fantasies of the adolescent girl, or if the thrill of thwarting her brother's tyranny overshadowed the experience of the book itself. We can only spin our own fantasies of the experience of a young girl's reading, project our own experiences of childhood censorship upon the forbidden books, and flesh out our own notions of what neither Freud nor his sister tell about what a woman might do with a book. Yet amid these three fantasies — Freud's fantasy of the exchange between a woman and a novel, Anna's fantasy about her encounter with the book, and our own fantasy about that scene of censorship — we have the contours of a story that recurs throughout the nineteenth century.

In this chapter and the two that follow, I investigate the exercise of control over reading and the fantasies of reading that accompanied that control. The reading of those who sought to discipline the woman and the reading of the woman herself overlap here, collaborate, blur at times into one set of reading practices, and yet they emerge distinct. In the process the novel becomes a transfer point for power relations but also, in a more striking sense, the impetus for a rethinking of the uses of the imaginary. Targeted as dangerous, the novel forces a reconsideration of the very real social concerns in which it would be implicated. Placed on trial, both figuratively and literally, the novel would try its society's values. In this chapter, we consider these fantasies about reading in order to see how the novel came to be targeted for dangers far beyond its reaches.

Censored Reading

In the early autumn of 1847 Flaubert's Deslauriers tallied the accounts for the censorship of the Monarchy of Louis-Philippe: " 'Since the establishment of this best of republics, we have undergone twelve hundred twenty-nine press trials, resulting in writers being sentenced to three thousand forty-one years in jail, with the trifling sum of seven million one hundred and ten thousand five hundred francs in fines. It's charming, isn't it?' " A decade and two governments before the trial of his own *Madame Bovary*, two other cases serve Flaubert as exemplary: the censorship of newspapers for publishing accounts of the "Praslin Affair" — the murder on August 18, 1847, of the Duchesse de Choiseul-Praslin by her husband, and, on the first days of July 1847, the seizure of a single newspaper three days in a row: *"La Démocratie pacifique* is on trial for its serial, a novel entitled *Women's Share."*[3]

" 'But what hasn't been forbidden?' " demands Deslauriers in a conflation of the stories of censorship of *texts* with other fears to which we will return. Whether or not we believe the figures Deslauriers rattles off, they serve as an ironic reminder of public sentiment about the regime's assault on the word.[4] His remarks reflect the common anguish elicited by press censorship in the months preceding the Revolution of 1848. The extent to which censorship invaded newspapers as well as other spheres—the theater, the *colportage* or book-peddling industry, printing and engraving, publishing, reading rooms— focused attention on the standards for all forms of state intervention.

Louis-Philippe's government had brought with it the promise in its Charter that "The French have the right to publish and print their opinions in conformity with the law; censorship can never be reinstated."[5] Even as it gave lip service to a new freedom of speech, the 1830 government allowed ample means for new restraints. Its primary improvement over the previous government's repressive tactics came through an elaborate bureaucratization of censorship. However, the new mechanisms made it just as easy to restrict freedoms of expression as to promote them. Even with censorship formally abolished, citizen juries were invested with the potentially repressive authority to "preserve their property from whatever dangers might threaten it, and from those fatal excesses by which everything is corrupted and destroyed."[6] Newspapers still had to put up caution money as a guarantee against fines they might incur for libel and other offenses. The September Laws of 1835 further widened the scope of censorship to include any mention of the king's name "either directly, indirectly, or by allusion when discussing actions of his government" as well as any expression of a wish for the overthrow of the constitutional monarchy—or even for a Bourbon restoration.[7] Obviously, such laws targeted a certain kind of text or image, both right- and left-wing, intent upon criticizing the government. And indeed, a high percentage of the works censored by government authorities were attacks on the monarchy. Like the famous caricatures of Louis-Philippe as a pear-head, they poked fun at an administration with little sense of humor, or like Raspail's *Réformateur*, they showed the weaknesses of a government terrified of the rumblings of the masses.[8] Increased means for censorship ultimately prepared the way for crackdowns both inside and outside the press.

As they chiseled away at the new guarantees of freedom, Louis-Philippe's ministers promoted a myth that their censorship was a purely *political* matter, intended only to protect the king from threats such as Fieschi's assassination attempt in 1835. Whereas Restoration censorship trials had transpired, according to Odile Krakovitch, "between the government and the opposition, between the royalists and other parties, between the court and the bourgeoisie, between the past and the present," the trials of the July Monarchy changed focus. The new regime shifted its interests from politics to that broad category of *la morale*: "the battle occurred on the one hand between the social class in power, satisfied with its position, and the elements of reform and change and, on the other hand, between the bourgeoisie and the proletariat, between the present and the unknown future."[9] The monarchy's widening concerns, coupled with disavowals that individual acts of censorship added up to a specific policy, translated into a plethora of incidents of repression without an accompanying legal apparatus that might give a unified meaning to the trials.

Despite its rhetoric of free speech, the new regime found ways to sap the energies of literary as well as nonliterary texts. As Krakovitch has shown, the theater became a particularly visible target. Although the July Monarchy censors took a much more liberal view of the publishing industry than had the previous regime, books still caught the censors' blame.[10] The forays of this government into literary censorship do not fit into easy categories. They cannot be dismissed as attempts to marginalize the pornographic, since the very definitions of pornography and literature were newly under scrutiny, and the possibility of such categories to permit censorship were as much in flux as notions of the politically threatening. Certainly, the government's investments in the censorship of literature are suggestive of the power attributed to literature in this era. What makes the July Monarchy's engagement with literary censorship particularly intriguing derives not from the scandalous scenes of censorship in which it engaged (for these would be far more numerous during the Second Empire), but rather from the censors' increasing dependency on the views of literary critics. The July Monarchy's reinstitutionalization of censorship in a way that touched the literary *and* the political in strangely similar ways had parallels in other spheres. It coincided with speculation about the role literature might be permitted to assume, about who should have access to the word, and about the ends of reading. What the censors could not repress, the critics would seek to put in its place.

In this and the following chapter, we examine the censor's traffic in literature, and consider the politics of these choices. At the same time, we investigate the collaboration of the censor and the literary critic — specifically in the discourse surrounding the novel from the July Monarchy to the early Second Empire. What were the desires that fed these attempts at control? What fantasies did the censor and literary critic share? Whose reading did they seek to place under surveillance? How did the novel put their readings — along with their fantasies — on trial?

The nineteenth-century novel had its share of run-ins with the law. Unlike plays, which had to be submitted to the censor in order to be staged in the first place, or caricatures, which could be printed only with prior approval, the novel simply sallied forth to take its chances with the public, the critics, and the government. For a number of reasons, the case we consider in chapter 7 is a unique one: the seizure of *La Démocratie pacifique* because of its *roman-feuilleton*, Antony Méray's *La Part des femmes*, takes a place in history not unlike the one it holds in Flaubert's account of 1847 as a pinnacle of July Monarchy repression. Although this case prefigures the Second Empire trials of Xavier de Montépin's *Filles de plâtre* (1856), Eugène Sue's *Les Mystères du peuple* (1857), and Flaubert's *Madame Bovary* (1857), during the 1840s few newly published novels were brought before the censor, let alone seized, either in their *feuilleton* or their bound form.[11] We will not find a batch of novels brought to trial at the same time as Méray's novel, or even a pattern of legal repression of fiction to which this case might belong. The seizure of this

Fourierist newspaper is nevertheless an incident in a larger pattern of proscriptions.

In his account of Flaubert's 1857 trial, Dominick LaCapra has argued that trials in general are "noteworthy instances of the social reception of cultural phenomena" since "they attest to the way these phenomena are read or interpreted in a decisive social institution and to the hermeneutic conventions operative therein."[12] Like the trials of exceptional criminals, censorship trials become invested with extraordinary signifying potential. They can, therefore, tell a multitude of stories about the concerns and fears of their time. The censorship trial is only one of many forms the indictment of literature took in the course of the nineteenth century. Although a much publicized trial like that of *La Part des femmes* stamps the targeted text and author with its intrigue and its stigma, it needs to be read in the context of other indictments, in terms of other taboos, and alongside other intrigues. In chapter 7, I contend that *La Part des femmes* brings together almost uncannily many of the concerns of those indictments, taboos, and intrigues. By thematizing the concerns, it makes them readable. In order to situate the proscriptions it would thematize and those to which it would be subjected, we should first look at some of the other ways literature—and the novel in particular—was placed on trial during the July Monarchy.

"*C'était les romans qui avaient perdu la France*," harps Stendhal's Duchesse de Miossens in 1829 ("It was novels that ruined France"). When this avid reader of *La Quotidienne* rails against fiction, she joins a regiment that has long waged war upon novels.[13] Even in Stendhal's own novel, the Duchess has company, as we learn when the teenaged Lamiel begins sneaking around with the likes of *Gil Blas:* "[Lamiel] had succeeded in getting all the books into the tower without being noticed by her uncle, who would certainly have flown into a rage at the sight of so many books, for, although he was a schoolmaster, he often repeated, 'It was books that ruined France.' It was one of the maxims of the terrible Du Saillard, the parish priest."[14] The terror, albeit ironic, this novel associates with fiction could just as easily have reflected views of the late 1830s as those of the Restoration in which it is set. Whether Stendhal was lashing out at the press of 1839–42 as he drafted this account of female criminality or poking fun at long-standing traditions of scapegoating the novel, his characters' hyperbole is a familiar trope.[15] His mockery of the novel's critics—the aristocracy, the schoolmaster, and the church—demonstrates how widely these formulas could circulate. As *Lamiel's* parodies of female *Bildung* suggest, the woman reader struck particular horror into the hearts of those who blamed books for social ills. Women readers—and especially adolescent girls—were seen as extraordinarily vulnerable to the seductions of the literary text. But the France these characters claimed had been lost by books was not yet a nation of women readers.

Although Rousseau steered his model students, Émile and Sophie, away from reading, he provided the French revolutionaries with a program for creating republicans by the book. Central to this myth of the educated and free man was the notion that virtue could be instilled—that education in its varied forms could be brought to bear upon the people.[16] Although schooling did not lead directly to literacy in eighteenth- and nineteenth-century France, as François Furet and Jacques Ozouf have shown, the belief that schools might influence reading abilities served for decades as the linchpin for philosophical and political struggles. The French Revolution crystallized the belief that people could gain their liberty only if they learned to read and could therefore educate themselves: "The school became the central figure of society's limitless powers over the happiness of the individual: under the *ancien régime* its job was to produce Christians, but under the new order it was expected to make men happy and free. The Revolution thereby multiplied the educational ambitions of the Church by infinity, by transforming their final purpose. As the melting pot of new values, tirelessly pedagogic, its dream was school for everyone."[17] This "new religion" resulted in a program for education that packaged the virtues of citizenship along with basic skills. Though the Revolution made no immediate material alterations in the school system, it placed education at the center of debates about social change, and promoted a myth of the free, virtuous, literate man capable of working for the good of the republican state.[18]

The revolutionaries thus vigorously embraced an ideal of literacy as a way of gaining control over the citizens of the new republic, as Maurice Crubellier has suggested.[19] Saint-Just's totalitarian republic of virtue seems only a step away from Rousseau's fantasy of prescriptive readings for the ideal citizen: "In every revolution, it is necessary to have a dictator to save the state by force, or censors to save it by virtue."[20] By giving Émile acceptable books to read, Rousseau's tutor would perform the work of the censors in advance. Well-guided, the educated man might learn to choose his own reading material. The promotion of literacy, then, decreased the need for censorship while also serving as a form of surveillance.

Owing more to that promotion of an ideal of education than to the success of the schools, literacy spread rapidly in the nineteenth century, completing a process, as Furet and Ozouf have shown, that began in the seventeenth century.[21] At the beginning of the Revolution, half of all French men and a quarter of all French women could sign their name on a marriage certificate. By the end of the nineteenth century, about ninety-five percent of men and women could demonstrate some capacity with the written word.[22] With the increase in numbers of "new readers" came changes in the materials for their consumption.[23] And necessarily, their taste ran in directions quite different from what Rousseau might have wished. In addition to *Robinson Crusoe* or *Télémaque*—or perhaps in place of these more "worthy" books—narratives about criminality and prostitution gained a large readership and, in turn, fueled anxieties about the results of widespread literacy.[24] Throughout the nineteenth century revolutionary models for education became the point of departure for new debates about how the powers of books might best be deployed. The book itself, along with the ways of reading it, became an object of scrutiny. The complaint that because of a book the kingdom was lost became the refrain of a song that might have verses of many different political persuasions.

Such indictments of the novel scapegoated the written word for ills far beyond its powers. At the same time, these complaints asserted the hopes that had been pinned to books in general and mass literacy in particular. The battle cry sung by Stendhal's representatives of power resounded in practice from camps even more diverse than those of the aristocracy, the Church, and the teaching profession. Such indictments targeted certain kinds of books, certain kinds of readers, and certain conditions of reading. Some, like Rousseau's snipes against reading, belonged to a tradition that congratulated itself on its classical roots. Some were grounded in a present obsessed with proscriptions against people as well as against texts. And, like Freud's injunctions against his sister's reading, they fed into a series of fantasies about the scene of reading. As they represented the dangers of the novel, they embodied fears that even the censorship of texts could not dispel.

Contagious Reading

If the ability to read spread contagiously in the course of the nineteenth century, the fear about the results of that literacy was proportionately infectious. Programs for the discipline of the reader aimed at keeping track of new readers and quarantining those contaminated by their new abilities. To place literary texts under surveillance—both in the form of censorship and in the guise of prescriptions—meant making certain assumptions about the way texts function. To pose the question of surveillance required theories of the reading process, as the debates over censorship from the seventeenth century onward show. A look at the contours of these debates enables us to see how radical changes in the reading public and its texts altered the terms and mechanisms for nineteenth-century reading dangers, even as certain concerns from previous centuries still echoed throughout society.

Near the end of his 1670 *Traité des origines des romans*, educator Pierre-Daniel Huet (1630–1721) took up familiar concerns about licentiousness in the French novel of his own era. The theory of the reading process he embraced was distinctly opposed to those of moralists—like Boileau and Bossuet—who believed all novels were dangerous for all people at all times. While Huet sympathized with Plato's contention that fables should undergo careful scrutiny (since they are educational materials for children), he insisted that the seventeenth-century novel had been unjustly policed. Even if occasionally novels shake some weak and poorly defended heart, forcing it to love, wrote Huet, these books can do little damage since they only work on the imagination, encouraging "empty love."[25] Unlike many of his contemporaries, who viewed any evil in the novel as grounds for rejecting it, Huet argued that the novel's *workings* undo whatever damage its characters might plot. The novel's virtue lay, accordingly, in its ability to depict "profligacy and vice followed by shame and unhappy success" at the same time as it showed "honor and virtue gloriously raised up." Huet therefore believed that the problems with even the more licentious novels lay *not* in the books themselves, but in their *readers*. Unlike his contemporary Boileau and many others who took up these same issues over the next two centuries, Huet contended that young people must read about such passions in order to learn to close their ears to whatever is criminal, to untangle themselves from its artifices, and to know how to conduct themselves toward an "honest and saintly end."[26]

Huet's analysis of the potential value of the novel was fraught with the tension between the notion of the reader as locus of meaning and the belief that texts themselves have effects. His desire to free novels like *L'Astrée* from the censor's grip led him to walk an uncertain path between these two possibilities. With a spirit strengthened by a superior moral education, Huet's young person might be immune to the novel's potential dangers. The novel would need no censors, for the pure of mind would experience only benefits, and the impure would find themselves simply practicing their depravity in a vacuum of imaginary flight. At the same time, the novel would still retain an ability to function as a causal agent: it could contribute to a superior moral education.[27]

Huet's imaginary reader might have been far more easily stereotyped than the readers with whom Rousseau or Stendhal's duchess reckoned. Because Huet's readers' class and education already conferred upon them a framework for reading, his theories of the reading process could emphasize the strictures of those frameworks. By the end of the Revolution of 1789, however, a critic could no longer assign traits to imaginary readers in hopes of programing them for virtue. The changes in reading conditions—increased literacy, widening availability of reading materials, greater choice of materials, and more affordable texts—radically altered the kinds of people who might take up books. Suddenly, readers might lurk almost anywhere and read almost anything. In turn, mid-nineteenth-century fantasies about reading took many new forms.

The tensions between a belief in the meanings inherent in texts and a belief that readers themselves *make* meaning—tensions that informed the discourse about the novel since the seventeenth century—generally seem to ride piggyback on social conflicts.[28] In this way, the theories of reading that authorized the surveillance of literature take up, in metaphoric ways, the issues of much larger social debates. When critics of the novel took up such theories, they forced the reader out of the shadows. Their resulting analyses provide a link between policies of textual censorship and the politics of social reform.

From the late seventeenth century through the French Revolution, theorists of reading echoed concerns about education—especially of female readers—and moralization. Although these theorists, whose work will be taken up later in this chapter, frequently scapegoated the novel, their discussions of reading tended to remain general, their prescriptions part of a program for an ideal moral education, rather than reactions to specific kinds of readers or books. Critics like Boileau, Bossuet, Fénelon, Grimm, Marmontel, Rousseau, and Madame de Genlis reiterated concerns like those of Huet about the results of reading. They reflected tensions similar to those of Huet between a belief in the power of the text and fears about the work of the reader. They tended nonetheless to focus on readers of their own class.[29] When such critics did write about the reading of the masses, their prescriptions frequently came out sounding like literary variations on "let them eat cake!"

By the early nineteenth century, all this had changed. The Restoration saw new kinds of readers, new forms of literary texts, and subsequently a new focus in the criticism of that literature. Huet's idealized notions about the well-prepared reader reappeared in new, more practical theories about the uses of texts. Concerns about the influence of books upon the French nation now translated into what Jean Hébrard has called "framing popular reading."[30] Critics, censors, and policymakers had turned from ideal readers to potentially aberrant readers and the havoc they might wreak.

Although much of this new criticism relayed an old obsession with the virtue of the citizens of France, it had taken a more instrumental turn: "To spread education among the poor classes without at the same time giving them good readings is to risk the growth of the depraved tendencies of the people who got that education, a force which could be a source of advantages for them as well as for the country" (*CD*, 2:114). In his enormous study of workers and their behavior, Police Prefect Honoré-Antoine Frégier turns to the *reading habits* of his subjects as a means to transform them into law-abiding citizens. Although Frégier's *Des Classes dangereuses de la population dans les grandes villes* included as its subtitle the humanitarian goal "the means to make them better," it requires that these so-called dangerous classes first be identified as threatening before they can be helped. In turn, it recognizes the threats of the reading material of the workers, policing their pleasures and representing a kind of reading that might possibly redeem these censored citizens. For this reason, Frégier's analysis provides a useful model through which to see the obsessions of those who, in the nineteenth century, sought to place reading under surveillance.

Frégier reminds *his* readers (who clearly belong to some other class than the dangerous ones) that the primary goal of the 1833 Guizot Law on primary education is "as much to moralize the nascent generation of laboring classes as to enlighten it" (*CD*, 2:115). Once Frégier's worker has been "moralized," however, he must have an outlet for passions that will be subjected to "the greatest liberty" of "disorder" and "licentiousness." Like bad advice and "certain spectacles," but. above all, *like prostitutes*, bad books surge up to turn the young citizen from the "path of order and duty":

> It is certain that this influence can profoundly alter the purity of morals of those who do not know how to protect themselves. Some men, pushed by greed or

hunger, and too often by a fatal depravity, write only to please the base and shameful passions of our nature; they boldly trade in corruption and, among a certain circle of people, enjoy a vogue similar to that of those vile beings who, speculating on the same passions, prostitute their ways or their acts to satisfy those whom they serve. (CD, 2:117)

Frégier would rout literary "filth" with a viciousness greater than the one he would have used upon its prostitute counterpart.[31] *She* at least might serve as a conduit for dangerous passions. In spite of his call for the eradication of these works, the police prefect shifts his focus. Instead of advocating a program for censoring bad books, he places his faith in the institution of criticism. As if in response to the needs of these workers who teeter on the brink of becoming dangerous, "criticism" and "enlightened people" will demonstrate such contempt for bad literature that it will simply disappear (CD, 2:120). In the place of this dangerous literature, Frégier would disseminate moralizing novels in accessible public libraries. Time spent reading "novels founded on a moral idea" would, he contends, be far preferable to time otherwise "given to idleness and too often to cabarets and debauchery" (CD, 2:121). As if by miracle, the novel's speculation on "base and shameful passions" would come to an end. In the place of the infection of these "immoral productions" (CD, 2:117), Frégier's imaginary libraries would offer the worker a dose of the most sanitary morality. Harnessed to these new ends, the novel would become an "incomparable boon" precisely because of its realism, the familiar nature of its subjects, and its novelty. The chaste fiction Frégier would give his workers in the place of their present whorish pap would nevertheless appeal to tastes he seems to view as unique to their class.

Unlike the reader Huet imagined, corrupted by the literary text because of his own moral turpitude, Frégier's worker cannot help himself. Neither good nor bad, he is always in danger of giving himself over to instincts stronger than his will. Incapable of choosing for himself, susceptible to spectacles, advice, books, and prostitutes, the worker can be subjected to censured plays, moral education, and good honest fiction. His imagination is always ready for whatever comes to feed it. This is why his theater must be censored and his books drugged with moral mickeys.[32] Always impressionable, the worker is fortunately malleable for good purposes as well as for bad.

For the "true literary police"[33] of the July Monarchy, the imaginations of an entire nation of readers were in jeopardy. Reducing the risk might take the form of formal censorship—seizures, editing, banning; it might imply prescriptions for the betterment of endangered readers or programs for the improvement of the works available to those readers; or it might require proscriptions against texts as well as against readers. While strategies for disciplining literature varied, they all required a convincing fantasy about what happened when one read literature and the use of that fantasy to place under surveillance books, printing methods, and people. Just as policing prostitutes enabled Parent-Duchâtelet to keep track of other "dangers," the surveillance of literary texts allowed Frégier to get at certain kinds of readers. In the work of Frégier and his allies, the worker, youth, girl, and woman—in short, all members of the classes labeled *endangered*—came to be represented in compromised positions—with novels. Despite its reformist language and ostensibly charitable goals, Frégier's representations of working-class readers wind up justifying repressive surveillance of *all* workers' behavior, since, in his opinion, these are people unable to control themselves. Police chiefs and bureaucratic reformists were not alone in their obsession with the dangers of the novel. Workers themselves, like the editors of *L'Atelier*, echoed censoring impulses as they set out to improve the lot of their own class:

> We wanted to flee the novel, but the novel comes to find us. These serials, these installments, these dramas, priced in reach of the most modest pocketbooks, are in the hands of everyone, young and old. If these readings were only a bad use of precious time, it would be nothing. They are, however, a poison that warps our minds, that in turns stimulates and debilitates our souls.

According to the workers' press, these proscribed novels not only depict a world far from that of the worker and his family, but they risk making him feel embarrassed by his lot. Worse yet, according to *L'Atelier*'s editors, they take away his taste for "serious study . . . the healthy and fortifying nourishment of the spirit."[34] In goals if not in spirit, the workers' project of self-improvement dovetailed remarkably with the reformist plan of prescriptive reading. Although the portrait of the reading worker differs drastically between the two texts, the fears of novels, the metaphors used to describe the effects of those texts, and the prescriptions themselves, emerge as extraordinarily similar. *Des Classes dangereuses* and *L'Atelier* also shared a striking disinterest in the reading matter of the working woman. In its place we find a common obsession by police chief and workers alike with what both refer to as her "condition." This obsession took the form of a fantasy not unlike the psychiatric ones with which we began the chapter—about uncontrollable bodies surrounded by dangers.

Because of the working-class woman's inadequate education, complain the workers of *L'Atelier*, she is driven into abject misery or else into prostitution. Her pittance of a salary and the conditions of the workroom conspire to expose her to "debauchery"—what we see repeatedly called "seduction." Although the editors of the working-class newspaper are most emphatic about improving the girl's education, like Frégier, they seem more concerned with her moralization. The utopia they embrace oddly resembles the happy families of Rousseau and Michelet:

> If the worker's salary was generally sufficient for supporting his family, as it should be, his wife would not be obliged to gad about the workrooms. She could, by working a little at home, raise her children, send them to school, care for them, and thus avoid later creating ne'er-do-wells. And therefore the mother of the family would be elevated in her own eyes. She would understand her dignity and

her duties, she would raise her daughters with the same feelings so that they too could one day be good mothers.

The reality of the workroom leaves *L'Atelier*'s authors scrambling for other solutions. In fact, they seem more concerned with finding ways to improve the working-class woman's *reputation* than with guaranteeing her better conditions:

> How can one demand from many working women habits of order and morality, of virtue and courage with which to resist poverty, when by the weakness of their organs, by the absence of any moral education, of any idea of duty or respect for themselves, they find themselves cast into workrooms from the tenderest age, in contact with people of all ages, exposed to bad company, hearing conversation that would make men blush? The good tendencies they may have are stifled by the jeering and mockery of other women, and especially by certain old working women who, instead of preaching and showing a good example, avenge themselves for not being able to continue to do evil, by inciting others to debauchery.

Like the prison, where a girl picked up for suspicion of clandestine prostitution might in reality learn the tricks of the trade, the workroom seems to set the working-class girl straight on the path to her fall. This fantasmatic representation of the dangers of the workroom—depicting, ironically, women's corruption of other women rather than heterosexual "corruption"—calls for improved conditions only because it shows girls irremediably susceptible to any bad influence. Like Frégier's male workers, these girls need to be rescued, for they haven't the wits to differentiate between a life of immorality and a path to happiness: "It doesn't take long for girls in such milieus to have their hearts and spirits corrupted since the nonexistence of their education cannot protect them from all the vulgarities and immoralities they hear that, because spoken so often around them, seem to them to be the ordinary and usual life one has to lead to be happy."[35]

Novels, like these oral "vulgarities," are imagined by the workers' press as an equally threatening influence. Like the language of the workroom, the novel was seen to debase women and offend modesty, leaving girls open to the dangers of other kinds of seduction. While they eagerly promote an ideal of an educated male worker, capable of making noble and virtuous choices among the influences around him, the editors of *L'Atelier* fail, however, to imagine a woman capable of self-determination. Instead, they take a protectionist stance toward both the workroom and the novel, demanding, on the one hand, women's retreat to the safety of the home and, on the other, the censorship of any reading that might recreate for girls and women the dangers of the streets.[36]

Whereas the editors of *L'Atelier* would corral women in the safe spaces of mothering, Frégier, strangely enough, pushes the wife and daughter of the fantasmatic worker to the margins of his program for moralization. They nevertheless play a central role in the urban drama of *Des Classes dangereuses*. As the inherently depraved female worker (*CD*, 1:102), the already dangerous prostitute, or the girl who will inevitably fall into debauchery and commodified sex (*CD*, 1:97), Frégier's women have no chance to lie back with a good book. The closest Frégier's prostitutes come to reading is to take as lovers the merchants of obscene books (*CD*, 1:167).[37] Like the male worker, the girl of what we might call the "endangered" classes must learn morality in accordance with the values of those who would put her under surveillance. Frégier will therefore create a program for her primary education resembling that of her brother, but including two hours of sewing a day. Although Frégier claims to wish to ensure that she will learn to read and write, his chapter on her education is consumed with preparing her for the workroom where her busy fingers will keep her off the streets.[38] The convent workroom, where she listens to amusing and moralizing stories, seems little more than a warehouse for the *Bureau des moeurs'* future stock. Frégier's girls don't have a chance: "Female workers, considered as a group, afford in Paris two well-marked divisions: those attached to shops and workrooms, and those employed in mills and factories. . . . Vice rules in both classes" (*CD*, 1:94). She may enter into concubinage only to be abandoned by her boyfriend or find herself flattered on the street by a passerby offering higher wages than she can make with her needle. Just as the worker, left to his own devices, will wander blindly into evil, the female worker, left to herself, will end up seduced into prostitution. Small wonder, then, that Frégier does not pause to worry about her reading. Whereas he attempts to imagine a private world of moralized distractions that would keep his male worker away from any form of vice, sexual or otherwise (*CD*, 2:111–12), Frégier seems unable to imagine the working-class woman in any space but a public one or in any role besides *fille publique*. At least in the workroom, as in the street, she could be observed, ordered, and policed. What she did behind closed doors could only threaten such a system of surveillance.

The marked increase in literacy in the first half of the nineteenth century was matched by the growing visibility of workers whose misery had become more and more conspicuous. Manifestos for social change, like those of Frégier and *L'Atelier*, depicted a reading process that could be transformed instrumentally, as if to control those workers' access to knowledge and, ultimately, to power. Through such discussions of literature, the critic could make visible the worker's desires and regulate his exposure to anything that might upset the delicate balance necessary to his labors. By putting literature on trial in this way, the critic managed to create a space of otherness where the endangered reader could be seen and known. The theories that permitted this surveillance of literature methodically targeted certain groups, certain conditions of reading, and certain kinds of books. Workers, young people, and especially women and girls—all of whom belonged to the newly literate of the July Monarchy—loomed up in the intrigues around reading like so many sleepwalkers on the cliffs of disaster. The new cheap literature, like that criticized by the *Atelier* writer above, proved repeatedly the instrument of these readers' downfall. The conditions in which these endangered groups would read novels—in newspaper *feuilletons* or in pamphletlike *livraisons*, rented in *cabinets de lecture*, or passed from one person to another—made the commodification of these works a subject of dispute. If the novel took the fall for bringing about widespread social decay, certain kinds of novels, such as the *roman-feuilleton*, and certain authors, for example, Sue, Balzac, Soulié, and Sand, lent themselves with particular ease to the target practice of the novel's critics.

The analysis of the novel in the nineteenth century was as much a province of social reformism as the domain of literary criticism. As we shall see, Sainte-Beuve had much in common with both Frégier and the editors of *L'Atelier*; like Jules Janin and Alfred Nettement, the censors of *La Part des femmes* were as preoccupied with the moral order of the working classes as with the vulnerability of women. The trials of the novel in the nineteenth century shared certain obsessions with reformists, police bureaucrats, and charity workers. By putting the novel on trial, literary critics, government censors, and others succeeded in penetrating and claiming control over hitherto secret spheres. Most importantly, the trials of the novel created a *visible* space of otherness where novel readers could be known.

As the analyses of Frégier and *L'Atelier* suggest, the reading process of endangered readers, such as workers, could be represented by means of several interchangeable metaphors. Their reading might be a process of sexualization, infection, or magnetism. The text might drug or poison them. They might find themselves, by contagion, diseased, sexually corrupted, criminalized, hysterical, or mad. Depending on the degree of complicity attributed to them, they could be seen as having indulged their corrupt nature with the food of literary debauchery, as having been seduced, or as having been violated. The results of this encounter might be short-term—a temporary insanity—or long-term—a thorough mania—or permanent—an unmitigated madness, poisoning, or even vampirization. All of these contaminations were represented in a frame of reference that dropped the literary text out of view. Instead, the fantasies of a worker's reading gained their force from the referential power of these metaphors. As soon as the worker could be framed in such a representation, he could be kept under surveillance. Most striking, all of these metaphors insisted on the visibility of effects on the worker, and many of these same metaphors translated female readers into a similar visibility. The fantasies that contained workers—each dependent on readable signs that, in the sphere of the social, had already been recognized as symptoms of social destabilization—spread quickly to other new readers as well. If literacy was contagious, its effects might be contagious as well. And so, therefore, might be the fantasies of that contagion.

Reading Difference

"Two opposing maladies today afflict French literature," declared Jacques-Joseph Virey in 1825, "convulsions or nervous spasms, and languor or atrophy."[39] This convulsive literature works like a drug, infusing the brain with "feverish emotion": "Its great art, or its inspiration, consists in warping the mind into a fiery delirium, and warping that of its readers or spectators through a storm of incoherent words crammed together, through which it crushes the imagination."[40] The hysterical literature Virey associated with Shakespeare, German Romanticism, and Madame de Staël seemed capable of acting on any reader, no matter how rational, healthy, or measured of will.

Yet for Virey, it was women who were particularly predisposed to this contagion of hysterical madness. Reading women were imagined to be like workers, believed incapable of protecting themselves from dangerous reading; like youths, women were viewed as endangered by their own prized innocence. Unlike workers or young men, however, women could never rise above their own susceptibility. They remained at risk regardless of their age, education, marital status, or class. The metaphor of hysterical contagion embraced by Virey and dozens of his contemporaries gave bodies to readers who would engage in such scenes of hysterical reading. It served to describe the uses of those bodies and became a paradigm not only representing fears that the body might get out of control but also alluding to an entire genre of bodies teetering on the brink of disaster. Just as those critics targeted a set of texts that might set off hysterical reactions among endangered groups, they circumscribed an optic in which certain readers were known by their reading difference.

Like the potential citizens of the bourgeois republic and the endangered classes who might become virtuous workers, the female reader focused the attention of an entire generation of moralists and state officials. The woman reader haunted the censors and critics of the July Monarchy just as her prostitute counterpart plagued the reformists of the working class. When theories about the results of reading became gendered, the obsessions set loose seemed to spill over, like the prostitute's excesses, from debates about the social sphere. Just as the metaphors for describing the dangers of reading echoed from debates about the conditions of the working classes, the gender differences reflected in the uses of those metaphors suggested different ways of representing women reading, and more significantly, different approaches to the policing of women's reading practices.

A Gavarni print from "Les Gens de Paris" (figure 6.1) shows a man seated at a desk looking down at a large book in front of him. Behind him, on the right, a curtain is pulled to reveal shelves full of books. A woman gazes down from behind him in consternation, seeming to try to attract his attention by playing with the fingers of the hand he uses to brace his head to read. The caption comments upon their failed interaction: "Ninie thinks that novels are bad books, not for what they add to our passions, but for what they take away."[41] The irony of this twist on the adage that novels spoil girls for marriage does not lie in the shift from a ruined female reader to a sexually ineffectual male reader, but rather in the insistence that the *woman's* desire is troubled by books. Whether *she* reads novels and comes to want more than her husband can provide, or *he* reads novels and ignores her desires, the myth and its parody

Figure 6.1

Engraving after Gavarni, "Les Gens de Paris" (1943–46).
(Bibliothèque Nationale)

both point to the woman's desire as excessive. Measured in relation to male desire, what a woman wants is always out of bounds.

All work and no play may well make the man of Paris a dull boy—like Balzac's Raphaël in *La Peau de chagrin*. It might drive him mad like Louis Lambert or earn him a place among the *femmelins* Proudhon labeled so ineffectual they could not keep the revolutionary ball rolling.[42] But the terror men's reading generates among those who comment on the novel does not compare to the fears about the dangers of women's reading. Unless the male reader is a worker or a young heir, his indulgence in books will simply keep him away from other kinds of mischief (gaming tables, brothels, adulterous affairs). It may feminize him, but its effects, except in the most exacerbated cases, seem to wear off. The girl who reads a novel is as irredeemably lost as if she had slept with the first suitor who dropped his glove in her path. The married woman who reads submits her fragile nervous system to potentially permanent shocks. Like magnetism or hysterical fits, the effects of the text may last a lifetime. Like poison, they may bring an end to a healthy body. Like seduction, they have categorized her as irretrievably "other."

"Never has a chaste girl read novels," insists the "editor" of Rousseau's *Nouvelle Héloïse*.[43] The assumption that reading, especially novels, is a sexualizing process echoed through a variety of texts in the eighteenth and nineteenth centuries. From Bienville, who cautioned parents to keep their daughters away from certain kinds of books lest they become nymphomaniacs, to Virey, who warned against educating women out of marriageability, to Mathieu, who viewed nearly all books as dangerous for the nerves of his oversensitive female patients, the medical profession embraced a model that targeted novels as one of the ultimate dangers for girls.[44] Like Rousseau, novelists exploited and played upon this paradigm. Madame de Tourvel in *Les Liaisons dangereuses* is prepared for her fall by reading *Clarissa*. After Lamiel turns up her nose at Fénelon and de Genlis, she discovers forbidden novels like *Les Quatre fils Aimon*, the bandit tales of Cartouche and Mandrin, and the titillations of trial reports in *La Gazette des tribunaux*. Balzac's *L'Envers de l'histoire contemporaine* summons Vanda de Mergi's rage to read as the source of both her father's debts and her hysterical neurosis. The Scott, Sand, Sue, Balzac, and *Paul et Virginie* on which Emma Bovary nourishes her illusions could have been picked from lists of novels targeted as dangerous by nineteenth-century moralists.[45]

The authors of medical and other advice manuals would find they had much in common with censors who sought to limit women's access to novels. If the reading girl fascinated eighteenth-century writers and their critics, nineteenth-century changes in literacy, reading practices, and the availability of new kinds of reading material only increased the obsession and enlarged the framework for repression.[46] Whereas eighteenth-century advice primarily concerned upper-class adolescent virgins like Rousseau's *"fille chaste,"* nineteenth-century remonstrances infringed upon the reading of women of all classes, ages, and levels of sexual experience.

The danger for the female reader lay, it seemed, in the desires she brought to fictions. Rousseau's "editor" shifts the blame from the book to the girl herself: "She who, despite this title, would dare to read a single page is a *fille perdue*. But she should not blame this book for her ruin, the damage was done long before. Since she has begun, let her finish reading: she has nothing more to lose." As far as he is concerned, a novel like *Julie* is better for women than books of philosophy and cannot harm girls who are already lost. Only the purest girl could be endangered by a novel, and any girl who reads a novel has already sacrificed her right to be seen as chaste.[47] What the double talk of Rousseau's "editor" avoids, however, is an account of what novels actually do to the "corrupted masses" for whom they are necessary. In a moment of passion, the girl might be drawn into a text and marked as forever lost, but how? Or why? And assuming she is chaste enough to know better or protected enough never to have been given a chance at such texts, then what *does* a *"fille chaste"* read? What can an angelic wife, already introduced into nuptial bliss, read with impunity? What are these women to do with themselves?

In 1829 Stéphanie de Genlis advised new brides to educate themselves: "In the hours of leisure that are left to you, cultivate your mind with solid readings; study books where human passions are superlatively painted." In addition to offering the young wife tips on running her household—managing servants, raising children, organizing private and public space—the education expert gives advice on furnishing "a little library" with works that develop "those lights of the spirit." Her list of required reading includes: "Fénelon's *Éducation des filles*; a selection of the letters of Mme. de Sévigné . . . ; selections from the letters of Mme. de Maintenon; the tragedies of Corneille and Racine; the most beautiful tragedies of Voltaire; Massillon's *Petit Carême*; Vauvenargues's *Pensées*; Rousseau's *Émile*; Bernardin de Saint-Pierre's *Paul et Virginie*; de Genlis's *Mlle de Clermont*."[48]

De Genlis embraced a model of reading already espoused by at least two of the authors, Fénelon and Rousseau, who would fill the bookcase of her model wife. The female reader, like the woman depicted in figure 6.2,[49] should aspire to *use* what she reads: "Wisdom and reason lie in taking from these writings everything that can be used." Unlike Fénelon and Rousseau, however, the governess of the royal children did not insist upon the physical, moral, or intellectual inferiority of the women she wished to educate. Following Fénelon's belief that women are the best police of the family,[50] de Genlis envisioned a means of preparing them for their special role of mother, spouse, and household manager. Behind this prescription for a well-armed police of virtue nevertheless lurked the fear, related by Fénelon, of the effects of a poorly educated woman:

It is given that the bad education of women does more harm than that of men, since the disorders of men often come from the bad educations they received from their mothers and from the passions that other women inspired in them at a later age. What intrigues history reports to us, what reversals of laws and morality, what bloody wars, what innovations against religion, what revolutions of the state,

(D'après un dessin de Greuze.)

Figure 6.2

This anonymous engraving after Greuze, "Une Scène de famille,"
from the January 1847 issue of the family periodical *Magasin
pittoresque* is accompanied by a story that asks women readers,
"Are you looking for happiness? Where do you expect to find it?
Outside your home, far away maybe. But look: here it is."

(BIBLIOTHÈQUE NATIONALE)

caused by the disorders of women! That's what proves the importance of raising girls well. Let us find the ways.[51]

Like Fénelon and Rousseau, de Genlis aspired to keep girls and wives away from certain kinds of fiction—fairy tales, for example—but she did not proscribe the novel as thoroughly as these earlier educators of girls. *Paul et Virginie* will somehow be "useful" to the model wife of de Genlis's book. The well-educated, well-disciplined, and well-mannered woman seems to exist at the expense of another, her monstrous shadow, the specter haunting nearly every work on women from Fénelon to Freud.

In the admission registers of the Salpêtrière asylum, in the space used to write down the source of the patient's ailment, a set of brief epithets marks the woes of nineteenth-century women: "sorrows from love; sorrows caused by the death of two children; sorrows caused by the death of her husband; loss of money; bad treatment by her husband; consequences of childbirth; poverty; old age; rape consummated at the age of fourteen, terror caused by the memory; abuse of strong liquors; abandonment." Below the name of a young woman who entered the hospital in 1845, one finds listed as the cause of madness: "bad readings" (*mauvaises lectures*).[52]

The belief that reading could drive women mad served as a fundamental tenet of nineteenth-century *aliénisme*. But unlike this unemployed woman whose reading left her "apathetic," or the other working-class women who populated the Salpêtrière with their "monomanias" and "partial deliria," the *bourgeoise* focused doctors' anxieties. Even in studies where virtually every case comes from the lower classes, the chapter devoted to prophylaxis revolved around the imagination of the bourgeois or aristocratic woman. Because she was supposedly all the more sensitive, her nerves proved the ideal model for the case studies out of which difference could be read.

Because she was all the more likely to *be* a reader, her involvement with literature became a regular topos for the medical advice manual as well as for case studies of hysteria. The *Dictionnaire des sciences médicales* advised forbidding hysterical girls "erotic readings and the sight of everything that exalts the senses and the imagination." Georget urged preventive action from early childhood for girls predisposed to hysteria: "Daily muscular exercises, frequently taken to a point of fatigue, manual work, the study of natural sciences, continual occupation of the mind. Avoid all those occasions, all those effects suited to exalt the imagination, excite passions, fill the head with illusions and chimeras." Repeating Tissot's warnings about novels and hysteria, Briquet called for strict discipline, limiting the upper-class girl to books that would in no way introduce her to feelings—"rudimentary books and . . . works of an ordinary devotion" (Br, 112, 608, 606).[53]

By representing the female reader as the exemplary touchstone for moralizing literature, critics of the novel provided a reading of female sexuality that made possible strategies of containment in spheres outside literature. Auguste Debay, whose most popular medical advice manual saw 173 editions, warned against any activity that might prevent women from enjoying their complete marital duties. Novels, he claimed, would not only occupy women's imaginations, but teach them "a thousand ruses for tricking a husband, where lying, perfidy, base plots, adulterous loves, implacable hatreds, vengeance and lessons about all crimes are hidden beneath literary flowers, so as not to show themselves in their horrible nudity." Women, he argued, needed to be single-mindedly poised for reproduction, not infected by literature: "From the hands of the mother, these novels fall into those of the daughter who reads avidly, poisoning herself with these readings. Blind mothers! Poor girls!"[54] The poison of novels like those Virey branded as hysterical was certainly seeping into the bloodstream of the daughters of the middle classes, for those girls were reading novels against all the experts' advice.

In his treatise on the education of women, Virey proposed solutions to "the irremediable evil" of corrupting novels whose "venom" penetrates everywhere, threatening the human species with extinction: "If I had the right, I swear that every woman who should turn to a novel instead of to her housework would be shut up for the rest of her life in a convent and forced to earn her living with her own hands." If novels are absolutely necessary, he continues, then they must be so clean that a respectable mother could read them to her daughter without blushing. As for the novels that would not meet his standards: "let all the others be annihilated and their authors hunted down."[55]

In the next two chapters, we will turn to trials that evoked a similar discourse of censorship. The novels on trial there, ranging from the *roman-feuilleton* to the works of Sand, would not have passed Virey's litmus test. Rather, they underwent trials that turned into more generalized trials of women. In chapter 8 we will examine the trials of the female reader at their most explicit by considering the debates surrounding Marie Cappelle-Lafarge, convicted in 1840 of poisoning her husband. Because the censorship trial we analyze in chapter 7 invoked an imaginary male as well as a female reader, it can show us in a more general way how concerns about reading encoded concerns about other social spheres. Ultimately, as the title of that chapter suggests, such a trial became very much a judgment of women's share.

7
The Politics of Seduction:
Trying Women's Share

"*La Démocratie pacifique* a un procès pour son
feuilleton, un roman intitulé *La Part des femmes.*"
—"Allons! bon!" dit Hussonnet. "Si on nous défend
notre part des femmes!"

"—*La Démocratie pacifique* has been prosecuted
because of its serial, a novel entitled *Women's Share.*"
—"Well, that's great!" said Hussonnet. "Are they going
to forbid us our share of women!"

—Flaubert, *L'Éducation Sentimentale*

*T*he literary trial sets off contagious reactions. Beginning with an
interpretive judgment by the government censors that a text
offends "public morality," other interpretations are called forth, other readings
set in motion. A *roman-feuilleton* that might otherwise have been read and
discarded by the several hundred contemporary subscribers of a leftist newspaper
instead makes headlines in the largest newspapers of its era. Its trial will be
read by thousands more readers than the novel ever might have hoped to reach.
The incident will generate incendiary commentary, finding its way into the
pages of canonized literature (Flaubert) and positioning the censored novel
alongside its illustrious cousins in catalogues of banned writings. This chapter
takes part in those contagious reactions, for it is the censors' work—and not
the author's or the newspaper's—that has brought us to examine this text. The
censors' attempt at exclusion, therefore, has ensured the survival of this novel;
the censors' prohibition has guaranteed this text further readings. The seizure
of two chapters of *La Part des femmes* has assured that this text will forever
put the censors' values on trial.

In May 1847, nine months before the Revolution of 1848 rocked France,
a Fourierist newspaper called *La Démocratie pacifique* began publishing a new
roman-feuilleton. Fourteen chapters of Antony Méray's *La Part des femmes*

had appeared when suddenly the state censors swept down, blocking the distribution of three separate issues of the newspaper. The first two issues contained sections of Méray's novel—sequences in which a young bourgeois is set up with a woman, and in which a "seduction" occurs. By the time of the third issue, the newspaper had suspended publication of the offending novel and was proceeding without a *feuilleton* to analyze government politics in its own customary—and previously never censored—way. Its editorial, "Two Categories of Offenses," accused the state of punishing the crimes of the poor while tolerating the crimes of the rich and powerful but made no mention of either Méray's novel or the censors' actions.

The trial that took place late that summer would explain the connection between these "three seizures in five days" as it linked the politics of censorship of literature with the politics of censorship of people. Meanwhile, nearly every newspaper in France took up arms against the state's censoring of this small newspaper founded in 1843 by Victor Considérant and François-Jean Cantagrel. The editorials of papers as diverse as *Le Constitutionnel, La Gazette de France,* and *Le Charivari* railed first against the literary censorship and then against the extraliterary seizure. Despite this incomparable show of public support, on September 2 the jury found the newspaper's editors and their author guilty as charged of "offenses against public morality and good morals." For their "crimes," Cantagrel and Méray were each fined one hundred francs and sentenced to one month in jail.

Unlike many papers targeted by Louis-Philippe's henchmen, *La Démocratie pacifique* would survive to report the turbulence of the February Revolution.[1] Though we can hardly attribute the success of the republicans to the incitement of a small leftist paper with a circulation of under two thousand,[2] the scandals surrounding this paper exposed an entire series of injustices and caused the government to make a farce out of its own policies of censorship. The concerns played out during this summer of scandal reemerged, not surprisingly, in republican discourse in the spring of 1848. In this sense, the February Days were among the reactions this trial was to unleash so contagiously.

The scandal of *La Part des femmes* stands in for the text itself, guaranteeing it incessant signifying potential, yet making the novel itself unreadable in both a literal and a figurative sense. In the place of the seized sections of the novel, *La Démocratie pacifique* and other papers produced detailed plot summaries, rehashed the circumstances leading to the censors' wrath, and reinterpreted the chapters almost no one had read in their entirety. The subscribers to *La Démocratie pacifique* never got their copies of these two chapters of their novel. They did not know until weeks later what the seized issues held. When the trial finally arrived to give substance to what had been banned, the novel's readers gained access only to selections out of context as an excuse for the censors' choices. In the place of the seized chapters, subscribers to the Fourierist newspaper could read the government's case against the novel, complete with the segments the censors found most scandalous. Instead of the missing chapters, readers of Méray's novel received an elaborated version of the scandal, framed by new interpretations and condemnations. They gained access to the original censored text only as a vehicle for state-sponsored literary criticism.

Yet those who began reading *La Démocratie pacifique*'s *feuilleton* in May 1847 could indeed read the *end* of the novel and might well have done so even before the trial began. Despite the seizure of its issues of June 30 and July 1, the paper resumed publication of the censored work. Although the censorship forced Méray to weigh his investment in his *original* version of the novel, he did indeed finish his story between July 21 and August 14, summarizing three chapters rather than risking further censorship. In this revised ending, the character who seemed particularly to have piqued the censors' interest, a *lorette* named Suzanne, had all but disappeared from the novel.

But the greatest change in Méray's text lay in how the censorship of the newspaper had transformed the ways this novel might be read. Although the novel continued for thirteen chapters after the confiscated issues, it gained an alternate ending in the form of the trial that reinstated portions of its excised middle chapters. In this *other* ending, which seems to double back to incorporate Méray's continuation of the novel, *La Part des femmes* became the basis for rereadings without end. We will be concerned here with these contagious interpretations and the readings they imposed, with the scandal around the text, and the contagious reactions it set off. This chapter considers the trial of *La Part des femmes* as a means for understanding the involvement of the French state of the July Monarchy in literary criticism, exclusion, and canonization. We will look first at the prosecution's framing of its case, then at the stakes for the defense's readings of the novel. The censored scenes will enable us to examine the fears of seduction in which both the novel and the censors engaged. Finally, we will turn to the broader continuum in which such a censorship case functioned and to the theories of dangerous reading implicit in the prosecution of all three issues of *La Démocratie pacifique*.

Seduction in Confinement

"Censorship is for Romanticism a torture, a prison, a dungeon," declared Victor Hugo not long after his play *Le Roi s'amuse* was closed down by the state.[3] Censorship not only puts authors and editors *into* prison[4] but also performs a disciplinary function on their works. The censorship trial asserts a continuity between a criminal and a moral offense. It stigmatizes the content of a work and criminalizes the production and consumption of texts it reads as stigmatized. As a result, the trial stigmatizes *readings* of the text as well.

Once a text is spotlighted by the censorship trial, one can no longer read it in isolation. Like the nineteenth-century women's prison Saint-Lazare, censorship has forever marked the victim who passes through it. Even today, we read such a text as police inspectors eyed women previously arrested on suspicion of clandestine prostitution, that is, for signs of suggestive behavior. Censorship has repositioned the text in a new framework of desire. The censors, like the police inspectors of the *Bureau des moeurs*, have a job of proving that the seized text is up to no good—and their trial of a text is as much consumed with endorsing their authority as it is with actually trying the work. This is why the readings put on display during a censorship trial can tell us so much about the investments of the state in certain strategies of surveillance. In the trial of a work like *La Part des femmes*, we are privy to the interpretations essential to a continued moral state of siege.

A censorship trial requires that the *reading* of the censors be able to open up a prison to which the literary perverse and textually marginal might be relegated. The state prosecution must be able to demonstrate that its interpretation is the only possible reading—just as a prosecutor in a murder trial must prove that no other verdict could be possible. The defense must show that other readings *are* possible and that the prosecution has misread the text. The trial therefore becomes a battle of theories of reading. What is at stake in this reading, the morality of the work, becomes a matter of interpretation and, ultimately, a question of frames of reference.

To analyze these interpretations we must redefine the boundaries of our text to include not only the novel on trial but also the text of the third confiscated issue of the paper as well as the trial transcripts, which appeared in *La Démocratie pacifique* between August 25 and September 1. By allowing the legal action to set the boundaries of our text, we broaden our inquiry to read this episode as the trial of the values of the Fourierists who published this newspaper, of the *roman-feuilleton* and the novel in general, of the readers the prosecutor sought to protect, and of the issues taken up by Méray's novel. We must also read this unbounded text as the trial of exemplary readings, and, for this reason, all accounts we give of the novel's content risk either replicating the prosecutor's vantage point or placing our own readings on trial. But the alternative—not retelling the story in any context—makes all readings impossible. My account focuses first on the portion of the novel that precedes the censorship, then concentrates on the readings given by the state to the censored episodes. After turning to defense rereadings of the novel and its censored scenes, we will look at the various endings of *La Part des femmes*.

La Part des femmes has the shares of a number of women in view. Juanna Dusable, poor but beautiful, loves young Léonce Lachaumelle, son of a provincial landholder who sees his children as chattel through whom he can increase his power and property. Léonce and Juanna watch sadly as teenage Ernestine Lachaumelle is engaged to a conservative deputy twice her age, yet Léonce goes on believing that his father will approve his passion for Juanna. What the novel calls *"les convenances"*—the constraints of society—assert themselves nonetheless: Léonce asks to marry dowryless Juanna. His father mocks him. In a chapter entitled "What is done to rich girls—What is owed to poor girls," part 1 of the novel culminates in the marriage of Léonce's sister (rich) Ernestine to the man of her father's choosing, and in Léonce's separation from his (poor)

beloved. Condemning the father who sends his daughter into "a forced prostitution, on the pretext of getting rid of her with a favorable return," the narrator
calls for a new morality in which poor girls get what they deserve and rich girls
are freed from paternal despotism.[5]

What comes next brings the novel temporarily to a stop. Part 2 of the novel
finds Léonce sent to study in Paris. His father's plot cuts to the heart of the
problem: his cousin Adelstan is to introduce the young heir to the pleasures
of the flesh. If the girl does not help Léonce forget his dowryless beloved,
Léonce's betrayals will surely suffice to show Juanna she has been forgotten.
The plot works and so do the censors: a drunken Léonce climbs into bed with
a poverty-stricken needleworker named Suzanne. The father's attempt at censoring his son's desires sends the state censors into action. The novel that
questions the values of the landholder comes to a sudden halt at exactly the
moment where those values seem to triumph.

What, then, according to the government censors, takes place in these two
chapters of *La Part des femmes* that so threatens "public morality"? Can we
recognize the "corruption" in these scenes alone, as the prosecutor contends,
or is the whole novel implicated by this censorship? To what extent is this the
trial of the novel in general, or of the *roman-feuilleton*, and not just the trial
of these censored sequences? What does the state prosecutor want his audience
to see in the scenes he so eagerly puts on display?

The censors of *La Démocratie pacifique* want to read this text into their
disciplinary powers by placing it in confinement. Unlike the 1857 case of
Madame Bovary, where the entire novel was put on trial, the prosecutor Bresson
puts the squeeze on this text by replaying its potentially felonious moments out
of context and in a kind of critical slow motion. He will set out to frame *La
Part des femmes* by likening it to a series of pornographic pictures:

> The *Démocratie pacifique* . . . has taken on a mission for the future and for
> reform . . . but it has overstepped all bounds in gathering together licentious
> pictures calculated to ruin the young. . . . The colorist writer has not made his
> pictures any less dangerous than those obscene engravings against which every
> day the law exercises severe penalties.[6]

Méray's text, argues the state prosecutor, deserves the maximum penalty in this
case because, like obscene pictures, it shows too much.

Bresson thus freezes five *tableaux vivants* for the court, demanding that the
audience see in them "all the details of an orgy" (8/30). The prosecutor's
framing of these scenes excises them from their context and places them into
his own frame of reference. By reading them out of context, he can no longer
easily label them pornographic, for they are now without beginning or end,
without continuity of characterization, without an apparent function, and without relation to any other elements of the text that might have given them
narrative or aesthetic coherence.[7] The trial, in fact, gives these scenes a new
beginning and end, assigns the characters its own continuity, and posits a read-

able function for the passages cited as immoral. More importantly, Bresson offers his own coherence to the five sections he chooses to cite—by emphasizing the different levels of *seduction* at work in the *feuilleton*.

For the censors of the July Monarchy, as we saw in chapter 6, the danger of a supposedly obscene image or explicit novel lay in the possibility that such a text could beguile an unsuspecting viewer or reader. Obsessed with the possibility that a text could breed contagion, Bresson metaphorically bodies forth the disease of seduction. The prosecutor imagines a scene of seduction that is not just the one performed by the text upon the reader but also, most significantly, the one depicted in the text. The prosecutor will return constantly to this metaphor of dangerous seduction to bolster his framing and his readings of the novel. His legal case as well as his authority depend on his ability to prove that the seduction *in* this text could create in its readers desires for just such pleasures. For the prosecutor, all *"séductions"* are dangerous, potentially capable of disseminating yet other horrors.

La Démocratie pacifique is dangerous, Bresson contends, because it stirs up passions with its ardent polemics. The novel in all forms is dangerous, and as a *roman-feuilleton* addressed to all ages and to all classes it represents even greater dangers. The novel in such an accessible form and in such a dangerous newspaper had already strained the boundaries of decency when it presented a seduction scene so explosive, Bresson contends, that it seemed capable of destroying the moral fiber of an entire nation. This trial represents the state's attempt to reestablish exemplary readings and to wrench the evil from the hands of readers before it can work its seductions everywhere. The five sequences cited by the prosecutor during the trial are supposed to show how the novel puts into action "ideas of libertinism that result in prostitution." In the course of the trial, he warns listeners, "we will find an offense against public morality, a lesson intended to defile principles and to lure those young people, under whose eyes the newspaper would fall, into licentious musings that might corrupt and ruin them" (8/30).

The perdition that terrifies Bresson is not that of the young woman whom the novel shows sinking into the form of prostitution that marks her as a *lorette*, willing to exchange her body for her keep. Unlike the corruption that marks this *fille perdue* once Léonce lays his hands on her, the "seduction" the prosecutor imagines depicted in the novel is the one the young heir's father has arranged: Léonce's initiation into the pleasures offered by women. And this seduction is precisely the one the prosecutor invokes as requiring censorship by all those members of the audience who, like himself, seek to "keep watch over the morals of our young people":

> Look, we are all fathers. . . . Well then, after these singular descriptions I have just given you, when each of you has to watch over his son, won't you be afraid that this page should fall into his hands, that he might become intoxicated by these lines, that he might *let himself be carried away by seductions, by the treacherous seductions* of a publication of that kind? (8/30, my emphases)

The slippage that marks the discourse of the prosecutor—from concern over the dangers that might befall "young people" to terror about the "treacherous seductions" that might beguile sons—elides one of the players in the scene of seduction while dispensing with the explicit theme of *La Part des femmes*. In Méray's words, quoted by the prosecutor as part of his case, this novel seeks to show "what dangers surround the young woman of the poor classes amid the bad examples and cynical words besieging her." Despite its author's self-censorship, Bresson reminds his audience, this text continues to betray "scenes of libertinism and practices of debauchery that the novel came to advocate and vindicate." It goes on disseminating "paintings fit to perturb the senses and to excite . . . evil passions." Suzanne, the working-class girl who has already been led astray into a "first seduction" by her envy of "the fate of young people richer than herself," is only the instrument of further immorality (8/30). The danger Bresson imagines lies in the seduction itself and therefore in the *seductions* such a text might work on its readers.

Yet, when Bresson reads these five carefully chosen fragments of Méray's novel, freezing the frames of what he labels lascivious paintings so as to brand each one with his own exemplary reading, the prosecutor seems to lose control. He goes far beyond simply isolating certain scenes as immoral. Rather, the excesses of his outrage, the extravagance of his call for repression, and the passion of his rhetoric suggest he reads something *into* the scenes he wants so desperately to see excised. The very reader who would free his society from textual seductions is himself led astray by the text he puts under surveillance.

The Spectacle of Morality

"In the second half of the nineteenth century, morality makes a spectacle out of itself," Jacqueline Rose declares in a reading of the Victorian novel.[8] For the July Monarchy as well—if not for the entire French nineteenth century—the visual became a matter of moral consequence. This is what authorized the prosecution, in the trial of *La Part des femmes*, to refer repeatedly to "obscene" images one might read, to paraphrase Rousseau, with one hand.[9] Erotic picture books like those proliferating in the late eighteenth century continued to be surreptitiously reproduced and marketed in such pleasure centers as the Palais-Royal. The nineteenth-century pornophile could also easily obtain individual reprints of the illustrations from works ranging from those by Sade and Louvet de Couvray to the likes of *Les Fouteries de bon goût*. Equally circulated in the underground were original mass-produced lithographs with titles like *Comment l'esprit vient aux filles*, *Seule? Hélas-oui!*, *La Femme qui n'y voit pas*, and *Plaisir sans crainte*.[10] By the mid-nineteenth century, the fascination with such pictures had even undergone a spectacular *mise-en-abime*, with the production of eroticized images of women reading (see figures 7.1 and 7.2).[11] Perhaps not surprisingly, Bresson's prosecution of the novel hinged upon his ability to draw

CONCLUSION DU ROMAN .

Figure 7.1

The prosecution and the defense in the trial of *La Part des femmes* could have been referring to images like this, which draw a causal relationship between the woman's reading of Louvet de Couvray's *Les Amours du Chevalier de Faublas* lying beside her on the ground, and her "seduction" by something other than books.

(BIBLIOTHÈQUE NATIONALE)

on the audience's fantasies about such licentious pictures. His entire case came to depend on the spectacle he made out of the scenes he framed.

Everyone knows, he tells the jury, about the insidiousness of the scenes of seduction in obscene engravings. Yet he never *shows* such images. Rather, he creates a fantasy of them by referring his audience to the literary scenes a prurient eye might fill in with its own graphic shading. He also never justifies the censorship of such prints or explains where the lines might be drawn between censored and uncensored pictures. Instead, he shows the audience how to read for the dangerous literary detail.

In four of the five scenes he reproduces in court, Bresson censors as smut the innuendoes that surround the body of the *lorette*. He condemns the novel for its refusal to gloss over the exposed body parts he eagerly unveils and for its contagious appeal to readers. He points to the obscene detail *in* these passages, as if these sequences would have deserved condemnation in any context. His first quote recounts Léonce's first perceptions of the *lorette*:

Figure 7.2

Charles Wheeler, *And So the Story Ends.* (Collection—Art Gallery of South Australia, Adelaide Morgan Thomas Bequest Fund 1927)

Suzanne was blond . . . with glints of gold, so joyous and so sweet to the gaze. Her dress, readied with skill, uncovered shapes of a splendor that purists might have found a little overstated; Léonce, to be sure, didn't think so. Besides her neck was so pure, her shoulders so softly curving downward and rounded; all that Suzanne let be seen was so white, so fresh, so young, so well-molded, with the object of catching the eye, the lips, and the hand, that you, to be sure, would not have judged any differently from him. (*PdF*, 6/30)

According to Bresson, this passage could not have uncovered more "nudities suited to stir up young people": "any such image is sure to have a definitively fatal effect upon the young imagination" (8/30). Yet we see remarkably little skin here. Can the prosecutor really be blustering about a neck described as "so pure," or shoulders depicted as "so softly curving downward and rounded"? Or does he take offense at the euphemism in this description of Suzanne that allows one to imagine that "all that Suzanne let be seen" descended below her neck and shoulders? But this "so white, so fresh, so young, so well-molded" portion of her body remains so thoroughly unnamed that even a reader looking for trouble would surely recall that this girl is on public display at a dinner party in a restaurant.

The prosecutor's second citation finds Léonce kissing Suzanne: "The voluptuous tepidity of this first touch of a woman's flesh produced in him a tremor of happiness, a quiver of sensuality. . . . He seized the astonished girl in his arms and began to cover her with kisses" (*PdF*, 6/30). According to Bresson, the author of this passage has not feared "setting fire to every element of passion" (8/30). What these elements might be remains uncertain, but Léonce's heated kiss, with its "tremor of happiness," has not been lost on the prosecutor. Bresson so focuses on the "veil" he sees stripped away that he skips over the next scene of the novel. In what the prosecutor elides, we learn that although Suzanne becomes Léonce's first lover that night, he will also be a first for her. Her own first lover has returned home to the provinces. Léonce will be the first man with whom she stays because she has economic needs. We will return later to Bresson's elision here, for the circumstances that led to Suzanne's second seduction are central to the scandal of *La Part des femmes*.

In Bresson's second citation as well as in the one that follows it, the prosecutor focuses with anguish on the awakening of passions in the body of the young bourgeois. The seduction that worries the censor is not that of the *lorette:* she has *already* been seduced; this text will only show her fall into prostitution. Rather, Bresson is concerned with what happens to Léonce. Although Suzanne's nubile body provides the temptation for the provincial landowner's son, the seduction related by the prosecutor is enacted by Léonce's cousin Adelstan, "a young man . . . who has followed the path where his passions have carried him, plunging himself into a life of libertinism and dissipation" (*PdF*, 6/30). The author of this novel, complains Bresson, has delivered Léonce into the hands of "artists of corruption," Adelstan and his mistress Juliette. Méray has predisposed his hero to such a seduction, claims Bresson, because the youth leaves home with a heart filled with "one of those passions born at age twenty" (8/30). In short, according to the prosecutor, the text shows how easily a young aristocrat might be seduced by a libertine when he has been allowed to nourish such a passion.

As Bresson retells the story amid his framing of the endangering episodes, this "homosocial" seduction depends upon an already awakened sensuality, as if Suzanne arrives on scene simply to release the "sexual misery" Léonce could not satisfy with his dreamgirl in the country.[12] In outlining the confiscated episodes of seduction, the prosecutor curiously conflates the roles of the author (who sets up the seduction), the libertine cousin Adelstan (who procures the seduction), the working-class Suzanne (who serves as the agent of the seduction), and the girl who stirred up all the excitement in the first place. Bresson's framing lets him place Juanna, the girl left behind, at the origin of the corruption, because these two chapters find Léonce repeatedly contemplating her. Such a framing also allows the prosecutor to elide a figure who is as much the source of this seduction as Adelstan, Suzanne, or Juanna, namely, Léonce's father. Bresson's moral condemnation of the text requires an elision of the father's role in these turpitudes. In the novel, however, the fate of all these characters turns on the duplicity of the father who *procures this seduction* in order to *censor* his son's desires.

In the prosecutor's third citation, bed arrangements are made, the seduction is prepared, and ultimately a candle is left flickering upon "the sparkling skin of the crazy virgin (*vierge folle*) who had entrusted herself to [Léonce]" (*PdF*, 6/30). Here again, the prosecutor must work hard to see beyond the protagonist's desire for Suzanne's "beautiful shoulders," for the chapter prudishly closes on that image: "We will leave this study of manners at the threshold that they have just crossed," the novel announces, censoring itself in advance of the first seizure, blocking our view with its reproach of Léonce's "weakness of the flesh" (*PdF*, 6/30). Only the hero's flash of regret for Juanna and the candleglow on her rival's skin will momentarily slow the chapter's fade to black. Bresson manages nevertheless to see a "lubricity" breaking out behind the curtain of the chapter ending, signaling "the swift invasion of vice which is accepted and deified" (8/30). Bresson's rereading of this passage sees Léonce enslaved to agents of evil. But how can we know this "invasion of vice" has been accepted, let alone deified, when the novel does not let its readers see beyond the flickering candle?

The agent of vice Bresson envisions in his third citation elicits his moral condemnation in his fourth. Gazing intently upon the figure of Suzanne as she lies in bed the next morning watching her sleeping lover, Bresson ignores the substance of the passage he quotes. There the girl expresses her dreams of marriage to the likes of Léonce, her sadness that no one like him will ever want her for more than her body, her realization that she has become as easy as her *lorette* friend Juliette, and her regret that in order to wrench herself from poverty she has been obliged to become a *"fille perdue."* Bresson appropriates Suzanne's own voice in order to condemn her:

> Here is the awakening of this girl of seventeen. Here begins her vindication. After all, what can one blame her for? She was easy; she wanted to lead a more refined life than that of the men around her. There's no fault in that. There is only weakness. That's how far morality is stretched. These are the principles which the novel tries to make honorable. (8/30)

The prosecutor's moral stance is unequivocal: he wants the *lorette* censored. Bresson complains that the text excuses her error as "a weakness," stretching "morality" beyond propriety and validating the principles of prostitution. But what does Bresson want his audience to reproach Suzanne for? What reason does he want her to give for her fall if not "a weakness"? What principles would he make *dishonorable?* He does not tell. Yet his framework suggests he has an investment in emphasizing Suzanne's seduction of Léonce and in leaving out the story of how *she* was herself first seduced: horrified by her father's plans to marry her to a brutal alcoholic, the young woman "contented herself with letting herself be forced to accept asylum in the room of her generous protector" (*PdF*, 7/1).[13]

Suzanne's remorseful recollections end when Léonce awakens and succumbs again to the *lorette*'s charms. Bresson reads this scene in its entirety—up to and including a paragraph in which the narrator invokes the censor: "Alas, alas," the novel intones, "What are moralists going to say about him? A lot of very judicious things without a doubt" (*PdF*, 7/1). Again Bresson will take up arms against seduction, gazing through the eyes of Léonce to see an orgy in detail: "Not only do they show you the young man succumbing to seduction, but still more, they push the reader to the very foot of the bed; they make him touch with a finger all his desires; they make palpable for him all the charms that they describe with pleasure" (8/30).

It is precisely at this moment, gazing through the reader's eyes at the many temptations in this text, that Bresson places himself at risk. In order to catch the reader at the foot of the bed, touching his desires with his fingertips, the prosecutor must figure himself as that reader—and look through the eyes of Léonce at the moment of his seduction. Bresson has to write between the lines of the novel his own fantasy of what Léonce has seen and touched—and he must do so taunted by a text that bares the hypocrisy of the moralist's stance.

Bresson's so-called paintings of the obscene, as we have seen, revolve around several isolated moments he invests with his own significance. Challenged by the defense for twisting the meaning of these passages, for giving them through his oral presentation "a perverse intention that was not the author's intentions" (8/30), Bresson will nevertheless focus on the obscene detail *in* these texts, as though nothing in their context could alter their immorality. According to the prosecutor, Méray does his damage by showing what should have remained *covered up.* Yet even if we imagine Bresson insinuating perverse details through voice inflections, we see less skin in the passages read aloud than in the prosecutor's comments on them. The scandal of this "exposure" begins to resemble that of Manet's *Olympia:* like the critics who swarmed angrily around Olympia's flexed hand,[14] the censor returns constantly to the moment when the chapter ends and the lights go off, as if he could see something in the darkness that we are left only to imagine. Somehow Bresson has glimpsed "sensual objects" in the twilight that have become for him "altogether palpable" (9/1).

In four out of five of the sequences he frames, Bresson describes the representation of the female body as a locus of sexuality. The gaze he evokes would seek visual pleasure in her represented body. The text has made her the lure for Léonce's gaze. By insisting on the power of "lascivious literary paintings" to seduce the reader, Bresson makes the *lorette* the lure for the reader's gaze as well.[15] In demanding a condemnation of Méray and *La Démocratie pacifique,* Bresson ultimately seeks to censor what later psychoanalytic theorists have come to call scopophilia; he wants to punish *the text* for representing a Peeping Tom whose look led to satisfaction. The fantasy he summons — of a libertine reveling at the keyhole in the sexual exploits of others — may initially seem to stigmatize the prosecuted work but the gazing eye begins to resemble his own far too closely.

What matters in looking, Teresa de Lauretis has argued, is as much the story we give to that process as the image we take in.[16] The voyeur who is always threatened by the possibility of being caught in the act of looking[17] is caught by the story his look gives him. He is ensnared by the other he imagines creeping up on him as he satisfies his scopic drive, but that other is as much a part of his gaze — and therefore of his desire — as the body he views through the keyhole. He is haunted by the possibility that the woman he watches will notice and censor his gaze. The narrative he gives to his voyeurism reverts to a censorship like the father's in the Freudian fantasy of castration, but the censoring look now comes from the female. If the voyeur is to regain control, he must put her under consideration in some other way and ensure that she cannot threaten his look with a desire outside his field of vision. He must retell the story in such a way as to recast the father as censor, even if at the expense of his own visual pleasure.[18]

Bresson's narrative of voyeurism deploys just such a scene of censorship, imposing from outside the "extra look" that overtakes the desiring viewer just at the moment of satisfaction.[19] The prosecutor's refusal of anything outside the frame, however, whether narrative closure or authorial intention, blocks those limits that might put a cap on the threatening desire. His represented viewer goes on looking, his gaze overtaken by the one who makes it known. Bresson must account for his own gaze and in doing so puts his motives on the line. His investments in the frame suddenly come into perspective as part of the picture.[20]

In order to prescribe such a spectacular morality, Bresson must himself reproduce the dangerous gaze as a part of a relay of looks. He must put on display the transgression he deems excessive. In casting Léonce in a transgressive role along with Méray, the newspaper editors, and even the endangered readers, the prosecutor must reproduce the voyeuristic gaze. This leaves him with a dilemma, for whether he wants to represent as dangerous the subjects seen by the voyeur or the transgressive results of Léonce's looking, in order to show the dangers of seeing Bresson must also look like a libertine.

Defending Moral Vision

The voyeuristic gaze endangers Bresson's rational scientific gaze while nevertheless placing the defense attorneys Favre and Hennequin in the awkward position of having to look at the novel through his fantasmatic frames of reference. Seeking to establish an alternative theory of reading, the defense insists on the importance of these censored scenes in the overall framework of the novel. Instead of defending the scenes Bresson has compared to obscene engravings, the Fourierists argue that the work could not achieve its moral aims without painting such scenes of passion. Bresson's frames are the problem, they contend, for these frames block the view of the whole novel, leading to a misreading of its intentions. Although Hennequin does insist that the "moment of infidelity" in Méray's novel is more "veiled" than Bresson imagines, the defense underscores the importance of *painting* vividly the temptations that the novel will go on to condemn. The novel cannot denounce the notion that Léonce should "sow his oats" (*PdF*, 6/19) without showing how bad that act can be.

The defense attorneys' case requires them to show that the real issues lie outside Bresson's bracketed scenes. By insisting on the inconsistencies in Bresson's framing strategies, they try to catch him in the snares of his own framework. Through careful argumentation, they successfully show that his theories of reading are tainted by politics and vengeance against their paper. Yet, they make the mistake of validating Bresson's views of dangerous engravings and contagious seduction. Their consensus on the potential dangers of any text ultimately gives Bresson the moral ground to continue trying *La Part des femmes*.

The prosecution fleshes obscene pictures out of the words and air. The defense brings pornography right into the courtroom, taunting Bresson with his own views:

> Here is a roll of engravings; I will not unroll it, I don't want to pollute my vision yet again; but gentlemen, the jury may cast a glance and they will recognize those images that they have already seen on our boulevards. Oh! the society that allows similar things to be exhibited does not have chaste ways, and literature, which is the expression of those ways, can certainly have some freedom. (9/1)

A novel in which one finds, even according to Favre, a few risqué pictures hardly deserves to pay for what multiplies around it. Besides, as both defense attorneys will insist, the novel uses these paintings of "passion" to order a moral vision:

> You have rightly spoken of this dangerous trade in obscene images, which come from the underground with a commercial intention to corrupt public morals. Ah! Be pitiless against those who give themselves over to this shameful trade; that is just, and we will, along with all honorable people, applaud your severity. But what similarity is there in the publication for which Cantagrel and Méray have been blamed? This is no clandestine publication, it is a moral work, and if there are some pictures that one might want more reserved, they are hardly as revealing as other writings that won their authors honors and rewards. (9/1)

In parts of the novel ignored by the court, the defense attorneys argue, the son's debauchery will be condemned by its results. Like Virgil's *Aeneid* and Richardson's *Clarissa*, Méray's plot will serve the moral aims embraced by the prosecutor himself for it will show that the wages of seduction are loss for all involved.[21] Insisting that Méray does not exalt vice, but rather punishes it, the defense seeks to demonstrate how these scenes of seduction work in the context of the whole:

> We counted on the temptations of Paris to make the young man reasonable; it is necessary for the direction of the novel, for the sincere moral that must come of it. But temptation, don't forget, has to be seductive. . . . Léonce therefore had to be seriously tempted; the paintings of seduction had to be vivid for us to understand how quickly this young man would forget his pledge of fidelity to Juanna. Otherwise the novel would become altogether unrealistic. (9/1)

According to the defense, this novel tells a typical story of "a thwarted love," but it does so "with all the incidents that might illuminate the vices of the society in which we live" (8/30). The paintings of seductions accompanying this story would therefore serve as a critique of social evils.[22] The moralist novelist can, in this view, only achieve his ends by offending "public morality." The painter of morals can only censor vice by depicting it. The good novelist could only seduce his reader with a scene that would demand censorship.

The intrigues of this circular logic figure Suzanne's body as requiring censorship from every angle. The confiscation of the three issues of *Démocratie pacifique* secures that censorship, for she has vanished when the novel resumes. In summaries of the three chapters censored in advance by their author, Suzanne's share in the novel is reduced to a bit of hearsay: she has become a prostitute locked away in Saint-Lazare.[23]

The novel's plot has thus turned in a number of ways from seduction to censorship. Both of the above-mentioned alternate endings of the text—each significantly different from the author's original plan—substitute discipline for titillation. The first of these endings ultimately framed the text with the scandal and trial, censoring seduction through bureaucratic means. The second ending, consisting of the concluding chapters published in late July and early August, occupied a liminal space between the confiscation and the trial of the novel.

And although Méray claimed to have changed only the three chapters concerning the *lorette*, the novel's actual handling of themes of censorship and literary seductions makes one wonder if the scandal transformed the novel into a kind of self-defense. During the trial, Favre and Hennequin used summaries of the rest of the novel to argue for its morality. As they suggested, the remainder of the novel can indeed be viewed as actively interrogating the censor's act.

The seduction at the beginning of part 2 of the novel gives way to the father's continuing efforts to censor his son's desires. Monsieur Lachaumelle fakes letters to his son in Paris that suggest to Léonce that his best friend, the Fourierist Louis-René, has seduced his beloved Juanna. His own infidelity justified, Léonce leads a life of remorseless debauchery in Paris. Meanwhile Lachaumelle makes sure Juanna finds out about her boyfriend's inconstancy. After intercepting his son's letters before they reach the girl, he stages a scene in which he violently reproaches his son's debauchery in front of Juanna and her mother. The impressionable Juanna falls violently into a hysterical madness the novel calls "accesses of hypochondria" (*PdF*, 7/29).[24] Her mother dies, leaving her daughter to the humiliations of Lachaumelle who continues to worry that his son will return to the now even poorer girl. Thoroughly mortified by Lachaumelle, Juanna sets out for Paris in a delirium to find out if the father has told the truth about Léonce forgetting her. She arrives in the middle of a party only to find Léonce dead drunk and unable to defend her against the libertine Adelstan. Léonce's old friend Louis-René arrives at the apartment just in time to rescue her from Adelstan's advances. As Lachaumelle plots anew to keep Juanna safely out of his son's reach, the young Fourierist Louis-René manages to reveal the father's duplicity to the son. He gets an uncensored letter through to Léonce who rushes home, hoping to make amends. As luck would have it, he arrives just as the melancholic Juanna performs suicidal feats in a boat. She misreads Léonce's concern for her safety as a confirmation that the youth no longer loves her and drowns despite his attempts to save her.

In an epilogue that resumes the story ten years later, Léonce meets his old friend Louis-René beside the very river where his beloved drowned. There he undergoes a conversion to Fourierism, which will enable him to join in the charity work of those who seek to improve the lot of girls like Suzanne, Ernestine, and Juanna.[25] Framing the novel with a political statement, the epilogue affirms that men working together can save women. It also affirms that the desire to do so can be contagious.

The defense attorneys argued that it is this contagious political discourse that has brought down the wrath of the censors upon their newspaper. Pointing to the "third seizure," of their political editorial—and not of the novel—Hennequin mocks the state censors for trying to use an accusation of immorality to get at the politics of *La Démocratie pacifique*. Hennequin correctly points to the prosecution's conflation of political questions (about property and propriety—*la propriété*—for example) and moral questions. Throughout, the prosecutor's case is tinged with contempt for the Fourierists' values he claims pervade the immoral sequences. The scandal the Fourierists choose to make out of the body of the prostitute, however, places the defense's most convincing arguments at risk.

The defense attorneys try to break open Bresson's frames by focusing our gaze on what occurs in and around the discourse of the *lorette*. Suzanne serves as the source and compulsion of their narrative as well, for it is upon her body that the stakes for seduction in this novel have been set. If she engenders smut, she also serves as the lure that traps the censoring gaze. She serves at the same time, however, as a snare for the defense lawyers, who need to read her as dangerous to justify the novel's "moral" purpose. Thus, her body is the one locus of contagion everyone seems to agree upon. The disagreement in this courtroom seems to derive from disagreements on how the woman's share, in her, should be put on trial.

According to Méray's attorney, the author of *La Part des femmes* uses Suzanne's body to indict society's treatment of women. With its vivid depiction of the young man's seduction into a life of debauchery, the novel claims to expose the results of a moral order based on exchanging women and wealth through marriage. Through its narrative of the *lorette*'s desires, it pleads for the elimination of arranged marriages *and* prostitution. By means of its representation of the libertine ways of the upper classes, it tries to undermine the values assigned to property at the expense of personal liberty.[26]

Yet even as the novel condemns prostitution of women inside and outside of marriage, it also performs a censorship of the women it claims to wish to help. Even as it puts the father's desires on trial, it forbids men the women they desire. Even as it questions the double standards surrounding seduction, the only kind of seduction it leaves in place is political.

The Politics of Seduction

Bresson reads the Fourierist politics as a call for libertinism and an approval of prostitution. He takes their purpose to be revolutionary (and therefore not at all *pacifique*) and links them with social upheaval in every domain. In fact, his description of the newspaper's views finds an ironic equivalent in the first half of *La Part des femmes*. When the novel's young Fourierist voices his beliefs at a dinner party, a conservative character condemns the phalansterian cause by asserting that "these men have as their goal the sharing of women and possessions." Surely, insists Mme. de Logny, Louis-René isn't one of those people whose doctrine wounds "all our feelings of modesty and maternal love by destroying the family" (*PdF*, 6/17). Bresson's facile misconceptions about Fourierism lead him to blur the newspaper's values in a similar way and to impute to the phalansterians almost every social ill.[27]

Since the novel broaches questions of the family, property, prostitution, sexuality, and even politics, Bresson can connect every impropriety to a political view and every political value to the framed scenes he calls obscene. He transforms this text into an extension of dangerous political values without ever acknowledging the defense's presentation of the narrative context for the scenes of seduction. He refuses to spar with the defense attorneys on the politics of the newspaper, repeating insistently that the real issue is in the scenes of seduction themselves. The brilliance of his case is that he indicts the margins and the marginal, all the while claiming that neither makes any difference.

The prosecutor milks for all its worth the novel's attempt to put women's share on trial. On the basis of the story of a *lorette* and a lovesick young man, he manages to put the values of an entire social movement on trial. He uses the novel's indictment of prostitution to condemn the text for incitement to debauchery. He exploits the narrative's protest of inequality for working-class girls to censor every reader who might find comfort in these views.

"They have represented us as the enemies of society, as the enemies of property, as men speculating on scandal," claims editor Cantagrel at the end of the trial (9/1). The defense attorney Hennequin has accused the prosecutor of knowing too little about their movement and therefore of lapsing into speculations without substance. In his final statement, Cantagrel invites the prosecutor to see the "spectacle" at their offices: "social regeneration by the very moral path of solidarity." He justifies the values of his movement as a defense of order, of liberty, of *la propriété*, and above all, of "upright and beneficial doctrines." He reminds the court of his movement's political support of the July Monarchy between 1832 and 1840, insisting that the Fourierists have only withdrawn their backing because the government has followed a path that compromises order, honesty, and propriety (9/1).

Speaking for himself as well as for the Fourierist author and editors, the defense attorney summarizes the goals of their movement:

> What we want are associations where the owner can enter freely into [industrial enterprises], which are at the same time less oppressive for the worker. We want a society that could create new values to reconcile the interests and the rights of all. Nurseries, asylums, communal bakeries and butchers, these are the germs of the community such as we understand it, such as we hope to realize it by persuasion alone, by constituting agricultural social colonies. (9/1)

The novel embraces these values, becoming a ploy for such persuasion and a plea for social change. Its Fourierist character not only delivers similar speeches, but its hero Léonce learns through his sorrows the need for such a community and the evils of the values that he has been raised to endorse.

But what of Suzanne amid all this proselytizing and conversion? What happens to the *lorette* when the moral values of the Fourierists have taken over? What role does she finally play, seduced and censored, in this carnival of dangerous reading? Should we assume that her author went to prison because her dangers were as excessive as the prosecutor tried to show? Should we read the outcome of the trial as a confirmation that the *lorette* enabled the stories of other injustices to be told? Or is her story only told in the place of other excesses—those in the government, for example? What are we to make of the guilty verdict in the trial of a novel that itself put the working girl's share on trial?

In his much applauded lectures at the Collège de France in Spring 1848, published as *Histoire morale des femmes* in the same year, the republican Ernest Legouvé demanded a new approach to the sexual intrigues we have seen thematized in Méray's novel. His chapter entitled *"Séduction"* opens with a hypothetical question: "If we said there is a country where chastity is given such a high value for women that it is called their honor," should we not expect a law that punishes any *"séducteur"* twice as severely as any girl who might be *"séduite?"* The conditions he protests recall those we have seen in the courtroom of 1847: "As to seduction, at least to the kind men practice, the law declares that it doesn't exist when a girl has reached the age of fifteen; from then on, she is the one who is always supposed to do the seducing." According to French law, Legouvé points out, no girl over fifteen could be "seduced"—whether that meant sweet-talked, coerced, or raped. No matter what her seducer might have promised, or what the man might have done to coerce her "accord," the girl had no legal recourse to demand either the punishment of her seducer or his responsible involvement in any results of the seduction. For lack of laws holding him responsible, the girl must silently endure social stigmas. For lack of state authorization of paternity suits, seduced women were left with sole responsibility for their children.[28] The regulations Legouvé would institute would shift the burden of protecting a woman's virtue away from her and onto the state. They would require the government to censor the man for the results of his duplicity.[29] While Frégier wanted to keep closer watch over women, shielding them from the workplace and the streets, Legouvé sought to hold men accountable for sexual encounters—one reason for his popularity among feminists in 1848.[30] Unlike Fourier, who demanded women's right to sexual pleasure, Legouvé called for women's right to be protected from the pleasure-seeking of men.

Fourier's followers in the 1840s—Considérant, Cantagrel, Méray, and Hennequin, among others—depended upon a fantasmatic scene of seduction closely resembling the one republicans like Legouvé touted in 1848. Like Frégier, they were far more concerned with maintaining a certain familial order than with improving the lot of women like Suzanne. The associations they embraced would seek to make divorce legal, but they would never take the risk of promoting female desire. Like the censors, the Fourierists sought to speculate on scandals in the woman's body but only insofar as those scandals helped men realize the necessity of phalansterian associations. The editors of *La Démocratie pacifique*, their censored author, and their attorneys wanted to put the *lorette* Suzanne back into the novel as a whole, but they only wanted her for her trade. They would put the scene of seduction back into the novel in order to censor the system that permitted traffic in her body.

Méray's novel, therefore, concerned itself with seduction in terms much like those that haunted Bresson. It embraced a version of censorship that traded upon the bodies of its whore and its hysteric and required the sacrifice of both — one to Saint-Lazare, the other to death — before it could achieve its political ends. If we believe the novel's defenders, the sex scenes in its center set up the novel's creation of a Fourierist moral order in a pastoral scene of redemption. Its Magdalen, the defense claimed, was as much a part of that redemption by virtue as her biblical equal. Although the novel actively thematized the moralists attempting to censor it, it took up their fears of contagion and seduction. Although it claimed to serve very different political ends, it nevertheless worked its seductions in a way that aggressively excluded women. Although this text claimed to protest the impossibility of love in a repressive society, it actualized that impossibility. The politics of the novel and those of the censor emerge with striking structural similarities: these are complaints exchanged between men. The scene of seduction appears in this light as a framework for other debates; it produces a locale for arguments about a seduction whose politics is far more than literary.

The Third Seizure

The political editorial says more than it means and means more than it says, setting off rhetorical reactions like firecrackers while only hinting at what might explode, threatening dangers it refuses to name. Although charges were dropped against *La Démocratie pacifique* for its seized editorial of July 4, the trial of Méray's novel continued to focus attention on the rhetoric of the editorial. The indictment of the literary text placed the motives of the "third seizure" on trial. Was the trial of Méray's novel only a ploy by the government, a safe way of harassing the Fourierists without having to take on more powerful, but equally provocative, editorialists? Was the defense right in claiming that the state was pursuing, "by means of the *feuilleton*, the political theories of a daily paper" (9/1)? Or was there a connection between the three confiscations that the defense lawyers could not admit without compromising their case? Did the Fourierist newspaper create an intentional relationship between its editorial views and its literary supplement? Did the censors pick up on that intertextuality, or did they overread a relationship between the rhetoric of the literary text and the rhetoric of the editorial? And if the connection created by the censors was entirely fantasmatic, then what projections enabled them to read the three texts as interrelated? What dangers did they name to justify the third confiscation?

"You are preparing France and Europe for new convulsions," warned the editors of *La Démocratie pacifique* in their censored editorial. "It is not ... the rich but the poor who have elevated you to power," the editorial reminds the government officials it labels "ungratefuls!"[31] The article, entitled "Two Categories of Offenses," accuses the state of punishing the crimes of the poor while it tolerates the other category of offense, the crimes of the rich and powerful. "While the poor plundered wheat stores, the rich looted the finances of the state and the purses of private individuals," the editorial declares. So why, it continues, has the government failed to bring the rich to justice? Since the state pursues pitilessly the crimes of the working class and crimes of hunger, the editors insist that the justice system of their country should equally rise up "to illuminate all these disorders and bring all these criminals to justice." Certainly, the editors continue, the government does not hesitate for lack of police: "It doesn't wait to act until these offenses are denounced by the papers and in court, or talked about in all citizen meetings. It pursues them, scrupulously and inquisitorially researching the least founded suspicion and the vaguest rumor." Although the editorial names the incidents where the working class has been brought to trial, it avoids pointing the finger at those who have committed the other "category of offense." Although the editors of La Démocratie pacifique invoke a special kind of justice in great detail, they allow the criminals in question to be as "chimerical" as the plots they contend the government has actually brought to trial. Despite softened reminders of their "peaceful and conciliatory efforts," the newspaper calls for a new terror to prevent the mass hysteria of another revolution.

One can easily read into this editorial what fears of censorship had forced out. For weeks in the pages of every newspaper in France a scandal had been unfolding that would in the long run contribute to the downfall of the July Monarchy. Two ex-ministers were charged with accepting bribes in exchange for government concessions during the division of stocks in the railway of the North. Cunin-Gridaine, minister of commerce and agriculture, and Mackau, minister of the seas, managed to escape charges, although the government pursued two of the other guilty parties, Teste (minister of public works and a Peer of France) and General Cubières (also a Peer and a former cabinet minister). Teste tried to commit suicide but failed and was condemned to prison and fines. Because one of the primary witnesses, Pellaprat, refused to appear in court, other clearly guilty parties went unpunished.[32]

The Teste-Cubières incident proved to be the first in a series of scandals that racked Louis-Philippe's government during the summer of 1847. The "Two Categories of Offenses" summoned by the editorial of La Démocratie pacifique quickly came to include a number of new crimes among those committed by the "rich and powerful" as well as a radical increase in the crackdowns on the press that reported and protested the inequities in governmental justice. In the course of August 1847, even before the trial of La Part des femmes, La Démocratie pacifique was again seized—this time for its reporting a further scandal in the upper echelons of Louis-Philippe's supporters. On August 18, 1847, the Duc de Choiseul-Praslin, a Peer of France, brutally murdered his wife, then committed suicide while in police custody, thereby escaping punishment. Three other newspapers, the satirical leftist Charivari, the right-wing Gazette de France, and the republican National equally caught the wrath of the censors. The last of these trials was still be underway when the February Revolution brought an end to the monarchy's version of justice.

Meanwhile Émile de Girardin, powerful editor of *La Presse*, continued his assault on the government's failure to punish the crimes in its own ranks. *La Presse*, which like *Le Siècle* and *Le Constitutionnel* had an average press run of over twenty-thousand, had turned in 1847 from supporting the regime to active opposition. Girardin's insults had already seen him conveyed before the Peers for remarks about the sale of peerages—but even then he was acquitted following testimony behind closed doors.[33] The editors of *La Démocratie pacifique* were not alone in supposing that the confiscation of their paper was related to government outrage over Girardin's editorial stances. Considérant and Cantagrel had replicated too closely the views of *La Presse*, argued many of their supporters. Rather than enter into combat with the editor of the largest newspaper in Paris, the government seemed to have censored one of the smallest—and most vulnerable—papers. *Le Courrier du Nord* contended that the third seizure was part of an attempt to silence all papers by making them think anyone could be persecuted: "War on the weak today, war on the strong tomorrow!" "Logically," commented *Le Constitutionnel*, "it wasn't *La Démocratie pacifique* that should have been seized."[34]

The validity of this hypothesis was tested on July 5 when Girardin reproduced *La Démocratie pacifique*'s censored editorial. Although news initially spread that *La Presse* had itself been confiscated, when this proved false, other papers quickly registered the inequities in the government's reaction: "the same article, published in a peaceful newspaper is guilty in the eyes of the court but innocent in a conservative newspaper," complained *La Réforme*.[35] In an ironic commentary upon Girardin's taunting of the censors, the editors of *La Démocratie pacifique* suggested that the real reason for the third confiscation lay in the list of plays they published on July 4. After all, sniped the editorial, theaters are nearly as immoral as the Ministry of Public Works, the Chamber of Peers, and the Bourse. *Marion de Lorme* was playing in the *Comédie Française*, as were a play by Molière and one by Schiller containing a *lorette*. "The most moral theater is definitely the most dangerous," the editors assert sarcastically, for this list of plays was the only thing in the confiscated issue that was not taken up by another paper. For the Fourierists, Girardin's ploy had become yet another example of the "two categories of offenses" discussed in their censored editorial. *La Presse* had joined the ranks of "the rich and powerful" capable of transgressing the law while offenses "committed by poor devils" like themselves were punished.[36]

The story of the novel *La Part des femmes* got in the way of this battle over the rhetoric of editorials. It interfered with the best of intentions of the government censors and with the best of defenses for the editors of *La Démocratie pacifique*. Like the prostitute who raised her skirts to the gunmen of the National Guard in 1848, the novel caught fire from every angle. Regardless of its relationship to other scandals, this literary work took the fall.

Whatever its author's intentions, the *feuilleton* assumed the force of an allegory amid these scandals over justice and equality. The Teste-Cubières scandal read intrigues into it. The editorial of July 4 made the *lorette* Suzanne into an emblem for the hungry worker who suffered punishment for wanting more. The third seizure—this time of that very editorial—transformed the editorial views of the newspaper into an extension of what the government would censor as immoral in a literary work. The response of other newspapers turned these three censored episodes into continuations of the same story. But which one? Of the novel, perhaps. Of the government ministry scandal, to be sure. But above all, these three confiscated issues testified to the inequities in the justice system, and bore witness to the inequitable censorship practiced by the state upon texts and people alike.

Whether or not the rest of the press approved of the *roman-feuilleton*, they rose up almost without exception in support of *La Démocratie pacifique.*[37] Some newspapers agreed that Méray's novel unclothed its characters a bit too much; others condemned the *feuilleton* genre, noting that Méray's work seemed tame by comparison; still others offered advice to Méray and the newspaper's editors to help them win their case. But with the exception of the *Journal des débats*, which supported the government, the press expressed outrage at the confiscations, reading the third one as part of a much larger scandal. *Le Charivari* depicted the king's prosecutor in search of a newspaper to sacrifice to the minotaur-like minister of justice.[38] *La Réforme* accused the attorney general of trying to reestablish government equilibrium by seizing the story of a student and a *lorette*.[39] The German *Grenzboten* read the censored literary episodes as an allegory of the political scandal brewing in the Ministry of France. It pointed out that even as Suzanne was seen selling her innocence for "a bit of luxury," peerages, laws, and even ministerial favors were being sold "for a bit of luxury too." *La Démocratie pacifique* erred in sacrificing old morals for new ones, exclaimed the German paper: "Heavens! How France needs the censors to defend decency!"[40]

Dangerous Seductions

The attorney general targeted *La Part des femmes* because, as almost every newspaper in France believed, it could try the values of the newspaper by means of a literary text more easily than by means of its editorial policy. To censor the political expression of this small newspaper while ignoring others that voiced the same views would, indeed, court greater scandals and even louder protests about injustice and inequality. Political censorship might send the government into a more terrifying spiral of public outrage. Moral censorship seemed as permissible as a father's attempt to protect his child from degradation. The state therefore gambled on current fears of the novel, bourgeois discomfort with the "new readers," and widespread desires to censor the reading matter of young people, workers, and women. The government depended on a commonly shared terror of dangerous pictures and dangerous readings. The prosecutors sought to capitalize on fears about seduction to censor political views as well as literary scenes.

Those fears of seduction were so widespread that the novel depended on one kind, that of a youth by a prostitute, to promote its political ends. It depended on another kind to ensure that its message would have the "right" effect. That second kind of seduction was one that occurs through books. The prosecutor had to prove that kind of seduction both dangerous and contagious if he was to win his case. In its insistence on the novel's power to enact change, the defense, like the novel itself, wound up validating that view.

The trial of *La Part des femmes* ultimately staged a trial of women—of their roles, their sexuality, and their desires—and of the uses to which women were put. But the novel did not try the women any less than the censors. Nor did the Fourierist defense enlarge women's share. Neither provided any alternatives to this spectacle of seduction. In fact, the novel's own commentary on reading and desire advances a theory about seduction so like the one embraced by the prosecutor that one wonders that the two are on different sides: "We are wrong," argues Méray's narrator, "to say questionable language and libertine insinuations leave no impression on chaste souls. There is an age where we should be especially afraid of exciting, through vulgar insinuations, instinctive desires produced spontaneously by the mysterious labor nature then works in us" (*PdF*, 6/5). According to Méray's narrator, the language of debauchery excites all individuals—whether it leaves them disgusted or sexually eager. For this reason, he argues, young people find themselves especially intrigued by libertine literature and art:

> Who among us, in reading these works full of luxurious paintings by [. . .] cynical poets, or in opening an album full of shameless themes, has not felt assailed by burning impulses? [. . .] Who among us, despite a more or less vivid sense of disgust, never feels at that moment the electrical jolt of a blazing fluid reddening the face and inflaming the blood. [. . .] In virgin hearts, it fascinates. (*PdF*, 6/5)

Méray's narrator therefore depicts the heroine Juanna as excited by the words alone of the libertine even though they are hardly as "strong"—he hastens to add—as this comparison to "an erotic book or a licentious picture album" might suggest. Small wonder that when Juanna sees Léonce, she falls eagerly into his arms. "Surrendering to his desires," she returns her boyfriend's "voluptuous kiss." Stimulated by the language of debauchery, she will follow him as far as he will lead her: "If Léonce had dared . . . Juanna would have been lost! . . ." comments the narrator with weighted ellipses (*PdF*, 6/5). Seduced by words and images alone, Juanna is easy prey for any man who would come along.

The *lorette* Suzanne has also endured far too much exposure to the licentious language of men, as we learn in the censored chapter that recounts her childhood: "She had heard the obscene talk of her brothers and their friends who told each other cynically their first adventures, without being at all bothered by her presence. . . . She learned to see the physical part of love as something with little importance and to give the final gift nearly the value of a simple kiss" (*PdF*, 7/1). Smut corrupts the *bourgeoise* and the *grisette* alike, Méray's narrator seems to insist. Profligate texts, language, and images lead to wanton ways and uncontrollable urges. In this sense, the trial of *La Part des femmes* was not a trial of a text or of a newspaper, but the trial of the ways texts might be imagined to affect people whose desires were already under surveillance.

Just as Bresson ignored Suzanne's seduction by Léonce, he did not appeal to the jury to protect girls like her from salubrious scenes in immoral novels. The *lorette* is neither honorable enough nor modest enough to merit his concerns. Though he stages an assault on the *lorette*'s seduction, his concern is not with the desires born in her but rather with the young bourgeois who beds her. The young man is the one who might be "intoxicated" by the seductions in the text, Bresson tells the court; he is the one who may be "lured" by the text's spoils.[41] By learning about passions from such a text, he might be as easily led astray by *lorettes* as Léonce under the spell of Juanna. The real danger, Bresson repeatedly affirms, lies in the passion this novel acknowledges and evokes.

The image of the young man, seething with desire borne of a book, does not in itself justify Bresson's measures. To wage war on the seductions he claims texts perform and to justify the censorship of those who read such newspapers, he must frame the female reader as well. Just as the prosecutor wants to protect the youth from *lorettes*, he claims to want to keep the honorable girl safely away from the seductions of fictions. She must not be allowed to get hold of a description showing Suzanne "put in contact with the seduction of riches, shown giving herself over to her first seducer, then to a second seducer." Fascinated by art, by riches, or by sexuality, such a girl might be lost. But to whom? Or from what? As I will show in chapter 8, this fantasy of the female reader was a powerful one indeed. At least in this trial, it seems to have seduced everyone into censorship.

Méray's novel leaves itself open to Bresson's accusations that such a text would be "poison thrown into young hearts." It anticipates the moralism of a censor who would ask: "Would an honorable and modest young girl handle such descriptions with impunity?" (8/30). It acknowledges that literary works and engravings alike can lead to improprieties by young people. It incites fears of the language of desire precisely because such language can seduce. By acknowledging the dangers of women's reading, it puts itself on trial.[42]

In this way, the defense of *La Part des femmes* repeatedly endangers its case by trying to cash in on the seductions of texts and images. By validating the dangers of texts, the defense attorneys put the Fourierist scenes on trial. By evoking dirty pictures along with Bresson, they validate his gaze. And like Bresson's imaginary dirty pictures, the ones they bring into the courtroom remain entirely fantasmatic. The defense lawyers remain fearful enough of the moral gaze to keep their obscene representations under wraps. Because they fail to unfurl their pictures, they share in Bresson's fantasies about the dangers of vision. Under other circumstances, their rhetorical tricks—of agreeing with certain premises of Bresson's argument in order to turn his argument against him—might have helped them show him up. In this case they only reproduce the tensions between the gaze of seduction and the gaze of rational investigation. They simply fall into their own traps. After all, if paintings can seduce, then surely so can a text.

Even more precariously, the defense makes its case on the redeeming values of its own moral vision. The defense attorneys attempt to show that the scenes of seduction at the center of this text serve only to underline the need for a change in morals. Yet in making such a case, they put their own values on the line. They seem to have forgotten that if a text can persuade politically, then it may, as Méray himself suggests, seduce its readers in other ways as well. By depending upon a moral vision that permits and even esteems political persuasion, the defense attorneys, the editors, and the novelist alike ally themselves with the seductions Bresson manages to show as dangerous. Even as they try to squeeze something else out of the moments Bresson frames, they empower the prosecutor to convince the court that the novel's scenes of seduction deserve to be cut away. Even holding out for another kind of censorship, another politics of seduction, another spectacle of morality, the Fourierists embrace undercover work. They want to believe that texts can seduce.

By creating contagious readings where the only possible interpretation is where seduction occurs, the state censors manage to push aside questions about morality and injustice and to replace them with debates about the effects of texts. In spite of Bresson's outraged overreadings, despite the frameworks that make his ideological bias far too obvious, and despite the unjust targeting of a literary text for political issues far beyond its margins, neither the novel nor the defense can avoid perpetuating his trial of women's share. The obsessive desire of all parties in the novel—and in the courtroom—to make female susceptibility a source of proscriptions ultimately bolsters the case of censors who want, for men and women, an end to any desire that does not pay.

Other Shares

To listen to Flaubert's characters in *L'Éducation sentimentale*, censorship during the July Monarchy was a matter of contagion that might spread beyond the press. Frédéric's allusion to the censorship scandals of 1847 leads to his friend's remarks on a contagion of interdictions: "Are they going to forbid us our share of women?" This slippage between the censorship of a novel and limitations that might be placed on male sexual satisfaction has more than just a rhetorical value. By shifting the political question of press censorship into a private domain, Hussonnet's joke performs a kind of censorship in its turn: it replaces concerns about the trial of *La Part des femmes* with bourgeois fears about not having one's share of women. Yet it also insists upon a correlation between censorship of represented sexuality and prohibitions that touch on sexual life. If Hussonnet's remark asserts, ironically perhaps, a belief in men's entitlement to a certain share of women, it takes up the thematics of the censorship trial and becomes a conduit for a slippage that is already performed and tried in the novel itself. Hussonnet's complaint thus replays the rhetorical question asked from the beginning by Méray's novel: "What is the woman's share?" And it does so with a vengeance—by substituting another question: "What share of women is men's due?"

The extent to which this second question recurs in the readings engendered by Méray's *roman-feuilleton* suggests that Flaubert is as much a conduit for a slippage inherent in the 1847 scandal as he is a commentator on it after the fact. This allusion in *L'Éducation sentimentale* that would send us in search of a footnote to tell us if Méray's novel ever existed confers value on the Fourierist *feuilleton*. Yet Flaubert so successfully situates this censorship trial in a larger pattern of proscriptions that we risk allowing the joke to perform in the *place* of a reading of the individual incident. This is nevertheless a moment where the embedded historical event transports disruptive potential. We might have caught the thread to unravel Flaubert's concerns here.[43] Instead, I have taken the reference to this censored novel as an invitation to read the seized text as well as its trial and therefore to consider the slippage each performs between investments in telling the woman's share and attaching her interests. The question I have been asking is, in a way, the same question posed by Flaubert's allusion: what does the censorship of a novel have to do with men's fears about not getting what they want from women? What desires—and whose—are on trial here?

As Flaubert's evocation of the *Démocratie pacifique* scandal suggests, the censors' attempt to control texts threatened to spread contagiously to other spheres. Méray's novel was perhaps targeted *because* it thematized the contagion of censorship and surveillance, because it drew correlations between fears about representation and fears about sexuality, and because it thematized the same fantasies about the workings of the imagination that permitted Tissot, Brachet, Briquet, and later Freud, to limit women's share in books. *La Part des femmes* exposed itself to the censors' gaze because it took risks, lashing out at a justice system that hovered ready to curtail its right to speak. It lent itself to a commotion that began long before and continued long after its condemnation. Its trial therefore became a kind of carnival in which the novel was made into a spectacle. This was not a subtle world of panopticons and transparent prisons, but rather a kind of Grand Guignol—exposing the absurdity of nineteenth-century surveillance mechanisms. Even as it came under the censors' gaze, Méray's *roman-feuilleton* seems to have chosen to make a spectacle of itself.[44]

By the time Méray answered his censors by registering his seductress among the prostitutes of Saint-Lazare, the *lorette* had an impressive literary standing. Although this kept woman was the subject of her own little book called a "physiology" and of an essay by Dumas père, the source of the myth in which Suzanne shared was as much visual as written.[45] Beginning in the early 1840s, Gavarni's caricatures of *lorettes* caused more titters than scandals when they appeared in *Le Charivari*. They showed, in any number of different contexts, pretty girls dressed up for balls, setting out into a public sphere to dance and drink and, above all, to be seen by men. Like Hussonnet in *L'Éducation sentimentale*, these lithographs seem to complain about the inaccessibility of the women pictured there. They serve as jokes between men about the impossibility of seduction, or at least as asides between men about unsatisfied desires.

Some of the women in the lithographs wear the latest fashions and are indistinguishable from any other woman on her way to the opera or the theater. Others wear men's clothing.[46] Yet whether they dress up or cross-dress, all of these women are putting themselves on display. Like their "fantasmatic origins,"[47] their clothing provides them with a masquerade; it gives them a cover. But these lithographs do not stage a show about what the *lorettes* wanted or what they needed. This is not even a spectacle that hides the lack that might make them undesirable. Rather it is a put-on, like their clothes. It makes a joke of *lorettes* in order to tell a story about what is wanted from them and winds up telling far more about what is seen in them.

The myth of the *lorette* makes her a needleworker, like Suzanne in Méray's censored novel, who has sold her body for luxuries. As the caption of one of Gavarni's lithographs (figure 7.3) puts it, she is one of those "little women who . . . —gain by being known."[48] But just as the myth makes her one of the trappings men buy to improve their own trade, her image sells. Admitting no disease, no poverty, no primal scene of seduction, she becomes a representation of seduction, and sells pictures, newspapers, and novels that try to speculate on her scandal. "Easy to take, impossible to keep,"[49] serves as an enticing title that would attach her interests for those who sell books and politics. Yet it also invites those who would try to keep her in view. Because there is always some other story to tell about her, her interests are always on trial. Her seduction is always a matter for surveillance.

One version of the *lorette*'s story makes her the flip side of the virtuous spouse and mother, as necessary to familial procreation as a double bed.[50] Yet the *lorette* is a pose, not an alternative. She may represent seduction, but hers is only posturing. She is a mask. She does not satisfy desire. She evokes its lack of satisfaction. She may represent, as a fantasy at least, currents of desire and commodification, but she is always just display. She is always spectacle. And we are always looking with the eyes of those who wanted her to show them wanting.

For a woman to make a spectacle of herself, someone has to be looking. For a text to make a spectacle of itself, there must be someone keeping watch. And that presupposes a desire, or at least a desire to censor, which in nineteenth-century France may come to the same thing.

Figure 7.3

The caption of this Gavarni lithograph records the conversation between men: "Lorettes? I like them: they are nice as anything, and they don't hurt anyone . . . . you know, those little women who . . . ." "—Who gain from being known."

(HOUGHTON LIBRARY, HARVARD UNIVERSITY)

8
Reading Dangerously:
The Memoirs of the Devil
and Madame Lafarge

*T*he novel drives women to murder. At least one novel, Frédéric
Soulié's *Les Mémoires du diable*, was accused of such a deed,
for one of its volumes was supposedly found next to Marie Cappelle-Lafarge's
bed when officials came to arrest her for the poisoning of her husband. Her
other reading would in turn be implicated in the trial that shook all of France
in 1840. For long after her condemnation, the novel itself would regularly be
put on trial. In this chapter, I consider how the novel came to be represented
as a danger and what dangers it did indeed contain.

In August 1839, a wealthy Parisian family pressured its orphaned niece to
accept the spouse they had found for her through a marriage broker. Within
only a few days, twenty-three-year-old Marie Cappelle found herself on the
road to a distant village in the Limousin, accompanied by this stranger who
had become her husband. A web of deception quickly unraveled around this
supposedly rich and respectable spouse. His castle turned out to be a monastery
in ruins; his advertised ironworks were in financial straits; he had wed her, it
seemed, to use her dowry of ninety thousand francs to ward off impending
bankruptcy.

Five months later Charles Lafarge was dead. Local authorities took his recent
bride into custody and charged her with murder. Her mother-in-law and other
members of her husband's family pointed an accusing finger at Marie. This
unwilling bride, they said, had mixed arsenic into cakes and then into "remedies"
for his illness: unhappy with the husband she had been given, she had stirred
up potions to make herself a widow. Townspeople joined the Lafarge family
and servants in gossip that Marie had both the motive and the opportunity to
poison her husband. The resulting scandal, relayed by the press, quickly cap-
tured national attention in the summer of 1840. Horrified to have her name
associated with that of her closest childhood friend, the former Mademoiselle
de Nicolaï came forward with a new accusation: Marie had stolen a diamond
necklace from her the previous summer. The police swooped down upon this
"crime" as well, forcing Marie to stand trial first for the theft of the necklace.

Within weeks of the guilty verdict in a trial full of adolescent intrigues, Cappelle-Lafarge went on trial for poisoning her husband.

By the time the murder trial began, the press had already tried Marie. Her childhood pastimes, her flirts, her obsessions, her reading, and even her letters to her husband had been displayed publicly. In a trial marked by hearsay and questionable medical testimony, determining whether Charles Lafarge had really been poisoned turned out to be less important than judging the character — and desires — of his wife. The trial had become, as Flaubert's narrator remarks in L'Éducation sentimentale, "the rage of its era."[1]

While the intrigues of the trial revolved around the character of the young bride, the central issue, the murder of Charles Lafarge, emerged as far less certain than his family initially contended. Part of the problem came from the difficulty of knowing if a crime had been committed in the first place. Although Lafarge's mother and sister provided elaborate details of what they believed was Marie's plot to rid herself of her husband and enjoy the independence of a well-to-do widow, the medical experts repeatedly came up with conflicting accounts — despite multiple efforts to make the body and bones of Charles Lafarge tell *their* story. With the exception of Orfila, the medical examiner whose testimony for the prosecution proved devastating though it was dubious in motivations, no one seemed sure if the small amount of arsenic found in Lafarge's body had anything to do with his death, or if it could have been given to him on purpose by a wife bent on his destruction.[2]

Marie's case was not helped by the fact that she would have had few alternatives if she had indeed been unable to endure life with this unkempt man in a village distant from her family and friends. Divorce had been outlawed since 1816. A separation would have dishonored all parties. A woman's adultery was even less acceptable in the countryside than in Paris. Provincials pointed to Marie's upper-class Parisian upbringing as proof that she might have simply chosen to write her own rules of conduct. Believed the great-granddaughter of Stéphanie de Genlis, the renowned educational expert and governess of the boy Louis-Philippe, Marie drew national attention in part because rumors held her maternal grandmother to be the king's half-sister — the illegitimate daughter of Philippe Egalité.[3] For those who proclaimed Marie's guilt, her trial represented a chance to preserve those institutions conservatives believed most endangered by the social changes of the July Monarchy: the family, marriage, property, and morality. Since many of those same conservatives sought to blame books for the fall of the ancien régime, they eagerly grasped this new opportunity to show writing in violation.

Marie Cappelle-Lafarge endured a trial by letters in three ways. First, her own education came to be questioned. Had it made her into an *empoisonneuse?* Did the educational values promoted by the likes of Rousseau and de Genlis predispose bourgeois daughters to dangers? Did a certain kind of education for women make them incapable of finding happiness beside the mates chosen by their families?

Second, her pleasure in reading made her a figurehead in already stormy debates over women's reading. Women's access to literature, and especially to serial novels and romantic texts, had been vehemently questioned in the years before her trial. Women's imaginations had undergone serious analysis by critics, censors, and doctors. Women's new literacy had made them objects of scrutiny. The books Marie read were placed on trial along with her. The novel I examine here, Soulié's *Les Mémoires du diable*, took the fall for a batch of novels Marie was supposed to have read. George Sand's *Lélia*, which Cappelle-Lafarge claimed as her favorite novel and which I discuss later in this chapter, became a further weapon against her. In this way, her trial put the novel on trial, and her reading was used to try her.[4]

Third, Marie's own writings took on a central role during the trial and after her conviction. Her letters to her husband, to her own family, and to a young man with whom she had flirted, were turned against her as evidence of her duplicitous nature. From prison Marie wrote and published her own *Mémoires* in an attempt to vindicate herself and gain a pardon. This account of her youth, marriage, and trial served only to revive the scandal and reopen her case. The dangerous text summoned like a specter during the early 1840s was as much her own as that of the novelists she may have read. The *Memoirs of the Devil* and those of Madame Lafarge might as well have been the same book.

In this chapter I look at how the trial of a woman put practices of reading on trial. We saw in chapter 7 how fears about seduction put women as well as texts on trial. In this chapter I examine how the trial of Cappelle-Lafarge focused debates about reading difference. By looking at the imbrication of the trials of Cappelle-Lafarge, of the novels she supposedly read, and of her own writings, we will see how theories of reading came to be viewed as gendered and what those readings in turn engendered. If indeed, as her critics suggest, Cappelle-Lafarge read in a criminal way, how does her duplicity emerge in her own texts? How do her critics imagine such a criminal reading? What duplicity must they embrace in order to believe they catch her in the act? In order to answer these questions about a woman's reading strategies, I would like to pose a double reading of *Les Mémoires du diable*. We will first follow Cappelle-Lafarge's critics as they read Soulié dangerously, as they imagine her criminal pacts with the text. Then we will oppose to this reading the strategies articulated in Cappelle-Lafarge's writings. Finally, we consider the trials to which women and novels alike were subjected.

Reading Dangerously

Near the beginning of Soulié's *Mémoires du diable*, the devil shows the protagonist a vision of a woman who has been locked up in a barren room by her fiancé and family. The Baron Armand de Luizzi looks on as Henriette Buré puts down her baby and exchanges it for a book she reads attentively. Equipped with supernatural vision, Luizzi realizes the book is Sade's *Justine*. Since Luizzi does not yet know *who* this woman is, why her family has placed her in this cell, or even why the devil is showing him this vision, he can only speculate on her desire for fictions and on what she reads into Sade. His fantasy of what drives such a woman to novels he thinks obscene resembles many of those meant to explain women's intercourse with the *roman-feuilleton:* "Wretched girl, thought he, if she was born with that frenetic delirium that medical science explains, but which our language cannot describe" (*Mdd,* 1:212–14). Gazing at this woman with pity and fright, Luizzi soon discovers that she has an alibi for her dangerous reading. Between the lines of this volume of Sade, given to her by her fiancé in hopes that she will be eventually sufficiently corrupted to wish to marry him, she has written in blood her painful life story. She has been reading her *own* story between the lines of *Justine.*

Alfred Nettement found no such excuses for Marie Cappelle-Lafarge. In his newspaper columns on the *roman-feuilleton,* the Catholic journalist holds up this convicted husband-murderer as a deterrent to men who let their wives read newspaper novels. According to Nettement, the wife who becomes an "addict" of the passion and drama of the novels of Balzac, Sue, Dumas, Soulié, and Sand will be tormented by her desires—and she will torment the man who does not satisfy them (*EC,* 2:434–39). The *roman-feuilleton* will make her bored, discontented with her duties, and dreamy. She will become a *"folle du logis"* (crazywoman of the hearth), her mind twisted by "the impassioned and romantic exaggerations of that evil literature" (*EC,* 2:449). Worse yet, she will begin to live the novels she has read. Like Madame Lafarge, Nettement reminds his reader, the corrupted girl may drag innocent victims into her novel-induced fantasies. Or she may simply become so obsessed with what she has read, that she may believe she has become one of the characters in the novel (a danger represented by Daumier in figure 8.1).[5]

Sharing the views of his contemporaries who were convinced that novel reading produced hysterical girls, Nettement produces a list of symptoms induced by reading serial novels that could have been lifted from the *Dictionnaire des sciences médicales:*

> Those kinds of strange ideas, those new feelings to which [novels] give birth, that exaltation they paint and communicate, those disordered passions, those frenetic raptures, those unknown excesses, that world of vice they reveal, those violent emotions, those corrosive sensations that develop a feverish sensitivity in the soul, are these not the infallible causes that necessarily beget the effects of which I tried to warn you by recreating a picture so incomplete? (*EC,* 2:440)

Once the novel has awakened in a woman a desire for passion, she will stop at nothing—not adultery, not madness, not even crime—to get more of what she has read between the lines of her books.

Nettement's fantasies about the female reader carry to logical extremes theories about reading proliferating in medical studies, advice literature, and other works of criticism of his time. Because Nettement's own readings of the

Le Roman.

Ils se battent pour moi.... Alfred m'enlevera...... nous nous marierons.

Figure 8.1

The woman reader in Daumier's lithograph imagines the characters in her novel coming alive around her: one man fights a duel for her. Another will carry her away and they will get married.

(HOUGHTON LIBRARY, HARVARD UNIVERSITY)

novels he indicts are so detailed, we can use them to pinpoint the strategies of containment necessary to theories that put reading women under surveillance. The dangerous readings he envisions tell a great deal about fears of what women read into books and about nineteenth-century practices of reading difference. Though he claims to show how women read, he winds up telling how he reads women. As we shall see, his version of her dangerous readings creates a space in which a woman reader might tell her own stories.

Henriette Buré's fiancé gave her novels like Sade's *Justine*, claims Nettement, because "the *roman-feuilleton* had not yet been invented and *Les Mémoires du diable* had not yet appeared" (*EC*, 1:387). Had Henriette read Soulié's eight-volume *feuilleton* novel she surely would have found yet more dangerous ways of coping with her imprisonment than writing her autobiography—or so Nettement would have his readers believe. As far as he is concerned, Madame Lafarge is guilty of poisoning her husband, but the *roman-feuilleton* made her do it.

Because Soulié's 1837 novel supposedly was found lying open on her table at the time of her arrest, Nettement and others made an example of it to demonstrate the dangers of reading for women.[6] Soulié's novel made a convenient target for it had everything: sex, madness, prostitution, criminality, even a woman's murder of her husband. It not only thematized the dangers of women's reading, but it developed the role of the moralist who would read women in(to) confinement. And it did so without skipping a beat in a battle cry against immoral literature. What galled the critics, or so their readings suggest, derived from the duplicity with which this novel took their stance.

Nettement's stages his reading of Soulié's work as a *defense* of Madame Lafarge. By showing *how* she read, he presumes to demonstrate that the novel deserves even greater blame. In this way Nettement places reading practices on trial. What is really at stake is not Cappelle-Lafarge's crime, but the possibility that a causal relationship exists between a text and its reader's actions. Perhaps even more important, with his fantasies about how Madame Lafarge read Soulié, Nettement places on trial certain assumptions about the workings of the female imagination.

How then, according to Nettement and others like him, did Cappelle-Lafarge read? What constitutes a dangerous reading of *Les Mémoires du diable*? What desires did Soulié's novel inflame in the young bride of Charles Lafarge? How could this novel turn to poison in the hands of its model reader?

There are books that must be read in secret. Of others we must simply keep secret our readings. The crumbling monastery called Glandier must have seemed cold and lonely those autumn nights of 1839 when Marie Cappelle sat alone in her room, wondering how much longer she could hold off the man who claimed his rights as her husband. Could any book have consoled her in her terrifying solitude? Far from relatives and friends, for the first time in her life absolutely alone, the memories must have at first helped pass the time. But the frigidity of this new family, the suspicion and jealousy of the woman she had hoped would take her mother's place, the dullness of the rest of them — that must have brought the kinds of memories that haunt. It would be a lonely time ahead. The dead would be with her for a long time. Reading in secret, perhaps she could let them go.

There are books that might give solace to a twenty-three-year-old orphan, huddled in a room that is all she can hope to call her own. The dowry she had believed would buy her the freedom to dream has been traded instead for this nightmare, this unfamiliar world, this family that will never know how differently she dreams. The books might help her keep the dreams. Like a crypt, she might cradle them inside her. Reading in secret, keeping secret her readings, Marie Cappelle-Lafarge could keep alive the other she would have wanted to become. Hoarding up the images she has savored, she might make a museum of secrets, a collection of places where she can let herself be.

There are desires that may be confided, in secret, to books. The readings we give — the stories we make out of those fictions — they are our stories. The books we read in secret teach us ways to keep what hurts us. They teach us mourning to go on. Or perhaps they only give us places to put the ghosts so they are no longer dead. Marie Cappelle-Lafarge must have known that no one else would care what desires she brought to her fictions as long as she put on the right performance. She could keep anyone she wanted on the inside as long as she did not make a spectacle out of herself.

But something went wrong. Was it that the inner spectacle grew too great? Could she simply not go on living the lie the books gave her? Or was this crime for which her accusers blamed her only another fiction, like the ones in the books? When they turned the books against her, as they did with her every gesture, at least for a change they made something really happen in her life. Her accusers would say she had been driven to crimes she had read about in books. She had, for the first time in her life, become really part of her fictions.

Still, when they began talking about the books, it must have seemed an unimaginable violation. No matter what she had done, her acts came from her and not from the novels she read or the education she had been given. But that wasn't what the press said. Or the lawyers. Or her mother-in-law who plundered her desk and stole her papers, keeping what was most precious, most secret, most fragile, most vulnerable. Her accusers would put her desires on trial. They would claim to find her desires in those books and papers, and they would use those desires to put *her* on trial.

It had been lonely at Christmas that winter at Le Glandier. She had written letters, trying to be cheerful, hoping to find someone who would help her believe that someday there would be more consolation than the books. That one day she would have a space where what she was and knew and wanted would no longer hurt her. She must have known she could not hold out forever. But that was her secret, like the diamonds, like the strangers she had loved from afar, like the men who loved her, like her dead grandfather's love, like what she knew about magnetism. And all those things kept her as much as she kept them. Inside. They became outside. And the others began to speak of poison.

What if there had been no poison, but only secret reading? What if there had been no theft, but only traded dreams? What if there had been no murderous urges, but only desires confided to books? What if there had only been a lonely girl, unable to breathe, terrified of the silence, afraid to speak her fears, closed up in a barren room, giving up her desires to books?

Madame Lafarge made herself into "the secretary of the devil," alleged Sirtema de Grovestins. By reading Soulié's *Mémoires du diable*, "She let herself be penetrated by the spirit of that novel. . . . She stopped on a fatal page of that book: she put the novel into action."[7] Her reading not only familiarized her with the crimes exposed in this novel, contended Sirtema along with Nettement, but it made a place for her to write her own continuation of the devil's memories. Even before she took up a pen to write her *Mémoires*, her "crimes" inscribed her into the novel from which she had, according to her critics, learned her trade.

"I have seen the poison: it was an immoral novel," proclaimed Nettement in his study of Madame Lafarge's dangerous reading. As far as he is concerned, she was simply a carrier for the poison of bad books: "Everything is a novel with that woman. She does not speak or think or act except through novels and with novels." Her adolescent flirts, her explanation for her "theft" of the diamonds, her relationship to her husband, Charles, even the letters she writes to him, are read by Nettement as part of this novel that Marie, through an adolescence of unbridled romantic reading, has put into action. When she wants to poison her husband, says Nettement, "she wraps arsenic in a dreamy and sentimental novel." Arrested, she will spin novels to defend herself and make a novel out of her trial, infecting her lawyers, the audience, and the newspapers with this "atmosphere of the novel" (*EC*, 1:355). For the moralist critic, the poison of the novel reveals itself everywhere, "in the feelings, ideas, words, and acts of Madame Lafarge," as obviously as the chemical analyses on the body of her husband showed the poison of arsenic (*EC*, 1:356).

The novel to which Nettement attributed the most venomous of these events, *Les Mémoires du diable*, had appeared in *feuilleton* in *Le Siècle* between June 1837 and March 1838, a seemingly endless set of stories bound together by a pact between the devil and the protagonist Armand de Luizzi. Like every member of his accursed family before him, Luizzi has ten years to choose the one thing in the world that might bring him true happiness. Otherwise he will be claimed by the devil. So that Luizzi may be better equipped to make a decision that will affect him for eternity, the devil allows him to see the interior life of others and to know their stories. Though the devil regales Luizzi with the secret lives of his acquaintances, Luizzi does not necessarily gain the privileged knowledge that will help him make an informed choice. The devil's gain depends upon his ability to lead Luizzi astray *with the truth*. For, if Luizzi arrives at the end of the ten years able to choose something that *would* make him happy, then the devil will come up empty-handed. The curse on Luizzi's family would be broken, and Luizzi would go free *and* happy.

In the course of what became 2750 pages in the eight-volume edition of 1838, the devil manages to stack the cards against Luizzi in every way. He tells the stories *he* wants to tell about the people *he* wants to expose. He tells their stories selectively so that Luizzi's decisions to act upon this privileged information constantly create havoc and ruin lives. He forces Luizzi to pay for information with coins representing a portion of Luizzi's lifetime, but he steals time from Luizzi without telling him and sets Luizzi up for disasters by with-holding Luizzi's memory of what has happened during the lost time. He re-peatedly changes the terms of pacts, playing Luizzi for a fool with promises and unresolved paradoxes. By the time Luizzi finds out what is really going on, it is always too late. When Luizzi at last makes sense of the devil's stories, the people in them are already dead or beyond rescue.[8]

Luizzi's plight sustains the *feuilleton* not so much because of the stories the devil tells him, but because of the turns given to the stories by the devil: a constant set of *dénouements* reverses everything Luizzi has assumed, or believed, or been told previously. A story about one woman always turns out to be a story about another. Everyone turns out to be related to Luizzi. Or else they are connected to Luizzi by some act of fate. Or else they have some reason to want to see Luizzi suffer. And when a story is told we can always assume that it will later be reread by the devil as a different story, with a different moral, and a different significance for Luizzi. In this way, the ploys of the devil create a play of duplicity that forces the listeners—Luizzi and the reader—into a kind of detective work with a twist. Untangling the double identities of the characters always involves Luizzi more fully in the stories he believed were unrelated to his own.

These stories are, in both their written as well as oral forms, the memoirs of the devil. Luizzi has obtained permission from Satan to write down and publish the stories he will get out of their pact, and though we never see him do so in the course of the novel, we assume that this set of texts comes to us mediated by Luizzi's hand. What we are reading then, turns out to be a kind of performance by the devil, an autobiography in duplicitous deeds. Luizzi is destined from the start to lose, but then he was also doomed because of his family history to endure a hell without end. Descendant of incest and adultery, Luizzi has little hope but to become a man of letters.[9]

Soulié's text turns out to be as much a work of philosophy or literary criticism as it is a novel. Its plots seem little more than ruses to justify commentary by the narrator, the devil, or Luizzi, about social classes, vice, virtue, the role of the *roman-feuilleton*, the dangers of reading, and the difficulties of reading virtue. The novel is not only concerned with the literature of the July Monarchy and the allegations against it, but it is also obsessed with women's reading. It parades out accusations against the novel as if to assimilate and coopt them. It revels in the difficulties of reading women as if to profit from the failings of its own stories. Just when this novel seems to have detected itself into self-censorship, it shifts gears to become another novel altogether, with other women to read, other pacts to fulfill, and another morality to espouse. Its slipperiness makes it hard to summarize, but it also invites readings, like Luizzi's own, that depend upon blindness. It plays at being double and generates duplicitous readings.

The "devil's memoirs" turn out to be a collection of background checks— the "true stories" of women of French society in the decade before the Revolution of 1830. Or at least these are the stories of the relationships of these women to one another and to Luizzi. The devil successfully masks these relationships with names that change through marriage, illegitimacy, the purchase of titles, and foul play. The double identities of the women in Luizzi's life not only generate the excitement necessary to keep the *feuilleton* in print, they also require constant rereadings of the circumstances (and morality) of the novel's actions.[10] Luizzi's blind reading must always be revised by the trickster readings of the all-knowing devil. The most virtuous women, the devil will constantly demonstrate, always have skeletons in their closets. The most scandalous turn out to have been compromised by their virtue.

It is this economy of reversals that proves so worrisome to the novel's critics. Nettement, like other conservative critics for whom his work stands here as exemplary,[11] wants fiction to conform to the most rigorous of moral systems. He wants his heroes moral, and he expects the immoral to be punished brutally for their deeds and desires. He wants his text readable in the most unequivocal of terms with no reversals, no doubts, no satire, and certainly no duplicity, for nothing terrifies Nettement more than the possibility that a text may generate duplicitous readings. With the venom of a hermeneuticist who demands that his texts mean and, above all, that their meaning be readable, this proponent of moral propaganda sets out to show how the novel may lead its reader astray. Yet this very demonstration requires that he reproduce the dangerous desires of another reader, or at least that he produce desires that are enough like hers to show the novel's dangers.

Nettement claims to derive "rules for judging the morality of literary works" right out of Soulié's own novel. First, he claims, Soulié is aware of the effects of literature upon the world and of the world upon literature (*EC*, 1:379). Second, he asserts that the novelist agrees that it is dangerous to present society "as a vast cesspool of vices and infamies in which there are everywhere only semblants of virtue, lies about innocence, and whose dominion is divided between shamelessness and hypocrisy" (*EC*, 1:380). Third, he argues that even Soulié would agree that "It is . . . a real moral wrong to show systematically in a work virtue not only always unfortunate, but always scorned, always debased, in face of vice not only prosperous, but honored and surrounded by esteem and glory" (*EC*, 1:383).[12]

The moral of the story, claims Nettement, is that virtue makes women unhappy—or, worse yet, shames them (*EC*, 1:393–94). This is the moral, he argues, that Madame Lafarge heeded as she read the novel that literally spelled out the steps for her crime. The reader Nettement fantasizes is endangered, above all, by her belief in the justice of the narrative. Bent over her volume of the *Mémoires du diable*, this reading woman assumes the text metes out rewards and punishments that correlate with the actions of the characters:

> Here is a young woman with a romantic mind, with a strong-willed and determined character, Madame Lafarge, for example, who reads the *Mémoires du diable*. She sees Henriette Buré unhappy, scorned, shut up in a dungeon, then put into a madhouse as a madwoman, ending up becoming mad, and suffering all those sorrows for having refused to marry Captain Ridaire except to trick him after the marriage. And opposite that lamentable fate, she sees the tranquil life of Hortense Buré, her sister-in-law, happy, loved, and respected, for having refused her spousal duties and later assassinating the man to whom she had surrendered. [Our reader] turns the page, hoping perhaps to escape temptation. . . . She sees Mme. de *** [du Bergh], as Mr. Soulié himself says, attaining happiness and renown for the highest devotion, by poisoning her husband and giving him through adultery an heir whose gestation she calculated with a heinous cold-bloodedness next to the corpse of the man she had just poisoned. (*EC*, 1:408–9)

In his extended fantasy of Madame Lafarge reading, Nettement plots the terms for a dangerous reading. First, he is obsessed with the criminality of the women in this novel and with their ability to pass themselves off as respectable members of society. His reader would take these plots and characters as evidence that such duplicity is not only possible but *desirable*. In such a way, Madame du Bergh's poisoning of her husband—however motivated or justified by the novel— becomes a lesson in murder for a reader like Madame Lafarge. Second, Nettement assumes that his reader will correlate the sorrows of the virtuous (like Henriette Buré) with their innocence and therefore eschew virtue because it leads to grief. Third, he assigns no powers of discretion to his reader. Unlike him, she will not differentiate ideology from plot element, or even understand that these events have no basis in fact. Like him, she will profess no interest in the philosophical digressions of the novel's characters but will leap to the conclusions of each story, able to read well enough to keep these characters straight but unable to make sense of their relationship to any representational framework.

Nettement even imagines his female reader having privileged communication with these characters. The reading relationship he fantasizes about goes beyond one of identification because the characters she reads about actually step out of the picture frame to cheer her on to a life of duplicity and crime.[13] Nettement depicts a kind of vampiristic reading in which one set of women sucks the lifeblood from the reader until she believes she takes pleasure in joining them. As if she had been hypnotized by the text, his fantasmatic reader appears defenseless against it. She introjects the desires of the novel's characters, incapable of differentiating them from her own, and acts upon her own desires with abandon. The book sets off contagious reactions because the reader serves as a conduit for dangerous desires she does not even understand.

Such a theory requires female readers to be incapable of controlling their own desires. It also depends upon a notion of femininity that would assign their difference to their defective theoretical skills. Women read dangerously (say the experts) when they are not kept under surveillance. Does this mean that they read in more acceptable ways when disciplinary mechanisms entrap them? Does this mean that women's reading practices are inherently different and, therefore, inherently defective? Are women more likely than men to read dangerously? Can a woman be trained to read Soulié in a way that will not risk her house, husband, and reputation? Or is Soulié so poisonous that even a few pages would ruin the chaste woman who dips into it?

Nettement's idea of "feminist" criticism exposes husbands to treacherous treatment at their wives' hands. It assumes that a guilty Madame Lafarge has learned her tricks from a novel full of murder, madness, seduction, prostitution, incest, and duplicity. Above all, it assumes that whatever "authorization" Cappelle-Lafarge may have gotten from this novel, she managed brilliantly to cover up her real desires and true motives under a cloak of deception. *Les Mémoires du diable* not only gave her the tools of her new trade, but it schooled her in double-dealing. This is, I believe, what terrifies Nettement the most about the novel he wants to reduce to its simplest formulas. Behind the rhetoric he espouses to fantasize one kind of dangerous reading, Nettement generates yet another representation of a woman's reading. Far less idiotic and inept than the literal reader, this female reader knows the score. For she has picked up on the novel's interpolation of its own project. Like Nettement, she knows how to rig the rhetorical game to find what she wants in a text. And like Nettement, she might have desires to cover up.

Nettement therefore inscribes two possible ways of reading dangerously into his analyses of Soulié: *haunted reading* and *duplicitous reading*. These two reading practices stand in for each other because they depend upon a certain ideal of femininity. Unlike men, whose roles may be diverse and who may reflect varied temperaments, the endangered woman Nettement and his cohorts fantasize about has one natural temperament and one correct *devoir*.[14] His *haunted reader* has so thoroughly come to embody the feminine ideals of the early nineteenth century, that her readings, like her hysterical body, get out of control. The *duplicitous reader*, in contrast, manages to project an absolute control even as she puts her desires to work like gremlins inside the machines of orderly, moral society. Should we assume that her options, even at their most idealized, are indeed so limited that even her captors begin to dream up modes of escape for her?

The haunted female reader begins by giving herself over to the expectations of others. Her very nature creates in her an exacerbated susceptibility to sensation, an innate pity, and an intensified sympathy.[15] The essential female imagined by Virey, Louyer-Villermay, Brachet, and other nineteenth-century "hysterizers" is always capable of acting out through her nerves the passions of others. This is, of course, why the world is such a dangerous place for her. The spectacles of public space, like those on the stage and in books, may induce in her the very reactions that serve her so well in private bonding. Because she can introject others with such ease, she is always in danger of overloading her own fragile system with the desires of others. Or, what is even worse, she risks learning from others the desiring practices that result in more than just longing. Exposed by her own affinities, she may harbor the ghosts of anyone who crosses her path. This is why, according to those who want to put her encounters with books under surveillance, her reading may take several dangerous forms.[16]

First, for such a woman in thrall to her nerves, reading may act as a magnetic agent, forcing her to serve as a medium for the novel's dangerous impulses.[17] To see the novel as a magnetizer whose seductions she has not accepted nevertheless exculpates the female reader from a yet more dangerous form of involvement with books, that of willfully engaging in a sexual encounter of sorts. In this second form of reading, the woman submits her body and nerves to the desires of the text, learning in turn to take pleasure in the sensations she encounters.[18] Her subsequent nymphomania, erotomania, *clitorisme* (penchant for masturbation), or hysteria would result from her addiction to the desires the books have awakened in her. Small wonder that she would be lost to her husband once her standards are elevated to the level of imagining herself as Luizzi's lover. Third, because it acts upon her somatically, working through her body to generate desires she did not even know she could have, reading may act as an agent of contagion. Like cholera or syphilis, the dangers of the text may make her the carrier of degeneracy for her family. Or the text may subject her to the identificatory miming of a contagion of hysteria: seeing the madness or degeneracy of the women in the text, she may be overcome by reactions she cannot control.[19] In a fourth vision of this woman's reading, she has been infected by texts that have acted upon her like a poison. Incapable of differentiating the good influences of a novel from what critics see as its bad influences, this woman indiscriminately devours whatever comes in serials, drugging herself into exhaustion, madness, idiocy, and mental degeneracy.

In every representation given to her reading practices, the woman haunted by novels comes to a new kind of desire. Whereas prior to her affairs with books she served as the passive receptacle of the desires around her, novels now fill her with new passions, teach her new sensations, and introduce her to women who act on their own initiative, in public, and in their own interests. Her reading has generated in her a desire that is not the one of the other but instead that of the others in books.[20] But this woman, whose reading mirrors her idealized feminine attributes, does little besides endanger her own body with the desires infused into it by texts. Though she may endanger her offspring with the degeneracy novels could shoot into her bloodstream and though she may not prove very useful to a father who wants to marry her to increase family power, the girl seduced by books has simply exchanged one kind of discipline for another. Like a vampirized woman, she can be known by her pallor and hypersensitivity. And since she can be recognized and quarantined, she is not likely to harm anyone besides herself.

The truly dangerous reader who lurks in the wings of Nettement's critique of Soulié is, however, the one who may escape recognition. The duplicitous *gynolectrice* pulls legs, pulls punches, pulls tricks, escalating herself into a space where her hysterized double would not dare to venture. This cookie knows what men want from her, and she reads in any way they like, keeping secret her other readings. Her covert actions are by their very nature a lie, and she takes pleasure in maintaining her cover. Drawing on the reading pleasures she cannot divulge, she shows her delight in the readings they assign her. Her duplicity is not just part of her style.[21]

She is a fantasy, just like the haunted hypersensitive, hysterical reader. But what she gets out of books, the critics seem to tell us, is real action. And it is from the vantage point of the actions they attribute to her that I would like to show her reading practices on trial.

Readings in Danger

"Many readings are perverse," teases Roland Barthes in *Le Plaisir du texte*. The kind of perversity Barthes has in mind differs, however, from what Nettement speculates upon. "The text is a fetish object," Barthes declares at another point in these fragments about reading pleasure, "and *this fetish desires me*." Barthes imagines a process of reading that would be split, in which "nothing is really antagonistic, everything is plural" regardless of the ideology of the text: "One might be astounded by the housewifely skill with which the subject is meted out, dividing its reading, resisting the contagion of judgment, the metonymy of contentment: can it be that pleasure makes us objective?"[22] The cleavage in reading would consist of the subject's insistence on going on reading even though he or she knows that the outcome will take pleasure away. Like Freud's fetishistic little boy who knows that his mother has no penis but who simultaneously makes believe she has one, this reader will embrace the illusions constructed by the text with the same *"je sais bien, mais quand même . . ."* Barthes fills in the ellipsis for this fetishizing reader with one version of the scenario that haunts Nettement: "I am moved as though these words were uttering a reality."[23] For readers to give texts the power to move them requires abandon and risk. For a reader to get pleasure from a text, he (or she) may have to read in danger.

But part of the terror for the nineteenth-century moralist, as we have seen, is that readers will take pleasure in texts. The worker may throw his money away on textual illusions that will only spend him emotionally and physically, inciting him to unattainable blisses, and reminding him of the misery of his plight. The youth may be drawn into desires that could compromise his family, name, and fortune. The girl may be violated by a text that is depicted—like Barthes' text-fetish—as desiring her. Once positioned within the structures of desire, the woman has no options left but to go on wanting. Marginalized by the excesses assigned to her body, she has nothing else to do but read. Nettement creates an image of the reading woman consumed by the text, lost into narrative, wasted by illusions she takes for reality. Yet the reader he fears far more than this violated wastrel is the one who lives a lie. His fantasy of Madame Lafarge's reading suggests that the perversity of reading that terrified him the most was precisely the kind that he, along with Soulié's Satan, seemed remarkably capable of sustaining. "Many readings are perverse, implying a split or cleavage," claims Barthes. The danger Nettement imagines in his model female reader consists precisely of the split or cleavage of such a perverse reader. She would not need to lose herself in the text, because like Barthes' fetishistic reader, she knows it is an illusion. But she keeps what she reads into it a secret and uses those illusions to keep her desires safe. Working under cover, she can have any reality she wants—even the one the books desired in her.

Whether she mixed arsenic potions or not, reading became Cappelle-Lafarge's *pharmakon*. Remedy and poison at once, it played her for her difference.[24] "Operating through seduction," according to Jacques Derrida, "the *pharmakon* makes one stray from one's general, natural, habitual paths and laws." Its danger, as in the kind of perverse reading described by Barthes, is that it lays you on the line. It lets you have it both ways, or else it has you both ways, which may count for the same thing. It makes order out of the differences it puts into play. The *pharmakon* takes over desire to fill it with its own spectacles of difference. Reading for Cappelle-Lafarge made possible a kind of double-dealing that might be read as duplicity.[25] What's more, her reading became a lure for those who wished to see her as duplicitous. It taunted moralists like Nettement with what they wanted to believe women did with books. It suggested to them that women might be able to hold out without their ever knowing the difference.

The female poisoner is the most hideous of criminals, wrote nineteenth-century criminologists, because she destroys the family with a smile on her face. Working under cover, she lives a lie, day by day, emptying the cups of her poison into her unknowing victim, teasing out secrets and money in her quest to produce an innocent-looking death. And no one knows the difference.[26]

The poisoner has engaged in a kind of insidious double-dealing, contend the pathologists who take up her case, for she needs to go undetected if she is to accomplish this most premeditated of acts. She cannot be mad, they argue, for she must bring to bear the most acute skills of rationality to perform as if she were really what everyone around her believed her to be. She must create in those who surround her an illusion that does not leave room for doubt. Putting on the garb of her deceit, she is no longer at play: this is pure determinacy. The risks she takes can cost her life if they do not save her. Her work is to be one woman but to have another inside her, perfectly, completely preserved, as if for later. She has to make sure she is not read at all, that no one cares what she's up to, that nobody wants to see beyond the ritual actions she has so carefully practiced that they have become like life to her. Her show must go on, unnoticed.

Poisoning is a woman's crime, the experts professed in the second half of the century.[27] It is the crime of a hysteric, argued many *aliénistes*.[28] Marked by their "affective perversity," the *empoisonneuses* will intrigue the medico-legal community with their aptitude for simulation.[29] Not masculine, monstrous, unnatural, or atavistic like most female criminals made into case studies in the course of the nineteenth century,[30] the *empoisonneuse* is an exacerbated version of the oversensitive *bourgeoise*—with a heart of steel underneath. While most female criminals are read within a paradigm that makes them defective men, the *empoisonneuse* is female, but with a difference:

> Everything in these abnormal beings is but contradiction: their imagination, fertile in ruses, abounds in blunders; their will, habitually absent, shows itself sometimes indomitable; their emotions are sometimes studded with infatuations and sudden and unjustified hatreds, and their feelings, changeable and fleeting, succeed and contradict one another endlessly under the influence of their passions, their desires, or the inspiration of the moment.[31]

Like the hysterics to whom they are often compared, *empoisonneuses* are read as possessing an extraordinary intellect and boundless imagination. Nanette Schoenleben, for example, is said to have read Goethe's *Werther* so avidly that she wished to kill herself; Marie Jeanneret, diagnosed as hysterical as well as "degenerate," was supposedly "very impressionable."[32] René Charpentier's description of the fertile imagination of the female poisoner seems almost to feed upon images of Cappelle-Lafarge circulating throughout the nineteenth century: "Their fertile imagination, placed in the service of that morbid egotism, results in this need for the marvelous, for the extraordinary, for that need to be noticed, that concern for the spectacle that is characteristic of these hysterical degenerates."[33]

Imagined as overtaken by their vanity, wickedness, and perversity, these female poisoners have chosen solutions that place them among the *causes célèbres* of their century.[34] Read through their weapon—the poison—they gain a privileged position in a gallery of criminals known otherwise for the relationship of their motives to their crime. What prevents the *empoisonneuse* from leaving behind explanations comes, it would seem, from the lies necessary to her crime. For even when she tells the truth, no one believes her anymore. Once she has been accused of manipulating poison, no one knows when she can be believed. One thing is certain, though, for those who read her: she knows her own crime.

The duplicity of the knowledge she hides makes unreadable the woman accused of poisoning. It makes whatever motives she may have had somehow irrelevant. It makes whatever innocence she might protest impossible for her accusers to swallow. Those who assign her feminine traits gone awry believe that the double-dealing might stop if only she could be given a place. Contained in the "physiological system of woman," she would have a knowable imagination within boundaries that had to be female. Whatever refuge reading might have given her could be invaded by the codifiers of female behavior and bodies. The doctors, criminologists, and moralists have, however, misjudged the nature of the reading processes in which a woman accused of poisoning her husband may have engaged.

"The possibility of reading can never be taken for granted," maintained Paul de Man. "It is an act of understanding that can never be observed, nor in any way prescribed or verified."[35] Yet critics like Nettement and the prosecutors of the Limousin depended on a kind of fantasmatic observation of Madame Lafarge's reading. They believed that the books she had taken like a poison might be, in turn, taken for granted as the source of her crimes. To that end they tried to show her reading the way they believed a woman could.

"Men confess; women deny," maintained the criminologist Raymond de Ryckère, holding Cappelle-Lafarge up as his example.[36] Although experts have studied her crime for a century and a half, no one has ever proved definitively that she fed Charles Lafarge arsenic.[37] Yet no one has ever ascertained her innocence either. Cappelle-Lafarge's crime was taken for granted by her contemporaries because it is perfectly unknowable. Her reading may be implicated because at least it tells something about what she imagined. Or at least it stakes out the parameters of a space in which she may have insinuated her desires. It gives those who wanted to know her mind a way of imagining themselves in her place. By trying to read like her, they would attempt to find out what she had to deny.

"I tried, but always vainly, to bend beneath that coat of lead thrown by society upon the shoulders of those who accept its yoke, and I found distractions only in the desire to educate myself" (*Mém.*, 1:170). Cappelle-Lafarge's *Mémoires* rehearse her entrapment and flight into books — especially after the deaths of her father, mother, and grandfather: "Because it was required, I kept silent; but I wrote and read with a passion" (*Mém.*, 1:154). More importantly, she says she learned to keep her reveries a secret (*Mém.*, 1:150). Her childhood joy in reading had been converted into a pursuit of knowledge and a preservation of what she came to know, imagine, and believe. As she tells it, from the time of her father's death, she was always in jeopardy of having that pleasure compromised by the desires and demands of others.

"Everything in education must, it seems to me, have a moral goal," she proclaims, cautioning educators against the hypocrisy that enslaves little girls to appearances.[38] Her own self-education was transacted through literature, she explains in her *Mémoires*. Her favorite book was Voltaire's *Histoire de Charles XII*, which sent the girl into passionate excitement.[39] She took special pleasure in history and travel accounts, though *Paul et Virginie*, that novel de Genlis believed would be "useful" to any housewife, "bored her to death" (*Mém.*, 1:98). Above all, she took pleasure in an act of doubled reading and writing— through copying extracts out of her books: "One single occupation remained my favorite, though required: that was the extracts that I made from my readings, the imaginary letters that I wrote to form my style and that I used also to say to my mother all that I did not dare express to her aloud" (*Mém.*, 1:96).

"One must then, in a single gesture, but doubled, read and write," proclaims Derrida of a "pharmacy" not unlike Cappelle-Lafarge's.[40] Young Marie's strategy of expressing through copied texts what she might have otherwise kept hidden lets her tell her own story between the lines of her books. Like the writing of Soulié's Henriette Buré in the volumes given to her by her captor, Marie's script lets her cover over dangerous desires with what she reads. In this prescribed exercise with a kind of *pharmakon*, she adds nothing, it would seem, but only takes up texts proper to a girl and reads them into her own hand.

Marie's vampiristic writing is accompanied by her haunted reading of the novels of Walter Scott:

> That reading bewitched me, I was no longer alone, my imagination had friends in Fergus, the Master of Ravenswood, Caleb, Flora, MacIvor and Diana Vernon, the noble and outspoken girl whom I had made the companion of my dreams and the sister of my thoughts. Each night before falling asleep, I called her to me or went to seek her, galloping next to her as she rode across the heathers of Scotland on her white mare. She told me her joys and her tastes, which were my joys and my tastes. She confessed her heart to me, and I felt that if I loved one day, I would love as she loved. (*Mém.*, 1:120)[41]

Scott remains with her "like a phantom friend" even in the prison where she writes these *Mémoires*. There, she continues to read: the Bible, *L'Imitation de Jésus-Christ*, Bossuet, Fénelon, Rousseau, Lamennais, Byron.[42] In a letter dated 1841, Marie thanks an anonymous correspondent for the "friends" he has sent to shorten her hours in prison: "I wept over *Geneviève*, I stretched out my arms to *Adolphe*, spent many days and many nights with that great and beautiful *Lélia*, whom society placed on its censored list, whom women repudiate and refuse to understand in that virtuous simplicity" (*Corr.*, 2:292). Should we take her tears over *Geneviève*, her embrace of *Adolphe*, and her hours with *Lélia* as evidence of the haunted reading of an adult Cappelle-Lafarge? Or ought we to read her fascination with Sand's much censored novel as the key to her duplicity?[43]

"Poor Lélia," she writes, "Poor woman who suffered all those sorrows, all those doubts, all those discouragements, who was nailed to the earth by evil passions, lifted to the heavens by sublime desires, who possessed equally the powers of good and evil, who did not want to be a weak woman, and who could not become an angel!" (*Corr.*, 2:292). What might her reading of *Lélia* tell us about how she read in general? Can we use the pacts she makes with texts as a way of questioning the reading practices of which she has been accused? Does she read this novel as they say she read Soulié? And if so, would the differences between the two novels account for any difference in reading practice?

According to Sand's most vituperative contemporaries, her work is dangerous because its purpose is to make its readers think: her novels initiate their readers into "all the mysteries of vice and the most unruly passions." Worse yet for Sirtema, what distinguishes Sand's writings is that "the women she depicts are never wholly women, anymore than the men are wholly men"[44] (see figure 8.2). Charles Lafarge's aunt assaults her nephew's young bride with similar condemnations of the literature she cherishes. Marie reports in her *Mémoires* that Sand, of course, figured prominently in this attack:

> Madame Ponthier talked to me a great deal about literature, about the bad taste of Victor Hugo, . . . about the insanity of Alexandre Dumas, about the sublime greatness of the poets of the Empire, and above all about the immorality of Madame Sand, who wrote like a cook and thought like a fishwife. My dear aunt assured me that *that woman* would never be admitted into any honorable salon in La Châtre, that respectable women did not even know her name, and that she [Madame Ponthier] had just quarreled with a subprefect who had tried to disgrace Monsieur Ponthier by loaning him an infamous work called *Lélia*. I dared to tell her that I had read *Indiana* and that I admired at least the magic and the seduction of its beautiful prose, splendid and graceful like a diamond hidden in the petals of a rose. She raised her eyes to the sky, astonished by so much perversity at such a tender age. (*Mém.*, 2:116)

What kind of perversity did Charles Lafarge's aunt think Marie would learn from reading Sand? How could *Lélia* corrupt a wife?

Lélia is double, claims one of the three men who love her: both spectacle and specter, one great and imposing, the other monstrous and demanding (Sand, 81–83). We learn her story as she tells it to her sister Pulchérie, the courtesan. She suffers, she tells the prostitute, from a split between her body and spirit. Her reading gave her too many dreams. Reality gave her too few. Inflamed by poetry, she became contemptuous of herself: "it was a great and arduous combat, because when intoxicating us, poetry does not tell us that it deceives us" (Sand, 167). Lélia practiced a kind of haunted reading:

> I loved to read the *Life of Saints*, those beautiful poems, those dangerous novels, where humanity appears so great and so strong that one cannot then lower oneself and look at men on earth such as they are. I loved those eternal and profound retreats, those pious sufferings hatched in the mystery of the cell, those great renunciations, those terrible expiations, all those mad and magnificent actions that compensate for the vulgar injuries of life with a noble feeling of flattered pride. (Sand, 195)

But, as she explains to Pulchérie, she was unable to sustain this life as a *spectacle*, this religious retreat from the world, this incessant betrayal by poetry. Her mobility drives her to other desires. Yet her options, as her prostitute double

Figure 8.2

Daumier's *Moeurs conjugales* depicts the irritation of the husband of the reading woman: "I don't give a damn about your Madame Sand who keeps women from mending men's pants! . . . Divorce has to be legalized again, and that author must be gotten rid of!"

points out, are always socially prescribed and limited to places outside the realms of the desire she has learned in books: "Beneath what mountain of shame and injustices must [a poor creature] learn to sleep and to walk, in order to be a lover, courtesan, and mother, the three conditions of the destiny of women from which no woman escapes, whether she sells herself by means of prostitution or with a marriage contract" (Sand, 153).

"Oh woman, you are only a lie," complains Sténio, one of the men who love Lélia (Sand, 290). He rages at her for being "a woman like any other" whom he has wished, after the example of Don Juan, to seduce precisely because she appeared so spectacular. Her exchange of masks with Pulchérie has redoubled Lélia's doubling and confused his desires to the point of jeopardizing them. He wants her "spectacle," but gets only her "specter." Putting aside the poetry that has haunted her, Lélia projects herself into the strategies of her far more duplicitous double.

As audience for Lélia's confession, Pulchérie provides the model for the reader of both the novel and the woman Lélia.[45] Her own mode of reading differs substantially from that of her sister:

> I read the poets; I read them to reconcile myself with the life they paint with such false colors and which has the detriment of being too good for them. I read them to know against what pretentious and scandalously erroneous ideas we must guard ourselves in order to be wise. I read them to take from them what is useful and reject what is bad, that is to say, to seize that luxury of expression that has become the usual language of the century and to keep myself from clothing it in the follies they teach. You should have contented yourself with that. You should have, my Lélia, used the fertility of your brain to poeticize things so as to better appreciate them. You should have applied your superiority of constitution to pleasure and not denial; for what good is enlightenment to you now? (Sand, 163–64)

Pulchérie can serve as the exemplary perverse reader. Like the pleasure-seeking fetishist described by Barthes, she knows how to divide up her readings to keep her illusions alive. Refusing to practice denial, she seeks instead *jouissance*. Taking her pleasure with the text, she knows how to get from it what she wants.

Reconciling herself with the life the poets paint, Pulchérie plays the text against itself. She uses her reading to preserve her cover. Her reading is duplicitous because she doesn't let herself be taken in by anything. The opposite of her sister, the courtesan would refuse to let texts move her. Instead, by accusing Lélia of a "hypocritical virtue" she induces the other woman's story (Sand, 154). By refusing to believe the morality of the spectacle Lélia presents to the world, she procures her sister's text.

The duplicity Pulchérie elicits in Lélia gives the novel's protagonist the force to leave behind the kind of reading that sapped her strength. The encounter with her double inspires Lélia to remember that Pulchérie praised her once for her beauty because she resembled a man, but it also helps her gain the force those around her already attribute to her (Sand, 158). Telling her story allows Lélia to reread her experiences as if they were being written. Though Lélia will never resolve the combats in her dual nature, as Cappelle-Lafarge noted, she will nevertheless gain the power to take control over the way she is read by those around her. She will begin to substitute her own story for the poetry that betrayed her with its illusions.

Cappelle-Lafarge describes her own reading processes in ways that parallel those of Sand's heroine. Her projection into Lélia's suffering, like her adolescent infatuation with Scott's Diana, or her adolescent desire to live out a novelistic fantasy, gives her a place to dream and a shape for her desires. The novel is never quite enough for Cappelle-Lafarge. As her *Mémoires* and letters repeatedly suggest, she needed a way to produce her own texts. Like Lélia, she will begin to supplement her reading with fantasies her books cannot contain: "If I want to read, . . . I must finish the thoughts of the book that seem to me incomplete. I bring them, with my imagination or my heart as a guide, . . . to a higher stage than the author conveyed them."[46] Writing her *Mémoires* and *Heures de prison* will give her a way of completing the novels she reads, just as they will give her a way to incorporate these fictions into her own experience.

But her writing also gives her a chance to put on a show. If Cappelle-Lafarge had taken lessons from Lélia, she might have learned that a woman could trade on a feminine performance. Had she read Sand's novel instrumentally, she might have recognized that as long as Lélia remained enigmatic she inspired desire. The mask of virtue, humility, and above all, of feminine morality could satisfy admirers, and elicit the support of those who might help her in her appeal for a pardon.[47] "I write to save my innocence from slander, I write for my honor, I write for my friends," she tells the editor of her *Mémoires* in 1841. But she also writes for public consumption: "Since the greatest publicity is necessary for the *moral effect* that is the goal and the ambition of my efforts, I confide myself to your experience for the announcement of the publication of this work," (*Corr.*, 2:248–49). Her only way out of this prison, this regime of silence, this increasingly narrow world of forced labor, is a "moral effect." She knows who *her* readers are.

Cappelle-Lafarge tells a story of double binds that may have led to desperate acts, of circumstances so confining that criminality or hysteria would have seemed logical ways of escaping.[48] Ultimately, she narrates strategies of reading that appeal to fantasies of women's mysteries and ideals of feminine sensitivity. She provides a seductive account of her intellectual aspirations because her desires remain always within the confines of the most rigorous nineteenth-century notions of women's roles. Even when she insists upon women's rights to be educated or to be loved in marriage, she does so with appeals to the most romanticized notions of her gender. Fearing censorship of her writings, she will adhere to moral ethics far stricter than those in the authors she admires—Sand, Dumas père, or Constant. The practices of reading she claims to have embraced emerge as acceptable, even desirable, within the criteria set by critics like Nettement. Though she represents herself in a kind of glorified *lecture féminine*, as if to ward off the critics' attacks, she nevertheless invites suspicions.

"People have spoken a great deal," writes her editor, "not without reason, of the seduction that Marie Cappelle works on all those around her. No one has gotten away from this irresistible charm; many have made it a crime, so absurd is the bias against it. But those who wanted to judge her with impartiality asked themselves if a body so pleasing, so attractive, could have devised and executed the infamous crimes for which she is blamed" (*Mém.*, 3:105). Because she is able to project herself as double, "child and man at the same time," Cappelle-Lafarge elicits terror in those who want to put women under surveillance (*Mém.*, 3:107). She summons up images of Lélia, "placed on the censored list," in all those who seek to keep female desire in view. She generates wild diatribes in those who censor women out of control. Her seductions make her critics all the more convinced that she had poison up her sleeve. As far as they are concerned, her writings are themselves readings in danger. They sought a way to put a stop to those undercover operations.

Taking it Like a Woman

The reading woman Nettement trails is operating under an alias. She has no other choice but to read like an other. Her name has effected a cleavage that no critics, no prosecutors, and no interpretations will suture. They will accuse her of duplicity, but she was already double-dealing when she rode that carriage to Le Glandier. They will make her out to be a criminal because she squirmed at the thought of living the lie Charles Lafarge asked of her, but she took on the lies and made the best of them. Double-crossed by her family, double-talked into this marriage of convenience, Marie Cappelle became Madame Lafarge. Operating under the name of another, she lived the lie they gave her. Haunted by the marriages she might have made, she took Charles Lafarge's name like a woman.

The masquerade of Marie Cappelle resembled those of the women in *Les Mémoires du diable*: taking the names of their husbands, they became unidentifiable to anyone but themselves.[49] The aliases of the women in the devil's stories serve to trick Luizzi. Their double identities draw him into their affairs and make him take their part. Operating under the names of others, these women have a critical edge over those who try to read them. The lies they live help them stay clear of danger. Their masquerades are so respectable no one knows the difference. Their masks fit so well no one even wonders who they were before they took on their husbands' names.

Divided by the name of Charles Lafarge, Marie Cappelle has no choice but to read perversely. Posing, Madame Lafarge will always perform her readings like another. She will have to read duplicitously, because she has taken a name that puts her forever under cover. Her put-on of femininity is just an extension of that cover-up. If she reads her books like a woman, then surely she is only operating according to what is expected; surely she is only taking orders like a woman.

I am insisting upon what Cappelle-Lafarge took on when she accepted her husband's name, because I want to emphasize the framework in which she was obliged to operate.[50] I want to demonstrate that the only kind of reading Marie Cappelle *could* perform was the kind her critics fantasized she might. Her reading had to be shifty because they confined her to reading like a woman. And that ensured that she would take every chance a woman might. As soon as they assigned her to a "woman's" appropriate role, they were asking her to pose. They were expecting her to play-act, presenting an image that would cast honor on her new husband. And that image was necessarily a duplicitous one. As Joan Rivière explained in her classic essay, womanliness could only be a masquerade: "Womanliness . . . could be assumed and worn as a mask, both to hide the possession of masculinity and to avert the reprisals expected if she was found to possess it—much as a thief will turn out his pockets and ask to be searched to prove that he has not the stolen goods."[51] For Rivière there is no difference between "genuine womanliness and the 'masquerade.' " They are both travesties—but of what?

Rivière seems to suggest that femininity covers up the woman's true masculinity. It hides the fact that she knows there is no difference. This notion of womanliness on parade depends upon an equation of the dangers of woman and the woman's hidden desires, suggests Stephen Heath. "What is *das ewig Weibliche?*" Rivière asks in Freud's place, claiming that "The conception of womanliness as a mask, behind which man suspects some hidden danger, throws a little light on the enigma."[52] One might think she almost wants him there suspecting that danger. As Heath remarks, "the masquerade is the woman's thing, hers, but it is also exactly *for* the man, a male presentation, as he would have her. . . . Which leaves Rivière where?"[53] Where is the pleasure in reading herself as posing when all she gets is permission to insist: "I must not take, I must not even ask; it must be *given* to me."[54] What does she get out of the man's reading her in danger?

With Lafarge's name given to her, Marie found ways to get pleasure without taking it. Or was her mistake that she confused the terms? Did she instead take pleasure without waiting for it to be given? What pleasure can there be in these fantasies of women reading like women? What do her critics get from their beliefs that what Marie Lafarge got out of books, she took like a woman?

"In the Limousin, women never write," protested Charles Lafarge when he got wind of his bride's epistolary relations. Cappelle-Lafarge writes of a husband eager to protect himself from scandal (*Mém.*, 2:295). During her murder trial, her husband's lawyer would describe Charles Lafarge's frustration with this wife who wanted far more than he knew how to give. "Don't forget that you are her husband," Chauveron says he advised the distraught husband. "You are, according to law, morality, and religion, entrusted with protecting her. It is up to you to combat the weaknesses, the mistakes, the deviations of an exalted imagination."[55] The husband's role, said his lawyer, was to make sure his wife put up the right front.

Lafarge's fears about his wife's education, reading, and writing come up repeatedly during the trial. The prosecutors in the rural Limousin are determined to prove that her contempt for her new family's educational limitations gave her the motives for murder. They will try to read into her very brilliance the signs of an imagination gone astray. They will read her for the powers of dissimulation that would dispose her to murderous acts.

Marie barricaded herself into her room the first night at Le Glandier, Charles confided to his lawyer. Locked up tight, she wrote her new husband a letter that made him sorry he had ever sought her hand.[56] She will not stand for this marriage, the letter says. Either Charles must give her an annulment, or she will kill herself. All she wants is to go home. Lafarge begs his lawyer to help bring his bride to her senses. Chauveron's intervention leaves him baffled: he had believed that he could get her to demonstrate her nervous symptoms — or at least to confide her misery, but instead, she agrees with everything he says. Her amicable nature drives him to conclude that his client's new wife is either extremely imbalanced, or, worse yet, amazingly duplicitous: "I told myself: either this young woman has a great mobility of feelings and ideas that make her forget the next day what moved her strongly the day before, or she possesses to the highest degree the great art of dissimulation."[57] Either way, the lawyer is sure that she is putting on a show.

Try to make her happy and comfortable in her new home, the lawyer tells his distraught client. Praising Marie's "merits, intelligence, and graces," Chauveron tells Lafarge "that he had the responsibility of using wise and enlightened control to guide his wife back onto the right path." Above all, the lawyer tells Charles, he must find a way to correct her education: "it was especially necessary to try to bring her around to ideas of religion and morality that, from her letters, did not appear to me to have been the foundation of her education."[58] Chauveron uses Marie's intimate correspondence with her husband to read her as endangered. He would diagnose her duplicity out of the disparity between her private writing and her public façade. He keeps referring to the kind of woman she is supposed to look and act like, as if her education or her husband could make her that way, as if a little time could accustom her to the right pose.

Chauveron is only the first of a steady stream of interpreters who try to read her danger in her own texts. Behind the duplicity they believe they find on the surface of her writing, they claim she hides dangers more dreadful than enigmatic. They assign her a mask of horror because the mask of their order repeatedly fails to fit. Upon the death of Charles Lafarge, Marie's mother-in-law — the other Madame Lafarge — breaks into the young woman's desk and steals her writings. Out of these letters, the family and the lawyers attempt to read Marie as a criminal. They try to reconstruct what she did with the arsenic, what may have been in the medicines Charles took, what she may have wanted that he could not give her. The prosecutors use these texts to put Marie on trial, not just for her imagination, or for her failure to live up to her duties, but for a murder that may never have happened in the first place. They read her letters and *Mémoires* against the image they have of women reading and writing. They compare her self-presentation with the representations they claim to find acceptable in women. They hold her reading practices up against their notions of what a reading woman is supposed to get out of books. They scour her writing for indications confirming that she is what they think she is. And again, the prosecutors and critics take her for a liar.[59]

"Madame Lafarge's entire book is an even greater lie than her declarations at the trial," claims Jules Janin in his review of her *Mémoires*. Janin's censure of Cappelle-Lafarge's writings depends on his sympathy for her husband—and not on any more vital knowledge he may have of the past she reports in her books. Although he points to discrepancies between the versions of the story of the diamond necklace told by Marie and by her childhood friend Madame de Léautaud, he cannot resuscitate Charles to demonstrate that Marie lied when she swore she did not poison her husband. Like the lawyer Chauveron, like her husband's family, like the prosecution at her trial, he ends up telling a story about the dangers of her education and the immorality of her reading. Janin's projection into Charles's place finds him overtaken by fears of what a woman might know: "I see him side by side on this long journey with an ill-bred girl who cries, who wails, who vomits, who doesn't eat, who appeals to the heavens and the stars, who turns her head away with disgust, who talks to him of all sorts of strange things—about Mozart, Beethoven, Meyerbeer, Lamartine—who *confesses* to him that she has read *Indiana*."[60] Janin's conclusions that Cappelle-Lafarge's writings are duplicitous seems to depend, above all, on his investments in preserving women from a certain kind of knowledge. If a woman is to read Sand, he seems to say, she should at least be wise enough to cover it up.

Should we assume that the way Cappelle-Lafarge says she read Scott, Lamartine, Chateaubriand, and Sand is just another masquerade? Is the story she tells of her reading only another convenient fiction, taken up to cloak the way she really read during her marriage of convenience? Were the pacts she made with her books far more dangerous ones than the enthralled readings she represents in her *Mémoires?* Did she take lessons from Lélia, or did she read, like Pulchérie, in ways designed to cover up her knowledge and desires? Is this why she never owns up to having read *Les Mémoires du diable*, not to mention having taken pleasure in its pages?

If we are to believe Janin, she would have had to read Soulié in a double way. Although, as Menche de Loisne noted, Satan's appeals were to women,[61] Soulié did not cut his female characters any slack. "Mr. Frédéric Soulié is, above all, the novelist of men," declared Janin. Unlike Balzac, the ladies' man, Soulié exposed women for what they really were, making sure women neither reigned nor governed: "In his books the woman arrives by chance, when she can and however she can. . . . The man commands and is obeyed." According to Janin, Balzac worked on the sly, setting up scenes with such subtlety that even murders seemed natural. Soulié was the exact opposite:

> Loud, animated, warm, pointedly brutal, he loves scandal and noise; when he has guessed a secret, well-hidden in the hundred thousand folds of the human soul, he climbs immediately on the roof and proclaims aloud the secret he has found. Women may faint, but what does it matter to him? He will not waste his time tapping softly into their hands—he will throw a big pail of well-water in their faces! . . . . Mr. Balzac is often a sucker for his heroines . . . Mr. Soulié is the opposite. He enters the house of the guilty woman. . . . If she wants to take his hand, he pushes her away; and when he has thoroughly crushed her, humiliated her, and disgraced her, he leaves her and goes on to another woman.[62]

For Cappelle-Lafarge to take pleasure in Soulié's *Mémoires du diable*, she would have to read it like a man. Her reading would have to divide her, leaving the womanly reader at best possessed by the vices of the characters Soulié paints so unsympathetically. She could only enjoy projecting into the roles of the women if she took them out of context. Reading blindly, transported so completely by the text that she could no longer find its boundaries, she could indeed suffer the pernicious effects Satan hopes for his women characters.

To read Soulié as a woman, then, would require that she selectively enter into complicity with the characters the text polices. She would have to give herself over to those the novel reads into confinement, puts under restraint, makes pay for crimes, and holds up as examples of the wages of sin. Such an identification would put society at risk, as Nettement contends, because once she takes the part of these characters, nothing would contain her anymore. Instead she would introject the bodies of the female characters, creating an army of multiple identities with which she might stage a defense against the policing strategies of the text. Her pact with the oppressed of literature would give them another body and a second chance at crime.

But what if, instead, the female reader identified with the male characters? What might happen to her then? What if she were to read Soulié like the men at whom Janin believes this novel was directed? What if she read like Nettement? Or like the devil? Or even, simply, like Charles Lafarge?

Soulié's novel set itself the task of demonstrating the duplicity of appearances. If it winds up making a show of policing the family or of giving women their just desserts, it nevertheless constantly undermines these spectacles with the devil's warnings against accepting anything on the basis of a superficial reading. If one way of reading this novel is thematized through Luizzi's "readings" of women and subsequent impassioned involvement with their relations, the novel tenders yet another way of reading. The double readings provided by the devil would serve, then, as a cue to another way this novel offers itself to its readers, male or female. At the same time, these double readings point to the duplicity of the interpretations by the moralists who condemn the *roman-feuilleton*. Like the devil in Soulié's text, the moralist can put a turn on appearances to find the underside of any woman's desire. And when Nettement does so, he uncovers an approach to reading that would make the woman's textual encounters dangerous indeed.

The readerly text can be "read, but not written," claims Barthes. The writerly text, however, makes the reader "no longer a consumer, but a producer of the text."[63] Nettement represents Madame Lafarge as consuming a readerly text, but as soon as he gives her another motive than the ones she would read out of the novel—when he imagines her dissimulating, lying, taking part in covert operations—he confers a writerliness on the text that surely she, too, must have seen. When he imagines her constructing plots of poison and making her own novels out of the *roman-feuilleton*, he transforms her passive consumption into an active production. He allows that she may have written her way out of what she read. He gives her the power to undo containing discourses.

For Nettement, Janin, and the prosecution in Cappelle-Lafarge's trials, reading like a woman was a matter of stepping into a mold, prescribed in advance, or else taking risks that would always put society in danger. Caught reading dangerously like a woman, Madame Lafarge would, in their book, turn out to have been reading like a man. Hooked on the paradoxes of their own reading models, these master-interpreters take even womanliness as a sign that danger lurks behind the woman's reading. Possessed by their readings, she is always shown as overtaken by lies.

Reading Theories

Soulié's devil has a theory about reading. He knows how people read each other and what investments they have in those readings. And no matter what reading a mortal seems to have of another, it always turns out to be a wrong reading—or at least an overinvested reading. The devil is always explaining that things are not the way they seemed.

He also knows how people read books and what they want from *that* kind of reading. People will run after the kind of literature Luizzi will write, the devil warns his protégé. They will devour "bad books" to satisfy "depraved tastes." (*Mdd*, 3:64–65). The only difference between Luizzi's book and the others, of course, will be that *Les Mémoires du diable* will be made up of true stories. And since novels gratify the desire for *vraisemblance* in hypocritical and duplicitous men, the *vrai* will undoubtedly give them similar pleasures (*Mdd*, 4:147).

The devil also has theories about reading women. He knows that men misread women's virtues, judging too eagerly their façades and missing the hypocrisy of their performances. He has their number, and he uses it to manipulate the likes of Luizzi. Playing the moralist, reading for his own pleasure, the devil performs divided readings. Everything is always readable in a different frame. When the new reading has been performed, every woman is always other than what she seemed. Every woman is always interchangeable with the others.

This is why the devil's theories about the way women read are so much a part of his overall strategies. When he says he wants to make sure his *Mémoires* are honest and moral, what would possess us to believe him? Shouldn't we assume that this is just another bluff, just another ploy to get men and women to turn to evil ways? What kind of reading should we give to this representation of reading?

The novel Luizzi will write, with its title *Les Mémoires du diable*, will recount with brutality—says his mentor—the criminality and the monstrosity of the people who want to read it. Incorporating all the stories the devil tells his pawn, it will be true, for these will be the *real* stories of the people Luizzi knows in the *real* world around him. And, the devil claims, it will be moral:

> May God always keep us from the two things for which society could pardon us, but for which we could never forgive ourselves: let him keep us from lying and immorality. Lying, for what purpose? Isn't real life more insolently ridiculous and depraved than we would know how to contrive? Little people and great men feed on immorality in the shadow of their solitude. Women of the world and *grisettes* swoon over immoral books in the secrecy of their boudoirs and garrets; and when their conscience is safely hidden with the book beneath a silk cushion or in a straw mattress, they hurl insults and scorn at the one who chatted with them for a moment about their sweetest infamies. (*Mdd*, 1:38–39)

The devil is not worried about corrupting ladies. Unlike Tissot, Virey, Briquet, or Nettement, he has no illusions about women. Unlike Rousseau, de Genlis, or even Freud, he is not afraid that bad books will make women less marriage-able. Rather, he is afraid of having his *Mémoires* read hypocritically.

The devil's models of reading replicate those we have already seen in Nette-ment—up to a point. Like the moralist critic, the devil imagines women driven by their desires for dirty books, hysterically fainting over these texts they devour in their bedchambers. He sees them giving themselves over body and soul to immoral novels, then putting on quite another show for the benefit of society: "All women act toward an immoral book like the countess of *Les Liaisons dangereuses* toward Préval; they abandon themselves entirely to it . . . and then they ring their servant to put it at the door like an insolent man who wanted to rape them" (*Mdd*, 1:39). Above all, the devil does not want to be the dupe for this kind of reading. Better, he insists, to be guilty than to be played for a fool. His book may be read lasciviously, but it will not be "taken."

The devil has theories about reading, and whether they are a trap or just a spoof, they warn the reader of this novel what not to make of it. They let readers know in advance that this devil is wise to them. As far as Satan is concerned, women can make anything they like out of his book as long as they don't try to cover up their readings. For he seems to know that there are some readings that remain secret. He is always extending those secret readings to the one who is willing to abandon himself to narration.

Luizzi is so taken by the devil's tales that he falls out of a window trying to rescue Henriette Buré, risks his life trying to restore Eugénie Peyrol's rightful name, winds up in an insane asylum trying to save Léonie de Cerny, and gives up his fortune trying to prevent his half-sister Caroline from being duped by the evil Jeannette. The ultimate haunted reader, Luizzi not only takes avidly to the new way of learning about women's "other" side, but he so delights in gaining a second sight into women's private lives that he inevitably comes to participate in their dramas and fates.[64] Like his victimized half-sister Caroline, he cannot tell the difference between virtue and vice, or even between one version of the story and another that sheds light upon the first. He cannot keep track of what he has read because he is so deeply involved in what he is reading. He blunders from one disastrous situation into another, giving himself progressively over to the devil, begging for yet another story to help him make sense of the world around him.

Like the endangered haunted reader imagined by Nettement, Caroline will give herself over to *Paul et Virginie, Romeo and Juliet,* and *La Nouvelle Héloïse*—and be lost (*Mdd,* 5:109–11). Irrevocably in love with the *colporteur* (traveling book salesman) who comes to deliver novels to a woman named Madame de Gélis, Caroline will not be able to see that the very letters her beloved sends to her are plagiarized and stacked to set her up. Henri has merely copied the productions of a vaudeville writer at the request of his actual lover Jeannette/Juliette, in order to secure Caroline's love and dowry. Neither Caroline nor Luizzi ever learn to read instrumentally. They never quite learn to tell the difference between texts and life, or between fake letters and real ones, or between duplicity and honesty. They become perfect dupes for the devil, for they do not cover up what they learn from him. They do not act in secret upon something they read in these stories. Rather, they take everything in, gradually corrupted by texts that hypnotize, seduce, infect, and poison. And they will be lost.

But the devil knows the other kinds of readers are more dangerous to his purposes than these reading dupes. He knows there are readers like Juliette who only *claim* to learn from texts. And readers like Madame du Bergh, who learn to desire from novels but never abandon themselves to the convulsions of fictions.[65] He knows there are readers far more like himself—and like Nettement—who will never let it be known what they really read or what they really want from those readings.

Moralist readers like the devil and Nettement need to present their readings as honorable and honest in order to preserve illusions. They need to present themselves as moral in order to keep on operating under cover. They need fantasies of haunted readers in order to ensure that no one will imagine they too have phantoms possessing their reading.

In *L'Écriture du désastre,* Blanchot imagines three kinds of reading. The first kind, explains Ann Smock, "is active, productive: it produces text and reader, *'elle nous transporte.'* It carries us away." This is something like the kind of reading I have been calling haunted reading. The second, as Smock explains, "is passive: it appears to submit to the text; but in this very submissiveness it is unfaithful, for it gives the illusory impression that the text exists objectively, and that it is *one*, a sovereign totality." This kind of reading emerges as a kind of duplicitous reading, but its mastery is tenuous because it depends upon texts that are given illusory powers. The third kind of reading is supposedly neither active nor passive, but "neutral." Smock reminds us that Blanchot sees this third kind of reading as "like insomnia, the nocturnal wakefulness that he often evokes: what there isn't won't let up; what isn't present will not depart."[66] This "forgetful reading knows neither pleasure nor the joy that transports; it escapes both comprehension and desire." Smock's fear is of having mistaken her readings for something other than this forgetful reading. The moralist's fear is of having not hidden well enough his investments in that process of forgetting.

Both the devil and Nettement have visions of a woman manipulating texts to produce meanings that suit her own interests.[67] They have nightmares of a woman refusing the lessons of novels to act as her own agent. When they assign dangers to the woman's reading, they not only engage in fantasies about reading, but they give free rein to their fantasies about women.[68]

Marie Cappelle-Lafarge's accusers gave her their dangerous readings: the books turned against her. The books made to betray her. A list of her readings like a litany in the press. And the trial made a mockery of her knowledge, of her education, of her aspirations to a noble spirit. They wanted to show the crime they accused her of had come from her books. They wanted to show she had learned her duplicity by reading.

The books, like Marie Cappelle, would resist. Only the dangerous readings of the critics would remain, betraying the investments the critics brought to her, making a mockery of the desires the critics brought to reading. That is what she must have known as she kept her own readings secret. That is what she must have used to console herself as the newspapers displayed her private world for everyone to read. Safe in her prison in Montpellier she could keep her readings safe. That would make her always able to show up those who claimed to read like her. All their readings would always betray something other than the secrets she had read into her books. They would always uncover some danger she had yet to dream about.

"What haunts are not the dead, but the gaps left within us by the secrets of others," wrote Nicolas Abraham.[69] Those who come to read Madame Lafarge's criminality, her hysteria, or her duplicity rehearse, one after another, the desire to have her secrets. She gives none up. She writes in the spaces they would use to confine her. She leaves no trace of her motives, or of her desires, or of what she took from reading. They censor her as a seductress. They contain her with their fantasies about dangerous readings. She gives up no secrets.

She haunts them. Her secrets haunt them. Their desires haunt them. They want to know what possessed her. But her readings leave them only phantoms. They want spectacles. Her writings leave them only masks. In the end she withholds herself. Despite all the words she poured into the spaces between their stories, Marie Cappelle-Lafarge remains a mystery, making believe someone might want what she knows how to give. She holds out to be a specter, doubled into fantasies of dangerous readings, keeping safe the ones they can never know.

PART FOUR
Scenes of Interpretation

9

Doubling Out of the Crazy House:

Gender, Autobiography, and the Insane Asylum System

*I*n September 1854, a thirty-nine-year-old Parisian musician was taken from her apartment, at the request of her half-brother, and committed to the private mental hospital at Charenton. From there she would later take her place in the dreaded public asylum, the Salpêtrière, then move through a series of institutions to which the authorities would consign her (figure 9.1). Labeled manipulative, dangerous, and sexually provocative by the doctors who examined her, she would find few resources—legal or otherwise—at her disposal. For the next fourteen years, Hersilie Rouy would attempt to write her way out of incarceration. She would first compose desperate letters to the authorities, then keep elaborate notes for her *Mémoires*, which she hoped would convince state officials that she had never been *aliénée*, or estranged of mind, but only the brunt of a terrible scheme by her family.[1]

As an unmarried woman with little wealth, Hersilie was doubly vulnerable: while the asylum system offered squalorous conditions and torturous "therapy" to men as well as women, it entrapped women with greater ease, kept them longer, and released them with less frequency than their male counterparts.[2] Furthermore, its investments in observing and representing female madness were linked to a refinement of gender-based social control and to an increasing medicalization of sexuality.[3] For these reasons, the circumstances surrounding Hersilie's *Mémoires* raise questions about gender and power in the nineteenth century, about the way the "police of the family"[4] enacted economic sanctions against women, and about women's access to the law. Against all odds, Hersilie broke through the wall of silence to which her gender, social position, and incarceration had doomed her. Unlike the hundreds who disappeared without a trace each year into the labyrinth of the psychiatric order, Hersilie did succeed in escaping. After over fourteen years of inscribing her condition on any surface she could use, with any ink she could obtain, Hersilie's writings gained her attention, hearings, and eventually protection under the law. Her *Mémoires*, published posthumously a decade after her release, testify to the horrors of the places she inhabited and to the terror of living in a world where writing one's

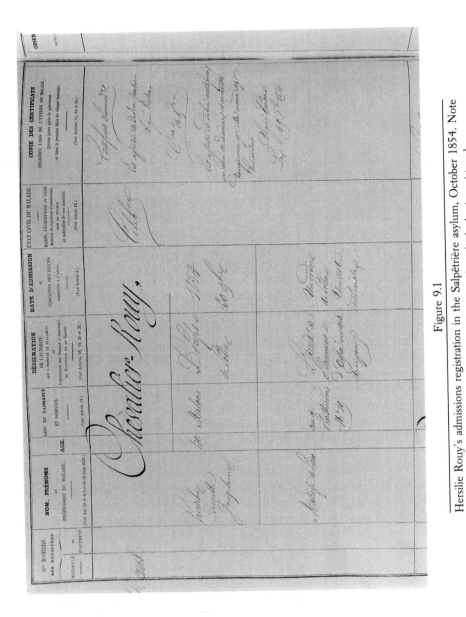

Figure 9.1

Hersilie Rouy's admissions registration in the Salpêtrière asylum, October 1854. Note the supposedly false name, "Chevalier-Rouÿ" under which she is registered.

(ASSISTANCE PUBLIQUE: HÔPITAUX DE PARIS: SERVICE DES ARCHIVES)

sanity only further confirms the diagnosis of insanity necessary for continued imprisonment.

Hersilie's autobiography represents her attempt to situate herself among the sane, to demonstrate her reason, and to protest the insane asylum system from a position of sanity. Her every attempt to do so, however, puts her goals at risk. Her self-defense threatens to reinstall her in a network that makes her readable only in the terms of the system that marked her as mad.[5] In paradoxical ways, Hersilie sets her own terms for analysis, leaving us unable to know whether she was sane or insane. Yet, through her solutions to the problem of writing her way out of the asylum system, she confides us with mysteries that ultimately put into question whatever terms we might use to read psychiatric difference. In this chapter, I consider the terms the testimony of an asylum inmate sets for itself in order to explore the more general problematic of writing in the system of *aliénation*. After examining Hersilie's writing and its maneuvers out of the mad-system, I will also consider how such writing destabilizes interpretative strategies, including theories of autobiography.

Hersilie's text is exceptional in every sense, and that is, I will contend, what allows it to stand in for the excluded and the marginalized. Indeed, its very survival as a text positions it in a rarefied space between the exclusion that engendered it and the exemptions that authorized it.[6] Because this text is intensely preoccupied with the process of becoming an exception, it interrogates the boundaries necessary to a discourse of exclusion. Because this work entangles itself with the discourse that might have silenced it, we must consider its complicity with the voices of reason. Because it rehearses with elaborate documentation the course of the internment, it forces a rereading of the terms of the *aliénation* system. Finally, because it offers itself endlessly as a case to be reinterpreted, we should consider the paradoxes of the readings that make it an object of knowledge. By restaging the clinical and administrative interpretations that led to its author's marginalization, it invites us as readers to entangle ourselves in the regions between madness and sanity, fiction and nonfiction, experience and representation, discourse and silence, the interpretable and that which resists interpretation.

Writing in the System of Aliénation

"I finally managed, here and there, to get hold of scraps of paper—like the margins of newspapers, or of books, or like tobacco wrappers. I glued them together or I sewed them to one another, then I wrote on them with my blood to the government official who was answerable, and I told him everything" (HR, 224). Writing in the asylum is always transgression. It is always an attempt to get beyond the asylum, to make sense out of being locked up, to reclaim an identity other than the one conferred by the system, to procure an inviolable space. The asylum system of the nineteenth century must ensure that no space exists where judgment is not passed, where sanctions are not applied, where its inmates are not watched and known and interpreted.[7] For this reason, all writing in the asylum is spied upon, supervised, and ultimately violated. "No one may enter into a division of the mentally ill without authorization from the director of the institution," proclaimed the Conseil général d'administration des hôpitaux in 1842.[8] The isolation of mental patients, embraced vigorously by *aliénistes*, supposedly removed them from habitual activities and family in order to shock them into "new impressions."[9] Once an individual had been committed to an asylum, he or she was effectively cut off from all contact with the outside world—except for what might pass through letters. According to law, the asylum administration had to allow an inmate to write a letter every two weeks, to carry on some contact with the outside to which the system claims she will be returned, cured, when she has learned its lessons well.[10] Some of the asylum doctors seemed, indeed, to revel in these missives: "There are lucid madpeople who reveal themselves only when they write. We let them write a great deal until we really know them," reported Ulysse Trélat, a prominent *aliéniste* who practiced in the Salpêtrière at the time of Hersilie Rouy's internment.[11] The letters Trélat reproduces in his case studies are only rarely addressed to the doctors. They are written to family members, to imagined acquaintances, to public figures, to friends. They invoke a world outside the asylum. Since they are caught in transit and reprinted as evidence of what Trélat calls *la folie lucide*, we cannot know if they arrived at their stated destination.

Whether it is reviewed and sent on, intercepted, or destroyed, all writing in the asylum is at risk. Hersilie recounts the story of an inmate who wrote her husband of the beatings she received in the asylum at Maréville: "The honorable doctors tore up her letters *seven* times" (HR, 149). Hersilie's own letter about this case, directed to the imperial prosecutor, returns to haunt her:

> The imperial prosecutor, according to the kind custom of these magistrates, sent my letter to the administration, who sent it along to Doctor X upon his return. He found nothing better than to announce to me that I was "extremely dangerous" and to have me sent to the ward of senile inmates. (HR, 149–50)

While Trélat copiously reproduces the confused banterings of his "monomaniacs," "nymphomaniacs," and "wicked lunatics" (*méchants*), he recoils from copying the portions of a patient's letters that criticize the asylum or the care she receives there: "What we find there, above all, are complaints and irony. No one escapes criticism, not the doctor, not the students, not the director, not the treasurer" (FL, 103). We see only an excerpt from the patient's criticism of a visitor to the asylum; we are supposed to be convinced of her madness simply because Trélat *tells* us she is a complainer. Here and elsewhere surveillance silences the substance of the protest. Hersilie recounts the injunction of a substituting doctor. What he tells the personnel is not new, just explicit, overheard, and transcribable: " 'Let all the letters be sent except those where the patients complain about the institution' " (HR, 149). In a world as closed and racked with prohibitions as the asylum, such an embargo might even seem reassuring. As long as she does not complain, the patient might get her word out.

Because all writing in the asylum is scrutinized, the letter becomes the arena of power struggles. The inmate may use letters to protest her treatment, to refute the doctors' diagnosis, to appeal for assistance, to tell her version of her condition, to attract attention, to make a bid for control. At the same time, because all writing in the asylum must pass through an acknowledged censor, each letter necessarily reenacts the drama of the powerlessness of its writer. Deprived even of the private sphere of writing, the asylum inmate inscribes each word in a register of interdiction. Hersilie even comes to envy criminals, since she believes she is already treated like one, stripped of her honor and persecuted in spite of her asserted innocence.[12] Differentiated from the criminal, placed in an asylum to herself, the madwoman has been certified as being outside the bounds of reason. Her writing is marked as *aliénée*, not to be believed, not worthy of delivery. No one wants her proofs, her witnesses, her defenses. If her keepers allow her to write at all, they do so only in order to turn her writing against her. The masters of the asylum permit her power struggle in order to reassert their control.

"In an oppressive society," Terry Eagleton has pointed out, "writing is the sole free self-disclosure available to women, but it is precisely this which threatens to surrender them into that society's power."[13] It is no accident that one of the most powerful Victorian fantasies of putting women under restraint, Wilkie Collins's *The Woman in White*, shuts two of its female characters up in asylums and allows a male eye to penetrate the private diary of the third. Female identity is jeopardized as much by the incursion of the censor into previously private spheres as by the man's right to designate any woman as mad who endangers his (familial) authority over her.[14] The asylum exchanges women by marking women's refusals to submit to traditional, socially accepted forms of exchange.[15] It registers them for attempting to challenge the forms of expression to which they have been assigned. The dossiers of the Salpêtrière swell with cases of women handed over by their husbands for flirting too much, of daughters turned over by their fathers for refusing chosen mates, of mothers committed by their sons for exhibiting too much religious fervor.[16] When a family member needs only a doctor's assent to rid himself of a troublesome relative, he can call on restrictive social codes of behavior to support his legal authority. The discipline of the asylum works better on women because women are already divested of the power to fight back.

In a society where a woman's word has no contractual value, she can be made a liar with ease and for profit. Her word may therefore count for more when it issues from places defined as outside the bounds of reason. In such a system, the asylum may even provide her first advocate in the form of the mad-doctor who wants her words. Philippe Pinel wrote, for example, of the importance of gaining his patients' confidence by listening to what they had to say. Like Trélat, Bénédict-Augustin Morel eagerly reproduced his patients' letters as well as verbal accounts of their experiences as evidence for his clinical findings.[17] Nevertheless, in a society where a woman's writing may serve as evidence to justify committing her to an asylum,[18] for her to accept the invitation to write in the system of *aliénation* becomes risky business. Even if endorsed by the authorities, such writing is always expected to lie outside of reason. Writing in the asylum thus reveals in an exaggerated way the dangers of writing anywhere in the nineteenth century from a female position. The woman's writing can always be read duplicitously: it can always be used to shackle her; it always courts danger. In this sense, what distinguishes the asylum from the rest of society are the specific ways a woman's writing may be turned against her and the greater stakes for her expression.

Hersilie's self-defense brings down intolerable punishment upon her: "It is usually against individuals who have their senses and know how to defend themselves or complain that they use these terrible means to break them" (HR, 190). The asylum portion of the *Mémoires* reads like a catalogue of torture: beatings, straitjackets, a shaved head, solitary confinement, imprisonment with dangerous patients, deprivation of food, water, heat, clothing, light, or medical treatment. Yet for Hersilie the worst punishment is being prevented from writing. The *Mémoires* obsessively recount this scene of censorship. The tortures are only mentioned in passing, like insults added to the injury of not being allowed to express one's reason.

Still, nothing stops her, though the doctors try everything imaginable, including the nineteenth-century version of a strip search (HR, 137–38). Hersilie depicts a struggle with the "omnipotent" doctors (HR, 136, 183, 191) in which every prohibition increases her resourcefulness and enables her to find new ruses to get her message through. Even in solitary confinement, she has an extraordinary ability to engage others in getting her letters in the mail:

> The patients who saw me from their little court had taken a liking to me and pitied me. They gave me scraps of paper, attaching them to a thread that I lowered from my window; others slipped them to me under the door as they passed through my corridor. . . . One patient named Ronard, who went out sometimes, put my letters in the mail. She was caught and the doctor had her placed under the shower. I was sorry and told her so. "Don't torment yourself," she told me, "I did it for you. I didn't feel it. Do you have other letters to mail? I am ready." (HR, 138)

The asylum administration walls up the window of her cell, bringing curious workers from nearby who, horrified by her detention, slip her writing tools and sent off her letters (HR, 138–39). Later, at the asylum of Maréville, she achieves a similar complicity with the servants. Locked in an attic room of a separate building because of her supposed pride (she has refused to play the piano for paying patients), she finds the servants eager to provide her with the means to get her letters out (HR, 163).

Although Hersilie is explicitly punished for writing, no prohibition seems sufficient to bring an end to this desperate scribbling. Using blood for ink (HR, 138, 164, 173, 214, 224) and stringing together fragments of paper (HR, 138, 214, 224), Hersilie mounts her assault on the system that has taken her name, her possessions, and her autonomy. Her challenge will be to put something together that gets her signal through; once delivered, however, her message must still convince its receiver that it does not belong in the system of *aliénation*. Stolen out of the asylum, her letters will always be read in the context of their origins. They can never arrive at the destination Hersilie imagines for them because they are always stamped in advance with a return address that risks sending them astray.[19]

Once an individual has been marked for interpretation in the order of madness, she or he is always readable as mad. The asylum structure taints the discourse of anyone who has passed through it: we are warned not to believe such an author too much. We are cautioned that she may try to dupe us, that her writing may seduce us with its lucidity, lure us with its plausibility, but that at any moment it may betray her for what she really is—a lunatic—and catch us trapped in her unreason. Shoshana Felman provides a lucid formulation of the dilemma: "What characterizes madness is . . . not simply blindness, but a blindness *blind to itself*, to the point of necessarily entailing an illusion of reason. But if this is the case, how can we know where reason stops and madness begins, since both involve the pursuit of some form of reason?"[20] What, then, do our readings betray?

In his paradigmatic act of reading madness, Freud claimed to read the psychosis of Daniel Paul Schreber out of his autobiographical book, the *Denkwürdigkeiten eines Nervenkranken*. According to Freud, a psychoanalytic investigation by means of such a text becomes possible because the paranoid always betrays precisely what other neurotics keep hidden. The paranoid may be read from his text because he always says precisely what he chooses to say.[21] Because Schreber's memoirs literally name its author as mentally ill (these are, after all, the "Notable thoughts of a man suffering from a nervous illness"), they invite us to read him for the *nature* of the illness and not for the possibility that he was wrongly incarcerated.[22] Unlike Hersilie, whose *Mémoires* begin with a preface stating that their goal is to improve the conditions under which patients are committed to asylums, Schreber begins his by announcing that his manuscript is designed to describe his "apparent oddities of behavior" to those "civilized men" with whom he hopes to live outside the asylum.[23]

Because Schreber's memoirs do indeed describe "oddities of behavior," they tempt us to read him as if he were mad as a hatter. After all, he wants to share his peculiarities with others beyond his family circle, and he remains as aware as anyone that his descriptions of intercourse with God, the incorporation of his doctor's soul into his body, his transformation into a woman, and the invasion of scorpions into his head are indeed very special responses to the world. Because of these "oddities," even if we read his text on its own terms, we read it mediated through the masterful interpretations of Freud who never met this "patient" but instead analyzed him only through his text. Thanks to historians who have supplemented both Schreber's and Freud's texts with background on Schreber's father, an extremist education expert, and Doctor Paul Emil Flechsig, the (literally) castrating nerve expert who treated Schreber in the asylum, we can speculate on a collusion of family interests and the psychiatric system not unlike the one responsible for Hersilie's internment. We cannot, however, use these experiences of "soul murder" as a gloss to read Schreber out of the insanity to which interpreters assigned him. Although Schreber's social class and high-ranking position as a federal judge allowed him to escape the asylum with relative ease, it is nevertheless tempting to read him as irreparably registered in an economy of alienation. He has managed to order his vivid fantasies of being penetrated by divine rays into an astonishing autobiography that takes its revenge upon the system that incarcerated and treated him, upon the doctor who experimented with him, and upon the society that placed controls on the expression of sexuality. But he does so, unlike Hersilie, by inscribing his difference from those who would claim a hold on reason.

Because Schreber's *Denkwürdigkeiten* seem so thoroughly outside reason, they reveal the delicacy of all readings we perform on texts from the insane asylum system. Our eagerness to free Hersilie Rouy from the shackles of *aliéniste* interpretations becomes, like Freud's determination to read Schreber back into psychosis, potentially suspect. We too read Hersilie from a text, sharing with her editor the task of making sense of these fragmented accounts, of these collected testimonies, of these letters and documents and diagnostic certificates and inquest reports. Reading from outside the system of *aliénation*, we are always testing to see if she belongs outside too. Hersilie's misfortune becomes the same as that of anyone who has passed through the order of madness: "The misfortune of the mad," writes Derrida in his discussion of Foucault's *Histoire de la folie*, "the interminable misfortune of their silence, is that their best spokesmen are those who betray them best; which is to say that when one attempts to convey their silence *itself*, one has already passed over to the side of the enemy, the side of order, even if one fights against order from within it, putting its origin into question."[24] Hersilie inevitably underwrites the legal system that will both free her and endlessly retry her. Explicitly intended to write her way *out* of the system of *aliénation*, her *Mémoires* nevertheless reinscribe her within it.

In ambitiously attempting to indict the system in which they originated, Hersilie's *Mémoires* renegotiate the boundary lines between regions of madness and sanity. Yet they position her endlessly in an interpretative cycle in which she always comes up short in her search for reparations. We are forever summoned to read her for her *folie lucide*, to seek the moments where she might betray herself, to put her back into the system of *aliénation*. Caught resisting her interpretations, we are forced over to the side of the enemy, trapped by the discourse that silences and engaged in silencing her yet again. Nevertheless, because Hersilie's text orchestrates these readings that silence by restaging them as internal scenes in her own text, she suggests we might find other ways of reading them. In inviting us to read her text through the diagnosing eyes of the twenty-five mad-doctors who imprisoned her, she allows us to see the folly of their interpretations. By presenting the readings that silence her as part of her documentation and therefore as part of the evidence against the insane asylum system, Hersilie manages to win us over to her side. This is, I believe, why her accounts of her confinement proved so destabilizing to the psychiatric order of nineteenth-century France. She manages, remarkably, to convince readers — among them ministerial investigators — that the only mad ones were the doctors and that the only lunacy was in the system itself. In a masterful gesture of refusal, Hersilie's *Mémoires* manage to contain the readings that would silence.

Thanks to the curiosity of those patients and asylum workers who helped her to write, Hersilie comes to tell more than just the story of her silencing: she tells the stories of her victimization in the insane-asylum system and especially of the retaliation against her when her letters did not get through. Her martyrdom, conveyed by her letters and memoirs, continues to make seductive subject matter; the *Mémoires* depend on our desire to know more about her victimization. Hersilie will let us, too, spy on her letters if only to make us desire her story on her terms. She will let us in on the ruses that drove the doctors to call her letters dangerous for "public morals" in order to force us to recognize the brutality she encountered when she sought to make some — any — connection to the outside.

Although Hersilie's letters submit her to nightmarish retribution and find her perpetually addressed in a place outside reason, they finally enable her to break out of the vicious circle of the asylum system. They launch her into a fairy-tale economy for which, as she points out, her mortification has already prepared her: "They made me play the part of those legendary heroines in fairy tales and medieval romances" (HR, 164), she remarks while describing her confinement at Maréville in the attic room she calls "the dungeon." After more than fourteen years of desperate pleas, Hersilie at last finds a protector; her knight-in-arms will ensure that she is given a hearing and that her words continue to get through. Her death in the midst of these hearings and before the publication of the *Mémoires* in no way dissipates the force this text carries across the decades.

At its most seductive, her text makes an appeal that no longer concerns just her case. At its most powerful, her work indicts an entire system from which she only barely escaped — in such a state of disintegrated health that she lived only long enough to leave behind this written legacy of her martyrdom. At its most persuasive, the *Mémoires* reassure us that even in the most horrifying conditions, a woman might empower herself with writing: "If I had not been able to write . . . to pour out the overflowings of my heart and the indignation with which it often boiled, I would have died or gone mad," her editor and defender reported her as saying (HR, 215n). This succinct formulation of the redemptive power of writing appears, curiously, not in the body of Hersilie's *Mémoires*, but in a footnote from her editor, a sort of caption that explains the fold-out illustration in the center of her book (figure 9.2). In this double-paged insert, Edouard Le Normant des Varannes has created a replica of Hersilie's journal, a lithographic "reproduction of a photograph" that purports to show the fragments of paper on which she kept her notes. Le Normant's footnote preserves the force of the facsimile:

> She was able to save part of her journal from the asylum of Orleans; it was written on a mass of little fragments of paper of all kinds and all colors, sometimes with ink, sometimes with diluted soot, sometimes with a reddish liquid that was none other than blood. We offer here a photograph of that sad evidence to her sorrows, such as they appeared at the time of the untying of the old handkerchief in which they were closed up and which undoubtedly protected them, for they would have been mistaken for a bundle of rags. (HR, 214n1)

On the fold-out, we find Le Normant's apology for the poor quality of this reproduction: "Since lithography cannot reproduce the writing traced on these countless little papers, we offer a facsimile of one of the largest ones." Only one fragment therefore is made readable. The rest are reduced to so many purposely illegible scribbles in little boundaries, all drawn by a lithographer so that we might get a sense of the texture of the writing that escaped the asylum.

But is this really her writing—or her signature, on that biggest piece of paper, made readable by the hand of a skillful copyist? Are these really her words about writing, quoted in the footnote by her defender, or are they, like the reproduced fragments of her journal, part of a seduction that gains power in her absence? The *Mémoires* obtain their "gripping, poignant, and true-to-life character" from the fact that Hersilie was able to draw on the accounts in her journal to compose them, Le Normant tells us (HR, 214–15). These simulated fragments pretend to represent the truth of the writing that has saved its author. As if to elevate this representation of writing in the *système d'alienation* to hagiographic heights, Le Normant transcribes his author's words in the footnote, letting her say what the very survival of this text has promised all along: writing has the power to save: "Si je n'avais pas pu écrire . . . je serais morte ou devenue folle."

Language defers madness, Derrida has contended.[25] How is it that, in this case, such an account of keeping madness at bay is itself also deferred and spoken by another? Should we read as consonant this conjuring up of the voice of the dead and the evocation of Hersilie in the title her champion gives her work—as it were, over her dead body—*Mémoires d'une aliénée?* Is there a connection between the legend, promoted by her protector, of a woman kept alive and sane by her writing and his renaming of that writing—"the memoirs

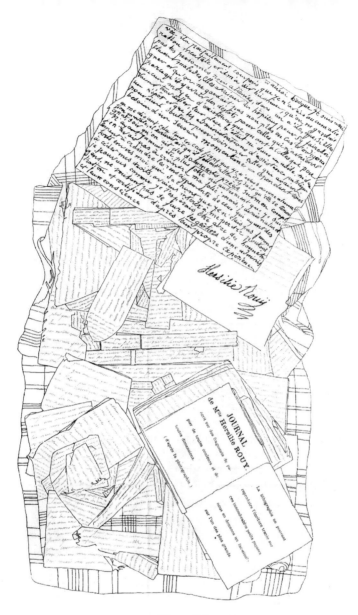

Figure 9.2

The Journal of Hersilie Rouy as recreated by her editor for a two-page foldout in her *Mémoires* (1883). The typescript by le Normant reads, "Journal of Mlle. Hersilie Rouy, written on fragments of paper of every color and every dimension (based on a photograph). Since this lithograph cannot reproduce the writing traced on those countless little papers, we give here a facsimile of one of the largest ones." The signature "Hersilie Rouÿ" and this large fragment are supposedly replicas of her own writing.

(Bibliothèque Henry Ey, Hôpital Sainte-Anne, Paris)

of a madwoman" — in terms that register her once again as mad? Has Le Normant des Varannes only unveiled the "defacement of the mind" of which autobiography, according to Paul de Man, is the cause?[26]

Hersilie Rouy's *Mémoires* actualize a threat she has made from the moment she is brought into the order of madness — to expose the system that refuses to redress its errors. She decides to publish her *Mémoires*, she contends, in a fury that marks her ironically as "crazier and madder than ever." The "madness" of publishing what she "only wrote in secret" responds to the *aliénistes'* insistence that despite the errors made in handling her case — although she was incarcerated without the proper documents and kept there without the required medical testimony and under a false name — she nevertheless fit their diagnosis of *aliénée*: "They kept you because you were mad, and they freed you because you were cured" (HR, 320). She will show, she believes, how egregiously false this appraisal is. At the same time, Hersilie plans to undo the system that refuses to believe those it has labeled crazy. If she is "cured," then her accounts must be reasonable. If her accounts are *not* reasonable, then either she has been released by error, uncured and potentially dangerous, or else, as she will argue, she was never mad at all, but only outraged by her illegal incarceration and desperate to have it known so that she might regain her name, her position, her possessions, her right to self-determination, some semblance of the life she once knew.

In the final analysis, Hersilie doesn't care that "no one believes madwomen" (HR, 321). She is not interested in repositioning the boundary lines between madness and sanity, though she worries that the interpretations are made too freely and the lines drawn too definitively. She only wants to be believed, to be noticed, to be heard. Astutely, she has long recognized that being heard depends on differentiating herself from the other *aliénés*. No wonder, then, that Trélat puts her in the chapter with those whose *folie lucide* he calls *orgueilleuse* or "haughty" (FL, 178–223). Although one of her attempts to set herself apart backfires, Hersilie's social class, profession as musician (whether recognized or not by her keepers), education, and refinement set her so much apart from other patients (*internées*) that she easily commands attention wherever she goes. In fact, nothing outrages Hersilie more than Doctor Payen's diagnosis of her in Orléans as suffering from a *folie d'orgueil* because she insists that she is an artist, a piano teacher, and a writer — all of which, of course, she *was* before her confinement:

> The conclusions of the doctor that were dictated by the Administration of the Seine prevailed, and the artist, that *intelligent, lucid* being, whose *madness could not have been appreciable in society*, was dragged among the most disgusting idiots, among the most dangerous lunatics; she was placed on the same level as prostitutes and habitual criminals who had become mad through debauchery or through crime and poverty; she was submitted to outrages, to blows, to the violence of crass attendants . . . by the doctors who were charged with returning to society

a wayward spirit, by the magistrates charged with protecting individual liberties and assuring the execution of the law! (HR, 213–14)

The folly of such a diagnosis, perhaps even more than the abuses of her rights under the Law of 1838, gives Hersilie a base of authority from which to speak. In order to get an inquest into her case she must consolidate that power base. She must grant that some of the incarcerated are indeed so *aliénés* that they are not to be believed:

> Because there are sick people who, in their ramblings, say things analogous to those I publish, does it follow that I am mad and that these facts don't exist? Can special medicine not tell the difference between a woman denouncing real acts, with composure, with evidence in hand, no matter how unbelievable they are— and the poor woman without her senses with whom you and your colleagues confuse me? (HR, 373)

What makes her different, she writes of her petition to the National Assembly, is her *responsibility* for her acts (HR, 415) and her ability to produce *written documents* on her own behalf.

The *Mémoires* restage this self-defense in which she tries to transform herself from a medical case into a legal one. Hersilie places herself under investigation: she explicitly prefaces her *Mémoires* with a note regarding the 1881 revision of the Law of 1838 for which she wished them to be evidence; she makes provisions to have all these documents and letters—as well as those fragments that constituted her journal—placed in an archive for future researchers; she adds an appendix of historical documents.

Because Hersilie's *Mémoires* were composed to justify her pleas for protection and justice, they put the reader in the position of those who would attempt to judge her sanity. Although we might collect archival evidence to bolster the case she makes against her half-brother, the *aliénistes*, and the asylum system, such an effort would simply retrace the ground she covers with ample documentation in her *Mémoires*. Regardless of the historical marginalia we might bring to her case, we cannot grant her text the status of truth. We cannot give her the identity she requests, or the reparations for which she pleads. Most importantly, we cannot give her what she has asserted as her central goal: proof that she never erred on the other side of reason. Because no research could ever give Hersilie the interpretation she desired, I would like instead to examine her solution to the problem of writing in a system of *aliénation*.

Erring on the Side of Reason

The asylum swallows the identity of its inmates, substitutes its diagnoses for their names, and denies their connections with the outside. In 1868 Hersilie Rouy writes to a hoped-for protector: "Look only at the goal I must attain. Forget the name, the identity, and see only the woman" (HR, 512). A month later she has attained the first of her goals: she is released from the asylum of

Orléans. She will wait nearly a decade more for the fulfillment of her second major goal: in 1876, the state-appointed investigator reports to the National Assembly that Hersilie's confinement in Charenton violated her rights under the Law of 1838 and was not motivated by any proof of her madness.[27] Hersilie will not stop with the reparations she receives from the National Assembly. She will pursue criminal complaints against her half-brother and against the doctor who entered into complicity with him—to no avail. She will attempt to discredit assorted *aliénistes*—among them Trélat, whose diagnosis of her at the Salpêtrière motivated the orders from Paris to detain her regardless of her mental health. She will try to unravel the power structures that enabled doctors to mark patients permanently with hastily procured diagnostic certificates. With her *Mémoires* she will seek to expose the abuses and tortures of the asylum system. Most importantly, in spite of her broken health and disintegrated talents as a pianist, she will attempt to reconstruct an identity for herself. She will try to find a place for herself on the other side of the walls that have so long identified her.

The *Mémoires* embrace this private goal even as they further all the public ones. They enable Hersilie to reclaim the name the asylum took from her when it registered her as Chevalier, a name she had never borne. They permit her to differentiate herself from the others of her family who tried to despoil her of her own name. They allow her to reassert her identity as an artist: although she can no longer play the piano, here she composes an account of her sequestration that makes sense of her loss of artistry. She substitutes artistry with language for the musical skills she has lost, orchestrating a connection between the identity of an applauded musician and that of a woman whose claims to be a pianist were derided by the *aliénistes*. The *Mémoires* give substance to her life in spite of the fourteen years the asylum took from her: by telling the asylum's tales, Hersilie can find her own meaning in her long ordeal. They allow her to give coherence to the fragments she has recorded in her journals and to draw together the contradictory strands of the letters she composed in the asylums. By restaging the inquests and trials of her sanity, they allow her to substitute her own diagnoses and to confirm the findings of the state investigator: she was never insane at all, she contends, only victimized, falsely imprisoned, and travestied by her enemies and the asylum doctors. The *Mémoires* permit her to give her version of the story out of which Trélat made her a case of *folie lucide*. Ultimately, and perhaps most important, the *Mémoires* enable her to write her way out of the alienation imposed by the asylum system.

In the place of one kind of *aliénation*, however, Hersilie's *Mémoires* embrace another. Although Hersilie uses her text to substitute a new identity for the diagnoses in the asylum registers, her self-representation emerges as anything but stable.[28] Rather, her passage through the mad-system seems to have left her unable or unwilling to resolve her identity into a narrative that would make her whole again. In spite of the redemption it rehearses, this text has other truths to tell. In particular, it has the truth of *others* to tell. And in that sense, the risk always remains that Hersilie is spoken outside reason.[29]

Hersilie's *Mémoires* harbor a central mystery regardless of the sanity we grant her. Even if we come to believe that she was mistakenly kept in these institutions, that her family imprisoned her to keep her from claiming her father's money and, therefore, that her plight relates to the economic powerlessness of women under the Napoleonic Code, we remain puzzled by the question of her identity, used first by those who locked her up and later by Hersilie *herself* in her attempt to escape.

There are two "Hersilies" we learn — or at least two women who exchange identity either in reality (one taking the place of the other) or in a fictional ploy embraced by Hersilie to seek her freedom. In one set of letters out of the asylum, Hersilie claims to have been incarcerated because of a murky relationship to the Duke of Berry. In another set of letters, she tells of trading places with the real Hersilie Rouy: "I was at Mademoiselle Rouy's. . . . They were supposed to take her away; I saved her: they took me away in her place, and they forced me to be her" (HR, 506). Throughout the autobiography, she tells of pleading that her captors wanted to lock someone up in an insane asylum, but since she is not that person, she is therefore sane. Yet, according to the author of the *Mémoires*, no one was *ever* insane.

The questions Hersilie forces us to ask emerge as questions of gender and power. What kind of reading can we perform on a text that inscribes gender in a crazy system, madness in a system of gender, fiction in a system of (autobiographical) truth? Can we read Hersilie's *Mémoires* as systematized duplicity, as an attempt to double her way out of the crazy house? Is this her attempt to dissolve her identity as a way of preserving something — anything — a writing, a text, a scrap of paper inscribed in blood that would convey the horrors of the trajectory, even if not the reliability of writing?

Shortly before her release from the asylum of Orléans, Hersilie Rouy begs her protectors to help prove that she was never insane:

> Whether I am personally Hersilie Rouy, or whether I am her shadow, it matters little, my good friends! What does my name or my identity matter? It is *me, me,* the being fatally chosen to walk in this dismal path that consists of unveiling before the eyes of all a whole series of *unbelievable, unexplainable* crimes. And to do so, the order of my cruel destiny is that no one should know *who I am or from where I come!* (HR, 511)

The asylum makes her a shadow of her former self. By registering her under the name "Chevalier" and obstinately refusing to admit that she possesses a name other than the one on her placement orders, the *aliéniste* system invites duplicity. It not only affirms the double-dealing of the men who tried to dispose of her in its hermetically sealed world, but it also disposes her to plays of identity.[30] Whether her interlocutors accept the identities she assumes, they nevertheless must address the crimes she unmasks.

In the early stages of her internment, Hersilie clings to the belief that if she can only expose the irregularities in the process through which she was committed, she will be allowed to go free with proof that the entire nightmare has been an administrative error. Progressively she learns that the administrative errors damn her: as soon as she reveals the absence of documentation about her identity, the authorities, eager to avoid scandal, reject her side of the story as the confabulation of a madwoman (HR, 100–18). Disabused of her hopes, Hersilie decides to turn their cover-ups to her own advantage. Her only way out of hiding, she believes, is through scandal:

> The need that they seemed to have to make me disappear, all the while saying that they cared for me; the pains they took to hush my identity, to keep from procuring any papers, any information; the silence of the administration charged with my guardianship; the way in which I was raised; a certain resemblance that people found in me with Madame the Duchess of Berry; the name of Chevalier, which corresponded to the name of a woman who, I was told, had given birth at the Tuileries Palace on the 29th of September 1820: all this summoned up rumors spread since that period about the birth of the Duke of Bordeaux, and made people say that I could well be the daughter of the princess. (HR, 106)

She therefore writes letters to the workers in her ward, playing on the familiar legend in which a son was substituted for the daughter actually born to the widow of the assassinated Duke of Berry.[31] The results, she later explains, are anything but what she had hoped. The workers jubilantly accept her messages, but at an enormous cost to her. The authorities censor her writing, she is placed in solitary confinement, and almost every diagnosis from this moment on will mention her "delirium" of a family relation to the Duchess of Berry. As she explains much later in the *Mémoires*, she played on this identity for the same reason the doctors and inspectors continue to use it against her—"because *it attracts attention*" (HR, 112).[32]

Hersilie says she embraces this account of her origins in order to be heard. By insisting upon the scandal of her confinement in a way that will make people talk, she believes she can draw attention to the smaller scandal, that she has been incarcerated without papers that show *who* she really is. Although Hersilie insists that she only used instrumentally the title "daughter of the Duchess of Berry," it nevertheless serves other purposes the *Mémoires* do not account for. As her prisonkeepers point out, it proffers a fantasy of power for someone reduced to absolute powerlessness. It gives her a story others want to hear that expresses *her* victimization. It allows her to harness for her own uses the kind of power her society endorses in women—the power of reproduction. Here, ironically, she has translated the power of being reproduced from a noble line out of a legend that exists only because women may reproduce but they may not reign.

Within the asylum, Hersilie's doubling gives her a cushion against scourge and selflessness even as the fiction closes in around her. It justifies her demands for better treatment from workers and fellow patients; it gives her an excuse from forced labor; and it enables her to distinguish herself from other inmates by explaining the already visible differences of class and education. Most importantly, by calling attention to the subterfuge surrounding her imprisonment, Hersilie focuses attention on the foul play of her own family. By forcing an investigation of her *real* identity, she appeals to the readers of her letters and, ultimately, of the *Mémoires*, to make sense of the family plots that enclosed her in a space where the family name would longer be recognized.

By making us privy to her own double-dealing, Hersilie would excuse herself from excesses that might otherwise prove damning.[33] Just as her *Mémoires* take an obsessive interest in the conditions of writing, they repeatedly account for what the doctors will diagnose as her "delirious letters" (*lettres délirantes*) (HR, 115–16). Just as Hersilie details the censorship and punishment that followed her writing, she will elaborately pursue the implications of her pseudonyms. By continually forcing those around her to ask about her relationship to the Bourbon monarchy, Hersilie believed she would reopen the question of her own identity. Like all questions in the asylum, however, the one she raises is twisted into the one her interpreters wish to ask. Her real name will not be verified for eight more years. Instead, the asylum doctors will mock her for her "delusions" (*idées fausses*) (HR, 92)—her contention that she is an artist and her refusal to accept the name they give her (Chevalier or Chevalier-Rouy). Although her protest induces some to ask if the authorities locked her up because she sanely claims her birthright, it also supports the *aliénistes*, who had long sought some proof of her madness.[34]

The asylum, she will show, has dissolved her identity as part of a pact with her family. When she renames herself—however scandalously—she is refusing that exchange. Deprived of her own name, Hersilie resorts to multiple identities in hopes of making someone care that the asylum system is trying to destroy her.[35] The *Mémoires* restage the trial that used the pseudonyms to put her sanity into question. They tempt us to follow the state investigators in finding that the illegal incarceration placed her under such duress that almost any aberration might have developed (HR, 377–78, 433). They urge us to skip over the accounts of her instability provided by her cornered and vengeful half-brother.[36] They encourage us to find the interpretations of twenty-five doctors ludicrous for, after all, the doctors only *relayed* a diagnosis that she suffered from delusions of grandeur.

Hersilie's autobiography seduces us with its justifications for her "*lettres délirantes*" and "*idées fausses.*" We know, after all, how easily words can be corrupted in the asylum system; we certainly would not want to perpetuate that betrayal of writing by doubting this woman's word. After all, we have the findings of a state investigation to prove that the asylum system wronged Hersilie Rouy, that it took her name, her possessions, her talent, and released her with only her story to tell.

"Whatever had I done to be locked up like a madwoman?" (HR, 117). Hersilie's haunting appeal defers all answers until after she has her say. Through such appeals, the *Mémoires* plead with us to entangle ourselves with the logic of an asylum inmate and to become advocates of her reason. Released as cured — or at least as no longer dangerous — Hersilie can claim that she speaks from the side of reason. Her words echo now on the other side of the order of madness. Her testimony has proved so threatening during her incarceration that the asylum doctors have repeatedly sought to shut her up — either by releasing her or by reducing her every utterance to madness under lock and key. Her accounts in the asylum of her identity, occupation, family relationships, and treatment could always be interpreted as the banterings of a madwoman. Outside the asylum, they continue to place her on trial, but, beside her now, the asylum is also placed in jeopardy.

Hersilie Rouy would double her way out of the asylum, using her writing to produce such scandals that her jailers might have no choice but to admit their errors. Her pseudonyms launch her into Ulysse Trélat's *Folie lucide*, thus inscribing her even more deeply in the alienation system. But in the end they are excused, legally at least, and she is allowed to disavow them in a gesture her *Mémoires* would finalize. At the same time, however, Hersilie has embraced another account of doubling. This "shadow" of Hersilie Rouy will remain with her, nagging, unexplained, and resisting interpretation, to the end of the *Mémoires*. While we might follow Hersilie's earlier disclaimer and read this alternate identity as just another ploy to get attention, her *Mémoires* make too much of this other for it to be so easily dismissed. Her other alternate selves — from "*l'Étoile d'Or*" (Star of Gold) to "*l'Antéchrist*" to "the daughter of the Duchess of Berry" — that appear in letters from the asylum generate repeated disavowals in the *Mémoires*. Her autobiography presumes to undo the damage the aliases have done her. Her other double, however, creeps in at the fringes of her text, suggesting that everything we have come to believe about her has yet another side to it. If Hersilie's text undoes the boundaries between madness and sanity, her continued doubling ensures that those lines will not be redrawn.

In this *other* version of the story, Hersilie Rouy has stolen herself away, leaving another to take the rap. After all her pleas to be recognized as Hersilie Rouy, she now seeks recognition as an *other* who has taken Hersilie's place:

> I don't want them to defile an angel; Hersilie was an angel. I want people to know that *she* was not the one who was dragged through the asylums; I want people to know that this Rouy family tossed her into grief, took away from her what she had earned with the sweat of her brow, degraded her, ruined her, dishonored her, disowned her, do you understand that, Madame? I want people to know that *I* am the one who saved her by sacrificing myself, and by bringing to everyone's attention the proof of the crimes of that family. (HR, 506)[37]

It is tempting to read this letter as an acceptance of the sanction the asylum has placed on her identity, to interpret Hersilie's refusal to be helped as the result of tortures that have "taught" her that no one calling herself Hersilie Rouy will ever get heard. Like her other doubling, this letter bids for attention, but its agonized disavowals of all identity return us to understand how she might call herself, nevertheless, "a heroine, a victim" (HR, 507).

Despite its writer's insistence that she is not Hersilie Rouy, the letter continues a story begun by the narrator of the other letters and of the *Mémoires:* the story of the crimes Hersilie Rouy's family committed against her. Even when she insists she is someone else, even when another speaks in Hersilie Rouy's place, that other will take Hersilie's part. "I am not a woman who goes back on my word," she warns her future protector. "I denounce the Rouy family before the law." As if encoded in this denial of identity, Hersilie Rouy's message still gets through. Hersilie will not have to denounce her half-brother, for she has made herself a double who will do it for her.

Fifteen years before her incarceration and nearly a decade before her father's death, Hersilie began to have visits—so she writes in her *Mémoires*—from a stranger she calls "the dark lady." According to Hersilie, this woman has given concerts in her name, "in order to increase my reputation and to pluck me from obscurity, which could be fatal to me in letting me be forgotten, and which would allow me to disappear for eternity" (HR, 29). The stranger claims to be the *real* Hersilie, but explains to our narrator that she has only come in good faith: "I had nothing to fear from her; that, on the contrary, she had come to warn me, in order that the blow, which could be brought to me by others, might be less severe and so that the means to shield myself might be available to me" (HR, 31). She offers Hersilie the opportunity to escape, but our narrator chooses to remain, to accept the dark lady's advice: to appear regularly in public, give concerts, publish an album of music with the added pseudonym *"L'Étoile d'Or,"*[38] and place a *tréma* on the *y* of Rouy to keep others from taking the name away.

The dark lady produces documents to back up her claims. These are the papers taken from Hersilie at Charenton and never returned. Hersilie will later attempt to reproduce them, insisting on their importance to proving her case. What never becomes clear—even when we study her "reproductions" of these papers—is how they bear upon her story. Hersilie recounts her first meeting with the dark lady in terms that suggest she remains equally confused about the meaning of these papers:

> It had happened, therefore, according to what was written there, that it was the bearer of that writing who was Hersilie, and not me, although I had possession of the status; that a change of a baby had been made in order to ensure the daughter of the astronomer a happy and tranquil existence and to preserve her from Pierre.
>
> I was astounded! This happened to me at the time when Claude-Daniel [her half-brother] wrote me to tell me to have myself declared a child of adultery. . . . When Désirée, his wife, told me that I had no right to the name Rouy. . . . And here it seemed that I was no longer at all the child of the astronomer, but an

unknown to all and to myself, substituted to conceal the traces of another and to mislead . . . whom? (HR, 30)

In letters included in the *Mémoires,* Hersilie will tell of encounters with strangers who inform her that she will be committed and made to pass for mad, then for dead, because, she writes, "they believed that I was in possession of secrets and papers concerning my godfather, Pierre, son of Pierre, who was the head of a formidable secret society whose divisions extended to all points on the globe" (HR, 514–15). A stranger, who comes to her as a doctor at Charenton, and who reappears even in a letter from Claude-Daniel's son (HR, 64) will contend that the important thing is to know *why* her name as Rouy has been placed in doubt and "why there had been a substitution and a seclusion" (HR, 63). Hersilie writes that this "Doctor Chevalier" takes the documents away, promising to use them to prove a plot has long been meditated to eliminate her.[39] Her handwritten transcriptions, he assures her, will always serve as proof, since they are "supported by authentic documents" (HR, 517–18).

On the basis of these documents, reproduced from memory and bearing an uncanny relationship to extant family documents, our narrator will insist that she is not the person she was raised to be. Regardless of who she really is, she will maintain, what counts is that her name has been taken from her, that she has been shut up in an asylum and kept there without appeal. What matters is that all the Hersilies have been made to pass for mad, or dead, or gone.

"It is my very self they are out to get; it's me they want to annihilate, whatever name I call myself" (HR, 517). Hersilie's doubles allow her a fragile alternate world that constantly threatens to collapse upon her. In the fantasy this account embraces, Hersilie Rouy has escaped the horrors of the asylum, while in the reality her text proposes, someone has tried to annihilate a woman called Hersilie Rouy.[40] Above all, the narrator is always reasonable, always sane, for she is not the woman who was declared mad. It will no longer matter who she is, for she can now tell the story of what Hersilie Rouy's family tried to do, how the *aliénistes* colluded, and how they all failed to prove anyone mad. It will not even matter which *one* she is, for both she and Hersilie now err on the side of reason.

Hersilie's text is haunted by an awareness that her family betrayed her, that her half-brother chose to pass her off as mad while he killed off her double in the outside world.[41] During her long imprisonment, Hersilie has learned well the lessons of the *système d'aliénation.* Her wardens have taken her name, her identity, her family connections, and passed her off as another. She has learned to be another. They have labeled her madness lucid. She has learned to tell her story in the madness they expect from her. They have called her duplicitous. She has learned to use that duplicity to temper the torments of the system that makes her no one at all. They have told her that documents don't matter, proof doesn't count, papers won't identify her. She has learned to fabricate her own documents, proof, papers—and in them, she has no identity. She has dissolved her identity, doubling her way out of it as she has doubled her way out of their system. She has scattered herself among the fragments of paper, and promised to be possibly everywhere herself Hersilie—or someone like her who knows the same pain.

Gender, Interpretation, and the Insane Asylum System

Hersilie Rouy wrote her way out of the order of madness, resisting the coercion that would have reduced her to another docile body. She writes her account *outside* the order that would have silenced her into an interpreted medical case. She claims to articulate her life, experiences in the asylum, and legal case from the side of the order of reason, determined to induce those who read her to invalidate the diagnoses that imprisoned her in the system of the *aliénistes*. Her documents, her proof, her writings separate her from the mad, she insists (HR, 373); yet she remains painfully aware that the asylum has taken from her the identity to which those papers entitle her. To prove illegal acts committed in her admission and detention will not mitigate the alienation she has undergone. But in order to write at all, Hersilie must situate herself on the side of reason. Her protests against the asylum system must ring out from the same interpretative sphere that confined her. Has her speech, then, been subsumed in the discourse of surveillance? Has she, even speaking against the confining system, been made its messenger? Does her text—this laborious staging of her trials, this risky restaging of her inquest—only reproduce the discipline that shackled her inside the system? Can one err on the side of reason without reducing oneself to silence? Can a woman raise her voice in resistance without underwriting the power that would reduce all protest to white noise?

"Where there is power, there is resistance," Foucault contends (HS, 95). Where disciplinary interpretation would summon the speech of the madwoman, it would induce her resistance as signs of its power over her. Hersilie Rouy's *Mémoires* stake out the space of such resistance, ever threatening to check that power with tactical maneuvers. Not content simply to *tell* her subjection, Hersilie creates a theater in which she stages the very readings that keep her imprisoned. She reproduces the actual diagnostic certificates of the doctors who attended her and describes the observations they made of her case. She provides copies of her letters that were construed as evidence of her madness, and duplicates the *aliénistes'* accounts of that proof. She transcribes all testimony (including her half-brother's damning letters) in the inquests surrounding her case and provides a detailed account of the proceedings. She reduplicates from memory documents she says were taken from her during her stay at Charenton even though these letters serve as much to bolster the doctors' case against her as to corroborate her version of the motives behind her imprisonment. Finally, by framing her text with her plans for her manuscript's use in further inquests, she stages a reading that will endlessly retry her after her death. Although she manages to control the *aliénistes'* readings of her by carefully reproducing them, she nevertheless creates for herself an "interrogation without end" (*DP*, 227).[42] Should we then assume, despite this text's ingenious defusing of the diagnostic powers of psychiatry, that its heroic resistance only makes it a more special, more individualized, better articulated addition to the casebooks of disciplinary power?[43] Although it outperforms the documents that would read Hersilie as mad, should we assume that it cannot undo their diagnoses? Or has Hersilie's text simply been trapped in its own double binds?

Hersilie Rouy manages to open up a space where she can represent herself. By speaking so convincingly and articulately against the asylum system, she deeply threatens the surveillance mechanisms for the ordering of madness. By not writing from the place it has authorized, she manages to destabilize the interpretative strategies of the system of *aliénation*, but she destabilizes as well any theory one might use to interpret her representations. Hersilie's play of identity lets her keep being, even if only on the borders of reason. It lets her go on resisting even if on the edge of madness. Her doubling places her outside interpretation, but it also gives her a play for what she has lost. Her *Mémoires* suggest that writing *can* be used to master the alienation system, yet this writing undoes her both inside and outside the system.[44] Alienated from her name and by her gender, she doubles her way out of the crazy house, scripting her resistances to its interpretations.

The *aliéniste* order founded its interpretations on readings of women like those in Trélat's *Folie lucide*. The Salpêtrière became a laboratory for the "invention of hysteria"[45] and the training of those who, like Freud, would establish rigorous techniques for telling and interpreting the self.[46] Theories of female aberrance, like those developed from the seventy-seven case studies in Trélat's work, anchored notions of "normal" selfhood.

Trélat turned Hersilie Rouy's truths into proof of her madness. He made his mockery of her side of the story into a guarantee of the power of his interpretations. Hersilie would nevertheless have the last word, in spite of all the others Trélat vampirized to make his own heard. Another text, however, came shortly afterward to subsume her again, reminding us of the ease with which the psychiatric order reduces even its best opponents to silence. About the same time as Freud published his analysis of Judge Schreber, Doctors Paul Sérieux and J. Capgras again took up the stories of duplicitous lunatics. Re-baptizing Trélat's subject "reasoning madnesses" (*les folies raisonnantes*), they gave their work a subtitle, "the delirium of interpretation" (*le délire d'inter-prétation*) suggestive of their approach to this special psychosis.[47] Sérieux and Capgras attach their analysis to the etiology of their era: this disability of the power to interpret results from hereditary degeneration. The parents' sins are visited upon their offspring in the form of an incurable disturbance in strategies of reading. Trading detailed case studies for a more philosophical treatment of the malady, they find, for example, that Rousseau suffered from just such an interpretative delirium. As if in excess, Hersilie turns up in a footnote. Attached to the last case in the volume, she is appropriated as part of *their* last word.[48]

Like Trélat, Sérieux and Capgras read Hersilie Rouy's *Mémoires* as proof of her madness:

> We see in this book the extent to which administrators and judges can let themselves be impressed by the intellectual acuteness of these "reasoning madpeople," by the propriety of their writings, and by the cleverness of their concealments. They even manage to justify a strange ambitious delirium established exclusively on the basis of interpretations. Expurgated in large part of all that gets too close to the system of delirium, these *Mémoires* let us nevertheless catch sight of the nature and richness of that system.[49]

According to these two doctors, editing cannot cover up the madness of Hersilie's interpretations. Her "novel of substitution" reveals the lunacy of her readings. What we have chosen to view as defensive tactics and compromises emerge here as a further justification of Hersilie's exclusion. Hersilie has reminded us of the dangers of believing her when she tells how her protector, Le Normant des Varannes, was accused of madness for his defense of her (HR, 439). Sérieux and Capgras nevertheless give her credit for duping those who found her sane.

With their summary of her case, Sérieux and Capgras would silence Hersilie once again. However, their insistence upon the power of her interpretations returns us to a question that has haunted us throughout this book. Are there ways of reading that might enable us to resist surveillance? Can one interpret one's way out of insane systems? And if so, must such interpretations only double the other madness, the other exclusion, the other discipline? Has Hersilie simply engaged us in mad readings? Or has she taught us a form of "delirious interpretation" that might help us defend *her* readings as well as our own?

As an alternative to the theories that have interpreted and excluded her, Hersilie Rouy poses her own text. By displacing the *aliéniste* discourse, Hersilie's text challenged the interpretive strategies that put women's expression under surveillance. It opens up a place where other theories might command attention. These theories must still read her, but on her own terms. Such a reading must begin with the conditions that permitted her exclusion—her family situation, her occupation, her class, but above all, her gender. Because her incarceration is an extension of the limited status of women in her society,[50] her self-presentation is suggestive of many of the problems we must confront in considering women's expression.

Wherever distinct gender roles separate women's experiences and possibilities, the conditions under which women write their own stories are, as Hersilie Rouy's text suggests, inevitably other. Nancy K. Miller has argued that "the textualization of a female 'I' means escape from the sphere inhabited by those 'relative beings' who experience the world only through the mediation of men."

Recognizing the cultural limitations for women's expression, Miller asserts the possibility of "the inscription of a *female* self: a cultural fabrication that names itself as such."[51] This analysis is particularly suggestive for reorienting auto-biographical theory in a way that would enable us to read Hersilie's *Mémoires*. It not only insists upon the gender differences that condition our readings, but it also points to the extent to which any expression of self is a cultural construction. As such, it makes way for the study of self-representation in terms of the marginalized.[52]

The challenge of gender, I would contend, should entail a reinterrogation of the conditions of writing and of the possibilities of any kind of representation — whether of the self or of others — under historical conditions of exclusion. I would like to believe that if Hersilie Rouy's autobiography is in any way exemplary, it marks the limits of the exclusion out of which a woman might attempt to represent herself. It affirms the possibility of resistance in terms that cannot be categorized again. It requires an investigation into the historical conditions for such exclusion. It destabilizes *all* interpretative strategies because it has made its way from the farthest reaches of victimization where there are no real names, no pacts, no truths, no selves, but only more interpretations.

10
Epilogue: Seductive Theories

*R*epublican Ernest Legouvé's lectures at the Collège de France in the spring of 1848 sought to analyze the "actual condition of French women according to laws and morals." His goal: to compare women's current condition to that of the past and imagine how it might change in the future.[1] In the book that enlarged upon those lectures, the much praised Legouvé laid out the trajectory of a woman's life, from "girl" to "lover" to "spouse," to "mother," concluding with a section on women's uniqueness. This proponent of biological, social, and political difference staked the dreams of the Revolution of 1848 on a difference that permeated all aspects of a woman's life, from her health to her mental states to her social aspirations. Neither a zealot nor a reactionary, Legouvé inspired feminists and leftists alike with his accounts of the special ways women might serve their society.

Like many of his era, Legouvé was equally concerned with the ways women's "distinctive qualities" might be compromised by the reigning social and political conditions. Adultery was depicted as an evil comparable to prostitution, which he assimilated into a category called "the free woman," in opposition to the liberties embraced by the Saint-Simonians of the early July Monarchy. In the place of these "abuses of marriage" (259), Legouvé advocated the temporary institution of divorce (outlawed between 1816 and 1884) and an enlargement of the rights of mothers. Just as adultery came to trouble the path of the "spouse" and infanticide to warp views of "the mother," in Legouvé's view, the single greatest danger for the "girl" lay in what he called "*la séduction.*"[2]

This story of seduction, which we have touched on repeatedly in the course of this book, holds a peculiar place in the discursive practices of nineteenth-century Europe. Just as we cannot read *seduction* today without hearing the resonance of Freud's theory of 1896 (or Baudrillard's theories of 1979),[3] Legouvé's readers would not have heard the word without recalling a series of associations relating, first, to debates over the Penal Code of 1810, second, to an ever growing specter of fear within cities due as much to the increasing numbers of single men in urban areas as to the profusion of prostitutes, and third, to an account of dangers lurking as much in books, newspapers, pamphlets, theaters, and prints, as in the shadows of the city.[4] Not surprisingly, the story of seduction told by Legouvé encompassed all three of these resonances, just as it bolstered an account of women's vulnerability that would underpin social, medical, and psychiatric theories for decades to come. By the time Freud found himself confronted with the women out of whose stories the 1895 volume *Studies in Hysteria* would emerge, seduction had become codified as an account of violation that evoked calls for punishment under the penal codes regulating rape, prostitution, or obscenity. It depended, as Katherine Cummings has remarked, upon a conflation of stories about allurement and those of molestation or rape.[5]

This book has sought to show that those stories of enticement and violation, so invested by Freud and his followers, had a complex discursive tradition in the nineteenth century. They are not simply stories that *structure* fantasy, but stories that give content to fantasy. Freud's rejection of the seduction theory must therefore be seen not just as a revised account of a hysteric's symptoms, but as a process through which those symptoms are emptied of their historical context. The woman who tells her story does so without being able to count on her listeners' belief in the history she tells or, perhaps even more important, on her listeners' awareness of the historical constraints in which and through which such a story might be told.[6]

If the scene of seduction became in Freud's early work the source of the hysteric's symptoms, that scene emerges, for nineteenth-century France, as a privileged space for the construction of difference. The imagined vulnerability of women, girls, and workers on which such a scene depended was translated repeatedly into scenes of surveillance and censorship. The violations imagined to result from novelistic, textual, and visual seduction were transformed into fuel for political crackdowns as well as into metaphors for social change. The powers of the discourse of seduction gave strength to reactionary moves of censorship as well as to utopian moves toward social transformation. Underpinning far more than the voluminous discourses about hysteria and prostitution, the scenes of seduction we have considered in this book became topoi for an imaginary in which *difference* held sway.

Underlying my account of scenes of seduction in this book has been the argument that the fantasmatic investments in difference—of class, race, and especially gender—in nineteenth-century France generated and even *required* a discourse of surveillance and narratives of containment. At the same time, as I have argued, that discourse and those narratives imploded on themselves, caught paradoxically in the very networks that seemed to sustain them. In this way, the discourse of tolerated prostitution monumentalized by Parent-Duchâtelet and other regulationists seemed to break down in the face of the tactical moves of charity ladies and prostitutes' desires, counterrevolutionary attacks on working women and their sexuality are destabilized by the discourse that surrounded prostitutes and their plight, terrors about upper-class prostitution are turned to embolden the causes of working-class women and republicanism. In this way, the narratives of difference that informed psychiatric accounts of women's madness and hysteria as well as debates over prostitution wound up creating a space for women's subjectivity. Thus, the strategies of containment that bolstered critiques of the nineteenth-century novel wound up making space for other stories to be told within and through those novels. Thus, the trial of the Fourierist *La Part des femmes* wound up interrogating the very discourse of censorship in which it was engaged, the critiques of Marie Cappelle-Lafarge's involvement with the *roman-feuilleton* turned out to enlist her dangerous reading strategies, the asylum structures that imprisoned Hersilie Rouy crumbled in the face of her powerful tactics of resistance.

Nancy Armstrong has recently argued that the English novel "helped to redefine what men were supposed to desire in women and what women, in turn, were supposed to desire to be."[7] I have argued here that the nineteenth-century French novel—particularly newly accessible forms of it, such as the *roman-feuilleton*—was inextricably caught up in social, political, medical, and psychiatric struggles over such desires. Neither remaking desire, nor simply representing it, the nineteenth-century French novel became a cultural battlefield where those struggles were mediated and transformed. As relayer of yet more scenes of seduction in a world littered with anxieties about both enticement and violation, the nineteenth-century French novel both elicited fears and made way for strategies of resistance to such fears. Even as it seemed to resolve the tensions that narrative desires evoked inside and outside its pages, the novel invited readers to imagine alternative desires in which their differences might be rewritten.

The dangers of the novel traced here are not so much dangers as invitations to desire differently. Hersilie Rouy's formidable psychiatrist, Ulysse Trélat, recorded in his *Folie lucide* the story of a woman suffering, like Hersilie, from a "madness of pride." From the moment of her wedding, this woman "discourages [her husband] in his hopes. . . . In his projects, she shakes his confidence" (*FL*, 218). In the first years of her marriage, her father-in-law died. The proof of her madness, according to the doctor, lay in her response to what "should have" deeply touched her. "What does she do?" asks Trélat rhetorically in a gesture that foregrounds his outrage at her response to loss: "Closed up in the sitting room adjacent to the deathchamber, she read *Les Mystères de Paris* and did not interrupt her reading until she had finished the volume" (*FL*, 219). Despite Trélat's certainty of the inappropriateness of such reading, it is hard to know what intrigues she found in Eugène Sue's novel. Nevertheless, in this passage, mediated through the *aliéniste* who would investigate her reading only to condemn her, we are given a peek at the fantasies that made women's reading a dangerous affair. We become privy to the desires that make a woman read madly to the end of the *feuilleton* novel. We are reminded that Sue knew how to enlist women in his charitable intrigues, and that they found something in this new genre that goaded them to improper revolts. We recall that, regardless of the limitations put on women in the works of Sue, Balzac, Sand, Dumas, and Soulié, these novels opened up spaces in which women could generate intrigues of their own.

Unlike the narratives of dangerous reading and theories of seduction embraced by *aliénistes* like Trélat, literary critics like Nettement, or state prosecutors like Bresson, there exists a nineteenth-century discourse about reading that seems to call for a far more positive appreciation of women's engagements with books. Burgeoning in the July Monarchy, along with the new readers who have so often served as the subject of discourses of surveillance and censorship, visual representations of reading, such as the image on the cover of this book (figure 10.1), suggest a counter-discourse to the stories of fear we have traced here. Grafted onto the visual discourse of absorption in which reading had been theatricalized as a private space since the eighteenth century,[8] the genre portraits of reading women of the Second Empire and Third Republic Salons differ radically from an earlier tradition of bawdy popular imagery that showed amorous encounters as the results of a stimulated imagination, or that suggested the sexual availability of its female readers. Unlike the July Monarchy lithographs of Daumier or Gavarni that were published in the popular press and gave a fantasmatic content to the text depicted as read or shared,[9] these later visual representations, by the likes of Henri Fantin-Latour, Edouard Manet, Auguste Renoir, Edgar Degas, and here, Berthe Morisot, gave their readers a private space in which the text is as unknown as the experience of reading.

In this way, Morisot's *Mother and Sister of the Artist* (1869–70) (figure 10.1) depicts a scene of reading that seems to be anything but a scene of seduction. In contrast to popular imagery that might have given a lubricious meaning to the represented book, this large canvas was destined for the respectable halls of the Salon. There, only a few years before, in 1865, Manet's *Olympia* had caused a scandal for her provocations. The scenes of seduction we have been considering in this book entail far more the women of Morisot's painting than those of Manet's. Although *Olympia* was imagined a threat to the women salongoers who were depicted as "turning their heads from the picture in fright,"[10] this naked woman on Manet's canvas was far less at risk for seduction than the observers she so boldly confronted with her gaze. Like the prostitutes of *Les Mystères de Paris* to whom she was compared,[11] Olympia was far more likely to be read for the difference that might support an ongoing story of marginality than she was to be read as herself endangered by her marginalization. Morisot's mother and sister entail quite another story—and quite another fantasy of seduction.

Like the women in many salon portraits of the late July Monarchy and Second Empire, Morisot's mother is engrossed in a book. We can only guess at what such a book may have been: a work of devotion like Adeline Hulot's *Imitation de Jésus-Christ* (CB, 189), perhaps, or one of those novels Stéphanie de Genlis might have offered to the ideal wife, like *Paul et Virginie*. We can

Figure 10.1

Berthe Morisot, *Mother and Sister of the Artist* (1869–70).
(NATIONAL GALLERY OF ART, WASHINGTON, D.C.)

be sure that Morisot's viewers would not have been pleased to learn that even this middle-aged matron was absorbed in reading Balzac or Flaubert.[12] Well into the Third Republic, debates raged over the proper kind of reading women might engage in and the kind of education girls were getting from their books (figure 10.2).[13]

Morisot's representation of the differences between her mother and her very pregnant sister, draped in a thick white dress and staring vacantly out into space,

Figure 10.2

Bourdet's "Bétises No. 10," *Le Charivari*, March 27, 1837.

(Houghton Library, Harvard University)

reminds us of the hierarchies through which the practices of reading could be imagined in the nineteenth century. Unlike that earlier reader, in the *Magasin pittoresque* engraving (figure 6.2), whom we saw bewitching her family by reading aloud, the mother's lips are closed: she is not sharing her book with her daughters. Privately, silently, she is absorbed in a world the painter purports to convey but does not penetrate. What daughter born into the *haute bourgeoisie* of mid-nineteenth-century France would not have known what this painting makes all too evident: the silent reader has become, even in her middle-aged drapery of mourning, a reader potentially at risk. Morisot's sister, idly dangling ribbons in her hand the color of those tying her hair, is left without anything that might engage her. No seductions there, only the trappings of ornamentation — among them the violets with which the painter herself will be associated in Manet's painting of 1872.[14] Unlike Morisot's mother, whose posed absorption closes the viewer out of the picture, the sister's accessible gaze into space invites visual intervention. This may be a married woman, but the painting shows her as a woman with time on her hands.[15]

Morisot's painting bears a striking resemblance to an earlier double portrait by Fantin-Latour (*The Two Sisters*; or, *The Embroiderers*, 1859; figure 10.3) that shows the painter's two sisters, one reading, the other staring off into space. Like Morisot's mother, Fantin-Latour's sister Marie seems to be reading silently, while her sister Nathalie sits idly. Unlike Morisot's sister Edma, however, who invites the viewer into the space of the painting with her luminosity and pensive availability, Nathalie is cut off behind a sewing table, half steeped in shadow. We cannot even see what she might be holding in her hands. James Smith Allen has recently read Fantin-Latour's image as a powerful statement of the changing nature of reading in the nineteenth century from a collective practice to a personal, private one.[16] Edma Pontillon and Nathalie Fantin-Latour, those

Figure 10.3

Henri Fantin-Latour, *The Two Sisters*; or, *The Embroiderers* (1859). Nathalie, at left, entered Charenton asylum shortly after this painting was completed and never again left the mental hospital. (SAINT LOUIS, MISSOURI, ART MUSEUM)

vacantly staring nonreaders, emblematize the potential readers whose engagements with books came to be seen as suspect in the course of the nineteenth century. As reading became ever more a private practice, its scenes of seduction were more and more imagined as endangering the ever growing population of women, girls, and workers who had gained access to its pleasures. But that story of private reading came hand in hand with yet another, equally linked to these two paintings, namely, the story of the growing powers of the medical and psychiatric profession in the reading of difference—of gender, race, and class. The reading woman may seem impenetrable to the viewers of these paintings, but she was not unknowable to the doctors of the Salpêtrière and their psychiatric contemporaries.

In October 1858, a few months after this portrait was painted, Nathalie Fantin-Latour was committed by her father to the asylum of Charenton and diagnosed as suffering from *"démence précoce"*—early senility. She remained there until her death in 1903.[17] Unlike Hersilie Rouy, who was committed to Charenton only a few years before Nathalie, Fantin-Latour's sister was unlikely to be able to write her own way out of the asylum. Her story, like so many others like hers, has been confided in the shorthand of a diagnosis to the dossiers of the faceless women whose cases make up the legacy of nineteenth-century psychiatry. Her portrait by her brother stands in the liminal space in which some other story might have been possible, or in which some other story seems to have existed all the same. But as Allen has poignantly suggested, that portrait seems to read her for a difference this later diagnosis makes only too easy—for the signs of mental disorder that would suggest she is estranged of mind.

Strangers to the streets in which any passerby might have taken them for a prostitute, these women sat erect in the interiors made of carved wood and embroidered cushions to which their class and gender had assigned them. Strangers to the world of higher education, to the spaces of commerce, and to the professional sphere in which they might have been encouraged as professional writers and painters, women like Edma Pontillon and Nathalie Fantin-Latour sat idle. But for all any viewer knew, they were calling up scenes from the novels they had been reading earlier that day, only posing now as idle. Perhaps they were awaiting some word that the pose could end, so that they might turn again to the pleasures with which their books had seduced them.

Notes

Introduction: Scenes of Seduction

1. De Montègre, *DSM*, 6: 363–64.

2. The French word *continence* immediately implies *sexual* containment. The *Petit Robert* (1972), defines it as "*état d'une personne qui s'abstient de tout plaisir charnel.*" The English equivalent, *continence*, excises the sexual aspect of the containment (See *Webster's Seventh New Collegiate Dictionary* [1972], first definition "self-restraint"; second definition, "the ability to refrain from a bodily activity"). I use the same word in French and English to maintain the etymological resonance and because no other translation would reinstate sexuality as what has been repressed.

3. The debate about whether a prostitute could be reformed (see chapter 1) almost never gave her the option of becoming an upright wife and mother. Prostitutes were encouraged to enter refuges where needlework and devotion could occupy their time (*PD*, 2: 5–36, 2: 546–86).

4. The Latin *continere* is defined by the Oxford *Latin Dictionary* as "to restrain, contain, or enclose."

5. On adolescents see Louyer-Villermay, *DSM*, 23: 257–68; Landouzy (1846). On widows see de Montègre, *DSM*, 6: 374–75; Louyer-Villermay; and Hatin, for whom continence caused nymphomania but not hysteria (1832: 329). On neglected spouses, see Landouzy (1846): 266, and Morel (1859) 2: 217.

6. Recent studies of hysteria insist on the illusory powers of the "disease." For Swain hysteria "functions as a scene where the truth of the female body, and the condition resulting from that truth, are unveiled and exhibited" (1983: 107). Didi-Huberman sees hysteria in the Charcot Salpêtrière as a matter of representation (1982). Beizer is exploring how hysteria's metaphors transcend medical and literary discourses, "revealing glimpses of the ideology in which both are enmeshed" (1988). Foucault used changing medical perceptions of hysteria to illustrate the powers of the gaze in *The Birth of the Clinic* (1975a: ix–xix). See also Carroy-Thirard (1979) and Trillat (1986).

7. On Parent-Duchâtelet's social scientific importance see Leuret's introduction, *PD*, 1: v–xx, as well as Chevalier (1973): 41–53, and La Berge (1974).

8. See *PD*, 2: 44–46, 525; and *FPP*, 1: 106–107, discussed in chapter 1.

9. Louyer-Villermay's suggestions for therapy allow some latitude about where the frictions are being applied (*DSM*, 23: 264–65). Sandras speaks with horror of those who have suggested

vaginal or vulval frictions ([1851] 1: 192–93). Briquet cites doctors recommending masturbation: Forestus, Louyer-Villermay, and Landouzy (Br, 137). Colombat suggests that reading novels may occasionally help—to excite an apathetic girl into menstruation (1838–43: 1085), but otherwise condemns such reading.

10. Georges Lanteri-Laura calls the failure to connect syphilis with mental illness a "kind of *nosophobie.*" Syphilis did not enter into mental pathology until the end of the century ("Folie et syphilis: Histoires," in Bardet [1988]: 314–27). Most of those who linked sexual excess to hysteria also thought continence predisposed women to nervous disorders. Medical popularizers like Virey and Debay, along with physicians like Louyer-Villermay, Lévy, Chomet, and Lisfranc emphasized *proper* quantities of sexual stimulation. When the female reproductive organs were seen as the source of hysteria, almost anything a woman did with her genitals or uterus could get her into trouble. See Virey (1825a); Debay (1850); Louyer-Villermay, *DSM*, 23: 226–72; Lévy (1845) 2: 690–92; Chomet (1846); Pauly (1836).

11. See Louyer-Villermay, *DSM*, 23: 229–30, 257, 263; Landouzy (1846): 184; Mathieu (1847): 469–71; Debay (1862): 18, 225–26; Virey (1825a): 89–11; Chomet (1846): 140; Lévy (1845): 2: 690 (who nevertheless cautioned against early marriages); Hatin, who believed continence caused chlorosis and nymphomania—but not hysteria (1832: 322, 329); and—as late as 1907—the article "Continence" in the *Dictionnaire de médecine* (Bouchut and Desprès, 7th ed., 1907), cited by Knibiehler (1976): 52. Marc (1840) 1: 320–27, also believed excessive incontinence and masturbation caused insanity, as did Lisfranc (Pauly [1836]: 289). Though Esquirol thought continence predisposed women to erotic deliria (*DSM*, 13: 186–92), he believed prostitution predisposed them to mental illness. On the rarity of nervous disorders among prostitutes, see *PD*, 1: 258–68, discussed in chapter 4, and Colin (1890): 39–41.

12. These views are rehearsed by Briquet, then refuted with statistics (Br, 105–9). Brachet, who rejected continence as a predisposing cause of hysteria, nevertheless thought the working classes less disposed to hysteria than the upper classes because he believed the most significant cause of hysteria was *"une éducation vicieuse"* (*JLB*, 212).

13. Georget (1824): 36, 39; Sandras (1851) 1: 193; Br, 126–42; JLB, 249–50.

14. Police commissioner Béraud believed women entered prostitution because of perverted passions as well as a bad education (*FPP*, 1: 2); Dubois did not believe hysteria was caused by continence but rather that professions that "have no other purpose than the pleasures of the senses" predispose women to nervous ailments (1833: 60). Esquirol, despite his implication in de Montègre's view that prostitution cures hysteria, believed libertinage a frequent cause of madness among the working classes ([1838] 1: 47); Brachet thought a poor education could lead women into an entire series of dangerous afflictions, among them prostitution, which in turn endangered the nervous system (JLB, 93); Morel developed elaborate theories about hereditary degeneracy (1862); Legrand Du Saulle (*AMP* [1860], 605–12) and Colin (1890: 37–38) held prostitutes to be hereditary degenerates. Lombroso and Ferrero's theories of the "born prostitute" proved influential in the 1890s (1896). The close relationship between hysteria and prostitution was forged by Briquet (Br, 124–26) and Rossignol (1856) though neither thought prostitutes inherently degenerate.

15. See *PD*, 2: 45–46, and *FPP*, 1: 149–56, discussed in chapter 1. As I argue in chapter 7, this fantasmatic scene recurred—with a few strategic differences—in the discourse of those seeking to extract women from betrayals by men who then abandoned them. See Mallet (1845): 76, 108, 115; Legouvé (1854): 68–82; Daubié (1866): 274–89. For nineteenth-century writers, the word *seduction* often has a valence resembling that of rape or assault. It is most often used in the etymological sense of being *led astray* and not at all in the Kierke-

gaardian sense of artful temptation (*Either/Or*, trans. David F. and L. M. Svenson [Princeton: Princeton University Press, 1959]), or in the Baudrillardian sense of a play of appearances (1979). Fournel (1781) established legal precedents for such usage. Caroline Ford (1992) has explored nineteenth-century "seduction" trials, which rarely involved unmarried women and male "betrayers," but rather drew on the *ancien régime* notion of *"rapt de séduction"* to bolster property claims. Seduction was not recognized as a valid legal accusation in any of these cases.

16. Béraud calls this scene, which he reproduces in novelistic detail, *"une scène de séduction"* (*FPP*, 1: 149–56). He imagines the fall of young women into prostitution who "would have been good spouses, excellent mothers, if they had not had the misfortune to please those corrupt beings for whom nothing is sacred" (1: 113), and he therefore demands improvements in the police system of regulating clandestine prostitution. Legouvé and Daubié, like the worker editors of *L'Atelier* (see chapter 6) wanted an improvement in the moral systems of men who lead women astray. Mallet and Frégier demanded an improvement in the moral education of women whom they believed too easily "seduced." The concerns of those demanding an improvement in the conditions of women overlapped uncannily with those who demanded an improvement in the *morals* of women and an amelioration in the workings of the Morals Police (*Bureau des moeurs*).

17. The stories psychoanalysis gave to hysteria at the end of the nineteenth century were extensions of these fantasmatic scenes. In opposition to Charcot who had sought to extract hysteria from these stories of sexualization, Freud and Breuer again insisted on the sexual origins of nervous disorders (1893–95). The scenes of seduction they imagined bore striking resemblances to those through which nineteenth-century French women came to be policed. Like the scenes evoked by de Montègre, Georget, Louyer-Villermay, and Briquet, their scenes generated debates about the responsibility of young women for their own bodies and treated women as incapable of managing their own desires.

18. Marie Marcel, "Émile Mathieu, *Études cliniques sur les maladies des femmes,*" *L'Opinion des Femmes*, I, no. 2 (March 10, 1849), 5–6. Debay (1849): 83–84. Freud (1963a): 80, 120–21.

19. Tissot (1770), cited in Br, 112; and Legrand Du Saulle (1883): 40.

20. D. A. Miller (1988): 2.

21. Corbin (1978).

22. I am indebted to Susanna Barrows for my formulation of these problems. See Foucault's call for a "history of bodies" that would account for "the manner in which what is most material and most vital in them has been invested" (*HS*, 152). On writing an archaeology of silence, see Foucault, *The Order of Things* (New York: Vintage, 1973): x–xi.

23. Although I was concerned with the ways literary texts were embedded in social contexts, I ultimately problematized these issues in ways more closely resembling the projects laid out by Chartier in *Cultural History* ([1988]: 1–16) or Hunt in "Introduction" to Hunt, ed., *The New Cultural History* (Berkeley: University of California Press, 1989), 1–24) than those of Greenblatt, to whom I am indebted for provocative discussions of these issues (cf. Greenblatt's first "naming" of "new historicism" in "Introduction," *Genre*, 13 [1982], 1–6; and reformulation of his work as "cultural poetics" in *The New Historicism*, ed. Aram Veeser [New York: Routledge, 1989], 1–14). It would be impossible to name all those from whom I have learned theoretical questions and models; nevertheless, this book was marked by discussions with Susanna Barrows, R. Howard Bloch, Charles Bernheimer, Alain Corbin, Catherine Gallagher, Jan Goldstein, Friedrich Kittler, Thomas Laqueur, and D. A. Miller as well as by the examples of Chartier, Hunt, Nancy K. Miller, Mary Poovey, Joan Scott, Naomi Schor, Richard Terdiman, and Judith Walkowitz.

1. Traffic in Mystery: The Roman-Feuilleton and the Tolerance System

1. Jeremy Bentham argued these benefits would emanate from his *Panopticon* (*Works*, 4: 39, cited in *DP*, 207).

2. *Cagney and Lacey* capitalized on techniques police departments had used since the late 1970s. Controversies surrounding the series' portrayal of women police officers saw it repeatedly preempted, canceled twice in its first year (1982), and one of its actresses replaced because CBS claimed the women were "not feminine enough, too aggressive" (Todd Gitlin, *Inside Prime Time* [New York: Pantheon, 1983], 9, 112). See *New York Times*, March 25, 1982; *Ms.*, April 1984, 23–25; *Ms.*, January 1987, 40, 86–88. NBC's *Miami Vice* further extended the masquerades of police officers as prostitutes. See Onc Wang, "*Miami Vice*: Sex and Drugs and Rock & Roll in the TV Market," *Jump Cut*, 33 (1988), 10–19.

3. The Manhattan Police Department began using decoy plainclothes policewomen to arrest "johns" in February 1978 (*New York Times*, July 4, 1978, p. 8). For protests, see *New York Times*, September 17, 1984, p. B16; January 24, 1985, p. B9.

4. In June 1990 Dr. Michèle Barzach, French Health Minister from 1986 to 1988 under Prime Minister Jacques Chirac called for a reopening of brothels and the establishment of new "sanitary controls," like those in effect from the early nineteenth century until 1946, when brothels and required medical exams were abolished. Ministers in the current government remain divided over what they see as a problem of stemming the spread of AIDS among male as well as female prostitutes (*New York Times*, June 17, 1990, p. 16; January 11, 1992, p. 4). In France, as of this writing, prostitution is legal although certain kinds of solicitation, together with pimping and brothel-keeping, remain punishable offenses. On the controversies and legislation surrounding prostitution in France from 1850 to the mid-1970s, see Corbin, *Les Filles de noce* (1978).

5. See Dennis Porter, *The Pursuit of Crime* (New Haven: Yale University Press, 1981); Stephen Knight, *Form and Ideology in Crime Fiction* (Bloomington: Indiana University Press, 1980); Geoffrey Hartman, "Literature High and Low: The Case of the Mystery Story," in *The Fate of Reading* (Chicago: University of Chicago Press, 1975); John Cawelti, *Adventure, Mystery, and Romance* (Chicago: University of Chicago Press, 1976); Ian Ousby, *Bloodhounds of Heaven* (Cambridge: Harvard University Press, 1976); Julian Symons, *Mortal Consequences: A History—From the Detective Story to the Crime Novel* (New York: Harper and Row, 1972); Tzvetan Todorov, "L'Histoire à Mystères," in *Théorie de la littérature* (Paris: Seuil, 1965), and "The Typology of Detective Fiction," in Todorov (1977).

6. Impressive attempts to unravel these networks may be found in Poovey *(1988)*; Armstrong (1987); Mary Kelley, "Sentimentalists: Promise and Betrayal in the Home," *Signs*, 4 (1979): 434–46; and Jane Tompkins, "*Uncle Tom's Cabin* and the Politics of Literary History," *Glyph*, 8 (1981): 79–102.

7. See, for example, Mogador (1854) and Pearl (1886). Rigolboche's memoirs were written by Ernest Blum and Louis Huart (Paris: Dentu, 1859). Marie Colombier's memoirs were faked by Maxime Formont (*Mémoires, fin d'Empire* [Paris: Flammarion, 1898]). Blanche d'Antigny's fictional autobiography was published in an attempt to launch her as an actress (See Briais [1981]: 36, 27n4, 21). A rare autobiography of a common prostitute is Böhme (1919).

8. Tristan (1840): 110.

9. On this army of social investigators—as well as Parent's role among them—see Chevalier (1973): 38–53, 135–44; La Berge (1974); and Coleman (1982).

10. Harsin (1985): 241; *FPP*, 1: 33; Zeldin (1973) 1: 307.

11. See Harsin (1985): 43–45, 312–13. Harsin provides a fine discussion of the police ordinances and ministerial sanctions of *tolérance*, but she sees Parent as far too charitable, thereby losing sight of the repressive nature of the regulatory system.

12. Henry Milton, "Paris, Its Dangerous Classes," *Quarterly Review*, 70 (1842): 20, cited in Walkowitz (1980): 36. For details on Parent's career, see François Leuret, "Notice sur A.-J.-B. Parent-Duchâtelet," in *PD*, 1: v–xx; Corbin, "Présentation," (1981b): 25–32; and B.-P. Lécuyer, "Démographie, statistique, et hygiène publique sous la monarchie censitaire," *Annales de démographie historique* (1977): 215–45. On Parent's enduring stature, see Corbin (1978): 36–37; and Corbin, "Présentation," (1981b): 9.

13. Leuret, in *PD*, 1: xiii. We have already met Esquirol and Marc (see introduction); Villermé wrote *Tableau de l'état physique et moral des ouvriers* (1840); Orfila was the consulting chemist in the Lafarge trial (see chapter 8).

14. See Corbin, "Présentation," (1981b): 12.

15. APP, DB407, Circular of June 14, 1823, p. 2.

16. This background is based on documents in APP, DB407–410, and reprinted police circulars in the *Recueil officiel* (1882). On the gradual institutionalization of the tolerance system, see Weston (1979), Clayson (1984), and Harsin (1985): 3–95.

17. European and American studies of prostitution routinely rehearse debts to Parent: William Acton, *Prostitution Considered in its Moral, Social, and Sanitary Aspects in London*, 2d ed. (London: Churchill, 1870), 99–161; Lombroso and Ferraro (1894): 530–88; Abraham Flexner, *Prostitution in Europe* (1914; Montclair, N.J.: Patterson Smith, 1969), 10, 21–22, 70, 73, 130–36; Iwan Bloch, *Die Prostitution* (Berlin: Marcus, 1912). On Russia, see Laura Engelstein, "Morality and the Wooden Spoon: Russian Doctors View Syphilis, Social Class, and Sexual Behavior, 1890–1905," *Representations*, 14 (1986): 189, 206.

18. Leuret, in *PD*, 1: xiii.

19. Janin, review of *Un Grand homme de province à Paris*, *Revue de Paris* (1839), cited in Chevalier (1973): 68.

20. Parent's early work revolved around the Paris sewers ("Rapport sur le curage des égouts," *Annales d'hygiène*, 2 [1829]). For a list of his publications, see *PD*, 1: xxi–xxiii.

21. Prison informants were called *mangeuses* because they supposedly got hold of their information by eating with the criminals they ratted on.

22. Donzelot points to the parallel histories of convents for the surveillance of girls, foundling hospitals, and supervised brothels, which he says served as "practices of collection and segregation" (1979: 23–24).

23. See Lecour (1872), Jeannel (1874), Martineau (1885), Reuss (1889), Commenge (1897), as well as Corbin (1978): 14–53.

24. "We will arrive at the height of possible perfection . . . when men, and in particular those who seek [prostitutes], can distinguish them from honest women; but when women, and especially their daughters, cannot make that distinction, or make it only with difficulty" (*PD*, 1: 363). Police regulations of this period explicitly require "decent" clothing and a covered head. See APP, DB407, ordinance of April 14, 1830, art. 3, reprinted, *FPP*, 1: 242–44.

25. On the nineteenth-century origins of moral economy, see Lynch (1988): 48–64.

26. Police circulars give no directives for making these decisions. Evidence suggests the police took their chances and covered their tracks easily in a system that denied women arrested for prostitution any right to a public hearing. The *instruction réglementaire* of No-

vember 16, 1843, (APP, DB407) provided for increasing safeguards to keep regular prostitutes from being confused with those women given to "dissolution," but it stopped short of clear guidelines. Paul Baum found chilling anecdotes of mistaken arrests in the abolitionist press of the 1870s (" 'Les Filles Inscrites': The Role of Writing in the Social Construction and Deconstruction of the Prostitute in France [1860–1890]," Honors Thesis, Harvard University, 1990). His archival research in Amiens also turned up compelling portraits of women who argued there had been no grounds for their arrest. Since, as Harsin notes, no denunciation of a woman as a prostitute was ignored by the police, one is not surprised to find that of the 13,007 women denounced between 1845 and 1854, 7234 were arrested. The other 5773 slipped from the grasp of the *Bureau des moeurs:* they were simply never found (Harsin [1985]: 265). Harsin's descriptions of the everyday workings of the police bureaucracy show how easily mistaken arrests might occur (19–21, 30–32). For denunciation figures see *PD*, 3d ed., 1: 574.

27. Among his stereotypes are the prostitute's plumpness, rough voice, love of flowers, alcoholism, and inability to save money (*PD*, 1: 103–245).

28. See *PD*, 1: 5–36; 2: 546–86, esp. 577–79.

29. See *PD*, 2: 546–86; 1: 104–9.

30. See Felman (1981) on Freud and Balzac's female subjects.

31. Corbin believes social pressures led to this elision (1978: 35).

32. Corbin (1978): 21. Béraud complains that the prostitute "plays at passion without feeling the least desire" (*FPP*, 1: 128).

33. *PD*, 1: 21. Parent requires discreet medical inspectors who must be either very old or married—i.e., desexualized (*PD*, 2: 93–96).

34. For views of the speculum exam, see Walkowitz (1980): 109, 110, 201–2.

35. *PD*, 1: 503, his emphasis. See also 1: 587, 1: 335, discussions of prison, 2: 253–373, and marking, 1: 355–56.

36. *PD*, 1: 352; *PD*, 3d ed., 2: 98; *PD*, 3d ed., 2: 111; *PD*, 2: 454. See also *PD*, 1: 353–54; 370–71; 490; 587.

37. *PD*, 3d ed., 1: 22, 309; *PD*, 1: 342–43.

38. Augustine, *De Ordine*, II, iv. 12 (cited in *PD*, 2: 527 in Latin).

39. Donzelot so characterizes the discourse that urged changes in the family hierarchy and pled for the preservation of children (1979: 12).

40. See Lynch on nineteenth-century differences between *political economy* and *moral economy:* "Political economy says to men: 'Work and you shall be happy.' Moral economy [says]: 'Behave well and you shall be happy' " (J. B. F. Marbeau, *Du paupérisme* [1847], cited by Lynch [1988]: 48). For most moral economists, argues Lynch, hard work was a necessary component of the good behavior that led to happiness (48). Regulationists could not promise prostitutes happiness in exchange for good behavior. They instead extended pledges of safety and health. They suggested a prostitute would gain solace from her knowledge that she was keeping *their* order and serving *their* morals.

41. See Donzelot (1979): 24.

42. For the threat of the working classes, see Chevalier (1973) and Perrot (1979b): 149–68. For the threat of the "dangerous classes," see Catherine Duprat, "Punir et guérir. En 1819, la prison des philanthropes," in Perrot (1980): 64–122; Perrot, "1848. Révolutions et prisons," in Perrot (1980): 277–312; and Chevalier (1973). For the threat of domestics, see McBride (1976) and Donzelot (1979). For women's threat, see Olafson (1980) and Donzelot (1979).

43. This term is Foucault's, *HS*, 98ff. The definition is my own.

44. See Donzelot (1979): 24ff.
45. Neuburg (1977): 12 uses this definition for popular literature.
46. See de Certeau on popular narrative in (1984): 85–86.
47. I here take issue with Umberto Eco, who contends that the only aspect of Sue's stories "not to have been 'inflexibly' planned is the reader" ([1979]: 8). My views on the workings of the popular novel owe much to Brooks (1976) and (1984) as well as to D. A. Miller (1981 and 1988). Brooks's Sue chapter in *Reading for the Plot* (1984), published in article form the year I drafted this chapter, was the first major study to rescue the *roman-feuilleton* from critical obscurity. I am grateful for his encouragement of my concurrent efforts.
48. See Brooks (1976): 41–42.
49. See de Certeau (1984): 77–90; Chevalier (1973): 405–6; Chartier (1988): 37–47.
50. Hall (1981): 239.
51. Balzac, cited in Bory (1962): 304–5.
52. Poitou (1858, 2d ed.): 15. The following works provided background for this section: Allen (1981); Grubitzsch, "Einleitung" (1977); Bory (1962); Marc Angenot, "Roman et idéologie: *Les Mystères de Paris*," *Revue des langues vivantes*, 38 (1972): 392–410; Chevalier (1973), especially pp. 59–69 and 394–408; and Neuburg (1977): 123–234.
53. *Universel*, June 6, 1829, cited in Allen (1981): 93.
54. According to Allen (1981): 139, a [male] day laborer earned more than two francs per day. A newspaper sold for six and later four sous—20–30 centimes (123). Three-volume titles had previously sold for 22 franc 50 centimes (105), and cheaper one-in-eight editions for 2 francs 50 centimes (107). The average female daily wage in 1840 was .81 francs, rising to 2 francs 41 centimes in 1850, with a salary range between 50 centimes and 10 francs per day. The average daily wage for men in 1850 was 4 francs 75 centimes, and men earned up to 20 francs per day (Sullerot [1968]: 90, 103).
55. *La Presse* began publishing *La Vieille Fille* in October 1836. Most of Balzac's subsequent works appeared in *feuilleton*, including *Illusions perdues*, *Splendeurs et misères des courtisanes*, and *Les Parents pauvres*. See Guise (1964): 283–338.
56. See Bory (1962): 671; and Chevalier (1973): 406. Bory cites the nameless critic in "Présentation" to *Les Mystères de Paris* (Paris: Pauvert, 1963), xiv.
57. Menche de Loisne (1852): 317–19.
58. Bory cites Alexandre Dumas's account of this legend, (1862): 244–52. See also 230–36, as well as John S. Wood, "La Mythologie sociale dans *Les Mystères de Paris* d'Eugène Sue," in *La Lecture sociocritique du texte romanesque*, ed. Graham Falconer and Henri Mitterand (Toronto: Hakkert, 1975), 89–100; Wood (1965): 78–94; Jean-Louis Bachellier, "Images de la biographie romanesque ('Les Mystères de Paris' d'E. Sue)," *Littérature*, no. 26 (1977): 32–39; René Guise et al., "Des 'Mystères de Paris' aux 'Mystères du peuple,' " *Europe*, no. 575–76 (1977): 152–67; and Eco (1979): 127–28.
59. Both *tapis-francs* and *garnis* were known as haunts of prostitutes (see *PD*, 1: 504–40). On Sue's "Rodolphisme," see Bory (1962): 248. No records exist of Sue's correspondence with or encounters with prostitutes. Schenda (1976) and Allen (1991) discuss the correspondence.
60. Chevalier (1973): 53.
61. Ernest Legouvé, cited in Bory (1962): 284.
62. Marx and Engels (1845, rpt. 1980); V. G. Belinski, in Grubitzsch (1977): 217–39; Antonio Gramsci, *Letteratura e Vita Nazionale, III: Letteratura popolare* (Turin: Einaudi, 1953); Marc Angenot, "Roman et idéologie: *Les Mystères de Paris*," *Revue des langues*

vivantes, 38 (1972): 392–410; Eco (1979); Marcelin Pleynet, "Souscription de la Forme: Pratiques d'Eugène Sue," in *Théorie d'ensemble* (Paris: Seuil, 1968): 326–37; and Chevalier (1973): 398–408.

63. Bory, "Présentation," *Les Mystères de Paris* (Paris: Pauvert, 1963), xiv. Foucault explicitly refers to Sue's *Mystères de Paris* in his discussion of the crime novel. He contends that the criminal *fait divers* made police supervision acceptable, while crime novels, such as *Mystères* or *Rocambole*, banished the delinquent first to "the lower depths of society," then to a world of madness, and later to the world of high-society crime (*DP*, 286). See Hall (1981): 228, 233; and de Certeau (1984): 78–81.

64. John Parker was thinking of *The Mysteries of London*, modelled on Sue, but his complaint sums up criticisms of opponents of this "literary prostitution" ("On the Literature of the Working Classes," *Meliora: of Better Times to Come*, ed. Viscount Ingestre [1853], 186, cited in Neuburg [1977]: 161). In Grubitzsch (1977), see Thackery, Belinski, Nettement, and Sainte-Beuve.

65. *La Mode*, September 15, 1842, cited in Bory (1962): 284. Restif de la Bretonne's *Pornographe* (1769, rpt. 1977) is considered the first proposal for a kind of *tolérance* system. Restif imagined state-regulated brothels with regular medical exams for prostitutes. Parent praised the work's farsightedness but condemned it as "the fruit of a delirious imagination" (*PD*, 1: 322).

66. De Certeau (1984): 47–49; 86–90.

67. Foucault's coherent description of panoptic strategies has the effect of mobilizing the success of the repressive apparatus he describes. In his final interviews and writings he suggested a move toward reformulating these problems. What he called "technologies of the self" promised to articulate ways individuals "transform themselves." See Foucault (1985): 365–72 as well as Foucault (1988a and 1988b).

68. De Certeau (1984): 36–37, 78, 89.

69. Fraser (1989): 28–33, esp. 29.

70. Flaubert (1857, rpt. 1966): 76, 92.

71. Sainte-Beuve, "M. Eugène Sue," in (1876) 3: 115–16.

72. There were 32 cabinets in 1820, 150 in 1830, 189 in 1840, and 226 in 1850 (Allen [1981]: 140, 31, 139–146; and Parent-Lardeur [1982]). On women readers, see Sauvy (1985), Crubellier (1985), Lyons (1985), Hébrard (1985), as well as Allen (1981): 31; and Bory (1962): 292. On works directed specifically at women, see Sullerot (1966), Smith (1981): 187–213, and Sally Mitchell (1981): esp. 1–21.

73. I am using Allen's statistics of the "estimated number of potential readers in Paris, 1817–1846." By 1846, notes Allen, newspaper circulation had risen to more than two hundred thousand readers, many of them workers ([1981]: 170–71).

74. Sauvy cites statistics showing a rise in minimal literacy for women from 27% in 1786–90 to 66% in 1871–75. In 1876 the literacy rate for women in the Paris area was 92.3. These figures represent the number of women able to sign their marriage register (Sauvy [1985] 3: 445–53).

75. Théophile Gautier, *Histoire de l'art dramatique en France depuis vingt-cinq ans* (Paris: Magnin, 1858–59) 3: 161, cited in Allen (1981): 168.

76. Parent-Lardeur (1982): 98–105.

77. *PD*, 3d ed. 1: 668–69, 306–9.

78. Zeldin (1973) 1: 307.

79. Corbin (1978): 287–88; Zeldin (1973) 1: 291–92. Debay (1848, 2d ed.): 88–90. See also Schor's conclusions (1976) that the idea of the mother's orgasm represented a supreme scandal. Corbin concurs (1978: 288).

80. Michelet (1859, rpt. 1981): 119–22, emphasis from Badinter (1980): 244–45.

81. Briquet contended, for example, that "woman is made to feel, and feeling is nearly hysteria" (Br, 50).

82. See Georges Cabanis, *Oeuvres complètes* [Paris: 1824] 3: 328–29, cited in Olafson (1980): 80, who presents a fine analysis of the promotion of the sensitive and hysterical woman (58–122).

83. Paul Janet, *La Famille. Leçons de philosophie morale* (Paris: 1855): 102, cited in Olafson (1980): 47.

84. Walkowitz (1980): 2. See Hellerstein (1981): 423–28, for the testimony of an English domestic servant wrongfully arrested for prostitution in 1880.

85. M. J. Brisset, "La Ménagère Parisienne," in *Les Français peints par eux-mêmes* (1841–43) 3: 17–18.

86. Olafson (1980): 40.

87. See Donzelot (1979): 21–22, and Badinter (1980): 253–64.

88. Donzelot (1979): 33; Pope (1977): 319.

89. Smith (1981): 148.

90. Donzelot (1979): 58–70. July Monarchy Police Prefect Delessert's wife was active in charity to help repentant prostitutes (Harsin [1985]: 263).

91. Pope (1977): 321.

92. On the Salpètrière, see Pottet (1912) and Henry (1922). By the 1840s bourgeois women with mental problems were unlikely to be placed there but were instead committed to private convalescent hospitals like those in Sue's *Juif Errant* (1844–45) and Balzac's *L'Envers de l'histoire contemporaine* (1848) or to the larger paying asylum, Charenton, where Hersilie Rouy began a journey through the asylum system that ultimately took her to the Salpètrière. See chapters 4 and 9.

93. Balzac, *La Femme de trente ans* (1832; Paris: Garnier, 1962), 16.

94. Cobb (1970): 5–6.

95. This definition of the detective's intrigue comes from Sue's contemporary Edgar Allen Poe, "The Murders in the Rue Morgue," *The Complete Tales and Poems* (New York: Modern Library, 1938), 141.

96. *The Oxford English Dictionary*, vol. 1 (Oxford: Oxford University Press, 1971), 1189.

97. Eugène Faure, "Les Mystères de Paris par M. Eugène Sue," *Revue indépendante*, 8 (1843): 186–296, reprinted in Grubitzsch (1977): 42.

98. Béraud reports the story of the discovery in 1838 of an *inscrite* who was still a virgin by a *Bureau des moeurs* doctor (*FPP*, 1: 251). She had registered as a prostitute, she told him, because of poverty.

99. See Michael R. Wisser, *Crime and Punishment in Early Modern Europe* (Atlantic Highlands, N.J.: Humanities Press, 1979), 6.

100. On the four spaces of *tolérance*, see Corbin (1978): 55–170.

101. See Cobb (1970): 22.

102. See Bory (1962): 277–79.

103. Grubitzsch, "Einleitung" (1977): 1.

104. Rodolphe even appropriates the narrator's role to convey this moment of risked revelation in a letter to Clémence—as if this moment must be even further brought under his gaze and into the framework of his law.

105. Marx and Engels (1845, rpt. 1980): 20.

106. Marx and Engels (1845, rpt. 1980): 199, 205.

107. See F. Zycglin von Zychlinski (Szeliga), "Eugen Sue: Die Geheimnisse von Paris," reprinted in Grubitzsch (1977): 105.

108. Marx and Engels (1845, rpt. 1980): 57.

109. I am borrowing my definition of hymen from Derrida (1972).

110. We turn to these engagements in chapters 6 and 7.

111. Donzelot (1979): 36–37. Walkowitz (1980), Pope (1977), and Corbin (1978) take a more positive view of this alliance. See especially Corbin, 339–44.

112. Nowhere is this more evident than in the legend with which we began our introduction, where prostitution cured a bourgeois girl's hysteria.

113. According to Parent, some prostitutes were as occupied with novel intrigues as their bourgeois counterparts. During their leisure time, he noted, some prostitutes read "stories and novels, particularly those describing tragic scenes capable of exciting strong emotions." Parent was amazed to find he "never encountered in their hands those licentious and obscene books that young people seek out with such ardor and that corrupt such a great number of them. . . . What is it really that these kinds of books could teach them? Doesn't satiety make dull and monotonous what under very different circumstances would be a strong stimulus?" (PD, 1: 124–26).

114. *Shield*, May 9, 1870, cited in Walkowitz (1980): 128.

115. See Walkowitz (1980): 146–47, 256.

116. Tristan (1840): 110–12.

2. Censored Bodies: Plots, Prostitutes, and the Revolution of 1830

1. Even those who did not *live* in the police-regulated brothels were expected to work there and forbidden to appear in the streets, except to go to work and then only after dark (APP, DB407, rpt. *FPP*, 2: 106–8). Prefect Debelleyme's regulations for more rigorous surveillance of prostitution—the increased bureaucratization of the dispensary, a larger staff for the *service des moeurs*, and greater pressure placed on women to live in the *maisons closes*—were now "completed" (*PD*, 1: 565) by his successor.

2. Circulars of April 27 and June 21, 1830, rpt. *FPP*, 2: 110–11. The decree of April 20 reorganized the system of surveillance (rpt., *FPP*, 2: 108–10). Police inspectors could earn bonuses for arresting an unregistered minor "proven" to "give herself habitually to debauchery," for finding an unregistered brothel, or for discovering such a brothel where minors worked. In June and July of 1830, 140 women were arrested, 91 of them for unregistered prostitution—a radical increase over prior years (*FPP*, 1: 287). In all of 1826, only 72 women were arrested as *insoumises*. In 1828, 224 *insoumises* were arrested over a twelve-month period (Harsin [1985]: 267).

3. Bertier de Sauvigny (1977) 7: 283; (1955): 242. Pinkney echoes Bertier, ascribing the crackdowns on prostitution to a series of short-sighted regulations on Mangin's part—of butchers, shop-closings, street vendors: "When [Mangin] forbade prostitutes to solicit in the streets, he alienated another special interest—one with important if concealed ramifications and influence" (1972: 62). Nineteenth-century historian Raisson attributed "*de grands effets*" to public discontent over the prostitution ordinances (1844: 316–18). Suzanne Huart takes the pamphlets to be the genuine protests of the prostitutes (1959: 606–7). Louis Girard's *Étude comparée des mouvements révolutionnaires en France en 1830, 1848 et 1870–71* addresses the incendiary power of Mangin's crackdowns (Paris: Centre de Documentation Universitaire, 1960), 95–97. Alphonse Esquiros cites Mangin's repression of prostitution as an invitation to revolution and further debauchery (1842: 153, 160–61).

4. Parent recounts his version of this liberation, *PD*, 2: 300. His editors tell how the "*souteneurs*" forced open the doors of the Prison of the Madelonnettes on July 29, 1830, and set free the *filles* inside (*PD*, 3d ed., 2: 113). See also *FPP*, 1: 288. This story is today available only through secondary sources because of the 1871 fire that destroyed city archives.

5. Cf. *PD*, 2: 497; *FPP*, 2: 85–92; Lombroso and Ferrero (1894): 557–58; Suzanne Huart (1959): 606–7; Harsin (1985): 44 recognizes the satire.

6. Cf. Bertier de Sauvigny (1977) 7: 283; (1955): 242; Pinkney (1972): 62; Suzanne Huart (1959): 606–7; *FPP*, 2: 85–92; Raisson: 317–18; and *50,000 Voleurs de plus à Paris* (1844) (1830).

7. Cf. the *History Workshop Journal* and *Representations* debates: Hobsbawm (1978); Agulhon (1979); Alexander, Davin, and Hostettler (1979); Richardson (1982); Hertz (1983); and Gallagher, Fineman, and Hertz (1983).

8. Gallagher analyzes the imbrication of these two kinds of representation in Britain, 1840–1870 (1985: 187–268). For a powerful analysis of the differences between aesthetic and political representation, see Spivak (1988).

9. Cf. Paulson (1984) as well as Brooks (1976), who relates melodrama to the Revolution of 1789, and whose analyses in *Reading for the Plot* (1984) inform many of the questions I ask in the following two chapters.

10. On the speech of the subaltern, see Spivak (1988 and 1990) as well as Ranajit Guha and Spivak, ed. *Selected Subaltern Studies* (New York: Oxford University Press, 1988).

11. A Napoleonic decree of 1806 had instituted a commission of censors; a Restoration ordinance of 1816 had set up a board to read plays and newspapers, and yet another in 1819 elaborated bureaucratic mechanisms through which, by 1821, censors would go over manuscripts before works appeared in print or on stage. This group of supposedly learned men scrutinized manuscripts, marking potentially offensive expressions, and excising scenes that were deemed offensive to "public morality," believed capable of inciting political unrest, or challenging to religious values. The play was then returned to its author for changes or entirely banned. See Krakovitch (1985): 30–43.

12. Because the censors' report and the play manuscript are missing, this account is pieced together from Hugo's preface and notes, and from Adèle Hugo (1863; rpt. 1985); Sainte-Beuve's critique, *ML*, 1405–6; and the press of 1829. See also Victor Hallays-Dabot, *Histoire de la censure théâtrale en France* (Paris: Dentu, 1862), 281–88; Nettement (1859) 2: 177–204; Menche de Loisne (1852): 134–36; Jolly (1851): 14–15.

13. Even in the July Monarchy, notes Krakovitch, the theater gave them only two possible stories: that of the decadents of the era of Louis XV or the Regent, or of the poor girl tricked into prostitution who dies in abandonment and repentance, usually after having a baby (1985: 191).

14. Nettement (1859) 1: 192.

15. Note that Mangin was Polignac's appointee. See Pinkney (1972): 62.

16. "The ardor of young people was already no longer the same as at *Hernani*; the political overstimulation created a powerful diversion from literature" (Adèle Hugo [1985]: 491). Despite widespread awareness that Hugo had written the play two years before its opening, several journalists accused him of plagiarizing Dumas's *Antony*, the theatrical rage of the moment. Political uprisings in September of 1831 led to the closing of the theater, thus ending the play's short run.

17. Hugo's friends complained in 1829 that the original play made Didier far too brutal. Hugo relented in 1831 when Madame Dorval, the actress who was to play Marion, begged for a more merciful lover (Adèle Hugo [1985]: 450–51, 491).

18. On the marginalization of abandoned children, see Daubié (1866): 277–81: "Illegitimate children are exposed to the outrages of petty villagers who abuse them, throw rocks at them, and brand them with the name *bastard*. As soon as they have enough sense to be conscious of the social oppression weighing on them, they revenge themselves for these abusive provocations by means of duels" (278). See Fuchs (1984) and Lynch (1988) for statistics on the increase in foundlings in France from 1784 (40,000) to 1830 (118,073) (121–54, 123).

19. When Laffemas contrives to get Marion into bed, the young woman anguishes: "Even if it were to save you, I could not return to that infamy!—Your breath has revived my soul, my Didier! With you nothing of me remained, and your love remade my virginity" (*ML*, 860–61). Didier's forgiveness near the end of the play's final 1831 version seems to have been to remake precisely that virginity not in spite of, but because of this moment of further sacrifice. The new lines read: "You would have to be a truly infamous and truly vile man— decidedly—to believe that a woman—yes, even Marion de Lorme!—after having loved the purest man that heaven ever made, after having been purified in that chaste flame, after having remade a soul with that soul, could fall so low as you from the height of that love so sublime and so sweet!" (*ML*, 835–36). For the rest of his life, Hugo remained wistful about the original lines and irritated about public sentiment (see note of 1836, *ML*, 860–61).

20. By 1832 censorship had been reinstituted, first by the protests of the critics, then by state prohibition of Hugo's *Le Roi s'amuse*. Within months, the trial of Hugo's new play had spurred the new monarchy to reestablish a board of censors similar to that of the previous regime. The freedom of literary and journalistic expression, so touted in the preface to *Marion de Lorme*, had become a vague memory. In 1838 *Marion* again went before the censors. Despite their reservations about the scene where Marion barters herself to Laffemas, a scene, they argued, that would be completely inadmissible under normal circumstances, they let the play go on. *Marion de Lorme*'s position in debates about politics, morality, and revolutionary freedom was far too invested for them to ban it once again: "considering the circumstances that had accompanied the presentations of this work," they wrote, "there would be reasons to authorize it notwithstanding the profound indecency of the situation" (AN, F-21, 966, cited in Krakovitch [1985]: 24, 192–93).

21. Jolly (1851): 15; 10–11; 14.

22. Menche de Loisne (1852): 135

23. Menche de Loisne (1852): 136. For Nettement, Hugo's play is a return to the Terror—"with its hateful gossip against the great houses and adulation for cottages." The king, cardinal-minister, and court, along with "all of France" are insulted and "sullied." In this play, only Marion has a noble soul: "In her, degradation become worthy and vice virtuous." The play's political choices seem offerings to popular passions ([1859] 1: 192). Its moral choices strip the drama of its "*vraisemblance*" and "dramatic truth" (1: 191). He is nevertheless won over by the dramatic beauty of Hugo's writing (1: 195n).

24. PD, 1: 407–18; FPP, 2: 154–56. In March of 1828, Debelleyme ruled out marriage as a justification for radiation (PD, 1: 412–14). Harsin's study of the arrest records of a series of repeat offenders from the Restoration and July Monarchy confirms the difficulties of radiation (1985: 212–37).

25. In April of 1831, 3131 prostitutes were registered in Paris (PD, 1: 569).

26. On classifications, see Dumas père (1842); "La Grisette" and "La Femme sans nom" in *Les Français peints par eux-mêmes* (1841) 1: 9–16; 245–56; A. Huart (1842); Alhoy [1841]; FPP, 1: 129–31; and PD, 1: 174; Goncourts (1853); Joëlle Guillais-Maury, "La grisette," in Farge and Klapisch-Zuber (1984): 233–50; and Gasnault (1986). Harsin discusses

police attempts to place courtesans under surveillance, which were abandoned in 1830 (1985: 17–18).

27. See Harsin (1985): 19–21, 30–32, 38, 264. Béraud published a series of denunciations as "proof" of the debauchery unleashed after the July Revolution, *FPP*, 1: 269–83.

28. See the July Monarchy forms used to record the arrest of a suspected prostitute, reprinted in Harsin (1985): 21–24.

29. Esther walks in Marion's shadow in *SMC*, 62, 104. Marguerite is compared to Marion by the narrator in *DC*, 66, and by Dumas fils in his 1868 preface, rpt. *DC*, 511. Zola claimed he wrote *Nana* to protest the rhapsodizing of vice in *Marion de Lorme* and *La Dame aux camélias*, which he called "dangerous for morals" and "a disastrous influence on the imagination of our poor girls," *Le Voltaire*, October 28, 1879, rpt. in *Les Rougon-Macquart* (1961) 2: 1686.

30. The Société de la Morale Chrétienne asked the new police prefect why the government had managed to control "infamous books" but failed so miserably to clean up the streets (cited in *PD*, 1: 560).

31. The *Bibliographie de France* for spring of 1830 lists twenty-one pamphlets and one print relating to the Mangin ordinances on prostitution. This account is based on a reading of twenty pamphlets, listed below with abbreviated titles by publication date, printer (named in the *Bibliographie*), and price (according to the *Bibliographie*). Although most pamphlets name a distributor (see bibliography) none lists its printer, and only one, *Plainte et révélations*, gives its date: "the month of May, that pretty month of love" (p. 6). May 15, 1830: *Epitre à M. Mangin* (Mie, no price); *Pétition des filles publiques* (Poussin, 50 centimes); *Le Tocsin* (David; no price); *A MM. les Députés* (Gaultier-Laguionie, 50 centimes). May 27, 1830: *Aux Ministres!!!* (Poussin, 75 centimes); *50,000 Voleurs* (David, 50 centimes); *Complainte authentique* (David, 75 centimes); *Deuxième pétition* (Gaultier-Laguionie, no price); *Doléances des filles* (Poussin, 50 centimes); *Les Filles en cage* (Sétier, no price); *Grande, véritable et lamentable complainte* (Gaultier-Laguionie, no price); *Plainte et révélations* (Poussin, 1 franc); *Projet d'un nouveau réglement* (Poussin, 50 centimes). May 29, 1830: *Projet de pétition d'un spartiate* (Gaultier-Laguionie, 50 centimes [2d ed. of *A MM. les Députés* . . .]; *Observations soumises* (Constant Chant pie à Saint-Denis, 40 centimes); *Prière romantique de Laure* (Poussin, 30 centimes) *Réponse de M. Englin* (Chassaignon, no price); *Réponse de M. le Préfet* (Poussin, 50 centimes); *Le Vrai Motif* (Charpentier-Méricourt, 40 centimes). June 5, 1830: *La Paulinade* (Charpentier-Méricourt, 50 centimes). I was unable to locate one pamphlet and the print, *Pétition d'un souteneur à M. le Préfet de Police de Paris* (Paris: Poussin, n.d.) listed as "*en prose*" and published May 22, 1830; *Une Maîtresse de maison: Empêcher ces pauvres créatures de prendre air, comme si la rue n'était pas à tout le monde* (Paris: Ardit), published May 29, 1830. *Plainte et révélations* includes a different color print (figure 2.1).

32. On the pamphlets of 1789, see Antoine de Baecque, "Pamphlets: Libel and Political Mythology," in Robert Darnton and Daniel Roche, ed. *Revolution in Print: The Press in France, 1775–1800* (Berkeley: University of California Press, 1989), 165–76; and Chantal Thomas, *La Reine scélérate: Marie-Antoinette dans les pamphlets* (Paris: Seuil, 1989).

33. *La Paulinade*, title page.

34. *50,000 Voleurs*, 7, 10.

35. For the surviving fragments of the censorship report on *Hernani*, see Victor Hugo, vol. 3, pt. 2 (1967): 1413–15. Like the report on *Marion de Lorme*, the *Hernani* dossier has disappeared from the AN (Krakovitch [1985]: 275n23). *Hernani*'s censors (October 29, 1829) were obsessed with the morality of the play: they complained that the daughter of a

great man of Spain "was nothing but a profligate," yet called for the play to be performed despite its bad examples without the change of a single word. (Hugo, vol. 3, pt. 2 [1967]: 1413-14). The minister of the interior took the same hardline approach here as with *Marion de Lorme*. The play would not be performed, he told Hugo, without major changes. Hugo bowed to all but minor changes, and the government allowed the curtain to rise on *Hernani* (Krakovitch [1985]: 41-45).

36. Cf. Peter Brooks, "An Oedipal Crisis" in Hollier (1989): 649-56.

37. *Hernani* tells the story of a young man with two goals—avenging his father and marrying Doña Sol. His father's executioner, Don Carlos, King of Spain, wants the hand of Hernani's beloved. He has banned Hernani and spends half the play pursuing him. As Hernani seeks to escape, he is saved by Don Ruy Gomez and pledges his life to this elderly protector of Doña Sol. Should Don Ruy ever call with his hunting horn, Hernani must be prepared to honor his pledge. Unfortunately for Hernani, Don Ruy also loves Doña Sol and, just as Don Carlos has finally pardoned the young man, restored his title, given up Doña Sol, and authorized the marriage, the sound of a hunting horn calls in the pledge. Doña Sol will not stop her husband from honoring his pledge: instead she grabs the vial of poison he has been given by Don Ruy, drinks a deadly portion, and passes the rest on to him for his suicide.

38. Victor Hugo (1967) 3: 2: 1413-14.

39. What the artisans at the barricades meant by *liberty*, explains Newman, was not the same thing the leaders of the new regime understood by that term (1975: 19-20, 28).

40. AN, F-7, 6772, cited in Chevalier (1973): 267.

41. See Pinkney (1972): 66-69.

42. Police report, October 1828, AN, F-7, 6772, cited in Chevalier (1973): 266.

43. *50,000 Voleurs*, 10; *La Paulinade*, title page.

44. Pinkney (1972): 252-73, discussed in Merriman, "Introduction," to Merriman (1975): 1-6, and further developed in Newman (1975): 17-40. The death list included two women, "apparently as unlucky spectators," reports Pinkney. Fifty-two women were listed as wounded. Their roles seem to have been limited to "pulling up pavements, throwing stones, and caring for the wounded" (256).

45. Pinkney (1972): 256-58; Merriman (1975): 6-7.

46. "The activists and the public disorders that they created ... were an expression of timeless economic complaints, of loyalties within traditional crafts, of popular resentment against symbols of the old regime, and of eighteenth-century ideas of liberty, equality, and fraternity" (Pinkney [1972]: 273).

47. Cf. Guizot, "The July Revolution raised only political questions.... Society was by no means menaced.... What has happened since? Social questions have been raised" (*Le Moniteur universel*, December 22, 1831, cited in Merriman [1975]: 7). On the workers' protests following the July Days, see Georges Bourgin, "La Crise ouvrière à Paris dans la second moitié de 1830," *Revue historique*, 198 (1947): 203-14.

48. Cf. Merriman (1975): 8.

49. Strangely oblivious to the articles in Merriman (1975) and to Pinkney (1972), Collingham recently embraced the old thesis that the "dangerous classes" fought the revolution (1988: 4).

50. Pinkney (1972): 68.

51. Collingham (1988): 5.

52. *Le Tocsin*, 3.

53. *Doléances des filles*, 6; *Le Tocsin*, 9-10; *Projet de pétition d'un spartiate*, 6-9.

54. *Plainte et révélations*, 4.

55. *50,000 Voleurs*, 5.

56. Parent also alludes to the pamphlets, *PD*, 2: 497.

57. *Plainte et révélations*, 13.

58. *Plainte et révélations*, 5.

59. *Aux Ministres*, 5. "Judge the effect, if such a thing happened to a great lady of name, titles, or whatever? (6).

60. *Aux Ministres*, 7; *50,000 Voleurs:* "Moreover, aren't you afraid that depraved men and foreigners might begin to mistake real seamstresses and milliners circulating in the capital for those false milliners, seamstresses, and maids to whom they are accustomed? What injury you would be inflicting on virtue, by exposing these young and virtuous girls to being attacked as *filles publiques!*" (13–14).

61. *Aux Ministres*, 9.

62. *Aux Ministres*, 8.

63. *Aux Ministres*, 9–10.

64. One Mademoiselle Pauline explains that her cousin has ensured her Mangin's ordinance cannot last because it is in open contravention of the rights of people. Because "All the French are equal before the law, thus 'one cannot challenge your freedom, because the Charter was not made for nothing.' And to my observation that in the article he was citing for me there was no discussion of French women, he answered that it didn't matter because the legislator meant both males *and* females" (*Pétition des Filles*, 6).

65. *Projet de pétition d'un spartiate*, 6–7, 9.

66. *Le Tocsin*, 9–10. See Parent's response, *PD*, 2: 494–500: "individual liberty is a right to which prostitutes cannot lay claim" (499).

67. Harsin (1985): 80–95.

68. AN-F7, 9304, report, c. 1819 and 1822, cited in Harsin (1985): 20.

69. La Petite Force was established as the prostitutes' prison in 1801, replaced in 1826 by Les Madelonnettes, and in 1836 by Saint-Lazare.

70. *Aux Ministres*, 5–6.

71. *Projet de pétition d'un spartiate*, 8.

72. Parent called for a return to Restoration ordinances because the very sight of prostitutes could lead the young astray (*PD*, 1: 566, 556, 561–62).

73. *Plainte et révélations*, 4. *Aux Ministres* sticks to a total figure of twenty-five thousand, similar to Béraud's for 1831 (6).

74. Cf. *FPP*, 1: 106–7: the purpose of tolerance is "to protect women of pure morals."

75. *Plainte et révélations*, 19.

76. See Valerie Steele, *Paris Fashion* (New York: Oxford University Press, 1988), 7. A widespread myth about prostitutes held that they entered the trade because of a love of luxurious clothes (cf. "Notice historique" in *FPP*, 1: 89).

77. *Aux Ministres*, 8.

78. On *Physiologies*, see Lhéritier (1966); Hans-Rüdiger van Biesbrock, *Die literarische Mode der Physiologien in Frankreich (1840–42)*, (Frankfurt: Peter Lang, 1978); Judith Wechsler, *A Human Comedy* (Chicago: University of Chicago Press, 1982).

79. Fewer than a half dozen other pamphlets appeared in this period. See the *Bibliographie de France* (1830) and pamphlet collections of the Bibliothèque Historique de la Ville de Paris.

80. That ten percent of the printers of Paris got into the act in a period of only four weeks suggests more than a snowball effect. Within a week of the publication of the first three pamphlets by three different printers, eleven more had appeared. The third and fourth

weeks saw increasing variations in tone and style—with a proliferation of theatrical and verse variations and a slight drop in cost to 30–40 centimes for three of the six pamphlets published the week of May 29. The week of June 5 saw the publication of only one pamphlet specifically related to the ordinances (*La Paulinade*), along with two pamphlets protesting other state policies (*Aux amis des moeurs et de l'ordre public* [Paris: Sétier, 1830] and *Épitre au chapeau neuf de chodrun duclos dit l'homme à la longue barbe sur la rentrée au ministère de M. de Peyronnet* [Paris: Poussin, 1830]. Then, as suddenly as they had first materialized, the prostitution pamphlets ceased to appear—just as the minister of the interior announced a press crackdown, which simultaneously declared war on every newspaper opposing the Restoration Monarchy.

81. AN, F-18, 567, no. 314 (October 30, 1833), on Chassaignon.

82. Although not produced by the same printer as any of the pamphlets, *Le Corsaire* leapt on May 13 to cite the first pamphlet and on May 18 to greet with approval the publication of the longest of the pamphlets, *Plainte et révélations*, which not only thanked this newspaper for its support but requested the same of seven other papers, among them the Monarchist *Gazette de France* and *La Quotidienne*. *Plainte et révélations* claims its authors are sending this letter to the editors of several newspapers: *Le Pandore* (a liberal satirical revue that folded in 1828), *Le Figaro* (a small liberal satirical paper), *Le Voleur*, *Le Courrier des théâtres*, *Le Nouveau Journal de Paris* (a small republican paper), *La Quotidienne* (the largest ultra paper), *La Gazette de France* (a royalist paper supportive of the current monarchy), and especially *Le Corsaire* (a liberal satirical paper), which they declare has befriended their cause (36–38). *Le Corsaire* published its pamphletlike text on May 10, 1830, following a series of articles protesting the Mangin ordinances (April 24, p. 3; May 3, pp. 3–4; May 6, p. 2) and preceding frequent protests of the police crackdowns (May 12, p. 4; June 7, p. 3; June 8, pp. 2–3; June 9, p. 3; June 10; June 12, pp. 2–3, etc.). *Le Corsaire* was published by Charles Dezauche, a printer deemed upright by press spies of 1833 (AN, F-18, 567, no. 314), unlike Poussin, the printer of *Plainte* and other pamphlets, who was viewed as suspect. Sétier and Chassaignon, each publisher of one pamphlet, were disparaged by July Monarchy spies, while Gaultier-Laguionie, a major source of pamphlets, was declared scrupulous—possibly because it printed *Le Courrier français*, the Orleanist paper where François Guizot once published political articles (Rader [1973]: 21–22). I am indebted to James Smith Allen for his help in tracking the pamphlets' ideological sources.

83. Articles of April 24, p. 3; May 3, p. 4; May 18, p. 4.

84. On June 7, just after the last pamphlet appeared, *Le Corsaire* announced an (imaginary) police ordinance against everyone who read that paper (p. 3). On June 9, editors chided the state along with the right-wing press that supported it: "To avoid any crowds in the Palais-Royal garden, Mangin recently decided to admit only the subscribers of *La Quotidienne* and *La Gazette de France*; it was effectively the best way to prevent a large assembly" (p. 3).

85. *50,000 Voleurs*, 6.

86. *Projet de pétition d'un spartiate*, 11, 12, 9, 12–13.

87. None seem to have been censored. Their appearance in the *Bibliographie de France* suggests all were legally published and deposited with the state.

88. Paulson (1983): 55.

89. Du Camp (1872) 3: 420.

90. Canler [1862]: 311.

91. Cf. Vidocq (1828) and Soulié (1837–38).

92. Raisson saw press support of the prostitutes' cause as an incitement to the criminal classes who lent support and fury to revolutionary demands (1844: 317–21).

93. Alphonse Esquiros (1842): 153, 160–61.

94. Terdiman (1986): 43.

95. Hunt (1990): 103–104.

96. Giles Gunn, *The Culture of Criticism and the Criticism of Culture* (New York: Oxford University Press, 1987), 74, cited in Hunt (1990): 109.

97. Cf. Jameson (1981): 10 et passim.

98. Cf. Hall (1981): 239.

99. Chartier (1988): 44.

100. It did not gain a popular following until after February 1848. See T. J. Clark (1982a): 20.

101. See Hamilton (1954); Adhémar (1954); Lüdeke (1965); T. J. Clark (1982a): 17–19, 25–26; Hadjinicolaou (1979); and Pointon (1990): 59–82.

102. Lee Johnson, *The Paintings of Eugène Delacroix* (Oxford: Oxford University Press, 1981), no. 144, cited in Pointon (1990): 64. See also Hamilton (1954): 62.

103. Lüdeke (1965): 15.

104. On Liberty poetry, see Hamilton (1954): 60, Pointon (1990): 68–69. On Amazon myths, see Anne Hollander, *Seeing Through Clothes* (New York: Avon, 1988), 199–202; Marina Warner, *Monuments and Maidens* (New York: Athenaeum, 1985), 278–93. On Delacroix's relation to the political culture of 1789, see Agulhon (1979a): 21–67.

105. Warner, *Monuments and Maidens*, 292.

106. See Heinrich Heine's reading of the painting discussed by Margaret Rose, *Marx's Lost Aesthetic* (Cambridge: Cambridge University Press, 1984), 18–20.

107. As Pointon notes, most earlier representations of Liberty keep her "'in an allegorical role, clean of violence; she enters the stage at a final point in the narration, as a divine witness to the goal having been attained." Here, "Liberty, for all her fine, wholesome, thrusting breasts, surmounts a pile of debris and bodies—male bodies. She is a powerful woman striding towards the viewer over the bodies of dead men" (1990: 73).

108. Maxime Du Camp, *Les Beaux-Arts en 1855* (Paris: Librairie nouvelle, 1855), 97, cited in Adhémar: "This hussy escaped from Saint-Lazare has nothing in common with the immortal and fertile virgin we adore" ([1954]: 91–92). Critics of 1831, cited by Hadjincolaou, frequently took her to be a prostitute: C. M. of *L'Avenir* (June 9, 1831) called her "*une femme de mauvaise vie*"; Ambroise Tardieu saw her as "a dirty and shameless woman of the streets"; Louis Peisse named her "a courtesan of the lowest rank"; and an anonymous critic of *La Tribune* called her "the most infamous courtesan of the dirtiest streets of Paris" ([1979]: 18, 23–24).

109. Like Du Camp, many commentators confuse the prostitutes' prison of 1830, Les Madelonnettes, with the later Saint-Lazare. See Alboize and Maquet (1845) 8: 83; *PD*, 2: 300; *FPP*, 1: 288. Another version has the women released by the masses: "During the July Days, the people opened the doors to the prisoners . . . and gave them temporary freedom" (Alhoy and Lurine [1846]: 420).

110. Landais's 1833 novel gives a striking description of this "spectacle": "That morning we saw from afar a crowd of women coming toward us, all debauched and shouting out our sublime rallying call of "long live the Charter! long live liberty! From their loud and shameless revelry, it was possible to recognize the class to which they belonged. It was a mob of prostitutes escaped from the cesspool of the depot of the Prefecture. . . . People laughed a lot as they saw this funny parade go by" (3: 90–91). See also Parent: "After the events of July 1830,

the fetters of the police having been necessarily loosened, one could see prostitutes spread out again in the streets and show themselves with all the insolence they had long restrained; it was, as I recall, for all honorable people, a subject of sorrow and pain" (*PD*, 1: 559). See also *FPP*, 1: 269–75.

111. Alboize and Maquet (1845) 8: 83.

3. Taking Liberties: Plots Around Prostitutes in 1848

1. Du Camp (1876, rpt. 1979): 90.

2. On the living allegories of the Revolution of 1789, see Ozouf (1976); Hunt (1984): 23–31; and Agulhon (1979a): 38–42.

3. Agulhon (1973): 228.

4. See Agulhon (1979a): 55–128.

5. Hunt (1984): 12–13.

6. Agulhon (1979a): 90.

7. Military officers may have used her parade to encourage revolutionaries to leave the Tuileries (Agulhon [1979a]: 89, 121n16).

8. Du Camp (1878) 2: 89.

9. One account of Mobile Guard enlistments claimed "Anyone was accepted, anyone enrolled: men over fifty, cripples, even women" (Traugott [1985]: 60). Strumingher (1987) discusses women's armed participation.

10. Tocqueville (1850); reprinted in English under the title *Recollections: The French Revolution of 1848* (New Brunswick: Transaction Books, 1987).

11. Caricatures by Cham and Edouard de Beaumont were published in *Le Charivari* between March and July 1848. See Strumingher (1987).

12. Scott (1988): 48. "It is not sexuality which haunts society, but society which haunts the body's sexuality. Sex-related differences between bodies are continually summoned as testimony to social relations and phenomena that have nothing to do with sexuality. Not only as testimony to, but also testimony for—in other words, as legitimation," writes Maurice Godelier ("The Origins of Male Domination," *New Left Review* 127 [1981]: 17, cited in Scott, 45). On politics and biological difference, see Laqueur (1986): 3–14, 18. On debates over gender in 1848, see Moses (1984): 117–41; Devance (1976); Offen (1986); and Strumingher (1987).

13. See Hertz (1983): 27; Hobsbawm (1978); Perrot (1979a); and Fraisse (1975).

14. Cf. Agulhon (1979b): 169; and Richardson (1982): 132–37.

15. Stern (1850–53) 1: 202.

16. Agulhon (1975): 43.

17. Stern (1850–53) 1: 204.

18. Flaubert (1869, rpt. 1964): 291.

19. Marx (1848, rpt. 1978): 69.

20. See Hobsbawm (1978); Agulhon (1979b); Richardson (1982); and T. J. Clark (1982a): 21. In Marx's analysis of the revolution, the prostitute epitomizes the dishonor of France who is "not forgiven the unguarded hour in which the first adventurer that came along could violate [her]" (1978: 599, 607).

21. Stern (1850–53) 1: 204–5. La Maillard played the Goddess of Reason in the living allegories of 1793 (*La Gazette des femmes*, October 21, 1843, p. 9).

22. Stern (1850–53) 1: 144. For an engraving of this scene, see Price (1975): 25. T. J. Clark analyzes a watercolor of a dead *man* raised to the crowd (1982a: 25).

23. On the prisons of 1848, see Lessellier (1982); Matter (1975); and Perrot, "1848. Révolution et prisons," in Perrot (1980): 277–312.

24. *Le National*, February 26, 1848, p. 3, col. 1.

25. Chevalier (1973).

26. On prison uprisings during other populist struggles, see Bizard and Chapon (1925); Pottet (1912); Alhoy and Lurine (1846); Légier-Desgranges (on 1792) (1950); and Pinkney (1972): 66–69.

27. *Le National*, February 28, 1848, p. 4, col. 1. The same issue reported: "The Innocents station was occupied by the people, who, in their rage, broke all the furniture of the police commissioner of the Halles quartier and made a barricade with it. Everything was destroyed, and we are afraid for the life of an individual who took a book. We destroy, said these brave people, but we do not steal. 'Death to thieves!'" (p. 3, col. 3). The *Journal des débats* declared, "The people are making unrelenting war on thieves" (February 28, 1848).

28. See *MP*, 955–1076 on La Force; and 606–657 on Saint-Lazare.

29. *La Gazette des tribunaux*, February 29, 1848, p. 436, col. 3.

30. Forstenzer (1981): 50.

31. See La Berge (1974); Sewell (1980): 219–42; and Chevalier (1973): 29–58.

32. See Michaud (1980) 2: 377–89. Conversations with Ian Burney helped focus this section.

33. See Faure and Rancière (1976).

34. See *La Tribune des femmes* (1832–34), *La Gazette des femmes* (1836–38), and, in 1848, *La Voix des femmes*, *La Politique des femmes*, and *L'Opinion des femmes*.

35. Chevalier's study of this construction of social reality makes a significant contribution to our understanding of the nature of this discourse even though it mistakes the loaded ideological terms used by the social scientists and novelists for confirmation that the working classes were in fact dirty, sick, disorderly, and criminal. See (1973): esp. 395–408, 409–33, 437–41.

36. "Various different classes will use one and the same language. As a result, differently oriented accents intersect in every ideological sign. Sign becomes an arena of class struggle" (Volosinov [1986]: 21–23).

37. See Legouvé (1854); Daubié (1866): 274–89.

38. See *FPP*, 1: 149–56; *CD*, 1: 89; Villermé (1840) 2: 52.

39. See Michelet (1981): 54–63; and Scott (1988): 139–63.

40. Buci-Glucksmann reads prostitution as the "interpretative principle of Modernity" (1984: 116–17).

41. See Harsin for the account of a woman denied police protection because she was believed a prostitute (1985: 197).

42. Mallet (1845): 144. According to Matter (1975), Saint-Lazare held 941 prostitutes in June of 1846.

43. Alhoy and Lurine (1846): 128–29, and 132, referring to Frégier.

44. Only Perrot discusses it, in "1848," in Perrot (1980).

45. Cf. Parent's views on 1830 (*PD*, 2: 300; *PD*, 3d ed., 1: 113).

46. *Gazette des tribunaux*, December 26, 1846.

47. Perrot, "1848," in Perrot (1980): 296.

48. See Jules Michelet, *Histoire de la révolution française* (1848–52; rpt. Paris: Gallimard Pléiade, 1952); and Du Camp (1872) 3: 420.

49. M. A. M, "Notice historique," in *FPP*: lxxxviii.

50. *Gazette des tribunaux*, March 3, 1848, p. 4; *Le National*, March 3, 1848, p. 3.

51. *Gazette des tribunaux*, March 3, 1848, p. 4.

52. *Gazette des tribunaux*, March 5, 1848, p. 3.

53. Alboize and Maquet (1845) 8: 83.

54. Perrot, "1848," in Perrot (1980): 286.

55. "How do you expect such a woman to live from the work of her hands?" asked members of the workers' movement (Cited in Perrot, "1848," in Perrot [1980]: 294). *La Voix des femmes* vehemently protested the decision to eliminate prison work (March 10, 1848, p. 3).

56. Esquiros (1840): 139–41. Esquiros's *"baisers"* are *"fiévreux"* in all editions after 1841.

57. As we saw in chapter 1, the novel allows that her presence in the tolerance system could be imagined as only "administrative." See *FPP*, 1: 251 on a virgin registered as a prostitute, and *PD* 1: 386ff.

58. See Schenda (1976).

59. The 1843–44 edition (Paris: Gosselin), vol. 2, p. 197 (illustrated by Duboulot and Nargeot), shows La Louve stripped, barebreasted, but not yet in a pose quite so closely resembling Delacroix's *Liberty* as the 1851 edition (Paris: rue du Pont-de-Lodi), illustrated by J.-A. Beaucé and Stahl, p. 151 (see figure 3.2).

60. In *"Les Mystères de Paris: Roman philanthropique,"* *L'Atelier* (November 1843), p. 27–29, the workers complain that Sue's novel suits bourgeois interests.

61. "Les Mystères de Paris," *L'Atelier*, November 1843, p. 27.

62. Landais (1833) 2: 143.

63. *Filles en cartes* were registered prostitutes living in regulated brothels; *filles en numéro* operated outside brothels (*PD*, 1: 174–78).

64. See Odile and Henri-Jean Martin, "Le monde des éditeurs," in Martin and Chartier (1985) 3: 181. Havard's illustrated *Manon* appeared in January 1848 and sold for 20 centimes.

65. For the complete censors' reports of August 28, September 1, and October 1, 1851, see Dumas fils [n.d.] 7: 415–22, discussed by Descôtes (1964): 320–24, and Krakovitch (1985): 238–39.

66. On Second Empire censorship, see Zévaès (1924).

67. Jules Janin, "Mademoiselle Marie Duplessis," in *DC*: 494.

68. Her possessions are sold on March 16, the day of a demonstration by elite companies of the National Guard followed, on March 17, by a massive demonstration by the Paris democratic clubs in rejection of their demands. See Traugott (1985): 19–20. On Duplessis, see Joanna Richardson, *The Courtesans* (Cleveland: World Publishing, 1967), 153–70. *La Dame aux camélias* was published in late July of 1848 and cost 15 francs for two in-octavo volumes.

69. Brooks (1976): 15.

70. She calls him "the only human creature who would have wanted to pity me" (*DC*, 161). Armand's fascination with her disease approaches obsession: "I was almost happy about her illness," he confides (*DC*, 98). When she is spitting up blood, he chases after her to confess his love (*DC*, 114–15).

71. See Michaud (1980).

72. See Barthes (1957): 182.

73. Dumas fils [n.d.] 7: 415.

74. Poitou (1857): 104–8.

75. Adèle Esquiros (1865): 92, 119–22, 92.

76. Legouvé (1854): 260.

77. See Hans-Jörg Neuschäfer, "Introduction," *DC*: 19–42.

78. *La Voix des femmes*, March 10, 1848, p. 1.

79. Pauline Roland, "Morale socialiste: Lettres d'une prisonière," *La Liberté de penser* (1851), cited in Moses (1984): 139.

80. *La Voix des femmes*, April 23, 1848.

81. Cited in Adler (1979): 130.

82. Legouvé's lectures nevertheless impressed *La Voix des femmes*, March 10, 1848, p. 4. See Offen (1986): 453. Because the French Civil Code did not authorize paternity suits or punish "seduction," illegitimate births became a matter of consequence for feminists and social reformers. One-third of the children in Paris between 1837 and 1846 (nearly one hundred thousand babies) were born out of wedlock; only 10% of them were recognized by their fathers (Moses [1984]: 28). Like Legouvé, the women of 1848 wanted changes that would force fathers to recognize their children and provide support.

83. *La Voix des femmes*, March 31, 1848.

84. *La Voix des femmes*, March 10, 1848, p. 1.

85. *La Voix des femmes*, March 10, 1848, p. 2.

86. Joséphine-Félicité, "Affranchissement des femmes," *Tribune des femmes*, August 25, 1832, p. 5, cited in Michaud (1980): 383.

87. Moses (1984): 145.

88. Between February and early June, 4580 of 8763 laundresses lost their jobs (Adler [1979]: 132).

89. Chénu, *Les Montagnards* (Paris: Giraud and Dagneau, 1850), 56, was discussing the "participation" of three hundred Vésuviennes in a Montagnard ball.

90. Thomas (1956): 152. The report also reproached her as an unwed mother.

91. "The criminality of woman is more dangerous than that of man because it is more contagious," wrote Charles Lucas, inspector of prisons in 1848 ([1858] 3: 395–96). Citing Parent on women's low salaries, he argued that "we must, in a word, *emancipate* the woman," not in terms of politics or marriage, but in order to ensure that her morality have contagious effects in the family and in society (3: 398, 421).

92. See *La Voix des femmes*, March 10, 1848, p. 4; Devance (1976): 88; Moses (1984): 136–42; and Offen (1986).

93. Summary of Legouvé's rationale given by *Le National*, March 6, 1848.

94. Hertz (1983): 27–54.

95. Gallagher argues that the texts cited by Hertz do not so much express a "fear of the weakness of the vagina, but a fear of its reproductive power" (1983: 55–57). On women's changing rights in 1848, see Devance (1976): 79–103.

96. Hunt (1980): 17.

97. Janin, *Journal des débats*, February 9, 1852, cited in Descôtes (1964): 320.

98. Daubié (1866): 267. Born in 1824, Daubié received a primary school education, became a governess, and on the basis of her own self-education, received the Lyons Academy prize for *La Femme pauvre* in 1858, received a baccalauréat in 1862 thanks to the Empress Eugénie's intervention, and was the first woman to obtain a *licence* in *lettres* in 1871 (See Scott (1988): 152–62).

99. Daubié (1866): 270, 273.

100. Moses (1984): 179–89.

101. Bidelman (1982): 174–75, 180.

102. Grandpré (1869): 79. Founder of the *Oeuvre des libérées de Saint-Lazare* in 1869, Grandpré eventually revealed herself as the book's author. The prison chaplain's niece, she was able to live in Saint-Lazare to collect women's experiences there. Her later works (1889,

1890) demanded improved education for women prisoners and an end to the prostitutes' prison. See Lesselier (1982): 372–76.

103. Zeldin (1973): 356–62.

104. DuBois and Gordon (1983); Donzelot (1979): 36–38; and Terdiman (1986): 72–74.

105. See Scott's comparison of Daubié to Jules Simon (1988): 139–63.

106. Proudhon viciously blamed Sand and other romantic writers (1875: 166, 250): "The reading of a *roman amoureux*, and the visit to the *maison de tolérance* that follows from it, do more damage than a week of hard labor." Flaubert (1869; rpt. 1964) mocked Sue by putting *Les Mystères de Paris* in the hands of the worker Dussardier in *L'Éducation sentimentale*. His appraisal of the revolution also particularly ridicules its feminist, La Vatnaz.

107. Poitou (1857): 290–91.

108. Poitou saw Dumas's novel as a sequel to *Marion de Lorme* (1857: 105).

109. Poitou (1857): 293–94.

110. "Lettres républicaines," *Le Courrier français*, June 28, 1848, p. 1.

111. Tocqueville (1987): 145.

112. *Le Lampion*, June 24, 1848; *La Démocratie pacifique*, June 24, 1848.

113. Hugo (1968) 36: 225–26.

4. Telling the Difference: Hysterics, Prostitutes, and the Clinical Gaze

1. Esquiros claims to take issue with Parent, but his findings parallel those of the regulationist (1841: 116–17, 9; 179; 182–83; 139–42).

2. Esquirol (1838) 1:47. Unlike Parent, whom he cites, Esquirol does not give dates for his statistics. The records of the Salpêtrière from the Esquirol years (1817–25) show a smaller proportion of *filles publiques* than his figures suggest. Could Esquirol be making assumptions about the "actual" occupations of the working women he encountered there? Did the registers simply leave off a woman's occupation when she was assumed to be a prostitute? Parent cites Esquirol as a personal source of information on the profession of prostitutes (*PD*, 1: 264). In statistics published between 1839 and 1845, Parchappe claimed more women were admitted into the Salpêtrière than men into Bicêtre because of the numbers of prostitutes in the area of Paris (Ripa [1983]: 296). That prostitutes wound up in the Salpêtrière seems to have been a widespread myth. Paul de Kock imagines *la femme entretenue* hocking her clothes at the state pawnshop "when the hour arrives for her to take the path to the Salpêtrière!" ([1842] 2: 113). In his 1840 novel, Frémy picks up Esquirol's statistic about the percentage of prostitutes in the Salpêtrière (1: 181). Esquiros later relays Esquirol's statistics, claiming Salpêtrière doctor Jean-Pierre Falret told him that they still hold true for the July Monarchy (1847: 126–27). *Insoumises* and *vénériennes* had not been routinely imprisoned at the Salpêtrière (cf. *Manon Lescaut*) since the turn of the nineteenth century. See also Trélat's 1848 examination of Julie Elisabeth T., a *fille publique* he does not believe either *aliénée* or "suffering from nervous attacks of any kind." He sends her back to the police, recommending she be treated at the Saint-Louis Hospital for a scalp malady (AAP, Salpêtrière, 6Q2–13, no. 16880).

3. Esquirol (1838) 1: 47.

4. AAP, Salpêtrière, 6Q2–8 and 6Q2–9 (1845). These statistics are consistent with my surveys for the years 1848 (6Q2–13), 1853 (6Q2–20), 1865 (6Q2–46), and 1869 (6Q2–

54). In surveys covering one month of admission records, prostitutes represented 2% (in 1853), needleworkers and seamstresses, 42%, domestics, 16%, *"journalières,"* 10%, shopgirls, 4%, and cooks, 4%. In 1865 prostitutes represented 4.71%, that is, they were the fourth largest professional group after needleworkers and seamstresses, who represented 26%, *"journalières,"* 12%, and domestics, 9.41%. In the six months of 1848 for which registers are available prostitutes represented 2% of involuntary admissions. In one hundred entries between July 19 and September 3, 1848, seamstresses and needleworkers represented 31%, *"journalières"* 12%, domestic servants 10%, merchants 4%, and cooks or bakers 4%, and prostitutes 2%. Prostitutes represented fewer than 1% of 396 involuntary admissions in 1865 and about 1% of 234 involuntary admissions in 1869. *Placements d'office* are involuntary admissions mediated by the police. *Placements volontaires* are voluntary not on the part of the patient but on the part of the patient's family. The latter group are far more prevalent before the Law of 1838, which required two doctors' medical certificates of mental problems for incarceration (see Ripa [1983]: 12, 14–94). In a study of the Salpêtrière registers from 1825 to 1833, Ripa found only *eight* women labeled as prostitutes (296). She also found prostitutes strikingly absent from registers in the period between 1838 and 1845 (212–14). The apparent decrease in the numbers of prostitutes in the Salpêtrière from the 1811–1815 period, which was discussed by Parent, and from the Esquirol years may be explained by the creation in 1836 of a special hospital (Lourcine) for prostitutes with venereal diseases.

5. Daubié (1866): 255. Ripa reproduces fantasmatic evidence about the depravity of seamstresses, linen maids, and laundresses (1983: 212–14).

6. Esquirol (1838) 1: 38. Goldstein contends Esquirol showed little interest in hysteria (1987: 331). Rather, his work suggests he saw hysteria as so omnipresent in women that one could hardly identify it. Goldstein rightly assumes Esquirol's ambitions led in different directions—toward an understanding of legal responsibility as it related to mental illness (128–51).

7. Parent warned that almost all hysterical attacks witnessed in prostitutes were either ruses designed to "escape the hands of inspectors and recover their liberty," or the result of "chagrins" or "fits of rage" to which such women were frequently disposed (*PD*, 1: 261–62).

8. Goldstein has astutely argued that the radically increased use of the hysteria diagnosis in Charcot's Salpêtrière of the 1870s has a political dimension relating to the *aliéniste* profession's anticlericalism and governmental connections to the Third Republic (1987: 322–77). What Goldstein has called the "political construction" of hysteria in the Charcot era (377) does not belie the convergence of other political factors in the construction of hysteria during the July Monarchy and the Second Empire. While government collaboration may have been crucial to Charcot's establishment of a psychiatric empire in the early Third Republic, the hysteria diagnosis making this possible had been nurtured in significant ways in *public hospitals* like La Charité and La Pitié throughout the July Monarchy and the Second Empire. The medical profession, which would eventually stake government connections on this diagnosis, had spent the previous fifty years formulating frameworks for the study of women's mental illnesses. The political aspects of these interpretative frameworks, as part 2 of this book argues, were less explicitly tied to the government than during the Charcot regime. They were, however, no less politically charged. Women's sexuality, reproductive ability, marriageability, education, work, and leisure activities, not to speak of class and professional qualifications, were all implicated in these interpretive struggles I am calling a poetics of hysteria. The translation of these poetics into strategies for watching, knowing, and disciplining women of all classes and circumstances is as politically charged as Charcot's anticlericalism. This was,

after all, a period in which women could not vote, obtain a divorce, control property, sign contracts, receive a high school diploma, or attend a university. The relationship of July Monarchy debates over the hysteria diagnosis to women's increasingly vocal demands for these rights is hardly accidental.

9. Foucault (1975a): xii, xviii–xix, xiv. Cf. Briquet's comments on "positive science" (Br, v).

10. Brooks (1984): 74.

11. Cf. Foucault (1975a): ix–xix.

12. Freud (1914) 14: 13–14, recounts Charcot's words ("dans ces cas pareils c'est toujours la chose génitale, toujours . . . toujours . . . toujours") from a conversation with his assistant Brouardel. "I said to myself," writes Freud, " 'Well, but if he knows that, why does he never say so?' " See also Roudinesco (1982) 1: 23, 32, who views Freud's development of the seduction theory as evidence of his disagreement with Charcot (Freud [1896] 3: 191–221).

13. Goldstein (1987): 166–67.

14. Major contributions to the study of hysteria in the mid-nineteenth century include Louyer-Villermay (1816b), Georget (1824), Voisin (1826), Dubois d'Amiens (1833), Brachet (1832), Girard de Lyon (1841), Landouzy (1846), Brachet (1847), Mathieu (1847), Sandras (1851), Briquet (1859), Morel (1859) 2: 185–227, Moreau de Tours (1865). Gynecological handbooks with a major chapters on women's nervous ailments include Colombat (1838–42); Auber (1841), who destines his work for the libraries of women (vi); Hatin (1832): 325–32; Lévy (1845); Chomet (1846); and Debay (1850). Roussel (1775; reed. 1845) gained a strange, new importance in this era of clinical observation. Like Virey (1815 and 1825a) and Moreau de la Sarthe (1803), Roussel drew more on popular fantasy than clinical experience.

15. Terrisse (1982) shows that between 1850 and 1860 three-tenths of psychiatric theses were on hysteria, that is, in the period before Charcot's first appointment as resident physician at the Salpêtrière in 1862. Charcot became professor of pathological anatomy at the Faculty of Medicine and *chef de service* in 1872. After a drop to two-tenths of theses between 1860 and 1870, in the period between 1870 and 1880 four-tenths of all psychiatric theses were again on hysteria and from 1881 to 1890 such theses represented three-tenths of all the ones on psychiatric disorders. However, between 1891 and 1900 only one-tenth of all psychiatric theses dealt with a form of hysteria (1982: 9–15). On Charcot's career see Silverman (1989): 79–106.

16. Goldstein (1987): 322–77.

17. A survey of admissions at Briquet's own La Charité shows that of approximately nine hundred women admitted in one month of 1845, twenty-seven (3%) entered with a diagnosis of hysteria, another 3%—thirty-three—were diagnosed with the related disorder chlorosis, and ten more were admitted with unnamed nervous disorders. If every woman diagnosed as hysteric at La Charité in 1845 had instead been sent to the Salpêtrière, the mental asylum would have harbored more hysterics in four months of 1845 than in all of 1882–83 put together (AAP, La Charité, 1Q2–102).

18. On the Law of 1838, see Castel (1976) and Goldstein (1987): 276–321.

19. See Pierre Marie, "Éloge de J.-M. Charcot, *Revue neurologique*, 41 (1925): 739–40. Veith takes Marie's account as the reason for a shift in emphasis in the Salpêtrière toward the study of hysteria (1965: 230). Goldstein contends that it begs the question of Charcot's interest in hysteria (1982: 215–17). The year 1871 represents less a point of rupture than a legendary reference point for an epistemological shift that occurred at about the time Charcot began his *Leçons du mardi* (1872). The Salpêtrière registers indicate that certain doctors were *always* primarily responsible for patients with epilepsy and hysteria. Even before this

supposed turning point in the asylum's organization, epileptics and other *aliénées* seem to have been clearly differentiated in the asylum, if not also kept separately from other patients. Moreau de Tours speaks of "several facts of physiology and of therapy of nervous disorders that I have had the opportunity to observe in the four years that I was in charge of the service of hysterics and epileptics in the Salpêtrière" (1865: 6). In January 1870, Delasiauve remarked that a patient was admitted as epileptic, but that she was instead *"aliénée"* —evidence that he wanted her transferred out of his ward (AAP, Salpêtrière, 6Q2–54).

20. Whereas the category of epilepsy had, between 1838 and 1871, been a "wastebasket" nosological category (Charles Lasègue cited by Cesbron [1908]: 198), hysteria took over this nosological burden in the early Third Republic. Redefined in terms of symptoms rather than in terms of causes, hysteria could be far more than it had ever been—and it could serve as a useful category for differentiating neurological disorders. This reconsideration of symptoms and their origins can account for the great statistical shift Goldstein found in the Salpêtrière, but it cannot explain the proliferation of hysteria studies in the first two-thirds of the century. On hysteria's importance for the development of neurological understanding, see Ellenberger (1970), Goldstein (1987), Veith (1965), Losserand (1978): 411–38, and Temkin (1945): 243–87, 317–23.

21. No English word can adequately render the concept of *aliénation* in terms of the individual who is absent from himself or herself. The use of the concept coincides, in fact, with the refinement of the clinical relationship in which the *aliéné* is given over to the other, the *aliéniste*. The *Robert Petit* (1972) dates the expression *aliénation mentale* from 1801 (when Pinel rejected the label *fou* in favor of the more scientific *aliéné*). Prior to this date, one spoke of those who were *aliénés d'esprit*. The doctors' name for themselves—*aliéniste*— dates from 1846. Recent scholarship on the history of psychiatry has adopted the anglicized French expressions *alienist, alienation,* and *alienism,* e.g., Scull (1981); Bynum, Porter, and Shepherd (1985). I adopt the French expressions wherever appropriate.

22. Béraud's belief that this naming process might even serve as a deterrent to prostitution shows how the label stood in for those attempting to give an order to sexuality (*FPP*, 1: 256). His editor writes, "When we force them to register as *filles publiques,* then we'll see a trace of modesty retain them on the road of goodness and preserve them from their fall" (*FPP,* 1: 5).

23. See Hoffmann [1977]: 130–41, 175–99; Livi (1984); Wilson (1982): 196–202, 291–341; and Foucault, *Histoire de la folie à l'âge classique* (Paris: Gallimard, 1972), 296–315.

24. This is Foucault's claim (*Histoire de la folie,* 315). The quantity of observations of hysteria in the early nineteenth century bears this out.

25. See Leuret, who surveys *aliénistes'* attitudes toward the "moral treatment" invented by Pinel. Leuret defines "moral treatment" as "the reasonable use of all the means that act directly on the intelligence and passions of *aliénés"* (1840: 156). On Pinel see Gauchet and Swain (1980).

26. Briquet (1796–1881) was considered the trailblazer in the study of hysteria in the mid-nineteenth century. Charcot cites him frequently.

27. Virey (1825a): 217. Some would say that the same impressionability predisposed her to prostitution as well as hysteria. Béraud wrote that the "new" and "interesting" facts in his book "will serve as salutary lessons and warnings to those unfortunate ones whose bad education or whose force of passions attracts them to depravity" (*FPP,* 1: 2). Esquirol cites women's education and sensory stimulation as the causes of their madness, which he notes is almost always complicated by hysteria. Libertinism and "the disorder of public and private morals" drive women to mental *aliénation* ([1838] 1: 38, 47).

28. This shift is nowhere more apparent than in the hysteria studies submitted for the 1833 Bordeaux Royal Society of Medicine prize: Dubois, who won, wrote a purely historical and theoretical account of hysteria: in his five-hundred-fifty-page *Histoire philosophique*, there are no reported observations. Brachet's 1832 study received honorable mention but did not actually win a prize until the 1847 Paris Académie de Médecine competition. Its five observations would be expanded substantially—to eighteen—to meet the expectations of the day.

29. Ripa contends that between 1838–1850, only 15% of those who entered did eventually leave (1983: 475). She also found that only one out of thirty-one patients (male or female) transferred from one asylum to another between 1844 and 1858 ever left the asylum system (483–513). The average stay for women in 1842 was two years, six months, seven days; for men it was one year, seven months, twenty-seven days. In 1852, the average stay for women was one year, seven months, twenty days; for men it was one year, one month, eight days (490). Single women had the least chance of leaving since asylum doctors were most likely to release patients because of familial demands (483–502).

30. In the 1880s Charcot opened a small wing for the study of men. See Ellenberger (1970): 437–42.

31. Charcot (1886–93) 3: 3–4.

32. Freud (1893) 3: 12.

33. Clarétie recounts anecdotes from one of these balls (1882: 128–29). Transformed by the personnel of the asylum into a reward for patients' submission, the ball excited inmates into discipline, Ripa contends (1986: 135–37). The balls served an equally important role as publicity for a medical regime with far-ranging ambitions. See Goldstein (1987): 321–77 and Micale (1985): 721.

34. Didi-Huberman (1982). On the spectacles of the Salpêtrière, see also Copjec (1981): 21–40 and Silverman (1989): 75–106.

35. Charcot (1887–88): 178.

36. Goldstein (1987): 324; Didi-Huberman (1982): 28; and Br, 5.

37. See Goldstein (1987): 369–75.

38. Charcot (1886–93) 9: 277, cited in Didi-Huberman (1982): 78. I owe the expression "storied body" to Peter Brooks. On the transformations brought about by medical iconography, see Salpêtrière photographer Londe's description of the uses of photographic observation to complete the written reports "that are called *observations*" (*La Photographie médicale. Application aux sciences médicales et physiologiques*, [Paris: Gauthier-Villars, 1893], 3–4, reprinted in Didi-Huberman [1982]: 278–79).

39. I have examined *placements d'office* records from AAP, Salpêtrière, 6Q2–38 (October 1861–March 1862), 6Q2–46 (January–June 1865), 6Q2–52 (May 1867–January 1868), 6Q2–54 (October 1868–February 1870), 6Q2–56 (December 1871–September 1972), 6Q2–60 (September 1875–August 1876), and the registers surveyed by Goldstein (1987): 6Q2–61 and 6Q2–62 (1882–83).

40. AAP, Salpêtrière, 6Q2–8, no. 14721 (May 19, 1945).

41. In 1845, all of the *placements d'office* of the Salpêtrière were either working-class or unemployed women. An occasional teacher (AAP, 6Q2–12, no. 16178, 6Q2–13, no. 17055) slipped in among these workers, but, as we see in chapter 9, an educated woman was a glaring exception to the rule. Women's average wage in 1840 was .81 francs, rising to 2.41 francs in 1850. In comparison, men earned an average wage of 4.75 francs in 1850 (Sullerot [1968]: 90, 103). According to an industrial survey of 1853, seamstresses earned between 50 centimes and 2 francs per day. *Corsetières* earned between 1 and 5 francs per day.

Culottières earned between 1 and 3 francs per day (Harsin [1985]: 85–87). On the basis of costs of necessities—food, clothing, wood, coal—provided in the same industrial survey, Harsin concludes that "some women did not earn enough to support themselves" (208–9). Simon assumed that in 1860 with subsistence-level rent of 100 francs, heat and light at 36 francs, and clothing at 115.50 francs, a working woman with a 500-franc annual salary would have only 60 centimes per day to eat, barely enough to buy bread (1862: 286–87).

42. This is based on a study of 607 *placements d'office* (AAP, Salpêtrière, 6Q2–8 and 6Q2–9) for 1845. No profession was listed for ninety-four of the women, thirty-seven are explicitly marked as "without position." Those with no profession listed seem frequently to have been unable to speak for themselves. For example, 6Q2–8, no. 14571 is a twenty-two-year-old married woman whom Falret diagnoses as suffering from "manic excitement following childbirth." Case 6Q2–8, no. 14874 is diagnosed as *"idiote"* (retarded). Her doctors know her age (twenty-eight) but not if she is married. Women listed as lacking a profession are either aged or suffering some form of mental retardation. Occasionally, *"sans profession"* seems to mask a past as a prostitute: Joséphine Cathérine B., age thirty-six, is described as having lived in Saint-Lazare for the past six months. Mitivié describes her as "ravaged and broken, as one is after debauchery or a dissolute orgy" (6Q2–9, no. 15079)

43. Of the ninety-four women *placements d'office* without a listed profession in 1845, thirty-six were single, ten widowed, and twenty-eight married. The marital status of another twenty was unknown. A large percentage of these women had ailments that would not have disposed them to be married (deaf-mute, epilepsy, retardation).

44. The majority of those who did leave the asylum did so at the request of a family member (e.g., 6Q2–12, no. 16197; 6Q2–46, no. 31226). Out of two hundred *placements d'office* in the first four months of 1845, seventy-four would be given *certificats de sortie* and allowed to leave. Of these patients, forty-six departed *with* a family member. One left with a fellow laundress. Of those twenty-eight who were not officially reclaimed by family members, another five were married; four were prostitutes *"remise à la police."* Only nineteen left on their own recognizance. Of these two hundred admissions, forty-four are listed as having died in the Salpêtrière. Thirty-four patients were transferred to another asylum or hospital (e.g., Lourcine). The status of ten others is unclear. For thirty-five of the patients, no further information was recorded. Three patients escaped.

45. Goldstein (1982): 211.

46. Ripa (1983): 23.

47. See Goldstein (1987): 152–96.

48. AAP, Salpêtrière, 6Q2–8 and 6Q2–9 (1845–46). The use of this diagnosis was entirely that of Jules Mitivié (1796–1871), nephew of Esquirol and Salpêtrière doctor from 1831 to 1865. Mitivié was also partial to the diagnosis *"lypémanie"* (melancholia), and occasionally described a hysterical patient as suffering from *"manie hystérique."* Falret tended to define patients in terms of *"aliénation partielle"* or *"aliénation générale"* and provided many more details of their condition than Mitivié who modified his diagnoses primarily with information about the patient's agitation or hallucinations. Girard de Cailleux criticized Mitivié for his sloppy "admissions certificates" and for the absence of observations. Falret was also criticized, but Trélat (see chapter 9) was considered more careful (1863b: 21–22).

49. Other forms of "manie"—"lypémanie," "manie ambitieuse," etc.—represent another 20% of all *placements d'office.* A survey of Salpêtrière register 6Q2–22 (October 1854–April 1855) demonstrates this. See also Ripa (1983): 135.

50. In 1864, for example, 75% of the patients admitted are listed as "dangerous."

51. AAP, Salpêtrière, 6Q2–8 and 6Q2–9 (1845–46).

52. Out of one hundred patients who were admitted in the same winter as Hersilie Rouy (see chapter 9, in November and December of 1854, three were diagnosed as suffering from hysteria (by Mitivié and Falret). Falret's patient suffered from "partial alienation" with "erotic ideas" and "hysterical convulsions." All three were young—sixteen, nineteen, and twenty-six—and single. Out of these one hundred patients, seven were categorized as suffering from epilepsy, fourteen as having "monomania," fifteen as afflicted with "lypémanie." Thirteen of them had some indefinite "mania." A total of fifty-five of those admitted were classed as "dangerous" (including Falret's patient with hysterical symptoms, but not including either of Mitivié's hysterics). This account of danger became a substitute for any story about causes or symptoms. Diagnosing doctors were Mitivié, Falret, Trélat, Baillarger, and Lélut (AAP, Salpêtrière, 6Q2-22 [1854]). A survey of 125 placements d'office in 1853 (October–December) found almost identical results: two patients were diagnosed as having hysterical symptoms; one had "attaques de nerfs" (all diagnosed by Mitivié). The two with "manie hystérique" were both young (twenty and seventeen) and single. Only five were diagnosed as having symptoms of epilepsy. Eleven of these patients had "monomanie." Fifteen of them had some indefinite "manie." Thirty-seven of the patients are aged women, fifty years old or more, many of them suffering from "démence" or "general paralysis." Of the total 125, ninety-four (or 75.2%) are described in terms of their "danger": 75% of these brief observations conclude with an assessment that the patient is in an "état qui peut être dangereux pour elle et pour les autres" (6Q2-20, no. 20580, for example). Diagnosing doctors were Baillarger, Trélat, Mitivié, and Falret. Lélut appears once (6Q2-19-20 [April 1853–April 1854]).

53. AAP, Salpêtrière, 6Q2-46 (January–June 1865). Charcot was not yet a diagnosing physician in these admissions. We might attribute this increasing rise in interest in hysteria to the work of Moreau de Tours, who replaced Lélut in the Service des épileptiques in 1861.

54. Significantly, in the same sampling of 269 patients, 113 of those not diagnosed as hysteric, epileptic, or suffering from "general paralysis" were aged (over fifty), and usually diagnosed as afflicted with "dementia." Fifty-eight patients were diagnosed as epileptic. The others, almost without exception, were children diagnosed as "idiots," or adolescents diagnosed as "imbéciles." Very few entering patients are labeled "non-aliénée." A few are diagnosed as suffering from "lypémanie," or melancholic mania. A handful have unclassifiable mental problems—"persecution deliria," etc. (AAP, Salpêtrière, 6Q2-54 [1868-70]).

55. "To treat those maladies that every writer saw as prototypes of instability, of irregularity, of fantasy, of the unexpected, as individuals governed by no law or rule, and as related by no serious theory—that was the task that revolted me the most. I resigned myself to it and set to work" (Br, v).

56. For gynecological treatises, see Roussel (1775), Moreau de la Sarthe (1803), Virey (1825a), Colombat (1838-43), Auber (1841), Chomet (1846), Debay (1850), etc. AMP studies suggest other hospitals were also dumping grounds for women designated as hysterical in the 1840s: see discussions of Louis at the Hôtel-Dieu (AMP [1846], no. 2, pp. 113-15); Piorry at La Pitié (AMP [1846], no. 2, pp. 421-22; [1848], no. 2, p. 109); Sandras at the Hôtel-Dieu (AMP [1845], no. 2, pp. 466-68; an unnamed physician at the Hôtel-Dieu (AMP [1847], no. 2, p. 460); and Briquet at La Charité (AMP [1848], no. 2, pp. 116-18).

57. AAP, Salpêtrière, 6Q2-8 and 6Q2-9 (January 1845–May 1846). Babet S., 6Q2-8, no. 14648. Another exception, Jeanne Adélaïde (6Q2-8, no. 14721), suffered from "chagrin" and monthly hysterical fits. Yet another exception, a seventy-nine-year-old widowed spinner was diagnosed as epileptic by Lélut, but he defined her epilepsy as related to hysteria (6Q2-8, no. 14866). Lélut's diagnoses frequently attempted to untangle hysterical and epileptic

symptoms. This resulted in descriptions like those of 6Q2-8, no. 14861, whom he defined as epileptic with symptoms of a hysterical character, and 6Q2-8, no. 14863, whose symptoms were categorized as "of a hysterical character." The causes in this latter case of a forty-three-year-old housekeeper were listed as "fear at the age of twenty-two." For similar confusion between epilepsy and hysteria, see 6Q2-12, Nos. 16146, 16197, and 6Q2-13, no. 17089.

58. Briquet, among others, saw chlorosis as a warning sign of hysteria (Br, 183). "Neuralgia" is frequently listed as a symptom of hysteria (JLB, 388). More detailed demographic readings would undoubtedly show that a single woman in her twenties had to have visible contusions or lesions to be admitted to the hospital as suffering from a disease other than hysteria, neuralgia, or chlorosis. If more details existed in hospital records on the symptoms read into these diagnoses, we might learn why this was so. With little more than ages, marital status, and occupations to tabulate here, it is hard to know whether the medical gaze of La Charité was so narrow as to prevent women from being seen as suffering from other ailments, or whether instead women defined their own symptoms in terms of these commonly known female conditions. Foucault in *DP* and Léonard (1981) suggest how these hospitals worked, but cannot reproduce the diagnostic circumstances leading to these demographic phenomena. What is most significant for us in the La Charité archives is that the ailments Charcot and his followers concerned themselves with were isolated in the 1840s in wards for female medical disorders. These wards held women with "nervous ailments" and unruly uteruses, but not epileptics or those with syphilitic conditions (even "general paralysis," later associated with syphilitic madness, was in the Salpêtrière).

59. Culler (1981): 178–79.

60. E. M. Forster, *Aspects of the Novel* (Harmondsworth: Penguin, 1962), 93, cited in Culler (1981): 183.

61. Scarry (1985): 4, 7.

62. AAP, Salpêtrière, 6Q2-8, nos. 14503, 14543, 14648.

63. AAP, Salpêtrière, 6Q2-13, no. 16797.

64. AAP, Salpêtrière, 6Q2-12, no. 16087.

65. AAP, Salpêtrière, 6Q2-13, nos. 17053, 16937, 17158.

66. AAP, Salpêtrière, 6Q2-13, nos. 17005, 16829. Patient 6Q2-13, no. 16794 suffers, they say, from "manic mental overexcitement resulting from the events of June." 6Q2-13, no. 16795 suffers from *"lypémanie"* as a result of her fear of being shot during the revolutionary uprisings. A forty-three-year-old day worker is listed as having delusions about the revolution (6Q2-13, no. 16816). A fifty-one-year-old seamstress has "predominating politico-religious ideas" due to the events of June (6Q2-13, no. 16764). A nineteen-year-old enters in September with "disorder" because of the June Days (6Q2-13, no. 16882). A "linen-maid," age forty-seven, is recorded as claiming that she is "a victim of great injustices . . . she stood up forcefully against the revolution of February, and believes she has the strength to repair all the harm she did" (6Q2-13, no. 16941).

67. AAP, Salpêtrière, 6Q2-12, no. 16238; 6Q2-13, no. 16833. Cf. 6Q2-12, nos. 16087, 16163, 16238; and 16335.

68. AAP, Salpêtrière, 6Q2-8, no. 14770. 6Q2-8, no. 14688 (1845) is listed as a *"fille publique, se disant couturière."* The admitting physician records that "she does not seem *aliénée."*

69. AAP, Salpêtrière, 6Q2-9, no. 14947.

70. AAP, Salpêtrière, 6Q2-9, no. 15079. Asylum doctors not only make assumptions about prostitutes, but seem so thoroughly to ignore them that they frequently reenter the asylum several times without ever being diagnosed as anything more detailed than "afflicted

with attacks of mania" (e.g. 6Q2-12, no. 16100). See 6Q2-8, Nos. 14646 (reappearing as no. 14818), 14664, and 6Q2-12, no. 16183. Asylum doctors are not alone in viewing prostitution as a scourge. A married seamstress, age thirty-seven, believes that she is accused of being "dishonest, a prostitute, and a poisoner." She even believes that these accusations are in the public papers (6Q2-13, no. 17054).

71. AAP, Salpêtrière, 6Q2-13, no. 17056.

72. AAP, Salpêtrière, 6Q2-13, no. 16775: Annette S. entered "in a state of melancholia with a penchant for suicide following convulsions resembling hysteria and epilepsy." Case 6Q2-12, no. 16321: Désirée V. is registered as "feeling alternative manic excitement and suicidal melancholia. This mental state seems to have begun eight months before when she had a fit of jealousy toward her husband so serious that she believed she saw women with him in the street when he was alone."

73. AAP, Salpêtrière, 6Q2-13, no. 16947.

74. Briquet found dozens of possible symptoms during his ten years at La Charité. At the Salpêtrière, Lasègue took each symptom individually to construct an infinitely fragmented hysterical body (see Goldstein [1987]: 328).

75. AAP, Salpêtrière, 6Q2-8 (1845).

76. Tissot's studies continued to have a major impact throughout the nineteenth century, as Briquet's citations suggest. Jean-François Bertrand-Rival even organized a horrific part of his anatomical wax museum around masturbation's scourges (*Précis historique physiologique et moral des principaux objets en cire préparée et coloriée après nature qui composent le museum* [Paris: Richard, an X]). For discussions of masturbation phobia see R. P. Neuman, "Masturbation, Madness, and the Modern Concepts of Childhood and Adolescence," *Journal of Social History* (Spring 1975): 1–27; Jordanova (1987); E. H. Hare, "Masturbatory Insanity: The History of an Idea," *Journal of Mental Science*, 108 (1973–74): 604–25.

77. AAP, Salpêtrière, 6Q2-8, 6Q2-9 (1845–46).

78. AAP, Salpêtrière, 6Q2-8, Nos. 14781; 14582; 14641; 6Q2-13, no. 17055.

79. AAP, Salpêtrière, 6Q2-8, no. 14799. See also 6Q2-8, no. 14770; 6Q2-12, nos. 16163, 16183; 6Q2-13, no. 16937.

80. AAP, Salpêtrière, 6Q2-8, no. 14704.

81. AAP, Salpêtrière, 6Q2-13, no. 17056.

82. "Physical pain does not simply resist language, but actively destroys it" (Scarry [1985]: 4).

83. Barthes, S/Z (Paris, Seuil, 1970).

84. AAP, Salpêtrière, 6Q2-13, no. 17089.

85. Unlike most of his predecessors, notably Landouzy, Briquet believed men could suffer from hysteria, though they were twenty times less likely to be afflicted than women. In Briquet's cases of male hysteria he is contemptuous of these men. A twenty-five-year-old baker, for example, is seen as having undesirable feminine qualities—he is "extremely impressionable, with a *romanesque* spirit, cries easily and is always extremely moved when he goes to the theater" (Br, 15–16).

86. De Certeau, "The Freudian Novel," in (1986): 24.

87. Phèdre's words, cited by Briquet appear in *Phèdre*, I, iii: 306.

88. Br, v–vi, 53–54. Landouzy (1847), whose clinical experience was limited, tabulated 351 observations from other treatises on hysteria. Briquet was especially fond of attacking Pomme, discussed in Foucault (1975a): ix–xx.

89. One-fourth of all girls whose mothers are hysterical will become hysterical themselves, said Briquet (Br, 605).

90. See Mathieu, repeatedly cited by Legouvé (1854) and reviewed favorably by Marie Marcel in the feminist *L'Opinion des femmes* (March 10, 1849), pp. 5–6.

91. Morel (1859) provides a rare set of asylum cases including hysteria.

92. Cf. the woman institutionalized because she saw the death of another woman, whose image she now sees everywhere (AAP, Salpêtrière, 6Q2–8 [1845]).

93. Report, Société médico-pratique de Paris, session of April 9, 1848, reprinted in *AMP* (1849): p. 458. Cf. "Clinique de M. Chomel," *AMP* (1843): 105–9.

94. Georget (1820): 55, 37. See also JLB, 199, discussed in chapter 5.

95. Morel (1859) 2: 43. Chatelain, "Considérations médico-légales sur l'état mental de la nommée Marie Jeanneret convaincue d'avoir commis neuf empoisonnements," *AMP*, (1869): 249. Jules Falret (1866): 407, 406.

96. Baillarger, "Quelques Observations pour servir à l'histoire de la médecine légale psychologique," *AMP* (1853): 466–73. Legrand Du Saulle (1860): 105. Despite his ambivalence about believing hysterics, Legrand refused to examine the hysteric to undercut her testimony. Jules Falret (1866): 406. Huchard (1882): 199–200.

97. See Coeurderoy (1847) where the father's account is played against that of the daughter. Although her Salpêtrière doctor seems to believe Jeanne Noël's story that her father's "immoral propositions" drove her from her home, the narrator of this account gives credence to the father's views and ultimately downplays this "insight" in an insistence that Jeanne's impressionability is primarily to blame for her attacks. In the place of a causal link between her father's mistreatment of her and her hysterical attacks, the *AMP* narrator recounts the endless repetitions of her symptoms—induced, due to her impressionable nature, by the very mention of her father, mother, or illness. Similarly, twenty-year-old Adèle F. was labeled hysterical by Trélat, who found the antecedents to her symptoms sufficiently "complicated" to leave them out of his report, in which he declared his suspicions that she was a prison escapee (AAP, Salpêtrière, 6Q2–46, no. 31091).

98. Esquiros (1841): 169; 174; Esquiros (1840): 96; 120–21.

99. Even doctors worried about the effects of continence remained divided over the issue of female pleasure, as Laqueur shows (1988, 1990). Moreau (1982) cites a number of medical doctors fiercely opposed to encouraging women to enjoy sexual pleasure, but she does not distinguish between semipornographic writers like Morel de Rubempré (1848) and those whose clinical experience might increase their authority. Le Doeuff links the early nineteenth-century discovery of female ovulation to a new popularity of Roussel's fantasmatic study of 1775 (1980: 196). Roussel's notion of the woman's physiological system anchored the denigration of female sexual pleasure, yet it also served those fighting the continence of clericalism because it insisted that woman's "true," "natural" function was reproduction.

100. Debay (1850) and Mathieu (1847): 255–63.

101. Doctors embracing these views included Virey, Louyer-Villermay, Chomet, Lisfranc, Lévy, Landouzy, Mathieu, and Debay, as well as *aliénistes* like Voisin, Marc, and Morel who spread their views.

102. "Clinique de M. Chomel" (1843). It might be tempting to read these isolated cases of hysteria following dog attacks as misclassified rabies cases. Yet something else seems to be happening here. Like the case of the girl suffering from an attack on her "modesty," this one encodes fears of sexuality in a register that acknowledges the girl's own account of her malady. What are we then to make of these repeated cases of attacks by dogs on young girls? Are these euphemisms for rapes, recounted in safe language by doctors unwilling to risk their reputations? Are they perhaps the girls' own revisions of sexual assaults into terms they can use in the doctors' presence? Are they displacements of fear from some other unnameable

and even forgotten incident onto the more narratable story of a dog attack? We cannot know. What we can know is that these girls transformed their fears into bodily symptoms, that the doctors gave names to these symptoms, and that they took their patients' word for the *causes morales* at the source of this pain. The attending physician makes the scene of this girl's seduction into hysteria the central concern of this case study of 1843. Though he names a dog as the agent of her hysterization, he grants credence to her account of victimization. He lets her be the subject for her own fears. On rabies, see Kathleen Kete, "*La Rage* and the Bourgeoisie: The Cultural Context of Rabies in the French Nineteenth Century," *Representations*, 22 (1988): 89–107.

103. Landouzy (1846) alone of authors of major studies between 1830 and 1872 believed prostitutes unlikely to be hysterical. Like him, Mathieu (1847) targeted continence as hysteria's source. Depot doctor and Charcot disciple Colin returned to this view, arguing that hysterics are smarter and more sensitive than prostitutes (1890: 39–41). Girard de Cailleux lamented the mixing of *filles inscrites* with other Salpêtrière patients, noting that "this deplorable confusion is morally revolting and casts a slur on the poor but honorable families among whom misfortune has most frequently produced madness, whereas the madness of prostitutes is almost the certain result of debauchery and a licentious life" (1863b: 17).

104. Rossignol (1856). See also Legrand Du Saulle's 1856 review.

105. Legrand Du Saulle (1883): 39–42.

106. See Voisin (1826): 67–68, 73; Chomet (1846): 38; JLB, 93; Br, 123–25; Legrand Du Saulle (1856): 606–7; and Esquiros and Frémy cited above.

107. Debay (1850): 88–90.

108. Felman argues, following Lacan, that Freud read "*his own unconscious*" *in* his patients' hysterical discourse: "The discovery of the unconscious is therefore Freud's discovery, within the discourse of the other, of what was actively reading within himself: his discovery, in other words, or his reading, of what was reading—in what was being read. The gist of Freud's discovery, for Lacan, thus consists not simply of the revelation of a new *meaning*—the unconscious—but of the *discovery of a new way of reading*" (1985: 164).

5. Pathological Masterplots: Hysteria, Sexuality, and the Balzacian Novel

1. Legrand Du Saulle (1883: 3, 4, 5) was not alone in his complaints about literary meddling in the physiological, anatomical, and psychiatric. Jean-Pierre Falret (1864) included novelistic observation among the kinds of studies of mentally ill patients pursued in his own era (109–10). Brierre de Boismont likewise deplored the number of *aliénistes* imitating novelists (review article, AMP [1850]: 692). Legrand was supplementing work by Tissot, Louyer-Villermay, Georget, Dubois, Brachet, Landouzy, Briquet, and Charcot, who he believed had neglected the hysteric's social relations.

2. "He pronounced again the word 'pornography' and went so far as to name the Marquis de Sade, whom he had never even read" (Zola [1961] 2: 114).

3. Zola (1961) 2: 113–14.

4. Henri Mitterand erroneously imagines Rougon referring to the Goncourts' 1864 *Germinie Lacerteux* or Zola's 1867 *Thérèse Raquin* (Zola [1961] 2: 1518). While both texts may have incited government ministers to hysteria, neither could have concerned a minister like Rougon when this scene is set—during the summer of 1857. *Madame Bovary* was published in the *Revue de Paris* in the fall of 1856 and tried and acquitted in February 1857. It appeared in book form in May 1857, just before this conversation would have transpired.

5. Poitou (1858): 17, 16–18. The Musée Dupuytren was founded in the École de Médecine in 1835 to honor surgeon Guillaume Dupuytren (1777–1835). I treat this museum in more detail in "Censoring the Realist Gaze," *Realism, Sexuality, and Gender*, ed. Margaret Cohen and Chris Prendergast (Minneapolis: University of Minnesota Press, forthcoming 1994).

6. Poitou (1858): 18–20. Attacks likening *Madame Bovary* to physiology, anatomy, and dissection were made by numerous critics, discussed by Weinberg (1937): 159–66, and in my "Censoring the Realist Gaze."

7. See Schor (1985): x–xi, 144–46; Waller (1989): 141–51; and Nancy K. Miller (1988).

8. The Salpêtrière and Bicêtre loom fantasmatically in the novels of Balzac and Sue, waystations or threats for Lydie Peyrade of *Splendeurs*, Reine in *Cousine Bette*, and Morel in *Les Mystères de Paris*. The private hospital turns up in Sue's *Juif Errant* (as prison for Adrienne de Cordoville) and Balzac's *L'Envers de l'histoire contemporaine* (as the place where Vanda de Mergi might be cured). Goldstein (1987): 152–53 notes Balzac's interest in psychiatric phenomena, particularly monomania.

9. Clarétie's *Les Amours d'un interne* (1881) and Lorde's *Théatre d'épouvante* (1909) explicitly thematize the Charcot Salpêtrière.

10. Apter (1991) uses the term "pathography" to designate the new genre that fused biography, fiction, and clinical case history (xi–xiii, 34–40). Early versions of the genre include the Goncourts' *Germinie Lacerteux* (1864), labeled a hysteric by critics; their *Madame Gervaisais* (1868), whose "mystical" madness is discussed by Apter, 124–46; Zola's *Thérèse Raquin* (1867), to which he compared the analytical work of surgeons on corpses ("Preface to the Second Edition," 1868; rpt. 1970: 60); and Huysmans's *Marthe*, whose alcoholic, Gingenet, is autopsied by Briquet (1876; rpt. 1975: 140–41).

11. Cf. Charles Bovary's *Dictionnaire des sciences médicales* with its uncut pages (Flaubert 1857; rpt. 1966: 66), discussed by Rothfield (1985): 57–81.

12. See Baudelaire (1976) 1: 76–86, and Flaubert's response in Baudelaire (1976) 1: 1120–21. See also Goldstein (1991): 134–165.

13. While novels like Balzac's *Lys dans la vallée* and Méray's *La Part des femmes* explore how the desires of women may have produced hysterical symptoms (as I will show later in this chapter and in chapter 7), they evoke these symptoms as part of an exploration of male prerogatives and subjectivity.

14. The novel became caught up in these debates in two other important ways. First, because it was repeatedly targeted as dangerous, tried, and censored (and the novels of hysteria were among the most brutally harassed by critics and the state censors), the novel became a transfer point for debates over the role of the literary in pathology. Second, because the novel was seen as dangerous for certain groups who were themselves pathologized, it regularly responded to moralistic, psychiatric, and police proscriptions against literature as well as against people. The investigations of difference pursued by the novel would be imbricated in uncanny ways with those pursued against the novelistic. Legrand's indictment of the novel became, in this respect, only one of many kinds of criticism levied against its pathological pursuits. The dangerous bodies that had become the subject of novels would focus struggles for decades—about the narration of pathology as well as about the women pathologized inside and outside the narrative.

15. Janin (1857) 5: 125–26. The reference to Balzac's women as *vaporeuses* summons a long tradition of medical accounts of hysterical symptoms. By the July Monarchy vapors are pathologized as hysteria, whereas in the eighteenth and early nineteenth centuries they were seen as only a fleeting complaint (Livi [1984]: 89–99; Veith [1965]: 168, 182, 210).

16. Schor (1985): xi.

17. Schor, "1833: The Scandal of Realism," in Hollier (1989): 656–61.

19. Soulié, Dumas fils, Feydeau, the Goncourts, and Zola were attacked for the vividness of their "pictures" of the world, or for their overly realistic approach to representation (cf. Weinberg (1937) and George Becker, *Master European Realists of the Nineteenth Century* [New York: Ungar, 1982]).

20. Mantegazza (1894) in the dedication and on page xv. Seventy years later, Freud worried that Dora had learned too much from Mantegazza (Freud [1963a]: 80).

21. Sainte-Beuve (1834): 441.

22. Al. de C., "Chronique littéraire," *Chronique de Paris* (November 9, 1835), p. 279; Chaudes-Aigues, "M. de Balzac," *Revue du XIXe Siècle*, 29 (October 1836): 411–15; Pelletan (1836): 449; Ozenne (1843): 147–71; Pelletan (1846): 3; Menche de Loisne (1852); Nettement (1854); Pontmartin (1857): 32–103; Sirtema de Grovestins (1859); Poitou (1856): 739–40; and Poitou (1858).

23. Sainte-Beuve (1834): 441.

24. Pontmartin (1857): 102, 99, 100.

25. Ozenne (1843): 170, 167, 168, 169–70.

26. Le Yaouanc argues for Brachet's influence on *L'Envers de l'histoire contemporaine* but also suggests that Balzac may have been familiar with Brachet's 1832 hysteria study (1959: 654).

27. Maron (1847): 242, 241.

28. *CB*, 27. Unlike the Pléiade *Cousine Bette* (*La Comédie humaine*, vol. 7 [Paris: Gallimard, 1977]), the Folio edition breaks the text into its original *feuilleton* chapters as it appeared in *Le Constitutionnel* between October 8 and December 3, 1846. My fairly literal translations were aided by Marion Ayton Crawford, trans. *Cousin Bette* (Middlesex: Penguin, 1965).

29. Phèdre's declaration, as we saw in chapter 4, resonates in nineteenth century medical studies as a description of the ravages of hysteria.

30. Lombroso and Ferrero (1894): 557–58. Valérie likewise served as the imagined source of "the putrid literature" of "a monstrous school of novelists" including the Goncourts and Zola in Ferragus's influential critique (*Le Figaro* [January 23, 1868], reprinted in Zola (1970): 40.

31. Jameson (1971): 245.

32. Valérie, even in repentance, even in death, somehow gets the better of the medical discourse that attempts to contain her. Bianchon and his colleagues gleefully await the autopsies they will perform on the two corpses, but they do not learn where this malady originated. Bette alone knows what we have already gleaned from the omniscient narrator's intervention in the private plotting of the rejected Montès. And Bette, too, soon becomes a corpse— though her tubercular condition leaves no physiological mysteries.

33. See Dowbiggin (1985) 1: 188–232.

34. Foucault *DP*, 97.

35. Lest parents of the upper classes think him too critical of the activities to which they destine their daughters, Brachet is reassuring. All those salons, balls, and social engagements can be risky for their daughters too, but parents ought not to "renounce the hope of seeing their daughters take the rank in the world that their merit ought to assign them": such a girl has a remarkable ability to "seize quickly the tone of the position in which she finds herself" (JLB, 93). Real class soon proves its own worth.

36. The frenzy of city life, court balls, salons, and receptions of Napoleon's court would therefore have been seen to endanger her. Cf. Louyer-Villermay, *DSM*, 23: 234–35 and Esquirol (1838) 1: 35.

37. On the dangers of reading and a sedentary life, see Louyer-Villermay, *DSM*, 23: 235, 232 and Esquirol (1838) 1: 35.

38. Georget embraced the theory that forceful emotions engender hysteria. Adeline's fear for Hortense, her terror for her uncle and husband, her embarrassment at Crevel's rejection, her mortification by Valérie's blackmail, her revulsion at Josépha's vices, her distress at the depravity of the people she meets as Lady Welfare Visitor, and her shock at Hulot's final betrayal could easily have converged as sources of hysterical convulsions (1824: 36, 50).

39. The remaining five include one man, three adolescent girls or unmarried women, and a nun.

40. The sources Brachet attributes to these women's hysteria vary widely. Madame F., a married laundress, suffered from hysteria as part of the complications of pregnancy (JLB, 141–43). Madame D.'s hysteria was set off by nursing her child. Madame de N. became hysterical at the birth of a child (JLB, 158–59). Madame Th. was a happy mother who became hysterical because of an aversion to something she ate (JLB, 127–29). Madame B. seemed predisposed to hysteria by her husband's political difficulties at the end of the Napoleonic Empire (JLB, 162). Madame Q. had hysterical crises after "great calamities of fortune and the loss of a beloved son" (JLB, 188). Madame A. was a recently married grocer whose sedentary work, lively imagination, and novel reading made her a logical candidate for hysterical attacks (JLB, 168–69).

41. Louyer-Villermay, *DSM*, (1816a) 23: 263.

42. Cf. Foucault *DP*, 107.

43. Jameson calls Adeline "the center of the work," "the framework of the novel," and the "representative and continuity of the family." In this view, Balzac makes her anchor a system in which this novel serves as an "object lesson: a warning against the kept mistress as the scourge of the legitimate family, a demonstration of the supreme responsibility of the wife, who ought to know how to be both wife and mistress in one, of the perfidy of servants as well, and the envy of the hostile outside world and of the family's own *'parents pauvres'* " (1971: 242). Jameson argues that she is transformed into "the point of view of the work, the consciousness across which the opposing instinctual forces struggle." Although the novel ultimately redeems Hulot's passion, Jameson argues that "she represents the only pole of human reality to which the civilizing claims, the dreams of the ideal, can attach" (253).

44. Brooks (1976): 4, 5, 13.

45. Laqueur (1989): 102.

46. Jameson (1971): 241–54.

47. See also the moralistic digression on women like Valérie: "This tirade will fly like an arrow to the heart of many families. We see Madame Marneffes at every level of society, even at Court; for Valérie is a sad reality, modeled from life in its slightest detail. Unfortunately, this portrait will cure no one of a mania for loving sweetly smiling angels with a dreamy air, an innocent face, and a strongbox for a heart" (*CB*, 173).

48. She is the only character in the book whose behavior is compared to that of a novel, her successful maneuvers with Hulot are depicted as *"sentimentales, romanesques, et romantiques"*—sentimental, novelistic, and romantic (*CB*, 122).

49. Jameson (1971): 246–47.

50. Cf. Brooks (1976): 20.

51. Alexandre Weill, "Revue littéraire: *Les Parents pauvres* par M. de Balzac," *Démocratie pacifique* (December 27, 1846) pp. 5-6.

52. Weill, *Démocratie pacifique* (May 9, 1847), p. 2.

53. Weill, *Démocratie pacifique* (December 27, 1846), pp. 5, 6.

54. Pontmartin (1857): 45.

55. According to Pontmartin, the edifying lines about the Catholic church near the conclusion of *Cousine Bette* leave the reader as shocked as if he had "found an obscene engraving in a devotional book" (1857: 46). A similar argument is made by Menche de Loisne (1852): 360 and Jolly (1851), who notes that Balzac has the modesty to declare that women ought not to read his books, yet throughout them paints the family and society in an immoral way (39).

56. Al. de C., "Chronique littéraire," *Chronique de Paris*, November 9, 1835, p. 279.

57. Cf. Menche de Loisne (1852): 370.

58. Nettement (1854) 2: 272.

59. Vicomte de Lovenjoul, *Une page perdue de H. de Balzac* (Paris: Ollendorff, 1903), 308, cited in *Lettres de femmes adressées à Honoré de Balzac* (1924) 3: vi.

60. On Balzac's female correspondents see *Lettres de femmes* (1924 and 1927); Bellos (1986): 253-62; and Allen (1991): 74-6. The original letters are in the Collection Spoelberch de Lovenjoul, Bibliothèque de France, A.312-18.

61. *Lettres de femmes* (1924) 3: 13-14.

62. *Lettres de femmes* (1927) 5: 16.

63. Cf. Kittler (1980): 47-48.

64. Jameson (1971): 251.

65. Balzac (1836, rpt. 1978) 9: 1630-31.

66. "Préface de la publication préoriginale," in Balzac (1836; rpt. 1978) 9: 915-16.

67. See Mozet (1986): 241-51.

68. Sirtema de Grovestins (1859) 1: 126, citing Poitou (1856): 743; Pelletan (1836): 451.

69. Critics attacked Balzac as a *séducteur* of female readers (Chaudes-Aigues, "M. de Balzac," *Revue du XIXe Siècle*, 29 (October 1836): 414; M. B., "Littérature.—Romans. *Le Lys dans la vallée*, par M. de Balzac," *La Gazette de France*, July 21, 1836, pp. 1-3; and A. G., "Etudes littéraires. *Le Lys dans la vallée* par M. de Balzac," *Le Siècle*, September 22, 1836, pp. 1-2.). Balzac's contemporaries claimed this novel was his revenge on Sainte-Beuve who was one of the first in 1834 to depict him as a favorite of female readers. See note to the later edition of that review ([1876] 2: 356-57).

70. Muret (1836): 3.

71. Pontmartin called it "the living, which is to say dangerous, part" of his works and compared it to *Cousine Bette* (1857: 67, 69, 80-81). "The *Lys dans la vallée* thus marks ... the extreme in immorality in Balzac's novels," claimed Pontmartin in a tirade on the novel's realistic qualities and seductions for its female readers. For those women, Madame de Mortsauf risked becoming "a patron ... to whom those inflamed hearts cling, proud of their secret wounds," Balzac had become a subtle tempter for these women, "infiltrating himself drop by drop, intoxicating with his perfidious aromas those whom he will lead astray or corrupt" (72, 71).

72. See Mozet (1986): 243. See also Balzac (1836, rpt. 1978) 9: 904-5; 1650-51. Roudaut's edition (Balzac [1836, rpt. 1977]) 326-32 gives a table comparing the two editions at the crucial moment of self-censorship. Nancy K. Miller notes that "even without the actual

suppression of the 'offensive' material, its potentially subversive content is undercut" by the positioning of Madame de Mortsauf's enunciation "under the sign of madness" (1980: 69).

73. Poitou (1856): 740; Sirtema (1859) 1: 123.

74. Poitou (1856): 741–42; Sirtema (1859) 1: 125.

75. Racine, *Phèdre*, I: iii, 306.

76. In a review lambasting Balzac's *La Marâtre*, *La Voix des femmes* called for the moralization of the theater, likewise naming Phèdre's passion in relation to the disturbing influence of Balzac on women: "The furors of Phèdre . . . are blessed bread next to all the pretty things Mr. Balzac spouts—'reading mothers will forbid to their daughters' " (June 4, 1848). Muret equally diagnoses as "hysterical" Madame de Mortsauf's husband (1836: 3, col. 1).

77. Brooks (1974): 155–56; Nancy K. Miller (1980): 74.

78. See Waller (1989).

79. Sirtema (1859) 1: 130, citing Poitou: "Like good, evil is contagious."

80. Charcot published sixty case studies on male hysteria between 1878 and 1892 (Mark Micale, "Diagnostic Discriminations: Jean-Martin Charcot and the Nineteenth-century Idea of Masculine Hysterical Neurosis," Ph.D. diss. Yale University, 1987). Offering seven cases of male hysteria, Briquet argues hysteria may strike men twenty times less often than women (Br, 11–51).

81. See Philip R. Slavney, *Perspectives on "Hysteria"* (Baltimore: Johns Hopkins University Press, 1990), 118, 158.

82. Kelly (1989): 50–55.

83. Sedgwick (1985).

84. *Lettres des femmes* (1924) 3: 29–30.

85. Edmond de Goncourt embraced medical stereotypes even as he traced his victim's trajectories out of *La Gazette des tribunaux* (see Ricatte [1960]: 81). Like Adeline, Emma Bovary, and a number of other women whom we examine in this book, Elisa has fallen into danger by reading too many books. Amid the "blows given by her mother, and the terrors of nights spent in the same bed," the narrator of Elisa's story counts "laziness only" as the "real determining cause" of her prostitution (Goncourt [1876, rpt. 1979]: 43). This special *"femme folle de [son] corps"* (54) sought distraction in novels: "Reading became a furor, a rage for Elisa. She did nothing except read. Absent in body and spirit from the brothel, the prostitute, as much as the low and limited ideals of her nature permitted, lived in a vague and generous upheaval, in the awakened dream of great, noble, pure actions, in a kind of homage of her brain to that which her profession made her profane every hour" (62). The madam of her bordello grows distressed about the prostitute's rage to read and demands an explanation: "The customers are complaining that you are no longer loving. . . . That's a reputation for my house to get! . . . It is those dirty books you read all day" (62). Yet the novels Elisa reads are not "dirty books" but *chaste romances* (60). Driven to Paris by the desires awakened in her by books, she finds herself increasingly disgusted with her trade. The outcome of this tension between desire derived from books and suffering in the flesh will be a hysteria that ends in murder—a scene of seduction so terrible Goncourt elides it from the novel.

86. "Narrative is constituted in the tension of two formal categories, difference and resemblance" (Todorov [1977]: 233).

87. Baudelaire (1976) 1: 81.

88. Baudelaire (1976) 1: 82.

6. Dangerous Reading: The Trials of the Nineteenth-Century Novel

1. Br, 112; Legrand Du Saulle (1883): 40, both citing Tissot (1770).

2. Anna Freud Bernays, "My Brother, Sigmund Freud," *The American Mercury*, 51 (November 1940): 357.

3. Flaubert (1869, rpt. 1964): 265. I consider the scandal of the Choiseul-Praslin murder in a work-in-progress, a version of which was presented as "The Dead Duke, the Dead Duchess, and Bette Davis: Twentieth-Century Readings of the Choiseul-Praslin Scandal," Nineteenth-Century French Studies, University of Oklahoma, October 1989.

4. Before the 1835 crackdown on the press, there were 520 press trials, 188 convictions and penalties of 106 years in prison and 44,000 francs in fines (Vincent [1968]: 52; and Bellanger [1969] 2: 103–4, 111). After September 1835, one finds a drop in condemnations of papers for political reasons (Bellanger 2: 138–41 and Irene Collins [1959]: 85–86). In 1841 Guizot again called for a press crackdown, but neither officials nor juries responded zealously.

5. See Krakovitch (1985): 15.

6. *Chambre des Députés*, 1, October 4, 1830, cited in Collins (1959): 63. These juries were drawn from the group of well-off men (whose property made them liable for 200 francs annual taxes) whose support was a mainstay of the bourgeois monarchy. Although citizen juries could be unpredictable, July Monarchy legal procedures allowed the state prosecutor great advantages (74).

7. The 1835 laws, the result of Fieschi's assassination attempt upon the king, raised the caution money for newspapers, allowed offenses to be tried in the Chamber of Peers instead of by juries (who might be more lenient than the Peers), submitted drawings to censorship, multiplied the kinds of offenses for which the press could be held accountable and increased the penalties for such offenses, and allowed the courts to suspend the publication of a newspaper that had been found guilty twice in a year. Although the censorship laws were explicitly intended to limit the criticism of the king that many saw as inciting the overthrow of the monarchy, the laws could be extended to far more than seditious discourse (see Bellanger [1969] 2: 113–14; Collins [1959]: 82–99; Krakovitch [1985]: 62–78; and Casselle [1985] 3: 46–55).

8. See Terdiman (1985): 188–89 and Collins (1959): 84.

9. Krakovitch (1982): 37.

10. The number of books prosecuted did drop after 1830: "During the Restoration, an average of twenty-six books a year were prosecuted successfully; during the July Monarchy twenty-three were annually brought to trial" (Allen [1981]: 184). Drujon (1879) bears out Allen's contention that censored books in the July Monarchy often had pornographic contents. The major exception to this rule seems to have been Auguste Luchet's *Le Nom de famille* (Paris: Souverain, 1842), which dealt with adultery among aristocratic families. Nevertheless, as we see in chapter 7, boundaries between the pornographic and the literary were fluid, and the positioning of those boundaries was blatantly political.

11. On censorship after 1851 see Krakovitch (1985), LaCapra (1982), Wing (1987): 114–33, Zévaès (1924), Spencer (1949 and 1956), and Maurice-Garçon (1931).

12. LaCapra (1982): 15.

13. The Bourbon *La Quotidienne*, founded in 1817, was edited from 1830 on by Alfred Nettement. With 5,800 subscribers in 1831 and an average press-run of 3,063 in 1846, it was one of the most regularly censored newspapers of the July Monarchy (Collins [1959]: 64; Bellanger [1969] 2: 146). Between 1830 and 1833, the *Gazette de France* and *Quotidenne* together suffered thirty-five prosecutions, with accumulated fines of 47,650 francs and three

years of imprisonment (Collins, 76). Although Nettement raged against newspaper novels, his paper published serial stories, claiming them high literature and not the immoral pap of the other papers.

14. Stendhal (1889, rpt. 1983): 79, 147.

15. Iknayan explores critical views of the connection between the Revolution of 1789 and the growth of the novel and provides highlights of the obsessive deprecation of the novel from the Restoration through the July Monarchy. She notes a transformation around 1830 in the debate relating the novel to society: rather than simply equate social mores and novelistic expression, critics begin to analyze the way such an equivalency is played out in practice (1961: 34–50). What changes, I would contend, is that the fantasy about dangerous reading is fleshed out in increasingly specific terms.

16. See Blum (1986): especially 116–117, 183–194.

17. Furet and Ozouf (1982): 83.

18. Although Furet and Ozouf argue that the Revolution did nothing to change the elementary school, it left the legacy of an imagined national school system that would gradually materialize over the course of the nineteenth century (1982: 97–99).

19. Crubellier (1985) 3: 25 cites Claude Lévi-Strauss: "The battle against illiteracy is confused . . . with control of citizens by Power" (*Tristes tropiques* [Paris: 1955], 344).

20. Saint-Just, *Oeuvres complètes*, vol. 2, ed. Charles Vellay (Paris: Charpentier and Fasquelle, 1908), 530, quoted by Blum (1986): 192. Because Rousseau believed that even men whose "moral habits" have been "purified" make mistakes in their choices of pleasures, he, too, advocated state censorship (*The Social Contract*, trans. Maurice Cranston [Middlesex: Penguin, 1968]), 174–76.

21. Crubellier writes of this moment: "It was a cultural contagion, initiated in the seventeenth century, extended in the eighteenth, completed in the nineteenth, beginning with a rural tradition and culminating in a bourgeois city model, moving from oral to written tradition, from gestual and ritual tradition to that of the book" ([1985] 3: 27–28).

22. Crubellier (1985: 25–26) and Hébrard ([1985] 3: 477–78) cite these generalizations from Furet and Ozouf (1982). Allen (1991): Table A.7 shows a 50% increase in literacy in France between 1831 and 1851.

23. For the concept of "new readers," see Hébrard (1985) 3: 477–83.

24. Defoe's and Fénelon's narratives are among Rousseau's choices for Émile (1762, rpt. 1969). On the reading of the masses, see Thiesse (1985) 3: 455–69 and Lyons (1985) 3: 368–97, who gives tables showing "best-sellers" from the period of 1811 to 1850. *Télémaque*, which was used in the schools (392) and *Robinson Crusoé* were among the best sellers for the entire era.

25. Huet (1670, rpt. 1942): 227–28.

26. Huet (1670, rpt. 1942): 225.

27. Huet safely evades mentioning the sex of these readers, but his applause of Scudéry suggests his neglect of their concerns derives more from his support for their education through fiction than from a wish to exclude them as readers. Huet even goes so far as to associate women's liberty in France with the excellence of the novel (Iknayan [1961]: 16–21, 39, 85–87).

28. See, for example, Darnton, "Readers Respond to Rousseau: The Fabrication of Romantic Sensitivity," in Darnton (1984): 215–56 and Joan de Jean, *Fictions of Sappho, 1546–1937* (Chicago: University of Chicago Press, 1989).

29. See F. C. Green, "The 18th Century French Critic and the Contemporary Novel," *Modern Language Review*, 23 (1928): 174–87; Wallace Kirsop, "Nouveautés: Théâtre et roman," in Martin and Chartier (1984) 2: 218–29; and Iknayan (1961): 34–50.

30. Hébrard (1985) 3: 486.

31. Frégier's views on prostitution parallel those of Parent-Duchâtelet (CD, 1: 153).

32. Frégier's terror about the theater's influence surpasses his fears about immoral literature. The theater serves as a kind of bad mother for the child of poverty, replacing the ideal mother who "neglects nothing to amuse her children and captivate their awakening imagination." The poor child must make his own amusements: his first theater will be the street, which develops his taste and readies him for the yet more vicious pleasures of the theater (CD, 2: 201). To ensure that apprentices will not be permanently debauched by plays passed over by critics and censors, Frégier projects industrial committees to provide a final check in this censorship process (CD, 2: 187–202).

33. Théophile Gautier, "Préface," Mademoiselle de Maupin, (1835–36; rpt. Paris: Garnier-Flammarion, 1966), 41.

34. "De l'Instruction de l'ouvrier," L'Atelier, November 1843, pp. 23–24.

35. "Enquête: De la Condition des femmes," L'Atelier, September 1840, p. 31.

36. L'Atelier attacked Sue's Mystères de Paris in ways resembling the Catholic and Monarchist press, railing against its "unspeakable chapters where the author shows us, with unbelievable complacency and daring, what horrible things debauchery and lust can beget." Their fears focused particularly on female readers: "We cannot believe that the simple thought that this work might fall into the hands of our wives or of our children did not stop him at the moment where he began to plot those repulsive scenes the equivalent of which one would perhaps search in vain in licentious books forbidden by the law" ("Les Mystères de Paris, roman philanthropique," November 1843, p. 28).

37. Parent argues that some prostitutes do read—"histories and novels," but never obscene works (PD, 1: 124).

38. Frégier insists upon the school's protective function: "So that schools fully attain the moral goal that we have proposed in founding them, they must give pupils a forever open refuge, a shelter against the temptations and traps of the streets. The influence of the streets is as dissolute and corrupt as that of the school is pure and productive (CD, 2: 79).

39. Virey (1825b): 7.

40. Virey (1825b): 9.

41. Le Diable à Paris (1845–46) 1: 311.

42. Proudhon (1875): 165–67.

43. Rousseau (1761, rpt. 1967): 4.

44. Bienville (1771, rpt. 1886): 78–79; Virey (1802): 90; Mathieu (1847): 471.

45. Pierre Choderlos de Laclos, Les Liaisons dangereuses (1782; rpt. Paris: Garnier-Flammarion, 1964), 245; Stendhal (1889, rpt. 1983): 67–68, 85; Balzac (1848, rpt. 1955): 367–68, 385–86, 397.

46. In 1801, 28% of French women over the age of fourteen were literate. By the end of the Second Republic, 52% of women over fourteen could read. Men's literacy increased in the same period from 50% to 60% (Allen [1991]: Table A.7). See also Sauvy (1985) and Hébrard (1985). Domestic manuals traditionally included a chapter on the dangers of certain kinds of reading, particularly citing novels and romantic literature. See Mme. Campan, De l'Éducation (Paris: Baudouin, 1824) 1: 206–14, 2: 400–401; J. B. Hullin, Le Mentor des jeunes demoiselles; ou, L'Art de se conduire dans le monde d'après les convenances sociales (Paris: Chaumerot, 1833), 56–57; the anonymous Conseils d'une maîtresse de pension à ses élèves sur la politesse et sur la manière de se conduire dans le monde (Lyon: Mongin-Rusad, 1841), 99–101; Mme. la Comtesse de Bassanville, Le Soir et le matin de la vie; ou, Conseils aux jeunes filles (Paris: Delesserts, 1850), 280–81; Mathilde Bourdon, Lettres à une jeune

fille (Paris: Casterman, 1859), 35–50; Comtesse Dash, *Comment on fait son chemin dans le monde* (Paris: Michel Lévy, 1868), 184–85.

47. Rousseau (1761, rpt. 1967): 4.

48. De Genlis (1829): 344–45; 39–41. Stéphanie de Genlis, governess for Philippe-Egalité's children, was widely believed to have been the great-grandmother of Marie Cappelle-Lafarge, whose murder trial I discuss in chapter 8.

49. The cover of *Magasin pittoresque*, 15 (January 1847), an engraving of Greuve's *La Lecture ou la Bonne éducation* (1776), suggests how successfully these ideals were translated into the new publications of the nineteenth century. As this image implies, the popular *Magasin pittoresque* (founded 1833) encouraged the reading of such women to enlarge its audience (Chollet [1983]: 36, 530n79). Delighting her family with the "happiness" of reading aloud, this girl seems to know what useful books to read. Her plain surroundings suggest she is one of those "new readers" who has already learned the moral scruples necessary to choose a new periodical.

50. "Society is not a phantom, it is the collection of all families; and who can police them with a care more exact than women—who, besides having the good fortune of natural authority and assiduousness in their homes, have even more so the advantage of being born painstaking, attentive to detail, industrious, ingratiating, and persuasive?" (Fénelon [1687, rpt. 1920]: 6, 141, 146).

51. Fénelon (1687, rpt. 1920): 7

52. AAP, Salpêtrière, 6Q2–8, no. 14993.

53. Louyer-Villermay (1816a): 254, (1816b) 1: 37–49. Georget (1824): 52. Among "causes of madness" Esquirol listed "the preference given to the arts of pure charm, novel-reading, which gives young people a precocious activity, premature desires, ideas of imagined perfections that they ["*elles*"] will find nowhere; frequentation of plays, clubs, the abuse of music, idleness" ([1838] 1: 35). Esquirol held women's taste for novels responsible for their "nervous illnesses," as well as for "disorder in public and private morals (1: 51). Voisin echoed Pinel's contention that reading novels was a source of *aliénation* (1826: 18); Hatin claimed that "voluptuous readings" led to hysteria and obscene pictures to nymphomania in women (1832: 325); Colombat warned against "licentious reading, especially passionate novels of the modern school" (1838–43: 1083); Morel argued that the romantic novel, particularly *Atala*, *René*, and *Obermann*, might destabilize young minds. He also believed newspaper accounts of crime might be traumatizing for women, citing the case of a woman driven to designs of infanticide after reading *causes célèbres* about maternal murder ([1859] 1: 241–42, 302).

54. Debay (1849): 83–84.

55. Virey (1802): 91–92.

7. *The Politics of Seduction: Trying Women's Share*

1. Other papers were not so lucky. Thirty republican newspapers folded because of the September Laws of 1835 (Jardin and Tudesq [1973]: 141). See also Irene Collins (1959) and Bellanger (1969) 2: 141–43.

2. In 1846 nineteen Paris dailies had larger circulations than *La Démocratie pacifique* whose pressrun averaged 1,165. *Le Siècle, Le Constitutionnel, La Presse* each had pressruns exceeding twenty thousand. Zeldin reports the Fourierist paper's circulation increased to 3,700 in 1848 ([1973] 1: 442).

3. Hugo, Préface, *Littérature et philosophie mêlées* (1834), cited in Krakovitch (1985): 43.

4. Spencer (1956) disturbingly romanticizes July Monarchy prison conditions.

5. Méray (1847). References to this novel appear in the text abbreviated as *PdF*, by date of publication, in this case, 6/19. In order to represent its Fourierist view of "the share of women," Méray's novel multiplies cases of female suffering. In addition to Juanna, an exotic half-Italian beauty, whose foreign origins and dowryless state prime her for disaster, and Ernestine, victimized daughter of the provincial landholder, its martyrs include Laure de Logny, lost love of Léonce's cousin Adelstan, married by her father to an aging libertine with whom he made a youthful pact; Léonce's mother, who silently suffers her greedy husband's tyranny; Adelstan's mistress Juliette, long since "lost" and dependent upon the libertine for support; Juanna's mother, whose early widowhood has left her on the edge of poverty, but who proudly seeks to marry her daughter honorably; and the censored Suzanne, the impoverished needleworker who has sought in a life of prostitution an improvement on the misery of her upbringing and freedom from her father's plans to marry her to a middle-aged drunk.

6. "Cour d'Assises de la Seine, Présidence de M. Jurien. —Audience du 24 août, affaire de *La Démocratie pacifique*," *La Démocratie Pacifique*, August 25, 1847. All further references to the trial reports in this newspaper will appear in the text abbreviated by date.

7. See Susan Sontag's "The Pornographic Imagination," in *Styles of Radical Will* (New York: Delta, 1981), 34–73; Deirdre English, Amber Hollibaugh, and Gayle Rubin, "Talking Sex: A Conversation on Sexuality and Feminism," *Socialist Review*, 11, no. 4 (1981): 43–62; Susanne Kappeler, *The Pornography of Representation* (Minneapolis: University of Minnesota Press, 1986); Alan Soble, *Pornography: Marxism, Feminism, and the Future of Sexuality* (New Haven: Yale University Press, 1986); Linda Williams, *Hard-Core: Power, Pleasure, and the Frenzy of the Visible* (Berkeley: University of California Press, 1989); and Andrew Ross, *No Respect: Intellectuals and Popular Culture* (New York: Routledge, 1989), 171–208.

8. "Morality is a sexual matter," argues Rose, "not just because of the reference to the prostitute and the explicit discourse of purity and vice. It is also because of the sexual fantasy, the relentless and punishing scrutiny of the woman, which supports it" (1986: 112).

9. Cited by J.-M. Goulemot, "Les livres érotiques," in Martin and Chartier (1984) 2: 226–27.

10. These titles translate as "Fuckings in good taste," "How spirit comes to girls," "Alone? Alas-yes!" "The woman who sees nothing there," and "Pleasure without fear." Drujon (1879) lists dozens of prints banned between 1814 and 1877.

11. Figure 7.1 suggests the dangers of one of the most popular banned books of the nineteenth century, Louvet de Couvray's *Les Amours du Chevalier de Faublas* (1787–90). For records of its bannings—and the censorship of its many obscene images, see Drujon (1879): 24–25. I discuss theories of pornographic vision surrounding this text in "Male Masquerades and Female Travesties: Body Politics and 'Pictures' of Revolutionary Minds," paper presented at the American Eighteenth-Century Studies Conference, Pittsburgh, April 10, 1991. Figure 7.1 represents a kind of culmination of this imagery, Charles Wheeler's (1881–1977) *And So the Story Ends*, which shows a naked woman from the back, curled languorously amidst draperies, reading—if we could call it that—a large book with pictures. Her partly closed eyes obscure her gaze, yet suggest she is looking at the caption of the picture on the right-hand page. While her body projects availability, her gaze betrays no excitement. The reader of the picture is invited to provide his own "end" to her story. Nies discusses several such "provocative readers" (1985: 97–106).

12. Sedgwick's analysis (1985) would suggest that the *"misère sexuelle"* described by Corbin (1978) was a fantasmatic concept generated to preserve dominant forms of male interaction.

13. Like Bresson, the novel elides the seduction and its implications for the girl it calls— even before her night with Léonce—a *lorette*. We learn only that the protector who saved her from the brutality of her father's choice, a young man named Jules, has left her three months before this dinner. Lacking financial assistance and a "protector," Suzanne agrees to stay the night "because [she] wanted to know luxury a little" (*PdF*, 7/1). What promises her first protector may have made and what seductions he may have worked on her are left unspoken. Suzanne's choice of *concubinage*, the novel simply tells us, was one in which she was "contented to let herself be forced" (*"elle se contenta de se laisser forcer à accepter un asile dans la chambre de son généreux protecteur"*).

14. See T. J. Clark (1985): 94–95.

15. The moments Bresson frames recall Freud's "scene of castration," in which a subject's *sight* of difference forever determines his psychic being. Having glimpsed the woman who lacks what he believes to be a critical organ, the little boy assigns the penis an overabundant signification and spends the rest of his life trying to assuage the anxiety the woman's lack produced in him. In the original scene, Freud's male child mobilizes all his resources to reconstitute that woman—with a difference and an excess. By representing her, the male viewer can produce her as *different* from himself, therefore as unthreatening, and as marked by *excesses*, which he must renounce in order to preserve himself from dangerous identification (Freud [1925; rpt. 1963c]; Laplanche and Pontalis [1964]: 1833–68). The parallels between Freud's account of the "scene of the male gaze" and the state prosecutor's production of framed sequences of looking link two central problematics of the nineteenth century: first, the investment of representation with sexuality, and second, the encroachment of the scientific gaze upon all forms of discourse. This is a gaze believed capable of rationally investing its objects, producing from them knowledge and therefore also power, without accounting for its own desire. The gaze that invests all representation with sexuality and the gaze that derives power and knowledge from its objects are not two different gazes, but rather two different *stories* surrounding the production of fields of vision. Just as the July Monarchy state seems to have needed a censorship trial to elaborate on its moral views, the gaze of the censor needs a narrative to propel its spectacle of morality into practice. It is this narrative that threatens to topple the entire system of nineteenth-century moral vision.

16. "The scopic drive . . . maps desire into a representation," de Lauretis has claimed, arguing that narrative pleasure *along with* visual pleasure together "constitute the frame of reference of cinema, one which provides the measure of desire." The *story* the voyeur gets out of looking is as important to him as his *view* (1984: 67). This analysis can be extended to the account of looking in this censorship trial of 1847 precisely because both cinema and the trial mobilize the gaze in a relay of glances, endowing it with a signifying function, yet jeopardizing its power at every turn.

17. See Lacan cited in Rose (1986): 193–94, 219.

18. The classic filmic parable of the voyeur's self-censorship is Michael Powell's *Peeping Tom* (1960), where the voyeur kills himself with the camera he has used to impale his victims. On the oedipal implications of voyeurism, see de Lauretis (1984): 140.

19. See Paul Willemen's notion of the "fourth look," he associates with pornography, where the viewer is explicitly addressed. The fourth look is "an articulation of images and looks which brings into play the position and activity of the viewer. . . . When the scopic drive is brought into focus, then the viewer also runs the risk of becoming the object of the

look, of being overlooked in the act of looking" ("Letter to John," *Screen*, 21, no. 2 [1980]: 56, discussed in de Lauretis [1984]: 148–49, 206n47).

20. Bresson and Freud both tell tales about looking. Both emerge as accounts of the sexual that attempt to justify the fears and obsession located in the female body. In Freud's story, which he holds up as a kind of allegory for understanding male desire, the little boy who looks gets more than he counted on. His fears and anxieties can be assuaged, but never eliminated. In Bresson's story, which he uses to justify for a model of well-funneled desire, the male reader who looks with Léonce sees more than his system can withstand. Both stories uphold a specular morality that would assure safe seeing. Freud would make sure his little boy never again sees anything that might jeopardize his "eye." Taking care of Oedipus means requiring that he see nothing that might incite him to violate taboos. Bresson tells the results of lascivious looking to keep potential transgressors away from contagious seduction. He compares his text to perverse views in order to demand stories that keep bodies safely under cover. Both Freud and Bresson would defend the right of a man to see nothing—if not their truth.

21. Bresson retorts that these great authors knew how to get at "what was the most burning and the most impassioned in the human heart without tearing those veils that must always remain intact" (9/1).

22. "It is impossible to paint the tumult of passions, to establish their tempests, to show the abysses in which they can drag someone who abandons himself to them, without coloring the story with certain details that provoke eloquent curses on the part of the moralist" (8/30).

23. Suzanne's fate in the novel is complicated by her absence in the wake of the censorship. In the summary that dispenses with her, Méray explains that she was to have come to Léonce's housing unit prostituting herself and, upon realizing that she did not just love him, Léonce was to have ended his affair with her. Juliette later reports hearing that Suzanne has been arrested and sent to Saint-Lazare. Much later in the novel, Juliette, Adelstan, and Léonce converse about her failed attempt to go straight. They claim she has wound up a *courtisane*, but is this a euphemistic concession to the censors, or a further transformation of her "share"?

24. "*Hypocondrie*" was considered the male form of "*hystérie*" during this era. See Louyer-Villermay (1816b) as well as entries on each condition in the *DSM*, 23 (1816). Juanna suffers from spasms, hallucinations, night agitations, and convulsions, her limbs in a state of "violent excitation." According to the doctor, Louis-René, "her sensibility is exalted beyond measure" and her illness resembles several, all equally "deriving . . . from the physical and moral." To cure her they must "exhaust this young and robust body and weaken this burning, loving imagination" (*PdF*, 7/28). The doctor's fight against her sickness might have been lifted directly from contemporary case studies of hysteria: "But the terrible illness, born from an exaltation that lacked the goal of loving passion, seemed to carry her away despite his care and good will." Even the doctor's prescription relates to current notions that marriage could cure hysteria: "A rich dowry would save her" (*PdF*, 7/29).

25. "We will seek to hurry, in uniting our hands, the arrival of those days of joy when . . . men of good will may understand that they must let bloom rather than suffocate, all those delicate instincts of women, all her tender affections, all her vital passions" (*PdF*, 8/14).

26. According to the defense, Méray is asking that "the bourgeois girl, rich in talents but stripped of a dowry, not be reduced to languish in celibacy. What he asks is that the young man finds early a companion he can acknowledge; that the worker, poor girl who likes to dress herself up and enjoy life a little, not be forced into evil by the scantiness of a salary

purchased through overwhelming work; that the woman be at last given circumstances of happiness and love—delicate, pure, unselfish love" (9/1).

27. On the Fourierist movement, see Moses (1984): 90–98; Pinkney (1986): 92–104; Jonathan Beecher, *Charles Fourier* (Berkeley: University of California Press, 1987); and Zeldin, who notes that Considérant abandoned Fourier's opinions on sex, a fact Bresson refuses to acknowledge (1973: 438–49).

28. Legouvé (1854): 68–82.

29. In her chapter on "Séduction," Daubié cites Raspail on the criminality of male seducers: "I would like it to be at last accepted that a man who has seduced a woman—in order to arrange himself the pleasure of dishonoring her—be more dishonored than her, because, finally, the woman didn't lie. He lied to her and lying is a crime. We are thus still in a savage state, we who honor the liar and scorn the weak being who was duped by him" (1866: 274).

30. The editors of *La Voix des femmes* praised his Collège de France lectures in 1848 (no. 1 [March 10, 1848], p. 4). See Offen (1986): 452–84.

31. Editorial, *La Démocratie pacifique*, (7/4).

32. For the unfolding scandal, see any Parisian newspaper of July 1847, including *La Démocratie pacifique* (7/13 and 7/25). Jardin and Tudesq (1973) note this scandal stimulated beliefs that the ruling groups of the July Monarchy were immoral. Wright calls the 1847 scandals evidence of "dry rot within the ruling elite" (1981: 129). See also Collingham (1988): 393–402.

33. Collins (1959): 98–99; Collingham (1988): 393.

34. Excerpts reprinted in *La Démocratie pacifique* (7/9).

35. Cited in *La Démocratie pacifique*, July 9, 1847.

36. Editorial, "Immoralités," *La Démocratie pacifique*, July 8, 1847.

37. *La Démocratie pacifique* reprinted daily collections of these articles: *La Réforme, La Patrie, Le Commerce, Le Charivari* (7/5–6); *Le Courrier français, Le National, La Presse, Le Corsaire, Le Constitutionnel, La Gazette de France, Le Siècle, La Réforme* (7/7); *L'Univers, La Voix nouvelle, Le Commerce, Le Constitutionnel, Le Siècle, La Réforme, L'Ami de la religion, Le Charivari, L'Echo du Nord, Le Courrier du Nord* (7/9); *La Gazette de France, Le Haro, Le Messager du Nord* (7/10). See also issues of 7/11, 7/15, 7/16, 7/25, 7/28, 7/30, 7/31, and 8/1.

38. *Le Charivari*, July 8, 1847, cited in *La Démocratie pacifique* (7/9).

39. "After the shameful scandals unveiled in the courts, after the hard blows to public morality, to feelings of honor and of probity, amid this overflowing of corruption that floods us; since ideas of right, of justice, and of virtue are outrageously debased, since lessons of debauchery, immorality, and the prostitution of the soul come down each day from the heights of society; since we seek to demonstrate to all that everything can be sold, that everything can be bought—votes, consciences, opinions, favors, jobs, honors—the court has understood the necessity of staying the shaken social order" (July 4, 1847, cited in *La Démocratie pacifique*, [7/5–6]).

40. *Grenzboten*, July 1847, cited in *La Démocratie pacifique* (7/25).

41. This view will be relayed by Nettement who fulminated that young male readers of the *roman-feuilleton* might be drawn to fall in love with a prostitute and to try to drag her out of the gutter (*EC*, 2: 500, 502, 490).

42. One might argue that *La Démocratie pacifique* appealed primarily to a male audience and that its *feuilleton* invokes a male reader both explicitly, through the narrator's asides, and implicitly, by asking him to relate to the protagonist Léonce. See, for example, the first

censored passage, where the narrator first asks the reader to play along: "judge the effect that she must have produced on this young male virgin," then reminds the reader that he too, would have had the same desire for Suzanne: "surely you too would not have judged any different from him" (*PdF*, 6/30). Likewise, in the second censored passage, the narrator appeals to the reader to admire Léonce's attempt to abstain from a second round with Suzanne, but when the hero fails to keep his pledge, the narrator digresses about prostitution, inviting his reader's participation in a group he calls "We men of the future." The novel seems very much to depend upon this kind of bonding with its male readers to play out its moral and political message. Nevertheless, it also invokes a female reader, particularly when Juanna's behavior might offend the morality of those who would relate to her. When Juanna sets out for Paris to seek Léonce, the narrator acknowledges that her acts are unreasonable and compromising, but asks the women in the audience: "after so many shocks, who among you, my ladies, would be sure to preserve her sanity?" (*PdF*, 8/6). Yet even here, like Louis-René, the narrator seems to protect women readers and Juanna alike from the acts that would compromise them.

43. What, for example, might this joke about sharing women have to do with the novel's plots around women's sexuality and with its view of Suzanne's descendant, the *lorette* Rosanette of *L'Éducation Sentimentale*? The intertextual function of *La Part des femmes* seems well represented by Rosanette's own first seduction: left alone by the man who has purchased her services, the young girl fell soundly asleep on a book of obscene engravings.

44. See Russo (1986): 213–29.

45. See Alhoy [1841] and Dumas père (1842). Alhoy's book makes a point of avoiding anything equivocal.

46. See Alhoy [1841]: 86–90.

47. Dumas père (1842): 11.

48. *Le Charivari*, July 23, 1843.

49. Dumas père (1842): 15.

50. See Lucette Czyba, *Mythes et idéologie de la femme dans les romans de Flaubert* (Lyons: Presses Universitaires de Lyon, 1983).

8. Reading Dangerously: The Memoirs of the Devil and Madame Lafarge

1. Flaubert (1869, rpt. 1964): 10. Sirtema de Grovestins complained, "That frightful drama of Le Glandier occupied all of Paris: some took the defense of Madame Lafarge; others railed against that woman without principals or heart; some even claimed there were duels for her honor and glory. Society was for a moment divided in *Lafargophiles* and *Lafargophobes*" ([1859] 2: 138).

2. This account is based on *Le Procès de Madame Lafarge* (1840), the *Mémoires de Marie Cappelle* (1841–42), and Cappelle-Lafarge (1913 and 1854). Volumes 3 and 4 of the *Mémoires* contain editor René's narrative of her side of the trial with accompanying documents and letters. See also Gelfand (1983): 153–75; Hartman (1977): 10–50; and the "Dossier Lafarge," Bibliothèque Marguerite Durand, Paris, which covers the controversy through the twentieth century. I am indebted to Alain Corbin for pointing out the relevance of this case to my project.

3. Some held that Louis-Philippe's obstinate refusal to pardon her derived from a desire to keep his father's affairs out of the press (Boyer d'Agen, "Le Secret du Berceau," in *Corr.*, 1: vii–xxii). In her *Mémoires*, Marie distanced herself from the family of the monarch—even

denying a family tie to Stéphanie de Genlis. She claimed her grandmother was the daughter of an English Colonel Campton and an unnamed woman who died when the girl was nine. Orphaned, "Hermine Campton" was taken in by de Genlis and educated with the royal children (*Mém.*, 1: 11). Given the criticism (see chapter 7) that Louis-Philippe tolerated crimes by nobles while the poor were censored, it was neither in Marie's interest nor the king's that she be associated with his family.

4. A number of other novels came up in the course of her trial and incarceration, some actually mentioned in her writings (Sand's *Indiana*, Benjamin Constant's *Adolphe*, Sophie Gay's *Anatole*, etc.), others foisted upon her by a press eager to pin her crime on texts already targeted as dangerous.

5. Nettement provides an example of a young girl who read Sue's *Le Juif errant*: "From her reading, the imagination of the poor girl is exalted; she is seized with strange insomnia, terrors without reasons. She hears noises that escape all ears, her gaze takes on a wild expression, a convulsive smile contracts her lips. Finally the day comes when the sad truth bursts forth before everyone's eyes: she is mad! She is mad, and since in her madness, she notices that precautions are being taken against the departure of her reason, she imagines herself to be Mademoiselle de Cardoville, prisoner in the madhouse of Doctor Baleinier" (*EC*, 2: 474–75). Among the novels he attacks as dangerous for the model wife are *Les Mystères de Paris*, *Les Drames inconnus*, *L'Hôtel Lambert*, *Mathilde*, *La Reine Margot*, *Le Comte de Monte-Cristo* (*EC*, 2: 430). His whirlwind tour of the literature he claims to have been the "school" of Madame Lafarge passes by the theater of Hugo, Dumas, Scribe, and Robert-Macaire before arriving at the characters of Soulié, Balzac's Vautrin, Sue's Atar-Gull, and Sand's Lélia.

6. Nettement and Sirtema de Grovestins report that the police found Soulié's novel in her bedroom. Anaïs de Reyneville claims to have visited Le Glandier, where a peasant girl told her "Madame Marie" used *Les Mémoires du diable* to teach her to read. In the bedroom, she finds a translation from German and a book of "rather unorthodox" poetry ("La Chambre à coucher de Madame Lafarge au Glandier," *Gazette des femmes*, July 16, 1841, p. 2).

7. Sirtema de Grovestins (1859) 2: 137, 146.

8. Although he ends up causing the death of a childhood friend, effecting the dishonor and subsequent death of a pure woman, and bringing about the corruption of his own sister, he continues to bumble along with a self-serving moralistic belief that he can reward the innocent and gain happiness for himself with his special knowledge of the private worlds around him.

9. Luizzi once accuses Satan of having all the appropriate qualities of a "veritable man of letters." Satan shrugs off the epithet insisting he is not "a maker of melodramas" (*Mdd*, 3: 109). The difference between the devil's representations and those literary ones to which he constantly alludes lies in the "reality" the devil claims to unveil. This doesn't make him any less willing to have Luizzi market his stories as that kind of literature that gives "easy pleasures" (*Mdd*, 3: 64–66).

10. Sophie Dilois turns out, for example, to be the same person as Laura Farkley, but by the time Luizzi knows this he learns that she is dead—because of his moralistic bungling. Lucy de Crémancé, married to the Marquis Du Val, turns out to be Sophie's sister. Eugénie Turniquel, supposedly the daughter of an illiterate mason and a second-hand dealer, is really the daughter of Madame de Cauny, alias Mme. Paradèze, daughter of the Vicomte d'Assimbret. The nun Angélique is really Caroline, Sophie's daughter and Luizzi's half-sister. Her friend Juliette Gélis, Luizzi's temptress, is really named Jeannette and is also his half-sister. As if these endless complications in naming were not confusing enough, the novel

repeatedly turns its stories inside out, undermining whatever understanding Luizzi has achieved with another version of the events. A woman (Laura Farkley) who is chased from the salons of high society for her supposedly scandalous past turns out to have been framed. The woman who has had her thrown out turns out to be a former brothel owner (Olivia). But lest readers join Luizzi in condemning her trade, the devil quickly demonstrates that she was driven into prostitution by necessity.

11. Cf. Sainte-Beuve, Janin, Sirtema, Menche de Loisne, Jolly, Poitou, etc.

12. Soulié does not, however, agree. In a response to Nettement published in the *Journal des débats* (August 18, 1841), pp. 1–2, he refutes the premises of the conservative critique, concluding with a final barb: "Although it pleases me sometimes to paint vice, it is not my habit to insult the guilty: that is a virtue I leave to the *Gazette de France.*"

13. "Hortense Buré passed beside her and said, 'A woman can be happy, respected by her family, and honored by society, after having given herself to a stranger and committed a murder.' Juliette leaned towards her and said, 'The infamy of morality only dishonors those who are not cunning enough to hide their vices.' . . . Mme. de *** [Du Bergh] said to her, 'this is how to pass for a religious and saintly woman after having poisoned one's husband and dishonored, beside his still warm body, the name he gave you.' At the same time Mme. Carin, the Marquise Du Val, Mme. Dilois, Mme. de Farkley, and Eugénie Peyrol cried to her with the voice of their humiliations: 'If you fear unhappiness, if you dread shame as more unbearable still, flee virtue for it ruined us.' Thus the case being heard in that woman's conscience was decided; evil won; she opened her hand and the poison fell into the drink; she gave way to her seducer, she betrayed her duties, she became a murderess" (*EC*, 1: 410–11).

14. See Roussel (1775) and Le Doeuff (1980).

15. See Virey (1825a), Roussel (1775), Mathieu (1847), etc.

16. Conversations with Avital Ronell helped me see what is at stake in reading with phantoms. See Ronell (1986) and Abraham and Török (1976 and 1987).

17. Queffelec (1986): 9–21 emphasizes this metaphor of magnetism.

18. Cf. Bienville's cases of nymphomaniacs who read too much and Debay's descriptions of overheated female readers.

19. See Goldstein (1984); Nye (1986) examines the translation of theories of hysterical contagion into theories of degeneracy.

20. Cf. Lacan's formulas about women's desire (1975).

21. Cf. Derrida's (1979) analysis of style, gender, and duplicity where the supposed doubleness of "woman" is essentialized into appearances.

22. Barthes, *The Pleasure of the Text* (New York: Hill and Wang, 1975), 47, 27, 31, 32.

23. Barthes, *The Pleasure of the Text*, 47. On fetishism and illusion, see Mannoni (1969).

24. Cappelle-Lafarge's books seem, at first glance, the inverse of Socrates's hemlock: she gave herself over to books as a kind of deliverance, but found herself poisoned by her reading in the eyes of those who might have defended her. Her position in relation to the *gift* of reading is far more complicated. See Derrida's plays at defining the *pharmakon*: "If the *pharmakon* is 'ambivalent,' it is because it constitutes the medium in which opposites are opposed, the movement and the play that links them among themselves, reverses them or makes one side cross over into the other (soul/body, good/evil, inside/outside, memory/forgetfulness, speech/writing, etc.). It is on the basis of this play or movement that the opposites or differences are stopped by Plato. The *pharmakon* is the movement, the locus, and the play: (the production of) difference. It is the difference of difference. It holds in reserve, in

its undecided shadow and vigil, the opposites and the differends that the process of discrimination will come to carve out." ("Plato's Pharmacy," in Derrida [1981]: 126–27).

25. See Smock (1985).

26. "There is a crime that hides itself in the shadows, that creeps into the family home, that terrifies society, that seems to defy by the artifices of its use and the subtlety of its effects the tools and analyses of science, that intimidates with doubt the consciences of juries, and that multiplies from year to year with a horrifying progress: this crime is poisoning," wrote Cormenin in 1842 (cited in Charpentier [1906]: 9). For criminological accounts of female poisoners, see Mallet (1845), Ryckère (1899), who devotes a chapter to Cappelle-Lafarge (ch. 4), Lombroso and Ferrero (1896): especially 430, 449, 451, 455, on Cappelle-Lafarge.

27. Legrand Du Saulle called poison "the special weapon of women, because it doesn't require physical force from those who wield it" (1883: 470). Mallet reports that in 1840, twenty-four out of forty—three individuals accused of poisoning were women. She sees patricide and poisoning as two crimes particularly frequently committed by women and justifies this by declaring, "The more premeditation the crime requires and the more it is outside of natural laws, the more often it is committed by a woman" (1845: 28). Granier (1906) reported from that seven out of ten poisonings were performed by women, whereas only twenty percent of "personal assaults" in general were committed by women (15). Hartman nuances this much-quoted statistic: "In the five year period from 1850 to 1855 in France poison accusations reached a high of 294, with roughly equal participation by men and women, a pattern which had held since the mid-1830s. Thereafter, the number of poisonings steadily declined to seventy-eight in the five years from 1875 to 1880, but interestingly, women's representation increased; in these years there were forty-one accused women and only nineteen men" (A. Laccasagne, "Notes Statistiques sur l'empoisonnement criminel en France," *Archives d'anthropologie criminelles et des sciences pénales*, 1 [1886]: 260–64, cited in Hartman [1977]: 271n9).

28. See Legrand (1883) and (1860): 95–110; Girard d'Auxerre (1848): 346; Gilles de la Tourette (1891): 528; Janet (1893). The question of the *hysteria* of the female poisoner gained importance in the Second Empire because the medico-legal community refused to categorize hysterics as "insane." Of all mental patients, only hysterics could be held legally responsible for their crimes.

29. On the *empoisonneuse*'s character, see Charpentier (1906): 9–14, 43–44.

30. See Gelfand (1983), especially chapters 1–3; O'Brien (1981); Guillais (1986); Barrows (1981): chapter 2; and Lesselier (1982).

31. Charpentier (1906): 92.

32. Charpentier (1906): 91.

33. Charpentier (1906): 93.

34. Charpentier (1906): 94. On female poisoners in the *causes célèbres*, see Hans-Jürgen Lüsebrink, "Les Crimes sexuels dans les 'Causes célèbres,' " *Dix-huitième siècle*, 12 (1980): 153–62; and *Kriminalität und Literatur im Frankreich des 18. Jahrhunderts* (Munich: Oldenbourg, 1983). Madame Lafarge appears favorably in Fouquier's later *Causes célèbres* (1858: vol. 1).

35. De Man, "The Rhetoric of Blindness," in De Man (1983): 107.

36. Ryckère (1899): 84. Mallet estimates that ninety-eight percent of the crimes committed by upper-class women remain unknown (1845: 50).

37. *Le Parisien*, March 21, 1979, reported proof brought by the Académie de médecine that declared Marie unjustly accused because Charles died of typhoid. Gelfand takes this new

finding to be a definitive exoneration (156n8); Adler's more recent analysis of the case (*L'Amour à l'arsénic* [Paris: Denoël, 1986]) turned up nothing so definitive.

38. These words will be made to double back upon her by critic Janin who reads her *Mémoires* with venom: " 'Everything in education ought to have a moral goal.' She says it, she prints it; her book is full of these virtuous formulas; you thought you were reading a story of the criminal court, you find yourself at a Senecan declaration. Such feminine minds, well made and well conforming in appearances, lack nothing except a moral sense. Something is deranged first of all in the brains of those women—neither the mind nor common sense, but integrity. They seek in vain in their skulls a bit of what makes honorable men, but they don't know what it is. . . . Bad daughters, bad wives, bad mothers, they don't even know how to attain the integrity of a prostitute" (1841: 1). According to Cappelle-Lafarge, women deserve far more in their education than society extends to them. Janin accused her for the lack of honesty she claims she learned at the convent school. According to the adult Marie, the absence of a moral goal in this education left the souls of these little girls untouched. Her prescription for educating girls might well come from Fénelon, Rousseau, or de Genlis, for she insists upon educating women in accordance with their "primitive nature." Cautioning against the hypocrisy into which girls may be compromised, she calls for educators to help girls turn their defects into virtues (*Mém.* 1: 40, 42–43).

39. "My cheeks reddened; my heart beat faster when I read all the victories of that hero, and I held back tears with difficulty as I arrived at his defeat and death" (*Mém.*, 1: 97–98).

40. Derrida (1981): 64. Derrida is here speaking of Plato's pharmacy—and Socrates' hemlock. See note 24 above.

41. Marie recounts another episode of haunted reading that figures prominently in her defense against the accusation of stealing her friend Madame Léautaud's diamond necklace. She claims to have entered into a pact with her friend that involved exchanging letters and love vows with a young man the two girls watched on the street during their afternoon walks. Serving as a go-between for Mademoiselle Nicolaï (who had not yet married Léautaud), Marie corresponded with the son of a Spanish schoolteacher and eventually became enamored with him. She explains that she was "taken by the romantic (*"romanesque"*) in this story . . . delighted to see in reality one of those novels that hardly exist except in the imaginations of poets" (*Mém.*, 1: 197). Clavé departed for Algeria in 1836 shortly after the intrigue, apparently brokenhearted that Mademoiselle de Nicolaï was unwilling to pursue their affair in letters or real life. Marie claimed during the trial that he later threatened to reveal the affair to Mademoiselle Nicolaï's new husband and that the frightened young wife gave her the diamond necklace to sell in hopes of paying him off.

Yet another episode of haunted reading involved Marie Cappelle in an intrigue that shamed her during her trial. Moved with desires for which she had no object, as a result of her role in the affair between her friend and Clavé, Marie began catching the eyes of strangers during her daily walks. Having sighted a comely young man in the Louvre, Marie discovered a model for her dreams in Sophie Gay's *Anatole*: "Those little romantic (*"romanesques"*) meetings, the memory of which came to brighten my bored thoughts . . . would have remained quite innocent and without danger if a novel, written with heart and spirit, had not fallen into my hands and made a vivid impression upon me. In this most interesting book, the hero Anatole follows everywhere the woman he loves, saving her life, surrounding her with the most delicate and most passionate love, writing her, making her love him without seeking to approach her, without trying to speak to her. After five or six hundred pages, when Anatole is adored, not only by the woman he loves, but also by those women who read him, one discovers that he is deaf and mute. . . . One cries, one would still be crying if *she* did not marry him, if they were not perfectly happy thanks to the Abbé Sicard, who teaches the language of signs to the beautiful and noble girlfriend of the hero. How do I dare say that I was mad enough to dream a deafmute as my stranger? That I wished him that grief, that I spied the symptoms of it in his face, in his sadness, in his eyes? Not able to understand the quizzical solicitude of my gaze, he showed himself happy to encounter it so often, and after we had followed one another for two hours, he waited two more hours beneath the windows of my aunt" (*Mém.*, 1: 275–76). Though Guyot was not a deafmute, Marie exchanged letters and vows with him for months. When her aunt discovered her letters and read them mockingly aloud in front of the family, Marie insisted she would marry the young man even though he was a druggist with a 600-franc annual income. She gave herself an out by claiming that her reading drove her to this *loveless* exchange of letters. Insisting in her *Mémoires* that she would have willingly married a man below her station, she could not bear to enter into a union like this one where there was no *love*. During her trial, claiming that Marie Cappelle had assassinated him, Guyot slit his throat with a razor.

42. Her editor seems to counter critics' allegations about her involvement with fictions: "She didn't like novels much; a few volumes of Walter Scott and George Sand are the only ones she read with pleasure" (*Mém.*, 3: 26).

43. Hartman comments upon this passage: "This was perhaps the closest Marie ever came to a confession" (1977: 50). Hartman's eagerness to view Cappelle-Lafarge as "sensitive and unbalanced" (49) prejudices her analysis of this case in ways not unlike nineteenth-century criminologists.

44. Sirtema de Grovestins (1859) 1: 533, 532. *Lélia* is the subject of constant attacks in the literature against the novel. Poitou accuses it of inciting women to view themselves as *"douloureuses exceptions,"* who believe they have the right to put themselves above *"des lois communes"* (1858: 352). Menche de Loisne devotes a chapter to it, commenting in particular upon Sand's rehabilitation of the prostitute as an emblem of modern woman (1852: 252, 248). Jolly uses it to indict Sand (1851: 40–42). Nettement unleashes his usual wrath on all Sand's works ([1854] 2: 255–70, and *EC*, 1: 343–44, 347, 353, 368–70). Esquiros quotes *aliéniste* Voisin as declaring that a great number of women *aliénées* have gone mad because of reading modern novels, particularly those of Sand "which they read without understanding" (1847: 119–20). Esquiros sees Lélia as herself emblematic of the modern *aliénée* (170–71).

45. *Lélia* opens with an unidentified voice asking, "Who are you? and why does your love do so much harm? There must be in you some horrible mystery unknown to men. . . . You are an angel or a demon, but you are not a human creature. Why do you hide your nature and your origin?" (Sand, 7). Sténio's demand that Lélia be *readable* is gratified only in the sections where she tells her story to her sister.

46. "Marie Cappelle à Alexandre Dumas," (1844), in *Corr.*, 2: 120.

47. Perhaps this is why the censorship she endures in the press takes such a toll on her. Her prison writings repeatedly articulate her concern with the critical reception of her *Mémoires*. She is particularly disturbed by Janin's 1841 censorship of her writings (*Corr.*, 1: 158–63, 257–61; and *Mém.*, 4: 336–48)

48. As Louis Blanc pointed out in an attack on laws preventing divorce, Cappelle-Lafarge's contemporaries could easily imagine her driven to murder because she had no other alternative to regain control over her existence. As a widow, she could have taken her dowry and gone back to Paris, enjoying, for the first time in her life, a kind of self-reliance possible *only* for women whose husbands were dead. She might then have achieved the kind of social power that we see in Soulié's *empoisonneuse*, Madame Du Bergh, who poisons her husband to save her father's life and who then takes part in the salon life of the aristocracy, holding sway over

the social fates of far more "virtuous" women. According to the devil, three drops of prussic acid have liberated her to the dreams she learned from that literature she read with too much abandon. She falls in with the devil because she has read herself into unfulfillable desires in a world where marriage is, as Blanc proclaims, "a market." More important, she winds up a partner to vice because she has found a way out of a double bind ("Madame Lafarge," *Revue de Progrès*, reprinted in *La Phalange*, October 9, 1849, pp. 305–06). On the status of widows in the nineteenth century, see Michèle Bordeaux, "Droit et femmes seules: Les Pièges de la discrimination," in Farge and Klapisch-Zuber (1984): 19–57.

49. In this way, Olivia leaves behind a life of prostitution by becoming Madame de Marignon. Mariette covers up her debauched past by taking the identity of Madame de Gélis. By transforming herself into Mme. de Fantan, the exposed Madame de Crémancé abandons her past as adulteress and possible husband-murderer. Eugènie Rigot masks her seduction and betrayal under the name of her husband Alfred Peyrol. Laura Farkley hides her trials behind the name Madame Dilois.

50. This is one of the reasons I have followed Gelfand (1983) in calling the protagonist of this drama Marie Cappelle-Lafarge instead of either Marie Cappelle or Madame Lafarge (used only when I appropriate the discourse of those who called her by that name). Her works are indexed at the Bibliothèque Nationale under Lafarge, yet their title pages offer variations on her given and married names. In a sense, I have given her another alias by providing her with this divided name. It nevertheless has the virtue of separating her from the other Madame Lafarge (Charles's mother) who accused her of murder.

51. Rivière (1929, rpt. 1986): 38.

52. Rivière (1929, rpt. 1986): 43.

53. Heath (1986): 50.

54. Rivière (1929, rpt. 1986): 43.

55. *Le Procès de Madame Lafarge* (1840): 228.

56. The prosecution used this letter during the trial as evidence of Marie's desire to murder her husband.

57. *Le Procès de Madame Lafarge* (1840): 249–50, 250.

58. *Le Procès de Madame Lafarge* (1840): 230–31.

59. The writings of Lady Audley in Braddon's *Lady Audley's Secret* (1862, rpt. 1974) are likewise used to incriminate her for her attempted murder of her husband. Read and therefore revealed in her duplicity, she seeks to be let off as mad instead of facing a murder trial. Cappelle-Lafarge explicitly refuses to plead insane. She holds to the end that she is innocent—and that she has only courted madness in the prison to which wrongful accusations condemned her. Before being pardoned by Napoleon III on June 1, 1852, she was nevertheless transferred to the Asile d'Aliénés of St. Rémy in February 1851.

60. Janin (1841): p. 2, col. 4.

61. "Pernicious for men, the book that we have just analyzed is even more so for women, because it is especially women that Monsieur Frédéric Soulié studied and depicted in his *Mémoires du diable*. It is especially to her that he addresses himself, it is especially her that Satan wants to tempt again" (Menche de Loisne [1852]: 344).

62. Janin (1857) 5: 125. Janin embraces a view of Soulié corresponding far more closely to the moral values of the protagonist of *Les Mémoires du diable* than to its overall economy. Like the Soulié represented by Janin, Luizzi incessantly jumps to conclusions about a woman's virtue, decides what she deserves, and rallies to distribute her reward or punishment, without ever considering there might be yet another side to the story. The moralist of this novel, the devil himself, plays a role like the one Janin here assigns to Balzac: mustering sympathy—

with ulterior motives to be sure—for his victims, the devil gives her a chance to show herself as other than she first appeared. In one sense, Janin is right about Soulié: his women are interchangeable; one of them might just as well be proclaimed guilty as another, for all of them are somehow double, all of them are somehow working under cover.

63. Barthes, *S/Z* (New York: Hill and Wang, 1974), 4.

64. Not surprisingly, his self-defense for "monomania" places him side by side in an insane asylum with the imprisoned reader, Henriette Buré.

65. She never had the chance: as soon as she was married, she discovered that her husband was plotting her father's death. A few drops of prussic acid delivered her into a widowhood where she could suffer no more illusions.

66. Smock (1985): 9–10, explicating Blanchot (1980): 157–58.

67. This formulation was suggested by Schweickert's "Reading Ourselves: Toward a Feminist Theory of Reading," in Flynn and Schweickert (1987): 48.

68. " 'Reading woman' necessarily entails both a theory of reading and a theory of woman—a theory of subjectivity and a theory of gender" (Jacobus [1986]: 5).

69. Abraham (1987): 427; "Notes on the Phantom: A Complement to Freud's Metapsychology," trans. Nicholas Rand, *Critical Inquiry*, 13 (1987): 287.

9. *Doubling Out of the Crazy House: Gender, Autobiography, and the Insane Asylum System*

1. The title on the cover page of Hersilie Rouy's *Mémoires d'une aliénée* seems to have been conferred by her editor, Edouard Le Normant des Varannes, named as *"receveur des hospices d'Orléans"* (HR, 527). In a letter in the book's preface and in her conclusion, she refers to the work she has confided to him for publication only as her *Mémoires* (HR, xi, 489). She died on September 27, 1881, two years before its appearance. In what follows, I refer to Hersilie Rouy by her first name for two reasons: first to avoid confusion with her half-brother and other relatives, and, second, because Hersilie loses her patronym within the asylum. From the moment she enters Charenton, her first name will be the only constant in the certificates of registration. The documents her half-brother Claude-Daniel Rouy used to procure her imprisonment at Charenton gave her the name Rouy, but when she was registered there, she was given the name Hersilie Chevalier. She reports in her *Mémoires* that when she was transferred to the Salpêtrière on November 30, 1854, authorities attempted to list her as Hersilie Chevalier, but ultimately agreed to register her under the hyphenated name Hersilie Chevalier-Rouy, in deference to her protests (HR, 96–98). On October 20, 1855, the authorities reregistered her at the Salpêtrière as Hersilie Chevalier-Rouÿ. According to her *Mémoires*, she was erroneously registered in the years that followed as Mademoiselle François and Madame Polichinelle (HR, 142–49). Her medical records are in AAP, Salpêtrière, 6Q2–22 and 6Q2–24, Nos. 21468 and 22225 (figure 9.1). In her death certificate, she was declared the legitimate daughter of Charles Rouy, and she was buried as a Rouy.

2. See chapter 4, note 29, on average asylum stays for men and women.

3. Cf. Foucault, *HS*. This chapter owes a great deal to discussions with Ripa (who shared her copy of Rouy's *Mémoires*), Alain Corbin, Michelle Perrot, and Susanna Barrows. Ripa's assessment of the Rouy case is in Ripa, "L'Affaire Hersilie Rouy," *L'Histoire* 87 (1986): 74–81.

4. See Donzelot (1979).

5. Behind my formulation of this problematic lies Derrida's masterful assessment of Foucault: "The unsurpassable, unique, and imperial grandeur of the order of reason, that which makes it not just another actual order or structure (a determined historical structure, one structure among other possible ones), is that one cannot speak out against it except by being for it, that one can protest it only from within it; and within its domain, Reason leaves us only the recourse to stratagems and strategies" ("Cogito and the History of Madness," in Derrida [1978]: 36).

6. All autobiographical texts arise, to some extent, out of the exceptional, though some disavow this more intently than others. See Kenneth Barkan, "Autobiography and History," *Societas*, 6, no. 2 (1976): 83–108; Mary Jo Maynes, "Gender and Class in Working-Class Women's Autobiographies," in Maynes and Ruth-Ellen Joeres, eds., *German Women in the Eighteenth and Nineteenth Centuries* (Bloomington: Indiana University Press, 1986), 230–46; George Landow, "Introduction," in Landow, ed. *Approaches to Victorian Autobiography* (Athens: Ohio University Press, 1979), xiii–xlvi; Patricia Mayer Spacks, "Selves in Hiding" in Jelinek (1980): 112–13, and Nancy K. Miller (1980): 258–73.

7. See Foucault, *Histoire de la folie*, 522–23.

8. Cited in Ripa (1983): 426.

9. Esquirol, "Question médico-légale sur l'isolement des aliénés," *Mémoire présenté à l'institut le 1er octobre 1832* (Paris: Crochard, 1832), 31, cited in Goldstein (1987): 288.

10. See Ripa (1983): 426–27.

11. *FL*, xv–xvi. Trélat's study sets out to demonstrate how "a great number of lunatics live in our midst, entangling themselves in our deeds, in our interests, in our affections, compromising them, disturbing them, or destroying them" (*FL*, 6). Trélat contends that because "these sick minds exert a deep and detrimental influence upon healthy minds," those who are "gifted with reason" must learn to recognize them and seek to protect others from these dangers (*FL*, 15). By entangling himself with the deeds, the interests, the affections, and especially the words of lunatic, the mad-doctor sought the information that would shield others from their dangers. His collection of seventy-seven cases of *folie lucide* are almost entirely women, culled from his experiences at the Salpêtrière, and produced as a guide for those who might otherwise fall in with such treacherous lunatics. It is in this collection that Trélat first transforms Hersilie into a written case: she is case number fifty (*FL*, 183–86). At the time of the publication of Trélat's book, Hersilie was still locked up.

12. "Aren't criminals better protected than madpeople, since they are allowed to produce their evidence and their witnesses in their defense?" Hersilie asks rhetorically. "They can defend themselves, justify themselves, they are even given a lawyer" (HR, 133–34).

13. Eagleton (1982): 49.

14. See Wilkie Collins (1859–60, rpt. 1974) as well as D. A. Miller (1988): 146–91.

15. Furthermore, it puts this exchange into writing in its registers and dossiers thanks to the Law of 1838, which required, for the first time, documentation about all patients kept in the national asylum system. The 1838 Law ostensibly made rules designed to help draw the line between the pathological and the normal. It created the spaces into which the pathological could be cordoned off and "protected"—a nationwide system of asylums. Unfortunately, this seemingly progressive law was unable to protect the likes of Hersilie Rouy. By establishing two processes through which an individual could be committed, the law supposedly shielded everyone from error. The patient gained the right to a medical verification of the reasons for internment. No one could put an individual away without first acquiring a medical opinion. The *placement d'office*, or involuntary admission, required official involvement from the state—a police document, usually declaring the individual a public

danger—and a letter from a medical specialist upholding the official opinion. The *placement volontaire* or "voluntary admission" implied that the individual was "volunteered" by yet another party (a family member, for example) along with the support of the medical observer. In spite of the protections such a law could offer, it nevertheless made way for countless abuses. The patient's right to be medically observed translated into the medical observer's right to dispose of patients on his own terms. Once the carceral space of the asylum had taken form, the asylum doctor asserted his right to practice his interpretations there undisturbed. The reason that had made this "moral world" possible now held sway virtually uncontested. Speaking in the place of the mad, the *aliéniste* ensured that his order would always have a space. On the 1838 Law, see Castel (1976): 316–24; Goldstein (1987): 276– 321. Hersilie is eminently concerned with the omnipotence of the *aliéniste* and with the abuses of the Law of 1838.

16. Ripa (1983) provides an excellent analysis of these issues.

17. Pinel (1801): 97; similar discussions appear in Esquirol, *Des passions considérées comme causes, symptômes et moyens curatifs de l'aliénation mentale* (Paris: Medical thesis, 1805), 80–81, discussed by Goldstein (1987): 85–89. For Morel's use of letters, see, for example (1859) 1: 322–23; 389–91. Taking Pinel and Esquirol's advice about gaining his patients' confidence, Morel frequently reports detailed conversations. Note his particular fascination with the loquacity of hysterics, 2: 211–12.

18. See, for example, Trélat, observation 58, of a woman who has a penchant for writing obscene stories (*FL*, 240–58). Mlle. Et's mystical writings led her family to place her in the Salpêtrière (*FL*, 203–10). Trélat's favorite *folle lucide* seems to have been Mlle. S. L., a cook with special abilities, whose pleasure at reading and writing has brought her into the asylum, though, according to her doctor, she might have been a "queen of a salon" had she come from another social class (*FL*, 200–203).

19. Whereas Lacan would insist that all letters arrive at their destination and Derrida that "it belongs to the structure of the letter to be capable, always, of not arriving" at its destination, the letters written by Hersilie threaten the kind of signifying system on which the debates over Poe's "Purloined Letter" are founded (See essays by Lacan, Derrida, and Barbara Johnson, collected in *The Purloined Letter*, ed. John Muller and William Richardson [Baltimore: Johns Hopkins University Press, 1988]). Even when postmarked outside the asylum, Hersilie's letters point to her position *within* the asylum. Even when literally addressed to administrators and bureaucrats, these letters always circulate back to cast doubt on the signifying power of their author.

20. Felman (1985): 36.

21. Freud (1963b): 104. Freud's analysis concerns Schreber 1903; trans. 1988. After finishing his analysis of Schreber, Freud wrote, "I have succeeded where the paranoiac fails" (Freud to Sandor Ferenczi, October 6, 1910, cited in C. Barry Chabot, *Freud on Schreber: Psychoanalytic Theory and the Critical Act* [Amherst: University of Massachusetts Press, 1982], 34). Freud would seem to contend here that his readings betray nothing, whereas the paranoid's writings betray all. Chabot is only one of many readers who question Freud's success. Other accounts by those incarcerated in asylums include Elizabeth Packard, *Modern Persecution or Married Women's Liabilities* (Hartford, Conn.: Case, Lockwood, and Brainard, 1873); Rachel Grant-Smith, *The Experiences of an Asylum Patient* (London: Allen and Unwin, 1922); Georgiana Weldon, *The History of My Orphanage; or, The Outpourings of an Alleged Lunatic* (London: 1878); and selections in Peterson (1982). Louis Renza asserts a connection between all autobiography and the workings of paranoia ("A Theory of Autobiography," in Olney (1980): 289.

22. Besides Chabot's study, see Morton Schatzman (*Soul Murder* [New York: Random House, 1973]) and William Niederland (*The Schreber Case: Psychoanalytic Profile of a Paranoid Personality* [New York: Quadrangle, 1974]). Kittler (1981) suggests ways our readings have betrayed Judge Schreber.

23. Schreber (1903): 1.

24. Derrida (1978): 58.

25. Derrida (1978): 84–85.

26. De Man points to an aspect of Lejeune's (1975) theory of autobiography that is particularly salient for our readings of Hersilie's writings. De Man argues that Lejeune's interchangeable use of "proper name" and "signature" signals his problematic desire that autobiography be "not only representational and cognitive but contractual, grounded not in tropes but in speech acts." For De Man, autobiography reveals contestations around proper names and identities, demonstrating the impossibility of a totalizing account of subjectivity. Prosopopeia, as the trope of autobiography according to De Man, confers a name and face to an "absent, deceased, or voiceless entity." A fiction of identity, it can confer meaning only through such an absence: "Autobiography," concludes De Man, "veils a defacement of the mind of which it is itself the cause" (1979: 919–30).

27. Aboville, the state investigator, concludes: "Without having committed any established act of madness, simply on the basis of the tales of her doorman, Mademoiselle Rouy, in the maturity of her life and at the time of her fullest demonstration of her talent as a pianist, was removed from her home by Doctor Pelletan, at the request of her half-brother by her father, Monsieur Claude-Daniel Rouy. She was received at Charenton in formal violation of the law, without any signed request and only on the basis of the medical certificate of the man who brought her there; registered under a name she had never used; stripped at Charenton and deprived for eight years of the papers that established her civil status; defrauded of her money and of her jewels; led subsequently for a period of fourteen years from asylum to asylum while in Paris her family passed her off as dead; kept three times in institutions against the wishes of doctors, on the basis of orders that came directly from the central administration of L'Assistance publique of Paris. For lack of administrative protection, her personal goods were in large part lost. In the asylums, she suffered shameful maltreatment; her talent disappeared and with it she lost her means of subsistence. Such were for her the terrible consequences of noncompliance with the laws. On this authority, she has the right to a reparation from the government" (HR, 412–13). Aboville's findings agree with Hersilie's arguments in her *Mémoires*.

28. One assumption of traditional autobiographical theory is that representation enables an author to anchor a self (Cf. Olney [1980]).

29. See Lacan's *Ecrits*, cited in Felman: "In madness . . . we must recognize . . . a discourse where the subject—can one say—is more spoken than speaking" (my translation [1985]: 48). Felman's embellishment on Lacan is particularly suggestive for Hersilie's text: "The question underlying madness *writes*, and writes itself. And if we are unable to locate it, read it, except where it already has escaped, where it has moved—moved *us*—*away*—it is not because the question relative to madness does not question, but because it questions *somewhere else*: somewhere at that point of silence where it is no longer we who speak, but where, in our absence, we are *spoken*" (55).

30. My allusions replay with thanks the notes of my reading of Smock (1985).

31. For an account of the auspicious beginnings and inauspicious ends of the Bourbon heir to the throne of France, see Merriman (1985): 53–57.

32. Hersilie is particularly adamant about showing that she only *adopted* a story others were telling about her. She even suggests her enemies fabricated this tale to embarrass her (HR, 517). Elsewhere she depicts her own doctors as the source of her temptation, claiming Mitivié was particularly taken with the idea that he was treating the dispossessed Bourbon heir (HR, 120), for he believed that such an identity might at least explain her family's actions against her. Claims of noble parentage are not alien to the asylum: a few years before Hersilie's internment, in July 1847, Jean-Pierre Falret treated a forty-two-year-old vestmaker who claimed to be the daughter of a very rich nobleman. His diagnosis resembled that given Hersilie: *"aliénation partielle"* (AAP, Salpêtrière, 6Q2–12, no. 16143). An 1843 visitor to the Salpêtrière told of a woman who claimed to be Marie-Antoinette (Vieuxbois [1843]).

33. See *FL*, 178–223.

34. Hersilie plays down her use of other pseudonyms. However, we know from documents she publishes in her *Mémoires* that the "Sister of Henri V" was not her only double. For lack of a legal name, she assumed outrageous names to mock the doctors who refuse to look into her civil status: "L'Antéchrist" (HR, 146), "Le Diable" (HR, 289), "Sathan" [*sic*] (HR, 212), "Dieu" (HR, 290). When her use of diabolic epithets causes a furor, she cons the doctors into asking her to sign "Polichinelle" (HR, 147)—a name that sticks to her for five years at Maréville (HR, 148).

35. The psychiatric account of multiple personalities would require us to read Hersilie's doubling as another symptom of her mental illness. See, for example, Jeremy Hawthorn, *Multiple Personality and the Disintegration of Literary Character* (London: Edward Arnold, 1983).

36. We know from countless details that Doctor Pelletan represented Hersilie's brother when he took her to Charenton. Claude-Daniel Rouy emerges, despite the doubt he manages to cast upon his sister's past, as the villain in this story. Everyone except the courts seems to conclude that he was up to no good. See, for example, his contentions that *she* took the name Chevalier (HR, 382), that the will he never let her see was burned by Prussians during the war, and that Hersilie was disowned by their father after the birth of her illegitimate child (HR, 404–6).

37. This is from a letter from Hersilie Rouy to Madame Le Normant des Varannes from the asylum, in which she refuses to be "that Hersilie whom you love without knowing" (HR, 507).

38. Trélat is particularly disturbed by this pseudonym (*FL*, 183–86). Hersilie explains it was her childhood nickname, the result of her haircolor and unrelated to her other claims about noble birth (HR, 32).

39. The subtext of secret societies, with its uncanny relationship to the legend about the substituted "miracle baby," might suggest that Hersilie has taken Collins's *The Woman in White* (1859–60) to the letter and tried to use its plot to explain her own. Yet from the earliest point of her incarceration (1854), her editor Le Normant des Varannes contends, she insisted that she has only taken the place of another and that her incarceration resulted from a plot involving her family but extending to much higher places. Le Normant seems to like the idea that a mysterious, romantic web of sensation enthralls Hersilie—going so far as to fictionalize her case into a novelistic intrigue in his earlier *Les Mémoires d'une feuille de papier* [Paris: Ollendorff, 1882]), written under the pseudonym Edouard Burton. For this reason, which we find almost hidden in his footnotes, we should recognize that the *Mémoires* may have been contaminated by an unscrupulous editor's ornamentation. I am more inclined to read Hersilie's *Mémoires* as her own work, however, if only because Le Normant makes such a production out of his footnotes, prefaces, appendices, and postscript. To a certain

extent, Le Normant has an investment in showing Hersilie as sane since he has served as her protector since 1868. For this reason, he should be more inclined to tidy up her *Mémoires* than to embellish or romanticize them. The text leaves far too many things unresolved to suggest that it has been radically edited. The editor's notes make attempts at resolving certain inconsistencies in the text, but they too fail. Hersilie seems, in spite of Le Normant, to give exactly the account she chooses. The *Mémoires* claim that her writings and all documents relative to the case had been turned over to the Archives du Loiret (Orléans) (HR, 529, 211); however those archives burned in 1940, leaving us without any way to differentiate the published text from original versions, journal entries, letters, or notes.

40. The family romance undergoes reversals and reinterpretations here: Claude-Daniel Rouy claims his sister is a bastard and tries to take away her name; Hersilie Rouy claims she is not his sister anyway but a substitute who has only taken the Rouy name to protect the real Hersilie.

41. It is perhaps then not remarkable that her destiny in the asylum changes from the moment she finds her young cousin. Laurency Rouy is both awe-struck to find her alive at all and eager to assist her. Hersilie gets out of the asylum within the year of their first contact.

42. Because she demands that her documents be read literally, she lends herself to readings like the very ones that imprisoned her for fourteen years. Without these documents, she cannot prove the abuses of the system. Yet the kind of literal reading of documents she demands is what found her initially marked with the false name "Chevalier" by the doctors at Charenton and the Salpêtrière. If we accept her invitation to read these reprinted documents literally, we can find much to doubt in her account. Too many reprinted papers contradict each other. We find too many gaps in what she contends will support her truths. She acts, for example, as though there had never been a Chevalier in her family; yet her mother's name was Chevalier. Confusion about *which* of two Chevalier sisters her mother really was— Jeanne-Henriette as one document attests or Maria-Enrichetta as the original Italian birth certificate states—also casts a shadow over Hersilie's accounts (HR, 492–96). Was she the daughter of the woman whom Charles Rouy claimed as his wife, or rather, the daughter of that woman's sister? And if the latter, who was her father? Was she the half-sister of Claude-Daniel Rouy or only the illegitimate daughter of his father's mistress? Hersilie contends that she and her siblings all have a mysterious "Pierre fils de Pierre" as godfather, yet her sister's birth certificate lists no such person. Oddly enough, that same sister is the only child of the four who obtains a legal recognition from her father. Most damning, at least for Hersilie's own quests for legal reparations, a literal reading of the documents proves unequivocally that Hersilie's mother was not married to her father (HR, 407). Regardless of his rights to have his half-sister locked up in an asylum, Claude-Daniel Rouy was within his rights to deprive her of their father's name. By revindicating an inquest of her family affiliations and of her brother's acts, Hersilie ultimately betrays her own goals (HR, 447). Her claims to her name are unraveled by the text she believes should repair what the asylum took from her.

43. Foucault notes that real-life cases have replaced adventure stories and romances. His examples include a biographical case (Little Hans), an autobiographical case (Mary Barnes), and a case that is both—Schreber (*DP*, 193–94).

44. Cf. Kofman (1975): 104–5. The text Kofman is reading bears uncanny resemblances to Hersilie's autobiography—E. T. A. Hoffmann's *Die Elixiere des Teufels*. Hersilie's play of identity rejects the names the asylum has given her and allows her to recuperate her family name, but with a difference: Rouy has become, at the encouragement of the mysterious dark lady, an artistic name. By putting a *tréma* on the *y*, Hersilie has guaranteed that no one can ever take her name again. If she gains hold on her family name, she does so, however, only

tenuously: it functions like all the other pseudonyms—in place of the name the asylum stole away. "I didn't recognize myself anymore" (HR, 327), she declares shortly after her release from the asylum. Hersilie Rouy is named elsewhere here—always other, always free—in a play of identity that makes this non-recognition a bid for power.

45. Cf. Didi-Huberman (1982).

46. On techniques of self-revelation, see Foucault, *HS*, 61–67.

47. They define this form of madness as "a false reasoning having as a point of departure a real feeling, a true fact, which, by virtue of the association of ideas related to tendencies and affections, takes, by means of erroneous inductions or deductions, a personal significance for the sick person who is invincibly driven to relate everything to himself or herself" (Sérieux and Capgras [1909]: 3).

48. Hersilie also turns up in Raymond Queneau's *Les Enfants du Limon* (Paris: Gallimard, 1938), 254–59, launched by Sérieux and Capgras. Queneau's narrator contends that "the 'case' of Le Normant des Varannes seems to me yet more interesting than that of Hersilie Rouy" (257). I am indebted to Ann Smock for drawing my attention to this literary extension of the chain of interpretations surrounding Hersilie.

49. Sérieux and Capgras, 386.

50. Cf. Elissa Gelfand, "Imprisoned Women: Toward a Socio-Literary Feminist Analysis," *Yale French Studies*, 62 (1981): 187.

51. Nancy K. Miller (1980): 266, 271.

52. Just as the system of *aliénation* circumscribed all writing its interpretations could not master, autobiographical theory has traditionally excluded all representations that fail to authenticate the selves it anchors. The notions of a self such interpretations embrace are fundamentally destabilized when we bring them to bear upon a text like Hersilie's. Although theorists of autobiography have often acknowledged the double-crossing of autobiographers, they frequently do so with leaps of faith that hold out for resolutions. Renza, for example, discusses how the autobiographical enterprise is alienated, but he assumes that the autobiographer *wants* to mitigate his alienation from his own activity (Olney [1980]: 268–95). Georges Gusdorf assumes that without a certain notion of self, autobiography cannot even exist. Despite his emphasis on the autobiographer's difficulty of coping with his own doubles, Gusdorf not only grants almost saintly honesty to his authors, but believes they are mobilizing the truth to save themselves ("Conditions and Limits of Autobiography," in Olney [1980]: 28–47). Lejeune has maintained that without the autobiographer's attempt to name himself—with a proper name—his writing will fail to engage in the autobiographical pact that is the condition of all self-representation. Otherwise, Lejeune claims, the text would become only a *"discours aliéné"* (1975: 7–46). We could only allow for the integrity of such a pact with Hersilie Rouy by reducing her again to singularity. We could only give her a single name by finding unreasonable her claims that there are two Hersilies. To refuse to believe her depiction of doubles would condemn her again to the space where being only one is being other, subjected, excluded. Only in the copy of her funeral announcement published near the end of the volume would Hersilie Rouy's *nom propre* contain her, and even there, she is spoken by another. Lejeune's more recent revisions of his theory do not alter these difficulties (1983: 416–34). Feminist theorists have considered women's alienation from their own discourse as a way of accounting for differences in women's fabrication of selves. Jelinek has pointed out the fragmentary, discontinuous, and understated nature of women's autobiographies ("Introduction" in Jelinek [1980]: 15–17). Mary G. Mason has lamented the "negative results" of women's autobiographies in confinement: lacking an other which she believes enables women to disclose a self, the imprisoned suffocate in their own selflessness ("The Other Voice:

Autobiographies of Women Writers," in Olney [1980]: 207–36). Patricia Meyer Spacks has analyzed the self-censorship in women's autobiographies in terms that account for historical determinants as well. She nevertheless generalizes this self-denial when she suggests that it both reflects a female dilemma and provides a female solution as women succeed in expressing themselves in spite of their doubts about the value of their female selves ("Selves in Hiding," in Jelinek [1980]: 132). Although these readings reject the limiting definitions of a self that circumscribed women *and* their expressions, they risk replacing the traditional autobiographical self with a female cultural construction.

10. Epilogue: Seductive Theories

1. Legouvé (1854): 1.

2. Like Legouvé, prison reformer Mallet argued that all women come to crime through seduction and that men are responsible for all women's crimes (1845: 115). See also Daubié (1966): 274–89; and Tristan (1840): 110.

3. Freud (1896) 3: 191–221; Baudrillard (1979).

4. Baudelaire depicts Madame Bovary as having an "excessive taste for seduction" ([1976] 1: 82), rendering her like a hysteric. Baudelaire claims Emma's problem is that she does not know "*la différence*." Mallet (1845: 74) claims male seducers use licentious novels to corrupt working-class girls

5. Cummings (1991): 1. Cummings's book, which appeared as I was completing this one, grows out of her own admitted seduction "by the origins of psychoanalysis" (12) and seeks to revise our understanding of Freud's seduction theory and to use this account to interrogate three canonical literary texts that "share the theory's structures of seduction and perversion" (13). I have taken the opposite approach: constantly aware of the resonances of seduction in Freud and later theorists, I sought to historicize the concept in the context of nineteenth-century accounts. Through this rewriting of nineteenth-century fantasies of scenes of seduction, I have nevertheless hoped that my own account could shed light on later investments in those scenes.

6. For an intriguing reading of this process, see Evans (1989), Török (1986), Andrew Benjamin (1988), and Laplanche and Pontalis (1964).

7. Armstrong (1987): 251.

8. See Fried (1980).

9. Cf. figures 6.1, 6.2, 8.1, 8.2. Allen (1991): 153 argues that imagery from the first half of the nineteenth century centers around the text, particularly on group images of public reading, while after mid-century imagery increasingly shows detached, self-contained readers engrossed in private reading.

10. T. J. Clark (1985): 84. Clark cites in particularly, Ego, "Courrier de Paris," *Le Monde illustré*, May 13, 1865, p. 291.

11. Jean Ravenel, *L'Epoque*, June 7, 1865, cited in Clark (1985): 296, n144.

12. Recall Poitou, cited in chapter 5. On the Morisot sisters reading *Madame Bovary*, see Higonnet (1990): 54.

13. Figure 10.3, which, like Morisot's portrait, depicts a mother reading and a daughter *not* reading, marks this difference as a matter of moral consequence: "Mama, give me something to read," says the underfed daughter who approaches her obese mother in the library where she is reading two books at a time. "My daughter, read the *Conseils à une fille*," she is told. "But Mama," the daughter protests, "I know them; reading nothing but boiled things is boring." "My daughter," insists her mother, "as long as you are single, you will have nothing else: your husband will give you roast if he wants."

14. See Edouard Manet, *Berthe Morisot with a Bunch of Violets*, reproduced in Stuckey and Scott (1987): fig. 32, p. 49; discussed by Higonnet (1990): 91–92.

15. Note the resemblance between Morisot's sister here and the position of the listening fiancé in Fantin-Latour's salon-painting of the same year, *Reading* (1870), which shows the admired future wife gazing alluringly out of the canvas as her older and far less attractive sister reads aloud (Stuckey and Scott [1987]: fig. 21, p. 36). Significantly, after the birth of the child with whom she was quite visibly pregnant in this painting, Edma Morisot Pontillon never again painted, leaving to her younger sister the dreams the two had once shared (see Higonnet [1990]: 30–31, 50–53, 77–85).

16. Allen (1991): 3–8.

17. Douglas Druick and Michael Hoog, *Fantin-Latour* (Ottawa: 1983), 92–93, discussed in Allen (1991): 3. In order to understand the uses of such a diagnosis, note that Hersilie Rouy was diagnosed as suffering from *"délire multiforme en voie de démence"* (AAP, Salpêtrière, 6Q2–22, no. 21468).

Selected Bibliography

Archives and Manuscript Collections

1. Archives Nationales

F^7 3884–3893 Bulletins of the Préfecture de Police, July Monarchy, 1846.
F^7 4179–4182 Rapports généraux de la Garde Municipale de Paris, July Monarchy, 1845–46.
F^7 11910–11921 Passeports d'indigens, 1830–33 (letters requesting the return to their home province of women who have been arrested for prostitution).
F^{18} III 41–42 Déclarations des imprimeurs, 1848.
F^{18} 567 no. 314, Rapport sur la situation des imprimeurs de Paris, October 30, 1883.

2. Archives de l'Assistance Publique

Archives of the Salpêtrière Hospital,
Registers of admission, "volontaires"
$6Q1_2$, $6Q1_7$, $6Q1_8$- $6Q1_9$ (1836–39, 1844–50, 1850–53)
Registers of admission, "aliénés d'office"
$6Q2_4$ - $6Q2_{20}$ (1841–54)
$6Q2_{22}$- $6Q2_{24}$ (1855–56),
$6Q2_{35}$, $6Q2_{38}$, $6Q2_{44}$ $6Q2_{46}$ (1860, 1861, 1864, 1865)
$6Q2_{52}$, $6Q2_{54}$, $6Q2_{56}$, $6Q2_{60}$ (1867, 1868–70, 1871–72, 1875–76)
$6Q2_{68}$ - $6Q2_{69}$ (1882–83)
Dossiers médicaux (Medical dossiers)
$6R_2$ (1856–61)
$6R_3$ (1852–56)
$6R_8$ (1868–71)
$6R_{22}$ (1856–59)
$6R_{23}$ (1868–71)
$6R_{56}$ (1855–58)
$6R_{75}$ (1851–55)

3. Archives of La Charité Hospital

1Q2 $_{102}$ (1845)
1Q2 $_{113}$ (1850)
1Q2 $_{122}$ (1855)

4. Archives of the Préfecture de Police

DB 407–410. Prostitution

5. Bibliothèque Marguerite Durand

Dossier 351—Prostitution.
Dossier 365—Prisons.
Dossier 360—Oeuvre des libérées de Saint-Lazare.
Dossier 360—Patronage des détenues.
Dossier Lafarge—Marie Cappelle-Lafarge.

Newspapers and Journals

Annales d'hygiène publique et de médecine légale, 1829–48
Annales médico-psychologiques, 1844–1865
L'Atelier.
Le Charivari.
Le Constitutionnel.
Le Corsaire. 1830.
Le Courrier français.
Le Courrier des théâtres. 1830.
La Démocratie pacifique. 1847–48.
Le Figaro. 1830.
La Gazette des tribunaux.
La Gazette de France.
La Gazette des femmes. 1836–38.
Le Journal des débats.
Le Lampion. 1848.
Le Magasin pittoresque.
Le Moniteur universel.
Le National.
Le Nouveau Journal de Paris. 1830.
L'Opinion des femmes. 1848–1849.
La Politique des femmes. June–August 1848.
La Presse.
La Quotidienne. 1830.
La Réforme.
Le Siècle.
La Tribune des femmes. 1832–34.
La Voix des femmes. March–June 1848.
Le Voleur. 1830.

Pamphlets

A MM. les Députés—Projet de pétition sur la liberté individuelle. Par un spartiate. Paris: Marchands des nouveautés, 1830.

Aux Ministres!!! Nouvelle Pétition des filles publiques de Paris . . . rédigée par Mlle Elisa C . . . ; Approuvée et signée par trois cents de ses compagnes. Paris: Libraires du Palais-Royal, 1830.

50,000 Voleurs de plus à Paris; ou, Reclamations des anciens marlous de la capitale contre l'ordonnance de M. le Préfet de police, concernant les filles publiques par le beau Théodore Cancan. Paris: Les Marchands de nouveautés, 1830.

Complainte authentique, originale, et seule véritable sur la grande catastrophe des filles de Paris. Paris: Les Marchands de nouveautés, 1830.

Deuxième pétition adressée à M. le Préfet par les filles publiques de Paris. Par une maîtresse de maison. Paris: Les Marchands de nouveautés, 1830.

Doléances des filles de joie de Paris. Paris: Les Libraires du Palais-Royal, 1830.

Epitre à M. Mangin, au sujet de l'ordonnance attentoire à la liberté des femmes. Par M. J. M. Paris: Mie, n.d. [1830]

Les Filles en cage; ou, Déguerpissons! Par un abonné au cachet des maisons de plaisirs de la capitale. Paris: Peytieux, 1830.

Grande, véritable, et lamentable complainte romantique de ces demoiselles écrites sous la dictée d'une ci-devant nymphe du no. 113, accompagnée de notes et commentaires. Par un moraliste du Palais-Royal. Paris: N.p., 1830.

Observations soumises par une fille de joie à M. le Préfet de Police sur le danger que les hommes et les honnêtes femmes ont à craindre . . . par Rosine, dite la Gracieuse. Paris: Les Marchands de nouveautés, 1830).

Pétition des filles publiques de Paris à M. le Préfet de Police . . . rédigée par Mlle Pauline. Paris: Libraires du Palais-Royal, 1830.

Plainte et révélations nouvellement adressées par les filles de joie de Paris à la congrégation contre l'ordonnance de M. Mangin . . . par une matrone, juriconsulte des dames. Paris: Garnier, 1830.

Prière romantique de laure. Paris: Les Marchands de nouveautés, 1830.

Projet de Pétition d'un spartiate, de ceux que vulgairement on nomme voleurs. N.p. n.d. [2d ed. of *A MM les Députés . . .*].

Projet d'un nouveau réglement concernant les filles publique et les maisons de prostitution. Par un ami de la Charte . . . . Paris: Les Libraires du Palais-Royal, 1830.

Réponse de M. Englin aux pétitions des filles publiques, suivie de 2 scènes historiques de révolte occasionées par la nouvelle ordonnance de Police. Paris: Les Marchands de nouveautés, 1830.

Réponse de M. le Préfet à toutes les pétitions et réclamations des filles publiques de Paris. Paris: Les Libraires du Palais-Royal, 1830.

Le Tocsin de ces demoiselles. Paris: Marchands de nouveautés, 1830.

Le Vrai Motif de la captivité des femmes soumises . . . par Frédéric. Paris: Charpentier-Méricourt, 1830.

Books and Articles

A., M. d.' *Cinquante années de visites à Saint-Lazare.* Paris: Fischbacher, 1889.

Abel, Elizabeth, ed. *Writing and Sexual Difference.* Chicago: Chicago University Press, 1982.

Abraham, Nicolas and Maria Török. *Cryptonomie: Le Verbier de l'homme aux loups*. Paris: Aubier Flammarion, 1976.

————. *L'Écorce et le noyau*. 1978. Reprint, Paris: Flammarion, 1987.

Abricosoff, Glafin. *L'Hystérie aux XVIIe et XVIIIe siècles (étude historique)*. Paris: Steinheil, 1897. Thesis in medicine.

Ackerknecht, Erwin H. *Medicine at the Paris Hospital, 1794–1848*. Baltimore: Johns Hopkins University Press, 1967.

Adams, Parveen. "Symptoms and Hysteria." *Oxford Literary Review* 8 (1986): 178–83.

Adhémar, Hélène. "La Liberté sur les Barricades de Delacroix." *Gazette des Beaux-Arts* 43 (1854): 83–92.

Adler, Laure. À *L'Aube du féminisme: Les premières journalistes, 1830–1850*. Paris: Payot, 1979.

Agulhon, Maurice. *1848; ou, L'apprentissage de la république*. Paris: Seuil, 1973.

————. ed. *Les Quarante-huitards*. Paris: Gallimard, 1975.

————. *Marianne au combat*. Paris: Flammarion, 1979a.

————. "On Political Allegory: A Reply to Eric Hobsbawm," *History Workshop Journal* 8 (1979b): 167–73.

Alboize and Maquet. *Les Prisons de l'Europe*. Vol. 8. Paris: Administration de Librairie, 1845.

Alexander, Sally, Anna Davin, and Eve Hostettler, "Labouring Women: A Reply to Eric Hobsbawm." *History Workshop Journal* 8 (1979): 174–82.

Alhoy, Maurice and Louis Lurine. *Les Prisons de Paris: Histoire, types, moeurs, mystères*. Paris: Havard, 1846.

Alhoy, Maurice. *Physiologie de la lorette*. Paris: Aubert, n.d. [1841].

Alibert, J. L. *Physiologie des passions; ou, Nouvelle doctrine des sentimens moraux*. 2d ed. Paris: Béchet, 1826.

Allen, James Smith. *Popular French Romanticism: Authors, Readers, and Books in the Nineteenth Century*. Syracuse: Syracuse University Press, 1981.

————. *In the Public Eye: A History of Reading in Modern France, 1800–1940*. Princeton: Princeton University Press, 1991.

Apter, Emily. *Feminizing the Fetish: Psychoanalysis and Narrative Obsession in Turn-of-the-Century France*. Ithaca: Cornell University Press, 1991.

Armstrong, Nancy. *Desire and Domestic Fiction: A Political History of the Novel*. Oxford: Oxford University Press, 1987.

Auber, Edouard Théophile. *Hygiène des femmes nerveuses; ou, Conseils au femmes pour les époques critiques de leur vie*. Paris: Baillière, 1841.

Auerbach, Nina. *The Woman and the Demon: The Life of a Victorian Myth*. Cambridge: Harvard University Press, 1982.

B., Victorine. *Souvenirs d'une morte vivante*. 1909. Reprint, Paris: Maspero, 1976.

Badinter, Elisabeth. *L'Amour en plus: Histoire de l'amour maternel—XVIIe-XXe siècle*. Paris: Flammarion, 1980.

Balzac, Honoré de. *Wann-Chlore*. 4 vols. Paris: Canel, 1825.

————. *Physiologie du mariage*. 1829. Reprint, Paris: Garnier-Flammarion, 1968.

————. *La Peau de chagrin*. 1831. Reprint, Paris: Garnier-Flammarion, 1971.

————. *Le Lys dans la vallée*. 1836. Edited by Jean Roudaut. Reprint, Paris: Presses de la Renaissance, 1977.

————. *Le Lys dans la vallée*. 1836. Vol. 9 of *La Comédie humaine*. Reprint, Paris: Gallimard Pléiade, 1978.

————. *Illusions perdues*. 1837–43. Reprint, Paris: Garnier-Flammarion, 1966.

————. *Splendeurs et misères des courtisanes*. 1838–47. Reprint, Paris: Garnier-Flammarion, 1968.

————. *Cousine Bette*. 1847. Reprint, Paris: Gallimard Folio, 1972.

————. *L'Envers de l'histoire contemporaine*. 1848. Vol. 7 of *La Comédie humaine*. Reprint, Paris: Gallimard Pléiade, 1955.

————. "Adieu." In vol. 9 of *La Comédie humaine*. Paris: Gallimard Pléiade, 1955.

Barbey d'Aurevilly, Jules. "La Vengeance d'une femme." In *Les Diaboliques*. 1874. Reprint, Paris: Garnier-Flammarion, 1967.

Bardet, Jean-Pierre et al., ed. *Peurs et terreurs face à la contagion*. Paris: Fayard, 1988.

Barrows, Susanna. *Distorting Mirrors: Visions of the Crowd in Late Nineteenth-Century France*. New Haven: Yale University Press, 1981.

Barthes, Roland. *Le Degré zéro de l'écriture*. Paris: Seuil, 1953 and 1972.

————. *Mythologies*. Paris: Seuil, 1957.

————. *Le Plaisir du texte*. Paris: Seuil, 1973. Translated by Richard Miller, under the title *The Pleasure of the Text*. New York: Hill and Wang, 1975.

————. *Sade/Fourier/Loyola*. Paris: Seuil, 1973.

————. *S/Z*. Paris: Seuil, 1970. Translated by Richard Miller, under the title *S/Z*. New York: Hill and Wang, 1974.

Baudelaire, Charles. "*Madame Bovary* par Gustave Flaubert." In vol. 1 of *Oeuvres complètes*, 76–86. Paris: Gallimard Pléiade, 1976.

Baudrillard, Jean. *De la séduction*. Paris: Galilée, 1979.

Beizer, Janet. *Family Plots: Balzac's Narrative Generations*. New Haven: Yale University Press, 1982.

————. "Uncovering Nana: The Courtesan's New Clothes." *Esprit Créateur* 25, no. 2 (1985): 45–56.

————. "The Doctors' Tale: Nineteenth-Century Medical Narratives of Hysteria." Unpublished manuscript. 1988.

————. "The Body in Question: Anatomy, Textuality, and Fetishism in Zola." *Esprit Créateur* 29, no. 1 (1989): 50–60.

Bellanger, Claude et al., eds. *Histoire générale de la presse française*. Vol. 2. *De 1815 à 1871*. Paris: PUF, 1969.

Bellos, David. *Balzac Criticism in France, 1850–1900*. Oxford: Clarendon, 1976.

————. "Reconnaissances: Balzac et son public féminin." *Oeuvres et critiques* 11, no. 3 (1986): 253–62.

Benabou, Erica Marie. *La Prostitution et la police des moeurs au XVIIIe siècle*. Paris: Perrin, 1987.

Benjamin, Andrew. "The Overflow of Words from Breuer to Freud." *New Formations* 5 (1988): 120–32

Benjamin, Walter. *Das Passagenwerk*. Edited by Rolf Tiedemann. 2 vols. Frankfurt am Main: Suhrkamp, 1982.

Béraud, F. F. A. *Les Filles publiques de Paris et la police qui les régit*. 2 vols. Brussels: Meline, Cans, 1839.

Bernheimer, Charles and Claire Kahane, eds. *In Dora's Case: Freud-Hysteria-Feminism*. New York: Columbia University Press, 1985.

Bernheimer, Charles. *Figures of Ill Repute: Representing Prostitution in Nineteenth-Century France*. Cambridge: Harvard University Press, 1989.

Bertier de Sauvigny, G. de. *La Restauration*. 2d ed. Paris: Flammarion, 1955.

——. *La Restauration, 1815–1830*. Vol. 7 of *Nouvelle Histoire de Paris*. Paris: Hachette, 1977.

Bibliographie de la France. Vols. 19–37. Paris: Pillet Aîné, 1830–1848.

Bidelman, Patrick Kay. *Pariahs Stand Up! The Founding of the Liberal Feminist Movement in France, 1858–1889*. Westport, Conn.: Greenwood, 1982.

Bienville, J.-D.-T. de. *La Nymphomanie; ou, Traité de la fureur utérine*. 1771. Reprint, Paris: Office de librairie, 1886.

Bizard, Léon and Jane Chapon. *Histoire de la prison Saint-Lazare du moyen âge à nos jours*. Paris: Boccard, 1925.

Blanchot, Maurice. *L'Écriture du désastre*. Paris: Gallimard, 1980. Translated by Ann Smock, under the title *The Writing of the Disaster*. Lincoln: University of Nebraska Press, 1986.

Blum, Carol. *Rousseau and the Republic of Virtue: The Language of Politics in the French Revolution*. Ithaca: Cornell University Press, 1986.

Böhme, Margarethe. *Tagebuch einer Verlorenen. Von einer Toten*. 1905. Reprint, Berlin: Fontane, 1919.

Bory, Jean-Louis. *Eugène Sue: Le Roi du roman populaire*. Paris: Hachette, 1962.

Boucher, Louis. *La Salpêtrière: Son Histoire de 1656 à 1790, ses origines, et son fonctionnement au XVIIIe siècle*. Paris: Delahaye et Lecrosnier, 1883.

Bourdieu, Pierre. *La Distinction*. Paris: Minuit, 1979.

Brachet, Jean-Louis. *Recherches sur la nature et le siège de l'hystérie et de l'hypocondrie et sur l'analogie et les différences de ces deux maladies*. Paris: Gabon, 1832.

——. *Traité de l'hystérie*. Paris: Baillière, 1847.

Braddon, Mary Elizabeth. *Lady Audley's Secret*. 1862. Reprint, New York: Dover, 1974.

Briais, Bernard. *Grandes Courtisanes du Second Empire*. Paris: Tallandier, 1981.

Briquet, Pierre. *Traité clinique et thérapeutique de l'hystérie*. Paris: Baillière, 1859.

Brooks, Peter. "Virtue-Tripping: Notes on *Le Lys dans la vallée*." *Yale French Studies* 50 (1974): 150–62.

——. *The Melodramatic Imagination*. New York: Yale University Press, 1976.

——. *Reading for the Plot*. New York: Knopf, 1984.

Buci-Glucksmann, Christine. *La Raison baroque de Baudelaire à Benjamin*. Paris: Galilée, 1984.

Buret, Eugène. *De la misère des classes laborieuses en Angleterre et en France*. 2 vols. Paris: Paulin, 1840.

Bynum, W. F., Roy Porter, and Michael Shepherd, eds. *The Anatomy of Madness*. 2 vols. London and New York: Tavistock Publications, 1985–86.

Canler, L. *Mémoires de Canler, ancien chef du service de sureté*. Paris: Hetzel, n.d. [1862].

Cappelle-Lafarge, Marie. *Mémoires de Marie Cappelle, Veuve Lafarge, écrite par elle-même*. 4 vols. Paris: A. René, 1841–42.

——. *Heures de prison*. Paris: Librairie nouvelle, 1854.

——. *Correspondance*. Edited by Boyer d'Agen. 2 vols. Paris: Mercure de France, 1913.

Carlisle, Robert. *The Proffered Crown: Saint-Simonianism and the Doctrine of Hope*. Baltimore: Johns Hopkins University Press, 1987.

Carroy-Thirard, Jacqueline. "Figures de femmes hystériques dans la psychiatrie française au 19e siècle," *Psychanalyse à l'université* 4 (1979): 313–24.

Casselle, Pierre. "Le Régime législatif." In *Histoire de l'édition française*, edited by Henri-Jean Martin and Roger Chartier, 3: 46–55. Paris: Promodis, 1985.

Castel, Robert. *L'Ordre psychiatrique: L'Age d'or d'aliénisme*. Paris: Minuit, 1976.

Cerise, Laurent. *Des Fonctions et des maladies nerveuses dans leurs rapports avec l'éducation sociale et privée, morale et physique*. Paris: Baillière, 1843.

Certeau, Michel de. *The Practice of Everyday Life*. Translated by Steven Rendall. Berkeley: University of California Press, 1984.

———. *Heterologies: Discourse on the Other*. Translated by Brian Massumi. Minneapolis: University of Minnesota Press, 1986.

Cesbron, Henri. "Histoire critique de l'hystérie." Thesis, Faculté de médecine de Paris, 1908.

Chambers, Ross. *Story and Situation: Narrative Seduction and the Power of Fiction*. Minneapolis: University of Minnesota Press, 1984.

Charcot, Jean-Marie. *Oeuvres complètes*. 9 vols. Paris: Progrès médical, 1886–93.

———. *Leçons du mardi à la Salpêtrière*. Paris: Delahaye and Lecrosnier, 1887–88.

Charpentier, René. *Les Empoisonneuses, dégénérescence mentale, et hystérie: Étude psychologique et médico-légale*. Paris: Steinheil, 1906.

Chartier, Roger. *Cultural History*. Translated by Lydia Cochrane. Ithaca: Cornell University Press, 1988.

Chesnais, Jean-Claude. *Histoire de la violence*. Paris: Laffont, 1981.

Chevalier, Louis. *Laboring Classes and Dangerous Classes*. Translated by Frank Jellinek. Princeton: Princeton University Press, 1973.

Chollet, Roland. *Balzac Journaliste*. Paris: Klincksieck, 1983.

Chomet, Hector. *Conseils aux femmes sur leur santé et sur leurs maladies*. Paris: Garnier, 1846.

Clarétie, Jules. *Les amours d'un interne*. 11th ed. Paris: Dentu, 1881.

———. *La Vie à Paris, 1881*. Paris: Havard, 1882.

Clark, Anna. "The Politics of Seduction in English Popular Culture, 1748–1848." In *The Progress of Romance: The Politics of Popular Fiction*, edited by Jean Radford, 43–72. London: Routledge, 1986.

Clark, T. J. *The Absolute Bourgeois: Artists and Politics in France 1848–1851*. 1973. Reprint, Princeton: Princeton University Press, 1982a.

———. *Image of the People: Gustave Courbet and the 1848 Revolution*. Princeton: Princeton University Press, 1982b.

———. *The Painting of Modern Life: Paris in the Art of Manet and His Followers*. New York: Knopf, 1985.

Clayson, Susan Hollis. "Representations of Prostitution in Early Third Republic France." Ph. D. diss. University of California, Los Angeles, 1984.

"Clinique de M. Chomel. Hystérie compliquée d'accidents épileptiformes. Réflexions sur l'influence des rapports sexuels sur l'hystérie." AMP 2 (1843): 105–9.

Cobb, R. C. *The Police and the People: French Popular Protest, 1789–1820*. Oxford: Clarendon, 1970.

Coeurderoy, E. "Hystérie épileptiforme et hémiplégie du côté droit du corps.—Rapports qui existent entre ces deux affections." AMP 1 (1847): 150–54.

Coffin, Judy. "Artisans of the Sidewalk." *Radical History Review* 26 (1982): 89–101.

Coleman, William. *Death Is a Social Disease: Public Health and Political Economy in Early Industrial France*. Madison: University of Wisconsin Press, 1982.

Colin, Henri. *Essai sur l'état mental des hystériques*. Paris: Rueff, 1890.

Collingham, H. A. C. *The July Monarchy: A Political History of France, 1830–1848*. London: Longman, 1988.

Collins, Irene. *The Government and the Newspaper Press in France, 1814–1881*. Oxford: Oxford University Press, 1959.

Collins, Wilkie. *The Woman in White*. 1859–60. Reprint, London: Penguin, 1974.

Colombat, Marc. *Traité des maladies des femmes, et de l'hygiène spéciale de leur sexe*. Paris: Labé, 1838–43.

Commenge, O. *Hygiène sociale: La Prostitution clandestine à Paris*. Paris: Schleicher, 1897.

Copjec, Joan. "Flavit et Dissipati Sunt." *October* 18 (1981): 20–40.

Corbin, Alain. *Les Filles de noce: Misère sexuelle et prostitution (19e siècle)*. Paris: Aubier, 1978. Translated by Alan Sheridan, under the title *Women for Hire*. Cambridge: Harvard University Press, 1990.

———. "L'Hérédosyphilis; ou, L'Impossible rédemption: Contribution à l'histoire de l'hérédité morbide." *Romantisme* 31 (1981a): 131–49.

———. *Le Miasme et la jonquille: L'Odorat et l'imaginaire social, 18e-19e siècles*. Paris: Aubier, 1982.

———. ed. *La Prostitution à Paris au XIXe siècle d'Alexandre P. Duchâtelet*. Paris: Seuil, 1981b.

———. "Le 'sexe en deuil' et l'histoire des femmes au XIXe siècle." In *Une histoire des femmes est-elle possible?*, edited by Michelle Perrot. Marseilles: Rivages, 1984.

Crubellier, Maurice. "L'Élargissement du public." In *Histoire de l'édition française*, edited by Henri-Jean Martin and Roger Chartier, 3: 24–45. Paris: Promodis, 1985.

Culler, Jonathan. *The Pursuit of Signs*. Ithaca: Cornell University Press, 1981.

Cumming, Katherine. *Telling Tales: The Hysteric's Seduction in Fiction and Theory*. Stanford: Stanford University Press, 1991.

Darnton, Robert. *Mesmerism and the End of the Enlightenment in France*. Cambridge: Harvard University Press, 1968.

———. *The Literary Underground of the Old Regime*. Cambridge: Harvard University Press, 1982.

———. *The Great Cat Massacre and Other Episodes in French Cultural History*. New York: Vintage, 1984.

Darrow, Margaret. "French Noblewomen and the New Domesticity, 1750–1850." *Feminist Studies* 5, no. 1 (1979): 41–65.

Daubié, Julie. *La Femme pauvre au XIXe siècle*. Paris: Guillaumin, 1866.

Daumard, Adeline. *Les Bourgeois de Paris au XIXe siècle*. Paris: Flammarion, 1970.

David-Ménard, Monique. *Hysteria from Freud to Lacan: Body and Language in Psychoanalysis*. Translated by Catherine Porter. Ithaca: Cornell University Press, 1989.

De Man, Paul. "Autobiography as De-Facement." *Modern Language Notes* 94 (1979): 919–30.

———. *Blindness and Insight*. 2d ed. Minneapolis: University of Minnesota Press, 1983.

Debay, Auguste. *Hygiène du mariage*. 2d ed. 1848. Reprint, Paris: Moquet, 1850; *Hygiène et physiologie du mariage*, 4th ed. Paris: Lantern, 1853; 21st ed. Paris: Dentu, 1860; 29th ed. Paris: Dentu, 1862; 57th ed. Paris: Dentu, 1872; 132d ed. Paris: Dentu, 1880; 133d ed. Paris: Dentu, 1882.

———. *Philosophie du mariage*. Paris: Moquet, 1849.

Delvau, Alfred. *Grandeur et décadence des grisettes*. Paris: Desloges, 1848.

Démar, Claire. *Textes sur l'affranchissement des femmes (1832–33)*. Paris: Payot, 1976.

Derrida, Jacques. *L'Écriture et la différence*. Paris: Seuil, 1967. Translated by Alan Bass, under the title *Writing and Difference*. Chicago: University of Chicago Press, 1978.

———. *Dissémination*. Paris: Seuil, 1972. Translated by Barbara Johnson, under the title *Disseminations*. Chicago: University of Chicago Press, 1981.

———. *La Carte postale*. Paris: Flammarion, 1980.

———. "The Law of Genre." Translated by Avital Ronell. *Glyph* 7 (1980): 202–32.

———. *Spurs: Nietzsche's Styles/Eperons: Les Styles de Nietzsche*. Translated by Barbara Harlow. 1981. Chicago: University of Chicago Press.

Descôtes, Maurice. *Le public de théâtre et son histoire*. Paris: PUF, 1964.

Devance, Louis. "Femme, famille, travail et morale sexuelle dans l'idéologie de 1848." *Romantisme* 13–14 (1976): 79–105.

———. "Le Féminisme pendant la révolution française." *Annales historiques de la révolution française* 229 (1977): 341–76.

Le Diable à Paris: Paris et les Parisiens. 2 vols. Paris: Hetzel, 1845–46.

Dictionnaire des sciences médicales. Paris: Panckoucke, 1812–22.

Didi-Huberman, Georges. *L'Invention de l'hystérie: Charcot et l'iconographie photographique de la Salpêtrière*. Paris: Macula, 1982.

Doane, Mary Ann. *Femmes Fatales: Feminism, Film Theory, Psychoanalysis*. New York: Routledge, 1991.

Donnard, J. H. *Balzac: Les réalités économiques et sociales dans la comédie humaine*. Paris: Armand Colin, 1961.

Donzelot, Jacques. *The Policing of Families*. Translated by Robert Hurley. New York: Pantheon, 1979.

Dowbiggin, Ian. "Degeneration and Hereditarianism in French Mental Medicine, 1840–90." In *The Anatomy of Madness*, edited by W. F. Bynum et al., 1: 188–232. London: Tavistock, 1985.

Drujon, Fernand. *Catalogue des ouvrages, écrits, et dessins de toute nature poursuivis, supprimés, ou condamnés depuis le 21 octobre 1814 jusqu'au 31 juillet 1877*. Paris: Rouveyre, 1879.

Du Camp, Maxime. *Episodes de la commune*. Vol. 2 of *Les Convulsions de Paris*. Paris: Hachette, 1878.

———. *Paris: Ses organes, ses fonctions, et sa vie dans la seconde moitié du XIXe siècle*. 3 vols. Paris: Hachette, 1872.

———. *Souvenirs de l'année 1848*. 1876. Reprint, Geneva: Slatkine, 1979.

Dubois d'Amiens, Frédéric. *Histoire philosophique de l'hypochondrie et de l'hystérie*. Paris: Deville Cavellin, 1833.

DuBois, Ellen Carol and Linda Gordon. "Seeking Ecstasy on the Battlefield: Danger and Pleasure in Nineteenth-Century Feminist Sexual Thought." *Feminist Studies* 9, no. 1 (1983): 7–25.

Dumas fils, Alexandre. *La Dame aux camélias*. Edited by Hans-Jörg Neuschäfer. Paris: Garnier-Flammarion, 1981.

———. *Théâtre complet avec notes inédites*. Vol. 7. Paris: Calmann-Lévy, n.d.

Dumas père, Alexandre. "Filles, lorettes et courtisanes." In *La Grande Ville*, edited by Paul de Kock. Paris: Magen, 1842.

Duveau, Georges. *1848*. Paris: Gallimard, 1965.

Eagleton, Terry. *The Rape of Clarissa: Writing, Sexuality, and Class Struggle in Samuel Richardson*. Minneapolis: University of Minnesota Press, 1982.

Eco, Umberto. *The Role of the Reader*. Bloomington: Indiana University Press, 1979.

Ellenberger, Henri F. *The Discovery of the Unconscious: The History and Evolution of Dynamic Psychiatry*. New York: Basic Books, 1970.

Esquirol, Jean-Étienne-Dominique. "Erotomanie." *DSM* 13 (1815): 186–192.

———. *Les Maladies mentales considérées sous les rapports médicaux hygièniques et médico-légaux*. 2 vols. Paris: Baillière, 1838.

Esquiros, Adèle. *Les Marchandes d'amour*. Paris: E. Pick, 1865.

Esquiros, Alphonse. *Paris; ou, Les sciences, les institutions, et les moeurs au XIXe siècle*. 2 vols. Paris: Comptoir des imprimeurs réunis, 1847.

———. *Les Vierges folles*. Paris: Le Gallois, 1840; 2d ed. Paris: Le Gallois, 1841; 3d ed. Paris: Delavigne, 1842; 5th ed. Paris: Dentu, 1873.

Evans, David-Owen. *Le Roman social sous la Monarchie de Juillet*. Paris: PUF, 1936.

Evans, Martha Noel. "Hysteria and the Seduction of Theory." In *Seduction and Theory*, edited by Dianne Hunter, 73–85. Urbana: University of Illinois Press, 1989.

Falret, Jean-Pierre. "Symptomatologie générale des maladies mentales." (1850) In *Des Maladies mentales et des asiles d'aliénés*. Paris: Baillière, 1864.

Falret, Jules. "De la folie raisonnante." *AMP* (1866): 382–426.

Farge, Arlette and Christiane Klapisch-Zuber, eds. *Madame ou Mademoiselle? Itinéraires de la solitude féminine, 18e–20e siècle*. Paris: Arthaud-Montalba, 1984.

Faure, Alain and Jacques Rancière. *La parole ouvrière, 1830–1851*. Paris: 10/18, 1976.

Feldstein, Richard and Judith Roof, eds. *Feminism and Psychoanalysis*. Ithaca: Cornell University Press, 1989.

Felman, Shoshana. "Rereading Femininity." *Yale French Studies* 62 (1981): 19–44.

———. "Women and Madness: The Critical Phallacy." *Diacritics* 5 (1975): 2–10.

———. *Writing and Madness*. Translated by Martha Noel Evans and the author. 1978. Reprint, Ithaca: Cornell University Press, 1985.

Fénelon, François de Salignac de la Mothe-. *De L'Éducation des filles*. 1687. Edited by Albert Cherel. Reprint, Paris: Hachette, 1920.

Flaubert, Gustave. *L'Éducation sentimentale*. 1869. Reprint, Paris: Classiques Garnier, 1964.

———. *Madame Bovary*. 1857. Reprint, Paris: Garnier-Flammarion, 1966.

Flynn, Elizabeth and Patrocina Schweickert. *Gender and Reading: Essays on Readers, Texts, and Contexts*. Baltimore: Johns Hopkins University Press, 1987.

Ford, Caroline. "Private Lives and Public Order in Restoration France: The Seduction of Emily Loveday." Manuscript, 1992.

Forrester, John. *The Seductions of Psychoanalysis: Freud, Lacan, and Derrida*. Cambridge: Cambridge University Press, 1990.

Forstenzer, Thomas. *French Provincial Police and the Fall of the Second Republic: Social Fear and Counterrevolution*. Princeton: Princeton University Press, 1981.

Foucault, Michel. *La Naissance de la clinique: Une archéologie du regard médical*. Paris: PUF, 1963. Translated by A. M. Sheridan-Smith, under the title *The Birth of the Clinic: An Archaeology of Medical Perception*. New York: Random House, 1975a.

———. *Les Mots et les choses*. Paris: Gallimard, 1966. Translated as *The Order of Things*. New York: Vintage, 1973b.

———. *Histoire de la folie à l'âge classique*. Paris: Gallimard, 1972. Partially translated by Richard Howard, under the title *Madness and Civilization*. New York: Vintage, 1973a.

———. *Surveiller et Punir: Naissance de la prison*. Paris: Gallimard, 1975b. Translated by Alan Sheridan, under the title *Discipline and Punish*. 1975. Reprint, New York: Vintage, 1979.

———. *La Volonté de Savoir*. Paris: Gallimard, 1976. Translated by Robert Hurley, under the title *The History of Sexuality, Vol. 1: An Introduction*. New York: Vintage, 1980.

———. "Sexuality and Solitude." In *On Signs*, edited by Marshall Blonsky, 365–72. Baltimore: Johns Hopkins University Press, 1985.

———. *Technologies of the Self*. Edited by Luther H. Martin et al. Amherst: University of Massachusetts Press, 1988b.

————. *Politics, Philosophy, Culture.* Edited by Lawrence Kritzman. New York: Routledge, 1988a.

Fouquier, Armand. "Madame Lafarge." In vol. 1 of *Causes célèbres.* Paris: Lebrun, 1858.

Fournel, Jean-François. *Traité de la séduction.* Paris: Demonville, 1781.

Fraisse, Geneviève. "Les Femmes libres de 48, moralisme et féminisme." *Les Révoltes logiques* no. 1 (1975): 23–50.

Les Français peints par eux-mêmes. Encyclopédie morale du XIXe siècle. 8 vols. Paris: Curmer, 1841–43.

Fraser, Nancy. *Unruly Practices: Power, Discourse, and Gender in Contemporary Social Theory.* Minneapolis: University of Minnesota Press, 1989.

Frégier, Honoré-Antoine. *Des Classes dangereuses de la population dans les grandes villes et les moyens de les rendre meilleures.* 2 vols. Paris: Baillière, 1840.

Frémy, Arnould. *Les Femmes proscrites.* 2 vols. Paris: Delessart, 1840.

Freud, Sigmund and Joseph Breuer. *Studies on Hysteria.* 1893–95. Reprint, New York: Basic Books, n.d.

Freud, Sigmund. "The Aetiology of Hysteria." (1896) *Standard Edition,* 3: 187–221.

————. "Charcot" (1893). *Standard Edition,* 3: 11–23.

————. *Dora: Fragment of an Analysis of a Case of Hysteria* (1905). New York: Collier, 1963a.

————. "On the History of the Psycho-Analytic Movement" (1914). *Standard Edition,* 14: 1–66.

————. "Psychoanalytic Notes upon an Autobiographical Account of a Case of Paranoia (Dementia Paranoides)" (1911). In *Three Case Histories.* Translated by James Strachey. New York: Collier Books, 1963b.

————. "Some Psychical Consequences of the Anatomical Distinctions Between the Sexes." (1925). In *Sexuality and the Psychology of Love,* 183–93. Translated by James Strachey. New York: Collier, 1963c.

Fried, Michael. *Absorption and Theatricality: Painting and the Beholder in the Age of Diderot.* Berkeley: University of California Press, 1980.

Fuchs, Rachel. *Abandoned Children: Foundlings and Child Welfare in Nineteenth-Century France.* Albany: SUNY Press, 1984.

Furet, François and Jacques Ozouf. *Reading and Writing: Literacy in France from Calvin to Jules Ferry.* 1977. Reprint, Cambridge: Cambridge University Press, 1982.

Gallagher, Catherine. "George Eliot and *Daniel Deronda:* The Prostitute and the Jewish Question." In *Sex, Politics, and Science in the Nineteenth-Century Novel,* edited by Ruth Bernard Yeazall, 39–62. Baltimore: Johns Hopkins University Press, 1986.

————. *The Industrial Reformation of English Fiction: Social Discourse and Narrative Form, 1832–1867.* Chicago: University of Chicago Press, 1985.

————. "More About 'Medusa's Head.'" *Representations* 4 (1983): 55–57.

Gallop, Jane. *The Daughter's Seduction: Feminism and Psychoanalysis.* Ithaca: Cornell University Press, 1982.

Garçon, Maurice. "Les Livres contraires aux bonnes moeurs." *Mercure de France* 230 (August 15, 1931): 5–39.

Gasnault, François. "Bal, délinquance, et mélodrame dans le Paris romantique: L'Affaire de la 'Tour de Nesle.'" *Revue d'histoire moderne* 29 (1982): 36–69.

————. *Guinguettes et lorettes: Bals publics à Paris au XIXe siècle.* Paris: Aubier, 1986.

Gauchet, Marcel and Gladys Swain. *La Pratique de l'esprit humain: L'Institution asilaire et la révolution démocratique.* Paris: Gallimard, 1980.

Gavarni (pseud. Guillaume-Sulpice Chevalier). *Oeuvres choisies de Gavarni*. 4 vols. Paris: Figaro, 1842.

Gelfand, Elissa. *Imagination in Confinement*. Ithaca: Cornell University Press, 1983.

Genlis, Stéphanie de. *Manuel de la jeune femme*. Paris: Charles Bechet, 1829.

Georget, Étienne-Jean. *De la Folie: Considérations sur cette maladie*. Paris: Crevot, 1820.

———. *De l'hypochondrie et de l'hystérie*. Paris: Rignoux, 1824.

Gilbert, Sandra and Susan Gubar. *Madwoman in the Attic*. New Haven: Yale University Press, 1979.

Gilles de la Tourette, Georges. *Traité clinique et thérapeutique de l'hystérie, d'après l'enseignement de la Salpêtrière*. 3 vols. Paris: Plon, 1891–95.

Gilman, Sander. *Difference and Pathology: Stereotypes of Sexuality, Race, and Madness*. Ithaca: Cornell University Press, 1985.

———. *Seeing the Insane*. New York: Wiley, 1982.

Girard d'Auxerre. "Rapport médico-légale . . . Langlois, femme Drouin," AMP 1 (1848): 346.

Girard de Cailleux, Jacques-Henri. *Considérations physiologiques et pathologiques sur les affections nerveuses dites hystériques*. Paris: Baillière, 1841.

———. *Études pratiques sur les maladies nerveuses et mentales*. Paris: Baillière, 1863a.

———. "Rapport sur les aliénés traités dans les asiles de Bicêtre et de la Salpêtrière," AAP, Pièce D-141 (manuscript, 1863b).

Girard, Louis. *Nouvelle histoire de Paris*. Vol. 9, *La Deuxième République et le Second Empire, 1848–1870*. Paris: Hachette, 1981.

Glazer, Catherine. "De la Commune comme maladie mentale." *Romantisme* 48 (1985): 63–70.

Goldstein, Jan. "The Hysteria Diagnosis and the Politics of Anticlericalism in Late Nineteenth-Century France." *Journal of Modern History* 54 (June 1982): 209–39.

———. " 'Moral Contagion': A Professional Ideology of Medicine and Psychiatry in Eighteenth- and Nineteenth-Century France." In *Professions and the French State, 1700–1900*, edited by Gerald Geison, 181–222. Philadelphia: University of Pennsylvania Press, 1984.

———. *Console and Classify: The French Psychiatric Profession in the Nineteenth Century*. Cambridge: Cambridge University Press, 1987.

———. "The Uses of Male Hysteria: Medical and Literary Discourse in Nineteenth-Century France." *Representations* 34 (1991): 134–66.

Goncourt, Edmond and Jules de. *La Lorette*. Paris: Dentu, 1853.

———. *Germinie Lacerteux*. 1864. Reprint, Paris: Librairie Générale Française, 1990.

Goncourt, Edmond de. *La Fille Elisa*. 1876. Reprint, Paris: 10/18, 1979.

Grandpré, Mme. Pauline de ("Editor"). *Les Condamnées de Saint-Lazare: Mémoires par Madame* ***. Paris: F. Curot, 1869.

———. *La Prison de Saint-Lazare depuis vingt ans*. Paris: Dentu, 1889.

———. *Démolissons Saint-Lazare*. Paris: Dentu, 1890.

Granier, Camille. *La Femme criminelle*. Paris: Doin, 1906.

Grisson, Georges. *Paris horrible et Paris original*. Paris: Dentu, 1881.

Grubitzsch, Helga, ed. *Materialien zur Kritik des Feuilleton-Romans: "Die Geheimnisse von Paris" von Eugène Sue*. Wiesbaden: Athenaion, 1977.

Guillain, Georges and P. Mathieu. *La Salpêtrière*. Paris: Masson, 1925.

Guillais, Joëlle. *La Chair de l'autre: Le Crime passionel au XIXe siècle*. Paris: Olivier Orban, 1986.

Guise, René. "Balzac et le roman-feuilleton." *L'Année Balzacienne* (1964): 283–338.

Hadjinicolaou, Nicolas. "La Liberté guidant le peuple de Delacroix devant son premier public." *Actes de la recherche en sciences sociales* 28 (1979): 3–26.

Hall, Stuart. "Notes on Deconstructing 'The Popular.'" In *People's History and Socialist Theory*, edited by Raphael Samuel, 227–40. London: Routledge, 1981.

Hamilton, George Heard. "The Iconographical Origins of Delacroix's 'Liberty Leading the People.'" In *Studies in Art and Literature for Belle da Costa Greene*, edited by Dorothy Miner, 55–66. Princeton: Princeton University Press, 1954.

Harris, Ruth. *Murders and Madness: Medicine, Law, and Society in the Fin de Siècle*. Oxford: Clarendon, 1989.

Harsin, Jill. *Policing Prostitution in Nineteenth-Century Paris*. Princeton: Princeton University Press, 1985.

———. "Syphilis, Wives, and Physicians: Medical Ethics and the Family in Late Nineteenth-Century France." *French Historical Studies* 16, no. 1 (1989): 72–95.

Hartman, Mary S. *Victorian Murderesses: A True History of Thirteen Respectable French and English Women Accused of Unspeakable Crimes*. New York: Schocken, 1977.

Hatin, Jules. *Cours complet d'accouchemens et de maladies des femmes et des enfans*. Paris: Baillière, 1832.

Heath, Stephen. "Difference." *Screen* 19, no. 3 (1978): 51–112.

———. "Joan Rivière and the Masquerade." In *Formations of Fantasy*, edited by Victor Burgin et al., 45–61. London: Methuen, 1986.

Hébrard, Jean. "Les Nouveaux lecteurs." In *Histoire de l'édition française*, edited by Henri-Jean Martin and Roger Chartier, 3: 470–509. Paris: Promodis, 1985.

Heitmann, Klaus. *Der Immoralismus-Proze gegen die französische Literatur im 19. Jahrhundert*. In *Ars Poetica*, vol. 9. Bad Homburg: Gehlen, 1970.

Hellerstein, Erna Olafson et al. *Victorian Women: A Documentary Account*. Stanford: Stanford University Press, 1981.

Henry, Marthe. *La Salpêtrière sous l'ancien régime: Les Origines de l'élimination des antisociaux et de l'assistance aux aliénés chroniques*. Paris: Le François, 1922.

Héricourt, Jenny d.' *La Femme affranchie*. 2 vols. Brussels: Lacroix, 1860.

Hertz, Neil. "Medusa's Head: Male Hysteria Under Political Pressure." *Representations* 4 (1983): 27–54.

Higonnet, Anne. *Berthe Morisot*. New York: Harper, 1990.

Hobsbawm, Eric. "Man and Woman in Socialist Iconography." *History Workshop* 6 (1978): 121–38.

Hoffmann, Paul. *La Femme dans la pensée des Lumières*. Paris: Ophrys n.d. [1977].

Hollier, Denis et al. *A New History of French Literature*. Cambridge: Harvard University Press, 1989.

Huart, Louis. *La Physiologie de la grisette*. Paris: Aubert, n.d. [1842].

Huart, Suzanne d'. "Le Dernier Préfet de police de Charles X: Claude Mangin." *Actes du 80e Congrès national des sociétés savantes*. Dijon (1959), pp. 603–16.

Huchard, Henri. "Caractère, moeurs, état mental des hystériques," *Archives de neurologie* 3 (February 1882): 187–211.

Huet, Pierre-Daniel. *Traité de l'origine des romans*. Edited by Arend Kok. 1670. Reprint, Amsterdam: Swets and Zeitlinger, 1942.

Hugo, Adèle. *Victor Hugo*. 1863. Reprint, Paris: Plon, 1985.

Hugo, Victor. *Choses vues*, vol. 2. Vol. 36 of *Oeuvres Complètes de Victor Hugo*. Edited by Jeanlouis Cornuz. Paris: Éditions Rencontre, 1968.

———. *Hernani.* In *Oeuvres complètes*, vol. 3, no. 2. Paris: Club Français du livre, 1967.

———. *Marion de Lorme.* In *Oeuvres complètes*, vol. 3, no. 2. Paris: Club Français du livre, 1967.

———. *Les Misérables.* Paris: Gallimard Pléiade, 1974.

Hunt, Lynn. "Engraving the Republic." *History Today* 30 (1980): 11–17.

———. "History as Gesture; or, The Scandal of History." In *Consequences of Theory*, edited by Jonathan Arac and Barbara Johnson, 91–107. Baltimore: Johns Hopkins University Press, 1991.

———. "History Beyond Social Theory." In *The States of "Theory": History, Art, and Critical Discourse*, edited by David Carroll, 95–112. New York: Columbia University Press, 1990.

———. ed. *The New Cultural History.* Berkeley: University of California Press, 1989.

———. *Politics, Culture, and Class in the French Revolution.* Berkeley: University of California Press, 1984.

Hunter, Dianne, ed. *Seduction and Theory: Readings of Gender, Representation, and Rhetoric.* Urbana: University of Illinois Press, 1989.

Huysmans, J.-K. *À Rebours.* 1884. Reprint, Paris: Garnier-Flammarion, 1978.

———. *Marthe: Histoire d'une fille.* 1876. Reprint, Paris: 10/18, 1975.

Iknayan, Marguerite. *The Idea of the Novel in France: The Critical Reaction, 1815–1848.* Geneva: Droz, 1961.

Jacobus, Mary. *Reading Woman: Essays in Feminist Criticism.* New York: Columbia University Press, 1986.

Jameson, Frederic. "*La Cousine Bette* and Allegorical Realism." *PMLA*, 86 (1971): 241–54.

———. *The Political Unconscious.* Ithaca: Cornell University Press, 1981.

Janet, Pierre. *Contribution à l'étude des accidents mentaux chez les hystériques.* Paris: Rueff, 1893.

Janin, Jules. *L'Ane mort; ou, La fille guillotinée.* Paris: 1829.

———. *Histoire de la littérature dramatique.* Vol. 5. Paris: Michel Lévy, 1857.

———. "Les Mémoires de Madame Lafarge." *Le Journal des débats*, September 20, 1841, pp. 1–2.

Jardin, André and André-Jean Tudesq. *La France des notables.* Paris: Seuil, 1973.

———. *Restoration and Reaction.* Translated by Elborg Foster. Cambridge: Cambridge University Press, 1983.

Jardine, Alice. *Gynesis: Configurations of Woman and Modernity.* Ithaca: Cornell University Press, 1985.

Jeannel, Julien. *De la Prostitution dans les grandes villes au 19e siècle et de l'extinction des maladies vénériennes.* Paris: Baillière, 1874.

Jelinek, Estelle. *Women's Autobiography.* Bloomington: Indiana University Press, 1980.

Johnson, Barbara. *The Critical Difference.* Baltimore: Johns Hopkins University Press, 1980.

———. *A World of Difference.* Baltimore: Johns Hopkins University Press, 1987.

Jolly, Jules. *De l'Influence de la littérature et du théâtre sur l'esprit public et les moeurs pendant les vingt dernières années.* Paris: Amyot, 1851.

Joly, Henri. *La France criminelle.* Paris: Cerf, 1889.

Jonghe, Elzélina Van Aylde (Pseud. Ida Saint-Elme). *Mémoires d'une contemporaine; ou, Souvenirs d'une femme sur les principaux personnages de la République Consulat de l'Empire.* 8 vols. Paris: Ladvocat, 1827–28.

Jordanova, Ludmilla. "The Popularization of Medicine: Tissot on Onanism." *Textual Practice*, 1, no. 1 (1987): 68–79.

Kahn, Gustave. *La Femme dans la caricature française.* 1907. Reprint, Paris: Méricant, 1911–12.

Kelly, Dorothy. *Fictional Genders: Role and Representation in Nineteenth-Century French Narrative.* Lincoln: University of Nebraska Press, 1989.

Kittler, Friedrich. *Discourse Networks 1800/1900.* Translated by Michael Metter et al. Stanford: Stanford University Press, 1990.

———. "Draculas Vermächtnis." In *Mit Lacan*, edited by Dieter Hombach, 103–36. Berlin: Rotation, 1982.

———. "Flechsig–Schreber–Freud: A Network of Discourses." Unpublished manuscript, 1981.

———. "Writing into the Wind, Bettina." *Glyph* 7 (1980): 32–69.

Knibiehler, Yvonne. "Le Discours médical sur la femme: Constantes et ruptures." *Romantisme* 13–14 (1976): 41–56.

Kock, Paul de. *La Grande Ville: Nouveau tableau de Paris comique, critique, et philosophique.* 2 vols. Paris: Magen, 1842.

Kofman, Sarah. *L'Énigme de la femme.* Paris: Galilée, 1980.

———. "Vautour Rouge." In *Mimesis: Desarticulations*, edited by Sylviane Agacinski, 95–164. Paris: Aubier-Flammarion, 1975.

Krakovitch, Odile. *Hugo censuré.* Paris: Calmann-Levy, 1985.

———. *Les Pièces de théâtre soumise à la censure (1800–1830).* Paris: Archives Nationales, 1982.

Kromm, Jane. " 'Marianne' and the Madwomen." *Art Journal* 48, no. 4 (1989): 299–304.

La Berge, Ann Elizabeth Fowler. "Public Health in France and the French Public Health Movement, 1815–1848." Ph. D. diss., University of Tennessee, 1974.

Lacan, Jacques. *Ecrits.* Paris: Seuil, 1966.

———. *Le Séminaire, XX. Encore.* Paris: Seuil, 1975.

LaCapra, Dominick. *Madame Bovary on Trial.* Ithaca: Cornell University Press, 1982.

Lambert, Juliette (pseud. Adam). *Idées antiproudhoniennes sur l'amour, la femme, et le mariage.* 2d ed. Paris: Dentu, 1861.

Landais, Napoléon. *Une Vie de courtisane.* Paris: Lachapelle, 1833.

Landouzy, Hector. *Traité complet de l'hystérie.* Paris: Baillière, 1846.

Laplanche, Jean and J.-B. Pontalis. "Fantasme originaire, fantasmes des origines, origine du fantasme." *Temps modernes* 215 (1964): 1833–68.

Laqueur, Thomas. "Amor Veneris, vel Dulcedo Appeletur." In *Fragments for a History of the Human Body.* Part 3. Edited by Michel Feher. *Zone* 5 (1988): 90–131.

———. *Making Sex: Body and Gender from the Greeks to Freud.* Cambridge: Harvard University Press, 1990.

———. "Orgasm, Generation, and the Politics of Reproductive Biology." *Representations* 14 (1986): 1–41.

Lasègue, Charles. *Écrits psychiatriques.* Reprint, Toulouse: Privat, 1971.

Lauretis, Teresa de. *Alice Doesn't: Feminism, Semiotics, Cinema.* Bloomington: Indiana University Press, 1984.

Lavirotte, J. C. *De la Femme à l'état physiologique.* Paris: Rignoux, 1844.

Lecour, Charles-Jérome. *La Prostitution à Paris et à Londres, 1789–1871.* 2d ed. Paris: Asselin, 1872.

Le Doeuff, Michelle. *Recherches sur l'imaginaire philosophique.* Paris: Payot, 1980.

Légier-Desgranges, Henri. "Les Massacres de septembre à la Salpêtrière," *Mémoires* published by the Fédération des sociétés historiques et archéologiques de Paris et de l'Ile-de-France, 2 (1950): 295–347.

Legouvé, Ernest. *Histoire morale des femmes* (1849). 2d ed. Paris: Sandré, 1854.

Legrand Du Saulle, Henri. Review of Stanislas Rossignol, *Aperçu médical sur la maison de Saint-Lazare. AMP* 3d ser., vol. 2 (1856): 605–12.

———. "Étude médico-légale sur l'hystérie et le degré de responsabilité des hystériques et des aliénés devant la loi à l'occasion des procès récents." *AMP* (1860): 95–110.

———. *Les Hystériques: État physique et état mentale.* Paris: Baillière, 1883.

Lejeune, Philippe. *Le Pacte autobiographique.* Paris: Seuil, 1975.

———. "Le Pacte autobiographique (bis)," *Poétique* 56 (1983): 416–34.

Léonard, Jacques. *La Médecine entre les savoirs et les pouvoirs.* Paris: Aubier Montaigne, 1981.

Lesselier, Claudie. "Les Femmes et la prison: 1815–1939." Ph. D. diss., Université de Paris VII, 1982.

Lettres de femmes adressées à Honoré de Balzac. Cahiers balzaciens. 3 (1924); 5 (1927).

Leuret, François. *Du Traitement moral de la folie.* Paris: Baillière, 1840.

Lévy, Michel. *Traité d'hygiène publique et privée.* 2 vols. Paris: Baillière, 1845.

Le Yaouanc, Moïse. *Nosographie de l'humanité balzacienne.* Paris: Maloine, 1859.

Lhéritier, Andrée. *Les Physiologies, 1840–45.* Paris: Service International de Microfilms, 1966.

Livi, Jocelyne. *Vapeurs de femmes.* Paris: Navarin, 1984.

Lombroso, Cesare and G. Ferrero. *La Femme criminelle et la prostituée.* Paris: Alcan, 1896. Originally published as *La Donna Delinquente,* 2d ed. Turin: Roux, 1894.

Lorde, André. *Théâtre d'épouvante.* Paris: Fasquelle, 1909.

Losserand, Jean. "Épilepsie et hystérie: Contribution à l'histoire des maladies." *Revue française de psychanalyse* 42 (1978): 411–38.

Louyer-Villermay, J. B. "Hystérie." *DSM* 23 (1816a): 257–68.

———. *Traité des maladies nerveuses en vapeurs et particulièrement de l'hystérie et de l'hypocondrie.* 2 vols. Paris: Méquignon, 1816b.

Lucas, Charles. *De la Réforme des prisons; ou, De la théorie de l'emprisonnement de ses principes, de ses moyens, et de ses conditions d'application.* 3 vols. Paris: Legrand et Descauriet, 1858.

Lüdeke, Heinz. *Eugène Delacroix und die Pariser Julirevolution.* Berlin: Deutsche Akademie der Künste, 1965.

Lukacher, Ned. *Primal Scenes: Literature, Philosophy, Psychoanalysis.* Ithaca: Cornell University Press, 1986.

Lynch, Katherine. *Family, Class, and Ideology in Early Industrial France.* Madison: University of Wisconsin Press, 1988.

Lyons, Martyn. "Les Best-sellers." In *Histoire de l'édition française,* edited by Henri-Jean Martin and Roger Chartier, 3: 368–401. Paris: Promodis, 1985.

———. *Le Triomphe du livre: Une histoire sociologique de la lecture dans la France du XIXe siècle.* Paris: Promodis, 1987.

Mallet, Joséphine. *Les Femmes en prison: Causes de leur chutes, moyens de les relever* 1843. 2d ed. Paris: Moulins, 1845.

Mannoni, Octave. *Clefs pour l'imaginaire.* Paris: Seuil, 1969.

Mantegazza, Paolo. *Physiologie de l'amour.* 4th ed. Paris: Fetscherin et Chuit, 1886.

Marc, C.-C.-H. *De la Folie considérée dans ses rapports avec les questions médico-judiciaires.* 2 vols. Paris: Baillière, 1840.

Maron, Eugène. "Critique littéraire: Année 1846." *La Revue indépendante* 7 (January 25, 1847): 237–54.

Martin, Biddy. "Feminism, Criticism, and Foucault." *New German Critique* 27 (1982): 3–31.

Martin, Henri-Jean and Roger Chartier, eds. *Histoire de l'édition française.* 4 vols. Paris: Promodis, 1982–86.

Martineau, Louis. *La Prostitution clandestine.* Paris: Delahaye, 1885.

Marx, Karl. "The Class Struggles in France." 1848. In Marx and Engels, *Collected Works,* vol. 10. Reprint, New York: International Publishers, 1978.

———. "The Eighteenth Brumaire of Louis Bonaparte." *The Marx-Engels Reader,* edited by Robert C. Tucker, 2d ed. New York: Norton, 1978.

——— and Friedrich Engels. *Die Heilige Familie* (1845). In vol. 2 of *Werke,* 5–223. Berlin: Dietz, 1980.

Mathieu, Émile. *Études cliniques sur les maladies des femmes.* Paris: Moquet, 1847.

Matter, Jacques. "Les Révoltes des prisonniers à Paris dans la première moitié du XIXe siècle," Mémoire de maîtrise, Université de Paris VII, 1975.

Mayeur, Françoise. *L'Éducation des filles en France au XIXe siècle.* Paris: Hachette, 1979.

McBride, Teresa. *The Domestic Revolution.* New York: Holmes and Meier, 1976.

McMillan, James F. *Housewife or Harlot: The Place of Women in French Society.* New York: Saint Martin's, 1981.

Meese, Elizabeth and Alice Parker, eds. *The Difference Within: Feminism and Critical Theory.* Amsterdam and Philadelphia: John Benjamins, 1989.

Menche de Loisne, Charles. *Influence de la littérature française de 1830 à 1850 sur l'esprit public et les moeurs.* Paris: Garnier, 1852.

Méray, Anthony. *La Part des femmes,* in *La Démocratie pacifique,* May 27–July 1, 1847; July 21–August 14, 1847.

Merriman, John, ed. *1830 in France.* New York: Franklin Watts, 1975.

———. "The Miracle Baby." In *For Want of a Horse: Choice and Chance in History,* edited by John Merriman, 53–57. Lexington, Mass.: Stephen Greene, 1985.

Micale, Mark S. "The Salpêtrière in the Age of Charcot: An Institutional Perspective on Medical History in the Late Nineteenth Century." *Journal of Contemporary History* 20 (1985): 703–32.

Michaud, Stéphane. "Esquirol et Esquiros." *Romantisme* 24 (1979): 43–52.

———. *Muse et Madone: Visages de la femme de la révolution française aux apparitions de Lourdes.* Paris: Seuil, 1985.

———. "La prostitution comme interrogation sur l'amour chez les socialistes romantiques (1830–1840)." In *Aimer en France,* edited by Paul Viallaneix and Jean Ehrard, 2: 377–89. Clermont-Ferrand: Publications de la Faculté des lettres et sciences humaines de Clermont-Ferrand, 1980.

Michelet, Jules. *L'Amour.* 1858. 8th ed. Reprint, Paris: Hachette, 1873.

———. *La Femme.* 1859. Reprint, Paris: Flammarion, 1981.

Miller, D. A. "Balzac's Illusions Lost and Found." *Yale French Studies* 67 (1984): 164–81.

———. *Narrative and Its Discontents.* Princeton: Princeton University Press, 1981.

———. *The Novel and the Police.* Berkeley: University of California Press, 1988.

Miller, Michael. *The Bon Marché: Bourgeois Culture and the Department Store.* Princeton: Princeton University Press, 1981.

Miller, Nancy K. *The Heroine's Text: Readings in the French and English Novel, 1722–1782.* New York: Columbia University Press, 1980.

———. "Tristes Triangles: *Le Lys dans la vallée* and its Intertext." In *Pre-Text/Text/Context: Essays on Nineteenth-Century French Literature*, edited by Robert L. Mitchell, 67–77. Columbus: Ohio State University Press, 1980.

———. "Women's Autobiography in France: For a Dialectics of Identification." In *Women and Language in Literature and Society*, edited by Sally McConnell-Ginet, Ruth Broker, and Nelly Furman, 258–73. New York: Praeger, 1980.

———. *Subject to Change: Reading Feminist Writing.* New York: Columbia University Press, 1988.

Mitchell, Juliet and Jacqueline Rose, eds. *Feminine Sexuality: Jacques Lacan and the École Freudienne.* New York: Norton, 1985.

Mitchell, Sally. *The Fallen Angel: Chastity, Class, and Women's Reading, 1835–1880.* Bowling Green: Bowling Green University Popular Press, 1981.

Mogador, Celeste. *Mémoires: Adieux au monde.* 2 vols. Pairs: Locard-Davi, 1854.

De Montègre, Antoine François Jenin. "Continence." *DSM* 6 (1813): 355–84.

Moreau de la Sarthe, Jacques-Louis. *Histoire naturelle de la femme.* Paris: Duprat, 1803.

Moreau de Tours, Jacques-Joseph. *De la folie hystérique et de quelques phénomènes nerveux propres à l'hystérie (convulsive), à l'hystéro-épilepsie, et à l'épilepsie.* Paris: Extrait de *L'Union médicale*, 1865.

Moreau, Thérèse. *Le Sang de l'histoire: Michelet, l'histoire, et l'idée de la femme au XIXe siècle.* Paris: Flammarion, 1982.

Morel de Rubempré. *La Pornologie; ou, Histoire nouvelle, universelle, et complète de la débauche de la prostitution et autres dépravations dans tous les pays du monde, notamment en France* . . . Vol. 1. Paris: Terry, 1848.

Morel, Bénédict-Auguste. *Traité des maladies mentales.* 2 vols. Paris: Masson, 1859.

———. *Traité des dégénérescences physiques, intellectuelles, et morales de l'espèce humaine.* Paris: Baillière, 1862.

Moses, Claire Goldberg. *French Feminism in the Nineteenth Century.* Albany: SUNY Press, 1984.

Mozet, Nicole. "Réception et génétique littéraire: Quand une lecture devient censure." *Oeuvres et Critiques* 11, no. 3 (1986): 241–51.

Mulvey, Laura. *Visual and Other Pleasures.* Bloomington: Indiana University Press, 1989.

Muret, Théodore. "*Le Lys dans la vallée*, par M. de Balzac." *La Quotidienne*, July 21, 1836, p. 3

Nettement, Alfred. *Études critiques sur le feuilleton roman.* 2 vols. Paris: Perrodil, 1845.

———. *La Littérature française sous le gouvernement de juillet.* 2 vols. Paris: Lecoffre, 1854. 2d ed. Paris: Lecoffre, 1859.

Neuberg, Victor. *Popular Literature: A History and Guide.* London: Woburn, 1977.

Newman, Edgar. "What the Crowd Wanted in the French Revolution of 1830." In *1830 in France*, edited by John Merriman, 17–40. New York: Franklin Watts, 1975.

Nies, Fritz. "Filles perdues und Femmes publiques: Für eine Sozialgeschichte der Literaturrezeption." *Romanistische Zeitschrift für Literaturgeschichte* 8 (1984): 394–403.

———. "La Femme-femme et la lecture: Un tour d'horizon iconographique." *Romantisme* 47 (1985): 97–106.

Nye, Robert. *Crime, Madness, and Politics in Modern France.* Princeton: Princeton University Press, 1986.

O'Brien, Patricia, *The Promise of Punishment: Prisons in Nineteenth-Century France*. Princeton: Princeton University Press, 1981.

——. "The Kleptomania Diagnosis: Bourgeois Women and Theft." *Journal of Social History* 17, no. 1 (1983): 64–77.

Offen, Karen. "Ernest Legouvé and the Doctrine of 'Equality in Difference' for Women." *Journal of Modern History* 58 (1986): 452–84.

Olafson, Erna. "Women, Social Order and the City: Rules for French Ladies, 1830–1870." Ph. D. diss., University of California, Berkeley, 1980.

Olney, James, ed. *Autobiography: Essays Theoretical and Critical*. Princeton: Princeton University Press, 1980.

Ozenne, Louise. *Mélanges critiques et littéraires*. Paris: Firmin Didot, 1843.

Ozouf, Mona. *La Fête révolutionnaire, 1789–1799*. Paris: Gallimard, 1976.

Parent-Duchâtelet, Alexandre-J.-B. *De la Prostitution dans la ville de Paris*. 2 vols. 1836. Reprint, Paris: Baillière, 1837. 3d ed. Paris: Baillière, 1857.

Parent-Lardeur, François. *Les Cabinets de Lecture: La Lecture publique à Paris sous la Restauration*. Paris: Payot, 1982.

Parry-Jones, William. *The Trade in Lunacy*. London: Routledge, 1972.

Paulson, Ronald. *Representations of Revolution (1789–1820)*. New Haven: Yale University Press, 1983.

Pauly, H. *Maladies de l'utérus, d'après les leçons de M. Lisfranc faites à l'hôpital de la Pitié*. Paris: Baillière, 1836.

Pearl, Cora. *Mémoires*. Paris: Lévy, 1886.

Pelletan, Eugène. "Revue critique: *Le Lys dans la vallée*, Roman de M. de Balzac." *La Nouvelle Minerve* 6 (1836): 449–52.

——. "Variétés: *La Comédie humaine*." *La Presse*, November 30, 1846, p. 3.

Perrot, Michelle. "L'Éloge de la ménagère dans le discours des ouvriers français au XIXe siècle." *Romantisme* 13–14 (1976):105–21.

——. "La Femme populaire rebelle." In *L'Histoire sans qualités*, edited by Christine Dufrancatel, et al. Paris: Galilée, 1979a.

——. "The Three Ages of Industrial Discipline in Nineteenth-Century France." In *Consciousness and Class Experience in Nineteenth-Century France*, edited by John Merriman, 149–68. New York: Holmes and Meier, 1979b.

—— ed. *L'Impossible prison: Recherches sur le système pénitentiare au XIXe siècle*. Paris: Seuil, 1980.

—— ed. *Une Histoire des femmes, est-elle possible?*. Marseilles: Rivages, 1984.

Peterson, Carla. *The Determined Reader: Gender and Culture in the Novel from Napoleon to Victoria*. New Brunswick: Rutgers University Press, 1986.

Peterson, D., ed. *A Mad People's History of Madness*. Pittsburgh: University of Pittsburgh Press, 1982.

Pinel, Philippe. *Traité médico-philosophique sur l'aliénation mentale, ou la manie*. Paris: Richard, Caille et Ravier, an IX [1801].

Pinkney, David. *The French Revolution of 1830*. Princeton: Princeton University Press, 1972.

——. *Decisive Years in France: 1840–1847*. Princeton: Princeton University Press, 1986.

Pointon, Marcia. *Naked Authority: The Body in Western Painting, 1830–1908*. Cambridge: Cambridge University Press, 1990.

Poitou, Eugène. "M. de Balzac, étude morale et littéraire," *Revue des deux mondes* (December 15, 1856), pp. 713–67.

————. *Du Roman et du théâtre contemporain et de leur influence sur les moeurs*. Paris: Auguste Durand, 1857; 2d ed., 1858.

Pontmartin, Armand de. *Causeries de samedi*. Paris: Michel Lévy, 1857.

Poovey, Mary. *Uneven Developments: The Ideological Work of Gender in Mid-Victorian England*. Chicago: University of Chicago Press, 1988.

Pope, Barbara Corrado. "Angels in the Devil's Workshop: Leisured and Charitable Women in Nineteenth-Century England and France." In *Becoming Visible: Women in European History*, edited by Renate Bridenthal and Claudia Koontz, 296–324. Boston: Houghton Mifflin, 1977.

Postel, Jacques, ed. *Nouvelle Histoire de la psychiatrie*. Toulouse: Privat, 1983.

Pottet, Eugène. *Histoire de Saint-Lazare (1122–1912)*. Paris: Société Française d'Imprimerie, 1912.

Prévost, Antoine François. *Histoire du Chevalier des Grieux et de Manon Lescaut*. 1753. Reprint, Paris: Havard, 1848; Paris: Garnier-Flammarion, 1967.

Price, Roger, ed. *The French Second Republic: A Social History*. London: Batsford, 1972.

————. *1848 in France*. Ithaca: Cornell University Press, 1975.

Le Procès de Madame Lafarge. Relation complète. Vol de diamants. Empoisonnement. 2d ed. Paris: Pagnerre, 1840.

Proudhon, Pierre-Joseph. *La Pornocratie; ou, Les femmes dans les temps modernes*. Paris: Lacroix, 1875.

Queffelec, Lise. "Le Lecteur du roman comme lectrice: Stratégies romanesques et stratégies critiques sous la Monarchie de Juillet." *Romantisme* 53 (1986): 9–21.

Rabine, Leslie. *Reading the Romance Heroine: Text, History, Ideology*. Ann Arbor: University of Michigan Press, 1985.

Rader, Daniel L. *The Journalists and the July Revolution in France*. The Hague: Martinus Nijhoff, 1973.

Raisson, Horace. *Histoire de la Police de Paris, 1667–1844*. Paris: Levasseur, 1844.

Recueil officiel des circulaires émanées de la Préfecture de police. 2 vols. Paris: Chaix, 1882.

Restif de la Bretonne, Nicolas. *Le Pornographe*. 1769. Reprint, Paris: Regine Deforges, 1977.

Reuss, Louis. *La Prostitution au point de vue de l'hygiène et de l'administration en France et à l'étranger*. Paris: Baillière, 1889.

Ricatte, Robert. *La Création romanesque chez les Goncourts*. Paris: PUF, 1958.

————. *La Génèse de la "Fille Elisa"*. Paris: PUF, 1960.

Richardson, Ruth. " 'In the Posture of a Whore'? A Reply to Eric Hobsbawm." *History Workshop Journal* 14 (Autumn 1982): 132–37.

Richer, Paul. *Études cliniques sur la grande hystérie ou hystéro-épilepsie*. 1880. Reprint, Paris: Delahaye et Lecroisnier, 1885.

Riot-Sarcey, Michèle. "La Conscience féministe des femmes de 1848: Jeanne Deroin et Désirée Gay." In *Un Fabuleux destin, Flora Tristan: Actes du Premier Colloque International Flora Tristan*, edited by Stéphane Michaud, 157–65. Dijon: Editions Universitaires de Dijon, 1985.

Ripa, Yannick. "L'Affaire Hersilie Rouy." *L'Histoire* 87 (1986): 74–81.

————. "Contribution à une Histoire des femmes, des médecins, et de la folie à l'âge d'or de l'aliénisme français, 1838–1860." Thèse de 3ᵉ cycle, Université de Paris, VII, 1983.

————. *La Ronde des folles: Femme, folie, et enfermement au XIXe siècle*. Paris: Aubier, 1986.

Rivière, Joan. "Womanliness as Masquerade." (1929) In *Formations of Fantasy*, edited by Victor Burgin et al., 35–44. London: Methuen, 1986.

Ronell, Avital. *Dictations: On Haunted Writing.* Bloomington: Indiana University Press, 1986.

Rose, Jacqueline. *Sexuality in the Field of Vision.* London: Verso, 1986.

Rosen, Ruth. *The Lost Sisterhood.* Baltimore: Johns Hopkins University Press, 1982.

Rossignol, A.-Stanislas. *Aperçu médical sur la maison de Saint-Lazare.* Paris: Rignoux, 1856. Thesis in medicine.

Rossum Guyon, Françoise von and Michel van Brederode, eds. *Balzac et les parents pauvres.* Paris: SEDES, 1981.

Rothfield, Lawrence. "From Semiotic to Discursive Intertextuality: The Case of *Madame Bovary.*" *Novel* 19, no. 1 (1985): 57–81.

Roudinesco, Elisabeth. *La Bataille de cent ans: Histoire de la psychanalyse en France: Vol. 1, 1885–1939.* Paris: Ramsay, 1982.

Rousseau, Jean-Jacques. *Du Contrat social* (1762). In *Oeuvres complètes.* Paris: Gallimard Pléiade, 1964.

———. *Émile; ou, De l'Éducation* (1762). In *Oeuvres complètes.* Paris: Gallimard Pléiade, 1969.

———. *Julie; ou, La Nouvelle Héloïse.* 1761. Reprint, Paris: Garnier-Flammarion, 1967.

Roussel, Pierre. *Système physique et moral de la femme.* Paris: Vincent, 1775. Reedited by Laurent Cerise as *De la femme considérée au physique et moral.* Paris: Fortin Masson, 1845.

Rouy, Hersilie. *Mémoires d'une aliénée.* Paris: Ollendorff, 1883.

Russo, Mary. "Female Grotesques: Carnival and Theory." In *Feminist Studies/Critical Studies*, edited by Teresa de Lauretis, 213–29. Bloomington: Indiana University Press, 1986.

Ryckère, Raymond de. *La Femme en prison et devant la mort.* Paris: Maloine, 1899.

Sabatier. *Histoire de législation sur les femmes publiques.* Paris: Gagniard, 1830.

Sainte-Beuve, Charles-Augustin. "M. de Balzac, 'La Recherche de l'Absolu,' " *Revue des deux mondes*, 4 (November 15, 1834), pp. 440–58.

———. *Portraits contemporains*, vols. 2 and 3. Paris: Calmann Lévy, 1876.

La Salpêtrière hier et aujourd'hui. Special issue of *L'Hôpital à Paris.* August 1982.

Sand, George. *Lélia.* 1833. Reprint, Paris: Garnier, 1960.

Sandras, C. M. S. *Traité pratique des maladies nerveuses.* 2 vols. Paris: Baillière, 1851.

Sauvy, Anne. "Une littérature pour les femmes." In *Histoire de l'édition française*, edited by Henri-Jean Martin and Roger Chartier, 3: 444–53. Paris: Promodis, 1985.

Scarry, Elaine. *The Body in Pain: The Making and Unmaking of the World.* New York: Oxford University Press, 1985.

Schenda, Rudolf. "Leserbriefe an Eugène Sue." In *Literatur für Viele*, edited by Helmut Kreuzer. Göttingen: Gandenhoeck and Ruprecht, 1976.

Schmolke-Hasselmann, Beate. "Manon—Marguerite—Nana oder: Was liest die literarische Kurtisane?" *Romanistische Zeitschrift für Literaturgeschichte* 8 (1984): 533–46.

Schnitzler, Arthur. *Therese.* 1928. Reprint, Frankfurt am Main: Fischer, 1992.

Schor, Naomi. "Le Sourire du sphinx." *Romantisme* 13–14 (1976): 183–97.

———. "Female Paranoia: The Case for Psychoanalytic Feminist Criticism." *Yale French Studies* 62 (1981): 204–19.

———. *Breaking the Chain: Women, Theory, and French Realist Fiction.* New York: Columbia University Press, 1985.

———. *Reading in Detail.* New York: Methuen, 1987.

———. "*Lélia* and the Failures of Allegory." *Esprit Créateur* 29, no. 3 (1989): 76–83.

Schreber, Daniel Paul. *Denkwürdigkeiten eines Nervenkranken*. Leipzig: Oswald Musse, 1903. Translated by Ida Macalpine and Richard Hunter, under the title *Memoirs of My Nervous Illness*. Cambridge: Harvard University Press, 1988.

Schulte, Regina. *Sperrbezirke: Tugendhaftigkeit und Prostitution in der bürgerlichen Welt*. Frankfurt am Main: Syndikat, 1979.

Scott, Joan. *Gender and the Politics of History*. New York: Columbia University Press, 1988.

Scull, Andrew, ed. *Museums of Madness: The Social Organization of Insanity in Nineteenth-Century England*. London: Allen Lane, 1979.

———. *Madhouses, Mad-doctors, and Madmen*. Philadelphia: Pennsylvania University Press, 1981.

Sedgwick, Eve Kosofsky. *Between Men: English Literature and Male Homosocial Desire*. New York: Columbia University Press, 1985.

Sérieux, Paul and J. Capgras. *Les Folies raisonnantes: Le Délire d'interprétation*. Paris: F. Alcan, 1909.

Sewell, William H., Jr. *Work and Revolution in France: The Language of Labor from the Old Regime to 1848*. Cambridge: Cambridge University Press, 1980.

Showalter, Elaine. *The Female Malady: Women, Madness, and English Culture, 1830–1980*. New York: Pantheon, 1985.

———. "Syphilis, Sexuality, and the Fiction of the Fin de Siècle." In *Sex, Politics, and Science in the Nineteenth-Century Novel*, edited by Ruth Bernard Yeazall, 88–115. Baltimore: Johns Hopkins University Press, 1986.

Silverman, Debora L. *Art Nouveau in Fin-de-Siècle France: Politics, Psychology, and Style*. Berkeley: University of California Press, 1989.

Silverman, Kaja. *The Subject of Semiotics*. Oxford: Oxford University Press, 1983.

Sirtema de Grovestins, Baron Charles Frédéric. *Les Gloires du romantisme appréciées par leurs contemporains et receuillies par "un autre bénédictin"*. 2 vols. Paris: Dentu, 1859.

Sivert, Eileen Boyd. "*Lélia* and Feminism." *Yale French Studies* 62 (1981): 45–66.

Smith, Bonnie G. *Ladies of the Leisure Class*. Princeton: Princeton University Press, 1981.

Smith-Rosenberg, Carroll. "The Hysterical Woman: Sex Roles and Role Conflict in Nineteenth-Century America." *Social Research* 39 (1972): 652–78.

Smock, Ann. *Double Dealing*. Lincoln: University of Nebraska Press, 1985.

Snitow, Ann, Christine Stansell, and Sharon Thompson, eds. *Powers of Desire: The Politics of Sexuality*. New York: Monthly Review Press, 1984.

Soulié, Frédéric. *Les Mémoires du diable*. 8 vols. Paris: Ambroise Dupont, 1837–38.

Spencer, Philip. "Censorship of Literature under the Second Empire." *The Cambridge Journal* 3 (1949): 47–55.

———. "Censorship by Imprisonment in France, 1830–1870." *Romanic Review* 47 (1956): 27–38.

Spivak, Gayatri Chakravorty. "Can the Subaltern Speak?" In *Marxism and the Interpretation of Culture*, edited by Cary Nelson and Lawrence Grossberg, 271–313. New York: Macmillan, 1988.

———. "Interview by Howard Winant: Gayatri Spivak on the Politics of the Postcolonial Subject." *Socialist Review* 90, no. 3 (1990): 81–98.

Stallybrass, Peter and Allon White. *The Politics and Poetics of Transgression*. Ithaca: Cornell University Press, 1986.

Staum, Martin S. *Cabanis. Enlightenment and Medical Philosophy in the French Revolution*. Princeton: Princeton University Press, 1980.

Stendhal (pseud. Henri Beyle). *Lamiel*. Paris: Gallimard, 1983.

Stern, Daniel. (pseud. Marie d'Agoult). *Histoire de la révolution de 1848*. 3 vols. Paris: Sandré, 1850–53.

Stora-Lamarre, Annie. *L'Enfer de la IIIe République: Censeurs et pornographes (1881–1914)*. Paris: Imago, 1990.

Strumingher, Laura. "The Vésuviennes: Images of Women Warriors in 1848 and their Significance for French History." *History of European Ideas* 8 (1987): 451–88.

Stuckey, Charles and William P. Scott. *Berthe Morisot: Impressionist*. New York: Hudson Hills, 1987.

Sue, Eugène. *Le Juif errant*. 1844–45. Reprint, Paris: Robert Laffont, 1983.

———. *Les Mystères de Paris*. 1842–43. Reprint, Paris: Robert Laffont, 1989.

Sullerot, Evelyne. *Histoire de la presse féminine en France, des origines à 1848*. Paris: Armand Colin, 1966.

———. *Histoire et sociologie du travail féminin*. Paris: Gonthier, 1968.

Swain, Gladys. *Le Sujet de la folie: Naissance de la psychiatrie*. Paris: Privat, 1977.

———. "L'Ame, la femme, le sexe, et le corps: Les Métamorphoses de l'hystérie à la fin du XIXe siècle." *Le Débat* 24 (1983): 107–27.

Temkin, Owsei. *The Falling Sickness*. Baltimore: Johns Hopkins University Press, 1945.

Terdiman, Richard. *Discourse-Counter-Discourse: The Theory and Practice of Symbolic Resistance in Nineteenth-Century France*. Ithaca: Cornell University Press, 1986.

Terrisse, Arnaud. "Évolution des thèses de médecine psychiatrique françaises au début du XVIIe siècle à 1934, d'après le fichier des thèses de médecine de la Bibliothèque Nationale." Thèse de 3ᵉ cycle, Université de Paris IV, 1982.

Thiesse, Anne-Marie. "Le Roman populaire." In *Histoire de l'édition française*, edited by Henri-Jean Martin and Roger Chartier, 3: 455–69. Paris: Promodis, 1985.

Thomas, Edith. *Les Femmes de 1848*. Paris: PUF, 1948.

———. *Pauline Roland: Socialisme et féminisme au XIXe siècle*. Paris: Rivière, 1956.

———. *Les Pétroleuses*. Paris: Gallimard, 1963.

Tiberge, Abbé (pseud. Hippolyte-François Régnier-Destourbet). *Louisa; ou, Les douleurs d'une fille de joie*. 1830. Reprint, Paris: Librairie centrale, 1865.

Tissot, Samuel A. A. D. *Avis aux gens de lettres et aux personnes sédentaires sur leur santé*. Paris: Herissant, 1767.

———. *De la Santé des gens de lettres*. Lausanne: Grasset, 1768.

———. *Essais sur les maladies des gens du monde*. Lausanne: Grasset, 1770. 3rd ed. (augmentée), Lausanne: Grasset, 1771.

Tocqueville, Alexis de. *Souvenirs*. 1850. Reprint, Paris: Gallimard, 1942. Translated by George Lawrence, under the title *Recollections: The French Revolution of 1848*. 1970. Reprint, New Brunswick: Transaction Books, 1987.

Todorov, Tzvetan. *The Poetics of Prose*. Translated by Richard Howard. Ithaca: Cornell University Press, 1977.

Török, Maria. "Unpublished by Freud to Fliess: Restoring an Oscillation." Translated by Nicholas Rand. *Critical Inquiry* 12 (1980): 391–98.

Traugott, Mark. *Armies of the Poor*. Princeton: Princeton University Press, 1985.

Trélat, Ulysse. *La Folie lucide étudiée et considérée au point de vue de la famille et de la société*. Paris: Adrien Delahaye, 1861.

Trillat, Etienne. *Histoire de l'hystérie*. Paris: Seghers, 1986.

Tristan, Flora. *Promenades dans Londres*. Paris: Delloye, 1840.

Trudgill, Eric. *Madonnas and Magdalens*. London: Heinemann, 1976.

Tulard, Jean. *La Préfecture de police sous la Monarchie de Juillet*. Paris: Imprimerie nationale, 1984.

Van der Gun, W. H. *La Courtisane romantique et son rôle dans la comédie humaine de Balzac*. Leiden: Van Gorcum, 1963.

Veith, Ilza. *Hysteria: The History of a Disease*. Chicago: University of Chicago Press, 1965.

Viallaneix, Paul and Jean Ehrard, eds. *Aimer en France, 1760–1860*. 2 vols. Clermont-Ferrand: Publications of the Faculté des lettres et sciences humaines de Clermont-Ferrand, 1980.

Vidocq, Eugène-François. *Mémoires de Vidocq, chef de la police de sureté*. 4 vols. Paris: Tenon, 1828.

Vieuxbois, Marquise de. "Les Folles de la Salpêtrière: Scènes contemporaines." *Gazette des femmes*, November 25, 1843, pp. 4–8.

Vigier, Philippe. *La Vie quotidienne à Paris pendant les journées de 1848*. Paris: 1982.

Villermé, Louis-René. *Tableau de l'état physique et moral des ouvriers*. 2 vols. Paris: Jules Renouard, 1840.

Vincent, Howard. *Daumier and His World*. Evanston, Ill.: Northwestern University Press, 1968.

Virey, Joseph-Julien. *De l'Éducation publique et privée des français*. Paris: Crapelet, an X [1802].

———. "Femme." *DSM* 14 (1815): 503–72.

———. *Des Maladies des la littérature française*. Paris: Ponthieu, 1825b.

———. *De la Femme, sous ses rapports physiologique, moral, et littéraire*. 2d ed. 1823. Reprint, Paris: Crochard, 1925a.

Voisin, Félix. *Des causes morales et physiques des maladies mentales et de quelques autres affections nerveuses, telles que l'hystérie, la nymphomanie, et le satyriasis*. Paris: Baillière, 1826.

Volosinov, V. N. *Marxism and the Philosophy of Language*. Translated by Ladislav Matejka and I. R. Titunik. 1973. Reprint, Cambridge: Harvard University Press, 1986.

Vovelle, Michel. *Idéologies et mentalités*. Paris: Maspero, 1982.

Walkowitz, Judith. *Prostitution and Victorian Society*. Cambridge: Cambridge University Press, 1980.

———. "Jack the Ripper and the Myth of Male Violence." *Feminist Studies* 8, no. 3 (1982): 543–74.

Waller, Margaret. "*Cherchez la femme*: Male Malady and Narrative Politics in the French Romantic Novel." *PMLA* 104, no. 2 (1989): 141–51.

Weber, Samuel. *The Legend of Freud*. Minneapolis: University of Minnesota Press, 1982.

———. "The Sideshow; or, Remarks on a Canny Moment." *MLN* 88 (1973): 1102–33.

Weinberg, Bernard. *French Realism: The Critical Reaction, 1830–1870*. 1937. Reprint, New York: Modern Language Association, 1971.

Weston, Elizabeth Anne. "Prostitution in Paris in the Late Nineteenth Century: A Study of Political and Social Ideology." Ph. D. diss., SUNY Buffalo, 1979.

Williams, Rosalind. *Dream Worlds: Mass Consumption in Late Nineteenth-Century France*. Berkeley: University of California Press, 1982.

Wilson, Lindsay Blake. "*Les Maladies des Femmes*: Women, Charlatanry, and Professional Medicine in Eighteenth-Century France." Ph.D. diss., Stanford University, 1982.

Wing, Nathaniel. *The Limits of Narrative*. Cambridge: Cambridge University Press, 1987.

Witkowski, Claude. *Monographie des éditions populaires: Les Romans à quatre sous, les publications illustrées à 20 centimes, 1848–1870.* Paris: Pauvert, 1981.

Wollstonecraft, Mary. *Mary: A Fiction.* 1788. Reprint, New York: Schocken, 1977.

Wood, John S. *Sondages: 1830–1848, Romanciers français secondaires.* Toronto: University of Toronto Press, 1965.

Wright, Gordon. *France in Modern Times,* 3d ed. New York: Norton, 1981.

Zeldin, Theodore. "The Conflict of Moralities: Confession, Sin and Pleasure in the Nineteenth Century." In *Conflicts in French Morality,* edited by Theodore Zeldin. London: Allen and Unwin, 1970.

————. *France: 1845–1945.* 2 vols. Oxford: Clarendon, 1973.

Zévaès, Alexandre. *Les Procès Littéraires au XIXe siècle.* Paris: Perrin, 1924.

Zola, Émile. *Thérèse Raquin.* 1867. Reprint, Paris: Garnier-Flammarion, 1970.

————. *Son Excellence Eugène.* 1876. In vol. 2 of *Les Rougon-Macquart.* Reprint, Paris: Gallimard Pléiade, 1961.

————. *L'Assommoir.* 1876–77. In vol. 2 of *Les Rougon-Macquart.* Reprint, Paris: Gallimard Pléiade, 1961.

————. *Nana.* 1879. In vol. 2 of *Les Rougon-Macquart.* Reprint, Paris: Gallimard, 1961.

Index